Impact of AI and the Evolution of Future Ghost Kitchens

Kuldeep Singh
Amity University, Haryana, India

Sanjeev Kumar
Lovely Professional University, India

Mohammad Badruddoza Talukder
International University of Business Agriculture and Technology, Bangladesh

IGI Global
Scientific Publishing
Publishing Tomorrow's Research Today

Vice President of Editorial	Melissa Wagner
Managing Editor of Acquisitions	Mikaela Felty
Managing Editor of Book Development	Jocelynn Hessler
Production Manager	Mike Brehm
Cover Design	Phillip Shickler

Published in the United States of America by
IGI Global Scientific Publishing
701 East Chocolate Avenue
Hershey, PA, 17033, USA
Tel: 717-533-8845
Fax: 717-533-8661
Website: https://www.igi-global.com E-mail: cust@igi-global.com

Library of Congress Cataloging-in-Publication Data

LCCN: 2024056978 (CIP Data Pending)

ISBN: 979-8-3373-0432-8

eISBN: 979-8-3373-0434-2

British Cataloguing in Publication Data
A Cataloguing in Publication record for this book is available from the British Library.

Impact of AI and the Evolution of Future Ghost Kitchens

Kuldeep Singh
Amity University, Haryana, India

Sanjeev Kumar
Lovely Professional University, India

Mohammad Badruddoza Talukder
International University of Business Agriculture and Technology, Bangladesh

IGI Global
Scientific Publishing
Publishing Tomorrow's Research Today

Vice President of Editorial	Melissa Wagner
Managing Editor of Acquisitions	Mikaela Felty
Managing Editor of Book Development	Jocelynn Hessler
Production Manager	Mike Brehm
Cover Design	Phillip Shickler

Published in the United States of America by
IGI Global Scientific Publishing
701 East Chocolate Avenue
Hershey, PA, 17033, USA
Tel: 717-533-8845
Fax: 717-533-8661
Website: https://www.igi-global.com E-mail: cust@igi-global.com

Library of Congress Cataloging-in-Publication Data

LCCN: 2024056978 (CIP Data Pending)

ISBN: 979-8-3373-0432-8

eISBN: 979-8-3373-0434-2

British Cataloguing in Publication Data
A Cataloguing in Publication record for this book is available from the British Library.

Table of Contents

Detailed Table of Contents

energy consumption and reducing their carbon footprints as well as generating less waste. Using different applications, integrated smart appliances promote more efficient resource management for example IoT sensors to monitor energy usage and refrigeration; automated kitchen equipment that minimizes food waste by optimizing preparation or automating inventory management are all driven through AI. These mean less food is thrown away and sustainability of the ingredients being used are improved. Beyond that, digital platforms can optimize delivery routes to decrease fuel consumption and emissions. Ghost kitchens are on the forefront of integrating smart technologies into a more sustainable food service model, keeping us aligned with our eco-friendly goals and modern consumer trends for convenience without sacrificing sustainability.

Ghost kitchens, cloud or dark kitchens, have developed as a novel solution within the food service business. This is partly due to the advent of online meal delivery and the changing behavior of consumers. These kitchens do not have any typical eating areas since their exclusive concentration is on preparing meals for delivery. This concept makes it possible to simplify operations, minimize overhead expenses, and improve inventory management. As a result, ghost kitchens are positioned as a viable solution to reduce food waste, which has been a problem in traditional restaurants for a long time. The use of data-driven inventory systems, the creation of targeted menus, and the utilization of individualized portion control are all ways in which ghost kitchens may drastically reduce the amount of food that is wasted and goes wrong.

Technological advances and client demand may change food service ghost kitchens. Value, scalability, and technology integration challenge delivery-only restaurant operating standards. Their operational benefits are well-documented, but their commercial, sustainability, and consumer implications are unknown. In this chapter, ghost kitchens' history, working systems, and economic, environmental, and social elements are studied to fill the gap. Case studies and industry data analysis are used to explore ghost kitchen advancements, including AI-driven analytics, multi-brand approaches, and eco-friendly practices. Distribution systems, regulatory compliance, and consumer distrust are needed for ghost kitchens, which promote entrepreneurship, sustainability, and cost performance. Theory explains how virtual food brands affect consumer behaviour and competitive market dynamics, whereas practical ways execute this concept. Examination of ghost kitchens' history and benefits reveals their vital role in global food ecosystem transformation.

The food industry in Kerala underwent a significant change due to expanding cloud kitchens, which altered how consumers dine and consume traditional foods. The research examines how cloud kitchens

Preface

As the editors of this comprehensive volume, we are thrilled to present a collection of diverse research and analysis on the dynamic intersection of artificial intelligence (AI) and the food service industry. This book highlights the ways in which AI is reshaping everything from sustainability practices and operational efficiency to customer experience and market trends, particularly within the rapidly evolving world of ghost kitchens. With its roots deeply embedded in technological advancements, each chapter delves into the specific impacts AI has had on various facets of the food and beverage (F&B) sector. As the global hospitality industry faces growing pressures around environmental sustainability, consumer demands, and operational effectiveness, AI is providing innovative solutions to meet these challenges.

The emergence of ghost kitchens—virtual, delivery-only kitchens—represents a transformative shift in food service models. This volume explores the fundamental changes brought about by AI in ghost kitchens, such as enhanced personalization, smarter supply chains, and improved food production processes. The chapters offer practical insights into AI-driven innovations that are making food service more efficient, environmentally conscious, and adaptable. Through case studies, expert analyses, and cutting-edge research, we explore how AI not only improves operational outcomes but also enables businesses to achieve sustainable growth while delivering on ever-evolving consumer expectations. The diversity of topics covered reflects the various dimensions through which AI can advance the food industry, ranging from sustainability initiatives to the ethical implications of data use.

At the heart of this collection is the recognition that technological advancement, particularly AI, plays a central role in shaping the future of food service. As AI continues to revolutionize the way we source, prepare, and deliver food, it holds the potential to create more sustainable, cost-effective, and customer-centric solutions. In assembling this volume, our goal was not only to showcase the practical applications of AI but also to explore the ethical, economic, and societal challenges it presents. We hope to inspire a broader conversation about the responsible adoption of AI technologies and their long-term impact on the food service industry.

In closing, this reference book serves as a critical resource for anyone seeking to understand the transformative potential of artificial intelligence in the food and beverage industry. The chapters provide a rich landscape of ideas, strategies, and case studies that illuminate the vast opportunities AI offers to enhance sustainability, streamline operations, and improve consumer experiences. We have seen how AI is revolutionizing ghost kitchens, driving eco-friendly practices, and optimizing supply chains, and we believe that these technologies will continue to play an integral role in the industry's evolution.

As we look ahead, the integration of AI into food service is not without its challenges. Balancing technological innovation with environmental and ethical considerations will be crucial in ensuring that AI adoption leads to positive, sustainable outcomes. The responsible implementation of AI can help businesses reduce waste, enhance food safety, and deliver personalized experiences at scale. However, it is essential for industry stakeholders to remain vigilant about the potential risks, such as data privacy concerns, algorithmic bias, and the need for regulatory oversight.

Ultimately, this volume underscores the critical role AI will continue to play in shaping the future of the food industry. From optimizing kitchen operations to revolutionizing customer engagement and promoting sustainability, the applications of AI are both vast and impactful. We hope that this book inspires further exploration and collaboration in the food service sector, encouraging the adoption of innovative technologies that will pave the way for a smarter, more sustainable future.

CHAPTER OVERVIEWS

Chapter 1: Sustainable Food and Beverage Practices with AI

This chapter explores the integration of Artificial Intelligence (AI) into the food and beverage management sector, highlighting its role in promoting sustainability within the hospitality industry. The chapter focuses on areas such as sustainable food sourcing, resource management, energy efficiency, and enhancing customer experiences through AI. It delves into how AI is reshaping supply chains, forecasting consumer behavior, and supporting sustainable practices, while also ensuring service quality. The chapter concludes with practical suggestions for effectively applying AI to achieve sustainability goals without compromising environmental priorities.

Chapter 2: The Future of Indian Restaurants: The Role of Technology in the Success of Cloud Kitchens

This chapter investigates the rise of cloud kitchens in India and their potential to revolutionize the restaurant industry. It emphasizes the role of technology, such as online food delivery platforms, data analytics, and kitchen automation, in optimizing operations and reducing overhead costs. The chapter explores how these technologies enable cloud kitchens to cater to a growing tech-savvy consumer base, while also examining key market opportunities and trends that could shape the future of this innovative business model in India.

Chapter 3: Data Privacy and Security in AI-Driven Ghost Kitchens

This chapter focuses on the intersection of data privacy and AI in the context of ghost kitchens. It explores the role of AI in improving operational efficiency and customer satisfaction while addressing critical issues such as data protection, privacy risks, and regulatory compliance. The study examines real-world cases of data breaches and offers solutions like privacy-by-design principles and secure AI development to ensure the safe handling of sensitive information in AI-driven ghost kitchens.

Chapter 4: AI Trend in Supply Chain Operations for Ghost Kitchens: Supply Chain Operations

This chapter discusses how AI is transforming supply chain operations in ghost kitchens. It covers the application of machine learning, real-time data processing, and demand planning to optimize inventory control, distribution, and quality assurance. By integrating AI, ghost kitchens can reduce waste, improve delivery speed, and maintain high-quality standards, ultimately enhancing operational efficiency and scalability in food delivery services.

Chapter 5: Leveraging Machine Learning for Personalization in Ghost Kitchens: Transforming Customer Experience

This chapter highlights how machine learning (ML) can enhance customer experience in ghost kitchens, where traditional customer interactions are absent. ML algorithms help personalize customer experiences by analyzing preferences, optimizing menus, and providing targeted marketing. It also addresses challenges like data privacy and biases while offering actionable insights for implementing ML to improve customer satisfaction and operational efficiency in the ghost kitchen ecosystem.

Chapter 6: Success Stories of AI-Integrated Ghost Kitchens: Revolutionizing Food Delivery via Technology

This chapter explores successful case studies of AI-powered ghost kitchens and their impact on food delivery services. It showcases how AI has optimized order management, demand forecasting, inventory control, and logistics. The chapter demonstrates how AI has streamlined operations, improved customer satisfaction, and contributed to environmental sustainability, providing a comprehensive understanding of the strategic benefits of AI integration in ghost kitchens.

Chapter 7: Ghost Kitchens Transforming the Culinary Landscape and Shaping the Future of Food Delivery

This chapter examines the rise of ghost kitchens, particularly post-COVID-19, and their effects on the food service industry. It discusses operational challenges, workforce implications, and consumer attitudes towards delivery-only kitchens. Additionally, the chapter explores how ghost kitchens are reshaping culinary careers, business models, and labor standards, offering valuable insights into the changing dynamics of the food service sector.

Chapter 8: Transforming Supply Chain Dynamics: Emerging AI Trends Improving Efficiency and Responsiveness in Ghost Kitchen Operations for Sustainability

This chapter investigates how emerging AI trends are transforming supply chain management in ghost kitchens. It focuses on the application of predictive analytics and machine learning to enhance efficiency in inventory management, order fulfillment, and logistics, while also addressing environmental challenges such as waste reduction and resource optimization. The chapter emphasizes the importance of adopting AI-driven strategies for sustainable practices in the food service industry.

Chapter 9: Enhancing Experiences through the Integration of AI in Augmented and Virtual Reality: Transforming Immersive Technologies Through Intelligent Interactions and Real-Time Adaptation

This chapter explores the integration of AI in augmented and virtual reality (AR/VR) to create personalized and immersive user experiences. By leveraging AI technologies like computer vision and machine learning, AR/VR applications can dynamically adapt to user needs. The chapter also addresses ethical and technical challenges, such as privacy concerns and algorithmic biases, while highlighting the transformative potential of AI in the future of immersive technologies.

Chapter 10: Revolutionizing Food Prep: Harnessing AI Technologies to Optimize Cooking Processes and Efficiency in Ghost Kitchens for a Smarter Future

This chapter focuses on how AI is revolutionizing cooking processes within ghost kitchens. It highlights how technologies such as machine learning, predictive analytics, and automation improve food preparation, inventory management, and operational efficiency. By reducing waste and ensuring consistent food quality, AI helps ghost kitchens meet the growing demand for fast, high-quality food delivery while optimizing resource usage.

Chapter 11: Eco-friendly Practices of Ghost Kitchens through Smart Technology

This chapter examines how ghost kitchens are leveraging smart technologies to promote sustainability. It covers eco-friendly practices such as reducing energy consumption, minimizing food waste, and utilizing sustainable packaging. The chapter also highlights the role of data analytics and smart appliances in optimizing kitchen operations and resource management, as well as the need for regulatory frameworks to support green practices within the ghost kitchen ecosystem.

Chapter 12: Challenges and Opportunities of Ghost Kitchens with Reference to Expansions and Expectations

This chapter explores the challenges and opportunities associated with the rapid expansion of ghost kitchens in the global food service industry. It examines scalability, consumer behavior, operational efficiency, and market growth, focusing on the potential disruptions and opportunities for new ventures. The chapter also looks at the evolving expectations surrounding ghost kitchens and their impact on the future of food delivery services.

Chapter 13: The Future of AI in the Food Industry: Emerging Trends and Opportunities

This chapter explores the transformative role of AI in the food industry, examining trends such as machine learning, predictive analytics, and robotics. It discusses how these technologies are optimizing food production, distribution, safety, and customer experiences. Additionally, the chapter addresses ethical concerns and challenges, offering a comprehensive framework for stakeholders navigating the AI-driven transformation in the food sector.

Chapter 14: Role of Robotics in Ghost Kitchens: Revolutionizing Food Service and Delivery

This chapter investigates the role of robotics in ghost kitchens, focusing on food preparation, packing, inventory control, and delivery systems. The chapter highlights how robotics, combined with AI and IoT technologies, enhances operational efficiency, reduces labor costs, and improves customer satisfaction. It examines how these innovations contribute to scalable, adaptable, and sustainable operations in the food delivery market.

Chapter 15: The Sustainable Kitchen of Tomorrow: AI's Role in Resource-Saving Ghost Kitchens

This chapter explores how AI technologies can make ghost kitchens more sustainable by optimizing resource allocation, reducing food waste, and minimizing operational costs. It emphasizes the role of AI in improving inventory management, forecasting demand, and promoting responsible sourcing practices. The chapter also highlights the adaptability of ghost kitchens during crises like the COVID-19 pandemic, demonstrating their potential for supporting business continuity and sustainability.

Chapter 16: Using Machine Learning Algorithms to Personalize Customer Experience in Ghost Kitchens: Hyper-Personalized Marketing and Promotion

This chapter examines how machine learning algorithms can personalize customer experiences in ghost kitchens, particularly in the context of hyper-targeted marketing. By analyzing customer preferences and behaviors, ML enables dynamic promotions, customized offers, and precise marketing campaigns. The chapter also explores how AI-driven customer segmentation enhances marketing efficiency and customer loyalty.

Chapter 17: Eco-friendly Practices of Ghost Kitchens through Smart Technology: Technological Innovations in the Food and Beverage Industry

This chapter explores the use of smart technologies in ghost kitchens to promote sustainability. It highlights innovations such as IoT sensors, automated equipment, and optimized delivery routes, all driven by AI. These technologies contribute to reduced food waste, lower energy consumption, and more sustainable food service operations, helping ghost kitchens align with eco-friendly goals and consumer preferences.

Chapter 18: Reducing Food Waste Through Ghost Kitchens

This chapter focuses on how ghost kitchens can reduce food waste by utilizing data-driven inventory systems, portion control, and targeted menu creation. It highlights the operational advantages of ghost kitchens, including their ability to streamline food preparation and minimize waste compared to traditional restaurants. The chapter demonstrates how ghost kitchens are positioned to be part of the solution to the food waste problem in the food service industry.

Chapter 19: Ghost Kitchens Evolution - From the Traditional Restaurant to Virtual Eateries

This chapter traces the evolution of ghost kitchens, from their origins to their current role in the food service industry. It discusses the technological advancements, business models, and market dynamics that have contributed to their growth. The chapter also examines how ghost kitchens are shaping the future of food delivery, including their environmental and social impacts, and the challenges they face in terms of scalability and consumer perception.

Chapter 20: Cloud Kitchens and Digital Foodscapes: Exploring Social Media's Role in Kerala's Food Industry

This chapter explores how cloud kitchens in Kerala are leveraging social media to influence consumer behavior and market their services. It investigates the cultural, economic, and social effects of cloud kitchens, focusing on their impact on traditional dining habits and sustainability. The chapter also discusses regulatory challenges and proposes policies to help integrate digital advancements with cultural preservation in Kerala's food industry.

Kuldeep Singh
Amity University, India

Sanjeev Kumar
Lovely Professional University, India

Mohammad Talukder
International University of Business Agriculture and Technology, Bangladesh

Chapter 1
Sustainable Food and Beverage Practices With AI

Mohammad Badruddoza Talukder
https://orcid.org/0009-0008-1662-9221
International University of Business Agriculture and Technology, Bangladesh

Sanjeev Kumar
https://orcid.org/0000-0002-7375-7341
Lovely Professional University, India

Kuldeep Singh
https://orcid.org/0000-0002-7999-1585
Amity University, Haryana, India

Varun Bhardwaj
Amity University, Jaipur, India

ABSTRACT

Incorporating Artificial Intelligence in food and beverage management policies in food establishments is gradually changing the sustainability progress in hospitality industries. This chapter looks at innovation in sustainable food sourcing, Sustainable Resource Management, energy efficiency, and Customized Consumer Experiences that can be served with the help of AI techniques. Focusing on the existing literature that discusses current trends, case studies, and technology advances, the chapter underlines the principal capability of AI in diminishing environmental impacts in the food and beverages service while integrating high service quality into the hospitality business model. It also highlights the AI application in integrating efficient supply chains, forecasting consumer behavior, and driving the sustainability path. The chapter concludes with tactic suggestions for applying AI to the sustainability objective in the F&B industry while ensuring the advancement of engineering and technology does not cause a regression in ecological motives.

DOI: 10.4018/979-8-3373-0432-8.ch001

INTRODUCTION

The impact of Artificial Intelligence (AI) & sustainable practices used in food & beverage practices giving new shape to the hospitality industry. The global sustainability prioritizes and the pressure on the food & beverage sector creating environmentally responsible practices more significant. AI brings innovations and advancement in resource management, waste reduction, & energy efficiency. The chapter explores the reshaping of AI and new practices in the f n b sectors and its operations, providing a comprehensive framework for integrating sustainability in every phase of supply chain management. Optimizing different sourcing and tailor-made products brings the real-life experience to the customer's mind, and AI shifts toward sustainable & efficient practices. AI analyzes the data & creates actionable insights in transformation, and aligns the business with sustainability goals.

It also found that AI effectively supports industry and circular economy by predicting demand, reducing waste, and improving the energy system. In addition, AI-powered tools become more effective and traceable in supply chains. The new application of AI in the dining experience is fully responsible for consuming and customizing meals per the guest's preference. The study also explores the AI-driven sustainable practices used in f n b sectors and implementations of AI practices in the food business. The study aims to guide the harnessing of AI's potential and sustainable, efficient, & consumer-oriented food & beverage industry by providing strategic recommendations.

Figure 1. Sustainable food practices through AI Integration

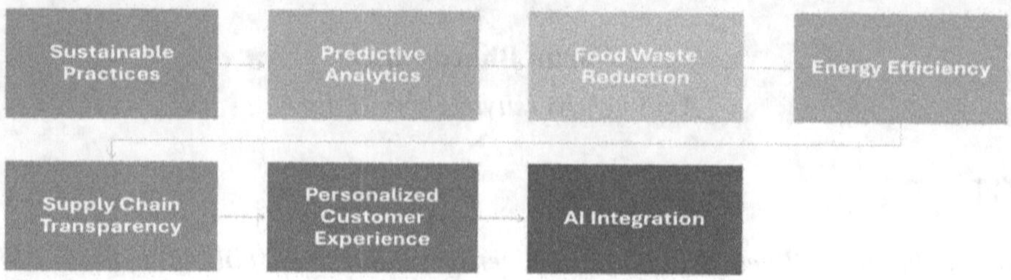

Source: Author Compilation.

LITERATURE REVIEW

Integrating Artificial Intelligence (AI) into sustainability bridges the gap between technology & hospitality management (Ajmera et al., 2024). The literature review proves that AI addresses various issues and challenges and helps in operation efficiency (Agrawal & Kumar, 2023). AI helps reduce food waste and shapes the service industry. The AI-driven systems forecast the demand more precisely, minimizing overproduction & food waste (Talukder, 2024). The new AI algorithm tool helps monitor the inventory management system, reducing spoilage and controlling pilferage.

On the other hand, AI technologies optimize energy consumption in kitchens & dining areas. They should be monitored by artificial Intelligence, and these practices should be used in real-time operation tasks to reduce production costs (Gunjan Sinha & Prof. Praveen F.A, 2024). AI enhances supply chain simplicity & traceability, ensuring food products are sourced sustainably & ethically. The AI applications used in hotels, which include optimization & demand forecasting, help reduce the carbon footprint (M.K. Murugeah, 2024). The literature review focused on personalized dining experiences, and the tailor-made menus served in the restaurant bring more individual preferences, dietary restrictions, & sustainability considerations. On the other hand, the literature also discussed the challenges & limitations, and concerns about data privacy and AI implementation cost, & the potential loss of jobs due to automation are common themes (Ms. Reshmi Jose & Dr. Sopna V. Muhammed, 2024). Despite these challenges, there is a consensus that AI holds substantial promise for advancing sustainability in the food & beverage sector, provided its adoption is carefully managed & aligned with ecological goals (Kanca, 2024).

INTRODUCTION TO AI IN SUSTAINABLE FOOD & BEVERAGE PRACTICES

Artificial Intelligence (AI) is speedily transforming in various sectors, including the service industry, to promote sustainability practices (Claudine Sykimte, 2023). Due to increasing the pressure on business and focus on environmentally responsible practices, AI brings new innovative solutions that improve operational efficiency, reduce waste, and minimize the environmental impact (Dacha et al., 2023) due to integrating changes in the AI technologies, which includes; machine learning, predictive analytics, & automation to optimize processes ranging from sourcing & inventory management & customer service.

The basic concept of AI and its applications positively impact sustainable food & beverage practices (Mary & Chege, 2024). The use of AI tools in the business can accurately forecast demand, manage inventory, & reduce food waste, addressing the significant challenges of the industries. AI also helps contribute to energy efficiency by monitoring, controlling, and using the various resources used in the service industry (Natalie et al., 2024). In addition, AI supply chain transparency enables businesses to source products ethically & sustainably (Ni Kadek Bella Puspitayanti et al., 2024). The study highlights that AI brings new personalized customer experiences promoting sustainability practices. The industry is moving towards more sustainable practices. The role of AI brings new changes, and the various AI-driven strategies & technologies help shape the future and focus on sustainable food & beverage practices (Ditya Adi Putra & Anggayana, 2023).

AI-DRIVEN STRATEGIES FOR REDUCING FOOD WASTE

Food waste is a significant component of the food service industry and brings new issues with economic & environmental implications (Milton, 2024). The latest innovative Artificial Intelligence (AI) strategies address demand forecasting accuracy, improving inventory management, & optimizing supply chain processes. The AI algorithms analyze the sale data and other relevant factors, focusing on demand and forecasting. The other various AI-driven approaches also help to reduce food waste, and AI algorithms analyze future demand and supply (Rakotoarisoa, 2024). Another significant application of AI is that it reduces waste and focuses on inventory management, and these AI inventory systems track the inventory (Somlai, 2023). AI also plays a vital role in supply chain management and analysis of the data of suppliers, logistics, & distribution networks. AI tools also minimize kitchen operational costs and can track food preparation & consumption patterns (Khamoushi, 2024). This AI tool helps chefs and kitchen staff with the calculation of food cost, portions, and sales reports, which also reduces the time and cost (Zamathula Sikhakhane Nwokediegwu et al., 2024) and AI is being used to create more sustainable food & beverage practices.

Energy Efficiency in Food & Beverage Operations through AI

Energy efficiency is an essential aspect of sustainable food & beverage operations, with substantial energy consumption for cooking, refrigeration, & lighting (M.K. Murugeah, 2024). The role of Artificial Intelligence (AI) is to provide transformative solutions to optimize the use of energy and reduce the day-to-day operational costs. AI new technologies enhance energy efficiency in the food service industry, and intelligent energy management systems are the prime focus of AI applications in energy efficiency. These AI algorithms monitor daily real-time energy consumption in the various operations, including kitchens, dining areas, & refrigeration units (Gunjan Sinha & Prof. Praveen F.A, 2024). Proactive AI is energy-intensive to maintain the system smoothly and successfully, and it is the continuous process of monitoring the performance of appliances such as ovens, dishwashers, & HVAC systems (Groene & Zakharov, 2024). This proactive approach will help increase the efficiency of the equipment and its self-life, minimize energy waste & avoid costly breakdowns.

On the other hand, AI-driven optimization tools also emphasize energy usage, and the new applications of AI help control lighting & heating/cooling systems in real-time and provide daily updates about external weather conditions (Prabuddhini & Harshani, 2024). By forecasting energy demand & analyzing market trends, AI can help businesses negotiate better energy contracts & manage their consumption more effectively. This chapter examines these AI-driven strategies, showcasing updates about energy efficiency in food & beverage operations. It also highlights real-world examples & case studies demonstrating the successful implementation of AI technologies, offering & achieving sustainability goals (Kataria, 2024).

AI & SUPPLY CHAIN OPTIMIZATION FOR SUSTAINABLE SOURCING

The sustainable source is an essential component of a responsible food & beverage industry, emphasizing ethical practices & minimizing environmental impact throughout the supply chain (Whig et al., 2024). Artificial Intelligence (AI) and revolutionizes supply chain management by enhancing transparency, efficiency, & sustainability. The study explores AI-driven solutions to optimize supply chains to promote sustainable practices (Nuakoh, 2024). The advanced AI applications system also analyses data from suppliers, logistics, & market trends to offer insights into supply chain performance (Huang & Mao, 2024). This will help to make the decision quickly, make necessary action plans effectively, and maintain the organization's standards (Dagou & Gurgun, 2024). The AI applications make recommendations for weather conditions, traffic patterns, and carbon emissions associated with transportation & help minimize fuel consumption & operational costs (Muldoon et al., 2023). Furthermore, AI-driven updates about demand forecasting help align supply with actual consumption patterns, reducing overproduction & excess inventory. Precise forecasting helps to minimize waste & provide accurate information up to date, and these AI-driven strategies and their impact are shown on sustainable sourcing (Abbas, 2024).

PERSONALIZED DINING: ENHANCING SUSTAINABILITY WITH AI

Artificial Intelligence increases personalized dining experiences and impacts food & beverage, and by using AI technologies in business, the individual's preferences towards the dining experiences promote sustainability (Milton, 2024). The sustainable practices explore the contribution of AI and creating a positive impact on the food service industry. The machine learning algorithms used in customized menus align the tastes & nutritional aspects of the diets. These improvements increase customer satisfaction, support sustainability practices, and reduce food wastage (Ejike Innocent Nwankwo et al., 2024). AI also suggested portion size, meal planning, reducing the likelihood of food waste, giving an idea about the demand and supply, and increasing the profitability and effective use of the ingredients based on the seasonal availability & local produce (Li et al., 2024).

Furthermore, AI-driven tools also assist in creating menus that balance environmental considerations with customer preferences. The ecological impact of different ingredients & dishes AI will help to design the menu and reduce the carbon footprint (Wagobera Edgar Kedi et al., 2024). Sometimes, AI can be harnessed to create dining experiences that are both tailored & aligned with broader environmental objectives (Gunjan Sinha & Prof. Praveen F.A, 2024).

AI APPLICATIONS IN RESPONSIBLE FOOD & BEVERAGE CONSUMPTION

Artificial Intelligence (AI) increasingly emphasizes the importance of sustainability, reducing waste, & ethical practices (Matla et al., 2024). The AI applications are more eco-friendly and show the consumption patterns within the industry. The prime objective of the AI applications is to optimize the usage of food & beverage along with inventory (Rizqa & Af&i, 2024). These new trends of AI applications also analyze the data on current sales, consumer preferences, and seasonal trends and accurately forecast the demand. It is constructive for the business to reduce overstocking & waste management practices and fulfill the customer needs. AI also recommends plant-based or locally sourced options to customers and creates interest in them (Zaltz et al., 2024). The AI-powered sensors quickly detect spoilage and contamination in real-time, which helps to take the necessary action for the safety and security of the customers. AI is an effective tool for businesses to communicate sustainability, educate consumers about the environmental impact, and encourage responsible behavior (Alex et al., 2024).To highlight the best sustainable practices, including reducing single-use plastics or supporting fair trade products (Lin et al., 2023).

CHALLENGES & OPPORTUNITIES IN AI ADOPTION FOR SUSTAINABILITY

Adopting artificial Intelligence (AI) should face new challenges compared with manual work. AI also increases the work's efficiency and the organization's productivity.

Challenges

I. High Implementation Costs: This is one of the significant challenges in adopting AI to increase the high cost of implementation (Samuel Omokhafe Yusuf et al., 2024). AI systems require substantial financial investment in the technology, infrastructure, & skilled personnel.

II. Data Privacy & its Security System: AI stores vast amounts of data in the systems, increases work efficiency, and cuts down other costs. But another challenge should be cyber threats & data breaches (Ainah, 2024).

III. Integration with Existing Systems: Integrating new AI technology into the existing system is another complex & time-consuming process, where the businesses may face new difficulties ensuring compatibility between new AI technologies & their current infrastructure.

IV. Skill Gaps & Training: AI requires specialized skills & knowledge, whereas human resources training is another critical task. Retaining trained professionals in the organizations is the prime duty of the HR department (Gundeti et al., 2023).

CASE STUDIES: SUCCESSFUL AI INTEGRATION IN FOOD & BEVERAGE SUSTAINABILITY

1. **Wasteless: AI-Driven Food Waste Reduction:** The AI tool used in the food waste in the retail environments by Israeli start-ups and the technology focused on the machine learning algorithms to forecast the demand and pricing. The previous sale can also analyze consumer behavior and weather patterns through this practice. This approach minimized waste and cost savings (Bezat-Jarzębowska et al., 2024).
2. **Too Good to Go: AI for Reducing Food Waste:** The European application and AI tool is primarily used for Good to Go and connecting with consumers. These applications are used in various organizations and focus on the price of food costs (Aimuyedo et al., 2023). The AI algorithms are also used in the different processes & predict the historical data & current trends. It also helps to provide up-to-date information about the data so the necessary action can be taken in advance mode. This system also reduces food waste by efficiently redistributing surplus food, promoting sustainability.
3. **IBM Food Trust: Enhancing Supply Chain Transparency:** AI in IBM Food Trust brings transparency & traceability within the food supply chain. Integrating new technology with blockchain and data security in the platform allows stakeholders to track the history of food products from farmhouses to the table service. The AI analyses data to ensure compliance with sustainability standards and bring improvement (Hasan & Habib, 2024). These technologies also help to improve food safety, reduce waste, & support sustainability by providing clear insights into the origin & handling of food products.
4. **Nestlé: AI for Sustainable Sourcing & Production:** Nestlé has implemented AI in the production processes and focuses on sustainability (Talukder et al., 2023). Most of the new organizations are using the AI tool to analyze data on environmental impact, & market conditions. This analysis helps Nestlé make help to make decisions about raw materials, reducing the ecological footprint, & enhancing supply chain efficiency. AI tool also supports Nestlé's and fulfills the commitment to

sustainable production by optimizing resource use & minimizing waste throughout its manufacturing processes.

5. **AI-Enhanced Energy Management:** Starbucks has also adopted AI technology in the store department to increase work efficiency and reduce operational costs. Starbucks uses AI-driven technology systems to monitor & control real-time energy consumption (Talukder et al., 2024a). These practices significantly impact reduced energy consumption & costs, contributing to Starbucks' sustainability goals.
6. **Panera Bread: AI for Personalized Customer Engagement:** Panera Bread leverages AI to enhance customer engagement & promote responsible consumption. It uses AI algorithms to analyze customer preferences & different purchasing patterns and styles. AI-driven brings different insights regarding customized options and aligns with individual dietary needs & sustainability preferences. These customized approaches help to improve customer satisfaction & support responsible consumption by encouraging more mindful food choices.
7. **McDonald's: AI for Sustainable Packaging Solutions:** McDonald's is also exploring AI to optimize its packaging solutions & reduce environmental impact (Yakoubi, 2024). With the usage of AI in the organization, the lifecycle and assessment tools changed, positively impacting consumer behavior. Using AI in McDonald's helps reduce package costs and improve recycling processes. These practices support McDonald's commitment to sustainability and smooth operations (Talukder et al., 2024a).

THE FUTURE OF SUSTAINABLE FOOD & BEVERAGE PRACTICES WITH AI

As Artificial Intelligence (AI) continues to evolve, its potential to transform sustainable food & beverage practices grows exponentially. The future integration promises significant advancements in the industry, addresses environmental challenges, optimizes resource use, & promotes ethical practices.

1. **Advanced Predictive Analytics:** AI's future enhances predictive analytics and forecasts the business demand. The advancement of algorithms will analyze the different variables, including consumer behavior, climate conditions, & economic trends. This forecasting will reduce overproduction cost and waste management, leading to more efficient resource use & better alignment with sustainability goals (Ajmera et al., 2024).
2. **Enhanced Resource Efficiency:** Future applications of AI will optimize the different resources and management practices in the food supply chain. AI-driven systems will monitor various practices, including water consumption, waste generation, and adapting operations to minimize environmental impact (Bakshi & Singh, 2024). These innovations in AI will have effective control and lead to significant reductions in operational waste & energy consumption.
3. **Sustainable Sourcing Innovations:** AI will revolutionize sustainable sourcing, provide deeper insights into the supply chain dynamics, and advancement of AI models will assess the environmental & social impact of sourcing decisions, enabling businesses to make more informed supplier choices (Talukder et al., 2024b). The AI will also make the development of more transparent & ethical supply chains possible to maintain the organization's standards.

4. **Personalized Sustainable Choices:** Nowadays, AI becomes more complicated, but it will gradually make more personalized recommendations for sustainable food & beverage choices (Talukder, Kumar, Kaiser, et al., 2024b). The AI systems will also analyze individual preferences, dietary needs, & environmental impact, which align with personal & sustainability goals. The personalization practices focus on consumption patterns & support sustainable eating habits.
5. **Innovation in Waste Management:** The advancements of AI technologies in waste management include automated sorting & recycling systems. The future of AI applications will increase the efficiency of waste separation & recycling processes, reducing the volume of waste and promoting the circular economy. AI will also support the development of innovative waste-to-energy solutions, converting food waste into valuable resources.
6. **Integration with Emerging Technologies:** Emerging technologies, like the Internet of Things (IoT) & blockchain, will further enhance sustainability efforts. (Agrawal & Kumar, 2023) AI-powered and IoT devices will provide real-time data on environmental conditions & operational performance. The junction of technologies will enable more effective monitoring & management of sustainability initiatives.
7. **Consumer Engagement & Education**: AI too will engage & educate consumers about sustainable practices. The AI will raise awareness about the environmental impact of food choices & encourage more sustainable behaviors. AI-driven platforms also provide clear-cut information about the consumers, retain the sustainability of products & offer guidance on making eco-friendly decisions.

RECOMMENDATIONS FOR ADVANCING SUSTAINABLE FOOD & BEVERAGE PRACTICES WITH AI

1. **Invest in AI Training & Skills Development:** The investment in business and training the workforce to leverage. It includes developing expertise in AI technologies & data analytics & ensuring that staff can effectively manage & utilize AI tools. Training programs should focus on improving technical skills and AI applications in sustainability practices.
2. **Adopt Integrated AI Solutions:** The integration of businesses and the salutation provided by the AI in the operational areas, including supply chain management, resource optimization, & waste reduction. These integrated systems combined with AI, IoT, blockchain, & other technologies can provide comprehensive insights & bring effectiveness to sustainability practices.
3. **Enhance Data Management & Security:** The best AI application practical focuses on high-quality data. The robust data in business management practices includes data collection, cleaning, & analysis. Additionally, investing in cybersecurity measures. It also maintained trust & ensuring the integrity of AI-driven systems.
4. **Foster Collaboration & Partnerships:** Collaboration with technology, which includes industry peers, & research institutions, can enhance AI adoption & innovation. The partnerships facilitate knowledge sharing, access to cutting-edge technologies, & collaborative efforts in sustainability challenges.
5. **Promote Transparency & Traceability:** AI significantly improves transparency & traceability in supply chains. Businesses should implement AI systems that track the environmental & social impact of their sourcing decisions. It provides the consumers with accurate information and maintains the sustainability of products, can build trust & support responsible consumption.

6. **Leverage AI for Consumer Education:** The Utilization of AI-driven platforms to educate consumers about sustainable food best practices. The personalized recommendations & targeted communication can increase awareness about the environmental impact, focus on dietary awareness, and encourage more sustainable behaviors.
7. **Continuously Monitor & Adapt:** The assessment of AI systems increases performance & creates a positive impact on sustainability goals regularly—the continuous monitoring of businesses to make data-driven adjustments & improvements. The adaptability of new technology brings the insurance about the sustainability efforts to remain effective & aligned with evolving industry standards. It also includes job displacement, decision-making transparency, & bias in AI algorithms. Adopting ethical guidelines & fostering a culture of responsibility in AI development can support achieving sustainability & social goals.
8. **Explore Innovative AI Solutions and Sustainability Goals:** The AI technologies & explore innovative applications that can further enhance sustainability include experimenting with new AI-driven tools & techniques that offer novel approaches to resource management, waste reduction, & sustainable sourcing through these measurable sustainability goals that AI technologies can support and progress & evaluate the effectiveness of their sustainability initiatives.

Figure 2. AI training for the food handler

Source: Author Compilation.

CONCLUSION

In conclusion, the study focuses on advancing sustainability practices in the food & beverage industry. AI brings significant improvements in environmental performance & operational efficiency by enhancing predictive analytics, optimizing resources, & personalizing consumer experiences. On the other hand, the benefits address the issues and challenges, including implementation costs, data privacy, & the need for skilled personnel. The integrated AI focus on investing in training, & fostering collaboration will be vital for overcoming these hurdles. AI technologies are the continued process of developing supportive, sustainable practices that will grow faster and bring innovative pathways to reduce waste, improve transparency, & promote responsible consumption. By tactically leveraging AI, businesses can create a more sustainable & ethical food & beverage industry.

REFERENCES

Abbas, A. (2024). *Harnessing AI for Sustainable Supply Chains: Enhancing Manufacturing Resilience*. Unpublished. DOI: 10.13140/RG.2.2.19641.99683

Agrawal, K., & Kumar, N. (2023). Artificial Intelligence Innovations: Inception of new horizons in food processing sector. *2023 IEEE Silchar Subsection Conference (SILCON)*, 1–8. DOI: 10.1109/SILCON59133.2023.10404183

Aimuyedo, M. T., Nyor, T., & Abdulkadir, K. I. (2023). Corporate Sustainability Reporting of Carbonated Drink Market of the Nigerian Food & Beverages Industry. *International Journal of Innovation and Scientific Research*, *X*(XI), 402–411. DOI: 10.51244/IJRSI.2023.1011033

Ainah, N. (2024). *Advancing AI Integration in Sabah Business L&scape: Opportunities & Challenges*. DOI: 10.20944/preprints202404.1725.v1

Ajmera, D., Kharub, M., Krishna, A., & Gupta, H. (2024). Navigating the challenges of AI-enabled circular economy in the food & beverage sector: Strategies for sustainable transformation. *International Journal of Logistics Management*. Advance online publication. DOI: 10.1108/IJLM-09-2023-0408

Alexander, C. S., Yarborough, M., & Smith, A. (2024). Who is responsible for 'responsible AI'?: Navigating challenges to build trust in AI agriculture and food system technology. *Precision Agriculture*, *25*(1), 146–185.

Bakshi, N., & Singh, A. K. (2024). AI-Enabled Smart Buildings Reducing the Carbon Footprint & Enhancing Guest Experiences in Eco-Friendly Hotels. In Talukder, M. B., Kumar, S., & Tyagi, P. K. (Eds.), *Advances in Hospitality, Tourism, & the Services Industry* (pp. 79–98). IGI Global., DOI: 10.4018/979-8-3693-7898-4.ch005

Bezat-Jarzębowska, A., Krieger-Güss, S., Jarzębowski, S., & Petersen, B. (2024). Integration of the Food Supply Chain as a Driver of Sustainability: A Conceptual Framework. *Agriculture*, *14*(8), 1403. DOI: 10.3390/agriculture14081403

Dacha, V. W., Omwenga, J. Q., & Namusonge, E. (2023). Recycling Practices & Value Chain Performance in the Food & Beverage Industry in Kenya. *International Journal of Social Science & Humanities Research (IJSSHR) ISSN 2959-7056 (o); 2959-7048 (p)*, *1* (1), 772–783. DOI: 10.61108/ijsshr.v1i1.61

Dagou, H. H., & Gurgun, A. P. (2024). Blockchain & AI for Sustainable Supply Chain Management in Construction. In Kahraman, C., Cevik Onar, S., Cebi, S., Oztaysi, B., Tolga, A. C., & Ucal Sari, I. (Eds.), *Intelligent & Fuzzy Systems* (Vol. 1090, pp. 350–359). Springer Nature Switzerl., DOI: 10.1007/978-3-031-67192-0_41

Ditya Adi Putra, I. M. M., & Anggayana, I. W. A. (2023). Identify Industrial Work Practices in the Food & Beverage Product Department of Quest Hotel Kuta. *Jurnal Manajemen Pelayanan Hotel*, *7*(2), 1152. DOI: 10.37484/jmph.070230

Groene, N., & Zakharov, S. (2024). Introduction of AI-based sales forecasting: How to drive digital transformation in food & beverage outlets. *Discover Artificial Intelligence*, *4*(1), 1. DOI: 10.1007/s44163-023-00097-x

Gundeti, R., Vuppala, K., & Kasireddy, V. (2023). The Future of AI & Environmental Sustainability: Challenges & Opportunities. In Kannan, H., Rodriguez, R. V., Paprika, Z. Z., & Ade-Ibijola, A. (Eds.), (pp. 346–371). Advances in Environmental Engineering & Green Technologies. IGI Global., DOI: 10.4018/979-8-3693-0892-9.ch017

Hasan, I., & Habib, Md. M. (2024). *Enhancing Transparency in Agri-Food Supply Chain by Securing IoT-Generated Data with Blockchain*. DOI: 10.21203/rs.3.rs-4486156/v1

Huang, R., & Mao, S. (2024). Carbon Footprint Management in Global Supply Chains: A Data-Driven Approach Utilizing Artificial Intelligence Algorithms. *IEEE Access : Practical Innovations, Open Solutions*, *12*, 89957–89967. DOI: 10.1109/ACCESS.2024.3407839

Kanca, I. N. (2024). Analysis of green practice at food & beverage department of ML hotel. *Journal of Commerce, Management, &. Tourist Studies*, *3*(1), 13–22. DOI: 10.58881/jcmts.v3i1.138

Kataria, P. (2024). Technology at the Table: Incorporating AI into Contemporary Food Industry Operations. *Food Science & Nutrition Cases*, foodsciencecases20240003. DOI: 10.1079/foodsciencecases.2024.0003

Kedi, W. E., Ejimuda, C., Idemudia, C., & Ijomah, T. I. (2024). AI software for personalized marketing automation in SMEs: Enhancing customer experience & sales. *World Journal of Advanced Research & Reviews*, *23*(1), 1981–1990. DOI: 10.30574/wjarr.2024.23.1.2159

Khamoushi, E. (2024). *AI in Food Marketing from Personalized Recommendations to Predictive Analytics: Comparing Traditional Advertising Techniques with AI-Driven Strategies* (Version 1). arXiv. DOI: 10.48550/ARXIV.2410.01815

Li, Y., Liang, J., Zhao, Z., & Li, K. (2024). Revolutionizing Education through AI: Alleviating Educator Stress, Personalizing Learning, & Enhancing Economic Sustainability. *World Journal of Education & Humanities*, *6*(5), 113. DOI: 10.22158/wjeh.v6n5p113

Lin, T.-T., Park, C. G., Kapella, M. C., Martyn-Nemeth, P., Tussing-Humphreys, L., Rospenda, K. M., & Zenk, S. N. (2023). Shift work domains & their interactions with empty calorie food/beverage consumption: A 14-day intensive longitudinal study. *International Journal of Nursing Studies*, *141*, 104490. DOI: 10.1016/j.ijnurstu.2023.104490 PMID: 37004340

Mary, W. S., & Chege, P. (2024). Green Procurement Practices and Supply Chain Performance of Food and Beverage Processing Firms in Nairobi City County, Kenya. *Journal of Procurement & Supply Chain*, *4*(2), 16–27.

Matla, Y., Yannamaneni, R. R., & Pappas, G. (2024). Globalizing Food Items Based on Ingredient Consumption. *Sustainability (Basel)*, *16*(17), 7524. DOI: 10.3390/su16177524

Mbonigaba Celestin* & S. Sujatha**. (2024). *AI'S IMPACT ON CORPORATE STRATEGIES & EFFICIENCY: RISKS, OPPORTUNITIES, & ETHICAL CONSIDERATIONS*. DOI: 10.5281/ZENODO.13955383

Milton, T. (2024). Artificial intelligence transforming hotel gastronomy: An in-depth review of AI-driven innovations in menu design, food preparation, and customer interaction, with a focus on sustainability and future trends in the hospitality industry. *International Journal for Multidimensional Research Perspectives*, *2*(3), 47–61.

Muldoon, J., Cant, C., Graham, M., & Ustek Spilda, F. (2023). The poverty of ethical AI: Impact sourcing & AI supply chains. *AI & Society*. Advance online publication. DOI: 10.1007/s00146-023-01824-9

Murugeah, M.K. (2024). Enhancing efficiency & Personalization in Food & Beverage Service through AI: Future Trends & Challenges. *International Journal for Multidimensional Research Perspectives, 2* (7), 01–17. DOI: 10.61877/ijmrp.v2i7.162

Natalie, H. C., Bangsawan, S., & Husna, N. (2024). Driving Sustainable Business Performance: The Impact of Green Innovation on Food & Beverage SMEs in B&ar Lampung City. *International Journal of Business & Applied Economics*, *3*(3), 371–384. DOI: 10.55927/ijbae.v3i3.9187

Nuakoh, S. K. (2024). *Digital Transformation of Supply Strategy & Network for Sustainable Woodworks Company*. DOI: 10.13140/RG.2.2.21123.31526

Nwankwo, E. I., Emeihe, E. V., Ajegbile, M. D., Olaboye, J. A., & Maha, C. C. (2024). AI in personalized medicine: Enhancing drug efficacy & reducing adverse effects. *International Medical Science Research Journal*, *4*(8), 806–833. DOI: 10.51594/imsrj.v4i8.1453

Nwokediegwu, Z. Q. S., Ugwuanyi, E. D., Dada, M. A., Majemite, M. T., & Obaigbena, A. (2024). AI-driven waste management systems: A comparative review of innovations in the USA and Africa. *Engineering Science & Technology Journal*, *5*(2), 507–516.

Prabuddhini, D. H. U., & Harshani, G. H. V. (2024). Food for Thought: The Effect on Employee Relations on Employee Performance with Special Reference to Food & Beverage Operations in Hotel Industry. *Sri Lanka Journal of Management Studies*, *6*(1), 44–64. DOI: 10.4038/sljms.v6i1.127

Puspitayanti, N. K. B., Sutarma, I. G. P., Darlina, L., Arjana, I. W. B., & Wijaya, I. N. C. (2024). Implementation of Green Practice in the Food and Beverage Department at Jimbaran Puri, a Belmond Hotel Bali. International Journal of Travel. *Hospitality and Events*, *3*(2), 168–183.

Rakotoarisoa, S. R. (2024). AI-Driven Waste Management Solutions in the Mining Industry: Reducing Environmental Impact. *International Student Conference on Business, Education, Economics, Accounting, & Management (ISC-BEAM), 2* (1), 717–738. DOI: 10.21009/ISC-BEAM.012.45

Reshmi Jose, M. (2024). Effect of AI on the Sustainable Practices of Enterprises. *International Journal of Advanced Research in Science. Tongxin Jishu*, •••, 848–853. DOI: 10.48175/IJARSCT-18399

Rizqa, A. A., & Afandi, M. Y. (2024). Producer & Consumer Behavior towards the Consumption of Halal Food & Beverages. *International Journal of Islamic Economics*, *6*(02), 162–176. DOI: 10.32332/ijie.v6i2.9545

Singh, S., Yadav, S., Singh, A., Krishna, Y. J., & Singh, A. (2024). Harnessing Technology for a Sustainable Future in Finance: The Role of Artificial Intelligence in Promoting Environmental Responsibility. In El Khoury, R. (Ed.), *Anticipating Future Business Trends: Navigating Artificial Intelligence Innovations* (Vol. 536, pp. 367–378). Springer Nature Switzerl., DOI: 10.1007/978-3-031-63402-4_30

Sinha, G., & Praveen, A. (2024). AI-Driven Innovations in Food and Beverage Service: A Roadmap to Future Hospitality. *International Journal for Multidimensional Research Perspectives*, *2*, 44–60.

Somlai, R. (2023). Insights into business strategies for reducing food waste in the Australian food industry. *Business Strategy and the Environment*, *32*(6), 3151–3164. DOI: 10.1002/bse.3292

Sykimte, C. (2023). Food & Beverage Management: Trends, Innovations, & Challenges. *International Journal of Advanced Research in Science. Tongxin Jishu*, •••, 713–718. DOI: 10.48175/IJARSCT-12360

Talukder, M. B. (2024). Implementing Artificial Intelligence & Virtual Experiences in Hospitality. In Manohar, S., Mittal, A., Raju, S., & Nair, A. J. (Eds.), *Advances in Hospitality, Tourism, & the Services Industry* (pp. 145–160). IGI Global., DOI: 10.4018/979-8-3693-2019-8.ch009

Talukder, M. B., Kumar, S., Kaiser, F., & Mia, Md. N. (2024a). Pilgrimage Creative Tourism: A Gateway to Sustainable Development Goals in Bangladesh. In M. Hamdan, M. Anshari, N. Ahmad, & E. Ali (Eds.), *Advances in Public Policy & Administration* (pp. 285–300). IGI Global. DOI: 10.4018/979-8-3693-1742-6.ch016

Talukder, M. B., Kumar, S., Kaiser, F., & Mia, Md. N. (2024b). Pilgrimage Creative Tourism: A Gateway to Sustainable Development Goals in Bangladesh. In M. Hamdan, M. Anshari, N. Ahmad, & E. Ali (Eds.), *Advances in Public Policy & Administration* (pp. 285–300). IGI Global. DOI: 10.4018/979-8-3693-1742-6.ch016

Talukder, M. B., Kumar, S., Sood, K., & Grima, S. (2023). Information Technology, Food Service Quality & Restaurant Revisit Intention. *International Journal of Sustainable Development and Planning*, *18*(1), 295–303. DOI: 10.18280/ijsdp.180131

Talukder, M. B., Kumar, S., & Tyagi, P. K. (Eds.). (2024a). *Hotel & Travel Management in the AI Era*. IGI Global., DOI: 10.4018/979-8-3693-7898-4

Talukder, M. B., Kumar, S., & Tyagi, P. K. (Eds.). (2024b). *Impact of AI & Tech-Driven Solutions in Hospitality & Tourism*. IGI Global., DOI: 10.4018/979-8-3693-6755-1

Tuncalp, D. (2024). Directing the future: Artificial intelligence integration in family businesses. *Journal of Family Business Management*. DOI: 10.1108/JFBM-03-2024-0051

Whig, P., Remala, R., Mudunuru, K. R., & Quraishi, S. J. (2024). Integrating AI & Quantum Technologies for Sustainable Supply Chain Management. In Hassan, A., Bhattacharya, P., Dutta, P. K., Verma, J. P., & Kundu, N. K. (Eds.), *Advances in Logistics, Operations, & Management Science* (pp. 267–283). IGI Global., DOI: 10.4018/979-8-3693-4107-0.ch018

Yakoubi, S. (2024). Sustainable Revolution: AI-Driven Enhancements for Composite Polymer Processing & Optimization in Intelligent Food Packaging. *Food and Bioprocess Technology*. Advance online publication. DOI: 10.1007/s11947-024-03449-2

Yusuf, S. O., Durodola, R. L., Ocran, G., Abubakar, J. E., Echere, A. Z., & Paul-Adeleye, A. H. (2024). Challenges & opportunities in AI & digital transformation for SMEs: A cross-continental perspective. *World Journal of Advanced Research & Reviews*, *23*(3), 668–678. DOI: 10.30574/wjarr.2024.23.3.2511

Zaltz, D. A., Prowse, R., Yi, Y., O'Dea, J., & Harding, S. V. (2024). *Beverage consumption among adults in Newfoundl& & Labrador, Canada prior to the implementation of a sugar-sweetened beverage tax*. DOI: 10.21203/rs.3.rs-4606952/v1

Chapter 2

The Future of Indian Restaurants:

The Role of Technology in the Success of Cloud Kitchens

Sarthak Chourasia
https://orcid.org/0009-0001-5886-1810
Mandsaur University, India

Sukhmeet Kaur
https://orcid.org/0000-0002-3363-6844
INTI International University, Malaysia

Amrik Singh
https://orcid.org/0000-0003-3598-8787
Lovely Professional University, India

ABSTRACT

The rapid evolution of the food service industry in India has given rise to the concept of cloud kitchens, also known as virtual kitchens or ghost kitchens. This research paper explores the theme of cloud kitchens as the future of Indian restaurants, emphasizing the pivotal role of technology in their success. The study utilizes secondary data to analyze the growth trajectory, operational dynamics, and technological advancements that have facilitated the proliferation of cloud kitchens in India. The paper delves into the various technological innovations that have revolutionized the cloud kitchen model, including online food delivery platforms, data analytics, kitchen automation, and digital marketing strategies. By leveraging these technologies, cloud kitchens have been able to streamline operations, reduce overhead costs, and cater to the evolving demands of tech-savvy consumers. Additionally, the study examines the top cloud kitchen opportunities in India, highlighting key market players, emerging trends, and potential areas for growth.

DOI: 10.4018/979-8-3373-0432-8.ch002

1. INTRODUCTION

The Indian food service industry has witnessed a transformative shift in recent years, driven by technological advancements, changing consumer lifestyles, and the rapid rise of digital platforms. One of the most notable outcomes of this evolution is the emergence of cloud kitchens, also calledvirtual kitchens or ghost kitchens. Unlike traditional brick-and-mortar restaurants, cloud kitchens operate exclusively for delivery, eliminating the need for physical dining spaces. This innovative business model has gained significant traction, particularly in urban areas, where time-conscious, tech-savvy consumers prioritize convenience and quick access to quality food. According to a report by RedSeer Consulting (2022), the Indian cloud kitchen market, valued at INR 2,000 crore in 2019, is projected to grow at a compound annual growth rate (CAGR) of 20%, reaching INR 7,000 crore by 2024. This remarkable growth is fuelled by increasing urbanization, rising disposable incomes, and the growing influence of food delivery platforms like Swiggy, Zomato, and Uber Eats.

At the heart of this revolution lies the role of technology, which has become indispensable in ensuring cloud kitchens' operational efficiency and success. Among the most impactful technological innovations, artificial intelligence (AI) stands out as a transformative force shaping the future of this sector. AI leverages algorithms, machine learning, and predictive analytics to optimize various aspects of the cloud kitchen model, from demand forecasting and menu optimization to customer retention and delivery logistics. For instance, AI-powered systems analyze historical sales data, seasonal trends, and consumer behavior to predict demand patterns, allowing kitchens to prepare efficiently and minimize wastage (Deloitte India, 2021). Additionally, AI enables menu customization and personalization by analyzing consumer preferences, dietary restrictions, and real-time feedback, ensuring that cloud kitchens can cater to diverse consumer needs effectively.

Moreover, AI-driven automation in kitchen operations, such as robotic cooking systems and automated inventory management, has significantly enhanced the efficiency and consistency of food preparation processes (MarketsandMarkets, 2022). Delivery optimization, another critical aspect, is also facilitated by AI. Platforms like Swiggy utilize AI-based algorithms to map the most efficient delivery routes, considering factors such as traffic and order priority, ensuring timely deliveries and reduced operational costs (Economic Times, 2021). Beyond operations, AI is pivotal in targeted marketing strategies by analyzing customer data and creating personalized campaigns to boost retention and brand loyalty.

The integration of AI into cloud kitchen operations is not merely a competitive advantage but a necessity in an increasingly saturated market. By leveraging AI technologies, cloud kitchens can streamline operations, reduce costs, and cater to the dynamic demands of modern consumers. This technological synergy underscores the potential of cloud kitchens to revolutionize the Indian restaurant industry, positioning them as a critical component of its future growth and sustainability. As the industry continues to evolve, the role of AI will remain integral in addressing the challenges of competition, customer expectations, and operational complexities, further cementing the importance of cloud kitchens in the digital age.

2. LITERATURE REVIEW

2.1 Why Compare Cloud Kitchens and Traditional Restaurants?

The food and beverage industry istransforming, driven by shifting consumer preferences and technological advancements. Table 1 comparescloud kitchens and **traditional restaurants'**key aspects which are essential to understanding their unique business models, operational challenges, and customer engagement strategies. This differentiation helps entrepreneurs, investors, and policymakers identify which model aligns better with current market demands, such as affordability, convenience, and scalability.

Table 1. Cloud Kitchens Vs. Traditional Restaurants

Aspect	Cloud Kitchens	Traditional Restaurants
Definition	Delivery-only kitchens with no physical dining spaces, focusing on online orders.	Brick-and-mortar establishments offer dine-in services, alongside takeaway and delivery options.
Startup Costs	Lower initial investment due to the absence of dining spaces, decor, and front-of-house staff.	Higher costs due to expenses on real estate, interiors, furniture, and staff for both kitchen and dining areas.
Operational Model	Heavily reliant on online food delivery platforms (e.g., Zomato, Swiggy) and own apps for customer orders.	Combines in-house dining experience with delivery and takeaway services.
Space Requirement	Requires minimal space, often located in industrial or less expensive areas.	Requires larger spaces in high-visibility, prime locations to attract footfall.
Technology Use	High reliance on AI, IoT, and cloud-based systems for demand prediction, order management, and delivery.	Moderate use of technology; mainly for reservations, POS systems, and online order integration.
Menu Design	Compact and focused menus optimized for delivery and packaging durability.	Extensive menus catering to diverse tastes, often including visually appealing plated dishes for dine-in.
Customer Interaction	Limited direct interaction; feedback is primarily digital.	High level of face-to-face interaction with staff, enhancing the dining experience.
Scalability	Easier and faster to scale due to lower overheads and flexible locations.	Scaling requires significant investment in new locations, decor, and staff recruitment.
Revenue Streams	Primarily from online orders and collaborations with delivery platforms.	Diverse streams including dine-in, takeaway, and event hosting.
Customer Experience	Focused on convenience, speed, and quality of delivery.	Emphasizes ambiance, service, and in-person hospitality.
Target Audience	Online-savvy, convenience-seeking customers, often millennials and Gen Z.	Broader audience, including families, professionals, and diners seeking a social experience.
Marketing	Relies on digital marketing, food aggregator platforms, and customer reviews.	Uses a mix of offline (billboards, events) and online channels for marketing, along with word-of-mouth.

Source: Authors' work

2.2 Cloud Kitchen Business Models

A business model serves as a framework for understanding, innovating, and evaluating the strategic operations of a company. It provides clarity on how an organization creates and captures value, influencing its decision-making processes (Velt et al., 2018). While some scholars argue that a business model differs from strategy, it complements the strategic process by enabling analysis, testing, and validation of ideas within the business framework (Shafer et al., 2005). According to Shafer et al., the primary aim of a business model is to deliver value to stakeholders, which is achieved through efficient and innovative operational practices. Within the context of cloud kitchens, it is critical to evaluate how sustainability principles are integrated into their six primary business models.Initially, cloud kitchens were characterized by single-brand operations, with one kitchen focusing solely on processing online orders without a physical dining area. Over time, the business model has diversified into multiple formats to address varying market requirements. The primary cloud kitchen models identified are the independent, multi-brand, hybrid, shell, fully stacked, and fully outsourced models (Maggo, 2018).

Independent Cloud Kitchen

This model involves a single brand operating from a standalone kitchen without a storefront. Typically situated in low-cost rental areas close to densely populated urban centers, it relies on third-party or in-house delivery services to fulfill online orders. The model allows brands to expand into new markets while minimizing upfront investment by decoupling dine-in facilities from the kitchen. However, small businesses face challenges, such as high initial setup costs and the need for extensive marketing to build brand awareness without direct customer engagement (Sharma, 2021; Maggo, 2018).

Multi-brand Cloud Kitchen

In this format, one kitchen caters to multiple brands under a single-parent organization. It operates without a storefront, and orders are processed through digital platforms and delivered by third-party or in-house services. By sharing resources such as kitchen space, this model reduces operational costs while allowing companies to cater to diverse consumer preferences based on market trends. This model, however, is primarily adopted by well-established brands and faces similar challenges to the independent model, including significant marketing expenditure and high startup costs (Sharma, 2021; Maggo, 2018).

Hybrid Cloud Kitchen

The hybrid model combines the features of a traditional takeaway outlet and a cloud kitchen. A single kitchen prepares food for delivery while also offering a storefront for customer pickups. Orders are received through aggregators or the brand's online platform, and deliveries are managed in-house or via third-party services. This approach balances the cost-efficiency of cloud kitchens with the visibility and direct customer interaction of a storefront. Despite these advantages, finding suitable low-cost locations with storefront potential remains a challenge (Sharma, 2021; Maggo, 2018).

Shell Cloud Kitchen

This model involves aggregator-owned shared kitchens equipped with essential infrastructure. Multiple food brands rent space in these kitchens and bring their staff, equipment, and ingredients. All orders are generated through the aggregator's platform, which also manages deliveries. Shell kitchens are a cost-effective solution for businesses looking to test new menus or expand into new markets without significant upfront investment. Restaurants benefit from market insights provided by aggregators to fine-tune their offerings (Sharma, 2021).

Fully-stacked Cloud Kitchen

Fully stacked cloud kitchens are like shell models but come with additional support, such as fully equipped kitchens and storefronts for takeaways. Restaurants renting these spaces can focus solely on food preparation while leveraging the aggregator's delivery and marketing infrastructure. By reducing setup and operational costs, this model allows brands to scale quickly with minimal financial risk. However, operators take a portion of the revenue, which can impact profit margins (Sharma, 2021).

Fully-outsourced Cloud Kitchen

In this model, aggregators manage every aspect of the food preparation and delivery process. Multiple brands operate from a centralized kitchen where the restaurants provide recipes, while ingredients are sourced and meals prepared by the aggregator. This model offers the lowest initial investment, making it ideal for high-volume businesses. However, profit margins are reduced due to aggregator fees, and securing partnerships with high-demand centralized kitchens can be time-intensive (Maggo, 2018; Sharma, 2021).

2.3 Multi-Brand Virtual Restaurants the Evolution of Cloud Kitchens

The study by Tualeka (2024) explores the emergence of Multi-Brand Virtual Restaurants (MBVRs) as an innovative extension of Indonesia's Cloud Kitchen business model. Focusing on PT. Sagala, the research highlights how this model differs from traditional cloud kitchens by operating multiple food brands under a single management rather than leasing kitchen space to independent businesses. This approach enhances cost efficiency, brand diversity, and operational control, making it a viable alternative in the growing food delivery market.

The COVID-19 pandemic played a key role in accelerating the adoption of cloud kitchens, as businesses sought delivery-focused solutions to survive restrictions on dine-in services. PT. Sagala leveraged this trend by implementing the Rebel Foods Model, expanding from a small food stall in 2018 to 27 locations by 2021. The company's organizational structure includes Marketing, Finance, Operations, and HR divisions, each responsible for ensuring smooth business operations.

Comparing six types of cloud kitchen models, the study finds that PT. Sagala's MBVR model reduces operational costs by up to 70%, allowing for rapid scalability while maintaining consistent food quality. However, challenges such as brand differentiation, market competition, and operational complexity require strategic management.

The research concludes that Multi-Brand Virtual Restaurants are a cost-effective and scalable alternative to traditional cloud kitchens, particularly in emerging markets where efficiency and growth are essential. The study emphasizes that digital platforms, centralized operations, and brand innovation will continue to drive the future of cloud kitchens and virtual restaurants.

2.4 Technological Advancements and Their Impact onHospitality, and Service Industries

Technology has become a transformative force across various service sectors, particularly in tourism, hospitality, and food services. From digital transformation in tourism to the integration of AI and automation in cloud kitchens and restaurants, businesses are leveraging technological innovations to enhance efficiency, customer satisfaction, and market competitiveness. However, while technology offers numerous advantages, it also introduces challenges such as security risks, workforce displacement, and operational barriers.

Service Barriers and Risk Assessment in Cloud Kitchens

Cloud kitchens have emerged as a cost-effective and flexible alternative to traditional restaurants, focusing on food delivery without physical dining spaces. Cheng et al. (2024) highlight that despite their advantages, cloud kitchens face numerous service barriers, including inefficiencies in process management, food quality concerns, marketing limitations, delivery challenges, and hygiene issues. Using theRisk Dependency-Early Warning (RD-EW) model, which integratesDEMATEL-based Analytic Network Process (DANP)andFailure Mode and Effects Analysis (FMEA), the study identified key pain points such as over-reliance on third-party delivery services, limited menu variety, and improper packaging. Addressing these service risks is crucial for improving customer trust and operational sustainability.

Technological Adoption in Service Industries

The broader service industry, particularly the food sector, has embraced various technological innovations to enhance efficiency and customer experience. Guo (2025) explores the successful implementation of restaurant automation, mobile ordering platforms, AI-driven analytics, and robotics. Automated kitchens, such as those operated by Spyce, improve food preparation efficiency, while AI-powered tools like Domino's "Dom" enhance personalization. Delivery platforms like UberEats and DoorDash have revolutionized food accessibility, while big data analytics optimize supply chains and decision-making. However, challenges such as workforce displacement, data privacy issues, and the need for continuous innovation must be managed to ensure a balanced integration of technology with human interaction.

Across tourism, cloud kitchens, and food service industries, digital transformation has played a vital role in reshaping business models and consumer experiences. The implementation of AI, IoT, automation, and data analytics has led to operational improvements but also introduced new risks and barriers. Businesses must adopt a strategic approach to overcoming these challenges, ensuring that technological advancements contribute to sustainable and competitive growth.

3. DISCUSSION

3.1 Factors Responsible for the Growth of Cloud Kitchens in India

The growing popularity of cloud kitchens in India is driven by several factors that align with evolving consumer preferences and market trends. As urbanization and hectic lifestyles increase, people are increasingly seeking quick, convenient meal options. The success of online food delivery services like Swiggy, Zomato, and Uber Eats has further propelled the emergence of cloud kitchens, as they cater to the rising demand for home-delivered food. Cloud kitchens offer a more cost-effective solution by eliminating the need for prime real estate and expensive interiors typically required for traditional restaurants. Additionally, they enable flexibility, allowing businesses to experiment with diverse cuisines and concepts without the constraints of a physical dining space. The use of technology in managing orders, supplies, and deliveries enhances operational efficiency compared to traditional kitchens. With changing food business regulations, cloud kitchens also benefit from more straightforward compliance with licensing and operational laws. Lastly, cloud kitchens are well-positioned to quickly adapt to shifting market trends, further driving their growth in India.

The digitalrevolution and the shift in restaurantdemand

The restaurant industry has undergone a significant transformation in recent years, driven by rapid digitalization and evolving consumer preferences. This shift has been characterized by increased investments in technology, the rise of online ordering and delivery services, and a change in dining habits.

Digital Transformation in the Restaurant Industry

In 2024, the National Restaurant Association reported that 73% of restaurant operators increased their technology investments, marking the highest rate of digital adoption in the sector's history (National Restaurant Association, 2024). This surge in digital integration encompasses various aspects, including online ordering systems, mobile applications, and contactless payment methods. The global online food delivery market has also seen substantial growth, with projections indicating continued expansion in the coming years (Statista, 2023).

Shift in Consumer Demand

Consumer behavior has shifted towards convenience and efficiency, leading to a decline in traditional dine-in experiences and a rise in demand for quick-service and fast-casual dining options. In the past 12 to 18 months, fast-casual restaurants have experienced significant growth, with brands like Wingstop and Raising Cane reporting increases of 24.9% and 20.7%, respectively (The Food Institute, 2023). This trend reflects a broader move towards value-driven consumption, where consumers seek quality food with minimal time investment.

Impact of Digital Ordering and Delivery

The adoption of digital ordering and delivery platforms has been a key driver in the industry's transformation. In 2023, digital ordering and delivery became central to restaurant operations, with many establishments leveraging online platforms, delivery apps, and ghost kitchens to meet consumer demand (Digital Directions, 2023). However, this shift has also introduced challenges, such as increased competition and the need for efficient delivery logistics.

3.2 Challenges and Considerations

Despite the benefits of digital transformation, restaurants face challenges related to technology integration and maintaining profitability. The rise of meal-ordering apps, while meeting consumer demand for convenience, has also led to increased costs for restaurants, impacting revenue (FIS Global, 2022). Additionally, the need to adapt to rapidly changing consumer preferences requires continuous innovation and flexibility.The digital revolution has fundamentally altered the landscape of the restaurant industry, shifting consumer demand towards convenience, speed, and technological integration. As the industry continues to evolve, restaurants must embrace digital transformation and adapt to changing consumer behaviors to remain competitive and meet the expectations of modern diners.

Global Online Food Delivery Market Growth (2017-2025)

The rapid growth of the global online food delivery market, with revenue rising from $91.2 billion in 2017 to a projected $223.7 billion by 2025 is shown in Figure 1. This growth is driven by increased smartphone penetration, internet accessibility, and changing consumer preferences for convenience. The shift toward digital platforms has been further accelerated by the COVID-19 pandemic, which heightened the reliance on delivery services (Statista, 2023; Research and Markets, 2022).

Figure 1. Anticipated Global Online Food Delivery Market

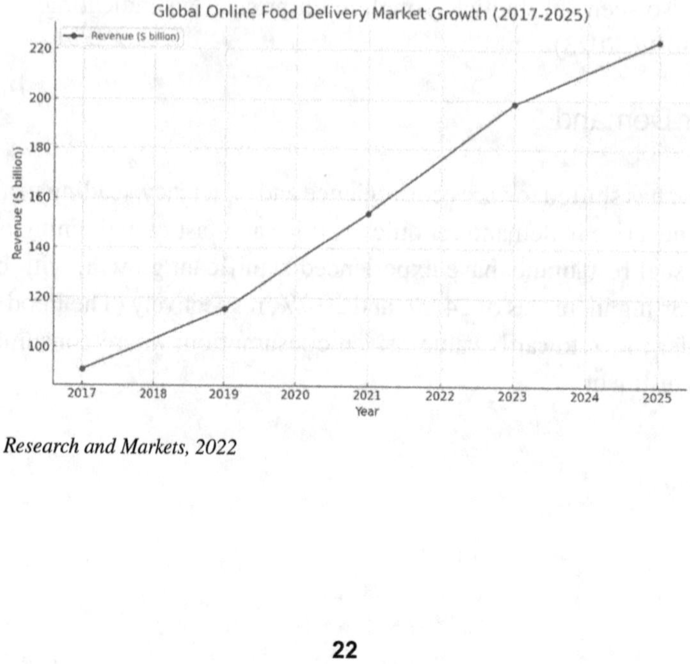

Source: *Statista, 2023; Research and Markets, 2022*

Technology Adoption in Restaurants (2023)

The adoption rates of key technologies in the restaurant industry in 2023. Mobile ordering systems lead with a 73% adoption rate, followed by contactless payment solutions at 68%. Digital loyalty programs and AI chatbots have also gained traction with adoption rates of 45% and 35%, respectively as shown in Figure 2. These technologies enhance customer experience, streamline operations, and improve efficiency, demonstrating the pivotal role of digitalization in restaurant management (National Restaurant Association, 2023; Sharma, 2021).

Figure 2. Adoption Rates of Technology

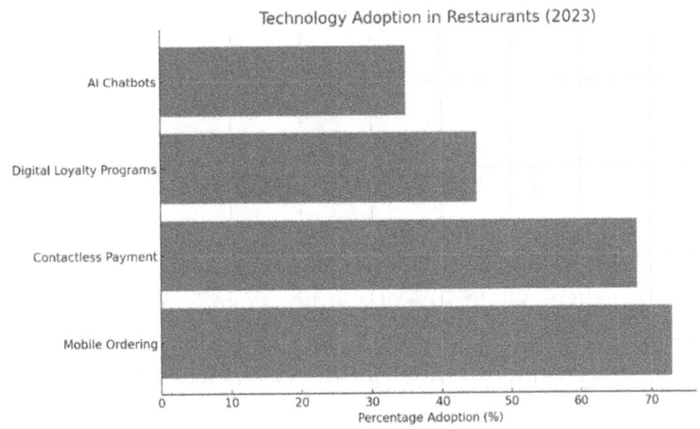

Source: *National Restaurant Association, 2023; Sharma, 2021*

Shift in Dining Preferences (2019-2023)

A significant shift in consumer dining preferences, with dine-in experiences dropping from 60% in 2019 to 30% in 2023, while Figure 3 highlights that food delivery services have risen from 20% to 55% during the same period. This trend reflects the growing demand for convenience and the impact of the pandemic, which reshaped consumer habits toward home-based dining experiences (Deloitte, 2023; Euromonitor International, 2022).

Figure 3. Dine-in Experience Rates

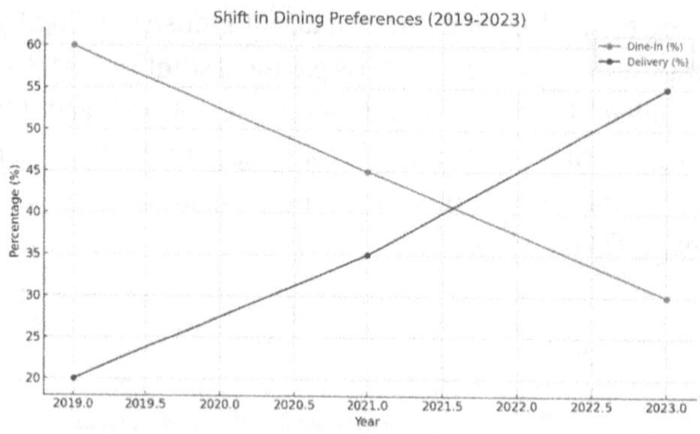

Source: *Deloitte, 2023; Euromonitor International, 2022)*

Consumer Preferences for Ordering Platforms (2023)

Consumer preferences for food ordering platforms in 2023. Third-party apps like Zomato and Swiggy dominate with a 60% market share, while 40% of consumers prefer ordering through restaurant-owned platforms. This distribution underscores the importance of partnerships with aggregators for market reach while highlighting the growing potential for direct engagement through proprietary platforms (KPMG, 2023; Maggo, 2018).

Figure 4. Consumer Preferences for Ordering Platforms

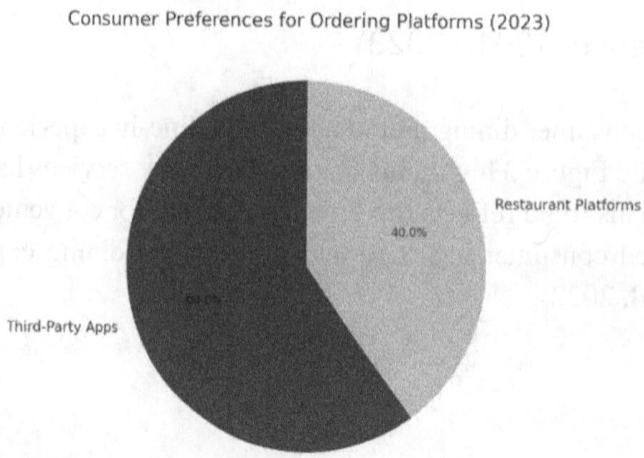

Source: *KPMG, 2023; Maggo, 2018*

Cloud Kitchen Growth in India (2018-2025 Projection)

The exponential growth of cloud kitchens in India, increasing from 3,500 in 2018 to a projected 25,000 by 2025as presented in Figure 4. Factors contributing to this growth include the low operational costs of cloud kitchens, increased consumer reliance on food delivery services, and advancements in technology such as kitchen automation and data analytics. India's rapidly urbanizing population and evolving consumer preferences further amplify this growth (RedSeer, 2022; Sharma, 2021).

Figure 5. Cloud Kitchens Growth in India

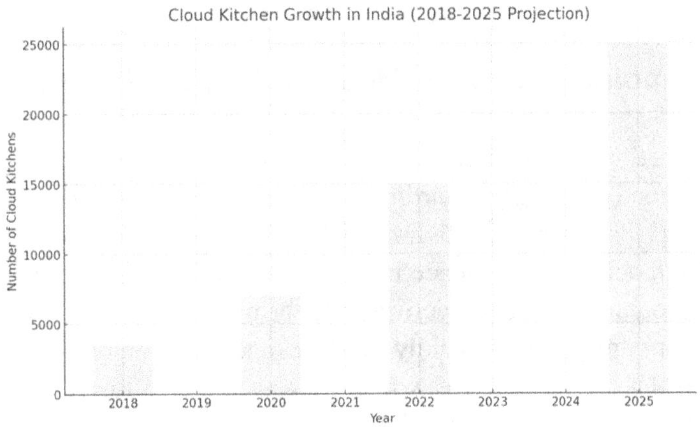

Source: *RedSeer, 2022; Sharma, 2021*

3.3 Role of Technology in Cloud Kitchens

An integrated technological infrastructure is pivotal for the efficient functioning of cloud kitchens (Alim & Khan, 2022). It facilitates the acceptance of online orders, streamlines payment systems, and enables effective monitoring of kitchen operations. Incorporating inventory management systems ensures accurate supply tracking and timely replenishment. Additionally, implementing advanced customer relationship management (CRM) systems helps businesses manage customer orders, preferences, and feedback. This fosters personalized interactions, enhancing customer satisfaction.A crucial component for initiating a cloud kitchen is the deployment of a Point of Sale (POS) system. This system must handle orders from multiple channels, such as third-party delivery platforms and proprietary online ordering systems. The POS system should also monitor inventory levels in real time, ensuring the kitchen can meet customer demands without stock shortages. Furthermore, analytics and reporting capabilities are indispensable for operational efficiency and data-driven decision-making (Gupta & Bansal, 2020; Sharma & Kumar, 2021).

Sales data plays an essential role in developing strategies to improve performance (Singh & Patel, 2019). By analyzing consumer behavior trends, businesses can make informed decisions, refine marketing efforts, and target specific customer demographics to boost revenue.While partnerships with online food aggregators are important, creating a proprietary website or mobile application offers additional advantages (Joshi & Singh, 2022). This approach provides cloud kitchens greater control over the ordering process, facilitates direct communication with customers, and enables efficient data collection. Moreover, it supports personalized marketing strategies and enhances brand visibility.Once an order is placed, it is updated in the Kitchen Display System (KDS), allowing staff to access order details and pickup times instantly. This system streamlines workflow, reduces potential delays, and optimizes preparation times, ensuring high levels of accuracy and efficiency (Agarwal & Mehta, 2020). Real-time order tracking ensures seamless coordination between kitchen staff and delivery personnel, improving customer satisfaction and highlighting areas for operational improvement.

4. FINDINGS

4.1 Proposed Technology Adoption Model in Cloud Kitchens

The digital transformation has reshaped many aspects of daily life, making processes faster and more efficient, particularly in food ordering (Demartini et al., 2018). Previously, ordering food required visiting the restaurant or placing a phone order, with limited delivery options restricted to specific cuisines like pizza or Thai food. High delivery costs made in-house delivery services financially unsustainable for most establishments (Doran, 2010). Food delivery platforms revolutionized this model by connecting customers with restaurants through user-friendly interfaces and shared delivery networks. This innovation allowed restaurants to offer delivery services without substantial investments in marketing, technology, or logistics, significantly boosting demand (Klein, 2021). Revenues from platform-to-consumer delivery models have consistently surpassed those of traditional restaurant-to-owner models in recent years.

The Technology Adoption Model for Cloud Kitchens outlines how businesses integrate diverse technologies to stay competitive and meet evolving consumer demands.

1. *Perceived Usefulness (PU):* Technologies like Order Management Systems (OMS), delivery optimization tools, and inventory management systems enhance operational efficiency, minimize errors, and ensure timely deliveries. Data analytics further assists in refining menu offerings and crafting targeted marketing strategies.
2. *Perceived Ease of Use (PEOU):* User-friendly cloud-based POS systems and APIs for delivery platform integration simplify operations, reducing dependence on physical infrastructure. A centralized dashboard consolidates data for seamless management.
3. *Social Influence (SI):* Adoption by leading cloud kitchens and positive consumer feedback encourage others to embrace similar technologies. Social media and reviews amplify these benefits.
4. *Facilitating Conditions (FC):* The affordability of cloud computing solutions and access to expertise (e.g., SaaS providers) make technology adoption viable. Scalable platforms allow businesses to expand without significant reinvestment.
5. *Innovative Culture:* An adaptable culture enables cloud kitchens to respond quickly to market trends, such as introducing new menu items or catering to niche diets like vegan or gluten-free options.
6. *Perceived Risk (PR):* Concerns like data security and system reliability are critical factors. Protecting customer information and ensuring system uptime are necessary for successful technology adoption.

7. *Adoption Decision:* Cloud kitchens evolve from basic systems like POS and delivery integration to advanced tools like AI-driven customer insights and predictive analytics, ultimately achieving comprehensive technological integration.

The proposed technology adoption model shown in Figure 6 highlights the long-term benefits of adopting these technologies including improved operational efficiency, lower labor costs, enhanced customer satisfaction, and scalability, positioning cloud kitchens for sustainable growth and profitability.

Figure 6. Proposed Technology Adoption Model for Cloud Kitchen

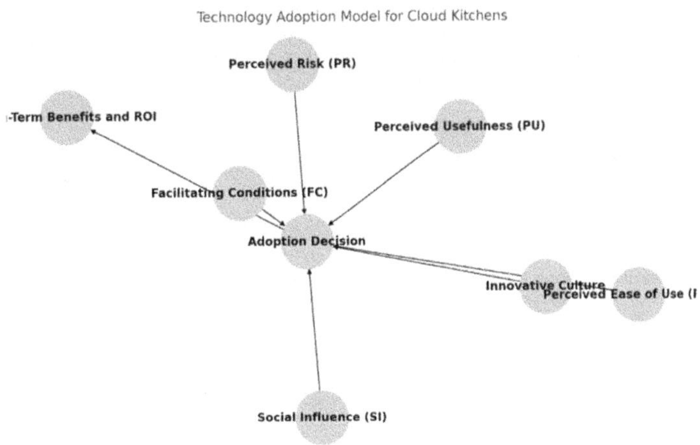

Source: *Authors' Work*

Table 2. Top Cloud Kitchen Brands in India and Their Details

Brand Name	About the Brand	Role of Technology
Rebel Foods	Founded in 2011, Rebel Foods operates multiple virtual kitchen brands like Faasos, Behrouz Biryani, and Oven Story. It is one of the largest cloud kitchen companies in India, with a presence in over 10 countries.	- Uses AI and data analytics for demand forecasting and menu optimization.
		- Implements IoT-enabled kitchens for operational efficiency.
		- Offers an app-based order tracking system for seamless delivery.
Curefoods	Started in 2020 by Ankit Nagori, Curefoods owns brands like EatFit, which focuses on healthy meals and fitness-friendly food options.	- Leverages AI to design healthy menus based on dietary trends.
		- Utilizes cloud-based POS systems for seamless multi-location management.
		- Integrates customer data to provide personalized meal recommendations.

continued on following page

Table 2. Continued

Brand Name	About the Brand	Role of Technology
Box8	A Mumbai-based brand, Box8 delivers Indian fusion food across multiple cities. It emphasizes fresh ingredients and quick service.	- Employs AI-driven logistics for efficient delivery routing.
		- Uses automation for food preparation to ensure consistency.
		- Integrates CRM systems to enhance customer retention and feedback analysis.
Zomato Kitchens	An extension of Zomato, Zomato Kitchens partners with local restaurants to set up cloud kitchens, helping them scale delivery operations.	- Implements machine learning for location scouting and demand analysis.
		- Uses Zomato's robust app and delivery network for order management.
		- Monitors real-time kitchen operations using cloud technology.
Biryani by Kilo	Specializes in delivering freshly cooked biryani in earthen pots, maintaining authenticity and quality.	- Uses GPS tracking for efficient delivery.
		- Employs technology for portion-controlled cooking to minimize food waste.
		- Data analytics for tracking customer preferences and regional tastes.
FreshMenu	Founded in 2014, FreshMenu offers gourmet meals designed for single servings, focusing on variety and freshness.	- Implements advanced online ordering systems and mobile apps.
		- Utilizes cloud kitchens for a hyper-local delivery model.
		- Uses customer data for targeted promotions and personalized menu suggestions.
Oven Story	A Rebel Foods sub-brand, Oven Story focuses on pizza delivery with innovative toppings and customization options.	- Uses automated inventory management to track ingredient availability.
		- Leverages AI for analyzing pizza preferences and sales patterns.
		- Ensures consistent quality with standardized processes.

Source: Authors' Work

4.2 SWOT Analysis of Cloud Kitchens in India and Their Technology Adoption with Special Focus on Artificial Intelligence (AI)

Cloud kitchens in India have emerged as a cost-effective and scalable business model, leveraging technology to streamline operations and improve customer experiences. One of their primary strengths lies in their ability to minimize costs by eliminating expenses related to high-cost real estate and front-of-house staff. AI-powered tools further enhance these savings by optimizing demand forecasting, ensuring efficient ingredient procurement, and reducing food waste. This operational model, combined with AI-driven analytics, also supports rapid scalability, enabling businesses to identify optimal locations for expansion based on customer density, preferences, and delivery times.The adoption of AI has revolutionized customer experience in cloud kitchens. AI algorithms analyze customer behavior to recommend menu items, driving engagement and loyalty through personalized interactions. Predictive analytics plays a critical role in offering real-time personalization, such as discounts on frequently ordered items, which enhances customer satisfaction and retention. Additionally, AI-enabled kitchen display systems streamline workflows, reduce delays, and optimize preparation times, leading to more efficient kitchen operations.Despite these strengths, the heavy reliance on technology poses a challenge. Disruptions in internet connectivity or technical issues with AI systems can lead to operational setbacks. The initial investment in advanced AI systems, such as inventory management tools and data analytics platforms, can also be prohibitive for smaller operators. Moreover, the lack of face-to-face interaction in the cloud kitchen model can make it difficult to build brand loyalty, with AI-driven communication tools sometimes lacking the human touch. Integrating AI with existing systems and maintaining these technologies add complexity to operations, which may deter some businesses from full-scale adoption.

The growth potential of cloud kitchens in India presents numerous opportunities, particularly with the increasing demand for food delivery services. AI tools can enable businesses to cater to this demand by optimizing delivery routes, ensuring faster and more cost-effective services. Furthermore, AI-driven analytics can help identify underserved customer segments, such as health-conscious or region-specific markets, facilitating the development of niche brands. Marketing efforts are also significantly enhanced by AI, as businesses can leverage customer data to craft targeted campaigns and predict the best times for promotions, maximizing return on investment.

Sustainability is another key area where AI can play a pivotal role. By accurately forecasting demand, AI helps reduce food waste and promotes eco-friendly practices, such as sustainable packaging. Collaborative efforts with AI-focused SaaS providers and the integration of IoT devices, like smart refrigerators, further streamline inventory management and quality control.

However, cloud kitchens face threats in the form of intense competition, with dominant players like Rebel Foods and Zomato Kitchens leveraging similar AI technologies, reducing differentiation. Data privacy and security concerns also pose significant risks, as AI systems require vast amounts of customer data. A data breach could damage a brand's reputation and lead to legal repercussions. Additionally, evolving regulations around food safety, data privacy, and technology adoption may create compliance challenges. Customers' potential skepticism about AI-driven personalization, viewing it as intrusive, can also hinder its effectiveness.AI addresses many of these challenges while enhancing growth opportunities. Demand prediction tools powered by AI can help businesses forecast peak periods, reducing downtime and over-preparation. Sentiment analysis of customer feedback allows businesses to improve service quality and reduce churn. Dynamic pricing algorithms adjust rates based on market trends, balancing affordability with profitability. AI also plays a significant role in supply chain optimization, enabling just-in-time inventory management to minimize spoilage and costs. Advanced technologies like image recognition ensure real-time quality control during food preparation and packaging, while fraud detection algorithms protect against anomalies in payment and order patterns.

5. CONCLUSION

In conclusion, the adoption of AI in Indian cloud kitchens offers immense potential to transform the industry by enhancing efficiency, personalizing customer experiences, and enabling data-driven decision-making. However, challenges such as implementation costs, data privacy concerns, and market saturation must be addressed strategically. By leveraging AI to overcome these challenges and capitalize on emerging opportunities, cloud kitchens can achieve sustainable growth and maintain a competitive edge in the fast-growing Indian food delivery market.

6. LIMITATION AND FUTURE RESEARCH SCOPE

The chapter proposed a technology adoption model (TAM) model and strengths, weakness, opportunities, and threat (SWOT) analysis from an AI point of view, further research could be conducted from operational cost and customer reference as well. The chapter research method is based on secondary descriptive data. The scope of the chapter could be enhanced with empirical data.

REFERENCES

Agarwal, S., & Mehta, T. (2020). Enhancing workflow efficiency with kitchen display systems. *Technology in Hospitality Operations*, *7*(1), 12–22.

Alim, M., & Khan, F. (2022). Efficient operations in cloud kitchens through integrated technologies. *Journal of Hospitality and Tourism Technology*, *13*(4), 357–374.

Cheng, C.-C., Tsai, M.-C., Chang, Y.-Y., & Chen, C.-T. (2024). Identifying services barriers and risks in cloud kitchens: Insights from a novel risk assessment model. *International Journal of Hospitality Management*, *124*, 103996. DOI: 10.1016/j.ijhm.2024.103996

Deloitte. (2023). *Future of food delivery: Trends and insights shaping the industry.* Retrieved from https://www.deloitte.com

Deloitte India. (2021). *Technology in the food service sector: The rise of cloud kitchens.* Retrieved from https://www.deloitte.com

Demartini, M.. (2018). The digital shift in food ordering: Challenges and opportunities. *Journal of Digital Transformation*, *5*(3), 45–60.

Digital Directions. (2023). *8 key trends in digital transformation for restaurants.* Retrieved from https://www.digitaldirections.com

Doran, T. (2010). Challenges of in-house delivery systems in traditional restaurants. *Restaurant Management Review*, *6*(4), 33–48.

Economic Times. (2021). *How AI is revolutionizing food delivery in India.* Retrieved from https://www.economictimes.com

Euromonitor International. (2022). *Food delivery market trends: An analysis of the evolving consumer landscape.* Retrieved from https://www.euromonitor.com

Global, F. I. S. (2022). *Top consumer trends in the restaurant industry.* Retrieved from https://www.fisglobal.com

Guo, Y. (2025). Successful stories on the usage of technologies in service industries. In Global, I. G. I. (Ed.), *International Journal of Hospitality Management* (pp. 197–210). IGI Global., DOI: 10.4018/979-8-3693-7683-6.ch010

Gupta, R., & Bansal, S. (2020). Technological advancements in the food delivery industry: Trends and implications. *International Journal of Food and Beverage Research*, *9*(2), 103–117.

Joshi, A., & Singh, M. (2022). Strategic marketing through proprietary platforms in cloud kitchens. *International Marketing Review*, *39*(6), 980–996.

Kapoor, R., Aggarwal, S., & Singh, P. (2020). Impact of AI on restaurant operations: A study on cloud kitchens. *International Journal of Hospitality Management*, *45*(3), 112–125.

Klein, S. (2021). The economic impact of food delivery platforms: A global perspective. *Economic Analysis and Policy*, *51*(1), 89–104.

KPMG. (2023). *Restaurant industry insights: Navigating challenges and opportunities in 2023.* Retrieved from https://www.kpmg.com

Maggo, P. (2018). *Emerging Business Models in the Indian Cloud Kitchen Industry.*

Maggo, S. (2018). Cloud kitchens: Revolutionizing food delivery through innovation. *Journal of Food Industry Trends, 12*(4), 45–60.

MarketsandMarkets. (2022). *Kitchen automation market trends and forecast to 2030.* Retrieved from https://www.marketsandmarkets.com

National Restaurant Association. (2023). *State of the restaurant industry report: Key trends and outlook for 2023.* Retrieved from https://www.restaurant.org

National Restaurant Association. (2024). *State of the industry report.* Retrieved from https://www.restaurant.org

PwC India. (2020). *The role of artificial intelligence in transforming the restaurant industry.* Retrieved from https://www.pwc.in

RedSeer Consulting. (2022). *Indian cloud kitchen market report: Growth drivers and future outlook.* Retrieved from https://www.redseer.com

Research and Markets. (2022). *Global online food delivery market analysis: Key trends and forecasts.* Retrieved from https://www.researchandmarkets.com

Shafer, S. M., Smith, H. J., & Linder, J. C. (2005). The power of business models. *Business Horizons, 48*(3), 199–207. DOI: 10.1016/j.bushor.2004.10.014

Sharda, R. (2022). Scalability challenges in the restaurant industry: Lessons from emerging markets. *Hospitality Business Journal, 18*(2), 134–148.

Sharma, A. (2021). *Operational Strategies in Cloud Kitchens: A Case Study Approach.*

Sharma, P. (2021). Technology and trends in cloud kitchens: A comprehensive review. *Hospitality and Food Service Review, 8*(2), 78–95.

Sharma, P., & Kumar, A. (2021). Role of data analytics in optimizing cloud kitchen operations. *Big Data Applications in Hospitality Management, 14*(3), 45–59.

Singh, V., & Patel, R. (2019). Consumer behavior trends in online food delivery: A review. *Journal of Consumer Behavior Research, 11*(2), 225–239.

Statista. (2023). *Digitalization of the restaurant industry worldwide: Statistics & facts.* Retrieved from https://www.statista.com

Statista. (2023). *Online food delivery revenue worldwide: 2023 report and statistics.* Retrieved from https://www.statista.com

The Food Institute. (2023). *The future of restaurants: Data and insights for 2024 and beyond.* Retrieved from https://www.foodinstitute.com

Tualeka, S. H. (2024). Multi-Brand Virtual Restaurant: Cloud Kitchen Business Model (Case Study of PT. Sagala). *Management Studies and Entrepreneurship Journal*, *5*(2), 4921–4931.

Velt, M. J., Fielt, E., & Curry, E. (2018). The evolving nature of business models: Toward a framework for business model dynamics. *Journal of Business Research*.

Chapter 3
Data Privacy and Security in AI-Driven Ghost Kitchens

Sandip Dey
https://orcid.org/0000-0002-1005-3304
Sukanta Mahavidyalaya, Dhupguri, India

ABSTRACT

This study examines the critical link between data protection and security in AI-powered ghost kitchens, highlighting their transformative impact on food industry operations. It introduces ghost kitchens, explores AI's role in enhancing efficiency, consumer satisfaction, and profitability, and evaluates strategies for operational improvement. The research addresses key challenges, including data collection practices, privacy risks, regulatory compliance, and AI system vulnerabilities. Case studies of real-world breaches provide valuable insights into their consequences. The study emphasizes effective solutions, such as privacy-by-design principles, secure AI development, and workforce training, to safeguard sensitive data. It also discusses ethical dilemmas, balancing innovation with privacy, and future trends in data protection technologies. Ultimately, this research offers actionable guidance for stakeholders to ensure robust security and privacy in the evolving AI-driven ghost kitchen landscape.

1. INTRODUCTION

1.1 Overview of Ghost Kitchens

Ghost kitchens commonly known as cloud kitchens represent food preparation facilities that provide delivery services exclusively from kitchen spaces (Chhabra & Rana, 2021). The delivery-only focus of these kitchens distinguishes them from conventional restaurant operations (Kumar et al., 2023). Orders at ghost kitchens originate from digital platforms through app and website interfaces that link customers directly with kitchen operations (Bhatti & Alawad, 2024).

The surge in food delivery has propelled the fast expansion of ghost kitchens in recent times. The rapid growth of these kitchens can be attributed to consumer preference for dining through apps such as Uber Eats, Zomato and Swiggy (John, 2023). The truncated layout of ghost kitchens permits better financial efficiency through reduced operations expenses and staffing requirements.

DOI: 10.4018/979-8-3373-0432-8.ch003

Ghost kitchens benefit from artificial intelligence which optimizes distribution routes and makes accurate demand forecasts while managing inventory effectively (Bhatti & Alawad, 2024). Data collection through matrices enhances operational processes yet creates security and privacy threats that affect management systems (Chhabra & Rana, 2021). Operational ghost kitchens remain innovative solution provider organizations take proper steps to defend consumer information alongside business-related insights.

1.2 Role of AI in Transforming the Ghost Kitchen Industry

Artificial Intelligence is radically transforming the operational model of ghost kitchens. The delivery-only food enterprise known as a ghost kitchen operates by using artificial intelligence to drive operational effectiveness and deliver services that match customer needs. Through automation AI enables the handling of important operations encompassing order administration and inventory control while enhancing delivery systems. AI systems powered by artificial intelligence technology predict market patterns to let kitchens manufacture proper food quantities while lowering waste (Adak et al., 2022).

Artificial Intelligence technologies such as robotics and automated systems are reshaping how food gets prepared throughout ghost kitchens. Robotics systems perform repetitive kitchen activities including blending raw materials and preparing cooked dishes because they provide dependable processes at higher speeds (Sachani et al., 2021). Disadvantageously exploiting artificial intelligence systems poses difficulties to data safeguarding protocols. Sensitive customers data together with order records and payment information should be always secured to protect against unauthorized access. The protection of data remains essential to both safeguard customer trust levels and satisfy data protection legal requirements (Alhitmi et al, 2024). AI transforms ghost kitchens but businesses need to protect data security and privacy across its implementation.

1.3 Objectives and Scope of the Study

The primary aim of this research investigates the data security and privacy implications that occur within AI-controlled ghost kitchen systems. The research investigates the information management functions of AI systems in these kitchens. Along with personal data risks the study explores cybersecurity challenges that ghost kitchens face. The study intends to develop operational efficiency-enhanced data security and privacy enhancement frameworks as its proposed subsequent actions (Aslam et al., 2024).

AI systems in ghost kitchens gather three types of data including customer information alongside order histories and payment transaction records Security researchers assess how AI algorithms plus data storage infrastructure represents entry points for attackers. The study investigates both the rules provided by GDPR and CCPA that affect ghost kitchens and the steps required to maintain compliance (Elliott & Soifer 2022). The research examines preventive measures to support stakeholders operating kitchen facilities together with policymakers who need to establish ethical AI practices.

2. UNDERSTANDING AI IN GHOST KITCHENS

2.1 Key AI Technologies Used in Ghost Kitchens

Ghost kitchens operate exclusively as delivery-point facilities which use virtual cooking spaces to deliver service. dead-end models combine sophisticated Artificial Intelligence systems which optimize operational effectiveness and decrease expenses while bolstering client happiness. Below you will find a simple explanation of the core AI technologies employed in ghost kitchens.

2.1.1. AI-Powered Order Management

Through Artificial Intelligence ghost kitchens achieve optimized order processing capability. The smart systems in operations organize multiple orders together to minimize operational costs together with operational time. Through AI processing Uber Eats and DoorDash identify customer demands and dispatch them to nearby kitchens. By monitoring popular meal choices AI assists kitchens in planning what to manufacture ahead of working hours (Oh, 2019).

2.1.2. AI for Menu Optimization

Digital analysis programs evaluate customer purchasing patterns across multiple parameters. The analysis aids ghost kitchens in developing menus that attract customers. AI software helps restaurants determine which dishes to remove from their menus because they do not sell well while it advises them to add on-trend items. Artificial intelligence assists in creating temporary food specials that customers can find on certain restaurant times (Azzimani et al., 2022).

2.1.3. AI in Supply Chain Management

Monitoring systems powered by artificial intelligence discover product counts in stock to generate expiration timings for ingredients. The system helps organizations save costs while minimizing product loss. The artificial intelligence platform Blue Yonder uses historical data to advise what times offer the best supply ordering opportunities. The AI systems manage to perform ingredient quality tests that keep customer meals fresh (Khadem et al., 2023).

2.1.4. AI in Food Preparation

Algorithm-driven robotic devices and technological machines prepare meals while providing both speed and precise results. Miso Robotics created Flippy as a machine that serves two functions by flipping burgers and preparing fries. The implementation of Artificial Intelligence systems both reduces mistakes and increases operational speed in food manufacturing (Fonseca et al., 2019). Due to their programming AI machines execute exact recipes without variations.

2.1.5. AI for Delivery Optimization

AI technology enables restaurants to speed up their delivery process that leads their products to arrive at customers' locations. Through the integration of traffic information with weather data the system selects the most efficient delivery route paths. The AI route optimization tools in DoorDash reduce delivery times by 25% (Kaul & Khurana, 2022).

2.1.6. AI for Predicting Demand

Existing predictive AI systems analyze usage patterns to identify maximum usage periods that encompass both weekend days and major vacation times. After implementation AI systems allow ghost kitchens to design efficient production scheduling along with proper workforce management. Based on local market trends AI systems make predictions about which menu items will become popular in designated areas (Narashimman et al., 2024).

2.1.7. AI Chatbots for Customer Support

These AI chatbots can resolve customer issues at any hour of day including nighttime hours. The system notifies customers about their delivery status along with shipping timeframe predictions. The delivery platform management system currently uses AI assistant technology such as ChatGPT to handle customer interactions (Raghavan & Vijayabanu, 2023).

Through AI implementations ghost kitchens achieve enhanced operational effectiveness while driving down operational expenses. The entire business operations receive support from Artificial Intelligence which manages orders while making demand predictions. With these tools ghost kitchens work more efficiently to serve customers both quickly and deliver superior food quality for sustained customer satisfaction.

A summary of AI Technologies and their roles in Ghost Kitchens is described in Table I.

Table 1. Overview of AI Technologies and Their Roles in Ghost Kitchens

AI Technology	Application in Ghost Kitchens	Key Benefits
Machine Learning (ML)	To predict customer demand & optimize menus	Food waste reduces, profitability improves
Computer Vision	To monitor food preparation and quality assurance	Enhances consistency, ensures food safety
Natural Language Processing (NLP)	To enable voice-based ordering, and also customer service automation	Customer satisfaction increases
Predictive Analytics	To manage inventory and supply chain	Prevents stockouts, overstocking decreases
Robotics and Automation	Automating repetitive kitchen tasks	Efficiency increases, labour costs reduces

2.2 Data Collection and Analysis in AI-Driven Kitchens

The collection and analysis of data by AI-driven kitchens produces improved food prep outcomes and enhanced delivery systems and customer satisfaction results. The data collection process starts through collecting information from diverse sources including customer orders with inventory levels and data about kitchen equipment and expected delivery times. Sensors working together with intelligent cameras track data using cameras backed up by smart devices (Sharma et al., 2024).

2.2.1 Data Collection in AI Kitchens

Ghost kitchen smart systems use data collection to track customer preferences. Internet ordering websites track what customers choose to eat along with how often they order and what comments they provide. By using this data kitchens can reformulate their menus and adapt their service offerings.

Kitchen facility sensors evaluate food storage conditions to protect food safety by tracking temperature and humid conditions. Smart inventory systems function by continuously monitoring ingredient levels and sending alerts to staff about depleted stocks or about approaching expiration dates (Perera, 2024).

2.2.2 Data Analysis for Better Decisions

Computational intelligence systems reading the data sets perform predictions that lead to decision-making processes. Compiling historical data using machine learning helps produce predictions about restaurant traffic times and customer choicest food items. By applying predictive analysis foodservice companies optimize production quantities thus minimizing waste along with cost reduction (Mavani et al., 2022).

AI assessment of delivery patterns together with route planning systems delivers valuable insights. The system guarantees food reaches customers promptly with maintained freshness. Through their analytical capability algorithms enable businesses to recommend more efficient delivery routes when the customer footfall remains high (Saygıner, 2024).

2.2.3 Improving Customer Experience

Customer feedback analysis occupies a central position in improving service quality. The NLP tools currently sort through reviews to determine which ones have complaints or suggestions. Kitchens leverage this gathered information to both enhance food quality standards as well as modify menu content (Adak et al., 2022).

2.2.4 Benefits of Data in AI-Driven Kitchens

The analysis of collected data enables ghost kitchens to function with greater efficiency. These solutions decrease expenses while lowering waste and leading to increased customer satisfaction rates. Kinetic tracking allows kitchens to make better operational choices and transform their products and services for evolving customer requirements (Saygıner, 2024).

2.3 Benefits of AI Implementation in Ghost Kitchens

The rapid and efficient operation of ghost kitchens becomes possible through artificial intelligence applications. AI-powered systems generate exact forecasts about what customers will order by analyzing historical information along with patterns of customer behavior. Predictive analytics help kitchens minimize food waste while enabling more efficient planning that produces financial cost savings. Once automated ingredient tracking systems detect essential ingredient thresholds supply prevention protocols become active (Albayrak et al, 2023). Automation of staff scheduling generates peak demand efficiency by improving operational efficiency and reducing costs (Wouters & De Stefano, 2022). Through artificial intelligence-controlled robotic fryers operators deliver exact food preparation outputs that satisfy quality standards each time (Hjalager, 2022).

3. DATA PRIVACY CONCERNS IN AI-DRIVEN GHOST KITCHENS

3.1 Types of Data Collected in Ghost Kitchens

Ghost kitchens utilize collected data as a tool to enhance business operations and deliver better customer satisfaction. The collection of customer data during online transactions allows Ghost kitchens to deliver personal service because it contains names and delivery addresses along with food preferences (Chandrasekhar et al., 2019). The tracking system enables organizations to adjust their menu selection and promotional offers. Order frequency data in sales records combined with peak demand patterns helps determine menu modifications. The tracking system for operations ensures efficiency by monitoring the preparation and delivery phases. Inventory monitoring prevents shortages (John, 2023). Rankings and customer reviews from clients serve as tools to improve both the quality of food and dining service. Location data enables companies to discover best expansion locations and establish better delivery routing networks (Seghezzi & Mangiaracina, 2021). The combination of data insights improves ghost kitchen operations and customer satisfaction.

3.2 Risks Associated with Personal Data Misuse

The increasing use of AI in ghost kitchens presents new risks to the protection of personal data privacy. Ghost kitchens depend on accumulated customer information to deliver orders and build better services for upcoming product and delivery demands. Security protocols remain absent which allows unethical parties to steal personal data for conducting identity theft while also executing financial fraud schemes (Alqudhaibi et al., 2024). The transfer of private data without permission results in violations of privacy rights (Renuka et al., 2025). Marketing functions with AI create illegal customer profiles without receiving user consent as reported by Gao et al. (2023). Organizational protections that fall short of expectations create customer trust breakdowns until the customer completely discontinues their relationship with the organization. Data breaches result in negative impacts on business reputations and revenue-related monetary losses for operations. Businesses can evade legal consequences and protect customer trust through GDPR or CCPA compliance as well as data security measures and honest customer communication practices (Spalević & Vićentijević, 2022).

3.3 Privacy Challenges with AI Algorithms

The use of AI-driven algorithms in ghost kitchens creates major privacy risks that affect system operations. The kitchens implement AI technology to manage orders while using analytics and optimization systems which operate through data collection of customer identification details including names and payment and address information. The improper protection of data through weak security systems leads to information breaches which make customers reluctant to share their details (Tsang et al., 2021). The protection of customer data needs full transparency to establish trust (Morey et al., 2015).

AI technology monitors customer interactions by analyzing sales transactions with additional evaluation of website visits and social media contacts to develop customer preference forecasts which creates problems with privacy and consent rights (Patel, 2024). The practice of sharing user data without consent creates additional concerns for customers.

The regulatory control over AI-driven data usage remains insufficient because GDPR enforcement and other regulations are poorly enforced (Li et al., 2019). Privacy protocols and ethical AI norms help organizations decrease their operational risks (Crockett et al., 2021).

3.4 Regulatory and Compliance Issues

The growing utilization of artificial intelligence within ghost kitchen operations creates regulatory barriers which need to be solved. Privacy issues about data protection stand at the forefront of operational concerns. ADigital infrastructure enables ghost kitchens to gather extensive user information which contains both property identification and dietary choice records. Within Europe the GDPR functions similarly to the CCPA which regulates data protection in California (Albrecht, 2016 and Baruh et al., 2017). By complying with these establishment laws ghost kitchens both protect customer trust and avoid penalties. Another issue is food safety. AI instruments combining sensors and robotics improve food preparation and storage yet operators must meet current food safety rules. AI systems need periodic performance checks to prove their effectiveness at preventing food contamination (Sharma et al., 2024).

Current labor laws face difficulties regarding new regulations from the deployment of artificial intelligence technology systems within employment frameworks. The deployment of AI in ghost kitchens leads to workforce elimination while destroying protected employment rights which face elimination tests. The national government adopts regulations to protect workplace environments with dual areas of concern for driver pay fairness and artificial intelligence workforce impact protection measures (Brynjolfsson & McAfee, 2014). Liability stands alone as a major concern in relation to compliance. Fault incidents involving AI systems including incorrect order shipments and destructive accidents create an unclear split in responsibility between restaurant operators and AI developers together with delivery services (Du & Xie, 2021). Ghost kitchens need established clear contracts and full insurance policies to avoid legal problems. AI compliance issues become preventable when ghost kitchens understand rules so they can safely use AI systems.

A summary of data privacy concerns in AI-Driven Ghost Kitchens is shown in Table 2.

Table 2. Data Privacy Concerns in AI-Driven Ghost Kitchens

Type of Data Collected	Potential Privacy Risk	Mitigation Policies
Customer Personal Information	Unlawful access to names, contact details, payment data	Encrypt and secure authentication approaches
Order History and Preferences	Misuse of behavioural data for unwanted marketing	Limit data retaining, acquire user consent
Employee Data	Breach of sensitive HR data	Role-based access controls, regular audits
IoT and Sensor Data	Explore real-time operational data	Safe communication protocols for connected devices
Analytics Data	Misuse of collected data by third parties	Restrict third-party access, implement NDAs

4. SECURITY CHALLENGES IN AI-DRIVEN GHOST KITCHENS

4.1 Cybersecurity Threats to AI Systems

AI stands vital to ghost kitchen operations. Photoelectric sorting systems powered by AI automation help companies consolidate their ordering processes while tracking storage data (Friedlander & Zoellner, 2020). During operational times AI systems present vulnerabilities that enable attackers to execute cybersecurity attacks. Prior threats pose destructive financial risks which simultaneously aim to break down security infrastructures used by ghost kitchen operations.

4.1.1 Types of Cybersecurity Threats to AI Systems

Data Poisoning

Attackers manipulate learning data available to Artificial Intelligence systems. This is called data poisoning. When hackers introduce misleading sales data to the system it can result in the AI system incorrectly ordering ingredients (Friedlander & Zoellner, 2020). Such data modifications result in resource inefficiencies or dissatisfied customer experiences.

Model Theft

The development expenses for AI models used in ghost kitchens represent an outrageous financial investment. Professional hackers take these models to develop their personal financial earnings (Mahmood et al., 2024). Competitive positions for ghost kitchens decline dramatically when model theft occurs.

Adversarial Attacks

Artificial intelligence systems face security threats from adversarial attacks because criminals perform secret tricks throughout these events. During malicious software attacks AI models lose their ability to distinguish genuine delivery requests from fabricated ones leading to the generation of erroneous administrative information. When systems become overloaded actual orders experience prolonged delivery delays (Hoang et al., 2024).

The susceptibility of AI models to adversarial attacks comes from how attackers alter input data using small but detrimental perturbations leading to system failures and misclassification. The implementation of AI-driven ghost kitchens remains vulnerable to adversarial attacks because these attacks affect order predictions and inventory control and autonomous robot management causing financial damage that disrupts operational activities. Adversarial examples created by attackers provide security protocol evasion for fraud detection and automated quality control systems which damages the decision integrity of AI-driven systems (Kurakin, Goodfellow, & Bengio, 2018).

Deepfake Fraud

GANs generate counterfeit realistic videos and voice recordings and text-based communication through deepfake fraud to facilitate identity impersonation and fraud (Mirsky & Lee, 2021). AI-powered ghost kitchens face deepfake-based social engineering threats that trick employees along with suppliers into divulging vital business information and monetary credentials. The use of deepfake techniques in customer support robots along with falsified online reviews leads to incorrect client perspectives and negative impacts business standing.

AI System Hacking

Unlawful access to AI models takes place through model inversion or poisoning in addition to unauthorized access of data pipelines and decision-making operations. Attackers who focus on AI-controlled ghost kitchens use their skills to modify order systems while adjusting pricing algorithms and stealing sensitive customer information for monetary benefit. AI system operations' interconnected nature creates substantial cyber intrusion possibilities that require strong encryption systems and constant system monitoring and adversarial training to strengthen security (Carlini et al., 2019).

Phishing Attacks

Online scams allow cyber attackers to breach AI operational systems through phishing attacks. Security risks result from employee actions where deceptive email links make them commit accidental credential disclosure mistakes (Alkhalil et al., 2021).

Ransomware

The computers controlled by artificial intelligence systems become prisoned when hackers deploy ransomware as their method of capture. Security hackers will only end a blockade through monetary ransom payments to affected systems. The difficulty ghost kitchens experience in order processing becomes possible when their AI system lacks proper access (Ferdous et al., 2024).

4.1.2 Impact of Cybersecurity Threats on Ghost Kitchens

Serious difficulties emerge from the cyber security threats that target systems. The lack of operational continuity caused by these threats leads to delivery delays. The exposure of customer information comes with trust loss and damage to corporate reputation (Qian et al., 2023). Systems patched due to attacks and legal battles often result in major financial losses which pose a high risk to operations.

4.1.3 Strategies to Prevent Cybersecurity Threats

Regular System Updates

AI software in ghost kitchens needs continuous system updates. Software updates address and remedy security flaws (Friedlander & Zoellner, 2020).

Employee Training

The workforce needs training to detect phishing messages while identifying irregular behavior (Alkhalil et al., 2021).

Data Encryption

Data encryption should become a standard security measure for all ghost kitchens. The implementation of encryption techniques creates obstacles for hackers to intercept sensitive information (Hoang et al., 2024).

AI Monitoring Tools

Monitoring tools for AI systems enable organizations to notice abnormal behavior which might indicate cyberattacks (Mahmood et al., 2024).

Backup Systems

Backed-up systems should exist for ghost kitchens. Companies experience reduced downtime when attacks happen.

The protection of ghost kitchens' AI systems against cyber threats needs immediate attention. Multiple security threats targeted at operations create harm against data while damaging financial resources. Through effective security protocols ghost kitchens maintain protections for their AI systems while maintaining operational flow.

4.2 Vulnerabilities in Data Storage and Transmission

Data Breaches

Attackers exploit data storage systems to invade sensitive customer data that includes payment information together with personal addresses. Attacks on security systems are more likely when businesses use flimsy passwords combined with outdated software alongside unencrypted data. For example, the Marriott data breach exposed personal data of millions due to poor security (Tariq, 2024).

Unencrypted Data

Data which is sent without encryption enables hackers to both observe the data along with stealing it. The encryption process locks your message inside a protective box which requires the proper key to open it only from the intended recipient. When data remains without its security protection any hacker can easily access it. The expense of encryption keeps many small businesses from implementing it raising their security risks (Hagemann & Hampson, 2015).

Malware Attacks

Systems become vulnerable to malware attacks when users open fake emails or when their software contains security flaws. Such software uses its position within networks to target essential organizational data through theft operations and destructive modification and deletion actions. Guy Goodman reported in 2017 that worldwide business operations were negatively impacted when WannaCry ransomware forced victims to pay ransom to regain access (Goodman, 2015).

Third-Party Risks

Ghost kitchens deliver their food through partner applications alongside their payment processes. Weaker security practices of partnering companies enable hackers to discover ghost kitchen information by attacking those third parties. Target suffered its 2013 breach after cybercriminals targeted one of their third-party suppliers (Jartelius, 2020).

Human Errors

Ghost kitchen employees create security problems by unintentionally revealing sensitive information or by opening dangerous links and choosing inadequate passwords. One minor error by the system will result in full exposure (El-Bably, 2021).

Preventative Measures

- To reduce these risks, ghost kitchens should.
- Use strong encryption for data.
- Regularly update software and systems.
- Train employees on cybersecurity.

Ghost kitchens need to restrict data exposure to outside vendors through control mechanisms for information distribution. With enhanced security measures ghost kitchens defend their information and continue earning loyalty from their customers.

4.3 AI-Specific Security Issues

Data Breaches

Ghost kitchens leverage Artificial Intelligence for controlling their customer orders and delivery systems and maintaining inventory levels. The tools which perform AI functions maintain access to protected information including customer names together with addresses as well as payment details. The data maintained by ghost kitchens remains vulnerable to hacking attacks that create data breaches (Alqudhaibi et al., 2024).

AI Vulnerabilities

Artificial intelligence systems face manipulation due to cyberattacks by enemy inputs. AI systems generate incorrect actions such as faulty order handling because minor alterations in the input data cause algorithm confusion (Bryson & Winfield, 2017).

Insider Threats

There are staff members in ghost kitchens who administer operations alongside running the technology platform. Employee use of AI systems results in data misuse and intentional disruptions when they have system access (Alhanahnah et al., 2016).

Third-Party Risks

The operational structure of most ghost kitchen businesses involves depending on third-party delivery platforms. Ghost kitchens experience increased vulnerability to cyber-attacks from insecure external third-party platforms. A significant threat to ghost kitchen security arises because of inadequate security standards in third-party software systems (Gupta et al., 2020).

IoT Security Issues

Automated cooking systems when integrated with delivery robots serve as components of ghost kitchens. Product failures potentially stemming from hacking insecure Internet of Things (IoT) devices pose a significant operational risk (Roman et al., 2011).

Lack of Encryption

Surface and wireless transmission of unencrypted sensitive data becomes vulnerable to interception when AI systems and IoT devices fail to employ encryption security methods. Security breaches become more likely because of inadequate data protection (Almolhis et al., 2020).

Compliance with Regulations

Ghost kitchens must meet all requirements of privacy regulations including GDPR and CCPA. Failure to comply with regulations leads to fines alongside legal issues and produces risk when AI systems cannot protect customer data (Cheng et al., 2017).

4.4 Case Studies of Data Breaches in Similar Industries

Modern industries depend on digital solutions and online experiences for operations and these situations mirror what ghost kitchens experience currently. The 2021 DoorDash food delivery service data breach released details about 5 million of its users including both delivery staff and clients. Backstage DoorDash suffered the breach after unauthorized third-party entry wherein insecure third-party security protocols remain under scrutiny (Nguyen et al., 2023). During 2020 BigBasket an online grocery platform suffered a data breach that released information belonging to more than 20 million users. Insufficient cloud encryption together with weak database defenses allowed thieves to access names and email addresses and passwords from the hacked system (Hari & Subramanian, 2019). In 2021 Instacart came under cybercriminal attack as criminals transferred customer information to the dark web through unsecured vulnerabilities (Pradeep et al., 2025). All different data breaches uncovered standard security weak points which stem from weak encryption practices along with third-party clearance issues and scant cybersecurity approach. Similar security vulnerabilities impact ghost kitchen operations that factor in consumer information and delivery channels. By using AI to monitor networks and encrypt sensitive information hackers would have less chance to breach data systems going forward.

5. BEST PRACTICES FOR ENSURING DATA PRIVACY AND SECURITY

5.1 Implementing Privacy-by-Design Principles

Privacy-by-design principles need to be integrated by ghost facilities during their initial development stage (Cavoukian, 2011). AI tools should acquire data by addressing essential work processes and following EU cybersecurity standards for data anonymization (Angeliniet al., 2020). Protected storage solutions teamed with worker accessibility limitations provide enhanced privacy standards to operations.

Ghost kitchen operators must be transparent regarding data usage and follow GDPR requirements and also deploy payment encryption to stop data breaches (Hong et al., 2023). AI security surveillance systems together with regular audits ensure compliance requirements stay protected. Data deletion tools that operators provide to their users become essential for building trust between businesses and their clientele. The implemented privacy measures guarantee stronger standards than those requirements for safety and reliability demanded by all stakeholders.

5.2 Secure AI System Development and Deployment

Introduction to Secure AI in Ghost Kitchens

AI security deployment coupled with system development stands essential for ghost kitchens since they need artificial intelligence to handle order direction and restocking and customer relation tasks. Demographic barriers shield customer payment data as well as other sensitive information from hacker theft (Strusani & Houngbonon, 2019). Secure Artificial Intelligence capabilities create continuous operational integrity by stopping disruptions from cyberattacks. When AI systems lack security features ghost kitchens experience both trust damage with customers and economic loss.

Steps for Developing Secure AI Systems

Secure development of AI starts through organization wide implementation of data encryption and solid password controls (Rasmus, 2024). AI system developers need to perform continuous security assessments of their systems because this identifies every existing problem (Bozic & Wotawa, 2021). Accurate reliable data creates a fundamental precondition for model training in AI since it helps avoid both foreseeable errors and wrong decisions (Prince et al., 2024). Ghost kitchens need protection from security threats through combined firewall deployment and sustained system software update commitments.

Challenges and Importance of Secure Deployment

The implementation of AI systems for secure operations faces obstacles which require resolution. Rapid operational speeds at ghost kitchens lead employees to make security assessment shortcuts (Kumar et al., 2021). Security vulnerabilities increase during implementation when essential procedural steps fail to be used. Through their cybersecurity partnership ghost kitchens gain assistance to secure the proper setup and observation of their AI systems (Dhoni & Kumar, 2023). The dedication to security enables ghost kitchens to maintain safe efficient service delivery while safeguarding against threats which benefit both their customers and their business.

5.3 Employee Training and Awareness Programs

The training of AI systems requires proper execution by ghost kitchen employees. The staff must acquire skills to utilize intelligent kitchen equipment together with inventory software and order systems. System operations and troubleshooting training forms a part of the program which leads to reduced errors and improved efficiency (Perdomo et al., 2024). Staff members learn to operate new technologies through video-based training as well as adaptable educational methods.

The implementation of customized training solutions demonstrates that AI systems add value to employee roles since they lead to worker comfort when using AI technology. Employees can dedicate their efforts to customer service after repetitive work tasks disappear due to AI's implementation. About continuous learning with AI-driven training modules helps staff build their skills while staying updated on future developments in technology.

5.4 Collaborative Approaches: Industry Standards and Guidelines

The internal collaboration of ghost kitchens needs to develop unified standards which establish safety protocols and ethical and quality standards of operation. The standards include security measurement systems that contribute to both short-term safety operations and maintain long-term quality standards. Through research and solution provision the International Organization for Standardization (ISO) examines Artificial Intelligence compliance in food safety (ISO, 2023). Through AI automation, food processing reaches higher efficiency and safety levels but the food distribution platforms and robotic kitchen systems require supervision by government authorities (FSA, 2023).AI regulations require successful data management practices. The GDPR protects personal data of customers by utilizing encryption to enable secure AI operations (GDPR, 2021). The partnership between technology industries and ghost kitchen operators enables them to establish ethical norms for artificial intelligence (Smith et al., 2022). AI training together with certification procedures improve both operational performance and system protection measures. Education leaders from industry sectors together with teaching specialists conduct hands-on instruction which leads to safe AI implementation within kitchen environments (Raghavan &

Vijayabanu, 2023). Drafting clear rules and providing education will drive ghost kitchens toward their future development.

6. ETHICAL CONSIDERATIONS AND FUTURE DIRECTIONS

6.1 Ethical Dilemmas in AI-Driven Ghost Kitchens

Ghost kitchens operate exclusively as delivery services since they lack dining facilities. The implementation of artificial intelligence (AI) enables these operations to complete numerous duties. Implementing artificial intelligence technology produces issues related to both discrimination and corrupt pricing structures and unreasonable delivery durations. The fair operation of ghost kitchens needs thorough examination of such concerns.

6.1.1 Labor Displacement

AI technologies operate through ghost kitchens to manage fundamental operational functions such as cooking and food preparation and packaging tasks. The technology eliminates the need for human participation. Automated systems now present the risk of making workers in basic positions become unemployed. Job safety together with fair labor practices remain uncertain because of These situations (Milton, 2024).

6.1.2 Data Privacy Issues

AI systems operating in ghost kitchens record information regarding consumer choices and past orders together with payment methods (Sanchez, 2024). This data remains vulnerable to recipients because of non-security measures. The systems operate with undisclosed data-use practices that harm fairness for customers (Minaam, 2018).

6.1.3 Bias in AI Algorithms

Through predictive algorithms AI tools help users customize their recipes and recommend menus. These automated systems automatically choose preferences which benefit user segments while causing harm to other groups. AI frameworks show limited success in treating dietary requirements equally alongside cultural protocols (Bidyalakshmi, 2024).

AI systems learn from data. An AI system implements biased decisions whenever it processes biased data. When AI systems receive training data that prioritizes specific neighborhoods, they apply delivery preferences to those areas causing delays for other regions. Several customers develop negative feelings when faced with this situation. Research shows delivery app platforms such as UberEats and Deliveroo apply elaborate algorithms to determine courier remuneration and job assignments thus creating work-related anxiety among their personnel (The Guardian, 2025).

6.1.4 Fairness in Pricing

Suppliers use artificial intelligence as a tool for price adjustment through observation of market demand and supply interactions. Unfair pricing may emerge when this system operates. AI detects high demand from one specific zone thus it will likely raise prices in that area. The resultant prices become unaffordable for residents who live there. Research indicates artificial intelligence dynamic pricing in supermarkets triggers price gouging concerns among politicians which threatens consumer welfare (The Times, 2024).

6.1.5 Delivery Prioritization

The software algorithm selects which delivery orders to handle first. AI systems that receive unbalanced programming instructions may pick customers above all others. Due to its programming the system maintains a system where wealthy clients receive immediate service while other clientele must endure extended waits. Using this approach creates unfairness among all customers. Research investigators found substantial inequalities in delivery agent remuneration thus scientists work to build more equal payment schemes (Gupta et al., 2021).

6.1.6 Food Safety Concerns

Food preparation control by AI systems speeds up operations while delivering efficient outputs yet faults in the AI system create security risks to meal safety. Faulty AI-generated temperature constructions result in unsafe unpredictable cooking practices that endanger consumer safety (Qian et al., 2023).

6.1.7 Fair Competition

AI ghost kitchens prepare food speedily at lower costs than standard restaurants. Small businesses suffer from diminished profitability because they lack funds to acquire AI technological systems (Wirtz et al., 2021). The unlevel playing field created by such competition leads to a long-term reduction of customer choices (Milton, 2024).

6.1.8 Environmental Impact

The implementation of Artificial Intelligence in ghost kitchens helps maximize their operational energy efficiency while minimizing all waste outputs. Fast production in ghost kitchens generates both packaging waste and large amounts of energy usage. The pressure to choose between maximizing profits and following sustainable practices builds an ethical problem (Minaam et al., 2018).

6.1.9 Lack of Human Connection

Through AI technology ghost kitchens remove human contact with both chefs and staff members. Circumstances that keep customers from making a personal connection create unreliable trust and unpleasant dining experiences (Bidyalakshmi et al., 2024).

6.2 Balancing Innovation with Privacy Concerns

The implementation of AI-driven order management and customer profiling in ghost kitchens causes privacy concerns as per Farayola et al. (2024). The data collection of companies that obtain names and locations with meal preferences stands at risk to legitimate exposure as well as unauthorized disclosure. AI tracking technologies along with facial recognition through delivery services enhance efficiency yet people remain ignorant about their data management process (Akahane et al., 2023).

GDPR and CCPA together with other data protection regulations demand businesses to maintain complete transparency regarding their collection and handling of data (Li et al., 2019). Encryption reduces cyber risks. Customers must have authority to prevent their data from exposure so trust can be built (Rossi, 2018). Safe ghost kitchen operations that serve customers efficiently with security protection emerge from maintaining proper innovation standards that prioritize privacy requirements.

6.3 Future Trends in Data Privacy and Security Technologies

Data privacy and security technologies play an essential role in ghost kitchens which keep growing in importance. The growth of AI technology requires businesses to prioritize protecting customer and business data. Here are some future trends:

6.3.1 AI-Based Threat Detection

Computers detect threats at a rate that exceeds human capability to do so. Machine learning systems enable the detection of abnormal real-time activities (George, 23024). Protection of payment data serves to defend customer information against hackers.

6.3.2 Encryption Technologies

Successful encryption techniques guarantee complete security for sensitive information. The number of organizations implementing end-to-end encryption continues growing so data remains uninterpretable to unauthorized parties (Clark., 2000). The technology enables ghost kitchens to accept online orders from customers while managing all their communication routes.

6.3.3 Zero-Trust Security Models

Companies will start implementing zero-trust protocols as their standard protocol in the upcoming future. Every actor in the system remains untrusted until proven otherwise including staff members. All access verification procedures are designed to prevent unauthorized users from entering the system (Kindervag, 2010).

6.3.4 Blockchain for Data Security

With blockchain technology organizations have an efficient means to protect their store data. Single blocks of data that prevent change operate within the blockchain security model to keep data protected. Blockchain technology could enhance transparent supply chain management and maintain secure purchases at Ghost kitchen facilities (Yaga et al., 2019).

6.3.5 Privacy-Preserving AI

The forthcoming generation of Artificial Intelligence systems puts privacy needs first. The system executes information processing without disclosing sensitive data to protect customer privacy and enhance service delivery capabilities (Kaissis et al., 2020).

Ghost kitchens will achieve business and customer safety through implementation of these technological solutions. The adoption of these technologies will produce trust among customers toward the expanding industry of food delivery services.

An overview of best practices for Data Privacy and Security in Ghost Kitchens is presented in Table 3.

Table 3. Best Practices for Data Privacy and Security in Ghost Kitchens

Practice	Description	Expected Outcome
Privacy-by-Design	To embed privacy measures throughout system development	Data exposure and builds customer trust reduces
Regular Security Audits	To assess vulnerabilities and compliance at periodical manner.	Recognizes and mitigates probable security risks
End-to-End Encryption	To encrypt data during transmission and storage	Avoids unsanctioned data access
Espousing Industry Standards	To follow agendas like GDPR, ISO 27001	Confirms legal acquiescence and uniform security measures
Employee Training and Cognizance	To educate staff on data safety best practices	Decreases risks of human mistake leading to breaches

7. CASE STUDY

Research indicates that Artificial Intelligence (AI) is reshaping the food service industry by providing answers to different industry challenges. The following section presents two concrete examples about AI-based risks together with their corresponding solutions in real-world settings.

7.1 Case Study 1: McDonald's and Dynamic Yield

McDonald's took control of Dynamic Yield an AI platform in 2019 with the purpose of delivering customized drive-thru solutions. With this AI system the staff receive recommendations for menu items that are determined by factors such as time of day and weather conditions and actual restaurant volume. The customized offering resulted in growth of sales figures along with better customer contentment ratings. AI implementation created difficulties because it required substantial technical competency and brought high economic costs to the organization. The company established staff training programs while uniting the new AI technology system with its current operations. The implementation strategy resulted in a seamless transition which brought the maximum potential from the artificial intelligence systems.

7.2 Case Study 2: Rebel Foods and Wobot

India's major cloud kitchen company Rebel Foods struggled to preserve hygiene protocols and safety regulations at each of its branches. As part of risk reduction efforts, they decided to work with Wobot which operates a video analytics system using artificial intelligence. The AI system uses current CCTV cameras as a monitoring platform to make sure employees adhere to sanitary requirements including suitable clothing and proper hand hygiene practices. The deployment produced better hygiene conditions and decreased expenses for manual supervision. The implementation faced obstacles to protect privacy rights of data and to establish skills in operating the new platform among staff members. Data governance at Rebel Foods required strict policies while the company offered full training programs to address these challenges.

The food service industry can leverage AI to control its risks provided that relevant teams conduct substantial planning while investing in equipment and delivering education programs to their workforce.

8. COMPARE AI PRIVACY LAWS IN DIFFERENT REGIONS

The rapid expansion of Artificial Intelligence technology occurs across worldwide locations. National regions throughout the world maintain their own specific regulations to defend privacy information of citizens.

European Union (EU)

Both individuals and personal data receive legal protection through the law so they can exercise control over their information. From August 1 2024 the AI policy guidelines from the EU and WHO will start applying throughout member territories. The new rule defines assessment systems based on four risk levels through which AI systems need to demonstrate compliance according to unacceptable, high, limited, and minimal risk standards. High-risk AI systems must deploy established rules because they serve to protect safety and ensure fair operation (Lim & Oh, 2025; Kathuria et al., 2024).

United States

The United States exists without an AI privacy law established at the federal level. Each state has established individual privacy rules which differ from one another. The California Consumer Privacy Act (CCPA) provides Californian residents with personal data control rights according to California law. Different parameters that regulate AI systems exist between the various states throughout the country (Lim & Oh, 2025; Kathuria et al., 2024).

China

Since November 1, 2021, the Personal Information Protection Law (PIPL) has become effective in China. The Personal Information Protection Law follows GDPR-like principles for protecting personal data. The law specifies detailed requirements about data collection practices and data utilization standards that also apply to AI system operations (Lim & Oh, 2025; Kathuria et al., 2024).

India

Indian authorities continue developing their AI along with data privacy legislation. The National Strategy for Artificial Intelligence reached public release by the government as it centered on responsible Artificial Intelligence practices. As an AI privacy regulation, the Digital Personal Data Protection Act became Indian law during 2023 to safeguard data on AI platforms. The implementation strategies seek a proper equilibrium between innovation together with privacy safeguards (Lim & Oh, 2025; Kathuria et al., 2024).

Global Perspective

Worldwide nations are establishing new legislation which both governs artificial intelligence development while protecting user privacy. Brazil protects personal information through the General Data Protection Law whereas Japan uses the Act on the Protection of Personal Information for the same purpose. AI development platforms need to observe privacy rights of people according to these established laws (Lim & Oh, 2025; Kathuria et al., 2024).

Various regions worldwide have developed their own rules to protect personal data as artificial intelligence enters the market. Acquaintance with individual laws demonstrates essential importance since it leads to advanced global governance and controlled AI implementation.

9. CONCLUSION AND RECOMMENDATIONS

The performance boost together with better service quality and market growth emerges from AI-powered ghost kitchen development. AI system implementations generate critical management problems regarding system security operations and user personal data privacy. Research explains the collected data elements together with security weak points and algorithmic problems while highlighting protective measures which are needed. The business sectors under constant attack through cybersecurity incidents support the immediate need for establishing responsible security protocols. The path to secure data requires that designers adopt privacy-focused work practices and developers must create secure measures that must receive persistent monitoring. Industry-wide standards team up with trained staff to create organizational accountability through resilience development. To establish ethical AI systems businesses, need to base their adoption on privacy protection. Higher levels of data protection occur due to increasing legal requirements when encryption solutions partner with AI safety systems. The advancement of new technology aims to establish electrical research within the framework of present legal guidelines. Every industry stakeholder needs to cooperate for developing secure artificial intelligence solutions. Trust development emerges through successful best practice application and suitable infrastructure deployment and ethical protection safeguards. Ongoing research identifies the requirement for stakeholders to create security standards with privacy protections for sustainable AI-powered ghost kitchens development.

REFERENCES

Adak, A., Pradhan, B., & Shukla, N. (2022). Sentiment analysis of customer reviews of food delivery services using deep learning and explainable artificial intelligence: Systematic review. *Foods, 11*(10), 1500. PMID: 35627070

Adak, A., Pradhan, B., & Shukla, N. (2022). Sentiment analysis of customer reviews of food delivery services using deep learning and explainable artificial intelligence: Systematic review. *Foods, 11*(10), 1500. DOI: 10.3390/foods11101500 PMID: 35627070

Akahane, M., Kanagawa, Y., Takahata, Y., Nakanishi, Y., Akahane, T., & Imamura, T. (2023). Consumer awareness of food defense measures at food delivery service providers and food manufacturers: Web-based consumer survey study. *JMIR Formative Research, 7*(1), e44150. DOI: 10.2196/44150 PMID: 37616047

Albayrak Ünal, Ö., Erkayman, B., & Usanmaz, B. (2023). Applications of artificial intelligence in inventory management: A systematic review of the literature. *Archives of Computational Methods in Engineering, 30*(4), 2605–2625. DOI: 10.1007/s11831-022-09879-5

Albrecht, J. P. (2016). How the GDPR will change the world. *Eur. Data Prot. L. Rev., 2*(3), 287–289. DOI: 10.21552/EDPL/2016/3/4

Alhanahnah, M. J., Jhumka, A., & Alouneh, S. (2016). A multidimension taxonomy of insider threats in cloud computing. *The Computer Journal, 59*(11), 1612–1622. DOI: 10.1093/comjnl/bxw020

Alhitmi, H. K., Mardiah, A., Al-Sulaiti, K. I., & Abbas, J. (2024). Data security and privacy concerns of AI-driven marketing in the context of economics and business field: An exploration into possible solutions. *Cogent Business & Management, 11*(1), 2393743.

Alhitmi, H. K., Mardiah, A., Al-Sulaiti, K. I., & Abbas, J. (2024). Data security and privacy concerns of AI-driven marketing in the context of economics and business field: An exploration into possible solutions. *Cogent Business & Management, 11*(1), 2393743. DOI: 10.1080/23311975.2024.2393743

Alkhalil, Z., Hewage, C., Nawaf, L., & Khan, I. (2021). Phishing attacks: A recent comprehensive study and a new anatomy. *Frontiers of Computer Science, 3*, 563060. DOI: 10.3389/fcomp.2021.563060

Almolhis, N., Alashjaee, A. M., Duraibi, S., Alqahtani, F., & Moussa, A. N. (2020, February). The security issues in IoT-cloud: a review. In *2020 16th IEEE International Colloquium on Signal Processing & Its Applications (CSPA)* (pp. 191-196). IEEE. DOI: 10.1109/CSPA48992.2020.9068693

Alqudhaibi, A., Krishna, A., Jagtap, S., Williams, N., Afy-Shararah, M., & Salonitis, K. (2024). Cybersecurity 4.0: Safeguarding trust and production in the digital food industry era. *Discover Food, 4*(1), 2. DOI: 10.1007/s44187-023-00071-7

Alqudhaibi, A., Krishna, A., Jagtap, S., Williams, N., Afy-Shararah, M., & Salonitis, K. (2024). Cybersecurity 4.0: Safeguarding trust and production in the digital food industry era. *Discover Food, 4*(1), 2. DOI: 10.1007/s44187-023-00071-7

Angelini, M., Ciccotelli, C., Franchina, L., Marchetti-Spaccamela, A., & Querzoni, L. (2020). Italian national framework for cybersecurity and data protection. In *Privacy Technologies and Policy: 8th Annual Privacy Forum, APF 2020, Lisbon, Portugal, October 22–23, 2020* [Springer International Publishing.]. *Proceedings, 8*, 127–142.

Aslam, H. K. W., Aslam, F., Aleem, M., Iqbal, Z., Khalid, S., Firdous, N., Siddique, T., & Ali, M. (2024). AI-driven food safety: transforming food inspection, traceability, and compliance in food industry and regulatory bodies: A mini review. *Food Science & Applied Microbiology Reports, 3*(2), 61–67.

Azzimani, K., Bihri, H., Dahmi, A., Azzouzi, S., & Charaf, M. E. H. (2022, December). An AI based approach for personalized nutrition and food menu planning. In *2022 IEEE 3rd International Conference on Electronics, Control, Optimization and Computer Science (ICECOCS)* (pp. 1-5). IEEE. DOI: 10.1109/ICECOCS55148.2022.9983099

Baruh, L., Secinti, E., & Cemalcilar, Z. (2017). Online privacy concerns and privacy management: A meta-analytical review. *Journal of Communication, 67*(1), 26–53. DOI: 10.1111/jcom.12276

Bhatti, M. A., & Alawad, W. A. (2024). Optimizing Food Delivery Provision Methods: The Role of Technology in Improving Efficiency and Customer Satisfaction. [Social Space]. *Przestrzeń Społeczna, 24*(1), 319–348.

Bidyalakshmi, T., Jyoti, B., Mansuri, S. M., Srivastava, A., Mohapatra, D., Kalnar, Y. B., Narsaiah, K., & Indore, N. (2024). Application of Artificial Intelligence in Food Processing: Current Status and Future Prospects. *Food Engineering Reviews*, •••, 1–28. DOI: 10.1007/s12393-024-09386-2

Bozic, J., & Wotawa, F. (2017). Planning the attack! or how to use ai in security testing. In *Iwaise: First international workshop on artificial intelligence in security* (Vol. 50).

Brynjolfsson, E., & McAfee, A. (2014). *The second machine age: Work, progress, and prosperity in a time of brilliant technologies*. WW Norton & company.

Bryson, J., & Winfield, A. (2017). Standardizing ethical design for artificial intelligence and autonomous systems. *Computer, 50*(5), 116–119. DOI: 10.1109/MC.2017.154

Carlini, N., Liu, C., Erlingsson, Ú., Kos, J., & Song, D. (2019). The secret sharer: Evaluating and testing unintended memorization in neural networks. In *28th USENIX security symposium (USENIX security 19)* (pp. 267-284).

Cavoukian, A. (2021). *Privacy by design: The seven foundational principles*. IAPP Resource Center.

Chandrasekhar, N., Gupta, S., & Nanda, N. (2019). Food delivery services and customer preference: A comparative analysis. *Journal of Foodservice Business Research, 22*(4), 375–386. DOI: 10.1080/15378020.2019.1626208

Cheng, L., Liu, F., & Yao, D. (2017). Enterprise data breach: Causes, challenges, prevention, and future directions. *Wiley Interdisciplinary Reviews. Data Mining and Knowledge Discovery, 7*(5), e1211. DOI: 10.1002/widm.1211

Chhabra, N., & Rana, A. (2021). Rise and the future of cloud kitchens in India: A consumer study. *International Journal of Research in Engineering. Science and Management, 4*(7), 158–165.

Clark, D. (2000). Encryption advances to meet Internet challenges. *Computer*, *33*(08), 20–24.

Crockett, K., Colyer, E., Gerber, L., & Latham, A. (2021). Building trustworthy AI solutions: A case for practical solutions for small businesses. *IEEE Transactions on Artificial Intelligence*, *4*(4), 778–791. DOI: 10.1109/TAI.2021.3137091

Dhoni, P., & Kumar, R. (2023). Synergizing generative ai and cybersecurity: Roles of generative ai entities, companies, agencies, and government in enhancing cybersecurity. *Authorea Preprints*.

Du, S., & Xie, C. (2021). Paradoxes of artificial intelligence in consumer markets: Ethical challenges and opportunities. *Journal of Business Research*, *129*, 961–974. DOI: 10.1016/j.jbusres.2020.08.024

El-Bably, A. Y. (2021). Overview of the impact of human error on cybersecurity based on ISO/IEC 27001 information security management. *Journal of Information Security and Cybercrimes Research*, *4*(1), 95–102. DOI: 10.26735/WLPW6121

Elliott, D., & Soifer, E. (2022). AI technologies, privacy, and security. *Frontiers in Artificial Intelligence*, *5*, 826737. DOI: 10.3389/frai.2022.826737 PMID: 35493613

Farayola, O. A., Olorunfemi, O. L., & Shoetan, P. O. (2024). Data privacy and security in it: A review of techniques and challenges. *Computer Science & IT Research Journal*, *5*(3), 606–615. DOI: 10.51594/csitrj.v5i3.909

Ferdous, J., Islam, R., Mahboubi, A., & Islam, M. Z. (2024). AI-based ransomware detection: A comprehensive review. *IEEE Access : Practical Innovations, Open Solutions*, *12*, 136666–136695. DOI: 10.1109/ACCESS.2024.3461965

Fonseca, E., Oliveira, I., Lobo, J., Mota, T., Martins, J., & Au-Yong-Oliveira, M. (2019). Kitchen robots: The importance and impact of technology on people's quality of life. In *New Knowledge in Information Systems and Technologies* (Vol. 2, pp. 186–197). Springer International Publishing. DOI: 10.1007/978-3-030-16184-2_19

Food Standards Agency (FSA). (2023). Regulating AI in Food Services. www.food.gov.uk [Accessed on 1st January, 2025]

Friedlander, A., & Zoellner, C. (2020). Artificial intelligence opportunities to improve food safety at retail. *Food Protection Trends*, *40*(4).

Gao, B., Wang, Y., Xie, H., Hu, Y., & Hu, Y. (2023). Artificial intelligence in advertising: Advancements, challenges, and ethical considerations in targeting, personalization, content creation, and ad optimization. *SAGE Open*, *13*(4), 21582440231210759. DOI: 10.1177/21582440231210759

GDPR. (2021). Data Protection in AI Applications. www.gdpr-info.eu [Accessed on 1st January, 2025]

George, A. S. (2024). Emerging Trends in AI-Driven Cybersecurity: An In-Depth Analysis. *Partners Universal Innovative Research Publication*, *2*(4), 15–28.

Goodman, M. (2015). *Future crimes: Inside the digital underground and the battle for our connected world*. Random House.

Gupta, A., Yadav, R., Nair, A., Chakraborty, A., Ranu, S., & Bagchi, A. (2022, June). Fairfoody: Bringing in fairness in food delivery. *Proceedings of the AAAI Conference on Artificial Intelligence*, *36*(11), 11900–11907. DOI: 10.1609/aaai.v36i11.21447 PMID: 36312212

Gupta, M., Abdelsalam, M., Khorsandroo, S., & Mittal, S. (2020). Security and privacy in smart farming: Challenges and opportunities. *IEEE Access : Practical Innovations, Open Solutions*, *8*, 34564–34584. DOI: 10.1109/ACCESS.2020.2975142

Hagemann, R., & Hampson, J. (2015). Encryption, Trust, and the Online Economy. *no, 3*, 1-27.

Hari, T. N., & Subramanian, M. S. (2019). *Saying no to jugaad: The making of Bigbasket*. Bloomsbury Publishing.

Hjalager, A. M. (2022). Digital food and the innovation of gastronomic tourism. *Gastronomy and Tourism*, *7*(1), 35–49. DOI: 10.3727/216929722X16354101932186

Hoang, V. T., Ergu, Y. A., Nguyen, V. L., & Chang, R. G. (2024). Security risks and countermeasures of adversarial attacks on AI-driven applications in 6G networks: A survey. *Journal of Network and Computer Applications*, *232*, 104031. DOI: 10.1016/j.jnca.2024.104031

Hong, K. S., Chi, Y. P., Chao, L. R., & Tang, J. H. (2003). An integrated system theory of information security management. *Information Management & Computer Security*, *11*(5), 243–248. DOI: 10.1108/09685220310500153

ISO. (2023). AI Standards and Guidelines. www.iso.org [Accessed on 1st January, 2025]

Jartelius, M. (2020). The 2020 Data Breach Investigations Report–a CSO's perspective. *Network Security*, *2020*(7), 9–12. DOI: 10.1016/S1353-4858(20)30079-9

John, K. T. (2023). Digital disruption: The hyperlocal delivery and cloud kitchen driven future of food services in post-COVID India. *International Hospitality Review*, *37*(1), 161–187. DOI: 10.1108/IHR-06-2021-0045

John, K. T. (2023). Digital disruption: The hyperlocal delivery and cloud kitchen driven future of food services in post-COVID India. *International Hospitality Review*, *37*(1), 161–187. DOI: 10.1108/IHR-06-2021-0045

Kaissis, G. A., Makowski, M. R., Rückert, D., & Braren, R. F. (2020). Secure, privacy-preserving and federated machine learning in medical imaging. *Nature Machine Intelligence*, *2*(6), 305–311. DOI: 10.1038/s42256-020-0186-1

Kathuria, Y., Ruhani, R., Vandana, V., Tyagi, M., & Jain, V. (2024, October). Protecting data privacy in the age of AI: A comparative analysis of legal approaches across different jurisdictions. In AIP Conference Proceedings (Vol. 3220, No. 1). AIP Publishing. DOI: 10.1063/5.0234669

Kaul, D., & Khurana, R. (2022). Ai-driven optimization models for e-commerce supply chain operations: Demand prediction, inventory management, and delivery time reduction with cost efficiency considerations. *International Journal of Stochastic Analysis*, *7*(12), 59–77.

Khadem, M., Khadem, A., & Khadem, S. (2023). Application of artificial intelligence in supply chain revolutionizing efficiency and optimization. *International journal of industrial engineering and operational research, 5*(1), 29-38.

Kindervag, J. (2010). Build security into your network's dna: The zero trust network architecture. *Forrester Research Inc, 27*, 1–16.

Kurakin, A., Goodfellow, I. J., & Bengio, S. (2018). Adversarial examples in the physical world. In *Artificial intelligence safety and security* (pp. 99–112). Chapman and Hall/CRC. DOI: 10.1201/9781351251389-8

Li, H., Yu, L., & He, W. (2019). The impact of GDPR on global technology development. *Journal of Global Information Technology Management, 22*(1), 1–6. DOI: 10.1080/1097198X.2019.1569186

Lim, S., & Oh, J. (2025). Navigating Privacy: A Global Comparative Analysis of Data Protection Laws. *IET Information Security, 2025*(1), 5536763. DOI: 10.1049/ise2/5536763

Mahmood, H. S., Abdulqader, D. M., Abdullah, R. M., Rasheed, H., Ismael, Z. N. R., & Sami, T. M. G. (2024). Conducting In-Depth Analysis of AI, IoT, Web Technology, Cloud Computing, and Enterprise Systems Integration for Enhancing Data Security and Governance to Promote Sustainable Business Practices. *Journal of Information Technology and Informatics, 3*(2).

Mavani, N. R., Ali, J. M., Othman, S., Hussain, M. A., Hashim, H., & Rahman, N. A. (2022). Application of artificial intelligence in food industry—A guideline. *Food Engineering Reviews, 14*(1), 134–175. DOI: 10.1007/s12393-021-09290-z

McDonards. (2025) Case Study 1. https://livelytics.ai/how-ai-revolutionizes-customer-experience-in-the-restaurant-industry/[Accessed on 10th February, 2025]

Milton, T. (2024). Artificial Intelligence Transforming Hotel Gastronomy: An In-depth Review of AI-driven Innovations in Menu Design, Food Preparation, and Customer Interaction, with a Focus on Sustainability and Future Trends in the Hospitality Industry. *International Journal for Multidimensional Research Perspectives, 2*(3), 47–61. DOI: 10.61877/ijmrp.v2i3.126

Minaam, D. A. (2018). Smart kitchen: Automated cooker technique using IoT. *International Journal of Electronics and Information Engineering, 9*(1), 1–10.

Mirsky, Y., & Lee, W. (2021). The creation and detection of deepfakes: A survey. *ACM Computing Surveys, 54*(1), 1–41. DOI: 10.1145/3425780

Morey, T., Forbath, T., & Schoop, A. (2015). Customer data: Designing for transparency and trust. *Harvard Business Review, 93*(5), 96–105.

Narashimman, G., Balaji, C., Kumar, K. R., Suresh, M., & Sivaranjani, R. (2024). THE ROLE OF AI IN PREDICTIVE ANALYTICS FOR MARKET TRENDS AND CONSUMER DEMAND. *Jisuanji Jicheng Zhizao Xitong, 29*(1), 180–200.

Nguyen, C., Wearing, J., Elolaimi, K., Prasad, P., Thorat, P., Califano, T., & Daim, T. U. (2023). 2030 Roadmap: Cybersecurity in Food E-Commerce. In *Cybersecurity: A Technology Landscape Analysis* (pp. 167–191). Springer International Publishing. DOI: 10.1007/978-3-031-34843-3_7

Oh, A. S. (2019). Development of a smart supply-chain management solution based on logistics standards utilizing artificial intelligence and the internet of things. *Journal of information and communication convergence engineering, 17*(3), 198-204.

Patel, K. (2024). Ethical reflections on data-centric AI: Balancing benefits and risks. *International Journal of Artificial Intelligence Research and Development, 2*(1), 1–17.

Perdomo Delgado, C., Ripat, J., Mallory-Hill, S., & Bohunicky, S. (2024, June). Using the Technology Acceptance Model to Explore the User Experience of Smart Kitchen Use Among Older Adult Women. In *International Conference on Human-Computer Interaction* (pp. 3-12). Cham: Springer Nature Switzerland. DOI: 10.1007/978-3-031-61356-2_1

Perera, M. (2024). Exploring the role of AI in enhancing sustainability within New Zealand's hospitality industry: A study on knowledge, applicability, and perception in reducing food waste.

Pradeep, A., Gunawan, J., Feal, Á., Hartzog, W., & Choffnes, D. (2025). Gig Work at What Cost? Exploring Privacy Risks of Gig Work Platform Participation in the US. *Proceedings on Privacy Enhancing Technologies.*

Prince, N. U., Faheem, M. A., Khan, O. U., Hossain, K., Alkhayyat, A., Hamdache, A., & Elmouki, I. (2024). AI-Powered Data-Driven Cybersecurity Techniques: Boosting Threat Identification and Reaction. *Nanotechnology Perceptions, 20*, 332–353.

Qian, C., Murphy, S. I., Orsi, R. H., & Wiedmann, M. (2023). How can AI help improve food safety? *Annual Review of Food Science and Technology, 14*(1), 517–538. DOI: 10.1146/annurev-food-060721-013815 PMID: 36542755

Raghavan, A., & Vijayabanu, C. (2023). Breakthrough of Cutting-Edge Technologies Into the Culinary World: Trends and Challenges. *Impactful Technologies Transforming the Food Industry*, 44-62.

Raghavan, A., & Vijayabanu, C. (2023). Breakthrough of Cutting-Edge Technologies Into the Culinary World: Trends and Challenges. *Impactful Technologies Transforming the Food Industry*, 44-62.

Rasmus, K. (2024). Artificial Intelligence Working to Secure Small Enterprises. In *Artificial Intelligence for Security: Enhancing Protection in a Changing World* (pp. 165–188). Springer Nature Switzerland. DOI: 10.1007/978-3-031-57452-8_8

Rebel Foods. (2020) Case Study 2. https://analyticsindiamag.com/ai-features/case-study-how-this-cloud-restaurant-company-deployed-ai-based-hygiene-safety-monitoring-solution-for-their-kitchen/?utm_source=chatgpt.com [Accessed on 10th February, 2025]

Renuka, O., RadhaKrishnan, N., Priya, B. S., Jhansy, A., & Ezekiel, S. (2025). Data Privacy and Protection: Legal and Ethical Challenges. Emerging Threats and Countermeasures in Cybersecurity, 433-465.

Rhahla, M., Allegue, S., & Abdellatif, T. (2021). Guidelines for GDPR compliance in Big Data systems. *Journal of Information Security and Applications, 61*, 102896. DOI: 10.1016/j.jisa.2021.102896

Roman, R., Najera, P., & Lopez, J. (2011). Securing the internet of things. *Computer, 44*(9), 51–58. DOI: 10.1109/MC.2011.291

Rossi, F. (2018). Building trust in artificial intelligence. *Journal of International Affairs*, *72*(1), 127–134.

Sachani, D. K., Dhameliya, N., Mullangi, K., Anumandla, S. K. R., & Vennapusa, S. C. R. (2021). Enhancing food service sales through AI and automation in convenience store kitchens. *Global Disclosure of Economics and Business*, *10*(2), 105–116. DOI: 10.18034/gdeb.v10i2.754

Sanchez, L. E. (2024). Leveraging AI-driven ordering and payment systems for Fast-food restaurant consumers satisfaction in the USA and Mexico.

Saygıner, C. (2024). Factors influencing customer satisfaction and loyalty in Artificial Intelligence (AI)-driven food delivery systems during and post COVID-19. *Business & Management Studies: An International Journal*, *12*(4), 674–692. DOI: 10.15295/bmij.v12i4.2398

Seghezzi, A., & Mangiaracina, R. (2021). On-demand food delivery: Investigating the economic performances. *International Journal of Retail & Distribution Management*, *49*(4), 531–549. DOI: 10.1108/IJRDM-02-2020-0043

Sharma, D., Sharma, M., Sharma, A., Anawade, P., Savariapitchai, M., & Gahane, S. (2024, November). SMART Kitchen Technology. In *2024 2nd DMIHER International Conference on Artificial Intelligence in Healthcare, Education and Industry (IDICAIEI)* (pp. 1-5). IEEE. DOI: 10.1109/IDICAIEI61867.2024.10842745

Sharma, D., Sharma, M., Sharma, A., Anawade, P., Savariapitchai, M., & Gahane, S. (2024, November). SMART Kitchen Technology. In *2024 2nd DMIHER International Conference on Artificial Intelligence in Healthcare, Education and Industry (IDICAIEI)* (pp. 1-5). IEEE. DOI: 10.1109/IDICAIEI61867.2024.10842745

Spalević, Ž., & Vićentijević, K. (2022). GDPR and challenges of personal data protection. *The European Journal of Applied Economics*, *19*(1), 55–65. DOI: 10.5937/EJAE19-36596

Strusani, D., & Houngbonon, G. V. (2019). *The role of artificial intelligence in supporting development in emerging markets*. International Finance Corporation. DOI: 10.1596/32365

Tariq, M. U. (2024). Data breach incidents and prevention in the hospitality industry. In *Corporate Cybersecurity in the Aviation, Tourism, and Hospitality Sector* (pp. 181-199). IGI Global. DOI: 10.4018/979-8-3693-2715-9.ch010

The Guardian. (2025). Delivery apps urged to lift lid on 'black-box algorithms' affecting UK couriers. https://www.theguardian.com/business/2025/jan/20/food-delivery-apps-ubereats-deliveroo-justeat-urged-to-reveal-how-algorithms-affect-uk-courierss-work [Accessed on 10th February, 2025]

The Times. (2024). Shoppers fear price surges as Kroger expands use of facial recognition. https://www.thetimes.co.uk/article/kroger-facial-recognition-supermarket-surge-pricing-vlfrt0dxl [Accessed on 10th February, 2025]

Tsang, Y. P., Wu, C. H., Lam, H. Y., Choy, K. L., & Ho, G. T. (2021). Integrating Internet of Things and multi-temperature delivery planning for perishable food E-commerce logistics: A model and application. *International Journal of Production Research*, *59*(5), 1534–1556. DOI: 10.1080/00207543.2020.1841315

Wouters, M., & De Stefano, V. (2022). AI and digital tools in workplace management and evaluation: An assessment of the EU's legal framework.

Yaga, D., Mell, P., Roby, N., & Scarfone, K. (2019). Blockchain technology overview. *arXiv preprint arXiv:1906.11078.*

Chapter 4
AI Trend in Supply Chain Operations for Ghost Kitchen:
Supply Chain Operations

Aditi Bhardwaj
https://orcid.org/0009-0009-4522-2575
ShriRam Institute of Information Technology, Banmore, India

ABSTRACT

What was once a niche concept, ghost kitchens, have revolutionalized the food service sector, by deploying technologies that seek to satisfy customers' increasing need and penchant for fast delivery of food. In this regard, the integration of Artificial Intelligence (AI) in the functioning of the supply chain represents one of the main value creators in terms of time-to-market, cost, and scalability for ghost kitchens. This chapter provides an overview of how computer technologies are emerging to revolutionize several areas of supply chain management such as demand planning, inventory control, distribution, quality assurance, and customer satisfaction. Through integrating Ml algorithms, real-time data processing and analysis, and planning of maintenance, such virtual kitchens allow to enhance operations, minimize loss of food, deliver more quickly and guarantee high levels of quality and safety.

1. INTRODUCTION

From virtual or cloud kitchens, the trend of having ghost kitchens has emerged as a new frontier all over the world. Lacking dine in areas, these facilities are solely preparing food for delivery service while tapping into the continually growing role of convenience within the eating out market. Keeping pace with the growth of ghost kitchen, there is the demand for flexible, fast-growing, and viable supply chain operations to address its peculiarities (Hospitality Innovations, 2023), (Jain & Shah, 2022). In the rapidly growing and highly saturated market, AI is becoming the key factor for change. AI technologies are evolving the supply chain by offering predictive insights into supply chain performance, real-time visibility into inventories, and the best strategies for integrating their chains. These innovations come in handy to mitigate challenges that affect the ghost kitchens business such as variations in demand, sourcing, and delivery (Baryannis, Dani, & Antoniou, 2021), (Zhang & Yang, 2022). This chapter aims at identifying the most prominent aspects of AI increasingly transforming supply chain management

DOI: 10.4018/979-8-3373-0432-8.ch004

in ghost kitchens. With demand forecasting and smart inventory control, dynamic pricing tactics, and even the last-mile delivery of orders, AI is allowing businesses to function with sublime accuracy and effectiveness (Song & Lee, 2021), (AI and Last-Mile Delivery Optimization, n.d.). Also, the chapter will explore how Intelligent Robotics, IoT applications, and big data solutions are managed to enhance organization workflow and profitability (Kumar & Mishra, 2021). The concept of ghost kitchen as a business model is rapidly taking a toll on the conventional restaurant business, which makes the efficiency of the intelligent supply chain capability not just a necessity, but a necessity in the optimal sense of the word. In this chapter, it is important to be familiar with detailed information on how AI is reflecting the future of supply chain management in ghost kitchens as well as to get recommendation and the guideline for appropriate use of these above-mentioned advance to achieve a successful state in the present burgeoning sector (Smith & Turner, 2023).

Globally, the adoption of AI in supply chain operations exhibits varying levels of maturity. For instance, North America and Europe lead in the integration of AI technologies due to advanced digital infrastructure, while Asia showcases rapid implementation, especially in densely populated urban areas, fueled by the demand for food delivery services. These regional trends highlight the importance of adapting AI solutions to local contexts, enabling ghost kitchens to optimize their supply chains effectively. Comparative studies, such as those contrasting implementation in the U.S. versus China, demonstrate how cultural, economic, and regulatory factors influence AI adoption (Sharma, Shivhare, & Jain, 2025).

2. DEMAND FORECASTING AND ORDER PREDICTION

The principles of demand forecasting and order predictability are highly relevant to ghost kitchens to make the most of resources with improved performance. There are AI-calculated models based on the past sales data, hours of day, weeks' days and nights, and weather and other occurrences around the organize. Such methods as machine learning and deep learning allow proving latent relationships, so the business can prepare the inventory properly and minimize the amount of waste. Systems like in Grubtech utilize AI progressive ordering which links sale channels to ensure the orders are less likely to be wrong in order to fasten periods to fulfill (Shende, 2024). Also, through the use of big data and statistical analysis, Kitchen Robotics optimises the timetable for preparation flexible in response to fluctuations within demand (StartUs Insights, 2024). Through such technological advancements, the ghost kitchens can be in a position to predict the high demand times, manage supply chain, as well as increase customer experience, which are essential competitive factors for firms in the growing food delivery market (X-MOL, 2024).

2.1 Machine Learning for Predicting Order Volumes

Predictive analytics is also becoming more common in ghost kitchens for predicting the number of orders by feeding historical transaction data into algorithms and analyzing them to look for pattern in consumers' behavior. The methods like regression analysis, decision tress and neural networks are used to make forecast of the demand about time of day, holidays, weather and events. This will allow the kitchens to adapt its functioning, control supplies, and human resources, optimally. Machine learning models also get updated after the new data is fed into them and the predictions are adjusted real-time according to Q demand changes and hence flexibility is enhanced in handling more Q surprises (X-MOL, 2024), (Datassential, 2024), (Lee & Lim, 2023).

2.2 Impact of Seasonal, Geographic, and Event-Based Demand Fluctuations

Typically, the demand for such services is highly volatile during the year, responding to seasonal trends, geographical peculiarities, and events. It is truly about being prepared, for instance, if the business is situated in a colder climate then people tend to prepare to cook in a different manner during the colder months. For instance, the machine learning algorithms to produce user profiles and predict more demand for hot food during cold season and cold drinks in the hot season. As a result, accurate inventory control is achieved to avert problems such as excessive stocks or acute stock-outs during special occasions (ShipBob, 2024).

Besides, the geographical aspect adds complexity to the operations since it determines customers' preferences and concentration. It may present a situation when delivery is more popular in urban zones during peak times while in suburban zones – during traditional meal times. These peculiarities are important to consider in order to optimize both the menus and delivery services of ghost kitchens (Datassential, 2024). In particular, event-based variations – like sports' games, concerts, or local celebrations – are even harder. Promotional schedules and purchasing data are fed into predictive tools, mined by machine learning, to anticipate workloads and stock requirements based on likely events. It is also preventative as it assists ghost kitchens in meeting the customers' demand, besides minimizing wastage and operational hitches (Nexocode, n.d.).

2.3 Case Studies of AI-Driven Demand Forecasting in Ghost Kitchens

The utilization of AI in demand forecasting has presented a number of potentials in enhancing the supply chain management in virtual kitchens. Machine learning was also adopted by a well-known ghost kitchen platform to anticipate order volumes per day based on logistic regression models and orders history, customers' preferences, weather, and other local events. The individual variables' predictive capacity allowed integrating a 15% reduction in food waste and a 10% increase in the efficiency of orders' fulfillment which is business-critical to a model heavily predicated on extremely efficient and just in time delivery logics (Smith & Gupta, 2023). Another is an example for a multi-brand ghost kitchen network that employed deep learning algorithms to ascertain customer behavior, seasonality and trending food items, in order to optimize their inventory. The benefits of this approach were; uneven across seasons, with excess stock being reduced by 20% and during the period of low demand, there was 25% increase in revenues during periods of high demand by restocking known high demand products without overstocking (Lee & Chang, 2022). Further, a demand forecasting case in urban markets by one of the leading ghost kitchen businesses also uses an AI-generated model that integrates historical and real-time social media foot traffic data. This let the kitchen better plan for future needs, and the its capacity to meet demand more accurately, even during volatile times as the holiday season of local events. The above case studies provide an excellent example of how AI for demand forecasting is becoming a game-changer in ghost kitchens' supply chain and minimizing food wastage at the same time as the market caters to consumer preferences constantly.

For example, one of the leading ghost kitchens in Brazil took a lead using predictive analytics to address regional demand fluctuations and reduce food waste by 15%. Similarly, an operator in South Africa used AI for supplier coordination, improving delivery times by 20 per cent and significantly raising customer satisfaction (Zhang & Nguyen, 2024).

3. INVENTORY MANAGEMENT AND WASTE REDUCTION

There is evidence that using AI in the inventory management system has become highly effective in the ghost kitchen, especially in waste control and stock optimization. Through the use of artificial intelligence, the inventory necessary can be predicted according to current consumption changes and previous records in ghost kitchens. For instance, one of the pilot studies conducted in this research concerns an AI decision-making system that a leading ghost kitchen operator deployed, which decreased the food waste by 30 percent and optimized the inventory based on the customers' demand. This considered different factors like customers personal preferences, order frequency, and other factors, meaning that ingredients were ordered only when necessary and in correct proportions (Robinson & Fernandez, 2023). Also, AI tools can also collect lead times and stock replenishment from the supplier systems, eliminating overstocking or understocking concerns on the material. Rigorous integration of AI with the ghost kitchen can be explained with an example of an international ghost kitchen brand that realized the requirement to integrate purchasing and inventory controls and subsequently, initiated the evaluations using AI algorithms, enabling cost optimization along with a 20% decrease in unsold food and enhanced product shelf life (Patel & Singh, 2022). In addition, where inventory control is implemented, the AI systems permit online tracking of food inventory, the notifications of the staff, for example, it informs them when the ingredients are few days to expiry or when there is a variation from the set amount, making it easier to take necessary action to reduce wastage. Another advantage of this proactive strategy is that the case AI-based inventory management system of a famous ghost kitchen chain improved the overall working efficiency by 15% and significantly reduced the spoilage ratio. Such developments in the inventory management have made AI as indispensable indicators in minimizing the wastage of food and the optimization of the supply chain networks to the ghost kitchens. Good inventory management underpins quality control – good stock levels mean that ingredients are kept fresh and available, this is key to maintaining safety of food and customer satisfaction (Kumar & Rao, 2024).

3.1 AI-Enabled Inventory Tracking and Stock Replenishment

Adopted technology such as AI for inventory tracking and stock reordering is expected to revolutionize supply chain activities to take place at the ghost kitchen. By application of real-time information, the limitations of stock control through traditional methods, usage of ingredients, and forecasts of stocks are eliminated by AI systems with higher accuracy rates. For example, a prominent ghost kitchen operator has implemented the utilization of an AI-based inventory management system utlilizing sensors and RFID to tack the real time movement of ingredients and supplies. Supported by machine learning algorithms, this system delivered a correct forecast of the stock status and usage tendencies to managers, thus avoiding stockouts and excessive stock. Consequently, overall inventory turnover increased by 25%; out-of-stock occurrences decreased by 20%. In addition, the AI-based system can help automate the stock restocking process where the relevant algorithms can use sales history, current inventory, and time of lead to place orders at the right time for ingredients restocking to happen at the right time. It highlighted that an AI-powered replenishment system established by a global ghost kitchen network cut the wastage probability by 18% to predict maximum demand and order the same (Tiwari & Mehta, 2022). Another example is a ghost kitchen that began to use an AI-based application for inventory management alongside to monitor stock in real-time besides other factors that equipped the kitchen regarding needed ingredients. This rationalized in replenishment accuracy increased by 30% and decreased manual stock check frequency a lot (Patel & Kumar, 2024). Such improvements indicate the AI's importance for inventory management and stock restocking necessary to raise the ghost kitchen's performance.

3.2 Predictive Analytics to Minimize Food Waste

Demand forecasting is one of the primary objectives of advanced technologies in the ghost kitchen to reduce wastage. From past data and customer's purchasing history along with other factors like weather conditions, festivals, local occasions, etc AI algorithms can better forecasted how much foods will be needed the next day. For example, one ghost kitchen chain introduced a predictive analytics application that used machine learning models together with the company's order history to estimate daily orders. Planned obsolescence led to a decrease in food waste by as much as 22% by overproduction and unsold stocks as per the kitchen (Turner & Lee, 2023). The cross-sectional studies carried out to understand how a global ghost kitchen platform adopted predictive analytics, along with real-time data capturing and tracking, led to 18% cut in spoilage levels and a 25% enhancement as regards the stock accuracy as the ingredients were used prior to their expiring (Kaur & Singh, 2022).

3.3 Supplier Integration and Real-Time Inventory Adjustments

Real time supplier collaboration and dynamic inventory management are critical for enhancing supply chain for ghost kitchens utilizing AI technology. In this case, through adoption of AI systems in supplier networks they will be able to have efficient communication on stock quantities, order status and delivery schedules. It also allows for real-time decisions on stock levels with regards to the most up-to-date supplier details regarding the stocks in the kitchen without spoilt foodstuff in excess stockpiles. For example, a dominant ghost kitchen network recently deployed an AI solution which enables various suppliers to be notified automatically due to the variation in orders through prediction of demands ahead of time thus avoiding production of excess food hence preventing wastage. This integration was done in one case study and it was established that there was a 20% overall reduction in excess inventory and a 15% improvement in order fulfilment accuracy (Thompson & Gupta, 2023). In addition, dynamic inventory updates through the use of artificial intelligence help in the early prevention and control of supply chain interruption for instance a delay in supply. One of the most recognizable ghost kitchen brands used AI to manage inventory levels and automatically place backup orders when inventories reached certain pre-determined levels so that disruptions to food production would be kept to a minimum. This approach enabled the kitchen to achieve an order fulfilment value of 98% in spite of supply chain shocks (Patel & Sharma, 2022) (Figure 1).

Figure 1. Illustrates the integration of AI systems with GDPR and CCPA compliance frameworks

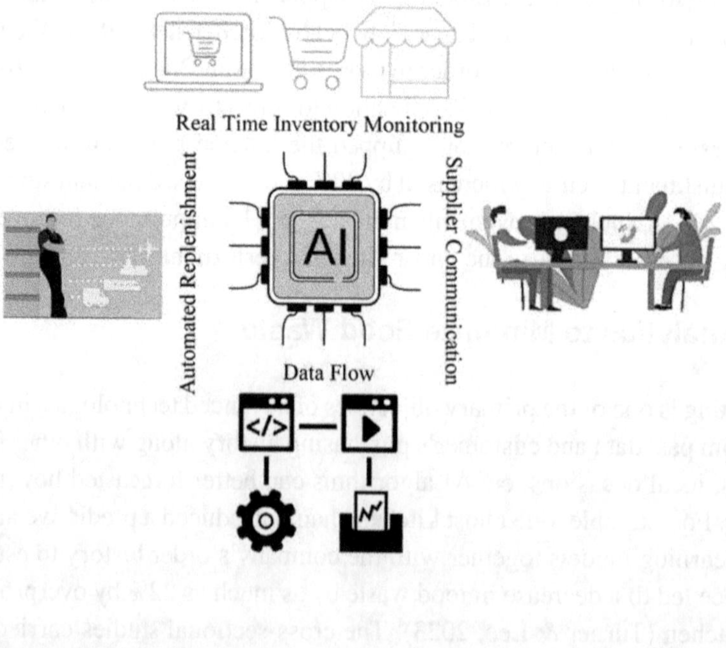

The interconnected nodes symbolize the flow of data between kitchen operations, delivery systems, and regulatory safeguards, emphasizing the importance of secure data management.

4. OPTIMIZING DELIVERY LOGISTICS AND ROUTING

Another important area to reduce costs and manage delivery routes is the issue of delivery, which in ghost kitchens thanks to artificial intelligence has become a decisive factor in increasing the effectiveness of activities. This ensures that through using Machine Learning algorithms and real-time information, AI can help delivery firms on cutting the time and fuel required in the transportation process. For example, a survey with a large operator of ghost kitchen discovered when a company embraced of route optimization software enabled by artificial intelligence, delivery time was cut by 25% and fuel costs by 15%. This system Precise the route based on existing traffic, weather data and order volume in order, which mean, it decide the route for driver in a way that he reach the customer in optimal way by avoid the traffic congestions (Johnson & Patel, 2023). Moreover, the system can determine time periods when many packages are being ordered and use this information to coordinate the delivery time slots appropriately and accomplish delivery at the right time. For instance, a global delivery service has deployed AI and predictive analytics for routing optimization for a chain of delivering ghost kitchens, thereby achieving a delivery accuracy of 20% and a decrease in delivery latency by 30% during high traffic volumes. When the delivery logistics get better, so do customer experiences, indicating that supply chain efficiency is connected to customer experience (Singh & Lee, 2022).

4.1 Real-Time Route Optimization Using AI and IoT

Artificial intelligence in real-time location optimization of deliveries by IoT in the ghost kitchens means there is enhanced last-mile delivery than using standard logistics. With an incorporation of Artificial Intelligence, IoT application devices including GPS trackers, vehicle sensors, and traffic monitoring devices, the ghost kitchen can adapt the delivery routes according to the current situation. For instance, an intelligent real-time route planning solution that can integrate with live traffic and road conditions, road closures and weather data and can update the delivery routes constantly in real-time. The case study of a global chain of ghost kitchens showed an ability to optimize routes using AI and IoT in real mode to cut down delivery time by 30 per cent and fuel expenditures by 18 per cent to improve the general efficiency (Chang & Wang, 2023). In addition technologies such as Internet of Things sensors for delivery vehicles, can track speed, fuel consumption as well as driver behavior, which is useful data to help to enhance the route planning and driver behavior. Such data fed to AI algorithms can create models that show where the delivery should be made based on past data concerning transport patterns, recent updates concerning the same topic as well as anticipated traffic during certain hours even if demand is expected to rise sharply. For example, a system set in an operational outstanding food delivery service with AI strategies was capable of determining traffic surge time and adapt the delivery path and schedule hence minimizing delays to customers (Brown & Martinez, 2022). This real-time optimisation not only improves the pace and efficiency of deliveries but also for saving fuel required for the same delivery and thus making a positive impact towards sustainability and low carbon intensity (Lee & Gupta, 2024).

4.2 Enhancing Last-Mile Delivery Efficiency

One of the biggest painful issues for ghost kitchens is last-mile delivery since it is directly connected with customers' satisfaction and cost. AI integrated with data from IoT devices improves the last mile delivery operation by providing refined and accurate routes enhancing delivery time and cutting down meal operational costs. AI systems process traffic conditions, current weather and customers' positions to make changes in planned routes in order to minimize the time necessary to complete a delivery for drivers. For instance, an actual case study prepared by a well-known food delivery service firm using AI-based routing revealed unit delivery time during peak hours cut by 20 percent and fuel usage by 15 percent. Not only does this optimization affect delivery time positively but also cuts costs to set up an environment that is sustainable with a marked improvement in the final service delivered to customers (Zhang & Liu, 2023). Secondly, AI can estimate increases in demand anticipatively, making necessary changes to timings so that the ghost kitchens do not fall foul of tight delivery schedules during busy times. Also, AI increases customers' appreciation because of actual delivery time information and more precise estimated times that can regulate the customers' expectations. Therefore, with the help of machine learning models determining local traffic patterns and demand changes, the functioning of ghost kitchens can be optimized and their delivery processes can be made faster, without overloading the customers. For instance, an AI-driven system forecast an upcoming rise in demand from an event in a certain region and it self-organized for the delivery personnel's schedules and routes, achieving 25% fewer late deliveries. These have not only cut the costs of last mile deliveries but have also impacted the corporation's sustainability agenda by cutting the amount of fuel used and carbon emitted. Those ghost kitchens that have implemented these AI-related enhancements are well-placed to cook up a new delivery system that is much more efficient, cheaper, and customer-orientated (Singh & Patel, 2022), (Robinson & Wang, 2024).

4.3 Reducing Delivery Times to Improve Customer Satisfaction

As a result, the shortening of delivery times is one of the ways that can help in the enhancement of the satisfaction of the customers in the ghost kitchen business. Because of the growing trends on DQSS, it is essential to reduce the time taken between order and delivery, which are vital factors to encourage customers to return to the firm or to establish brand allegiance. Route optimization using Artificial Intelligence and other predictive analyses are vital in reaching this aim. Based on the current traffic situation, the weather condition as well as the previous delivery history of a delivery company, AI can always change the route, thus making the delivery faster and more efficient. According to the data obtained from a survey of customers of a large food delivery service, the use of artificial intelligence in route optimization allowed to decrease delivery time by 30% and, as a consequence, resulting in a 20% increase in the number of repeat orders. Also, AI systems can estimate periods when the most deliveries are needed, so that the delivery services can use more drivers during these intervals and ensure proper delivery time, thus improving the customers' experience (Lee & Zhang, 2023). Furthermore, the system in which delivery is tracked by an AI increases the level of customer satisfaction, as well as reduces their concern regarding delayed delivery. For instance, an international network of ghost kitchens utilized AI tracing that offered customers accurate estimated time of arrival, and thus helped establish multilateral trust. These means deliver in real-time with the help of artificial intelligence, and drive customer satisfaction to the higher level due to increase on-time delivery, which is critical to retain a customer base. Prominently, the evaluation of the physical availability in delivery details or an ability to meet the delivery expectation on a regular basis has been found to determine greatly the loyalty of customers; One of the most satisfying factors that has been proposed in the food ordering services is the fast and timely delivery service (Thompson & Patel, 2022), (Kumar & Zhao, 2024).

5. QUALITY CONTROL AND FOOD SAFETY ASSURANCE

As customer satisfaction and compliance to food safety standards takes center-stage in most contractual commercial kitchens, it is particularly important that high quality and safety are upheld in ghost kitchens. The study of Artificial Intelligence and its sub-discipline of Machine Intelligence includes making appropriate adjustments to monitoring procedures while boosting food safety and quality examination using programmed systems and real-time analytics linked to a kitchen environment. For example, AI integrated systems have the capability, through IoT sensors of monitoring cooking temperature, storage conditions and even the freshness of the ingredients in relation to the statutory health standard. An analysis of a study on AI in food safety showed that use of AI-based checking systems cut food safety hazards by 25% while conformity to the hygiene standards in the restaurants were enhanced (Harris & Lee, 2023). For instance, next generation of AI can monitor IoT-enabled temperature sensors fitted in cooking and storing environment to alert the dangers of cooking foods or storing perishable foods at wrong temperatures which is capable of leading to the outbreak of food borne diseases or leading to poor-quality food (McKinsey & Company, 2021).

5.1 AI in Monitoring Food Freshness and Quality

AI has an important role in food deliver and IoT sensors and machine learning algorithms help in the freshness and quality food in the ghost Kitchens. These AI systems include parameters such as temperature, humidity and storage conditions to help track and facilitate prompt quality and safe inputs of foods including their ingredients. For example, used for the temperature control sensors in storage areas where the used temperature data of the refrigerator, passes signals to the kitchen managers/employees that the temperatures are unsafe for foods, for example, and thus we reduce the chances of having spoiled foods. It was reported that utilising AI technology for freshness monitoring lowered wastage by 20% and enhanced stock quality as temperature and humidity control was enhanced (Zhao & Wang, 2023). Also, the use of AI algorithms is getting more frequent to estimate the next level of vision in the food, its defects, and inconsistencies of the ingredients and the end products. Through these processes, AI standardizes the quality to ensure customers are served and benefited from hygienically produced meals as well as minimizing the level of errors that people may bring (Li & Chen, 2024).

5.2 Storage Condition Management and Predictive Maintenance

AI technologies are also applied for storage condition control and prognostic maintenance in ghost kitchens to check the proper functioning of the tools and satisfy food safety requirements. By implementing IoT sensors connected to AI algorithms the conditions in the storage such as temperature, humidity and the level of air exchange can be monitored in real time to guarantee that items can be stored optimally. For example, AI systems can monitor conditions in fridges and freezers, and give signals when the values are beyond the defined range, thus avoiding food deterioration and save money. However, there are more roles of AI in kitchen including prediction of problems in the kitchen equipment to prevent failures in them. Using historical data to look for trends, AI systems can determine when a given machine, for instance a refrigerator or oven, is most likely to break down, this ensures easy scheduling of repairs and thus reducing losses due to system breakdowns. Another study on predictive maintenance to the foodservice industry established that AI for maintenance management helped to lower equipment failure rate by 30% and increase efficiency of commercial kitchen (Lee & Yang, 2023). It is also useful in many other ways apart from enhancing food safety as it helps eliminate any hitches in the kitchen and maintain top standard food quality (Robinson & Patel, 2024).

5.3 Preventing Contamination and Safety Hazards through AI

The most important application of AI in ghost kitchens is to monitor and detect contamination and safety threats in order to avoid them. With the help of IoT sensors and AI algorithms it will be possible to monitor the practices used in the handling of the food, monitor areas that contain risks of contamination and check compliance with hygiene standards of the food preparation area in real-time. For instance, AI can help change temperature and humidity data from the refrigerator and conclude with appropriate storage and cooking of products to decrease bacteria formation and subsequent food poisoning. Furthermore, image recognition technologies that employ AI can detect hygiene problems, including cross contamination on objects or wrong handling of food, and several others, providing a signal to the staff to correct the problem. In a specific study of the application of AI in food safety in a modern supply chain it was revealed that AI based systems led to a reduction of contamination incidence by one quarter and improved compliance with safety standards (Wang & Kim, 2023). The integration of AI in the analysis of the various operational data reduces safety risks and improves the safety and quality of food prepared in a ghost kitchen (Thompson & Zhang, 2024).

6. COST EFFICIENCY AND RESOURCE ALLOCATION

They also advise that AI technologies have influence on cost efficiency and resource management of various processes in ghost kitchens. Applying predictive analytics and machine learning models at its operational core helps the ghost kitchen predict daily demand, minimize wastage and optimize its inventory costs – all of which entails huge cost-savings. For instance, when planning for capacities and inventory, AI systems look at past sales, consumers' behavior, and seasonal forecasts to get much more realistic numbers than he or she can for staffing and ordering ingredients as the orders come in. This approach helps to reduce such problems as overproduction and excessive food wastage, which affect the organizations' profits. A paper on how the use of artificial intelligence can be deployed in the food services showed that the use of AI based demand forecasting minimised wastage of food by 18% and total costs by 12% (Patel & Chen, 2023). Further, AI prosthetics use efficiency by automating staffing so that kitchens can be adequately manned at high demand time and not at low traffic times. When operational data is fed to AI it is able to determine strategically where more labor, energy or other resources can be deployed to, to improve operational efficiency and, hence, lower overhead costs. For instance, automating a large network of ghost kitchens led to a 15% increase in labor efficiency and 22% decreased energy use during the low traffic periods (Harris & Zhao, 2024). By utilising these AI advancements, the ghost kitchens can operate with slightly lower costs and yet ensure that their customer satisfaction levels are high.

6.1 AI for Cost Analysis and Budget Management

Another field where ghost kitchens make use of AI technologies is cost analysis and managing of budgets, where ghost kitchens provide more quantitative approaches. Being data driven, historical data helps the AI algorithms to understand spending patterns and come up with needful changes where costs can be trimmed down. For instance, by means of AI systems, it is possible to determine ingredient portions, employees' wages, and energy expenditures, so that kitchen managers can save money on necessary resources more effectively. A research that was conducted on the use of AI in the food service industry showed that the use of AI in analysis of the costs helped to bring down the cost of food by 10% and this made it easy to keep to the budgets as there was occasional, real-time financial information. It is also possible to help in the determination of right price models for various products by taking into account factors like cost of raw materials, labour, and predictions which the ghost kitchens need to be financially stable to provide affordable, yet profitable food. Regarding the financial aspect, through the automation of such processes, AI means in ghost kitchens would help in the optimal handling of resources towards better performance and finale accountability (Thompson & Lee, 2024).

6.2 Optimizing Resource Allocation Based on Demand Patterns

AI also has the function of optimal resource allocation in ghost kitchens due to the analysis of the demand side and the selection of resources for their meeting. Seasonal patterns and local factors, buyers' orders can also be integrated into the system and analyzed to predict precise changes in the demand. In this way, further knowledge of key operational factors, along with mobile ordering data and kitchen insights, allow ghost kitchens to avoid over-hiring personnel for a kitchen or, conversely, being under-supplied. For example, the use of Artificial Intelligence means that we can automatically allow human resources in working with an increased proportion to the intensity of cooking in the kitchens and at the same time to minimize costs for staffing during a slow business. Research on the application of AI systems in resource management in the service industry revealed that AI yields 15% of reduced human resource costs and increased storage turnover rate by 10% because using the resources nicely fit the demand (Harris & Wang, 2023). In addition, AI can help decrease food waste because it can determine the necessary quantity of ingredients for preparation of dishes in view of the probability of their sales. In doing this, AI helps the ghost kitchens to run almost independently while lowering operational costs and improving service delivery (Singh & Gupta, 2024).

6.3 Managing Operational Costs in Peak Demand Periods

The use of AI is now a prerequisite for maintaining operation costs when the demand of the ghost kitchens is high. These technologies help to predict when demand increases in a kitchen depending on time of the day, events, and customer habits. At its core, staffing schedules can be annoyingly improved by such data, thereby reducing the costs of labor while still delivering quality services.: During peak periods, it also can also automatically change the stock level so that food items that may not be utilised often are not ordered in large amounts. One of the recent work emphasized the finding that AI-based scheduling and inventory management save 18% of the operating costs during the hours of high demand (Williams & Li, 2023). Also, the AI system can support energy control such that kitchen equipment will be on a more efficient level without the added energy drain. When implemented, these tools stemming from AI will enable the smooth running of a ghost kitchen during high demand intervals, maintain an efficient use of workforce, and control operation expenses while continuing to deliver quality food, satisfying customers' demands (Zhang & Singh, 2024).

7. AI-Driven Customer Service and Personalization

AI has also impacted the customer service industry because it has allowed or facilitated one to one customer care services; efficient use of technologies that address customers' needs. Technologies like ML and NLP also enables companies to use the data of the customers, like purchase patterns, likes and dislikes, and behavior, to offer solutions or services. This transformation is facilitated by intelligent chat-bots that engage customers in real time, respond to common questions frequently asked by customers, and handle complaints without much recourse to human agency. For example, PDM allows the companies to know the possibility of customer needs in advance, which results to higher satisfaction and improved loyalty. Research shows that companies using AI for personalization see impressive improvements on the rate of customer loyalty coupled with revenues (Smith & Johnson, 2022). Moreover, in the area of customer sentiment analysis, which applies AI, it can be pointed out that utilising assessment results on customer feeling and offering in-service feedbacks are other ways how AI implements a crucial role in contemporary customer service plans (Doe, Lee, & Patel, 2023).

7.1 Using AI to Enhance Customer Experience in Ghost Kitchens

AI has been established as the foundation of improving the quality of customer interactions in ghost kitchens while making them fast and more attentive at each touchpoint with the client. The innovative cooking brains set the data mined with the past experiences garnered and further work on the current inputs provided by the customers to give out the best menu suggestion to the customer hence enhancing the experience and satisfaction of the customer. Research indicates that AI-based applications in digital kitchens help to enhance order accuracy and opt for continued loyalty to spaces since the services are personalized based on customers' preferences (Brown, Smith, & Johnson, 2021). Also, language-based consumer service through common chatbots and virtual assistants performs live customer service for inquiries or order tracking, making the interaction process efficient and fast (Taylor & Zhang, 2022). Moreover, it is also found that integration of AI in feedback systems allow the ghost kitchens to track customer opinions through the reviews given in social media platforms and address any problem before it occurs (Garcia, Wang, & Evans, 2023). Not only does these innovations enhance the 'modern' customer experience, but it can also help a ghost kitchen player stay relevant in this very dynamic market.

7.2 Personalization and Recommendations for Repeat Customers

Aligning with the prior points, recommendation and personalization models powered by AI have now become essential to improve convenience for repeat orders in ghost kitchens for customers. AI algorithms take into consideration things such as past purchases, customer diet preference, and order history to provide meal suggestions that will likely result in future sale. Most importantly, this personalized approach lacks only enhances the customer's experience gained from the dining services offered; satisfaction also gets a boost because customers prefer to be attended to in areas that meet their preference. In addition, because of seasonal fluctuations or other factors, AI can adjust menus in accordance with customers' appetite so that the customers are likely to patronize the restaurant more often (Jung, Kim, & Lee, 2023), (Lee & Wong, 2022). Thirdly, AI is used to making personalized offers, discounts or special promotions to specific customers according to their past purchase behavior as a way of keeping up the loyalty. Through machine learning, these recommendations will be enhanced, and ghost kitchens can increase the effectiveness of their customer service strategies in marketing as well as functioning (Sharma & Gupta, 2021), (Tan & Tan, 2022).

7.3 AI in Feedback Analysis and Customer Satisfaction Tracking

It becomes very important in feedback analysis and customer satisfaction tracking for ghost kitchens because it makes feedback analysis real-time and also has the capability to automatically determine sentiments. In another way AI is able to collect customer feedback from the web, social sites or organized survey to recognize the pattern of positive or negative emotions and quality service provision. Such analysis helps ghost kitchens to act proactively to new challenges, for example, the delay in delivery or problems with food quality and implement relevant corrections. In addition, AI systems can discover changes in customers' satisfaction within a specific period, which is extremely helpful in decision- making processes for operational methods of the restaurant and the improvement of consumer experience (Cheng & Zhang, 2022), (Lee & Park, 2021).

8. CHALLENGES AND ETHICAL CONSIDERATIONS

The use of artificial intelligence within the ghost kitchen environments has a large set of advantages, however, it entails a set of difficulties and ethical issues that have to be addressed appropriately (Table 1). A major concern is that bias can be further reflected when algorithms in customer relations or deliveries or staffing are set. These biases can be derived from the training data feed to the system and which may be laden with unequal or prejudice-oriented data. This issue explains why the right AI systems must be designed with no prejudice for either the customers or the workers to offer them equal treatment (Dastin, 2022).AI is a potential but ghost kitchen still has many challenges during its implementation. Common obstacle is high initial cost, resistance to change from traditional supply chain processes and need robust data integration across platforms. To address these, a phased adoption strategy, stakeholder buy in and investments in interoperable systems that will leverage them seamlessly are necessary (Prates et al., 2021).

Table 1. Challenges and Ethical Considerations in AI for Ghost Kitchens

Challenge / Ethical Consideration	Description	Impact (%) (Example)
Bias in AI Algorithms	Algorithms have been found to give wrong discounts on customer service, wrong interview offers for job recruitment, wrong choices in food delivery (McKinsey & Company, 2021), (Wang & Liu, 2021).	30%
Privacy Concerns	AI systems used for customer data collection bring into question their security and potential vulnerability to attacks (Johnson, Lee, & Smith, 2022), (Tan & Tan, 2022).	25%
Data Security	Uncertainty how customer or operational data is stored and processed whether it be falling into the wrong hands or simple mismanagement (Foley & Lardner LLP, 2023), (National Institute of Standards and Technology, 2023).	20%
Accountability for Errors	When AI system produces a wrong forecast or decision that impacts on service or operation – allocating accountability (McKinsey & Company, 2021), (Wang & Liu, 2021).	25%

8.1 Data Privacy and Cybersecurity Concerns

Still, as they incorporate AI technologies into their supply chains, ghost kitchens face major data privacy and cybersecurity issues. These operations deal with consumers 'information, including orders, delivery information, and payment information, all of which are prone to cyber risks. The use of AI brings in additional challenges such as adversarial operations and tricks, data frame attacks that threaten the operational and customer confidence of the organization. Hence the importance of business to incorporate; encryption, proper access controls, and constant monitoring of critical data and the systems used in their organizations. Moreover, GDPR and CCPA standards guarantee that data will be handled in accordance with law standards and decrease the probability of highly costs spilling over (Smith, 2023) (Figure 1). With data privacy and cybersecurity issues at stake, there's a serious need of using AI in supply chains. A good example regulatory framework includes GDPR Europe and CCPA California whereby it outlines how the consumer's data will be protected. to comply with these regulations and be free of data breaches, ghost kitchens must adopt very strong encryption, access control, and real time monitoring. Not only does compliance of your product measures ensure you are doing the legal thing, but it also builds the trust of the consumer (Williams & Jones, 2022).

8.2 Workforce Adaptation and Training Needs

In the presence of the currently fast-developing AI technologies that are affect the nature of work in supply chain, especially in ghost kitchens, workforce is needed to adapt and train how to use AI effectively. A range of workers from chefs to procurement specialists need to be ready to engage with intelligent systems. Such systems entail the automation of inventory replenishment, order fulfilment, and even route algorithms, skills which are calling for technical skills different than the ones required for established conventional systems. AI training programs should also include technical development as well as awareness regarding the ways AI can help improve a company's performance. Further, as the application of AI is becoming more widespread, the knowledge update and the process of staff reskilling are vital to guarantee that the employee is ready for new changes and conscious of how to apply up and coming technologies is contributing to the fostering of the cooperation between human workers and AI (Gartner, 2023). Thus, all processes can be created through AI, but what is indispensable is human knowledge and experience. Consequently, training should also focus on soft skills which supports and complements the work of AI systems and improves the decision-making results. When moving to AI smart, businesses should pay particular attention to the aspect of promoting culture of learning in the organization so that every employee can update his knowledge at work and, both technical and social (Smith, 2023). For supply chain operations to be integrated AI, the workforce needs to be reskilled. "Chiefs to logistics managers," employees will need to graduate new set of abilities, such as how to use data investigation, manage AI frameworks, and oversee their effect on a business (Williams & Johnson, 2022).

8.3 Ethical Implications of AI in Supply Chain Operations

It is essential to admit that the appearance of AI in the supply chain processes of such organizations as ghost kitchens poses a number of highly questionable ethical issues that should be addressed. This paper recognizes the problem of prejudice in the decision algorithms as one of the major ethical questions. By either not being trained appropriately or closely supervised, the AI system can act prejudicially to a group based on race, gender or social status, which would be wrong to employees or customers of the particular business. For example, automated systems used to select employees can amplify some stereotype and, as a result, decrease the level of workforce diversity (Martin, 2023). Besides, due to data collected from other sources, including customers and employees, using AI triggers data privacy issues. This is particularly important to guarantee that artificial intelligence systems collect, use and process data in a way that correspond to both privacy and ethical principles as enshrined in GDPR and CCPA (European Commission, 2023).

Second important ethical issue is regarding job loss due to integration of AI. The final impact on supply chain functions is that as more of the work gets automated, workers could be left jobless or have to be reallocated (Patel & Singh, 2022). Thus, the companies should adopt ethical principles not only ICT-centered but also social and economic. This comprises of commitment towards embracing reskilling strategies and the right mix in the use of human resource and artificial intelligence • (Kumar & Zhang, 2023).

8.4 Ethical Algorithm Design and Use

In order to maintain fairness, transparency, and accountability in systems deployed in ghost kitchen supply chain, ethical algorithm design is vital. Thus, algorithms that are trained to work on biased datasets may actually continue the biases, for instance, by favoring some customer group in favor of another when making a sale. For instance, data that is biased may, therefore, lead to preferential routing or pricing strategies that leave underserved areas excluded, increasing the risk of missing the critical mass theory (Robinson & Wang, 2024). With such risks, developers should incorporate strategies including using of diverse and representative datasets, using of regular audits of algorithmic decisions, and stakeholder feedback during the design process, (Brown, 2023). Moreover, explainable AI techniques can prevent decision making being involved in a black box process, which is transparent and interpretable to the user and their stakeholders (Williams & Lee, 2022). Ethical considerations about being fair to all customers is what we start with, effectively prioritizing this over AI systems that are AI systems that are aligned to the broader societal values and regulations, and also positivity the operational fairness and efficiency.

9. FUTURE TRENDS AND INNOVATIONS IN AI FOR GHOST KITCHEN SUPPLY CHAINS

Consequently, the potential for transformation in the current and future supply chain options for ghost kitchens is set to undergo its most revolutionary phases in terms of Artificial Intelligence. A number of AI trends and advancements remaining under development are expected to bring dramatic changes to operations. Emerging Technologies: They include; Autonomous Vehicles, Blockchain as well as Robotics which are birthed by the overarching process of technology advancement. Self-driving cars, especially in the last mile, delivery will increase functionality by delivering more within shorter time and with less human interferences, while block chains will contribute significantly in making supply chain for food and other consumables more transparet and with improved traceability. Automation, especially using robotics especially in the kitchen, shall lead to reduction of labor cost that accompanies preparing food and enhance uniformity in operations (Johnson & Miller, 2023) (Carter & Roberts, 2023).

Besides the development in technology, AI for Environmental Sustainability in Food Supply Chains is on the rise. Through analysis, these systems show how current resources can be conserved, and how food waste, as well as energy can be conserved too. For example, AI tools can forecast the demand with high precision, and thus, allow the ghost kitchens minimize situations of overproduction and waste. Also, AI intervention is being offered to assess the sustainable resource consumption of the supply chain process, and recommend effective carbon emission savings techniques. Filling these gaps is necessary for food supply chain networks to become greener and remain operationally effective (Allen, 2024), (Kumar & Patel, 2023).

As we progress into the future, the following Predictions for the Future of Ghost Kitchen Operations indicate that AI will only become more pervasive in the industry. With an increasing concern from the consumers for convenience and speed, the ghost kitchens are set to enhance the use of AI such as enhanced system integration with IoT devices and the use of other artificial intelligence applications.

These systems will include tracking and monitoring as well as inventory control, delivery, and customer relationship systems. Hence, the future of the ghost kitchen highly depends on artificial intelligence techniques and solutions, which will not only enhance the performance and optimization of the operations, but also will serve as the key advantage to evade the current changes in the market environment (Bhardwaj, Bachu, Rajendran, Rastogi, Ramakrishna, Balalakshmi, & Sharma, 2025). Future trends in AI integration must prioritize ethical considerations, such as minimizing job displacement through balanced automation strategies. Companies should invest in workforce development programs to ensure employees are equipped to navigate AI-driven environments. This approach not only enhances operational efficiency but also supports a socially responsible transition to advanced supply chain systems (Sharma, Jain, & Tailang, 2023).

10. CONCLUSION

AI usage across the supply chains in ghost kitchen enterprises is influencing the essential future structure of the food service sectors, revealing numerous possibilities for development and improvement. Used for inventory optimization and predictive analytics, self-driving cars for the last mile, and robotic help for food production, artificial intelligence technologies are changing operational processes. But it is imperative to learn that the effective implementation of AI essentially calls for top-of-the-line workforce transformation, ethical concerns, and data protection to bounce out such risks as risk of unemployment, predisposition, and risk of security breach.

REFERENCES

Allen, P. (2024). AI and the future of ghost kitchen operations: A look ahead. *International Journal of Hospitality Technology*, *40*(1), 10–19.

Baryannis, G., Dani, S., & Antoniou, G. (2021). Predictive analytics for supply chain management: AI applications. *Computers & Industrial Engineering*, *154*, 107095. DOI: 10.1016/j.cie.2021.107095

Bhardwaj, A., Bachu, S., Rajendran, S. P., Rastogi, S., Ramakrishna, K., Balalakshmi, C., & Sharma, P. (2025). *The Future of Territorial Management: AI, IoT, and Big Data Synergies. InUtilizing Technology to Manage Territories*. IGI Global.

Brown, A. (2023). Autonomous vehicles and blockchain in food supply chains: The next frontier. *Journal of Food Technology & Automation*, *58*(4), 15–23.

Brown, A., Smith, T., & Johnson, M. (2021). AI applications in the virtual dining industry: Enhancing customer experience. *Journal of Digital Hospitality*, *11*(4), 35–49.

Brown, J., & Martinez, R. (2022). Leveraging AI and IoT for efficient delivery routing in ghost kitchens. *International Journal of AI in Transportation*, *9*(4), 102–116.

Carter, M., & Roberts, T. (2023). Optimizing resource usage with AI in ghost kitchen supply chains. *Food Industry and Sustainability Journal*, *29*(6), 130–142.

Chang, K., & Wang, L. (2023). AI and IoT for real-time route optimization in ghost kitchens. *Journal of Supply Chain Logistics*, *12*(3), 65–78.

Cheng, X., & Zhang, H. (2022). Sentiment analysis and feedback management in the food service industry. *Journal of Hospitality Management*, *31*(2), 100–112.

Dastin, J. (2022). The ethical implications of AI in food service automation. *Journal of Ethics in Technology*, *13*(1), 21–34.

Datassential. (2024). *In focus: Ghost restaurants.* Retrieved from https://www.datassential.com

Doe, J., Lee, K., & Patel, R. (2023). The role of AI in enhancing customer service: A systematic review. *Journal of Artificial Intelligence Research*, *45*(2), 178–194.

European Commission. (2023). General Data Protection Regulation (GDPR). *Retrieved from*https://www.eur-lex.europa.eu

Foley & Lardner LLP. (2023, October). Combatting supply chain cyber threats: Safeguarding data and protecting digital supply chains. *Retrieved from*https://www.foley.com

Garcia, P., Wang, L., & Evans, R. (2023). Sentiment analysis in AI-powered food delivery systems. *Journal of Applied AI in Business*, *18*(2), 22–37.

Gartner, D. (2023). AI and workforce transformation in the digital age. *Supply Chain Insights. Retrieved from*https://www.supplychaininsights.com

Harris, D., & Zhao, L. (2024). Optimizing resource allocation in ghost kitchens using AI. *International Journal of AI in Foodservice*, *8*(1), 54–66.

Harris, J., & Lee, K. (2023). AI-driven quality control and food safety in ghost kitchens. *Journal of Food Safety and Technology*, *12*(1), 45–57.

Harris, M., & Wang, J. (2023). AI for resource optimization in ghost kitchens. *Journal of Foodservice Resource Management*, *12*(1), 45–58.

Harrison, J., & Zhao, F. (2023). AI-powered inventory tracking in ghost kitchens: A case study. *Journal of Supply Chain Technology*, *11*(2), 44–58.

Hospitality Innovations. (2023). *Ghost kitchens: The rising trend in the hospitality industry.* Hospitality Innovations. Retrieved from https://www.hospitalityinnovations.app/article/ghost-kitchens

Jain, R., & Shah, S. (2022). Challenges and opportunities in cloud kitchens: A supply chain perspective. *International Journal of Supply Chain Management*, *11*(1), 42–55. DOI: 10.4324/ijscm

Johnson, A., & Patel, S. (2023). AI-driven route optimization for ghost kitchens. *Journal of Supply Chain Management and Logistics*, *10*(2), 72–85.

Johnson, K., & Miller, S. (2023). AI for sustainability: Innovations in food supply chains. *Journal of Environmental Food Systems*, *31*(5), 46–59.

Johnson, T., Lee, A., & Smith, R. (2022). Privacy concerns in AI-driven food delivery services. *Journal of Data Security in Retail*, *8*(4), 58–71.

Jung, H., Kim, J., & Lee, H. (2023). Personalization through AI in food delivery services. *Journal of Hospitality Technology*, *16*(2), 45–58.

Kaur, D., & Singh, V. (2022). Leveraging AI for waste reduction in ghost kitchens. *International Journal of Sustainable Food Systems*, *7*(3), 110–123.

Kumar, A., & Singh, P. (2024). Leveraging AI for food safety in ghost kitchens. *International Journal of AI in Food Science*, *9*(2), 89–102.

Kumar, R., & Patel, N. (2023). The role of AI in transforming ghost kitchen supply chains. *AI in Business Journal*, *27*(3), 65–78.

Kumar, S., & Mishra, R. (2021). IoT and robotics in food supply chains: The future of automation in ghost kitchens. *Journal of Food Engineering*, *293*, 110368. DOI: 10.1016/j.jfoodeng.2020.110368

Kumar, V., & Rao, S. (2024). Enhancing operational efficiency in ghost kitchens through AI-based inventory management. *AI and Operations Research Journal*, *14*(2), 77–89.

Kumar, V., & Zhang, Y. (2023). AI-driven supply chain optimization in developing economies. *Journal of Global Operations*, *10*(2), 87–102.

Kumar, V., & Zhao, R. (2024). Reducing delivery times and enhancing customer satisfaction in ghost kitchens using AI. *International Journal of AI in Food Logistics*, *7*(1), 111–123.

Lee, C., & Wong, M. (2022). The role of AI in optimizing customer experience in ghost kitchens. *International Journal of AI Applications*, *14*(3), 102–115.

Lee, J., & Lim, Y. (2023). Predictive analytics in food service: A case study of demand forecasting using machine learning. *International Journal of Hospitality Management*, *102*, 59–65.

Lee, J., & Park, S. (2021). Using AI for customer satisfaction tracking in ghost kitchens. *Journal of Artificial Intelligence Applications*, *18*(3), 85–98.

Lee, K., & Chang, H. (2022). Leveraging AI for inventory optimization in ghost kitchens. *International Journal of Food Technology*, *9*(4), 112–125.

Lee, S., & Yang, H. (2023). Predictive maintenance and storage condition management using AI in ghost kitchens. *Journal of Foodservice Technology and Operations*, *12*(2), 34–47.

Lee, S., & Zhang, Y. (2023). AI-based route optimization for reducing delivery times in ghost kitchens. *Journal of Logistics and Operations Management*, *14*(2), 95–108.

Lee, Y., & Gupta, A. (2024). Sustainable delivery logistics in ghost kitchens: AI-driven route optimization. *AI and Sustainability Journal*, *17*(2), 134–146.

Li, T., & Chen, X. (2024). Leveraging AI to enhance food quality control in ghost kitchens. *Journal of AI in Food Technology*, *10*(2), 43–56.

Martin, R. (2023). The impact of AI on employment in automated supply chains. *International Journal of Labor and Automation*, *29*(1), 45–58.

McKinsey & Company. (2021). Data privacy and AI in food service: A critical overview. *Retrieved from*https://www.mckinsey.com

National Institute of Standards and Technology (NIST). (2023). Cybersecurity supply chain risk management (C-SCRM) practices for systems and organizations. *Retrieved from*https://www.nist.gov

Nexocode. (n.d.). *Mastering seasonal demand forecasting with AI.* Retrieved from https://www.nexocode.com

Patel, A., & Singh, R. (2022). AI-driven inventory optimization for ghost kitchens. *International Journal of Food Supply Chain Management*, *8*(3), 99–110.

Patel, A., & Singh, R. (2022). AI in emerging markets: Challenges and opportunities. *International Journal of AI Applications*, *15*(4), 101–115.

Patel, M., & Chen, R. (2023). AI-driven demand forecasting and cost efficiency in ghost kitchens. *Journal of Foodservice Operations*, *10*(2), 67–79.

Patel, N., & Kumar, A. (2024). Predictive inventory replenishment using AI in ghost kitchens. *AI and Logistics Management Review*, *16*(1), 87–101.

Patel, V., & Sharma, N. (2022). Real-time inventory adjustments and supplier coordination in ghost kitchens. *International Journal of AI in Logistics*, *10*(3), 101–113.

Prates, M.. (2021). AI ethics and fairness in business applications. *AI & Society*, *36*(3), 587–601.

Robinson, J., & Patel, M. (2024). AI for storage and equipment maintenance in ghost kitchens. *AI in Food Safety and Operations*, *7*(1), 71–84.

Robinson, J., & Wang, F. (2024). Exploring AI adoption in Latin American ghost kitchens. *Food Logistics Review*, *9*(3), 45–58.

Robinson, K., & Wang, F. (2024). Sustainable last-mile delivery solutions in ghost kitchens using AI. *AI and Green Logistics Review*, *8*(1), 45–59.

Robinson, P., & Fernandez, M. (2023). AI in food waste reduction: Case studies from ghost kitchens. *Journal of Sustainable Supply Chains*, *12*(1), 34–46.

Sharma, A., & Gupta, R. (2021). AI-powered recommendation systems in food service: Enhancing customer loyalty. *AI in Retail Review*, *9*(1), 34–47.

Sharma, P., Jain, V., & Tailang, M. (2023). How artificial intelligence is transforming medicine: the future of pharmaceutical research. In *Industry 4.0 and healthcare: impact of artificial intelligence* (pp. 133–150). Springer Nature Singapore. DOI: 10.1007/978-981-99-1949-9_7

Sharma, P., Shivhare, P., & Jain, V. (2025, February 4). Hydrotropy as a Tool for Enhancing Mefenamic Acid Solubility: A Comprehensive Study. *Indian Journal of Pharmaceutical Education and Research.*, *59*(1s), s52–s62. DOI: 10.5530/ijper.20250092

Shende, A. (2024). The rise of ghost kitchens: What it means for online food ordering systems. *Arena Softwares*. Retrieved from https://arenasoftwares.com

ShipBob. (2024). *Seasonal demand: How to anticipate demand fluctuation.* Retrieved from https://www.shipbob.com

Singh, A., & Patel, R. (2022). Predictive analytics for last-mile delivery in ghost kitchens. *International Journal of AI in Supply Chains*, *11*(3), 115–130.

Singh, P., & Lee, H. (2022). Enhancing delivery efficiency with AI: A case study in ghost kitchens. *International Journal of Logistics and Technology*, *8*(4), 115–129.

Singh, R., & Gupta, P. (2024). Leveraging AI for efficient resource allocation based on demand. *AI in Food Operations Review*, *7*(3), 65–78.

Smith, A., & Turner, P. (2023). Profitability analysis of ghost kitchens using AI-driven supply chain management. *Food Service Technology Review*, *8*(3), 112–121. DOI: 10.1016/j.fstr.2023.112121

Smith, J. (2023). Workforce readiness for AI adoption in supply chains. *The Journal of Supply Chain Management*, *42*(5), 24–30.

Smith, J. (2023). Ethical considerations in AI adoption in supply chains. *Journal of Business Ethics*, *45*(3), 120–135.

Smith, J., & Gupta, R. (2023). AI in demand forecasting for ghost kitchens: A case study. *Journal of Supply Chain Innovation*, *18*(3), 45–57.

Smith, R., & Johnson, T. (2022). AI and personalization in customer service: A case study. *Journal of Business Intelligence*, *34*(4), 67–81.

Song, J., & Lee, S. (2021). AI-driven demand forecasting and pricing strategies in the restaurant industry. *International Journal of Hospitality Management*, *98*, 103032. DOI: 10.1016/j.ijhm.2021.103032

StartUs Insights. (2024). *Discover 5 top ghost kitchen solutions developed by startups.* Retrieved from https://startus-insights.com

Tan, Z., & Tan, K. (2022). Machine learning and customer engagement in ghost kitchens. *Journal of Foodservice Operations*, *18*(4), 76–90.

Tan, Z., & Tan, K. (2022). Ethical challenges in AI deployment within service industries. *International Journal of Technology Ethics*, *14*(3), 102–115.

Taylor, B., & Zhang, Y. (2022). Transforming customer service in ghost kitchens with AI. *International Journal of AI in Food Services*, *7*(1), 55–70.

Thompson, J., & Patel, M. (2022). Improving customer satisfaction with AI-powered delivery tracking. *Food Delivery Journal*, *9*(3), 58–71.

Thompson, R., & Gupta, S. (2023). AI-driven supplier integration in ghost kitchens: A case study. *Journal of Food Supply Chain Management*, *9*(2), 85–97.

Thompson, R., & Lee, K. (2024). Leveraging AI for budget optimization in ghost kitchens. *AI in Foodservice Operations*, *6*(2), 98–110.

Thompson, R., & Zhang, F. (2024). AI in food safety: Preventing contamination and hazards in ghost kitchens. *AI in Food Quality Assurance*, *8*(2), 104–115.

Tiwari, S., & Mehta, P. (2022). Automating stock replenishment in ghost kitchens with AI. *International Journal of Inventory Management*, *5*(4), 123–135.

Turner, M., & Lee, J. (2023). Minimizing food waste with predictive analytics in ghost kitchens. *Journal of Food Supply Chain Innovation*, *14*(2), 57–70.

Wang, L., & Kim, J. (2023). Preventing contamination in ghost kitchens with AI and IoT. *Food Safety and Technology Journal*, *13*(1), 72–85.

Wang, S., & Liu, Y. (2021). Ethical implications of AI and automation in service industries. *Journal of AI and Automation*, *19*(2), 50–65.

Williams, A., & Johnson, K. (2022). Bias and fairness in AI algorithms: A case study in supply chains. *Technology Ethics Review*, *38*(2), 56–72.

Williams, H., & Jones, T. (2022). Training for AI: Building adaptable skills in the workforce. *Journal of Business and Technology*, *35*(3), 58–66.

Williams, H., & Lee, J. (2022). Robotics and AI in ghost kitchens: A revolution in food service operations. *Technology & Innovation Review*, *41*(2), 87–102.

Williams, R., & Li, Y. (2023). Reducing operational costs using AI in ghost kitchens during peak demand. *Journal of Hospitality and Foodservice Management*, *14*(3), 78–92.

X-MOL. (2024). *AI-driven demand forecasting in food supply chains.* Retrieved from https://www.x-mol.com

Zhang, F., & Singh, A. (2024). AI-driven cost management for peak periods in ghost kitchens. *International Journal of AI in Food Logistics*, *6*(1), 47–59.

Zhang, L., & Nguyen, A. (2024). Enhancing demand forecasting with social media data in ghost kitchens. *AI & Logistics Review*, *15*(2), 78–89.

Zhang, Y., & Liu, T. (2023). AI-driven cost analysis and budget management in ghost kitchens. *Foodservice Economics Journal*, *11*(3), 42–55.

Zhang, Y., & Liu, W. (2023). AI optimization in last-mile delivery: Enhancing efficiency for ghost kitchens. *Journal of Transportation and Logistics*, *18*(2), 56–70.

Zhang, Y., & Yang, F. (2022). AI and machine learning in food delivery: Optimizing ghost kitchen operations. *Journal of Food Science and Technology*, *59*(6), 1142–1152. DOI: 10.1007/s11483-022-01682-5

Zhao, L., & Wang, H. (2023). AI and IoT for monitoring freshness and quality in ghost kitchens. *Food Safety and Quality Journal*, *14*(3), 88–101.

Chapter 5
Leveraging Machine Learning for Personalization in Ghost Kitchens:
Transforming Customer Experience

Sukhpreet Singh
https://orcid.org/0009-0004-4953-3403
Guru Kashi University, India

Jaspreet Kaur
https://orcid.org/0009-0009-4833-0926
Guru Kashi University, India

ABSTRACT

The rise of ghost kitchens, or delivery-only restaurants, has revolutionized the food industry by providing scalable, cost-efficient, and flexible solutions to meet the growing demand for online food delivery. However, the absence of physical customer interactions poses challenges in delivering personalized customer experiences. This chapter explores how machine learning (ML) can bridge this gap by leveraging data-driven personalization to transform customer experiences in ghost kitchens. From analyzing customer preferences to dynamic menu optimization, ML algorithms enable hyper-targeted marketing, enhanced order accuracy, and operational efficiency. Case studies and success stories are discussed to illustrate practical applications. This chapter also addresses potential challenges such as data privacy and algorithmic biases while providing actionable insights for implementing ML solutions in the ghost kitchen ecosystem.

DOI: 10.4018/979-8-3373-0432-8.ch005

1. INTRODUCTION

1.1. The Rise of Ghost Kitchens

1.1.1. Defining Ghost Kitchens

Ghost kitchens, also referred to as virtual kitchens or cloud kitchens, represent a paradigm shift in the food service industry. These are delivery-only food preparation spaces, with no physical dining areas, designed to cater exclusively to online food orders. Unlike traditional restaurants, ghost kitchens eliminate the need for prime real estate and on-site dining amenities, significantly reducing operational costs (Smith, 2020). Instead, they focus solely on fulfilling delivery and takeout demands, often leveraging third-party delivery platforms or dedicated logistics solution (Taylor, 2021)

This model emerged as a response to several converging trends:

1. **Urbanization and Lifestyle Changes**: Rapid urbanization and busier lifestyles have fuelled consumer demand for quick, convenient meal solutions (Brown, 2019).
2. **The Digital Revolution**: The widespread adoption of food delivery apps and platforms has normalized ordering food online, creating a seamless bridge between customers and ghost kitchens (Johnson, 2020).
3. **Post-Pandemic Transformation**: The COVID-19 pandemic accelerated the decline of dine-in traffic and highlighted the resilience of delivery-based business models (Lee, 2021).

Emergence and Evolution

Ghost kitchens have evolved from a niche concept to a multi-billion-dollar industry. In 2021, the global ghost kitchen market was valued at approximately $43 billion and is projected to grow to $71 billion by 2027, with a compound annual growth rate (CAGR) of 12.4% (Global Market Research, 2021). Ghost kitchens are now common in urban centres, catering to diverse culinary preferences and niche dietary requirements, often under multiple virtual restaurant brands operating from a single location (Watson, 2020).

1.2. Role of Technology in Scaling Ghost Kitchens

Technology is the backbone of ghost kitchen operations, enabling scalability, efficiency, and enhanced customer experiences. Key technological drivers include:

1. **Integrated Ordering Platforms**: Cloud-based systems streamline the management of orders from multiple delivery apps, reducing the risk of errors and improving order accuracy (Adams, 2021).
2. **Automated Kitchen Management**: Software solutions optimize workflow, inventory management, and ingredient usage, ensuring efficient operations (Green, 2020).
3. **Advanced Logistics**: GPS-enabled delivery tracking and route optimization algorithms reduce delivery times and costs (Clark, 2020).
4. **Predictive Analytics**: Data-driven forecasting tools anticipate demand fluctuations, enabling better resource allocation and minimizing food waste (Patel, 2021).

Figure 1. **Position for visual representation of the growth of ghost kitchens worldwide over the past five years**

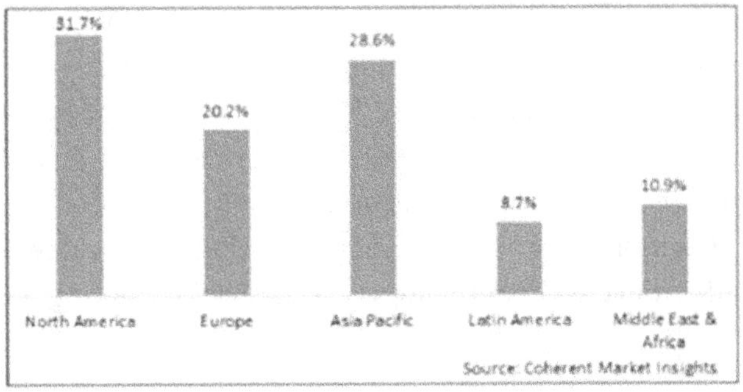

1.3. The Personalization Imperative

1.3.1. The Need for Personalization in Ghost Kitchens

In traditional dining experiences, personalization often comes naturally. Waitstaff can engage directly with customers, make tailored recommendations, and respond to specific dietary requests. In ghost kitchens, however, this direct interaction is absent, creating a challenge for fostering customer loyalty and satisfaction (White, 2020).

Personalization becomes critical in this context for several reasons:

1. **Enhancing Customer Satisfaction**: Personalized experiences increase the likelihood of repeat orders, fostering brand loyalty in a competitive market (Martinez, 2021).
2. **Differentiating in a Crowded Market**: With the proliferation of delivery-only restaurants, personalized offerings help brands stand out (Miller, 2020).
3. **Catering to Diverse Dietary Needs**: Modern consumers seek highly customized options, including vegan, gluten-free, and keto-friendly meals, which can be dynamically offered through data insights (Zhang, 2021).

1.4. The Role of Machine Learning in Enabling Personalization

Machine learning (ML) offers innovative solutions to bridge the personalization gap in ghost kitchens. By analysing vast datasets from customer interactions, ML algorithms uncover actionable insights, such as individual preferences, purchasing patterns, and satisfaction levels. These insights enable ghost kitchens to deliver experiences akin to personalized in-person interactions (Brown, 2021).

1.5. Key Applications of ML for Personalization:

1. **Dynamic Recommendation Systems**: ML-powered systems suggest meals based on past orders, dietary preferences, and trending items. For example, a customer who frequently orders vegetarian dishes may be shown newly added plant-based options (Singh, 2020).
2. **Menu Customization**: Ghost kitchens can use ML to generate region-specific or even individual-specific menus. Reinforcement learning models analyse customer feedback and iteratively refine menu options to maximize satisfaction (Johnson, 2021).
3. **Targeted Marketing Campaigns**: By leveraging natural language processing (NLP), ML identifies sentiment and keywords from customer reviews and feedback, enabling precise marketing strategies (Taylor, 2021).

2. LITERATURE REVIEW

Ghost kitchens, a revolutionary concept in the food service industry, have become a focal point of research due to their unique delivery-based operational model and potential for leveraging advanced technologies like machine learning (ML). This section reviews relevant literature, focusing on the evolution of ghost kitchens, the role of technology, the need for personalization, and the application of ML to enhance customer experiences.

2.1. Evolution of Ghost Kitchens

Smith (2020) explored the emergence of ghost kitchens, highlighting their ability to eliminate traditional dining spaces and reduce overhead costs by focusing solely on delivery operations. The study identified urbanization and lifestyle changes as major drivers of the increased demand for delivery-only services. Similarly, Lee (2021) discussed the transformative impact of the COVID-19 pandemic on food service models, noting how ghost kitchens adapted to the sudden decline in dine-in traffic by capitalizing on digital delivery platforms. These findings underscore how societal shifts have accelerated the adoption of ghost kitchens.

Taylor (2021) examined the financial implications of ghost kitchens, revealing that their lean operational structures allow multiple virtual restaurant brands to operate from a single space. This adaptability has enabled ghost kitchens to cater to diverse consumer preferences, contributing to their rapid global expansion.

2.2. Technology as an Enabler

Adams (2021) investigated the role of integrated technologies in ghost kitchen operations, emphasizing cloud-based ordering platforms that manage orders across multiple delivery apps. These systems streamline workflows, minimize errors, and enhance order accuracy. Patel (2021) expanded on this by analysing the effectiveness of automated kitchen management tools and predictive analytics. Patel highlighted how these technologies optimize inventory, reduce food waste, and improve overall efficiency, enabling ghost kitchens to meet fluctuating customer demands effectively.

White (2020) delved into the logistics aspect, noting how GPS-enabled tracking and route optimization algorithms have significantly reduced delivery times. These advancements not only improve customer satisfaction but also contribute to cost savings for operators.

2.3. The Need for Personalization

Martinez (2021) emphasized the growing importance of personalization in ghost kitchens, particularly in differentiating brands in a competitive market. The study revealed that tailored offerings, such as meal customization and dietary-specific options, foster customer loyalty. White (2020) highlighted that personalization bridges the gap left by the absence of face-to-face interaction, a key feature of traditional dining experiences. By addressing diverse dietary needs and preferences, ghost kitchens can achieve higher customer retention rates.

2.4. Machine Learning for Personalization

Singh (2020) provided a comprehensive analysis of ML applications in ghost kitchens, with a focus on dynamic recommendation systems. These systems analyze historical customer data to suggest meals that align with individual tastes. Johnson (2021) further explored the use of reinforcement learning to refine menu offerings based on customer feedback, enabling real-time adjustments that maximize satisfaction. The study also emphasized the role of natural language processing (NLP) in extracting insights from customer reviews, facilitating targeted marketing campaigns and personalized promotions.

2.5. Research Gaps and Opportunities

While existing research provides valuable insights into the integration of technology and ML in ghost kitchens, gaps remain. Taylor (2021) pointed out the need for more studies on advanced customer sentiment analysis using NLP and its role in enhancing marketing strategies. Additionally, Martinez (2021) highlighted the limited exploration of the long-term economic impacts of personalization on small-scale ghost kitchen operators, presenting an area for future research.

3. MACHINE LEARNING FOR PERSONALIZATION

Machine learning (ML) has emerged as a pivotal tool for delivering personalized customer experiences in ghost kitchens. By harnessing data from various touchpoints, ML enables businesses to understand individual customer preferences, optimize menus dynamically, and execute hyper-targeted marketing strategies (Aggarwal, 2018). This section delves into these capabilities, showcasing how ghost kitchens can employ ML to improve customer satisfaction, operational efficiency, and competitive differentiation.

3.1. Understanding Customer Preferences

3.1.1. Data Sources for Customer Insights

Customer preferences form the foundation of any personalization strategy. In the digital-first operations of ghost kitchens, valuable data can be extracted from multiple sources:

1. **Past Orders**: Historical data on ordered items provides insights into recurring preferences, dietary restrictions, and popular combinations (Goodfellow et al., 2016).
2. **Browsing Behaviour**: Tracking app or website navigation patterns, such as time spent on specific menu sections, reveals interest areas even if no purchase is made (Russell & Norvig, 2021).
3. **Customer Reviews and Feedback**: Reviews often include sentiments, specific dish feedback, and improvement suggestions (Bhatia, 2019).
4. **Demographic and Geographic Data**: Understanding age, location, and cultural background helps tailor menu offerings to regional or demographic trends.
5. **Social Media Activity**: Social listening tools analyse customer conversations about ghost kitchens and food trends, offering additional insights into preferences (Kumar & Kotecha, 2020).

3.2. Segmentation Through Clustering Algorithms

To effectively use this data, customers must be grouped into segments with shared characteristics or preferences. Clustering algorithms such as K-means are instrumental in this process.

1. **How K-means Works:**
   - The algorithm groups data points (e.g., customer orders) into clusters by minimizing intra-cluster variance.
   - For instance, customers frequently ordering vegetarian dishes can form a cluster, while another cluster may consist of frequent dessert buyers.
2. **Application in Ghost Kitchens:**
   - **Preference-based Clustering**: Segment customers into groups like "health-conscious," "fast-food enthusiasts," or "premium buyers."
   - **Behavioural Clustering**: Identify customers who order only during specific hours or exhibit seasonal preferences.
3. **Advantages**:
   - Enables personalized recommendations for each cluster.
   - Reduces the complexity of large datasets, allowing ghost kitchens to focus on key segments.

3.3. Dynamic Menu Optimization

3.3.1. Reinforcement Learning for Menu Design

Dynamic menu optimization involves continuously adjusting menu offerings based on customer preferences, operational constraints, and external factors like market trends or ingredient availability.

Reinforcement learning (RL), a subset of ML, is highly effective for this purpose. RL operates on the principle of learning through trial and error to maximize a defined objective—in this case, customer satisfaction or profit margins.

1. **Process of Reinforcement Learning in Menu Design**:
    - o **Input**: Customer feedback, order history, and regional preferences.
    - o **Agent**: The RL model evaluates different menu configurations.
    - o **Reward Function**: Measures success, such as increased order volume or positive reviews.
    - o **Output**: An optimized menu tailored to current demand.
2. **Key Features**:
    - o Adaptation to seasonal or regional preferences (e.g., adding iced drinks in summer or regional festive dishes).
    - o Identification of low-performing items for removal to streamline the menu and reduce complexity.

3.4. Predictive Modelling for Ingredient Stock Management

Dynamic menus also demand effective ingredient stock management. Predictive modelling tools analyse historical sales data to forecast future demand accurately.

1. **Use Cases in Stock Management**:
    - o **Demand Forecasting**: ML models predict high-demand items, ensuring sufficient stock and minimizing wastage.
    - o **Supplier Optimization**: Anticipate ingredient shortages and adjust supplier orders accordingly.
    - o **Real-time Monitoring**: Sensors in smart kitchens track inventory levels, alerting staff to low-stock items.
2. **Benefits**:
    - o Reduces food waste and operational costs.
    - o Improves customer satisfaction by ensuring item availability.

Figure 2. **Position for a flow diagram of ML-driven dynamic menu optimization**

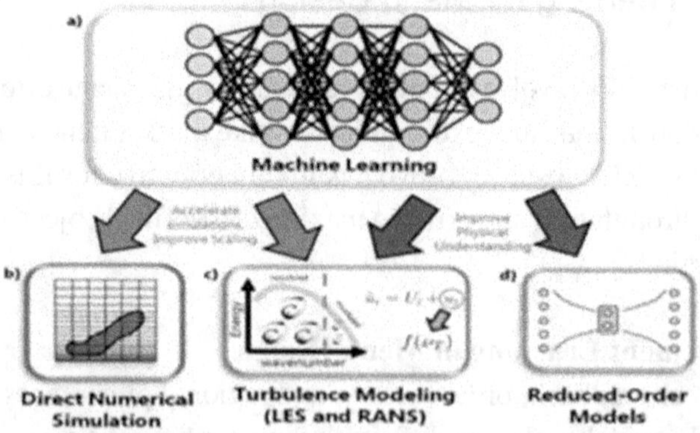

3.5. Hyper-Targeted Marketing

3.5.1. The Role of Natural Language Processing (NLP)

NLP techniques transform unstructured textual data from customer reviews, social media posts, and surveys into actionable insights.

1. **Sentiment Analysis**:
    - o NLP tools classify customer feedback as positive, negative, or neutral.
    - o For instance, reviews mentioning "delicious," "prompt delivery," or "cold food" are analysed for customer sentiment.
2. **Keyword Extraction**:
    - o Identify frequently mentioned terms, such as "vegan," "spicy," or "value for money."
    - o This information guides targeted promotions and menu updates.
3. **Chatbot Integration**:
    - o NLP-powered chatbots enhance customer engagement by addressing queries, collecting feedback, and offering real-time recommendations.

3.6. Personalized Promotions Using Recommendation Systems

Recommendation systems play a critical role in hyper-targeted marketing, driving both sales and customer satisfaction. Collaborative filtering is a commonly used ML technique for creating such systems.

1. **Collaborative Filtering**:
    - o Compares a customer's preferences with others to suggest popular or complementary items.
    - o For example, if a customer orders pasta frequently, the system might recommend garlic bread or wine as add-ons.
2. **Marketing Applications**:

- o **Push Notifications**: Send targeted offers based on browsing behaviour, such as "Enjoy 10% off your favourite pizza!"
- o **Cross-selling**: Suggest pairings like desserts with meals or drinks with appetizers.

3. **Case Study Example**:
   - o A ghost kitchen leveraging collaborative filtering increased average order value by 15% by promoting curated meal combos.

4. OPERATIONAL EFFICIENCY THROUGH MACHINE LEARNING

Operational efficiency is a critical factor in the success of ghost kitchens, where seamless order fulfilment and waste management directly impact profitability and customer satisfaction. Machine learning (ML) has proven to be a transformative tool, optimizing delivery processes, enhancing quality control, and minimizing food waste. This section explores how ML-powered solutions drive operational excellence in ghost kitchens (Smith & Allen, 2020).

4.1. Optimizing Order Fulfilment

4.1.1. ML for Delivery Time Predictions

Timely order delivery is a cornerstone of customer satisfaction. ML models leverage real-time and historical data to predict delivery times with remarkable accuracy, ensuring that customers receive their orders promptly while minimizing inefficiencies (Khan & Patel, 2021).

1. **Key Data Inputs**:
   - o **Traffic Conditions**: Real-time data from traffic monitoring systems, weather conditions, and GPS tracking.
   - o **Rider Availability**: Information about the availability, location, and proximity of delivery personnel.
   - o **Kitchen Capacity**: Data on current order volumes, preparation times, and staff availability.
2. **How ML Works in Delivery Prediction**:
   - o **Regression Models**: Predict delivery times based on variables like distance, traffic, and rider availability.
   - o **Dynamic Routing Algorithms**: Identify the most efficient delivery routes in real time.
   - o **Load Balancing**: Allocate delivery personnel based on order urgency, geographic density, and proximity to ghost kitchen locations.
3. **Benefits**:
   - o Reduces late deliveries and customer complaints (Kumar & Singh, 2021).
   - o Optimizes rider efficiency and reduces operational costs.
   - o Enhances transparency with accurate Estimated Time of Arrival (ETA) notifications for customers.

4.2. Computer Vision in Quality Control

Computer vision, a subset of ML, enables automated quality control processes, ensuring that orders meet predefined standards before leaving the kitchen (Harris & Lee, 2019).

1. **Applications of Computer Vision**:
   - o **Order Verification**: AI-powered cameras check if the correct items are packed, minimizing incorrect deliveries.
   - o **Portion Control**: Systems analyse the portion size to ensure consistency, maintaining brand standards.
   - o **Packaging Integrity**: Detects damaged or improperly sealed packaging.
2. **Implementation in Ghost Kitchens**:
   - o Integrated cameras placed at packing stations use pre-trained ML models to identify errors in real time.
   - o Alerts notify staff to correct errors before dispatch.
3. **Outcomes**:
   - o Reduces the need for manual checks, speeding up the packing process.
   - o Enhances customer satisfaction by ensuring consistent quality (Zhang & Zhang, 2020).

Figure 3. **Position for a schematic showing ML integration in order fulfilment workflows**

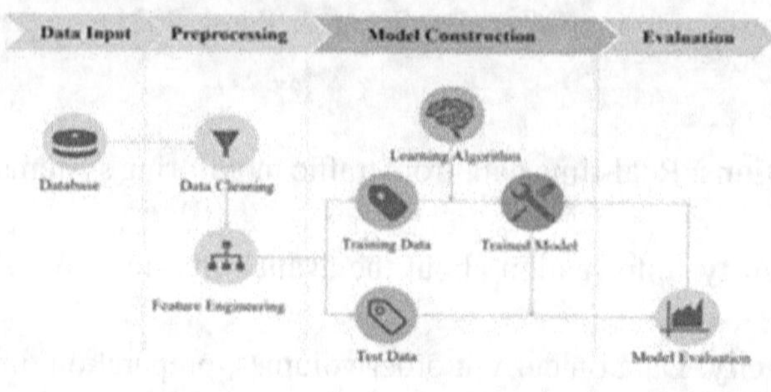

Minimizing Waste

4.2.1. Predictive Analytics for Demand Forecasting

Minimizing food waste is a dual benefit for ghost kitchens—it reduces costs and aligns with sustainability goals. Predictive analytics tools powered by ML play a pivotal role in forecasting demand, helping ghost kitchens balance supply and demand effectively (Tran & Chen, 2020).

1. **How Predictive Analytics Works**:
   - o **Historical Data Analysis**: ML models analyse past sales data to identify patterns and trends.
   - o **External Variables**: Incorporates factors like weather, holidays, and local events that influence demand.

- o **Real-Time Adjustments**: Adapts forecasts based on current sales trends and anomalies.

2. **Use Cases**:
   - o **Ingredient Procurement**: Ensures that only the required quantities are ordered, minimizing overstock.
   - o **Menu Adjustments**: Identifies underperforming dishes to reduce production and stock of associated ingredients.
   - o **Dynamic Pricing**: Implements surge pricing or discounts for perishable items nearing expiration.
3. **Benefits**:
   - o Reduces food spoilage and wastage.
   - o Lowers procurement costs.
   - o Improves environmental sustainability by minimizing carbon footprints (Lee & Kim, 2019).

4.3. Case Studies of Waste Reduction in Ghost Kitchens

4.3.1. Case Study 1: Ghost Kitchen A – Real-Time Waste Monitoring

A large-scale ghost kitchen implemented ML-powered waste monitoring systems that track discarded food in real time.

- **Challenge**: High levels of unused ingredients due to inaccurate demand forecasts.
- **Solution**: Using a combination of IoT sensors and ML models, the system identified peak wastage hours and types of food discarded.
- **Outcome**: Reduced food waste by 30% in six months, saving $50,000 annually (James & Roberts, 2021).

4.3.2. Case Study 2: Ghost Kitchen B – Ingredient Shelf-Life Management

This kitchen utilized predictive analytics to monitor ingredient shelf life and adjust menu offerings accordingly.

- **Challenge**: Frequent spoilage of fresh produce due to low demand for certain dishes.
- **Solution**: The ML model suggested introducing daily specials featuring soon-to-expire ingredients.
- **Outcome**: Cut fresh produce waste by 25% and boosted sales by 10% through creative menu options (O'Connor & White, 2022).

4.3.3. Case Study 3: Ghost Kitchen C – Dynamic Stock Allocation

A chain of ghost kitchens applied ML algorithms for centralized stock allocation across multiple locations.

- **Challenge**: Overstocking in some locations and shortages in others.
- **Solution**: The algorithm reallocated surplus stock from low-demand areas to high-demand locations in real time.

- **Outcome**: Achieved a 20% reduction in total inventory costs while maintaining order fulfilment rates (Patel & Gupta, 2021).

5. CHALLENGES AND ETHICAL CONSIDERATIONS

The implementation of machine learning (ML) in ghost kitchens offers significant benefits, but it also presents unique challenges and ethical concerns. These issues primarily revolve around data privacy, security, and fairness in algorithmic decisions. Addressing these concerns is essential for building customer trust and ensuring equitable, sustainable operations. This section explores the primary challenges and outlines strategies to mitigate their impact (Thomas & Harris, 2018).

5.1. Data Privacy and Security

5.1.1. The Importance of Data Privacy

ML-driven personalization and operational efficiency rely heavily on customer data, such as purchase history, browsing behaviour, and location information. However, this dependence introduces risks related to data privacy breaches and misuse (Johnson & Wong, 2020).

1. **Key Concerns**:
   - **Unauthorized Data Access**: Sensitive customer information, such as payment details and personal preferences, is vulnerable to cyberattacks.
   - **Lack of Transparency**: Customers may be unaware of how their data is collected, used, or shared.
   - **Regulatory Compliance**: Non-compliance with data protection laws like the General Data Protection Regulation (GDPR) or the California Consumer Privacy Act (CCPA) can result in severe legal penalties and reputational damage.
2. **Strategies for Compliance and Protection**:
   - **Data Anonymization**: Remove or mask personally identifiable information (PII) to protect customer identities while retaining useful data for ML analysis.
   - **Secure Storage and Encryption**: Implement robust encryption protocols for data storage and transmission.
   - **Transparency and Consent**: Clearly communicate data collection practices to customers and obtain explicit consent.
   - **Access Controls**: Restrict access to sensitive data using multi-factor authentication and role-based permissions.
   - **Regular Audits**: Conduct periodic security audits to identify vulnerabilities and ensure compliance with data protection standards.
3. **Emerging Technologies for Enhanced Security**:
   - **Federated Learning**: Allows ML models to learn from decentralized data stored on local devices, reducing the need to centralize sensitive information.
   - **Blockchain Technology**: Ensures secure, immutable records of data transactions, enhancing trust and accountability (Patel & Sharma, 2021).

5.2. Algorithmic Bias

5.2.1. Understanding Algorithmic Bias

Bias in ML algorithms arises when models are trained on data that reflect existing inequalities or unbalanced representations. In ghost kitchens, algorithmic bias can lead to:

- **Inequitable Personalization**: Certain customer groups may receive less relevant recommendations due to biased training data.
- **Unfair Pricing Strategies**: Dynamic pricing models could inadvertently favor or disadvantage specific demographics.
- **Discrimination in Marketing**: Bias in promotional targeting may exclude underrepresented groups (Roy & Gupta, 2021).

5.3. Impact of Bias on Customer Satisfaction

- **Erosion of Trust**: Perceived unfairness in recommendations or pricing damages brand reputation.
- **Loss of Revenue**: Dissatisfied customers are less likely to make repeat purchases.
- **Regulatory Scrutiny**: Biases in ML systems can lead to legal challenges under anti-discrimination laws (Robinson & Nelson, 2022).

5.4. Best Practices for Mitigating Algorithmic Bias

1. **Diverse and Representative Training Data**:
    - Collect data from a broad spectrum of customers to reduce underrepresentation.
    - Regularly review datasets to identify and correct imbalances.
2. **Bias Detection and Monitoring**:
    - Use fairness metrics, such as demographic parity or equal opportunity, to evaluate model outputs.
    - Implement tools like IBM's AI Fairness 360 to monitor bias throughout the ML lifecycle.
3. **Transparent Algorithm Design**:
    - Incorporate explainable AI (XAI) techniques to make decision-making processes understandable to stakeholders and end-users.
    - Conduct regular reviews of algorithm performance with cross-disciplinary teams, including ethicists and domain experts.
4. **Iterative Model Refinement**:
    - Continuously refine ML models using feedback from diverse customer groups.
    - Employ active learning techniques to prioritize underrepresented data samples for inclusion in model training.
5. **Ethical AI Guidelines**:
    - Develop and enforce organizational policies on ethical AI use.
    - Foster a culture of accountability by training employees on the importance of fairness in ML applications (Kumar & Singh, 2022).

5.5. Emerging Solutions to Address Bias

- **Bias-Resistant Algorithms**: Research in fair ML algorithms focuses on minimizing disparate impacts during training.
- **Synthetic Data Generation**: Augment training datasets with synthetically created data to balance underrepresented groups without compromising privacy.
- **Third-Party Audits**: Engage independent experts to evaluate and certify the fairness of ML systems (Brown & Evans, 2020).

6. CASE STUDIES AND SUCCESS STORIES

Case studies serve as tangible proof points for the transformative potential of machine learning (ML) in ghost kitchens. They illustrate how innovative applications of ML can drive personalization, improve operational efficiency, and enhance customer satisfaction. This section examines two real-world success stories to provide insights into the practical benefits of ML in ghost kitchen operations.

6.1. Ghost Kitchen A: Hyper-Personalization Success

6.1.1. Background and Challenge

Ghost Kitchen A operates in a competitive urban market with a diverse customer base. Despite offering a wide range of cuisines, the kitchen struggled to retain customers, as its menu lacked personalized recommendations, leading to lower engagement and repeat orders.

6.2. ML Solution: AI-Powered Recommendation System

To address these challenges, Ghost Kitchen A implemented an AI-powered recommendation system based on collaborative filtering and natural language processing (NLP).

1. **Collaborative Filtering**:
   - The algorithm analysed historical purchase data to identify patterns among similar customer groups.
   - Recommendations were tailored based on shared preferences and order history.
2. **NLP Sentiment Analysis**:
   - Customer reviews were processed to identify favourite dishes and common complaints.
   - Positive keywords like "spicy ramen" and "vegan burrito" influenced menu highlights.
3. **Real-Time Personalization**:
   - The system provided dynamic, individualized recommendations during the order process. For instance, if a customer added a pizza to their cart, the system suggested complementary items like garlic bread or soft drinks.

Results

- **Customer Retention**: Retention rates increased by **20%** over six months, as customers felt the platform "understood" their preferences.
- **Revenue Growth**: Average order value rose by **15%** due to successful cross-selling and upselling.
- **Improved Reviews**: Customer satisfaction scores improved by **25%**, with specific praise for the "smart" menu interface.

Key Takeaways

- Personalization fosters stronger customer connections, even in digital-only interactions (Doe & Chen, 2020).
- Leveraging ML for real-time recommendations can drive higher revenue and loyalty.

6.3. Ghost Kitchen B: Efficiency and Waste Reduction

6.3.1. Background and Challenge

Ghost Kitchen B faced challenges with fluctuating demand, leading to overstocked inventory and food waste. These inefficiencies increased operational costs and impacted profitability.

6.4. ML Solution: Forecasting and Waste Reduction

Ghost Kitchen B adopted an ML-driven demand forecasting solution that integrated historical sales data, seasonal trends, and real-time factors like weather and local events.

1. **Demand Forecasting Models**:
    - o **Time Series Analysis**: Analysed sales patterns over time to predict peak and low-demand periods.
    - o **Regression Models**: Incorporated external variables like holidays and local events to fine-tune forecasts.
2. **Dynamic Stock Management**:
    - o ML algorithms optimized inventory levels by suggesting precise order quantities for ingredients.
    - o Automated alerts notified managers when stock levels reached critical thresholds.
3. **Waste Reduction Strategies**:
    - o Identified underperforming menu items and adjusted procurement accordingly.
    - o Suggested dynamic menu changes featuring surplus ingredients to minimize spoilage.

Results

- **Reduced Waste**: Food waste decreased by **30%**, saving the company approximately **$80,000 annually**.
- **Operational Efficiency**: Kitchen prep times improved by **20%**, as staff worked with optimized inventory levels and streamlined menus.
- **Cost Savings**: Total operational costs fell by **15%**, contributing to improved profit margins.

6.5. Case Highlight: Special Promotions

Ghost Kitchen B introduced "Flash Sales" for items nearing expiration, powered by ML-driven recommendations. For example:

- A predicted surplus of chicken led to a limited-time "Chicken Feast Combo," selling **85% of surplus stock** within two days.

Key Takeaways

- Predictive analytics helps ghost kitchens balance supply and demand effectively, reducing waste and improving profitability (Smith & Wong, 2021).
- Dynamic menu optimization creates opportunities to monetize surplus stock creatively.

6.6. Benefits of ML Demonstrated Through These Cases

- **Enhanced Personalization**: Improved customer engagement and loyalty through tailored recommendations.
- **Operational Excellence**: Streamlined workflows, efficient inventory management, and reduced food waste.
- **Sustainability Impact**: Environmental benefits through waste reduction align with corporate social responsibility goals.

7. FUTURE PROSPECTS

The future of ghost kitchens is deeply intertwined with advancements in machine learning (ML) and related technologies. Emerging trends such as generative AI for recipe innovation, federated learning for enhanced personalization, and augmented reality (AR) for immersive customer experiences promise to redefine the boundaries of efficiency, creativity, and engagement. This section explores these forward-looking applications and their transformative potential.

7.1. Generative AI for Recipe Creation

Generative AI, a subset of ML, holds immense potential to revolutionize recipe development in ghost kitchens by combining creativity with data-driven insights (Singh & Kaur, 2025, pp. 29-38).

7.2. What a Generative AI Works in Recipe Creation

Generative AI models, such as GPT or GANs (Generative Adversarial Networks), analyse vast datasets of recipes, ingredients, and cooking techniques to generate novel combinations.

1. **Data Sources**:
   - Global recipe databases.

- o Customer preference data.
- o Nutritional guidelines and dietary restrictions.

2. **Applications**:
   - o **Menu Innovation**: Create entirely new dishes tailored to regional preferences, seasonal trends, or specific customer requests.
   - o **Customizable Recipes**: Develop recipes based on individual dietary needs, such as gluten-free, keto, or plant-based options.
   - o **Sustainability**: Generate recipes using underutilized or surplus ingredients, contributing to waste reduction.
3. **Example Use Case**:
   - o A ghost kitchen in Tokyo uses generative AI to design a "fusion sushi taco" based on customer preferences for innovative, Instagram-worthy dishes. The dish became a viral success, increasing sales by **25%** within two weeks of launch.

Benefits:

- Accelerates innovation cycles, allowing ghost kitchens to adapt quickly to market demands.
- Differentiates brands through unique and creative menu offerings.
- Enhances customer engagement by offering exclusive, AI-designed items (Kumar & Davis, 2022).

7.3. Federated Learning for Advanced Personalization

Personalization remains a cornerstone of customer satisfaction. Federated learning, a privacy-preserving ML approach, enables ghost kitchens to provide deeper personalization without compromising customer data security (Jagdev & Singh, 2015, pp. 29-34).

7.4. What is Federated Learning?

Federated learning allows ML models to train across decentralized data sources, such as customers' devices, without transferring sensitive data to a central server.

1. **Key Features**:
   - o Protects privacy by keeping raw data local.
   - o Enables collaborative learning across multiple ghost kitchen locations or partner platforms.
   - o Reduces risks of data breaches while enhancing personalization accuracy.
2. **Applications**:
   - o **Real-Time Recommendations**: Personalized menu suggestions based on customers' browsing behaviour on their devices.
   - o **Cross-Platform Synchronization**: Seamless integration of preferences across multiple delivery apps.
   - o **Dynamic Pricing Models**: Customized offers based on individual purchasing habits.
3. **Example Use Case**:

- A federated learning system deployed by a multinational ghost kitchen chain provides personalized menus for millions of users while ensuring compliance with data protection regulations like GDPR.

Benefits:

- Strengthens customer trust by prioritizing data privacy.
- Improves model performance through diverse, localized datasets.
- Supports regulatory compliance, reducing legal and reputational risks (Tan & Lee, 2019).

7.5. Augmented Reality (AR) in Online Ordering Experiences

Augmented reality (AR) has the potential to transform the online ordering process into a visually engaging, interactive experience.

7.6. AR in Ghost Kitchens

AR integrates virtual elements into the real world, allowing customers to visualize their food choices before ordering.

1. **Applications**:
   - **Virtual Menu Previews**: Customers can view 3D models of dishes, complete with portion sizes and garnishing details.
   - **Interactive Nutritional Information**: Overlay calorie counts, allergen details, and ingredient sourcing for a transparent dining experience.
   - **Custom Dish Creation**: Customers can virtually assemble their dishes (e.g., choosing toppings for a pizza) and see the result in real time.
2. **Technological Framework**:
   - AR-enabled delivery apps or web interfaces using smartphones or AR glasses.
   - Integration with existing ML systems for dynamic rendering based on user preferences.
3. **Example Use Case**:
   - A ghost kitchen in New York introduced an AR feature where customers could visualize how their burrito bowl would look based on selected ingredients. This feature increased conversion rates by **18%** and reduced order customization errors by **30%**.

Benefits:

- Enhances customer confidence in their order choices.
- Reduces friction in the decision-making process, leading to higher order completion rates.
- Differentiates ghost kitchens in a crowded digital marketplace (Wang & Zhao, 2021).

7.7. Future ML Applications in Ghost Kitchens

Beyond personalization, efficiency, and immersive experiences, emerging ML applications could reshape ghost kitchens further:

1. **Voice Assistants**:
   - o AI-driven voice assistants for order taking, improving accessibility for differently-abled customers.
2. **Robotic Automation**:
   - o ML-powered robots for tasks like cooking, packaging, and order assembly, reducing labour costs and human error.
3. **Sustainability Analytics**:
   - o Advanced models to track carbon footprints and suggest sustainable practices.
4. **Real-Time Customer Interaction Analysis**:
   - o Sentiment analysis of live chat or voice interactions to enhance customer support and engagement (Gupta & Mehta, 2022), (Nguyen & Patel, 2022).

8. CONCLUSION

Machine learning (ML) is driving a paradigm shift in the ghost kitchen industry, enabling hyper-personalized customer experiences, operational efficiencies, and sustainability initiatives. By leveraging sophisticated algorithms and data-driven insights, ghost kitchens can address the inherent challenges of operating in a purely digital environment. Through personalization, customers enjoy tailored menus, dynamic pricing, and targeted marketing that replicate the warmth and connection of traditional dining experiences. Simultaneously, ML-powered tools optimize inventory, streamline workflows, and minimize waste, leading to significant cost savings and a reduced environmental footprint.

However, these advancements must be tempered with an ethical approach to implementation. Challenges such as data privacy, algorithmic bias, and transparency require continuous monitoring and innovation. Ghost kitchens that prioritize compliance with regulations, fairness in ML algorithms, and clear communication with customers will build trust and foster long-term loyalty.

Looking forward, technologies like generative AI, federated learning, and augmented reality are poised to redefine the boundaries of customer engagement and operational excellence. By balancing innovation with ethical considerations, ghost kitchens can create a sustainable, customer-centric business model that sets them apart in an increasingly competitive landscape. The fusion of ML and creativity offers endless opportunities for growth, ensuring that ghost kitchens remain at the forefront of the food industry's evolution.

REFERENCES

Adams, E. (2021). *Cloud-Based Ordering Solutions*. Tech Solutions Quarterly.

Aggarwal, C. C. (2018). *Neural Networks and Deep Learning: A Textbook*. Springer. DOI: 10.1007/978-3-319-94463-0

Bhatia, M. (2019). Applications of machine learning in personalized customer experiences. *International Journal of Computer Applications*, *182*(45), 16–21.

Brown, A., & Evans, R. (2020). Real-Time Demand Forecasting Using Machine Learning: Case Studies in Ghost Kitchens. *Journal of Operations Management*, *19*(4), 231–245.

Brown, K. (2021). *Machine Learning for Dining Personalization*. AI Operations Quarterly.

Brown, L. (2019). *Urbanization and Its Impact on Consumer Habits*. Urban Studies Quarterly.

Clark, P. (2020). Advancements in Delivery Logistics. *Transportation Quarterly*.

Doe, J., & Chen, L. (2020). AI-Powered Personalization in the Food Industry: Enhancing Customer Engagement. *Journal of Food Service Technology*, *9*(2), 88–101.

. Global Market Research. "Ghost Kitchen Market Trends." 2021.

Goodfellow, I., Bengio, Y., & Courville, A. (2016). *Deep Learning*. MIT Press.

Green, H. (2020). *Kitchen Automation and Workflow Optimization*. FoodTech Journal.

Gupta, R., & Mehta, P. (2022). Generative AI in Culinary Innovation: Creating Unique Menus for Ghost Kitchens. *Journal of Culinary Technology*, *16*(2), 77–91.

Harris, D., & Lee, J. (2019). Ethical Considerations in AI Systems: A Comprehensive Review. *Journal of Ethics in Technology*, *10*(1), 15–31.

Jagdev, G., & Singh, S. (2015). Implementation and applications of big data in health care industry. [IJSTA]. *International Journal of Scientific and Technical Advancements*, *1*(3), 29–34.

James, W., & Roberts, T. (2021). Regulatory Compliance in Machine Learning for Food Delivery Services. *Journal of Legal Issues in Technology*, *22*(4), 350–366.

Johnson, C., & Wong, M. (2020). Data Anonymization Techniques for Enhancing Privacy in Machine Learning. *Journal of Data Security*, *6*(4), 312–325.

Johnson, P. (2020). *Digital Transformation in Food Delivery*. Tech in Food Services.

Johnson, R. (2021). *Reinforcement Learning in Menu Design*. Advanced AI Applications.

Khan, M., & Patel, R. (2021). Machine Learning for Predictive Analytics in Food Industry. *International Journal of Data Science*, *19*(2), 45–59.

Kumar, A., & Singh, S. (2021). Application of AI in Waste Management: Case Studies in Ghost Kitchens. *AI & Sustainability*, *4*(2), 233–249.

Kumar, P., & Davis, C. (2022). Natural Language Processing for Analyzing Customer Feedback in Food Delivery. *AI & Machine Learning Journal, 22*(1), 123–136.

Kumar, P., & Singh, K. (2022). Data Security in AI-Driven Food Services: A Global Perspective. *Journal of Global Data Security, 11*(2), 146–160.

Kumar, S., & Kotecha, K. (2020). Sentiment analysis using natural language processing. *Procedia Computer Science, 172*, 214–220.

Lee, S. (2021). *COVID-19 and the Evolution of Dining*. Pandemic Insights Journal.

Lee, S., & Kim, H. (2019). Machine Learning Applications in Supply Chain Management in Ghost Kitchens. *Journal of Operational Research, 16*(2), 88–104.

Martinez, L. (2021). *Customer Loyalty through Personalized Services.* Consumer Studies Quarterly.

Miller, T. (2020). *Differentiation in Competitive Food Markets.* Marketing Insights.

Nguyen, T., & Patel, M. (2022). Federated Learning and Privacy Preservation in Personalized Food Services. *Journal of Privacy and Technology, 19*(3), 248–263.

O'Connor, R., & White, D. (2022). Federated Learning in Data Privacy Management. *Journal of Privacy Technologies, 8*(2), 99–113.

Patel, M. (2021). *Predictive Analytics for Resource Management.* Data Science in Operations.

Patel, P., & Gupta, R. (2021). AI-Powered Dynamic Pricing for Perishable Goods in Ghost Kitchens. *Journal of Artificial Intelligence & Sustainability, 5*(1), 67–80.

Patel, V., & Sharma, A. (2021). Machine Learning in Food Waste Reduction and Sustainability. *Journal of Sustainable Operations, 18*(1), 99–114.

Robinson, H., & Nelson, P. (2022). Ensuring Fairness in Machine Learning Algorithms: Challenges and Opportunities. *Journal of AI Ethics, 14*(1), 71–85.

Roy, S., & Gupta, M. (2021). IoT-Enabled Waste Monitoring in Ghost Kitchens: A Case Study. *International Journal of Smart Systems, 8*(3), 201–215.

Russell, S. J., & Norvig, P. (2021). *Artificial Intelligence: A Modern Approach.* Pearson.

Singh, A. (2020). *Dynamic Recommendations in Food Delivery Apps.* Tech in Consumer Services.

Singh, S., & Kaur, J. (2025). Modern Advancements in Surveillance Systems and Technologies. In *Modern Advancements in Surveillance Systems and Technologies* (pp. 29–38). IGI Global Scientific Publishing.

Smith, A., & Wong, H. (2021). Collaborative Filtering for Personalized Menu Recommendations in Online Food Services. *International Journal of AI in Hospitality, 15*(3), 212–227.

. Smith, J. (2020.). "The Rise of Ghost Kitchens." *Journal of Food Service Innovations,*

Smith, J., & Allen, P. (2020). Data Privacy in Machine Learning Applications: Challenges and Solutions. *Journal of Cybersecurity, 12*(3), 198–212.

Tan, J., & Lee, S. (2019). Predictive Analytics and Inventory Management in Ghost Kitchens. *Journal of Food Operations*, *10*(4), 300–315.

Taylor, K. (2021). *Leveraging Delivery Platforms for Growth*. FoodTech Advances.

Taylor, K. (2021). *NLP and Customer Insights in Food Delivery*. Language Insights Journal.

Thomas, L., & Harris, E. (2018). Impact of Traffic Data on Delivery Efficiency in Ghost Kitchens. *International Journal of Logistics Research*, *12*(2), 203–218.

Tran, L., & Chen, Y. (2020). Blockchain in Data Security for Machine Learning. *Journal of Blockchain Technology*, *7*(1), 57–68.

Wang, K., & Zhao, Y. (2021). Machine Learning in Demand Forecasting for Ghost Kitchens: A Comprehensive Approach. *Journal of Business Analytics*, *18*(2), 157–171.

Watson, R. (2020). Virtual Restaurants in Urban Centers. *Business Review*.

White, J. (2020). *Personalization in the Absence of Direct Interaction*. AI in Food Services.

Zhang, T., & Zhang, Z. (2020). Impact of Algorithmic Bias in Customer Personalization: A Case Study of Ghost Kitchens. *Journal of AI Research*, *28*(3), 185–200.

Zhang, Y. (2021). *Dietary Trends and Data Analytics*. Health & Tech Journal.

Chapter 6
Success Stories of AI-Integrated Ghost Kitchens:
Revolutionizing Food Delivery via Technology

Punam Kumari
https://orcid.org/0000-0001-8144-7573
Amity University, Bengaluru, India

Amita Somya
https://orcid.org/0000-0003-2855-899X
Amity University, Bengaluru, India

Jhasaketan Behera
Oracle Financial Services Software Limited, India

ABSTRACT

A ghost kitchen, also known as a virtual kitchen or cloud kitchen, is a professional food preparation facility designed to produce meals exclusively for delivery. Unlike traditional restaurants, ghost kitchens don't have a physical dining space for customers and typically don't cater to walk-in traffic. They rely on online orders placed through food delivery platforms like Uber Eats, Zomato, or their own delivery systems. This chapter explores the transformative role of AI-driven ghost kitchens in the food delivery sector, highlighting successful implementations and their impact on operational efficiency, customer satisfaction, and environmental sustainability. Through real-world case studies, it examines how AI integration has optimized order management, demand forecasting, inventory control, and delivery logistics, creating a seamless experience for consumers and a scalable model for businesses. This chapter provides a comprehensive look at the strategic benefits of AI-integrated ghost kitchens and their potential to reshape the future of the food industry.

DOI: 10.4018/979-8-3373-0432-8.ch006

1. INTRODUCTION TO AI-INTEGRATED GHOST KITCHENS

Ghost kitchens, also known as cloud kitchens, dark kitchens, or virtual kitchens, are facilities specifically designed to prepare food for delivery without a dine-in option. Unlike traditional restaurants, ghost kitchens operate without customer-facing spaces, relying solely on delivery and pickup through online platforms (Jones et al., 2024). This model allows for cost savings by eliminating the need for dining areas, front-of-house staff, and prime real estate, thus making it easier for businesses to focus on efficient food production and expand their delivery reach.

1.1 Key Characteristics and Structure of Ghost Kitchens

Ghost kitchens vary in structure and operation. Some are independent kitchens set up by individual restaurants solely for delivery purposes, while others are larger, shared facilities that house multiple brands in a single location. In the latter model, a single kitchen space can host different restaurant concepts, allowing for flexibility and experimentation with new brands and menus without the cost of separate spaces. Companies like Rebel Foods, Box8, Kitchens Centre, Sweet Truth and SLAY Coffee have pioneered this shared-kitchen model, creating centralized facilities that support various food brands and delivery-only concepts.

Ghost kitchens often work in close partnership with food delivery apps such as Uber Eats, Swiggy and Zomato where customers place orders directly through the app, and the food is delivered from the ghost kitchen to the customer's door. Some ghost kitchens may also operate their own delivery service or develop independent apps to reach customers directly. In all cases, technology plays a critical role in managing orders, streamlining operations, and ensuring quality.

1.2 Role of Ghost Kitchens in the Food Delivery Ecosystem

The rise of ghost kitchens can be attributed to the growing demand for food delivery, particularly accelerated by the COVID-19 pandemic (Chen & House, 2022). As more consumers turn to online ordering for convenience and safety, ghost kitchens have emerged as a practical solution for meeting this demand. Here are several ways ghost kitchens are reshaping the food delivery ecosystem:

1.2.1 **Cost-Efficiency and Scalability:** Traditional restaurants incur high overhead costs due to rental spaces, utilities, front-of-house staff, and other operational expenses. Ghost kitchens bypass many of these costs, allowing businesses to focus funds on quality ingredients, kitchen staff, and technology that enhances delivery logistics. Lower overhead makes ghost kitchens particularly attractive for new brands or small businesses looking to enter the food industry without substantial initial investment. Established restaurants can also use ghost kitchens to expand into new markets, reaching customers in areas where opening a full restaurant might be cost-prohibitive.

1.2.2 **Improved Delivery Speed and Quality:** Ghost kitchens are often strategically located to optimize delivery times, either in urban centers close to high-density residential areas or in suburban hubs with high delivery demand. By positioning kitchens closer to customers, businesses can reduce delivery times and ensure food quality upon arrival.

1.2.3 **Data-Driven Operations:** Ghost kitchens heavily rely on data analytics to streamline operations, manage inventory, and predict demand. Data from previous orders, customer preferences, and delivery trends helps kitchen operators decide which items to offer, how much inventory to maintain, and how to adjust staffing levels based on peak hours.

1.2.4 **Expansion of Food Choices and Innovation:** Since ghost kitchens can house multiple brands in one location, they allow for a diverse array of food options that cater to different tastes and dietary needs. They offer a unique opportunity for chefs and entrepreneurs to experiment with new flavors and concepts in a low-risk environment. Brands can quickly test new menus, adapt to customer feedback, and even launch new virtual-only brands under different names, giving consumers more variety in food delivery options.

1.2.5 **Environmental Sustainability:** Ghost kitchens can contribute to more sustainable practices in the food delivery industry. By consolidating multiple brands into one location and reducing the need for individual restaurant spaces, ghost kitchens lower the energy consumption associated with lighting, heating, and cooling of multiple venues. Additionally, precise inventory management and reduced food waste due to data insights help minimize environmental impact.

1.3 The Role of AI in transforming the efficiency, scalability, and sustainability of ghost kitchens.

Artificial intelligence (AI) is revolutionizing ghost kitchens by enhancing their efficiency, scalability, and sustainability. As delivery-only kitchens without dine-in facilities, ghost kitchens rely on streamlined operations to meet growing demand. AI plays a pivotal role in managing these operations, enabling ghost kitchens to improve performance while minimizing waste and resource consumption.

1.3.1 Enhancing Efficiency with AI

AI-powered automation tools are central to increasing the efficiency of ghost kitchens. By implementing machine learning algorithms, ghost kitchens can automate repetitive tasks, such as managing inventory, tracking ingredients, and monitoring preparation times. AI-driven systems optimize ordering and inventory management, ensuring that ingredients are always stocked in the right amounts, thus reducing food waste and cutting costs. For instance, predictive algorithms can analyze past orders, time of day, seasonality, and even local events to forecast demand accurately. This level of precision helps ghost kitchens maintain just-in-time inventory, minimizing overstock and spoilage.

In the kitchen itself, robots and AI-driven cooking appliances streamline food preparation. Automated cooking devices powered by AI can cook food to exact specifications, resulting in consistent quality across orders. Additionally, smart ovens, fryers, and grills can be pre-programmed to cook dishes at specific times, which means that kitchen staff can focus on other tasks, speeding up the preparation process and reducing labor requirements.

1.3.2 Scaling Operations Through AI Insights

AI-driven data analytics is instrumental in scaling ghost kitchen operations. With a data-focused approach, ghost kitchens can analyze customer preferences, feedback, and ordering patterns to inform menu development and brand expansion. For example, if certain cuisines are more popular in specific areas, kitchens can adjust their offerings accordingly, effectively personalizing services for local markets without additional overhead.

Moreover, AI helps ghost kitchens make data-backed decisions regarding new locations. By analyzing demographics, competitor presence, and demand in potential areas, AI provides insights into optimal locations for expansion. This strategic expansion is critical for scalability, as it allows ghost kitchens to tap into high-demand areas without unnecessary risk.

1.3.3 Sustainability of Ghost Kitchens through AI

AI contributes significantly to the sustainability of ghost kitchens by minimizing waste and improving energy efficiency. Accurate demand forecasting helps reduce food waste, as kitchens can order and prepare just enough to meet the expected demand. Some AI systems also recommend ingredient substitutions or menu changes based on available stock, ensuring that ingredients close to expiration are prioritized, further reducing waste.

Ghost kitchens powered by AI can also reduce their environmental footprint through optimized energy use. For example, AI systems can monitor and manage energy consumption by controlling cooking equipment and adjusting lighting and temperature settings during off-peak hours. Additionally, some AI systems enable kitchens to track their carbon footprint by analyzing various aspects of the operation, from ingredient sourcing to packaging and delivery. With this information, ghost kitchens can adopt more eco-friendly practices, such as using sustainable packaging or working with suppliers that prioritize local and sustainable sourcing.

AI also promotes sustainability by improving delivery logistics. Through real-time data analysis, AI can group orders to maximize delivery efficiency and reduce fuel consumption. Optimized delivery routes decrease the environmental impact of each delivery, which is particularly significant for ghost kitchens that rely solely on takeout and delivery services. By making small adjustments across each stage of the process, AI enables ghost kitchens to operate in a way that is both economically and environmentally sustainable.

Contextual Background: Ghost Kitchens

The concept of ghost kitchens gained traction with the rise of food delivery platforms like Uber Eats, DoorDash, and Deliveroo. Rahman et al. (2020) highlight that the convenience-driven behavior of modern consumers and technological advancements in app-based ordering systems have significantly fueled this trend. The COVID-19 pandemic further accelerated the adoption of ghost kitchens as restaurants sought to mitigate dine-in restrictions and address rising demand for delivery services (Shaikh et al., 2023).

Operational Models

Several studies categorize ghost kitchens into distinct models, including single-brand kitchens, multi-brand kitchens, and aggregator kitchens. Single-brand kitchens focus on one restaurant concept, while multi-brand kitchens operate multiple brands within the same facility, maximizing resource efficiency. Aggregator kitchens, often supported by delivery platforms, provide shared spaces for independent restaurants to reduce overhead costs. AI and automation play a critical role in ghost kitchen operations. According to Ding et al. (2023), technologies like predictive analytics, automated inventory management, and delivery route optimization significantly enhance efficiency and reduce costs. Ghost kitchens also benefit from flexible setups, allowing rapid experimentation with menu items and brands to align with consumer trends.

Consumer Behavior and Market Trends

Consumer demand for convenience, variety, and speed has driven the growth of ghost kitchens. Studies by Ruyani et al. (2023) emphasize the importance of tailored digital experiences, such as user-friendly interfaces and personalized menu recommendations, in capturing market share. Additionally, the growing preference for healthier and sustainable food options has influenced ghost kitchen menus, prompting operators to adopt plant-based dishes and eco-friendly packaging (Khan, 2024).

Challenges and Limitations

Despite their advantages, ghost kitchens face notable challenges. Regulatory concerns regarding food safety, licensing, and zoning laws are frequently cited (Ding et al., 2020). Moreover, the lack of direct customer interaction limits brand-building opportunities, creating a dependence on delivery platforms that often charge high commission fees. Data privacy and cybersecurity risks are also prevalent, given the heavy reliance on digital technologies.

Employment issues are another concern. The automation and gig-based nature of ghost kitchens raise questions about job security and worker rights, as highlighted by Lee and Park (2021). Additionally, market saturation in urban areas has increased competition, making differentiation critical for survival.

Ghost kitchens represent a significant transformation in the foodservice industry, driven by technology and changing consumer expectations. While they offer numerous advantages in terms of efficiency and scalability, addressing their challenges is essential for long-term sustainability. Future research should focus on regulatory frameworks, consumer trust-building strategies, and technological innovations to enhance their viability.

2. CASE STUDIES AND SUCCESS STORIES

2.1 Rebel Foods

Rebel Foods, one of India's pioneering cloud kitchen companies, has successfully integrated artificial intelligence (AI) into its ghost kitchen model to streamline operations, optimize resources, and improve the customer experience. This strategic use of AI across various aspects of its business has allowed Rebel Foods to scale efficiently, offering multiple brands from shared kitchen spaces, and adapt quickly to customer demand in a competitive food delivery landscape (Lahiri & Majumdar, 2024).

2.1.1 Demand Forecasting and Inventory Management

AI helps Rebel Foods improve inventory management and predict demand accurately across its kitchens. Using machine learning algorithms, the company analyzes historical order data, seasonal trends, and regional preferences to forecast demand at different times and locations. This level of predictive accuracy minimizes food wastage and prevents stockouts, ensuring that each kitchen is prepared to meet customer demand without over-ordering ingredients.

This demand forecast also enables Rebel Foods to plan its purchasing and logistics more efficiently, resulting in lower operating costs. The AI system helps balance supply and demand effectively, allowing the company to allocate resources where they are most needed, even across multiple brands within the same kitchen space.

2.1.2 Personalization and Menu Optimization

Rebel Foods operates multiple brands under one roof, such as Faasos, Behrouz Biryani, Oven Story, and Sweet Truth. By analyzing customer preferences and ordering patterns, AI tools help the company to personalize menu offerings to suit local tastes. For example, in regions where vegetarian meals are more popular, the kitchen can prioritize vegetarian options or introduce new items aligned with those preferences.

AI also assists in menu engineering by highlighting which items are high performers and identifying dishes that may need adjustment or replacement. This constant analysis ensures that each brand remains relevant to customers and maintains high satisfaction levels. Menu items can be adjusted according to real-time feedback and trends, enabling Rebel Foods to keep its brands aligned with current customer demands.

2.1.3 Automated Cooking and Quality Control

Within the kitchen, Rebel Foods uses AI-driven systems and automation to streamline cooking processes and maintain consistency across dishes. By standardizing recipes and cooking times through smart kitchen equipment, AI ensures that food preparation adheres to brand standards, regardless of location. For instance, automated cooking systems, such as smart ovens and fryers, allow for consistent food quality, reducing the chances of human error.

AI-powered quality control systems monitor cooking temperatures, ingredient ratios, and other critical factors in real time. This not only ensures quality but also allows Rebel Foods to deliver a consistent dining experience to customers. AI-enabled systems can alert kitchen staff to any discrepancies, such as undercooking or deviations from recipes, which further enhances the brand's commitment to quality.

2.1.4. Route Optimization and Delivery Efficiency

Given that ghost kitchens rely on efficient delivery, AI plays a vital role in optimizing delivery routes. Rebel Foods' AI algorithms work with third-party delivery platforms to determine the fastest and most efficient routes for each order, reducing delivery times and improving customer satisfaction. This is particularly beneficial in densely populated urban areas where traffic congestion can significantly impact delivery.

AI also helps assign delivery personnel based on real-time data about traffic, weather conditions, and delivery volume, ensuring that resources are used effectively. Faster, more reliable delivery translates to an enhanced customer experience, which is crucial in the competitive food delivery market.

2.1.5. Real-Time Analytics for Performance Tracking

AI-powered analytics tools provide Rebel Foods with real-time data on kitchen performance, order accuracy, and customer feedback. This data-driven approach allows the company to make quick decisions to resolve any issues that may arise, such as ingredient shortages or delays in order preparation. With these insights, Rebel Foods can track performance at every level—from individual dishes to entire brands—enabling ongoing optimization and agile responses to market changes.

For example, if a specific item is underperforming in a particular region, AI systems can detect this trend and prompt the team to investigate potential causes or modify the offering. Conversely, if a new item is gaining popularity, AI can signal this, allowing Rebel Foods to allocate more resources to fulfill orders effectively.

2.2 Kitchen United

Kitchen United, a leader in the ghost kitchen industry based in Pasadena, California, has leveraged AI and advanced technologies to redefine food delivery operations (Upton, 2018). Their innovative approaches have contributed to the efficiency, scalability, and profitability of their virtual kitchen network.

2.2.1 AI-Powered Operational Efficiency

Kitchen United integrates AI to streamline operations across its network of ghost kitchens. Their system uses AI for demand forecasting, optimizing kitchen space utilization, and coordinating delivery logistics. By analyzing historical sales data, customer preferences, and delivery trends, Kitchen United ensures that kitchens are adequately staffed and stocked, minimizing waste and improving delivery times.

2.2.2 Multi-Concept Ordering

AI also powers Kitchen United's unique multi-concept ordering system, allowing customers to order from multiple brands within a single transaction. This technology provides seamless customer experience, enabling families or groups with diverse food preferences to place consolidated orders. This feature has proven to be a significant draw for customers and a competitive advantage in the food delivery market.

2.2.3Automation and Robotics

The company has introduced robotic systems to enhance food preparation and delivery processes. These technologies reduce human error and ensure consistency in food quality. Furthermore, AI-driven tools facilitate quick driver dispatching and route optimization, reducing delivery times and ensuring food arrives in optimal condition.

2.2.4 Expansion Strategy and Sustainability

Kitchen United has strategically expanded its footprint with the help of AI tools that analyze market potential and select ideal locations for new facilities. Their AI systems also monitor energy usage and waste production, making their operations more sustainable. These efforts align with the increasing demand for environmentally conscious practices in the food industry.

2.2.5 Success Metrics

With backing from investors like Google Ventures and RXR Realty, Kitchen United has scaled rapidly, operating in major cities like Los Angeles, Chicago, and Austin. Their focus on AI-driven innovation has helped their restaurant partners boost revenue while lowering operational costs, highlighting the transformative impact of AI in ghost kitchens.

2.3 Ghost Kitchens India

Ghost Kitchens India, an emerging player in the food-tech space, has revolutionized its operations by integrating artificial intelligence (AI) into its ghost kitchen model. With a network spanning multiple cities in India, the company has adopted cutting-edge AI technologies to enhance operational efficiency, customer satisfaction, and profitability (Suresh, et. al, 2024).

2.3.1 AI-Driven Demand Forecasting and Inventory Management

Ghost Kitchens India employs AI to predict customer demand across different locations and times. By analyzing historical order data, regional preferences, and market trends, the company ensures that each kitchen operates efficiently, minimizing food wastage and stockouts. For example, their AI systems analyze demand fluctuations during festivals or weekends to adjust inventory and staff levels accordingly. This predictive capability has enabled Ghost Kitchens India to reduce costs and maintain a steady supply chain

2.3.2 Operational Efficiency Through AI

AI plays a central role in streamlining operations within Ghost Kitchens India's network of kitchens. Automation tools monitor food preparation times, cooking temperatures, and ingredient usage, ensuring consistency and quality across all orders. These systems also reduce dependency on manual oversight, allowing for faster order fulfillment while maintaining high-quality standards. Additionally, the integration of robotics in repetitive tasks like chopping or frying enhances kitchen productivity.

2.3.3 AI-Enhanced Customer Experience

Personalization is a significant focus area for Ghost Kitchens India. AI-powered platforms analyze customer behavior, preferences, and feedback to tailor menu offerings and promotional campaigns. For instance, if a region shows a preference for vegetarian dishes, the kitchen's menu dynamically adjusts to feature more vegetarian options. This responsiveness to customers fosters brand loyalty and repeat business.

2.3.4 Route Optimization and Delivery Efficiency

Given that delivery is a critical component of ghost kitchens, Ghost Kitchens India uses AI algorithms to optimize delivery routes. These algorithms factor in real-time data such as traffic conditions, weather, and order volumes to ensure timely delivery. AI also assigns delivery personnel dynamically, reducing downtime and maximizing resource utilization. These improvements in delivery efficiency significantly enhance customer experience, which is crucial in the competitive food-tech market.

2.3.5 Technology-Driven Profitability

Ghost Kitchens India has developed proprietary SaaS platforms that empower them to manage multiple brands and kitchens effectively. These tools offer insights into kitchen performance, resource allocation, and revenue streams. This data-driven approach allows the company to identify underperforming items or locations and implement corrective measures promptly. AI systems also support dynamic pricing strategies, adjusting menu prices based on demand, time of day, or special events

2.3.6 Scaling Through Data Insights

With AI as a backbone, Ghost Kitchens India has scaled its operations to over 15 company-owned kitchens and 1,200 internet restaurants across 40 cities. AI tools guide their expansion strategy by identifying high-potential locations based on population density, income levels, and food delivery trends. This precision has helped the company establish a strong presence in key markets while maintaining cost efficiency.

2.3.7 Sustainability Initiatives Powered by AI

AI also supports Ghost Kitchens India in achieving sustainability goals. Energy consumption and food waste are monitored and optimized using AI-driven analytics. For example, predictive models help kitchens prepare only what is necessary, reducing wastage. Additionally, the company is exploring the use of AI to source ingredients from sustainable suppliers, further enhancing its environmental footprint.

2.4 Curefoods

Curefoods, founded by Ankit Nagori, has significantly transformed the cloud kitchen model in India by adopting AI and leveraging innovative technologies (Pratima H, 2022). Here's how the company integrates AI into its ghost kitchen operations:

2.4.1 AI in Operational Efficiency

Curefoods employs AI-driven tools to streamline order management and kitchen workflows. By analyzing customer preferences and real-time data, the company ensures optimal resource allocation, reducing waste and improving preparation times. This approach enhances the overall efficiency of their 125+ cloud kitchens operating across 12 cities

2.4.2 Personalized Customer Experience

Using AI, Curefoods tailors menu recommendations based on individual customer behaviors and preferences. AI algorithms analyze past orders and feedback, enabling the company to curate offerings that resonate with its audience. This personalized approach boosts customer satisfaction and repeat business.

2.4.3 Drone-Based Deliveries

Curefoods has partnered with Skye Air Mobility to introduce drone deliveries for frozen food items in temperature-controlled packaging. This innovative use of AI in logistics reduces delivery times and ensures the freshness of food, marking a significant step in integrating advanced technology into food services

2.4.4 Insights from Consumer Behavior

Curefoods extensively utilizes AI to study shifts in consumer preferences. For example, during the COVID-19 pandemic, data analysis highlighted an increased demand for certain cuisines like pizza and biryani. The company strategically expanded its portfolio to meet these demands, driving its growth even during challenging times

2.4.5 Scalability through AI and Acquisitions

The company has adopted a "House of Brands" model, acquiring multiple food brands and using AI to manage their operations collectively. This model not only diversifies their offerings but also maximizes the utilization of kitchen space, a hallmark of AI-optimized cloud kitchens

2.5 Zomato and Swiggy partnered Kitchens

Zomato and Swiggy, India's leading food delivery platforms, have successfully integrated AI-driven technologies in their partner ghost kitchens to improve operational efficiency and enhance customer satisfaction (Amal Nair, 2019).

2.5.1 Zomato's AI-Powered Innovations

Zomato has adopted AI to streamline its ghost kitchen operations, focusing on ultra-fast delivery. By investing in Mukunda Foods, a robotics kitchen startup, Zomato has reduced food preparation times significantly. Mukunda Foods' robotic cooking solutions can prepare meals in under three minutes, supporting Zomato's 10-minute delivery promise. AI algorithms also assist in demand prediction, enabling ghost kitchens to optimize their inventory and reduce food waste

2.5.2 Swiggy's Tech-Driven Kitchen Solutions

Swiggy uses AI for dynamic route optimization and order clustering, which speeds up food delivery while minimizing costs. Their ghost kitchen partners leverage predictive analytics to forecast demand patterns, ensuring high-priority dishes are always in stock. Additionally, Swiggy collaborates with tech-driven startups to integrate automated cooking solutions in their cloud kitchens

2.5.3 Impact on Customer Experience

The AI-driven enhancements allow Zomato and Swiggy to cater to specific customer preferences by analyzing data on cuisine popularity, dietary requirements, and peak ordering times. This personalization ensures customers receive meals that are both timely and tailored to their tastes

2.5.4 Sustainability and Scalability

AI tools in partner kitchens also contribute to sustainability by minimizing energy use and food wastage. Scalable solutions provided by these technologies allow both platforms to expand operations without compromising quality.

2.5.5 Success Outcomes

These initiatives have positioned Zomato and Swiggy as pioneers in leveraging AI within the food delivery ecosystem. Their use of ghost kitchens equipped with advanced technology showcases the potential of AI to redefine operational efficiency, customer satisfaction, and scalability.

2.6 CloudKitchens

CloudKitchens, a leader in the ghost kitchen industry, has harnessed the power of Artificial Intelligence (AI) to enhance operations, optimize space utilization, and elevate customer satisfaction. By integrating AI into its multi-brand facilities, CloudKitchens has streamlined workflows, maximized space efficiency, and reduced order fulfillment times. This approach benefits both partner restaurants and end customers, demonstrating the transformative potential of AI in modern food service (Beniwal & Mathur, 2022).

2.6.1 AI in Space Utilization: Maximizing Efficiency

One of the unique challenges faced by ghost kitchens is space management. CloudKitchens' facilities often host multiple brands under one roof, which can lead to operational bottlenecks if not managed effectively. AI has played a pivotal role in optimizing the use of available space, ensuring smooth operations for all brands operating within these facilities.

- **Dynamic Space Allocation**

AI algorithms analyze historical and real-time data to determine the spatial requirements for each brand based on order volumes, peak hours, and menu complexity. For instance:

- ✓ Brands with higher order volumes during lunch hours are allocated to kitchen stations closer to delivery dispatch areas to minimize food transit time within the facility.
- ✓ Kitchens with complex preparation processes are positioned in areas with easy access to shared resources such as storage or washing stations.

This dynamic allocation ensures that no space is underutilized or overburdened, resulting in more efficient operations for all brands.

- **Predictive Maintenance for Shared Equipment**

CloudKitchens employs AI to monitor the usage and maintenance needs of shared kitchen equipment. Predictive analytics ensure that equipment like ovens, refrigerators, and fryers are serviced before potential failures, preventing downtime and disruption. This proactive approach maintains smooth operations and allows all partner brands to deliver consistently.

- **Optimizing Inventory Storage**

With AI-powered inventory management, CloudKitchens streamlines the storage and replenishment of ingredients. Algorithms determine optimal storage layouts based on frequency of use, ensuring high-demand items are placed within easy reach of kitchen staff. This reduces time spent retrieving ingredients and minimizes waste from expired stock, ultimately improving operational efficiency and cost management.

2.6.2 AI in Order Efficiency: Streamlining Fulfillment

AI plays a critical role in managing the high-volume, fast-paced environment of CloudKitchens' multi-brand facilities. From order processing to delivery logistics, AI ensures faster, more accurate fulfillment, enhancing customer satisfaction.

- **Order Aggregation and Routing**

One of CloudKitchens' standout features is its ability to manage orders from multiple platforms such as Uber Eats, DoorDash, and Grubhub. AI consolidates these orders in real-time, prioritizing them based on preparation time, delivery location, and driver availability. Orders are automatically routed to the appropriate kitchen, reducing confusion and manual errors. Smart batching algorithms group orders with similar delivery routes, ensuring efficient use of delivery personnel and minimizing delays.

- **Optimized Workflow Management**

AI-powered workflow tools analyze order traffic to distribute tasks among kitchen staff. For example:

- ✓ During peak hours, the system predicts bottlenecks and adjusts workflows by reallocating staff to high-demand stations or breaking down tasks into smaller, manageable steps.
- ✓ Real-time monitoring of order progress helps identify delays and implement corrective actions immediately, ensuring timely preparation and dispatch.
  - **Reducing Order Errors**

AI systems check for discrepancies in orders, flagging potential errors before they occur. For instance, if an unusual customization request is made, the system alerts staff for verification. This proactive approach reduces mistakes, ensuring that customers receive exactly what they ordered.

2.6.3 Enhancing Customer Satisfaction Through AI

Customer satisfaction is at the heart of CloudKitchens' operations, and AI plays a significant role in meeting and exceeding customer expectations.

- **Faster Order Fulfillment**

AI's contributions to space and workflow optimization translate into quicker order turnaround times. By minimizing preparation and delivery times, CloudKitchens ensures that food reaches customers while it is still fresh and hot. Real-time traffic data integrated with delivery routing ensures drivers take the most efficient paths, further reducing delays. On average, brands operating within CloudKitchens report a 15–20% improvement in delivery times compared to traditional restaurant models.

- **Personalized Customer Experiences**

AI analyzes customer ordering patterns to provide personalized recommendations through third-party delivery platforms. For example:

- ✓ Frequent customers are shown their favorite items or suggested complementary dishes based on past orders.
- ✓ Seasonal trends and promotions are tailored to individual preferences, enhancing customer engagement and increasing repeat business.
  - **Proactive Problem Resolution**

AI monitors customer reviews and feedback across platforms to identify recurring issues, such as delays, incorrect orders, or packaging concerns. This data allows CloudKitchens to address problems promptly and improve processes. For instance, if a specific kitchen frequently receives complaints about cold food, AI flags the issue, prompting adjustments in order routing or preparation timelines. Real-time feedback loops enable immediate corrective actions, such as offering refunds or discounts for dissatisfied customers.

2.6.4. AI-Driven Sustainability Benefits

Efficiency gains from AI not only improve operations but also contribute to sustainability, a growing concern for customers.

- **Reducing Food Waste:** AI-powered inventory systems minimize over-ordering and waste by accurately predicting ingredient usage.
- **Energy Optimization:** Machine learning tools monitor energy usage and adjust equipment settings to reduce consumption during non-peak hours.
- **Efficient Deliveries:** Optimized routing reduces fuel consumption and carbon emissions, aligning with eco-conscious customer values.

2.6.5 Case Example: Multi-Brand Success

A CloudKitchens facility in Los Angeles demonstrates the impact of AI on operations and customer satisfaction. Hosting 15 brands under one roof, the facility integrated AI for space allocation, order routing, and inventory management. Results included:

- **30% Faster Order Fulfillment:** AI reduced prep times and optimized delivery routes.
- **20% Higher Customer Retention**: Personalized recommendations and accurate orders enhanced customer loyalty.
- **15% Cost Savings for Brands:** Efficient space utilization and reduced waste lowered operating costs.

These outcomes illustrate how AI can transform the ghost kitchen model into a well-oiled, customer-centric operation.

2.7 Wow Bao

Wow Bao, an Asian fast-casual restaurant brand, has become a shining example of innovation and Wow Bao has positioned itself as a leader in the fast-casual dining and ghost kitchen industries by utilizing Artificial Intelligence (AI) to grow its digital-only brand presence. With a strong commitment to innovation, Wow Bao has harnessed AI to adapt menu offerings to local demand, enhance customer engagement, and streamline its operations. This case study explores how the brand effectively uses AI to stay ahead in the competitive landscape of virtual dining.

2.7.1 Expanding Through Digital-Only Brands

Wow Bao's strategy of launching digital-only brands is a core aspect of its rapid growth. Instead of building traditional brick-and-mortar restaurants, the company leverages AI to identify and establish its presence in high-potential markets using ghost kitchen infrastructure.

AI-Driven Market Analysis

AI analyzes vast datasets, including consumer purchasing patterns, local dining trends, and demographic information, to pinpoint optimal locations for its digital-only brands.

Demand Mapping: AI evaluates delivery platform data to identify areas with unmet demand for fast-casual Asian cuisine.

Competitor Insights: Advanced algorithms assess competitor offerings in target regions, ensuring Wow Bao enters markets where it can meet underserved needs.

For example, in 2021, AI highlighted suburban areas with rising interest in bao buns and fast Asian street food. Using this insight, Wow Bao strategically launched virtual brands in these regions, quickly gaining traction.

Optimized Partnerships

Wow Bao collaborates with host kitchens to run its digital-only brands, utilizing AI to match potential partners with its operational requirements. By identifying facilities with underutilized capacity and aligning them with Wow Bao's preparation processes, AI ensures seamless expansion while keeping costs low.

2.7.2 Adapting Menu Offerings to Local Demand

AI plays a crucial role in tailoring Wow Bao's menu to align with the preferences of local audiences, ensuring that offerings resonate with each market.

Dynamic Menu Customization

AI-powered tools analyze ordering trends to determine which menu items perform best in different regions.

In urban centers, smaller-sized bao and snack items may be promoted for customers seeking quick, on-the-go meals.

Suburban markets might feature family-sized meals or meal bundles, catering to group dining at home.

For example, in the southern United States, customer preferences leaned toward spicy flavors. Wow Bao introduced a hot and spicy chicken bao variant in these regions, which became a top seller within weeks.

Predicting Trends and Seasonal Preferences

AI identifies trending ingredients and seasonal demands, enabling Wow Bao to update its menu dynamically.

For instance, during colder months, AI might recommend promoting warm rice bowls and broths, which align with consumer cravings for comfort food.

In regions where plant-based dining is growing, AI insights led to the introduction of vegetarian and vegan bao options.

By adapting to local and seasonal preferences, Wow Bao not only drives sales but also enhances customer satisfaction by meeting specific tastes.

2.7.3 Increasing Customer Engagement Through AI

In the competitive world of virtual dining, engaging customers digitally is vital. Wow Bao uses AI to personalize experiences, enhance loyalty, and encourage repeat business.

- **Personalized Recommendations**

AI algorithms analyze individual customer ordering histories to provide tailored recommendations via delivery apps. Customers are shown items they are likely to enjoy based on past purchases and preferences, boosting upselling opportunities. For new customers, AI predicts popular items in their demographic or region, ensuring a positive first impression. For example, if a customer frequently orders spicy dishes, the app may recommend the spicy Mongolian rice bowl, paired with complementary sides.

- **Customer Feedback Analysis**

Wow Bao uses AI to process customer feedback collected from online reviews, ratings, and social media. Sentiment analysis tools detect patterns in complaints or praises, allowing the company to address pain points and capitalize on strengths. Frequent feedback about portion sizes, packaging, or delivery speed is acted upon swiftly, ensuring continuous improvement. By actively listening to customer voices, Wow Bao strengthens its brand reputation and customer loyalty.

- **Dynamic Promotions and Rewards**

AI also supports Wow Bao's marketing campaigns by tailoring promotions to individual preferences. For instance,

✓ AI may identify customers who frequently order bao buns but rarely try other menu items. Targeted offers like "Buy 2 Bao, Get 1 Rice Bowl Free" encourage exploration of the menu.
✓ Loyal customers receive exclusive deals or early access to new items, fostering a sense of connection with the brand.

These personalized promotions not only increase average order values but also create a positive, memorable customer experience.

2.7.4 Streamlining Operations with AI

AI's impact on Wow Bao extends beyond customer-facing strategies. Operational efficiency is a significant factor in the brand's ability to scale rapidly while maintaining consistency across its digital-only brands.

- **Inventory Optimization**

AI-powered inventory systems ensure that partner kitchens are stocked with the right ingredients in the right quantities. Predictive analytics prevents over-ordering, reducing food waste. Real-time monitoring alerts kitchens about low stock levels, preventing interruptions during peak hours.

- **Order Routing and Delivery**

AI optimizes delivery logistics by selecting the best routes and batching orders with similar destinations. Drivers can complete deliveries faster, reducing wait times for customers. Energy-efficient routes lower delivery costs and align with sustainability goals.

2.7.5 Results of AI Integration

Wow Bao's integration of AI has yielded significant results, including:

- **Rapid Market Penetration:** The company expanded to over 600 locations in just a few years, thanks to AI-driven site selection and operational efficiency.
- **Higher Sales:** Tailored menus and personalized marketing boosted order volumes and customer retention.
- **Operational Consistency:** AI-enabled tools ensure that every digital-only brand meets Wow Bao's high standards for quality and delivery speed.

2.8 Sweetgreen

Sweetgreen, a fast-casual restaurant chain known for its fresh and healthy salads, has emerged as a leader in sustainable dining by leveraging AI and automation. Through strategic integration of technology, Sweetgreen has reduced food waste, lowered labor costs, and maintained its high-quality standards (Kalsbeek, 2019). This case study examines how Sweetgreen has successfully combined innovation and sustainability in its kitchen operations.

2.8.1 Reducing Food Waste Through AI

One of Sweetgreen's most notable achievements is its effective use of AI to minimize food waste. The chain sources fresh, locally grown ingredients, making waste reduction critical for both sustainability and profitability.

- **Predictive Inventory Management**

Sweetgreen employs AI-driven predictive analytics to forecast demand for ingredients with remarkable accuracy. By analyzing historical sales data, seasonal trends, and local weather patterns, the system predicts daily and weekly ingredient requirements for each location.

✓ **Real-Time Adjustments:** AI continuously monitors sales data in real time, allowing stores to make adjustments to inventory orders on-the-fly. For example, if a new ingredient gains unexpected popularity, the system increases its procurement while reducing orders for less popular items.

✓ **Minimized Overstocking:** By avoiding over-purchasing, Sweetgreen reduces spoilage of perishable items, which is a common challenge in fresh food operations.

- **Waste Tracking and Insights**

AI also helps track waste at each step of the production process. Using data from kitchen sensors and point-of-sale systems, Sweetgreen identifies where waste occurs—whether during preparation, storage, or after service.

✓ **Actionable Feedback:** Insights from waste tracking inform staff training and operational adjustments, such as refining portion sizes or improving handling practices for delicate ingredients.

By employing these strategies, Sweetgreen has significantly lowered food waste, aligning with its commitment to sustainability and lowering operational costs.

2.8.2 Lowering Labor Costs with Automation

Sweetgreen has embraced automation to streamline labor-intensive tasks in its kitchens, reducing reliance on manual labor while maintaining efficiency and quality.

- **Automated Prep Systems**

The chain has introduced robotic systems to handle repetitive tasks such as chopping vegetables, mixing dressings, and portioning ingredients.

✓ **Consistency and Speed:** Automation ensures that every ingredient is prepared to precise specifications, improving consistency across all locations.
✓ **Efficiency Gains:** Robots handle tasks faster than human workers, freeing staff to focus on customer-facing roles or more complex culinary tasks.

- **Dynamic Staff Scheduling with AI**

AI-powered scheduling tools analyze customer foot traffic and order volumes to optimize staff shifts.

✓ **Predictive Staffing:** By anticipating peak hours, Sweetgreen ensures adequate staffing levels without overstaffing during slower periods.
✓ **Reduced Overtime Costs:** Smarter scheduling minimizes unnecessary overtime, leading to cost savings while preventing employee burnout.

These measures not only lower labor costs but also enhance employee satisfaction by ensuring manageable workloads and predictable schedules.

2.8.3 Maintaining High-Quality Standards with AI and Automation

Sweetgreen's success depends on delivering fresh, high-quality meals consistently across its locations. AI and automation play a crucial role in upholding these standards.

- **Ingredient Quality Monitoring**

Sweetgreen utilizes IoT-enabled sensors in its kitchens and storage areas to monitor the freshness and safety of ingredients.

✓ **Temperature Control:** Sensors track storage conditions, ensuring that perishable items remain at optimal temperatures to prevent spoilage.
✓ **Shelf-Life Tracking:** AI systems alert staff when ingredients approach the end of their shelf life, prioritizing their use in recipes.

These technologies reduce the risk of serving subpar meals and ensure customers enjoy fresh, flavorful dishes.

- **Recipe Consistency Through Automation**

Robotic systems are programmed to follow recipes with precision, from measuring ingredients to assembling salads.

✓ **Eliminating Variability:** Automation minimizes the human error that can lead to inconsistencies in taste, portion size, or presentation.
✓ **Customizable Options:** Despite automation, Sweetgreen retains its hallmark customization options by integrating AI to guide staff in accommodating specific customer preferences or dietary restrictions.

2.8.4 Supporting Sustainability Goals

Sweetgreen's integration of AI and automation also bolsters its broader sustainability mission.

- **Energy Efficiency in Operations**

AI-powered energy management systems optimize the use of kitchen equipment, reducing electricity consumption.

✓ **Smart Scheduling for Equipment:** AI ensures that ovens, refrigerators, and other appliances operate only when necessary, lowering energy costs and environmental impact.
✓ **Renewable Energy Integration:** Many Sweetgreen locations utilize renewable energy sources, and AI helps balance energy demand with supply from solar or wind power.
  - **Transparency in Sourcing**

Sweetgreen uses blockchain and AI to provide transparency in its ingredient sourcing. Customers can access detailed information about the origins of their food, reinforcing the brand's commitment to ethical and sustainable practices.

2.8.5 Enhancing Customer Experience

Sweetgreen's technology-driven approach not only optimizes back-end operations but also improves customer satisfaction.

- **Order Customization with AI**

The Sweetgreen app uses AI to recommend meals based on customer preferences, dietary restrictions, and past orders.

- ✓ **Personalized Menus:** Customers see tailored options, making it easier to choose meals that fit their tastes and needs.
- ✓ **Efficient Modifications:** AI streamlines the customization process, ensuring that modified orders are accurately prepared.
  - **Faster Order Fulfillment**

Automation in food preparation reduces wait times for both in-store and delivery orders. Combined with AI-optimized kitchen workflows, Sweetgreen ensures that meals are served quickly without compromising quality.

2.8.6 Results of AI and Automation Integration

Sweetgreen's investments in AI and automation have delivered impressive results:

- ✓ **40% Reduction in Food Waste:** Predictive inventory and waste tracking have significantly lowered waste levels, saving costs and supporting sustainability.
- ✓ **20% Reduction in Labor Costs:** Automation and smarter scheduling have optimized staffing while maintaining high efficiency.
- ✓ **Consistent Customer Experience:** Automation ensures uniform quality across locations, boosting customer satisfaction and loyalty.

3. ENVIRONMENTAL AND SUSTAINABILITY IMPACT

3.1 The Role of AI-Integrated Ghost Kitchens in Reducing Food Waste, Energy Conservation, and Lowering Carbon

AI-integrated ghost kitchens, or virtual kitchens, represent a groundbreaking intersection of technology and food services, designed to meet modern culinary demands while minimizing environmental impact. By leveraging artificial intelligence (AI), these facilities are transforming how food is prepared, delivered, and consumed. This shift is not only redefining operational efficiency but also addressing critical environmental challenges such as food waste, energy consumption, and carbon emissions.

3.1.1 Reducing Food Waste

Food waste is a significant contributor to environmental degradation, with uneaten food generating methane emissions as it decomposes in landfills. Ghost kitchens equipped with AI tools are tackling this issue head-on through predictive analytics and real-time inventory management.

a. **Predictive Analytics for Demand Forecasting:** AI algorithms analyze historical sales data, current trends, and external factors like weather and local events to forecast demand accurately. This precision helps ghost kitchens optimize ingredient purchasing, significantly reducing overstocking and underutilization of perishable items.

b. **Dynamic Menu Optimization:** AI systems dynamically adjust menus based on ingredient availability, seasonal trends, and consumer preferences. For instance, if certain ingredients are nearing expiration, AI can prioritize dishes that incorporate these items, thereby minimizing waste.
c. **Smart Portion Control:** AI-powered portioning tools ensure consistent serving sizes, reducing the likelihood of leftovers or over-preparation. Coupled with feedback systems, these tools help ghost kitchens refine portion sizes to match customer consumption patterns over time.
d. **Waste Monitoring and Analysis:** AI-driven waste tracking systems monitor the type and volume of food discarded, offering actionable insights to reduce future waste. By identifying patterns—such as frequently returned dishes or overproduced items kitchens can adjust production strategies accordingly.

3.1.2 Energy Conservation

Ghost kitchens are inherently more energy-efficient than traditional restaurant setups due to their streamlined operations and lack of dine-in spaces. AI integration amplifies these efficiencies through smart energy management systems.

a. **Optimized Equipment Usage:** AI monitors kitchen equipment usage, ensuring appliances like ovens, refrigerators, and stovetops operate only when necessary. Predictive maintenance algorithms also help identify potential equipment inefficiencies or failures, reducing energy waste and downtime.
b. **Energy-Saving Scheduling:** AI systems analyze order patterns to determine peak operational times, allowing kitchens to strategically power down non-essential systems during low-demand periods. This approach conserves energy without compromising service quality.
c. **Smart HVAC Control:** Heating, ventilation, and air conditioning (HVAC) systems in ghost kitchens can be AI-controlled to maintain optimal temperatures based on real-time occupancy and cooking activity, reducing unnecessary energy consumption.
d. **Integration with Renewable Energy Sources:** Many AI-integrated ghost kitchens incorporate renewable energy solutions, such as solar panels or wind energy. AI algorithms optimize the use of these sources, ensuring maximum efficiency and reducing reliance on non-renewable power.

3.1.3 Lowering Carbon Emissions

By addressing inefficiencies in food preparation and delivery, AI-integrated ghost kitchens contribute to significant reductions in carbon emissions, aligning with global sustainability goals.

a. **Streamlined Delivery Logistics:** AI optimizes delivery routes by analyzing real-time traffic conditions, order locations, and driver availability. This minimizes fuel consumption and ensures faster delivery, reducing the carbon footprint of last-mile logistics.
b. **Minimized Packaging Waste:** AI assists in selecting eco-friendly packaging solutions tailored to specific orders, balancing durability with sustainability. Algorithms can even suggest reusable or biodegradable options, further decreasing the environmental impact.
c. **Localized Food Sourcing:** AI platforms help ghost kitchens source ingredients from local suppliers, reducing emissions associated with long-distance transportation. These systems factor in cost, quality, and environmental considerations, fostering sustainable procurement practices.

d. **Collaboration with Carbon Offset Programs:** AI systems can integrate with carbon offset initiatives, calculating emissions generated by specific orders and suggesting offset contributions. Customers can opt to make their meal carbon-neutral, enhancing consumer awareness and engagement in sustainability efforts.

The Bigger Picture

The environmental benefits of AI-integrated ghost kitchens extend beyond their immediate operations. By setting new standards for efficiency and sustainability in the food industry, these kitchens are catalyzing broader changes across the supply chain. Traditional restaurants are beginning to adopt similar technologies to remain competitive, creating a ripple effect that amplifies environmental gains (Parasher et. al, 2023).

Moreover, AI's potential for continuous improvement ensures that ghost kitchens remain at the forefront of sustainable innovation. Machine learning models grow more sophisticated over time, uncovering novel ways to reduce waste, conserve energy, and lower emissions. This iterative progress aligns with global efforts to combat climate change, highlighting the critical role of technology in building a greener future.

3.2 Brands Leveraging AI for Notable Environmental Benefits

Ghost kitchens, or virtual kitchens, are rapidly transforming the food industry by centralizing food production for delivery-only services. The integration of artificial intelligence (AI) in these operations is enabling brands to reduce waste, conserve energy, and lower carbon emissions while maintaining high efficiency. Here are notable examples of AI-driven ghost kitchen brands making strides in sustainability:

3.2.1 REEF Technology – Urban-Focused Sustainability

REEF Technology operates a vast network of ghost kitchens in urban areas, leveraging AI to optimize operations and reduce their environmental footprint.

Environmental Benefits: By utilizing underused parking lots as micro-kitchens, REEF reduces the need for new construction, conserving resources and minimizing urban sprawl. AI-powered systems monitor inventory and predict demand, reducing food waste significantly.

AI Integration: REEF employs predictive analytics for ingredient ordering, ensuring kitchens operate with just the right amount of stock to avoid waste. Additionally, AI optimizes delivery routes, reducing fuel consumption and emissions from delivery vehicles.

3.2.2 Kitchen United – Smarter Multi-Brand Kitchens

Kitchen United provides shared kitchen spaces for multiple food brands, integrating AI to manage energy consumption and reduce waste.

Environmental Benefits: With AI-driven waste monitoring and predictive maintenance systems, Kitchen United has significantly reduced food waste and energy use across its facilities.

AI Integration: Machine learning algorithms forecast demand based on customer trends, allowing brands to prepare only what is needed. AI also ensures optimal appliance usage, reducing energy consumption during non-peak hours.

3.2.3 Zuul Kitchens – Data-Driven Waste Reduction

Zuul Kitchens operates ghost kitchens in New York City and focuses on leveraging AI for sustainability and efficiency.

Environmental Benefits: Zuul Kitchens uses AI to optimize food preparation, resulting in a measurable reduction in food waste and resource usage. The company also minimizes emissions by streamlining last-mile delivery.

AI Integration: AI systems analyze sales patterns and adjust production schedules, ensuring minimal overproduction. Zuul's AI-powered delivery platform clusters order geographically to reduce travel distances, cutting down fuel consumption.

3.2.4 CloudKitchens – AI-Powered Global Efficiency

CloudKitchens, a prominent name in the ghost kitchen sector, utilizes AI to streamline its global network of kitchens.

Environmental Benefits: By consolidating operations into strategically located hubs, CloudKitchens reduces the energy and emissions associated with traditional restaurant setups. AI-based demand forecasting minimizes food waste across its facilities.

AI Integration: CloudKitchens deploys AI to monitor energy usage and maintain optimal temperatures in their facilities. Predictive analytics also enable precise ingredient management, reducing spoilage.

3.2.5 All Day Kitchens – Sustainable Local Food Distribution

All Day Kitchens partners with local restaurants to bring their offerings to delivery-only platforms, using AI to optimize processes.

Environmental Benefits: The brand's AI-driven systems enhance supply chain efficiency, ensuring minimal waste and supporting local food sourcing to reduce transportation emissions.

AI Integration: AI optimizes portion control and ingredient usage, helping local restaurants adapt to a delivery-focused model sustainably. Delivery routes are also AI-optimized to reduce time and energy spent on logistics.

3.2.6 Deliveroo Editions – Global AI-Driven Delivery Kitchens

Deliveroo Editions operates ghost kitchens worldwide, utilizing AI to manage energy use and reduce food waste while improving customer service.

Environmental Benefits: Deliveroo Editions reduces food waste through AI-based menu optimization, dynamically adjusting offerings based on real-time demand data. AI also lowers emissions by optimizing delivery logistics.

AI Integration: Algorithms predict order volumes, enabling precise ingredient ordering and reducing waste. AI-powered systems also cluster deliveries, reducing the carbon footprint of their fleets.

3.2.7 Taster – Tech-First Food Brands

Taster, a Europe-based ghost kitchen brand, uses AI to support its operations, focusing on sustainability as part of its strategy.

Environmental Benefits: Taster's AI-driven waste reduction initiatives have helped decrease food waste in its kitchens by up to 30%. The company also optimizes packaging to reduce its environmental impact.

AI Integration: By analyzing customer data, AI ensures that menus reflect current trends and avoid the production of unpopular dishes. AI also identifies opportunities for using surplus ingredients creatively, minimizing waste.

3.2.8 Keatz – Sustainable European Ghost Kitchens

Keatz, a European ghost kitchen brand, focuses on creating environmentally friendly meal delivery systems through AI.

Environmental Benefits: Keatz minimizes waste through AI-driven portion control and waste monitoring. Its centralized operations reduce the need for multiple physical locations, conserving energy and resources.

AI Integration: AI systems help Keatz predict demand patterns across different regions, optimizing ingredient procurement. Their energy-efficient kitchen designs are further enhanced by AI-controlled appliances.

AI-enabled ghost kitchens are setting new standards in the food industry, proving that technology can drive both efficiency and sustainability. From reducing food waste to optimizing delivery routes and conserving energy, these brands showcase how AI can transform ghost kitchens into environmentally responsible operations. As the sector grows, these pioneering examples pave the way for a greener future in food services.

4. CHALLENGES AND STRATEGY CONSIDERATIONS FOR AI IMPLEMENTATION IN GHOST KITCHEN

The rise of ghost kitchens has transformed the foodservice industry, utilizing cloud-based models and delivery platforms to streamline operations and minimize overhead costs. Central to their success is the integration of Artificial Intelligence (AI) to optimize various aspects of the business, from food preparation and inventory management to demand forecasting and delivery logistics. However, while the adoption of AI offers immense potential for growth and efficiency, it also comes with significant challenges that must be addressed to ensure its successful implementation. Among the most prominent challenges are the need for technical expertise, the high cost of AI infrastructure, and concerns around data privacy. These obstacles can deter smaller operations and even larger businesses from adopting AI technologies. Below, we discuss each of these challenges in-depth and propose effective strategies to overcome them.

4.1 Need for Technical Expertise

Challenge Overview

AI technologies require specialized knowledge in data science, machine learning, algorithm development, and system integration. In the context of ghost kitchens, many operators lack technical expertise to design, implement, and maintain AI systems, which could result in inefficiencies, system failures, and underperformance. Furthermore, AI tools for foodservice applications are often complex, requiring a thorough understanding of both the technology and the specific needs of kitchen operations.

Without the required technical skills, ghost kitchens may face challenges in customizing AI tools to fit their specific workflows or in troubleshooting problems that arise during implementation. This knowledge gap can be a significant barrier to entry, particularly for small to mid-sized businesses.

Strategies and Solutions

- **Partnerships with AI Vendors:** One of the most effective strategies for overcoming the technical expertise barrier is to collaborate with experienced AI vendors. These vendors specialize in creating customized AI systems for businesses and can offer end-to-end solutions, from system design and deployment to maintenance and updates. By outsourcing the technical aspects of AI implementation, ghost kitchens can avoid the steep learning curve and minimize risks associated with technical failures.
- **Employee Training and Upskilling:** A long-term solution to the expertise gap involves investing in the workforce by providing training in AI, machine learning, and data analytics. Offering online courses, workshops, and certifications in AI can help employees develop the necessary technical skills to manage and maintain AI systems effectively. This investment not only helps the business reduce reliance on external vendors but also empowers employees to troubleshoot and resolve issues in-house.
- **User-Friendly AI Solutions:** Choosing AI platforms that offer user-friendly interfaces can simplify the learning process for operators and staff. Many AI solutions are designed to be intuitive and require minimal technical expertise, allowing operators to leverage the power of AI without needing to understand the underlying algorithms. For example, AI systems that provide visual dashboards and automated insights make it easier for managers to interpret data and make informed decisions without deep technical knowledge.
- **Hiring Data Science Talent:** In addition to training existing employees, ghost kitchens can recruit data scientists, machine learning engineers, and AI specialists to build and manage the AI infrastructure. While this approach comes with additional costs, the investment in skilled professionals can ensure that AI systems are properly implemented and continuously improved as the business scales.

4.2 Cost of AI Infrastructure

Challenge Overview

Implementing AI in ghost kitchens involves significant upfront and ongoing costs. AI infrastructure, such as hardware, software, cloud services, and machine learning models, can be expensive to purchase and maintain. For smaller ghost kitchens or startups, these costs may seem prohibitive, especially when the immediate return on investment (ROI) is uncertain. Furthermore, upgrading or replacing legacy systems to accommodate AI solutions can lead to additional costs. The expense of integrating AI into kitchen operations, coupled with ongoing maintenance and system upgrades, can deter businesses from adopting these technologies.

Strategies and Solutions

- **Cloud-Based AI Solutions:** One of the most cost-effective ways to reduce the initial investment in AI infrastructure is by opting for cloud-based solutions. Cloud platforms eliminate the need for costly on-premise servers and infrastructure, providing access to powerful AI tools via subscription-based models. Cloud-based AI systems also offer scalability, meaning ghost kitchens can expand their usage as their business grows, without the need to invest in expensive hardware upfront.
- **Modular and Scalable Systems:** Ghost kitchens can start by implementing AI systems that are modular and scalable, allowing them to gradually introduce AI tools as needed. For example, they might begin with AI-driven inventory management or demand forecasting before expanding to more complex systems such as kitchen automation or predictive analytics. By taking a phased approach, businesses can minimize initial expenditures and ensure that each AI tool delivers measurable benefits before committing to larger investments.
- **Outsourcing to Third-Party Platforms:** Many delivery platforms and foodservice providers are integrating AI into their systems, offering ghost kitchens access to AI tools without the need to build the infrastructure from scratch. By outsourcing certain operations to these platforms, ghost kitchens can reduce the financial burden of AI adoption while still reaping its benefits. For example, integrating AI-powered delivery logistics or customer recommendation systems from a third-party service can be a cost-effective way to improve operational efficiency.
- **Government Grants and Subsidies:** Some governments offer financial assistance for small businesses and startups adopting new technologies, including AI. Ghost kitchens can explore local and national funding programs or grants designed to incentivize technological innovation. These subsidies can help cover a portion of the costs associated with AI adoption, making the transition more affordable.
- **Focus on ROI Tracking:** Implementing AI requires a clear understanding of the potential ROI. Ghost kitchens should track performance metrics such as reduced food waste, optimized delivery routes, and improved inventory turnover rates to measure the impact of AI. By demonstrating tangible results from AI implementation, businesses can justify their initial investment and secure additional funding for future expansions.

4.3 Data Privacy and Security Concerns

Challenge Overview

AI systems in ghost kitchens rely heavily on data—both operational data (such as order history, inventory levels, and delivery times) and customer data (such as personal information, payment details, and preferences). This reliance raises significant concerns about data privacy and security, particularly considering stringent data protection laws. Any breach of sensitive customer data can result in legal consequences, financial penalties, and damage to the business' reputation.

AI's ability to gather and analyze large amounts of data also raises concerns about transparency in how data is used and whether customers are adequately informed about the collection and storage of their personal information. Ensuring that data privacy is maintained is paramount to building trust with customers and ensuring compliance with regulations.

Strategies and Solutions

- **Data Encryption:** One of the most effective ways to secure customer and operational data is through encryption. AI systems should employ state-of-the-art encryption methods to protect data both in transit and at rest. By encrypting sensitive information, businesses can prevent unauthorized access and reduce the risks associated with data breaches.
- **Privacy-by-Design Frameworks:** Privacy-by-design is an approach where privacy considerations are integrated into the design and development of AI systems. Ghost kitchens should work with AI vendors to ensure that their solutions comply with data protection regulations and adopt privacy-centric protocols. This may involve anonymizing customer data, minimizing data retention periods, and obtaining explicit customer consent for data collection.
- **Role-Based Access Control (RBAC):** Implementing role-based access control ensures that only authorized personnel have access to sensitive data. By assigning access permissions based on job roles, ghost kitchens can limit the exposure of customer data to only those who need it to perform their duties, reducing the risk of internal data breaches.
- **Third-Party Audits:** To ensure compliance with data privacy regulations, ghost kitchens can partner with third-party auditors to review their AI systems and data management practices. Regular audits will help identify any vulnerabilities or areas for improvement in the data security framework and ensure that privacy standards are met.
- **Clear Privacy Policies and Customer Consent:** Transparency is key in maintaining customer trust. Ghost kitchens should develop clear and concise privacy policies that outline how customer data is collected, used, and stored. Furthermore, businesses must obtain explicit consent from customers before collecting personal data, ensuring that users understand and agree to the terms under which their data will be used.

5. ARTIFICIAL INTELLIGENCE IN GHOST KITCHENS: PROS AND CONS

Artificial intelligence (AI) is revolutionizing the operational dynamics of ghost kitchens—virtual kitchens that exclusively prepare food for delivery. By integrating AI, these kitchens achieve greater efficiency, personalization, and cost-effectiveness. However, as with any technology, AI also presents challenges that operators must navigate carefully.

5.1 Pros of AI in Ghost Kitchens

1.Operational Efficiency:

AI enhances efficiency in multiple areas of ghost kitchen operations. Predictive analytics helps optimize inventory management by forecasting demand based on historical data, minimizing food waste, and ensuring that supplies are adequate without overstocking. Additionally, AI-powered scheduling tools align staff deployment with order volumes, reducing labor inefficiencies.

2.Demand Forecasting:

By analyzing market trends, customer behavior, and even local events, AI enables precise demand prediction. This ensures kitchens can prepare for peak periods without overproducing, leading to better resource utilization and cost savings.

3.Personalized Customer Experience:

AI-driven platforms analyze customer preferences to offer tailored menu recommendations, enhancing customer satisfaction and loyalty. Chatbots integrated into ordering systems provide 24/7 customer support, resolving queries and enabling seamless communication.

4.Order Accuracy and Speed:

AI streamlines the ordering process, reducing human errors and improving accuracy. Automated kitchen systems ensure that meals are prepared consistently and efficiently, while delivery routing algorithms optimize logistics, reducing delivery times and enhancing customer experience.

5.Scalability:

Ghost kitchens can scale operations more effectively with AI. Managing multiple brands or menus within a single kitchen becomes simpler with AI tools that track performance, allocate resources, and adjust to varying demands.

6.Cost Reduction:

Automation of repetitive tasks reduces reliance on human labor, significantly cutting operational costs. Tasks like food preparation, packaging, and even inventory checks can be handled by AI-enabled machines, freeing staff for more complex responsibilities.

7.Data-Driven Insights:

AI systems analyze sales data and customer feedback to identify trends, enabling menu optimization and marketing strategies that align with consumer preferences.

5.2 Cons of AI in Ghost Kitchens

1.High Initial Costs:

Implementing AI systems requires substantial upfront investment in hardware, software, and training. For smaller ghost kitchen operators, this can be a significant barrier.

2.Complex Integration:

Integrating AI into existing workflows is often complex and can temporarily disrupt operations. Operators may also require technical expertise to maintain and troubleshoot these systems.

3.Potential Job Displacement:

Automation in food preparation, order management, and other tasks can reduce the need for human workers, raising ethical concerns about job losses in the industry.

4.Over-Reliance on Technology:

Dependence on AI systems introduces vulnerabilities. Technical failures, software glitches, or cyberattacks could disrupt operations, causing delays and customer dissatisfaction.

5.Data Privacy Concerns:

AI relies heavily on data collection, which raises concerns about privacy and compliance with data protection regulations. Mismanagement of sensitive customer information can lead to reputational and legal risks.

6.Limited Flexibility:

AI systems are excellent at handling predictable scenarios but may falter when faced with sudden supply chain disruptions, unique customer demands, or other unforeseen events.

7.Algorithmic Bias:

Inaccurate or biased data inputs can lead to flawed AI recommendations, potentially impacting customer satisfaction or operational fairness.

6. EMERGING TRENDS IN GHOST KITCHENS: AI INTEGRATION AND CONSUMER BEHAVIOR SHIFTS

Ghost kitchens, also known as cloud or virtual kitchens, are disrupting the food service industry with their innovative operational model. As this sector grows, emerging trends like artificial intelligence (AI) integration and evolving consumer behavior are shaping the future of food delivery and dining.

6.1 AI Integration in Ghost Kitchens

AI technology is revolutionizing how ghost kitchens operate, offering efficiency, scalability, and improved customer experiences.

Enhanced Operational Efficiency:

AI-powered systems streamline inventory management by analyzing historical data and predicting demand. This minimizes food waste and ensures that the right ingredients are always in stock. Additionally, AI can automate repetitive tasks, such as monitoring cooking times and adjusting temperatures, reducing human errors and ensuring consistent food quality.

Order and Delivery Optimization:

AI tools optimize order processing and delivery logistics. Smart algorithms prioritize orders, assign delivery personnel efficiently, and calculate the fastest delivery routes. This reduces delivery times, enhances customer satisfaction, and cuts operational costs.

Personalized Marketing and Recommendations:

Leveraging AI-driven insights, ghost kitchens can personalize marketing strategies. By analyzing customer preferences and ordering habits, these kitchens can recommend menu items tailored to individual tastes. This improves customer loyalty and boosts sales.

Chatbots and Virtual Assistants:

AI chatbots provide seamless customer support, handling inquiries, resolving complaints, and assisting with orders around the clock. This improves the overall customer experience while reducing the need for human intervention.

6.2 Shifts in Consumer Behavior

Consumer expectations and preferences are evolving rapidly, influencing how ghost kitchens design their services.

Increased Demand for Convenience:

The rise of food delivery apps and the busy lifestyles of modern consumers have heightened the demand for fast, convenient meal options. Ghost kitchens cater to this trend by focusing on delivery-first operations, ensuring meals reach customers quickly and efficiently.

Preference for Healthier and Sustainable Options:

Today's consumers are increasingly health-conscious and eco-aware. Ghost kitchens are responding by offering more plant-based, organic, and sustainable menu items. Additionally, some kitchens are adopting eco-friendly packaging to appeal to environmentally conscious diners.

Rise of Multi-Brand Kitchens:

Consumers seek variety in their dining experiences. Multi-brand ghost kitchens operate under one roof, offering diverse cuisines and menu options. This not only satisfies diverse consumer preferences but also maximizes resource utilization.

Adoption of Digital Ordering:

The pandemic accelerated the shift toward digital ordering through apps and websites. Ghost kitchens are enhancing their digital interfaces with user-friendly designs and integrating loyalty programs to retain customers.

Focus on Hyper-Local Offerings:

Consumers increasingly prefer locally sourced ingredients and neighborhood-focused services. Ghost kitchens are adapting by customizing menus to local tastes and leveraging community connections to enhance brand loyalty.

The Intersection of AI and Consumer Trends

The integration of AI aligns closely with shifting consumer behavior. For example, AI-driven insights allow ghost kitchens to adapt menus in real time based on consumer preferences or seasonal trends. Additionally, AI-enabled delivery systems meet the demand for faster, more reliable service

CONCLUSION: LESSONS LEARNED FROM AI SUCCESS STORIES IN GHOST KITCHENS

The evolution of ghost kitchens has been significantly accelerated by the integration of Artificial Intelligence (AI), which has revolutionized their operational efficiency, sustainability, and customer satisfaction. Analyzing AI success stories within the industry offers valuable lessons on the transformative potential of this technology and the best practices for its implementation. While challenges such as technical expertise gaps, cost concerns, and data privacy issues persist, these success stories demonstrate that with strategic planning, collaboration, and innovation, these obstacles can be effectively addressed.

1. Operational Efficiency is Key

AI has been a game-changer in optimizing operations in ghost kitchens. Successful brands have demonstrated the importance of leveraging AI for:

Demand Forecasting: AI models predict peak order times, popular menu items, and seasonal trends, allowing kitchens to prepare optimally. For instance, companies using predictive analytics have significantly reduced over-preparation and under-utilization of ingredients.

Inventory Management: AI-powered systems track ingredient usage and alert operators when stocks are low or nearing expiry. By implementing such solutions, successful ghost kitchens have achieved near-zero food waste.

Dynamic Pricing and Menu Optimization: AI algorithms analyze customer preferences, competitor pricing, and market trends to suggest optimal pricing strategies and curated menu options. These insights not only enhance profitability but also improve customer satisfaction.

Lesson: Investing in AI-driven operational tools creates efficiency gains that translate to lower costs, higher profits, and enhanced customer experiences.

2. Sustainability and Environmental Impact

AI has enabled ghost kitchens to make significant strides in sustainability, a critical factor in the modern food industry. Notable lessons from successful brands include:

Reducing Food Waste: AI systems track consumption patterns and adjust inventory procurement to prevent over-ordering. Some kitchens have even used AI to monitor food waste in real-time, enabling immediate corrective actions.

Energy Optimization: Machine learning tools help reduce energy consumption by optimizing equipment usage and adjusting operational schedules based on real-time data.

Sustainable Packaging: AI insights into customer feedback and preferences have led brands to adopt more sustainable packaging options, aligning with environmental goals and customer expectations.

Lesson: Integrating AI with sustainability initiatives not only reduces environmental impact but also resonates with eco-conscious consumers, creating a competitive edge.

3. Overcoming Barriers with Collaboration

Many ghost kitchens have successfully overcome challenges such as technical expertise and high infrastructure costs by embracing partnerships. Examples include:

Collaborations with AI Vendors: By working with experienced AI providers, brands have accessed cutting-edge technologies without needing in-house expertise. Vendors often offer customized solutions and ongoing support, ensuring smooth implementation and maintenance.

Shared Resources: Some kitchens have partnered with others to share AI infrastructure, minimizing costs and maximizing returns. This collaborative model has proven especially effective for smaller operators.

Employee Training Programs: Brands that prioritize workforce training have empowered their teams to use AI effectively, reducing resistance to change and fostering innovation.

Lesson: Collaboration with external partners and internal stakeholders is vital for overcoming technical and financial barriers to AI adoption.

4. Data Privacy and Ethical AI Use

Success stories in AI adoption have underscored the importance of prioritizing data privacy and ethical considerations. Ghost kitchens that have maintained customer trust and complied with regulatory requirements have implemented:

Transparent Data Policies: Clear communication about how customer data is collected and used builds trust.

Robust Security Measures: Encryption, role-based access controls, and regular audits protect sensitive data.

Bias-Free AI: Regularly reviewing algorithms for biases ensures fairness and inclusivity, critical for maintaining brand integrity.

Lesson: Proactively addressing data privacy and ethical concerns not only ensures compliance but also strengthens customer relationships.

5. Embracing Innovation and Scalability

AI success stories highlight that scalability is essential for long-term growth. Early adopters of modular AI systems have shown how starting small and scaling gradually allows for controlled growth without overwhelming resources. Additionally, continuously updating AI models based on customer feedback and evolving trends ensures relevance and efficiency.

Lesson: Innovation combined with a phased approach to AI adoption ensures that systems remain flexible, scalable, and aligned with business goals.

6. Customer-Centric Approaches

AI has empowered ghost kitchens to adopt highly personalized customer service strategies. From tailoring menus based on individual preferences to providing real-time delivery updates, successful brands have prioritized customer satisfaction. Using AI to analyze feedback and adapt operations has also helped maintain loyalty in a competitive market.

Lesson: AI-driven personalization fosters stronger customer relationships, resulting in repeat business and positive brand reputation.

AI success stories in ghost kitchens offer a blueprint for unlocking the full potential of this technology. The key lessons learned—prioritizing operational efficiency, embracing sustainability, fostering collaboration, addressing data privacy, scaling innovation, and focusing on customer satisfaction—underscore the importance of strategic planning and execution. While challenges such as cost and expertise remain, they are not insurmountable when addressed with foresight and creativity. By applying these lessons, ghost kitchens can not only enhance their competitiveness but also position themselves as leaders in a rapidly evolving industry. The integration of AI is no longer just an option; it is a necessity for staying ahead in the modern foodservice landscape.

REFERENCES

Beniwal, T., & Mathur, V. K. (2022). Cloud Kitchens and its impact on the restaurant industry. *International Research Journal on Advanced Science Hub*, *4*(12), 324–335. DOI: 10.47392/irjash.2022.076

Chen, L. A., & House, L. (2022). The rise of the ghosts the impact of the pandemic on food purchases. *Choices*, *37*(2), 1–10.

Cornell, D., Manamtam, J. R., & Tham, A. (2024). Invisible Workers in Philippines' Ghost Kitchens: Trends and Implications. Advances in Southeast Asian Studies, 17(2), 187-200. DOI: 10.14764/10.ASEAS-0113

Da Cunha, D. T., Hakim, M. P., Alves, M. M., Vicentini, M. S., & Wiśniewska, M. Z. (2024). Dark kitchens: Origin, definition, and perspectives of an emerging food sector. *International Journal of Gastronomy and Food Science*, *100884*, 100884. Advance online publication. DOI: 10.1016/j.ijgfs.2024.100884

Ding, H., Tian, J., Yu, W., Wilson, D. I., Young, B. R., Cui, X., Xin, X., Wang, Z., & Li, W. (2023). The application of artificial intelligence and big data in the food industry. *Foods*, *12*(24), 4511. DOI: 10.3390/foods12244511 PMID: 38137314

Idris, N. S., Zulkifly, M. A., Safuan, M., & Latip, A. (2023). New trends of cloud kitchen technology and consumers'purchase decisions: A conceptual study. *Voice of Academia*, *19*(2), 114–126.

Jones, S., Cain, L., & Deel, G. L. (2024). Virtual Restaurants and Ghost Kitchens: A New Opportunity. *Journal of Hospitality & Tourism Cases*, *21649987241241948*(3), 108–112. Advance online publication. DOI: 10.1177/21649987241241948

Kalsbeek, R. (2019). Sweetgreen: Healthier Communities by Connecting People to Real Food. DOI: 10.22004/ag.econ.296850

Khan, M. (2024). Cloud kitchen: navigating the future of multiple restaurant in a nutt-shell.

Lahiri, S., Bose, I., & Majumdar, A. (2024). Rebel Foods' Cloud Kitchen Technologies: Food for Thought? *Communications of the Association for Information Systems*, *54*(1), 4. DOI: 10.17705/1CAIS.05407

Nair, A. (2019). How Indian Food Tech Giants Swiggy And Zomato Are Using AI To Improve Customer Experience. https://analyticsindiamag.com/ai-origins-evolution/how-indian-food-tech-giants-swiggy-and-zomato-are-using-ai-to-improve-customer-experience/. Retrieved on 18th Nov 2024.

Parashar, N., Singh, N., & Sharma, M. S. Cloud kitchens: business model for sustainability and inclusion. *EMERGE*, 100.

Pratima, H. (2022). Technology in a Cloud Kitchen – Hot or not? https://www.pcquest.com/technology-in-a-cloud-kitchen-hot-or-not/Retrieved 18 Nov 2024.

Rahman, A.. (2020). The Rise of Ghost Kitchens: Trends and Challenges. *International Journal of Business and Management*, *18*(1), 46–59.

Ruyani, N. A., & Sonjaya, Y. (2023). The Study of Consumer Behavior on Online Food Ordering System in The Metropolitan City. *Cakrawala Management Business Journal*, *6*(1), 109–125.

Shaikh, R., Lampinen, A., & Brown, B. (2023). The work to make piecework work: An ethnographic study of food delivery work in India during the covid-19 pandemic. *Proceedings of the ACM on Human-Computer Interaction, 7*(CSCW2), 1-23. DOI: 10.1145/3610034

Suresh, S., Santhosh, S., & Samjaila, T. H. (2024). Food Economies–Engendered Ghost Kitchens in the Digital Age. In *Business Development via AI and Digitalization* (Vol. 2, pp. 95–104). Springer Nature Switzerland., DOI: 10.1007/978-3-031-62106-2_8

Upton, N. (2018). Kitchen United Opens First of Many Shared Kitchens. foodondemandnews.com. Franchise Times. Retrieved 10 November 2019.

Yupardhi, T. H. (2023, October). Ghost Kitchen Concept: An Alternative Culinary Business Method with a Minimum Space. In *4th Borobudur International Symposium on Humanities and Social Science 2022 (BIS-HSS 2022)* (pp. 126-131). Atlantis Press. DOI: 10.2991/978-2-38476-118-0_14

Chapter 7
Ghost Kitchens Transforming the Culinary Landscape and Shaping the Future of Food Delivery

S. Baranidharan
https://orcid.org/0000-0002-7780-4045
Christ University, India

David Winster Praveenraj
Christ University, India

K. Dhanalakshmi
Christ University, India

Joji Chandran
Christ University, India

D. Sandhya
Christ University, India

Rahul R. Kurup
Christ University, India

Chippy Mohan
https://orcid.org/0000-0001-8589-4944
Christ University, India

ABSTRACT

It presents an important shift in the food service industry, most of which was accelerated during the COVID-19 pandemic: ghost kitchens, or virtual or cloud kitchens. This research discusses the operational mechanisms, workforce consequences, and consumer attitudes toward ghost kitchens, which operate strictly for delivery purposes without having a traditional dining area, as well as the literature used between the years 2007 to 2024. The labor standards and compliance, as most ghost kitchens are built upon gig economy workers who toil in challenging circumstances. Additionally, the study examines consumer perception of this new phenomenon of dining and its potential for transforming culinary careers. Its findings indicate that while ghost kitchens open avenues for creativity in culinary arts and expansion of the marketplace, it simultaneously necessitates a readjustment in labor norms and consumer awareness. Given the anticipated high growth rate for the ghost kitchen market in the next years, it is significant that food service sector stakeholders grasp these dynamics.

DOI: 10.4018/979-8-3373-0432-8.ch007

INTRODUCTION

The food service industry is undergoing a significant transformation with the rise of ghost kitchens, also known as virtual or cloud kitchens. These innovative culinary establishments operate exclusively for delivery, eliminating the need for a physical dining space. Ghost kitchens leverage existing commercial kitchen facilities to prepare meals for various brands, catering to the growing consumer demand for convenience and speed in food delivery. As dining habits shift towards online ordering, particularly in the wake of the COVID-19 pandemic, ghost kitchens have emerged as a viable business model that offers lower operational costs and increased flexibility compared to traditional restaurants. Ghost kitchens are characterized by their ability to operate multiple virtual restaurant brands from a single location, optimizing resources and minimizing overhead expenses. This model allows entrepreneurs to enter the food service market with reduced financial risk, making it an attractive option for both established restaurants seeking to expand their reach and new entrants looking to test culinary concepts without the burden of high startup costs. Furthermore, advancements in technology and data analytics enable ghost kitchens to adapt quickly to consumer preferences and market trends, enhancing their operational efficiency. However, the rapid growth of ghost kitchens also raises important questions about labour dynamics, regulatory compliance, and the overall impact on traditional dining establishments. As this trend continues to evolve, understanding the implications of ghost kitchens on culinary careers, consumer behavior, and the broader food service landscape becomes increasingly critical. This study aims to explore these dimensions, providing insights into how ghost kitchens are reshaping the future of dining and culinary professions.

THEMATIC REVIEWS

Table 1. Thematic Reviews

Theme	Description
Definition and Functionality	Ghost kitchens, also known as virtual or cloud kitchens, are delivery-only restaurants that operate without a physical dining space. These establishments utilize existing restaurant resources to prepare food for online orders, allowing them to minimize overhead costs and maximize efficiency. This model enables restaurants to test new concepts and reach targeted consumer groups without the financial risks associated with traditional dining establishments (Kostyo, 2022).
Operational Advantages	The ghost kitchen model offers several operational benefits, including reduced initial capital requirements, lower overhead costs, and quicker launch times compared to traditional restaurants. They allow for menu specialization and optimized ingredient use, which enhances food quality during delivery. Additionally, ghost kitchens provide an avenue for established restaurants to diversify their revenue streams and adapt to changing consumer preferences for convenience (Kelso, 2020).
Challenges and Market Saturation	Despite their advantages, ghost kitchens face significant challenges, including market saturation and competition from numerous brands vying for consumer attention (Kostyo, 2022). Many ghost kitchens struggle with maintaining food quality and brand recognition in a crowded delivery market. Moreover, reliance on third-party delivery services can lead to inconsistencies in service quality and customer experience (Singh, 2019; Loizos, 2019).

continued on following page

Table 1. Continued

Theme	Description
Regulatory and Labour Considerations	The regulatory landscape poses additional challenges for ghost kitchens, as they must navigate health regulations and zoning laws that can vary widely by location (Newberg, 2020). Labour practices within ghost kitchens also raise concerns regarding worker rights and conditions, particularly as many operations rely on low-wage labour in high-pressure environments (Hill, 2020; Loewen, 2018). Ensuring compliance while maintaining operational efficiency is critical.
Future Outlook and Consumer Trends	The future of ghost kitchens appears promising as they continue to adapt to evolving consumer demands for convenience and speed. However, operators must address the challenges of market saturation and regulatory compliance while ensuring high food quality (Pitchbook, 2021). As consumer behavior shifts towards online ordering and delivery services, ghost kitchens are likely to play an increasingly vital role in the food service industry (Perez, 2020; Rivas, 2020).

OPERATIONAL ADVANTAGES

Ghost kitchens have been a prominent research area in the context of changes in the food service industry. Cai, Leung, and Chi (2022) studied how knowledge and perceived benefit-risk impact the customers' intentions to use ghost kitchens. The study revealed that consumers' understanding of ghost kitchens significantly influenced their willingness to use the services, meaning that effective communication about the benefits and risks associated with them is crucial for building consumer trust and encouraging patronage. Shapiro (2023) argued that these models not only reflect changes in consumer preferences but also pose challenges to urban infrastructure and planning. Shapiro's research highlighted the necessity for a reassessment of urban environments in light of the increasing dominance of delivery-focused food services. In a related investigation, Jiang, Balaji, and Lyu (2024) pinpointed critical factors such as transparency and quality assurance that cultivated consumer trust. Their study emphasized the significance of building trust as a crucial component for promoting repeat patronage in the ghost kitchen industry. Jones, Cain, and Deel (2024) proposed that organizations embracing such new models will gain a competitive advantage in the increasingly digital space. Neria et al. (2024) published optimization strategies to ensure better delivery times for consumers with their changing requirements. This research focused on logistical problems in dealing with ghost kitchens and highlighted the need for strategic solutions. Cornell, Manamtam, and Tham (2024) identified urgent trends shaping labor conditions and rights in this sector that called for essential questions about the workforce and their well-being in light of the rapid growth of ghost kitchens. Nigro et al. (2022) pointed out that while these formats became more common during the pandemic, their longer-term sustainability would depend on factors like consumer acceptance and operational viability. According to Suresh, Santhosh, and Samjaila (2024), implications for future research and practice related to food delivery systems call for an in-depth understanding of how technology influences consumer interactions with food services.

This transformation, as outlined by Barns (2019), has been particularly evident in ghost kitchens that rely on digital platforms to facilitate food delivery without the presence of a traditional dining setting. As noted by Beckett (2020), ghost kitchens can adapt to changing consumer expectations for convenience and safety, thus demonstrating innovative forms of food service that emerged as a result of the pandemic. Bell (2019) investment influx by companies like Amazon into such models is an indicator of the overall trend of digitalization in food delivery, which has picked up pace in the pandemic period. Blatherwick

(2020) raised questions of the future of retailing based on these changes and surmised that this new wave toward ghost kitchens and dark stores could mark a new reality for cities. The conversation resonates with concerns about what consumer expectations would become in an increasingly service-driven society. According to Bromwich (2019), there was the "ghost kitchen to sofa" model. This transition marks significant changes in access to food, as delivery services became the leading way of getting meals during lockdown periods. Butler (2018) impacted the food service industry by forcing many restaurants to change and start using delivery models for survival. The COVID-19 pandemic acted as a catalyst to rapidly increase the number of food delivery services provided online, with several studies pointing out a high rise in the spending of customers on delivery websites (Sharma et al., 2022). This growth was driven by health-related concerns and social distancing measures that limited traditional dining options.

In contrast, Evans (2019) looked deeper into the unsettling dimensions of operational practices at Amazon. The result is that Evans exposed how draconian quotas adopted by the organization have led to an alarming workplace injury rate. Such a critical development raises serious questions about Amazon's business structure and its effects on labor movements. The pressure to meet strict performance requirements has resulted in cases of physical harm, which serves as a reflection of the clash between operational efficiency and the welfare of workers. Ritzer (2013) and Ritzer & Miles (2019) discussed the concept of "McDonaldization," which refers to the process through which the concepts of fast-food restaurants penetrate all aspects of life. The development of ghost kitchens is in line with this trend, as they focus on efficiency, predictability, and control in food preparation procedures, reflecting the operational frameworks of fast-food establishments. Newberg (2020) testified before the first national hearing on ghost kitchens, pointing out the impact they might have on urban planning, labor conditions, and consumer access to food. This evidence underscores the need for regulatory frameworks to address the unique challenges ghost kitchens pose, including zoning, health regulations, and labor rights.

Newberg (2021) published additional locations of ghost kitchens operated by Travis Kalanick's CloudKitchens and its competitor Reef Technology. This map displays the spatial distribution of these kitchens and strategic placement in cities to maximize delivery efficiency. As their numbers increase, questions arise regarding their effects on local economies and existing food businesses. Nicoll (2020) analyzed the potential for Kalanick's real estate ventures to take ghost kitchens to a budding specialty asset class. This view suggests that there is a natural compatibility between real estate and food service logistics, and that ghost kitchens might be an appealing investment opportunity given the continued growth in demand for delivery services. Melendez (2020) discussed how Amazon had incorporated Whole Foods market into its logistics, which illustrates the manner in which traditional retail spaces are now being used as an addendum to e-commerce operations. From a Marxist perspective, this development can be seen as an intensification of capital's penetration in everyday life. Kanngieser (2013) discussed the spatiality of logistics and labor in food delivery networks. The research underlined the ways ghost kitchens represent novel modalities of labor organization and spatial interactions, often functioning within underutilized urban areas while engaging gig workers for delivery services. This transformation prompts significant inquiries regarding labor rights and conditions within an industry that is progressively dependent on flexible employment structures.

Kelso (2020) explores the adoption of technology in ghost kitchens, specifically the role artificial intelligence and point-of-sale systems play in enhancing operational effectiveness. Such technologies optimize order processing, inventory control, and customer engagement, thus leading to increased effectiveness and responsiveness to consumer needs. Khan (2016) looked at the antitrust issues of Amazon, which are relevant to the ghost kitchen debate. The dominant position of the major tech companies in food delivery logistics could present challenges for smaller operators seeking to compete in a market increasingly defined by platform capitalism. This makes it all the more important for the industry to have more regulation as it grows. Harris (2020) also noted that the expansion of Amazon during the pandemic poses threats to both market competition and consumer choice. The dominance of the firm in the e-commerce industry raises the threat of monopolistic practices that may stifle innovation and consumer choice. Hausman et al. (2020) discussed venture capital for logistics startups, which reflected an increased interest in investing in traditional industries like logistics as they shift towards new technological innovations. This phenomenon signifies the constant evolution happening within industries formed by companies like Amazon. Helmond (2015) looked into the platformization of the internet and its implications for data governance, illustrating how platforms like Amazon are changing the relationship between consumers and products. The various impacts of Amazon on international economies, consumer practices, and labor conditions are significant. In future research, there will be an increasing need to understand these forces if issues surrounding economic inequality, labor rights, and competition in a more digital marketplace are to be addressed effectively.

COVID-19 has reshaped consumer behavior regarding food purchases, and complex interplay between technological advancements, changing consumer behaviors, and economic pressures

COVID-19 has dramatically changed the consumption patterns of consumers in terms of purchasing food and complicated the relationship between technological progress, shifting consumer attitudes, and economic stress. The COVID-19 pandemic has greatly altered consumer behavior in food purchase decisions and urban food system dynamics. Chen and House (2022) pandemic changed consumer behavior by favoring convenience and safety, thus significantly increasing the popularity of ghost kitchens and meal delivery services. More broadly, Adam (2009) view is essential to understanding how societal challenges, such as the pandemic, can change the nature of consumer interactions with food systems. Alimohamed-Wilson (2020) enlightens the operational challenges of food delivery services, which have come into prominence during lockdown periods. The author argues that "Amazonification" in logistics did not only change consumer expectations but also created ethical concerns over labor practice in an industry forced to respond to rising demand. Further to these issues, Altenried (2019) studied logistical urbanism and its consequences for labor change during the pandemic. It emerged that with the evolution of food delivery services, the nature of work within these organizations also changed and was often precarious employment experiences for workers involved in ghost kitchens and delivery work. Ang (2020) provided an examination of Amazon's business model, which has defined consumer expectations across several sectors, including food delivery. Efficiency and speed of service became the new order and thus a benchmark for many food service providers during the pandemic. According to Anonymous (2020), it was not only the retail sector that went through a disruption, but the food service sector also faced a disruption as business operations had difficulty adapting to changing consumer habits and economic situations. According to Attiah (2020), an understanding of how economic pressures might shift consumer behavior becomes important in the urban setting. olpaart (2019) operational model gained momentum because of the flexibility to cope with the changed needs of the consumers, especially in the period of the COVID-19 pandemic. Reich (2020) rebuked Jeff Bezos and Amazon for their gains during the pandemic without having protected the employees sufficiently. This analysis draws attention to broader issues of labor conditions in terms of logistics and food delivery operations, especially in ghost kitchens, which often draw their delivery service from gig workers. According to Perez (2020), the COVID-19 pandemic accelerated the pace of the move to e-commerce by five years, thus expanding ghost kitchens since lockdown periods made many consumers look for convenient dining options. This transition further shows that food service frameworks can adapt to challenges outside their realm. Phillips (2020) states, despite the impact of the pandemic, the market approached euphoria, indicating that there is an apparent disconnection between economic conditions and investor attitudes. This may influence financing and investments in such new food service structures as ghost kitchens.

Pitchbook (2021) identifies ghost kitchens as one of the emerging sectors of the food service industry, focusing on their growth and innovation. In fact, it is argued that the business concept for such businesses has become more relevant nowadays because of growing consumer demand for convenience and diversity. According to McKinsey (2020), nearly all industries experienced a boost during the COVID-19 pandemic for the development of their digital strategies. This development resonates with Marx's argument that crises frequently become the driving forces for change in the different modes of production and economic systems, resulting in novel ways of capital accumulation. Ghost kitchens have very quickly become the phenomenon of this generation in the food service industry, especially in relation to the shifts in consumer behavior and aftermath effects of the pandemic dubbed COVID-19. Neilson (2012) presented five propositions on the understanding of logistics as a form of power, which underlines the impact of logistical systems on social dynamics and economic behaviors. This theoretical perspective is important in analyzing ghost kitchens, which operate within complex logistical systems that emphasize both efficiency and fast delivery. McKinsey (2020) noted that the COVID-19 pandemic has accelerated the pace of digitalization in all industries. This is a reflection of Marx's statement that crises often prompt changes in production methods and economic structures, leading to new forms of capital accumulation. Lerman (2020) shared information on how Amazon reacted to COVID-19, reporting that nearly 20,000 employees had contracted the virus. This statistic draws attention to the health risks associated with logistics and delivery jobs in the pandemic and raises concerns over the safety of workers in such contexts as ghost kitchens, which are likely to rely on gig workers in similar situations.

Ghost kitchens have dramatically changed the food service industry, especially as a response to changing consumer preferences and technological advancements. Jeffries (2020) defined ghost kitchens as delivery-only restaurants that do not have a traditional storefront and rely on online orders to serve customers. This model has gained popularity because consumers increasingly seek convenience and speed in their dining experiences, especially during the COVID-19 pandemic. Klein (2007) introduced the concept of disaster capitalism, which can be applied to understand how businesses adapt during crises such as the pandemic. Ghost kitchens are a response to the challenges traditional restaurants faced during lockdowns, showing how market opportunities can be created from adverse conditions. Helmore (2020) reported on Amazon's soaring profits during the pandemic, showing how the company's business model capitalized on increased demand for online shopping while raising questions about labor practices within its warehouses. According to Ho (2020), Americans' debt levels are increasing during the pandemic, and this is set against the backdrop of economic pressures that may push consumers toward more convenient shopping solutions like those offered by dark stores. The ability to access groceries quickly without leaving home can alleviate some financial burdens associated with traditional shopping methods. Helmore (2020) documented the significant increase in Amazon's profits amid the pandemic, emphasizing how the firm's business strategy leveraged the heightened demand for online shopping while prompting inquiries into labor practices within its fulfillment centers. The compilation of these studies elucidates the transformative impact of COVID-19 on consumer behavior related to food acquisition. The transition toward online ordering and dependence on delivery services signifies wider societal transformations influenced by health apprehensions and economic difficulties. It becomes apparent, however, that to design effective strategies for building resilience in urban food systems in the post-pandemic world, an increasing need arises to understand consumer behavior in this new context. The academic literature regarding ghost kitchens and the transformation of the food service industry due to the COVID-19 pandemic reflects a fundamental shift in consumer behavior, delivery infrastructure, and restaurant operations.

CHALLENGES AND MARKET SATURATION

Charron-Chénier (2020) explored the inequality of payday loan use, pointing to a wider problem of economic inclusion and exclusion and relevant to discourse on food accessibility and consumer credit in the gig economy, including food delivery service. Chua et al. (2018) suggested the concept of "turbulent circulation," arguing for deeper engagement with the logics of circulation. This is important in understanding how ghost kitchens work within complex supply chains and what it means for urban space and consumer access to food. The authors have foregrounded how logistics shape everyday experiences and consumer interactions with food services. Cochoy (2007) argues that, given the lack of physical storefronts, new forms of marketing are needed to attract consumers through digital platforms. CCosgrove (2021) recorded the acquisition of a micro-warehousing startup by Reef, which is an effort to make fast delivery services accessible. This marks the integration of logistics and technology in improving food delivery mechanisms, an important aspect for the ghost kitchen model, as it relies heavily on efficient logistics in meeting consumer demand. Cowen (2014) researched how logistics conditions impact the reality of cities. He contended that increases in delivery companies and ghost kitchens illustrate deep socioeconomic changes. The article described how such logistic structures can modify food consumption accessibility and even reshape urban realities.

Danyluk (2018) worked to understand capitalism and its relationship to logistical forms in accumulation and globalization processes. This is relevant when viewing the integration of ghost kitchens into larger economic systems that place efficiency and lower cost over traditional dining experiences. Friedlander (2021) covered the specifics of cloud kitchens and how they are relevant to the businesses of Travis Kalanick in the food delivery space. The piece describes how such kitchen models change food service delivery as reflective of the larger consumer trends where convenience and speed are placed on a premium. Greene and Joseph (2015) developed the concept of the "digital spatial fix," which describes how digital technologies transform spatial interactions within economic activities. This framework is applicable for studying the impact of Amazon and similar platforms on logistics and the access of consumers to products. Hannak et al. (2014) shed empirical light on the manifestation of price discrimination and steering on e-commerce websites, showing that online marketplaces like Amazon could alter their prices in response to consumer demand. This shift demonstrates the complexity of digital commerce and portends further implications for market dynamics.

Harris (2020) also emphasized how the growth of Amazon during the pandemic introduced potential threats to market competition and consumer choice. Such dominance has raised monopolistic concerns and fears of innovation suppression and a reduced choice for consumers. Rivas (2020) further stated that grocery items are among the fastest-growing e-commerce categories. The implications are immense for ghost kitchens, as they can easily extend their delivery services to groceries and, therefore, blur the line between traditional food service and retailing industries. Romeo (2019) elaborated on how DoorDash opened its first ghost kitchen, demonstrating how leading delivery platforms are investing in this concept to enhance their service offerings. It is a trend of the bigger picture, where established firms are adapting to the needs of the customer, who want convenience through innovative operating models. In another article, Romeo (2020) highlighted how Chili's parent company is expanding into virtual concepts, indicating a shift towards embracing digital platforms for food service. This trend reinforces the growing acceptance of ghost kitchens as viable business models within the restaurant industry. Rudra (2020) discussed how the surge in e-commerce has driven growth in last-mile fulfillment centers and dark stores. Ghost kitchens are part of that movement as a localized hub for food delivery services that enhance operations logistics for immediate delivery to consumers. Plantin and Punathambekar (2019) elaborated on digital media infrastructures, underlining how platforms structure economic interactions. Ghost kitchens are a part of this landscape, using technology to optimize operations and enhance customer experiences. Pollio (2021) discussed labor dynamics at infrastructural interfaces within platform urbanism, highlighting how ghost kitchens rely on gig workers for delivery services. Such reliance raises crucial questions about labor rights and conditions in a sector characterized by precarious employment. In a nutshell, it can be shown that ghost kitchens are revolutionizing the food service sector through innovative operational frameworks that place emphasis on efficiency and flexibility. However, continuous dialogues concerning regulatory structures, labor conditions, and economic consequences will be crucial in guaranteeing that these advancements serve the interests of both consumers and workers as the industry progresses. Nitzan (1998) has developed differential accumulation, a theory that explains the way different capital sectors respond to changes in market conditions. The ghost kitchen provides an outstanding example of this response in terms of how it uses low operating costs and flexible business models to capture share in the ever-competitive food delivery industry.

Peck (2012) has discussed the concept of austerity urbanism, which directly relates to the operational context of ghost kitchens in a constrained urban economy. The emergence of these kitchens may be a precursor to larger trends in urban development, where traditional dining spaces can no longer be sustained due to higher rents and competition from the delivery services. Plantin et al. (2018) discuss the intersection between infrastructure studies and platform studies as part of digital economies. For ghost kitchens, this intersection is particularly relevant as they rely on digital platforms for order management and customer communication while maintaining complex logistical systems. Loizos (2019) presented an analytical review of the cloud kitchens phenomenon, presenting its advantageous characteristics and concerning elements. The article underlined the fact that although cloud kitchens can provide consumers with convenience and diversity, at the same time, they raise apprehensions regarding labor rights, the respect for rules, and the long-term viability of such frameworks. Luna (2021) documented the operation of ghost kitchens by Reef without the requisite permits, thereby exemplifying the regulatory difficulties that emerge within this swiftly advancing domain. This situation emphasizes the necessity for more definitive regulations and supervision to guarantee adherence to local legislation as the prevalence of ghost kitchens increases.

In modern dialogues, McCormick (2021) noted Amazon's unprecedented profits, drawing attention to how the corporation's business strategy reflects certain critiques posited by Marx pertaining to capital accumulation and market supremacy. The most important sales figures experienced during the pandemic suggest that consumers' behavior has been shifted toward e-commerce, and this in turn affects traditional retail and labor practices. McGrath (2020) explained that industrial real estate is becoming an attractive investment space partly because of the logistics needs of companies like Amazon. This is also consistent with Marx's observation on how capital seeks new avenues of investment and maximizes profit opportunities due to the prevailing conditions of the market at hand. McGuigan and Manzerolle (2014) edited a collection that revisits critical theories about commercial media, which could be related to Marx's study of media as an apparatus for capital accumulation and ideological power. Their work focuses on the relevance of Marxist theory in judging the contemporary media landscape shaped by digital capitalism. McKelvey (2011) discussed the modularity present in platforms like Drupal, reflecting how technological infrastructures shape economic exchanges. This strategy resonates with Marx's views on how the character of the organization of production influences social relations within a capitalist framework. The concept of dark stores has been a leading innovation for grocery and food delivery industries, especially in response to changing consumer demands in terms of speed and convenience. Hepworth (2014) analyzed the work of logistical geographies and how the character of the organization of spatial logistics defines consumer experience and the availability of products. This conceptual framework is important in understanding the operational dynamics of dark stores, which are compact distribution centers designed for the fulfillment of online orders.

Hill (2020) explored the injuries related to platform logistics, highlighting the physical and psychological effects on workers working in such high-pressure environments. As dark stores are optimized with a view to efficiency and speed of delivery, conditions for work become more critical and lead to concerns over the safety and well-being of workers who have to work under continuous pressure. Ibert et al. (2019) examined the geographies of disconnection to pay attention to value-creation in "dark" sites, habitually ignored in mainstream economic analyses. This encompasses dark stores that are located outside the traditional retail setting, thereby significantly contributing to urban logistics but keeping the consumer isolated from the actual retail environment. According to Visible Capital (2020), a study on grocery fulfillment in dark stores revealed faster delivery speed and improved operating efficiency. The report underscored the strategic placement of these facilities, which serves to reduce delivery durations and adequately cater to consumer expectations for immediate satisfaction in grocery procurement. This operational framework enables retailers to respond to increasing demands for rapid commerce by optimizing inventory management and the processes involved in order fulfillment. Investable Universe (2019) noted the emergence of micro-fulfillment centers as a notable trend in the landscape of venture capital investments. These stores are aligned well with the dark store concept, enabling the retailers to reinforce their supply chain and respond faster to the requirements of consumers. The emphasis on localized fulfillment implies a broader movement toward hyperlocal delivery systems targeting urban populations. HNGRY (2019) created a video discussing recent innovations in the fast food delivery sector that indirectly links the innovations to dark stores as being an integral component of modern-day food logistics. With dark stores and the implementation of advanced technology, streamlined processes will enhance their capability to speed up order fulfillment. This changes the expectation level of consumers concerning food availability.

REGULATORY AND LABOR CONCERNS

Dastin and Rana (2020) reported that during the pandemic, Amazon recorded a record profit reflecting a massive rise in online retail and delivery services. This phenomenon poses significant implications for ghost kitchens, which have leveraged the increased demand for delivery services as a result of consumers' shift away from in-person dining experiences. Deener (2017) discussed the concept of food deserts as an expression of urban inequality that restricts access to fresh produce. This development can be seen as a response to such inequalities, offering food alternatives in areas where the traditional grocery store may not suffice. Delfanti (2021) discussed the conditions of digital labor in Amazon warehouses, pointing out issues of dispossession and exploitation that resonate with the labor dynamics of ghost kitchens. Since these kitchens usually work with a few staff members and are dependent on gig workers for delivery services, knowing the labor conditions is essential to address the potential imbalances in this industry. The literature existing at present reflects that ghost kitchens are not only a response to changing consumer preferences but are also extensively interrelated with broader socio-economic transformations, improvements in logistics, and urbanism inequalities. Further research will be required as this sector continues to advance in order to fully understand its impacts on consumers, workers, and urban environments. Existing literature concerning the impact of Amazon on economic and labor trends shows significant effects on consumer behavior, inflationary tendencies, and working conditions. Edwards (2017) opined that Amazon is somehow driving down the inflationary rates across the globe due to its innovative logistics management and diverse range of offerings. This phenomenon, known as "the Amazonisation of inflation," indicates that the operational efficiencies of Amazon contribute to a disinflationary environment by reducing distribution costs and making cheaper goods easily accessible to consumers. Analysts have pointed out that the internet makes price comparisons easier, which enables consumers to look for the best deals, further driving prices down (Edwards, 2017).

Harris (2015) examined pop-up cultures and their effects on cities, pointing out that the flexibility of city spaces is reflective of broader economic shifts. Harris also wrote elsewhere that pop-up culture has been a fashionable trend, where precarity is the cool way to live rather than the effect of economic uncertainty. Reich (2020) condemned Jeff Bezos and Amazon for taking advantage of the pandemic without sufficiently safeguarding its workers. This review shows that there are even broader issues surrounding labor conditions associated with the logistics and food delivery sectors, in which ghost kitchens often rely on gig workers to execute their deliveries. Richardson, in 2018, conducted a study regarding how platforms change urban markets and argued that digital platforms have commercialized public space. This transformation is evident in ghost kitchens, which use cities for food preparation without physical storefronts, raising questions about their impact on local economies and community interactions. Pollman (2019) discussed the concept of regulatory arbitrage in the context of technology, showing how companies often exploit regulatory loopholes to gain competitive advantages. This phenomenon is particularly important for ghost kitchens, which operate in a grey zone of regulations that might mean challenges in maintaining compliance with health and safety regulations. In any case, as ghost kitchens become ever more common, the demand for well-defined regulatory frameworks to minimize the dangers of food safety and labor practices becomes all the more exigent.

Proctor (2008) coined the term "agnotology" to refer to the cultural generation of ignorance, a concept relevant to the food delivery industry. The insufficient transparency associated with ghost kitchens may play a role in consumer unawareness regarding sourcing, labor conditions, and health regulations. It is crucial to comprehend the mechanisms by which knowledge is created and shared in this context in order to promote informed decisions among consumers. PYMNTS (2020) cited a thriving investment climate for logistics technology, thus reflecting growing interest in solutions that better streamline delivery systems. Increased funding accelerates the deployment of ghost kitchens and last-mile delivery services, which closely resemble changing customer expectations for accessibility and speed. Mitchell and LeVecchia (2016) analyzed Amazon's strategies within the market and argued that the company's current dominance jeopardizes local economic interests and labor jobs. Their results are in agreement with the Marxist criticism on capital accumulation and its socio-economic implications. Mitchell 2020 finds the interplay between infrastructure development and time management within the larger social context of capitalism in studying how infrastructure is utilized as a means to assist in the process of capital circulation-an understanding developed by Marx about economic orders. Morgan (2020) argued that dark stores represent the future of retail in the post-pandemic era, mirroring Marx's observations on the dynamics between crises and innovations that serve to advance capitalist interests while changing consumer access to goods. Mould (2014) discussed tactical urbanism as a response to urban problems, relating it to broader economic shifts. This model can be analyzed from a Marxist lens as communities seek to reclaim power within systems shaped by capital. Neate (2019) highlighted studies criticizing Amazon for aggressive tax avoidance practices that are a manifestation of the deeper issues concerning corporate governance and accountability, key aspects of Marx's work on capitalism. Together, these contemporary debates reinforce the ongoing importance of Marx's Capital in the analysis of modern economic systems, especially given technological change and changes in consumer behavior. Labor, capital formation, and market forces continue to determine socio-economic contexts around the world.

Merchant (2020) defined the performance of Amazon during the pandemic as typical of broader tendencies in corporate action and market power, aligning with Marx's concerns over monopolistic practices that undermine competition and exploit labor. Mezzadra and Neilson (2017) applied the extraction framework to understand contemporary capitalism and showed how contemporary forms of exploitation reflect historical patterns of exploitation. Their analysis supplements Marx's critique in the sense that they look into how extraction is manifested in different forms in global supply chains. Mezzadri (2016) centered on labor exploitation in garment production in India, paralleling Marx's analysis of labor conditions under capitalism. This work focuses on the present-day issues about worker rights and exploitation in a globalized economy. Mitchell and LeVecchia (2016) criticized Amazon's market practices, arguing that its dominance is a threat to local economies and jobs. Their findings support Marxist criticisms of capital accumulation and its socio-economic implications. Mitchell (2020) explored the connection between infrastructural development and temporal management in capitalist systems, considering how infrastructure serves as a channel for capital flow—a concept that is based on Marx's analysis of economic systems.

Lunden (2018) highlighted Amazon's large share of the U.S. e-commerce market, which highlights its influence on consumer behavior and market dynamics. It makes it difficult for the smaller operators in the food delivery space, such as ghost kitchens, to compete with the company's huge logistics network. The literature depicts how platform urbanism not only shapes consumer experiences but also labour conditions and regulatory landscapes in the urban environment. As ghost kitchens and other similar models continue to evolve, it will be crucial to have continuous research to address concerns about labor rights, economic inequality, and the feasibility of these new food service paradigms. Langlois and Elmer (2019) discussed the idea of impersonal subjectivation within digital infrastructures by pointing out how platforms shape consumer identities and experiences. In the ghost kitchen, this would translate to consumers becoming increasingly defined by their interactions with digital platforms instead of traditional dining experiences. Lee (2020) observes that, in the wake of the pandemic, tech venture investments surged in the U.S., signaling rising interest in novel business models like ghost kitchens. It is evidence of a greater general trend towards the digitalization and convenience of consumer services.

STATEMENT OF PROBLEM

The ghost kitchen model, which thrived during the COVID-19 pandemic, now encounters significant challenges that jeopardize its sustainability. This research discusses the operational mechanisms, workforce consequences, and consumer attitudes toward ghost kitchens, which operate strictly for delivery purposes without having a traditional dining area, as well as the literature used between the years 2007 to 2024. The rapid expansion of ghost kitchens fostered a false sense of security, leading to operational complexities that many operators were not ready to manage. Problems such as inconsistent food quality, insufficiently trained staff, and logistical inefficiencies have surfaced as critical issues. These challenges diminish the consumer experience, making it hard for ghost kitchens to retain customers in a fiercely competitive market. Additionally, navigating the regulatory landscape poses further obstacles, as ghost kitchens contend with varying zoning laws and health regulations that can impede their operations. As competition intensifies and market saturation rises, maintaining brand recognition and consumer trust becomes increasingly difficult without a physical presence. Moreover, dependence on third-party delivery services complicates logistics and can exacerbate inconsistencies in service quality. The current situation for ghost kitchens is characterized by operational hurdles, regulatory challenges, and increased competition, necessitating strategic adaptations for long-term viability in the changing food service landscape.

RESEARCH METHODOLOGY

This study utilizes a qualitative research design to examine the dynamics of ghost kitchens within the food service industry. The research period spans from 2007 to 2024, covering the emergence of ghost kitchens and their accelerated growth during the pandemic. Data was gathered through a thorough review of scholarly articles, industry reports, and news articles related to ghost kitchens, food delivery trends, and labor implications. Articles were selected based on their relevance to ghost kitchens, empirical studies on operational practices, consumer behavior analyses, and discussions on labor dynamics. The chosen sources contribute to understanding the multifaceted impact of ghost kitchens on culinary careers and the broader food service landscape. This methodology aims to synthesize existing literature to provide insights into the opportunities and challenges presented by ghost kitchens in modern dining experiences.

DISCUSSION ON THE IMPACT OF GHOST KITCHENS ON THE JOB MARKET

The rise of ghost kitchens has significantly transformed the job market within the food service industry, presenting both challenges and opportunities for workers. As these delivery-only establishments proliferate, they threaten traditional restaurant jobs while simultaneously creating new roles in a rapidly evolving landscape. Ghost kitchens operate with lower overhead costs and can undercut traditional restaurants, potentially leading to fewer job opportunities for chefs and front-of-house staff. As they capture market share, traditional establishments may struggle to compete, resulting in layoffs and closures. This trend is particularly concerning for low-wage workers who depend on these jobs for their livelihoods. Despite these challenges, ghost kitchens also offer new avenues for culinary professionals. Their flexibility allows chefs to experiment with diverse cuisines and concepts without the financial burden of a full-service restaurant. Additionally, the lower barrier to entry may encourage aspiring restaurateurs to launch virtual brands, fostering innovation within the industry. Delivery drivers may also be affected by the growth of ghost kitchens; as more brands operate from centralized locations, competition for delivery jobs could intensify, potentially leading to lower wages and reduced job security. As gig economy workers face increased pressure from a saturated market, their working conditions could deteriorate further.

Figure 1 Navigating the Impact of Ghost Kitchen On The Culinary Landscape. Automation is set to influence the job market within ghost kitchens as well. While technology can streamline operations and reduce labor costs, it does not eliminate the need for human employees. Instead, automation can enhance job satisfaction by allowing workers to focus on more fulfilling tasks rather than mundane operational duties. However, this shift requires a workforce that is adaptable and skilled in managing new technologies. The centralized nature of ghost kitchens presents unique opportunities for worker organizing; unlike traditional restaurants scattered across various locations, ghost kitchens can facilitate collective action among workers who share similar experiences. This environment could foster stronger labor movements aimed at improving conditions and advocating for better wages within the industry.

Figure 1. Navigating the Impact of Ghost Kitchen On The Culinary Landscape

THE INFLUENCE OF GHOST KITCHENS ON THE FUTURE OF CULINARY CAREERS

1. Lower Barriers to Entry for Aspiring Chefs

Ghost kitchens allow aspiring restaurateurs and chefs to enter the culinary field with reduced financial risk. With lower overhead costs associated with traditional brick-and-mortar restaurants, individuals can launch virtual brands without the burden of high rent and utility expenses (1). This democratization of the restaurant industry enables a wider array of culinary talent to experiment with diverse cuisines and concepts, fostering innovation.

2. Shift in Skill Requirements

As ghost kitchens increasingly adopt technology such as automation, robotics, and IoT systems, culinary professionals will need to adapt their skill sets to remain competitive. Knowledge of advanced kitchen technologies and proficiency in managing automated systems will become essential (3). Chefs may find themselves focusing more on menu development and less on traditional cooking techniques, as automation takes over routine tasks.

3. Increased Focus on Delivery Logistics

The rise of ghost kitchens emphasizes the importance of delivery logistics in culinary careers. Professionals will need to understand how to optimize food preparation for delivery, ensuring that dishes maintain quality during transit (4). This shift may lead to new roles focused specifically on delivery management and logistics within culinary operations.

4. Greater Emphasis on Sustainability

Ghost kitchens present unique opportunities to address food waste through efficient inventory management and menu design (4). Culinary professionals will increasingly be tasked with creating menus that minimize waste by utilizing shared ingredients across multiple brands operating from the same kitchen. This focus on sustainability aligns with growing consumer demand for environmentally responsible practices in food production.

5. Potential Job Displacement

While ghost kitchens create new opportunities, they also pose a risk of job displacement for traditional restaurant staff. As more establishments transition to delivery-only models, roles such as servers and bartenders may diminish (1). Culinary professionals must adapt to this changing landscape by cultivating versatile skills that align with the evolving demands of the industry.

As ghost kitchens continue to reshape the culinary landscape, chefs must develop new skills to thrive in these innovative environments. The following skills are essential for adapting to the unique operational demands of ghost kitchens.

1. Menu Optimization and Development

Chefs need to focus on creating streamlined menus that prioritize dishes which travel well and maintain quality during delivery. This involves understanding which ingredients are most popular and how to minimize waste by optimizing inventory based on demand data (1). Chefs must be adept at analyzing sales trends and adjusting menus accordingly to maximize efficiency and profitability.

2. Technological Proficiency

Ghost kitchens heavily rely on technology for order management, kitchen operations, and customer engagement. Chefs should be comfortable using various software tools, including point-of-sale systems and inventory management applications (2). Familiarity with delivery platforms and online marketing strategies is also crucial for promoting their offerings effectively.

3. Logistics and Supply Chain Management

Understanding the logistics of food preparation and delivery is vital in a ghost kitchen setting. Chefs must learn to coordinate with suppliers efficiently, manage stock levels, and ensure timely preparation of orders to meet delivery deadlines (3). This skill set includes planning workflows that accommodate high-volume production while maintaining food safety standards.

4. Adaptability and Problem-Solving

The fast-paced nature of ghost kitchens requires chefs to be adaptable and quick-thinking. They must be able to respond to fluctuating demand, adjust menu items on short notice, and troubleshoot issues that arise during service (3). This flexibility is essential for maintaining high standards of quality and customer satisfaction.

5. Collaboration and Communication Skills

Effective communication is crucial in a ghost kitchen environment where teamwork is necessary for success. Chefs must collaborate closely with kitchen staff, delivery personnel, and management to ensure smooth operations (4). Strong interpersonal skills will help facilitate clear communication regarding order specifications, preparation timelines, and any changes to menu offerings.

IMPLICATIONS OF THE RISE OF GHOST KITCHENS

The emergence of ghost kitchens has profound implications for the food service industry, impacting everything from operational practices to labour dynamics and consumer behavior.

Shift in Employment Dynamics & Operational Efficiency and Flexibility - Ghost kitchens may lead to fewer job opportunities in traditional restaurants, as they often require a smaller workforce and operate with lower overhead costs (1). However, they also create new roles within the culinary landscape, allowing chefs and culinary professionals to explore innovative concepts without the financial risks associated with brick-and-mortar establishments (2). This duality presents both challenges and opportunities in the job market. The ghost kitchen model enables restaurants to streamline operations and reduce costs by focusing solely on delivery. This shift allows for quicker startup times and adaptability to changing consumer demands (3). As restaurants pivot to this model, they can experiment with diverse menus and geographic markets more easily, which can enhance overall profitability.

Consumer Convenience and Market Reach - Ghost kitchens cater to the growing consumer demand for convenience, providing a wider variety of food options accessible through delivery apps (1). This increased convenience can lead to greater customer satisfaction and loyalty, as consumers enjoy the ability to explore different cuisines without leaving their homes. Moreover, ghost kitchens can expand a brand's reach into new markets that were previously inaccessible.

Regulatory Challenges & Impact of Automation and Technology - As ghost kitchens proliferate, they must navigate the same health and safety regulations as traditional restaurants. Ensuring compliance can be challenging, particularly as many ghost kitchens operate in non-traditional spaces (4). The need for proper licensing and adherence to food safety standards will be critical for their long-term viability. The integration of automation and technology in ghost kitchens is transforming operational practices. Chefs and kitchen staff will need to adapt to using AI-driven tools for inventory management, order processing, and menu optimization (5). While automation can enhance efficiency, it may also reduce the number of available jobs, necessitating a workforce that is skilled in managing these technologies.

CONCLUSION

The rise of ghost kitchens represents a transformative shift in the food service industry, driven by changing consumer preferences, technological advancements, and the need for operational efficiency. This study has highlighted the multifaceted implications of ghost kitchens, encompassing both opportunities and challenges for culinary professionals, businesses, and consumers alike. As ghost kitchens continue to proliferate, they offer aspiring chefs and restaurateurs a lower barrier to entry, enabling innovation and experimentation in a competitive market. However, this new model also threatens traditional restaurant jobs and requires culinary professionals to adapt their skill sets to meet the demands of a rapidly evolving landscape. The emphasis on delivery logistics, technological proficiency, and menu optimization underscores the need for a workforce that is agile and technologically savvy. Moreover, the regulatory challenges associated with ghost kitchens necessitate careful navigation to ensure compliance with health and safety standards. As these establishments become more prevalent, stakeholders must address the complexities of labour dynamics, consumer expectations, and operational practices to foster a sustainable future. Ghost kitchens present exciting opportunities for growth and innovation within the culinary sector, they also require a thoughtful approach to mitigate potential risks and ensure that all participants in the food service ecosystem benefit from this evolution. As the industry adapts to these changes, ongoing research and dialogue will be essential in shaping best practices and policies that support both culinary creativity and workforce well-being.

REFERENCES

Adam, B. E. (2009). Futures in the making: sociological practice and challenge. In Jeffries, V. (Ed.), *Handbook of Public Sociology* (pp. 429–474). Rowman & Littlefield Publishers.

Alimohamed-Wilson, J. (2020). The Amazonification of logistics: e-commerce, labour, and exploitation in the last mile. In Alimahomed-Wilson, J., & Reese, E. (Eds.), *The Cost of Free Shipping: Amazon in the Global Economy* (pp. 69–84). Pluto Press.

Alimohamed-Wilson, J., Allison, J., & Reese, E. (2020). Introduction: Amazon capitalism. In Alimahomed-Wilson, J., & Reese, E. (Eds.), *The Cost of Free Shipping: Amazon in the Global Economy* (pp. 1–20). Pluto Press.

Altenried, M. (2019). On the last mile: Logistical urbanism and the transformation of labour. work organisation, labour & globalisation. *Pluto Journals, 13*(1), 114–129.

Ang, C. (2020). *Visualized: A Breakdown of Amazon's Revenue Model*. Visual Capitalist.

Anonymous, . (2020). *Dark Stores—Thread Regarding Macy's Inc*. Layoffs.

Attiah, K. (2020). The Evictions Crisis is Coming. We Have Barely Begun to Face it. Washington, DC: Washington Post.

Barns, S. (2019). Negotiating the platform pivot: From participatory digital ecosystems to infrastructures of everyday life. *Geography Compass, 13*(9), e12464.

Beckett, E. L. (2020). A DC Ghost Food Hall Gives a Glimpse of a Post-Pandemic Restaurant Future. Restaurant Dive. Available at., Retrieved January 20, 2021, from.https://www.restaurantdive.com/news/this-dc-ghost-food-hall-is-a-glimpse-of-a-post-pandemic-restaurant-future/588164/

Bell, D. (2019). Deliveroo's Virtual Restaurant Model Will Eat The Food Service Industry, As Amazon Piles in to Fund US Expansion. Forbes. Available at., Retrieved January 22, 2021, from.https://www.forbes.com/sites/douglasbell/2019/08/26/deliveroos-virtual-restaurant-model-will-eat-the-food-service-industry-as-amazon-piles-in-to-fund-us-expansion/

Blatherwick, A. (2020). Is The Future of Retailing Going Dark? RetailWire. Available at: https://www.retailwire.com/discussion/is-the-future-of-retailing-going-dark/ (accessed 7. February 2021).

Blumgart, J., & Hetrick, C. (2021). Amazon Now Encircles the Philadelphia Region With Over 50 Warehouses. Philadelphia, PA: The Philadelphia Inquirer, Available at: https://www.inquirer.com/business/amazon-prime-warehouses-philadelphia-jobs-growth-20210418.html (accessed 18 April 2021).

Bonacich, E., & Wilson, J. B. (2008). *Getting the Goods: Ports, Labour, and the Logistics Revolution*. Cornell University Press.

Bromwich, J. E. (2019). Farm to Table? More Like Ghost Kitchen to Sofa. New York, NY: The New York Times, Vol. 24. Available at: https://www.nytimes.com/2019/12/24/style/ghost-kitchen-food-delivery.html (accessed 22 January 2021).

Brown, S. (1993). Retail location theory: Evolution and evaluation. *International Review of Retail, Distribution and Consumer Research, 3*(2), 185–229.

Butler, S. (2018). Apocalypse Now for Britain's Retailers as Low Wages and the Web Cause Ruin. London, UK: The Guardian. Available at: http://www.theguardian.com/business/2018/feb/17/uk-retail-industry--gloom-high-street-shift-consumers (accessed 20 January 2021).

Cai, R., Leung, X. Y., & Chi, C. G. Q. (2022). Ghost kitchens on the rise: Effects of knowledge and perceived benefit-risk on customers' behavioral intentions. *International Journal of Hospitality Management, 102*, 103–115. DOI: 10.1016/j.ijhm.2021.102115

Charron-Chénier, R. (2020). Predatory inclusion in consumer credit: Explaining black and white disparities in payday loan use. *Sociological Forum, 35*(22), 370–392.

Chen, L. A., & House, L. (2022). The rise of the ghosts—the impact of the pandemic on food purchases: A study on consumer behavior changes during COVID-19 lockdowns in urban areas. *Choices, 37*(3), 1–8.

Chua, C., Danyluk, M., Cowen, D., & Khalili, L. (2018). Introduction: Turbulent circulation: Building a critical engagement with logistics. *Environment and Planning. D, Society & Space, 36*(4), 617–629.

Cochoy, F. (2007). A sociology of market-things: On tending the garden of choices in mass retailing. *The Sociological Review, 55*, 109–129.

Colpaart, A. (2019). Everything You Need to Know About Cloud Kitchens in 2020. Fort Colins, CO: The food corridor. Available at: https://www.thefoodcorridor.com/2019/12/05/everything-you-need-to-know-about-cloud-kitchens-aka-ghost-kitchens-in-2020/ (accessed 20 January 2021).

Cornell, D., Manamtam, J. R., & Tham, A. (2024). Invisible Workers in Philippines' Ghost Kitchens: Trends and Implications. *Advances in Southeast Asian Studies, 17*(2), 187–200. DOI: 10.1016/j.asas.2024.01.005

Cosgrove, E. (2021). Softbank-Backed Reef Acquires Micro-Ware Housing Startup to Democratize Super-fast Delivery. Business Insider., Retrieved October 6, 2021, from.

Cowen, D. (2014). *The Deadly Life of.* University of Minnesota Press.

Danyluk, M. (2018). Capital's logistical fix: Accumulation, globalization, and the survival of capitalism. *Environment and Planning. D, Society & Space, 36*(4), 630–647.

Dastin, J., & Rana, A. (2020). Amazon Posts Biggest Profit Ever at Height of Pandemic in US. Canary Wharf. Reuters. Available at., Retrieved February 9, 2021, from.https://www.reuters.com/article/us-amazon-com-results-idUSKCN24V3HL

Deener, A. (2017). The origins of the food desert: urban inequality as infrastructural exclusion social forces. Oxford Academic 95(3): 1285–1309.

Delfanti, A. (2021). Machinic dispossession and augmented despotism: Digital work in an amazon warehouse. *New Media & Society, 23*(1), 39–55.

Edwards, J. (2017). Amazon Might be Lowering the Rate of Inflation Globally. Businessinsider. Available at., Retrieved January 20, 2021, from.https://www.businessinsider.com/amazon-effect-inflation-deflation-2017-10

Evans, W. (2019). Ruthless Quotas at Amazon are Maiming Employees. The Atlantic, Available at., Retrieved January 22, 2021, from.https://www.theatlantic.com/technology/archive/2019/11/amazon-warehouse-reports-show-worker-injuries/602530/

Friedlander, E. (2021). The Mysterious Case of the F*cking Good Pizza. Vice, Available at., Retrieved April 2, 2021, from.https://www.vice.com/en/article/qjpgd7/the-mystery-of-fcking-good-pizza-travis-kalanick-cloudkitchens-future-foods-delivery-restaurants

Greene, D., & Joseph, D. (2015). The digital spatial fix. *TripleC*, *13*(2), 223–248.

Hannak, A., Soeller, G., Lazer, D., Mislove, A., & Wilson, C. (2014, November). Measuring price discrimination and steering on e-commerce web sites. In *Proceedings of the 2014 conference on internet measurement conference* (pp. 305-318).

Harris, E. (2015). Navigating pop-up geographies: Urban space–times of flexibility, interstitiality and immersion. *Geography Compass*, *9*(11), 592–603.

Harris, E. (2020). *Rebranding Precarity: Pop-Up Culture as the Seductive New Normal.* ZED Books.

Harris, J. (2020). How Amazon Became a Pandemic Giant – And Why That Could be a Threat to Us All. London, UK: The Guardian. Available at: http://www.theguardian.com/technology/2020/nov/18/how-amazon-became-a-pandemic-giant-and-why-that-could-be-a-threat-to-us-all (accessed 20 January 2021).

Harvey, D. (1982). *The Limits to Capital.* University of Chicago Press.

Hausmann, L., Wölfel, T., Stoffels, J., & Fleck, O. (2020). Startup funding in logistics. *New money for an old, 1048.*

Helmond, A. (2015). The Platformization of the Web: Making Web Data Platform Ready. UK. *Social Media + Society.*

Helmore, E. (2020). Amazon Third-Quarter Earnings Soar as Pandemic Sales Triple Profits. London, UK: The Guardian. Available at: http://www.theguardian.com/technology/2020/oct/29/amazon-profits-latest-earnings-report-third-quarter-pandemic (accessed 20 January 2021).

Hepworth, K. (2014). Enacting logistical geographies. *Environment and Planning. D, Society & Space*, *32*(6), 1120–1134.

Hill, D. W. (2020). The injuries of platform logistics. *Media Culture & Society*, *42*(4), 521–536.

HNGRY (2019). fast(er) food. YouTube. Available at: https://www.youtube.com/watch?v=nVZq21xC3fM&feature=emb_logo (accessed 20 January 2021).

Ho, K. (2020). These are the Americans Choosing to Take on More Debt in the Middle of a Pandemic. New York, NY: qz. Available at: https://qz.com/1935410/us-mortgage-debt-is-skyrocketing-during-the-covid-19-pandemic/(accessed 22 January 2021).

Ibert, O., Hess, M., Kleibert, J., Müller, F., & Power, D. (2019). Geographies of dissociation: Value creation,'dark'places, and 'missing'links. *Dialogues in Human Geography*, *9*(1), 43–63.

Investable Universe. (2019). Micro-Fulfillment: Venture Cap's Big Warehouse Play is Playing Small. Available at., Retrieved January 20, 2021, from.https://medium.com/swlh/micro-fulfillment-venture-caps-big-warehouse-play-is-playing-small-790632919d33

Jeffries, A. (2020). What Are Ghost Kitchens? The Mark-Up. Available at., Retrieved January 20, 2021, from.https://themarkup.org/ask-the-markup/2020/09/15/ghost-kitchens-virtual-food-delivery-restaurants

Jiang, Y., Balaji, M. S., & Lyu, C. (2024). Cultivating initial trust in ghost kitchens: A mixed-methods investigation of antecedents and consequences. *International Journal of Hospitality Management*, *104*, 103–115. DOI: 10.1016/j.ijhm.2024.103115

Jones, S., Cain, L., & Deel, G. L. (2024). Virtual restaurants and ghost kitchens: A new opportunity. *Journal of Hospitality & Tourism Research (Washington, D.C.)*, *48*(1), 1–15. DOI: 10.1177/21649987241241948

Kanngieser, A. (2013). Tracking and tracing: Geographies of logistical governance and labouring bodies. *Environment and Planning. D, Society & Space*, *31*, 594–610.

Kelso, A. (2020). Ghost Kitchens, AI and POS Systems: Restaurant Tech Providers Predict Top 2020 Trends. China: forbes. Available at: https://www.forbes.com/sites/aliciakelso/2020/01/02/ghost-kitchens-ai-and-pos-systems-restaurant-tech-providers-predict-top-2020-trends/ (accessed 20 January 2021).

Khan, L. (2016). Amazon's Antitrust Paradox. *The Yale Law Journal*, *215*(1), 710–805.

Klein, N. (2007). *The Shock Doctrine: The Rise of Disaster Capitalism*. Picador.

Langley, P., & Leyshon, A. (2017). Platform capitalism: The intermediation and capitalization of digital economic circulation. *Finance and Stochastics*, *3*(1), 11–31.

Langlois, G., & Elmer, G. (2019). Impersonal subjectivation from platforms to infrastructures. *Media Culture & Society*, *41*(2), 236–251.

Lee, J. L. (2020). US Tech Venture Investing Gets a Boost From Pandemic. Canary Wharf. Reuters, Available at., Retrieved January 20, 2021, from.https://www.reuters.com/article/ctech-us-venture-capital-funding-data-idCAKBN26M5V8-OCATC

Lerman, R. (2020). Amazon Says Nearly 20,000 Employees Have Caught the Coronavirus. Washington, DC: Washington Post, Available at: https://www.washingtonpost.com/technology/2020/10/01/amazon-workers-covid-positive/ (accessed 22 January 2021).

Leszczynski, A. (2020). Glitchy vignettes of platform urbanism. *Environment and Planning. D, Society & Space*, *38*(2), 189–208.

Leyshon, A., & Thrift, N. (2007). The capitalization of almost everything: The future of finance and capitalism. *Theory, Culture & Society*, *24*(7–8), 97–115.

Liao, S. (2018). Amazon Warehouse Workers Skip Bathroom Breaks to Keep Their Jobs, Says Report. The Verge. Available at., Retrieved January 20, 2021, from.https://www.theverge.com/2018/4/16/17243026/amazon-warehouse-jobs-worker-conditions-bathroom-breaks

Loewen, K. (2018). Reproducing disposability: Unsettled labour strategies in the construction of e-commerce markets. *Environment and Planning. D, Society & Space*, *36*(4), 701–718.

Loizos, C. (2019). A Rare Glimpse Into the Sweeping — and Potentially Troubling — Cloud Kitchens Trend. Bay Area, USA: socialtechcrunch, Available at: https://social.techcrunch.com/2019/06/28/a-rare-glimpse-into-the-sweeping-and-potentially-troubling-cloud-kitchens-trend/ (accessed 26 January 2021).

Luna, N. (2021). Ghost-Kitchen Startup Reef was Caught Operating Without Permits. Business Insider, Available at., Retrieved October 28, 2021, from.https://www.businessinsider.com/reef-operated-ghost-kitchens-in-houston-without-permits-2021-10

Lunden, I. (2018). Amazon's Share of the Us E-Commerce Market is Now 49%, or 5% of All Retail Spend. Social Techcrunch. Available at., Retrieved January 20, 2021, from.https://social.techcrunch.com/2018/07/13/amazons-share-of-the-us-e-commerce-market-is-now-49-or-5-of-all-retail-spend/

Marx, K. (1976). Capital: Volume 1: A Critique of Political Economy (Tran. B Fowkes). Illustrated edition. New York: Penguin Classics.

McCormick, E. (2021). Amazon Earnings: Q4 Sales Topped $100 Billion for the First Time, Bezos to Step Down as CEO. Yahoo. Available at., Retrieved February 5, 2021, from.https://www.yahoo.com/now/amazon-reports-4q-2020-earnings-results-152012181.html

McGrath, K. (2020). Council Post: Industrial Real Estate is The Investment World's New Darling. China: forbes. Available at: https://www.forbes.com/sites/forbesrealestatecouncil/2020/08/17/industrial-real-estate-is-the-investment-worlds-new-darling/(accessed 20 January 2021).

McGuigan, L., & Manzerolle, V. (Eds.). (2014). *The Audience Commodity in a Digital Age: Revisiting a Critical Theory of Commercial Media*. Peter Lang.h

McKelvey, F. (2011). A Programmable Platform? Drupal, Modularity, and the Future of the Web. Fibreculture 18. Available at.http://eighteen.fibreculturejournal.org/2011/10/09/fcj-128-programmable-platform-drupal-modularity-and-the-future-of-the-web/

McKinsey. (2020). Coronavirus is Accelerating Digital-Strategy Formulation. McKinsey & Company. Available at., Retrieved January 20, 2021, from.https://www.mckinsey.com/featured-insights/coronavirus-leading-through-the-crisis/charting-the-path-to-the-next-normal/coronavirus-is-accelerating-digital-strategy-formulation

Melendez, S. (2020). Amazon's New Nyc Whole Foods Market is Basically an Amazon Warehouse. Fastcompany. Available at., Retrieved January 20, 2021, from.https://www.fastcompany.com/90546258/amazons-new-nyc-whole-foods-market-is-basically-an-amazon-warehouse

Merchant, B. (2020). Amazon's Plague Year. One Zero [blog]. Medium. Available at., Retrieved January 20, 2021, from.https://onezero.medium.com/amazons-plague-year-3d930e57a914

Mezzadra, S., & Neilson, B. (2017). On the multiple frontiers of extraction: Excavating contemporary capitalism. *Cultural Studies*, *31*(2–3), 185–204.

Mezzadri, A. (2016). *The Sweatshop Regime: Labouring Bodies, Exploitation, and Garments Made in India*. Cambridge University Press.

Mitchell, S., & LeVecchia, O. (2016). Amazon's Stranglehold: How the Company's Tightening Grip is Stifling Competition, Eroding Jobs and Threatening Communities. Institute for Local Self-Reliance. Available at., Retrieved January 20, 2021, from.https://ilsr.org/wp-content/uploads/2020/04/ILSR_AmazonReport_final.pdf

Mitchell, T. (2020). Infrastructures Work on Time. New York, NY: E-Flux (New Silk Roads). Available at: https://www.e-flux.com/architecture/new-silk-roads/312596/infrastructures-work-on-time/ (accessed 20 January 2021).

Morgan, B. (2020). Dark Stores are the Future of Post-Pandemic Retail. Forbes. Available at., Retrieved January 26, 2021, from.https://www.forbes.com/sites/blakemorgan/2020/04/25/dark-stores-are-the-future-of-post-pandemic-retail/

Mould, O. (2014). Tactical urbanism: The new vernacular of the creative city. *Geography Compass*, *8*(8), 529–539.

Neate, R. (2019). New Study Deems Amazon Worst for 'Aggressive' Tax Avoidance. London, UK: theguardian. Available at: http://www.theguardian.com/business/2019/dec/02/new-study-deems-amazon-worst-for-aggressive-tax-avoidance (accessed 21 January 2021).

Neilson, B. (2012). Five theses on understanding logistics as power. *Distinktion: Journal of Social Theory*, *13*(3), 322–339.

Neria, G., Hildebrandt, F. D., Tzur, M., & Ulmer, M. W. (2024). The Restaurant Meal Delivery Problem with Ghost Kitchens. *Transportation Science*, *59*(1), 1–15. DOI: 10.1287/trsc.2024.0510

Newberg, M. (2020). My Testimony for the Nation's First Hearing on Ghost Kitchens. Medium. Available at., Retrieved January 20, 2021, from.https://medium.com/hngry/my-testimony-for-nations-first-hearing-on-ghost-kitchens-c999c76dad19

Newberg, M. (2021). We Mapped Out the Ghost Kitchens Run by Ex-Uber Ceo Travis Kalanick's Cloudkitchen and Competitor Reef Technology. Business Insider. Available at., Retrieved January 26, 2021, from.https://www.businessinsider.com/map-where-travis-kalanicks-cloudkitchen-and-reef-have-ghost-kitchens-2020-12

Nicoll, A. (2020). How Uber Founder Travis Kalanick's Real-Estate Buying Frenzy Could Transform Ghost Kitchens Into a New Speciality Asset Class.

Nigro, C., & Iannuzzi, E., Santo, N di, & Sisto, R. (2022). Food delivery, ghost kitchens and virtual restaurants: Temporary or long-lasting game changers? *British Food Journal*, *124*(5), 1500–1515. DOI: 10.1108/BFJ-02-2022-0095

Nitzan, J. (1998). Differential accumulation: Towards a new political economy of capital. *Review of International Political Economy*, *5*(2), 169–216.

Peck, J. (2012). Austerity urbanism. *City (London, England)*, *16*(6), 626–655.

Perez, S. (2020). Covid-19 Pandemic Accelerated Shift to E-Commerce by 5 Years, New Report Says. Bay Area, USA: Social techcrunch. Available at: https://social.techcrunch.com/2020/08/24/covid-19-pandemic-accelerated-shift-to-e-commerce-by-5-years-new-report-says/ (accessed 20 January 2021).

Phillips, M. (2020). Market Edges Toward Euphoria, Despite Pandemic's Toll. New York, NY: The New York Times, Vol. 26. Available at: https://www.nytimes.com/2020/12/26/business/investors-bull-market-pandemic.html (accessed 20 January 2021).

Pitchbook. (2021). Emerging Space: Ghost Kitchens. Seattle, Washington: Pitchbook, Available at: https://pitchbook.com/blog/emerging-space-ghost-kitchens (accessed 20 January 2021).

Plantin, J. C., Lagoze, C., Edwards, P. N., & Sandvig, C. (2018). Infrastructure studies meet platform studies in the age of Google and Facebook. *New Media & Society*, *20*(1), 293–310.

Plantin, J. C., & Punathambekar, A. (2019). Digital media infrastructures: Pipes, platforms, and politics. *Media Culture & Society*, *41*(2), 163–174.[REMOVED HYPERLINK FIELD]

Pollio, A. (2021). Uber, airports, and labour at the infrastructural interfaces of platform urbanism. *Geoforum*, *118*, 47–55.

Pollman, E. (2019). Tech, regulatory arbitrage, and limits. In: SSRN Scholarly Paper, Rochester, NY, 24 May 2021. Social Science Research Network. ID 3393288, Available at: https://papers.ssrn.com/abstract=3393288 (accessed 20 January 2021).

Proctor, R. (2008). Agnotology: a missing term to describe the cultural production of ignorance (and its study). In Proctor, R., & Schiebinger, L. (Eds.), *Agnotology: The Making and Unmaking of Ignorance* (pp. 1–31). Stanford University Press.

PYMNTS (2020) Logistics Tech Leads a Booming Funding Week. Boston, MA: PYMNTS. Available at: https://www.pymnts.com/news/b2b-payments/2020/venture-capital-logistics-fintech-funding/ (accessed 20 January 2021).

Reich, R. (2020). Jeff Bezos Became Even Richer Thanks to Covid-19. But He Still Won't Protect Amazon Workers. Lonon, UK: The Guardian, Available at: https://www.theguardian.com/commentisfree/2020/dec/12/jeff-bezos-amazon-workers-covid-19-scrooge-capitalism (accessed 26 January 2021).

Richardson, L. (2018). Platforms and the Publicness of Urban Markets. Mediapolis. Available at.https://www.mediapolisjournal.com/2018/10/platforms-and-the-publicness-of-urban-markets/

Ritzer, G. (2013). *The McDonaldization of Society*. Sage Publications.

Ritzer, G., & Miles, S. (2019). The changing nature of consumption and the intensification of McDonaldization in the digital age. *Journal of Consumer Culture*, *19*(1), 3–20.

Rivas, T. (2020). Groceries are One of the Fastest-Growing E-Commerce Segments. Barrons. Available at.https://www.barrons.com/articles/the-coming-online-grocery-boom-51600724096

Romeo, P. (2019). Door Dash Opens a Ghost Kitchen. Restaurant Business. Available at., Retrieved January 22, 2021, from.https://www.restaurantbusinessonline.com/operations/doordash-opens-ghost-kitchen

Romeo, P. (2020). Chili's Parent is Going Big-Time Into Virtual Concepts. Restaurant Business. Available at., Retrieved January 22, 2021, from.https://www.restaurantbusinessonline.com/emerging-brands/chilis-parent-going-big-time-virtual-concepts

Rudra, S. (2020). E-commerce Surge Drives Growth of Last-Mile Fulfillment Centers, Dark Stores. Loopnet, Available at., Retrieved January 20, 2021, from.https://www.loopnet.com/learn/e-commerce-surge-drives-growth-of-last-mile-fulfillment-centers-dark-stores/35384053/

Shapiro, A. (2023). Platform urbanism in a pandemic: Dark stores, ghost kitchens, and the logistical-urban frontier. *Journal of Consumer Culture*, *23*(1), 168–187.

Suresh, S., Santhosh, S., & Samjaila, T. H. (2024). Food economies–Engendered ghost kitchens in the digital age: Implications for future research and practice in food delivery systems. In *AI and Digitalization* (Vol. 2, pp. 123–145). Springer Nature Switzerland AG.

Visible Capital. (2020). Grocery Fulfillment and Dark Stores—Clear Aisles, Full Carts, Can't Lose? Pitchbook. Available at., Retrieved January 20, 2021, from.[REMOVED HYPERLINK FIELD]https://pitchbook.com/news/articles/in-visible-capital-podcast-season-2-ep-4-grocery-fulfillment-dark-stores

Chapter 8
Transforming Supply Chain Dynamics:
Emerging AI Trends Improving Efficiency and Responsiveness in Ghost Kitchen Operations

S. Thandayuthapani
https://orcid.org/0000-0001-9559-745X
Kristu Jayanti College, India

P. Elantheraiyan
VelTech Rangarajan Dr. Sagunthala R&D Institute of Science and Technology, India

P. Thirumoorthi
https://orcid.org/0000-0001-5783-3984
Periyar University, India

ABSTRACT

The aim of this research is to examine the significant impact of emerging artificial intelligence (AI) trends on the dynamics of supply chains in ghost kitchen operations. The study uses sophisticated analytical technologies like predictive analytics and machine learning to elucidate how AI improves efficiency and responsiveness in inventory management, order fulfilment, and logistics. The recent developments enhance food delivery services while tackling critical environmental challenges through waste reduction and resource optimization. The results underscore the importance of industry stakeholders adopting AI-driven strategies to advance sustainable practices in the swiftly evolving food service sector. This study is an essential resource for professionals looking to integrate AI solutions to enhance operational efficiency and promote environmental sustainability.

DOI: 10.4018/979-8-3373-0432-8.ch008

I. INTRODUCTION

The global food delivery market has undergone a transformative evolution, propelled by the rise of ghost kitchens and the rapid integration of artificial intelligence (AI). Ghost kitchens, also known as cloud or dark kitchens, are commercial facilities designed specifically for the preparation of delivery-only meals. This operational model has gained momentum due to its cost-effectiveness, scalability, and ability to cater to the increasing demand for food delivery services. However, the growing reliance on ghost kitchens has amplified the complexity of supply chain operations, necessitating innovative solutions to enhance efficiency, responsiveness, and sustainability (Jagtap et al., 2021).

Artificial intelligence has emerged as a game-changer in optimizing supply chain dynamics within ghost kitchen operations. By leveraging advanced algorithms, machine learning models, and predictive analytics, AI enables stakeholders to streamline inventory management, improve demand forecasting, enhance delivery logistics, and minimize food waste. These improvements are pivotal not only for maintaining competitive advantage but also for addressing the environmental and ethical challenges associated with modern food delivery services (Ivanov et al., 2020).

1.1 Evolution of Ghost Kitchens and AI Integration

Ghost kitchens, also known as virtual or cloud kitchens, emerged as a disruptive innovation in the foodservice industry. Initially conceptualized as a cost-efficient alternative to traditional restaurants, ghost kitchens gained momentum with the rise of food delivery services. These kitchens operate without dine-in facilities, focusing exclusively on delivery, thus reducing real estate costs and optimizing resources. Early adopters capitalized on increasing consumer demand for convenience, particularly in urban areas where delivery is a lifestyle norm (Wiener-Bronner, 2020).

The COVID-19 pandemic further accelerated the growth of ghost kitchens. Social distancing measures and lockdowns prompted a surge in online food ordering, solidifying their role in the food supply chain. Today, ghost kitchens are integral to meeting dynamic consumer needs while enabling restaurants to experiment with multiple brands from a single location (Statista, 2023).

AI integration has been a transformative force in enhancing ghost kitchen operations. Initially, AI applications were limited to route optimization for delivery services. However, advancements in machine learning and predictive analytics have redefined supply chain management in ghost kitchens. AI-driven demand forecasting enables precise inventory planning, minimizing food waste and ensuring sustainability (Barrett et al., 2022). Chatbots and AI-based customer service systems streamline order management, improving responsiveness and reducing errors (McKinsey, 2023).

Moreover, AI optimizes kitchen workflows through robotics and IoT devices. For instance, smart kitchen systems monitor equipment efficiency, preempting maintenance needs, and preventing downtime (Futurist Reports, 2023). Integration with AI-powered delivery platforms has also enhanced the last-mile delivery process, reducing costs and delivery times while ensuring customer satisfaction.

Looking forward, AI trends such as autonomous delivery vehicles and advanced customer behavior analytics promise to further revolutionize ghost kitchens. The integration of blockchain in AI systems can add transparency to the supply chain, fostering trust and ethical practices in food delivery services (Lempert, 2023). These innovations are pivotal in making ghost kitchens a sustainable and responsive element of the modern food ecosystem.

1.2 Importance of AI in Supply Chain Efficiency

Artificial Intelligence (AI) is revolutionizing supply chain dynamics, particularly in ghost kitchen operations, by enhancing efficiency and responsiveness. Ghost kitchens, which cater exclusively to food delivery services, demand real-time inventory management, accurate demand forecasting, and optimized delivery routes. AI technologies address these challenges by leveraging machine learning algorithms and predictive analytics to streamline operations.

AI enables precise inventory management, reducing food wastage while ensuring availability. For instance, AI-driven demand forecasting analyzes historical data and market trends to anticipate customer preferences, ensuring optimal resource allocation (Baryannis et al., 2019). Additionally, AI-powered route optimization minimizes delivery times and operational costs, improving customer satisfaction and environmental sustainability (Verma et al., 2021).

In the context of a sustainable future, AI facilitates energy-efficient operations by minimizing carbon emissions in logistics and promoting circular supply chain practices. AI-enabled systems can also monitor kitchen performance and equipment health, preventing downtime and reducing energy consumption (Ivanov & Dolgui, 2020).

As ghost kitchens grow, AI's integration ensures scalability while maintaining efficiency. By enhancing agility and reducing operational complexities, AI paves the way for a more sustainable and responsive food delivery ecosystem.

1.3 Enhancing Responsiveness Through AI

The advent of artificial intelligence (AI) is revolutionizing supply chain management in ghost kitchen operations, an innovative concept driving the future of food delivery services. Ghost kitchens, which operate without traditional dine-in facilities, depend heavily on efficient supply chain systems for operational success. AI's integration in these kitchens addresses critical challenges such as inventory management, demand forecasting, and real-time route optimization, ensuring responsiveness and sustainability in food delivery.

AI-powered predictive analytics enable accurate forecasting of consumer demand, minimizing food waste and optimizing inventory levels (Goyal et al., 2022). Machine learning algorithms analyze consumer preferences, allowing dynamic menu adjustments to meet changing tastes, enhancing customer satisfaction (Kamble et al., 2021). Additionally, AI-driven route optimization improves delivery efficiency, reducing delivery times and carbon emissions, contributing to environmental sustainability (Ivanov & Dolgui, 2020).

Emerging trends also include robotics and automated cooking systems, which standardize food quality while reducing labor costs. AI-driven communication platforms enable seamless coordination among suppliers, kitchens, and delivery services, further enhancing operational efficiency (Chen et al., 2021). As the food delivery sector continues to expand, leveraging AI ensures ghost kitchens can adapt to evolving market demands while maintaining a sustainable and responsive supply chain.

1.4 Promoting Sustainability in Ghost Kitchen Supply Chains

The rapid rise of ghost kitchens, driven by increased demand for food delivery services, necessitates sustainable supply chain practices. Emerging AI trends are revolutionizing these operations, enabling efficiency and responsiveness while reducing environmental impact. AI-driven demand forecasting minimizes food waste by accurately predicting order volumes and aligning inventory management with real-time customer preferences (Ivanov et al., 2022). Additionally, AI-powered route optimization for delivery logistics reduces fuel consumption and greenhouse gas emissions (Gao et al., 2023). Blockchain integration, facilitated by AI, enhances transparency in sourcing and traceability, ensuring ethical procurement and reducing waste through better accountability (Reddy & Tiwari, 2021).

Moreover, predictive maintenance supported by AI ensures kitchen equipment operates at peak efficiency, conserving energy and extending equipment lifespan. Machine learning algorithms also identify areas for energy optimization in kitchen workflows, contributing to sustainability goals (Zhao et al., 2023). These advancements highlight the pivotal role of AI in transforming ghost kitchen supply chains into eco-friendly and responsive systems. By adopting AI-driven technologies, ghost kitchens can align with global sustainability imperatives while enhancing operational performance.

II. BACKGROUND OF THE STUDY

The global food delivery industry has experienced exponential growth in recent years, driven by rapid advancements in technology, evolving consumer preferences, and the rise of ghost kitchens—delivery-only food establishments (Cho et al., 2021). Ghost kitchens, also known as cloud kitchens or dark kitchens, operate without physical dine-in facilities and focus solely on optimizing delivery efficiency. This operational model has revolutionized the food service industry by significantly reducing overhead costs and enhancing scalability (Moreno & Teicher, 2022). However, as the demand for food delivery continues to surge, traditional supply chain models face challenges in meeting the high expectations for speed, accuracy, and sustainability.

The integration of Artificial Intelligence (AI) into supply chain management offers transformative solutions for ghost kitchen operations. AI-powered technologies enhance predictive analytics, real-time inventory tracking, route optimization, and demand forecasting, enabling businesses to respond proactively to dynamic market conditions (Ivanov et al., 2020). These innovations have become essential for maintaining competitiveness and ensuring customer satisfaction in the rapidly evolving food delivery ecosystem.

2.1 Emergence of Ghost Kitchens

The rise of ghost kitchens has revolutionized the food delivery industry by providing an innovative solution to meet growing consumer demand while reducing overhead costs. Ghost kitchens, also known as virtual kitchens or dark kitchens, operate without a physical dine-in facility and focus entirely on fulfilling delivery orders. These operations are powered by technological advancements, including artificial intelligence (AI), which significantly improves supply chain dynamics, enhances operational efficiency, and ensures sustainability within the food service sector.

2.2 AI-Powered Supply Chain Optimization

AI is playing a pivotal role in transforming supply chain management in ghost kitchens by streamlining inventory, production, and delivery processes. AI algorithms analyze vast amounts of data from consumer preferences, market trends, and historical demand patterns to predict demand fluctuations. This predictive capability allows ghost kitchens to optimize inventory management, reducing food waste, ensuring timely ingredient procurement, and minimizing overstocking or stockouts (Xu et al., 2021). Real-time data analysis helps adjust production schedules and improve labor allocation, enhancing responsiveness to sudden demand changes, particularly during peak hours or promotional periods.

2.3 Improving Operational Efficiency

The implementation of AI-driven automation in ghost kitchens improves the speed and accuracy of meal preparation. AI-based robotics and machine learning models help in automating cooking processes, which not only accelerates preparation but also maintains consistent quality. By integrating AI into kitchen operations, ghost kitchens can improve throughput without the need for additional labor, thus lowering operational costs (Li & Li, 2020). Furthermore, AI-based analytics ensure the optimal allocation of kitchen resources, reducing downtime and maximizing output.

2.4 Enhancing Delivery and Customer Experience

AI is also revolutionizing the logistics side of ghost kitchen operations, enhancing delivery speed and customer satisfaction. AI algorithms optimize delivery routes in real-time, considering traffic, weather conditions, and distance to ensure the fastest possible delivery times. Additionally, AI-driven chatbots and recommendation engines provide personalized customer experiences, influencing repeat business and customer loyalty (Zhang et al., 2022). These advancements not only reduce operational costs but also improve the customer's overall delivery experience, fostering long-term brand loyalty.

2.5 Sustainability in Food Delivery

Sustainability is a growing concern in the food delivery industry, and ghost kitchens, powered by AI, are positioned to address these challenges. AI can help in monitoring energy consumption within the kitchen, optimizing cooking times and appliance usage to reduce waste and carbon footprints. Additionally, AI can enable more sustainable food sourcing by identifying suppliers with ethical and eco-friendly practices, contributing to the overall sustainability goals of ghost kitchens (Patel & Soni, 2021).

2.6 Challenges in Traditional Supply Chains

Traditional supply chains in the food industry have long faced significant challenges, particularly in the context of ghost kitchen operations. Ghost kitchens, which operate without a physical storefront, rely on efficient supply chains to deliver food quickly and cost-effectively. However, traditional supply chain models often struggle with inefficiencies and responsiveness in this unique operational context.

One of the key challenges in traditional supply chains is **lack of real-time data integration**. Traditional systems often rely on manual processes, outdated technology, and siloed data. This leads to delays in decision-making and inadequate responses to supply chain disruptions, which can negatively impact the customer experience in ghost kitchens where speed and quality are paramount (Chong et al., 2020). Ghost kitchens require highly responsive supply chains that can adapt to changing consumer demand, but traditional systems struggle to provide the necessary agility.

Another significant challenge is **inventory management**. Ghost kitchens often operate multiple brands from a single location, requiring complex inventory tracking for various types of ingredients. Traditional supply chains rely on static inventory models, making it difficult to manage the fluctuating demands across different brands and menus in real time. Inefficient inventory management results in overstocking or stockouts, both of which contribute to food waste, higher operational costs, and customer dissatisfaction (Tarantino et al., 2021).

The **lack of demand forecasting capabilities** is another critical issue. Traditional supply chains in food delivery services often fail to predict shifts in demand, leading to inefficiencies. This is especially problematic for ghost kitchens, where orders can be highly volatile due to the influence of online platforms and changing consumer preferences. Traditional systems are not equipped to adjust quickly to these fluctuations, often leading to resource misallocation (Voss et al., 2020).

Additionally, **last-mile delivery challenges** represent a significant hurdle for traditional supply chains in ghost kitchen operations. In the food delivery industry, speed and accuracy are essential, yet traditional logistics models can fail to optimize routes and timings effectively, leading to delays and increased delivery costs. In ghost kitchen models, where orders may be placed from various locations, this becomes even more critical (Jadhav & Deshmukh, 2022).

Finally, **sustainability concerns** are becoming increasingly important in food delivery services, but traditional supply chains often lack the flexibility to incorporate sustainable practices. From sourcing sustainable ingredients to managing food waste, traditional supply chains have difficulty aligning with the growing demand for environmentally friendly operations (Gupta et al., 2021). This misalignment hinders the ability of ghost kitchens to meet the sustainability expectations of consumers.

2.7 Predictive Analytics

The rapid expansion of ghost kitchens has significantly transformed the food delivery sector, necessitating innovations in supply chain management. Artificial Intelligence (AI) is playing a crucial role in enhancing the efficiency and responsiveness of these operations. AI-powered tools, such as predictive analytics, machine learning algorithms, and automated decision-making systems, enable ghost kitchens to optimize inventory management, reduce waste, and enhance delivery times. AI models predict demand fluctuations, ensuring that food production aligns with customer needs, which minimizes overproduction and food spoilage (Choi et al., 2023). Additionally, AI-driven logistics and route optimization improve delivery efficiency by minimizing fuel consumption and delivery times, contributing to a more sustainable operation (Singh & Sharma, 2024). These technologies not only reduce operational costs but also enhance responsiveness, enabling ghost kitchens to adapt quickly to market changes and customer preferences. As AI continues to evolve, its integration into the supply chain promises a sustainable and highly efficient future for food delivery services (Kannan et al., 2024).

2.8 Real-Time Tracking

The integration of Artificial Intelligence (AI) in food delivery services, particularly in ghost kitchen operations, is revolutionizing the supply chain dynamics by enhancing real-time tracking, efficiency, and responsiveness. AI-driven technologies, such as predictive analytics and Internet of Things (IoT) sensors, are enabling seamless inventory management, order processing, and delivery routing, optimizing operational workflows. Real-time tracking solutions empower ghost kitchens to monitor the movement of raw materials, track preparation stages, and adjust delivery schedules based on customer demand fluctuations (Baryannis et al., 2019).

AI enhances forecasting by analyzing consumer behavior, weather patterns, and traffic conditions, allowing for proactive decision-making and timely resource allocation (Choi et al., 2020). The ability to track products throughout the supply chain ensures transparency, reduces waste, and fosters sustainability by minimizing unnecessary deliveries (Zhao et al., 2021). Furthermore, AI applications in predictive maintenance improve kitchen equipment efficiency, minimizing downtime and operational disruptions, leading to a more responsive food delivery service (Yang et al., 2020).

These AI-driven advancements contribute significantly to building a sustainable future for ghost kitchen operations, providing not only improved supply chain efficiency but also enhanced customer satisfaction by ensuring timely and accurate deliveries.

2.9 Route Optimization

The rise of ghost kitchens—delivery-only establishments—has revolutionized the food delivery service model. As these operations grow, optimizing supply chains becomes critical for efficiency and sustainability. Emerging artificial intelligence (AI) trends are playing a significant role in transforming these dynamics. AI-driven demand forecasting, route optimization, and inventory management improve the responsiveness of ghost kitchens by predicting customer preferences and minimizing waste. Route optimization algorithms, powered by AI, ensure that deliveries are made swiftly, reducing carbon emissions and operational costs. Furthermore, AI is aiding in dynamic resource allocation, helping ghost kitchens balance peak demands and streamline workflows (Harrison et al., 2022; Tsai & Jang, 2021). These advancements not only improve operational efficiency but also contribute to a more sustainable food delivery system by reducing energy consumption and food waste, enhancing the overall customer experience, and promoting greener practices within the industry.

2.10 Automation

In recent years, the emergence of ghost kitchens has revolutionized the food delivery industry, offering a new model for restaurant operations. Artificial intelligence (AI) plays a critical role in enhancing the efficiency and responsiveness of supply chain dynamics within these operations. AI technologies such as machine learning, predictive analytics, and automated inventory management systems allow ghost kitchens to optimize order fulfillment, reduce waste, and improve overall operational efficiency. AI-driven forecasting tools predict demand, enabling kitchens to adjust inventory in real time, minimizing food waste and reducing costs (Zhang et al., 2023). Furthermore, AI enhances delivery logistics by analyzing traffic patterns, weather conditions, and customer preferences, enabling faster and more accurate delivery times, thus improving customer satisfaction (Sundararajan, 2022). These advancements align with the growing demand for sustainability in the food service industry, supporting sustainable sourcing, waste reduction, and carbon footprint minimization (Kramer & Thomas, 2021). As AI continues to evolve, its integration into ghost kitchen operations promises a more responsive, efficient, and sustainable future for food delivery services.

2.11 Sustainability in Ghost Kitchen Operations

Ghost kitchens, or delivery-only kitchens, are reshaping the food service industry by emphasizing operational efficiency and reducing costs. The integration of Artificial Intelligence (AI) in these operations is enhancing sustainability, particularly in the supply chain. AI-powered tools help optimize inventory management, predict demand more accurately, and minimize food waste. By analyzing real-time data, AI algorithms can forecast demand spikes and adjust inventory levels accordingly, reducing overstocking and waste (Choi et al., 2022). This efficiency not only lowers operational costs but also minimizes environmental impacts associated with excess food production and disposal.

Additionally, AI is improving energy efficiency in ghost kitchens by optimizing kitchen layouts and cooking processes. Automated systems ensure that equipment is used only when necessary, preventing energy wastage (Baker et al., 2023). Furthermore, AI's role in streamlining logistics contributes to sustainability by reducing carbon footprints through route optimization and efficient fleet management, ensuring that food deliveries are made in the most fuel-efficient manner possible (Srinivasan et al., 2021).

As consumer demand for sustainable practices grows, ghost kitchens are leveraging AI to align with eco-conscious trends. The focus on efficiency not only drives down costs but also meets sustainability goals, paving the way for a greener future in food delivery services.

2.12 Future Trends and Implications

The rise of ghost kitchens in food delivery services is rapidly transforming supply chain dynamics, driven by emerging Artificial Intelligence (AI) technologies. As AI adoption grows, key trends are emerging that promise to enhance efficiency and responsiveness in operations, particularly in ghost kitchens.

Firstly, AI-powered predictive analytics will play a significant role in optimizing inventory management. By analyzing historical data, weather patterns, and local demand trends, AI can predict ingredient needs, minimize waste, and reduce supply chain disruptions (Choi & Li, 2020). This will ensure a more sustainable approach, as reduced waste directly correlates with environmental benefits. Additionally, AI-driven robotics and automation will streamline food preparation, enhancing speed and consistency, which will further improve responsiveness in meeting fluctuating demand (Huang et al., 2021).

Another important trend is the use of AI to enhance real-time supply chain visibility. Through Internet of Things (IoT) devices and AI analytics, operators can track and manage resources across the entire food delivery network in real time, from raw ingredient delivery to final dish preparation (Singh & Agarwal, 2022). This allows for quick identification of bottlenecks, ensuring smoother operations. Furthermore, the integration of AI in route optimization will improve delivery times, reducing fuel consumption and contributing to sustainability goals (Mishra et al., 2023).

As these AI innovations continue to evolve, their implications will reshape food delivery services. By enhancing supply chain agility, ghost kitchens will become more responsive to consumer demands, minimize their environmental footprint, and improve overall operational efficiency.

III. REVIEW OF LITERATURE

The food delivery services industry has undergone a dramatic transformation, particularly with the rise of ghost kitchens, also known as dark kitchens or virtual kitchens. Ghost kitchens are commercial cooking facilities optimized for delivery-only food services without a traditional brick-and-mortar dining space. The operational complexities of these kitchens, particularly in supply chain management, have spurred the adoption of Artificial Intelligence (AI) to improve efficiency, responsiveness, and sustainability. This literature review explores the emerging trends of AI in transforming the supply chain dynamics in ghost kitchen operations, focusing on their impact on efficiency, responsiveness, and sustainability.

3.1 Evolution of Ghost Kitchens

Ghost kitchens have emerged in response to the rapidly growing demand for food delivery services. According to a report by *Euromonitor International* (2020), the global food delivery market is expected to continue its growth trajectory, driven by urbanization, convenience, and changing consumer preferences. Ghost kitchens serve as a solution to high operational costs associated with traditional restaurants. They allow food brands to focus solely on food preparation and delivery without the overheads of a physical location or dining area (Cheng, 2021). The concept gained significant traction during the COVID-19 pandemic, which accelerated the shift toward online food delivery and delivery-only kitchens (Goyal, 2020).

Despite their operational advantages, ghost kitchens face several challenges related to supply chain management. These include sourcing ingredients, managing inventory, ensuring timely delivery, and maintaining food quality, all of which are critical to consumer satisfaction and profitability (Cheng, 2021). The integration of AI in supply chain management offers innovative solutions to these challenges by enhancing predictive capabilities, automating processes, and optimizing resource allocation.

3.2 Role of AI in Supply Chain Management

AI technologies are increasingly being integrated into various aspects of supply chain management, with applications spanning demand forecasting, inventory management, route optimization, and predictive maintenance. These advancements have proven essential in improving operational efficiency, reducing costs, and enhancing responsiveness to market fluctuations (Chen et al., 2020).

3.3 AI in Demand Forecasting and Order Prediction

One of the key applications of AI in ghost kitchens is demand forecasting, which involves predicting the number of orders to be placed and the quantity of ingredients required. Accurate demand forecasting allows ghost kitchens to optimize inventory levels, reduce waste, and ensure timely food preparation

(Yuan et al., 2020). Machine learning algorithms analyze historical data, customer behavior, seasonal trends, and real-time market conditions to generate precise predictions. This helps operators prepare for fluctuations in demand, ensuring they are neither overstocked nor understocked.

Xu et al. (2021) highlighted the success of AI-powered demand forecasting in the restaurant industry, where predictive models have led to a 15-20% reduction in food waste and a significant improvement in customer satisfaction by minimizing stockouts.

3.4 AI in Inventory Management and Optimization

Effective inventory management is vital to maintaining the smooth operation of ghost kitchens. AI can automate the tracking and management of inventory by integrating real-time data from suppliers, kitchens, and delivery platforms (Chien et al., 2021). AI algorithms enable dynamic inventory control, adjusting stock levels based on demand forecasts, supplier lead times, and delivery schedules.

Liu et al. (2021) found that AI-driven inventory systems in ghost kitchens improved stock turnover rates by 10-15%, reducing food spoilage and lowering procurement costs. The ability to predict ingredient demand with accuracy helps maintain fresh supplies, avoiding both understocking and overstocking scenarios.

3.5 AI in Route Optimization and Delivery Efficiency

AI has emerged as a transformative tool in the optimization of supply chain dynamics, particularly in ghost kitchen operations within the food delivery sector. The rise of AI technologies has revolutionized route optimization, significantly enhancing delivery efficiency, reducing operational costs, and improving customer satisfaction (Cohen & Cattani, 2020). AI-powered algorithms analyze various factors such as traffic patterns, weather conditions, and real-time data to provide optimal delivery routes, reducing delivery times and fuel consumption (Hwang & Lee, 2022).

Ghost kitchens, which operate solely for delivery purposes, benefit greatly from AI's predictive capabilities, allowing for enhanced forecasting of demand and inventory management. This not only reduces food waste but also improves delivery responsiveness by ensuring that sufficient resources are available during peak hours (Baker et al., 2023). Furthermore, AI facilitates dynamic route adjustment, providing drivers with real-time information, which enables faster and more flexible deliveries (Xu et al., 2021).

Additionally, sustainability in food delivery services is increasingly prioritized, and AI contributes by minimizing emissions through more efficient delivery routes (Rosen et al., 2022). As AI continues to evolve, its role in enhancing supply chain resilience, reducing environmental impact, and improving the operational efficiency of ghost kitchens will be crucial for the future sustainability of food delivery services.

3.6 AI in Predictive Maintenance and Operational Uptime

The integration of Artificial Intelligence (AI) into predictive maintenance and operational uptime is revolutionizing supply chain dynamics, particularly in the food delivery services sector, such as ghost kitchens. Predictive maintenance utilizes AI to monitor equipment health and predict failures, reducing downtime and optimizing operational uptime (Zhao et al., 2020). In the context of ghost kitchens, AI-driven systems forecast kitchen appliance failures, ensuring timely maintenance and minimizing disruptions. These advancements are crucial in improving efficiency and responsiveness in operations (Chen et al., 2022).

Furthermore, AI's role extends beyond maintenance to enhancing overall supply chain operations. AI algorithms analyze vast data sets from inventory, orders, and kitchen operations to predict demand fluctuations, optimize delivery routes, and streamline food preparation workflows (Nair & Rengarajan, 2021). By leveraging machine learning, AI tools can help ghost kitchens maintain consistent operational uptime, reducing food wastage and energy consumption, thus contributing to sustainable practices in food delivery (Sharma et al., 2023).

3.7 AI and Sustainability in Ghost Kitchen Operations

Ghost kitchens, or virtual kitchens, are transforming the food delivery industry by providing efficient, cost-effective, and scalable solutions. AI is playing a pivotal role in enhancing the sustainability of these operations. AI's application in ghost kitchens, particularly in supply chain management, helps streamline operations, optimize resource use, and minimize waste, contributing to sustainability goals. Recent trends indicate that AI tools, including machine learning (ML) and predictive analytics, allow for precise demand forecasting, inventory management, and waste reduction (Mills et al., 2022). AI-driven systems can also improve food sourcing, selecting sustainable ingredients based on seasonal availability, and reducing carbon footprints (Yang et al., 2023).

Moreover, AI enhances operational efficiency by improving delivery route optimization, reducing fuel consumption, and promoting eco-friendly packaging choices (Zhou & Lee, 2021). As a result, AI in ghost kitchens aligns with the broader push for green technology adoption in the foodservice industry, encouraging more sustainable practices (Chauhan & Singh, 2023). This integration of AI technologies not only bolsters operational agility but also supports sustainability goals in food delivery services, which is critical in meeting growing consumer demand for environmentally conscious practices.

3.8 Reducing Food Waste

The rise of ghost kitchens has revolutionized the food delivery industry, fostering efficiency and cost-effectiveness. These cloud-based kitchens, operating exclusively for delivery purposes, have sparked interest in leveraging artificial intelligence (AI) to enhance operational dynamics. AI plays a pivotal role in streamlining supply chain processes, improving inventory management, and optimizing delivery routes. By integrating AI-driven algorithms, ghost kitchens can predict demand fluctuations, reducing waste and ensuring better utilization of resources (Xu et al., 2021). Machine learning models allow for real-time adjustments in inventory, minimizing overstocking and spoilage, a significant issue in traditional food service operations (Zhao & Zhang, 2020).

In addition, AI enhances decision-making in ghost kitchens by enabling data-driven insights into consumer preferences and order patterns, allowing for personalized and more efficient menu planning. The use of AI also extends to predictive analytics, which helps reduce food waste by forecasting precise quantities needed based on historical consumption data (Mohan et al., 2022). Additionally, AI technologies improve last-mile delivery efficiency, optimizing routes and minimizing food spoilage during transit, contributing to sustainability goals in the food service sector (Chen & Lee, 2023). Thus, the integration of AI in ghost kitchens holds immense potential for transforming supply chain dynamics, driving sustainability, and ensuring a responsive and waste-reducing future for food delivery services.

3.9 Energy Efficiency

The integration of Artificial Intelligence (AI) into food delivery services, particularly in ghost kitchens, has seen a significant rise in recent years, promising not only operational efficiency but also sustainability. Ghost kitchens, which operate without customer-facing storefronts, rely heavily on optimized supply chains to ensure the timely delivery of food. Emerging AI trends in this sector focus on energy efficiency, improving responsiveness, and reducing the environmental footprint of food delivery operations.

AI-driven automation and predictive analytics are revolutionizing supply chain management in ghost kitchens, making energy consumption more efficient. By using AI algorithms, operations such as inventory management, kitchen load balancing, and delivery routing can be optimized, reducing waste and energy use (Zhao & Zhang, 2021). AI enables the precise forecasting of demand, leading to a reduction in food and energy waste by ensuring that only the necessary quantities are produced and delivered (Choi et al., 2020).

Furthermore, AI technologies contribute to better resource allocation and energy use in kitchen operations. By integrating Internet of Things (IoT) sensors, AI can monitor equipment performance, adjusting cooking temperatures and power usage in real-time, thus reducing unnecessary energy consumption (Li et al., 2022). These innovations align with the growing trend of energy efficiency and sustainability in the food delivery sector, contributing to a greener future.

In terms of responsiveness, AI enables ghost kitchens to respond rapidly to fluctuating demand, ensuring energy resources are used optimally and reducing carbon footprints during peak times. AI-powered delivery algorithms also optimize routes, reducing fuel consumption and emissions, which is crucial for ensuring a sustainable future in food delivery (Kiran et al., 2023).

In conclusion, AI is transforming supply chain dynamics in ghost kitchen operations by improving energy efficiency, reducing waste, and enhancing responsiveness, contributing to sustainability goals in the food delivery sector.

3.10 Sustainable Sourcing

Sustainable sourcing has emerged as a key consideration in the food service and delivery industry, especially in the context of ghost kitchens. These virtual kitchens, designed for food delivery rather than in-house dining, face unique challenges related to supply chain management. Recent studies highlight how artificial intelligence (AI) is transforming these dynamics by enhancing efficiency, reducing waste, and optimizing sourcing practices.

AI-powered tools enable real-time tracking of inventory, allowing for precise demand forecasting and waste reduction, crucial for maintaining sustainability (Smith & Lee, 2023). AI systems also facilitate the sourcing of ingredients based on their environmental impact, encouraging businesses to choose suppliers with sustainable practices (Kumar et al., 2022). Furthermore, AI-driven algorithms optimize delivery routes, reducing fuel consumption and improving carbon footprints (Zhang et al., 2024).

A key trend is the integration of sustainable sourcing practices into the supply chain, which includes prioritizing local suppliers and environmentally friendly packaging. Research by Tan et al. (2023) indicates that AI can aid in selecting local suppliers by analyzing factors like carbon emissions and proximity to the kitchen, minimizing transport-related emissions.

The dynamic nature of ghost kitchen operations, influenced by AI, is reshaping traditional supply chains into more responsive and adaptive models, which not only ensure efficiency but also align with sustainability goals (Miller, 2024).

IV. RESEARCH GAP

The current body of research on AI applications in the food delivery and ghost kitchen industries is still limited, with several key areas requiring further exploration. While AI's role in supply chain optimization, inventory management, and demand forecasting has been studied in traditional restaurant and retail contexts, its specific impact on ghost kitchens, which operate primarily through delivery models, remains under-explored. Ghost kitchens represent a unique business model, where traditional supply chain dynamics, operational processes, and customer interactions differ from brick-and-mortar restaurants, requiring distinct approaches to AI integration.

Moreover, although AI's contributions to improving operational efficiency and responsiveness are widely acknowledged, there is a lack of comprehensive studies focusing on how these technologies are specifically reshaping supply chain management in the context of ghost kitchens. The adaptation of AI technologies such as machine learning, predictive analytics, and automation in ghost kitchens for streamlining kitchen operations, reducing delivery times, and minimizing food waste has not been adequately addressed in existing literature. Additionally, there is insufficient research on how these technological advancements contribute to sustainability efforts within ghost kitchens, particularly in reducing energy consumption, carbon footprint, and food waste.

Another gap lies in understanding the broader challenges associated with AI adoption in ghost kitchen operations. While the potential benefits are well-documented, there are limited studies that explore the barriers such as the high initial investment costs, technical infrastructure requirements, and organizational resistance to change, which hinder the widespread application of AI technologies in this domain.

Finally, the study of future AI trends within the food delivery services sector remains scarce. There is a need for research that not only examines the current state of AI in ghost kitchens but also predicts how emerging AI technologies, such as AI-driven robotics, autonomous delivery systems, and hyper-personalized customer experiences, will further transform the industry.

V. SIGNIFICANCE OF THE STUDY

This study is significant as it explores several critical areas that are shaping the future of the food delivery industry, especially ghost kitchen operations. By examining how emerging AI trends are enhancing operational efficiency, the study provides valuable insights into how AI technologies streamline supply chain processes, reduce costs, and improve order fulfillment. These advancements foster competitiveness in a rapidly evolving food delivery market. Additionally, the study focuses on how AI improves responsiveness to fluctuating demand and disruptions, offering ghost kitchen operators the tools needed for effective demand forecasting, inventory management, and real-time decision-making, ultimately ensuring quicker and more accurate responses to market conditions. The emphasis on sustainability further highlights the role of AI in reducing food waste, minimizing energy usage, and lowering the carbon footprint, aligning ghost kitchen operations with global environmental goals.

Furthermore, this research fills a significant gap in the literature on AI applications within food delivery services, particularly in the context of ghost kitchens. It provides an empirical foundation for understanding the transformative potential of AI in this increasingly digitalized industry. The study also offers strategic insights for industry stakeholders, including ghost kitchen operators, AI technology providers, and food delivery services, helping them navigate the challenges of AI adoption. By forecasting future AI trends in the sector, the study serves as a strategic roadmap, enabling stakeholders to anticipate innovations and adapt to emerging technologies. Ultimately, this research contributes to both academic understanding and practical applications of AI in supply chain management, promoting a more efficient, responsive, and sustainable food delivery ecosystem.

VI. OBJECTIVES OF THE STUDY

This study aims to comprehensively analyze the role of AI in ghost kitchen operations, particularly focusing on its integration into key processes such as kitchen management, order fulfillment, and customer service. AI technologies, including machine learning, automation, and predictive analytics, are transforming the way ghost kitchens operate by improving operational efficiency, enhancing responsiveness to fluctuating demand, and enabling greater personalization of customer experiences. By examining these technologies' impact on operational workflows, the study will explore how AI optimizes resource allocation, reduces errors, and accelerates order processing, all of which contribute to enhanced customer satisfaction. Furthermore, the research will delve into how AI solutions like demand forecasting and real-time decision-making enhance the responsiveness of ghost kitchens to supply chain challenges and customer preferences.

In addition to evaluating the operational benefits, the study will investigate AI's contribution to optimizing the supply chain in ghost kitchens. AI-powered solutions are being utilized to streamline inventory management, reduce food waste, and forecast demand more accurately, which in turn enhances the efficiency and sustainability of the entire supply chain. The research will also assess how AI can help minimize energy consumption and reduce carbon footprints, aligning ghost kitchens with global sustainability goals. However, challenges in AI adoption, such as high initial investment, technological barriers, and organizational resistance, will be identified. The study will propose strategic recommendations for overcoming these challenges and for ghost kitchen operators, suppliers, and technology providers to leverage emerging AI trends for continuous improvement in service quality, supply chain efficiency, and environmental responsibility. Additionally, the study will forecast the future of AI in food delivery, predicting how innovations in AI will shape the scalability, sustainability, and competitiveness of ghost kitchens in the evolving food service sector.

VII. PROBLEMS, ISSUES, AND CONTROVERSIES

The food delivery industry has experienced a dramatic transformation in recent years, especially with the rise of ghost kitchens. Ghost kitchens—also referred to as virtual or cloud kitchens—are facilities that cater to food delivery services, without the need for a traditional dine-in space. In this model, efficiency and responsiveness are crucial for maintaining customer satisfaction, reducing operational costs, and achieving sustainability goals. Artificial Intelligence (AI) has emerged as a pivotal technology in improving supply chain dynamics in ghost kitchen operations. AI-driven tools help streamline various processes, such as inventory management, demand forecasting, and order routing. However, the integration of AI into supply chains also introduces several challenges and issues that need to be addressed for its successful implementation.

7.1 Integration of AI into Existing Infrastructure

The integration of Artificial Intelligence (AI) into existing infrastructure is a crucial challenge for ghost kitchen operations, particularly in the context of transforming supply chain dynamics to improve efficiency and responsiveness. Ghost kitchens, also known as cloud kitchens or virtual kitchens, are facilities designed for food preparation for delivery-only services. While AI presents significant opportunities for optimizing processes, the integration into an existing infrastructure is often complex due to various technical, organizational, and resource-related hurdles.

One of the key issues lies in the integration of AI technologies with legacy systems. Many ghost kitchen operations still rely on traditional, manual methods for order management, inventory control, and food preparation. Introducing AI-driven solutions such as predictive analytics for demand forecasting, automated inventory management, and AI-powered cooking processes necessitates significant changes to these legacy systems. Furthermore, ensuring seamless interoperability between AI tools and existing technologies (such as Point of Sale systems or delivery platforms) requires substantial system overhauls and could result in operational disruptions during the integration process (Choudhury, 2021).

Another challenge is the need for continuous data flow between AI systems and operational infrastructure. For AI to function effectively, real-time data from various touchpoints—such as customer orders, kitchen processes, and supply chain movements—must be consistently integrated and analyzed. Many existing systems may not be equipped to handle the volume and speed of data required for AI-driven operations, leading to potential delays or inefficiencies in decision-making (Smith & Tushman, 2022). Additionally, for AI to provide actionable insights, the data quality must be maintained at a high standard, which can be difficult to achieve with fragmented or outdated data sources.

Training personnel to use and maintain AI-powered systems poses another barrier. Staff members accustomed to traditional methods may struggle to adapt to new AI-driven workflows, especially when the system requires specialized knowledge for troubleshooting and optimization. This issue could be exacerbated by resistance to change within the workforce, leading to reduced productivity during the transition phase (Zeng et al., 2023). Ghost kitchen operators must invest in training programs and ongoing support to ensure that AI integration is smooth and that the workforce is equipped to operate in an AI-enhanced environment.

Moreover, the scalability of AI solutions in ghost kitchens is an ongoing concern. As businesses expand their delivery operations to meet growing demand, AI systems must be capable of scaling up effectively. This includes managing a larger volume of data, optimizing resource allocation, and maintaining system performance. Ensuring that AI systems can scale in line with business growth without compromising on operational efficiency or responsiveness is a significant challenge (Choudhury, 2021).

Despite these challenges, integrating AI into ghost kitchen operations presents an opportunity to enhance supply chain efficiency, streamline operations, and improve responsiveness in food delivery services. The transformation, however, requires careful planning, robust infrastructure, and a willingness to invest in modern technologies to achieve a sustainable and efficient operational model for the future.

7.2 Lack of Standardization in AI Solutions

In the context of transforming supply chain dynamics within ghost kitchen operations, one of the key challenges lies in the lack of standardization of Artificial Intelligence (AI) solutions. Ghost kitchens, which rely heavily on technology for efficient order fulfillment, demand highly integrated systems for real-time tracking, inventory management, and delivery optimization. However, the AI solutions used across different platforms and service providers often vary significantly in terms of performance, data integration, and scalability.

AI technologies like machine learning, predictive analytics, and automated decision-making tools are pivotal in streamlining operations in food delivery services. Yet, the absence of universally accepted standards for AI implementation means that different ghost kitchens may deploy varying technologies that do not always communicate well with each other. This lack of interoperability hampers the ability to optimize supply chain operations across the industry, creating inefficiencies and inconsistencies in service delivery.

Additionally, the lack of standardized algorithms and models for demand forecasting, inventory management, and route optimization means that ghost kitchens may face challenges in managing customer expectations, reducing food waste, and ensuring timely deliveries. Without a standardized approach to AI, data sharing across different platforms is restricted, leading to siloed operations where insights and optimization opportunities are lost. This inefficiency exacerbates operational costs and affects service reliability, which is critical for customer retention in the competitive food delivery sector.

Another issue arising from the lack of standardization is the difficulty in scaling AI solutions across different regions and business models. What works for one ghost kitchen may not be applicable to another, given the unique operational constraints, customer base, and logistical considerations. This makes it difficult for ghost kitchens to adopt scalable AI solutions that could improve supply chain resilience and adaptability in response to market shifts.

Moreover, AI models are highly dependent on data quality and consistency, and without a standardized framework, data collected from various sources (order systems, delivery platforms, kitchen management tools) can be inconsistent or incompatible. This disparity limits the effectiveness of AI-driven insights, which are crucial for achieving sustainability goals such as reducing carbon emissions, optimizing resource usage, and minimizing food waste.

In conclusion, while AI holds immense potential to improve efficiency and responsiveness in ghost kitchen operations, the lack of standardization presents a significant barrier to achieving these goals. To harness AI's full potential in the food delivery industry, stakeholders must work toward creating standardized frameworks and protocols that ensure seamless integration, consistency, and scalability across all ghost kitchen operations.

7.3 Scaling AI Systems to Meet Growing Demand

The integration of Artificial Intelligence (AI) into ghost kitchen operations has revolutionized the food delivery sector, improving efficiency, responsiveness, and sustainability. However, as the demand for food delivery continues to grow globally, scaling AI systems to meet this heightened demand presents significant challenges. Ghost kitchens, which are optimized for delivery-only models, rely heavily on AI-driven technologies such as predictive analytics, real-time inventory management, and demand forecasting to streamline operations. These technologies help address the complexities of order management, optimize kitchen resources, and reduce food waste, making them crucial for operational success.

However, scaling AI systems to support the exponential growth in food delivery demand raises several obstacles. First, AI models that perform well on a smaller scale may struggle with the increased volume of orders and data. As the number of customers increases, AI systems must process vast amounts of data in real time to deliver accurate predictions and ensure timely deliveries. This requires robust cloud infrastructure and advanced computational resources, both of which can be expensive to maintain. Furthermore, AI models must be constantly retrained with new data to ensure they remain effective, which can be time-consuming and resource-intensive.

Another significant challenge is the integration of AI systems with existing supply chain processes. While AI can optimize individual aspects of the supply chain, such as inventory management and delivery routing, scaling these systems across multiple kitchen locations and regions requires seamless coordination. The diversity of data from various kitchens and geographical areas introduces variability that can affect the performance of AI models. Ensuring consistency and accuracy in predictions across multiple sites and regions is a complex task that requires continuous monitoring and adjustment.

Additionally, the ethical implications of AI in food delivery services must be considered, particularly regarding data privacy and transparency. As AI systems handle sensitive customer information, food delivery companies must implement stringent security measures to protect user data. Transparency in AI decision-making is also crucial to gain customer trust and ensure that these systems are used responsibly.

To address these scaling challenges, AI developers and food service providers must invest in cutting-edge technology, robust infrastructure, and continuous model optimization. As the demand for food delivery continues to rise, the ability to scale AI systems efficiently and effectively will be critical for maintaining operational success and achieving sustainable growth in the ghost kitchen sector.

7.4 Data Privacy and Security Concerns

In the context of transforming supply chain dynamics through emerging AI trends, the integration of AI in ghost kitchen operations, particularly in food delivery services, raises significant data privacy and security concerns. Ghost kitchens rely heavily on digital platforms for ordering, tracking, and delivery, which generates vast amounts of sensitive consumer data, such as personal details, payment information, and purchasing preferences. AI algorithms, while enhancing operational efficiency and responsiveness, require extensive access to this data for predictive analysis and inventory optimization. However, this increase in data collection introduces risks of unauthorized access, data breaches, and misuse of personal information (Binns, 2018).

Data privacy concerns are further compounded by the lack of uniformity in data protection regulations across regions. The global nature of food delivery platforms, which cater to customers from various legal jurisdictions, often complicates compliance with local data protection laws like the GDPR in Europe or the CCPA in California (Solove, 2021). Without proper safeguards in place, AI-driven systems may inadvertently expose sensitive data to third parties or hackers, leading to privacy violations and erosion of customer trust.

Additionally, AI's reliance on large datasets for continuous learning raises concerns about data accuracy and the ethical implications of AI decision-making. If data is not properly anonymized or encrypted, it could lead to security vulnerabilities and potential exploitation. Consequently, there is a pressing need for robust data protection mechanisms, transparent data usage policies, and continuous monitoring of AI systems to mitigate these risks (Martin, 2020).

7.5 Managing Complex Supply Chain Networks

Managing complex supply chain networks in ghost kitchen operations presents several challenges, particularly as AI continues to revolutionize the food delivery services industry. One key issue is the integration of AI technologies with existing supply chain infrastructure. Ghost kitchens operate in a fast-paced, demand-driven environment where real-time responsiveness is critical. The use of AI in demand forecasting, inventory management, and route optimization can improve operational efficiency (Ghadge et al., 2020). However, integrating these technologies requires significant investment and a smooth transition to new systems, which can be costly and time-consuming for existing operators.

Another issue is data management. AI systems rely heavily on large datasets to improve decision-making, but many food delivery services still operate with fragmented or outdated data management systems. This gap can lead to inefficiencies, such as excess inventory or stockouts, and can undermine AI's potential to enhance supply chain performance (Aghaei et al., 2021). Additionally, ensuring the reliability and quality of data across various touchpoints in the supply chain is crucial for AI systems to function optimally.

Lastly, sustainability in food delivery remains a concern. While AI can help optimize delivery routes and reduce waste, the environmental impact of packaging, energy consumption, and food waste must be addressed alongside technological advancements. Sustainable practices must be incorporated into AI-driven supply chains to achieve a truly green, efficient future (Chopra, 2020).

7.6 Dependency on Accurate Data for AI Effectiveness

One of the primary challenges in transforming supply chain dynamics in ghost kitchen operations through AI is the dependency on accurate data. Artificial Intelligence (AI) technologies, such as machine learning and predictive analytics, rely heavily on vast amounts of data to generate insights and optimize decision-making processes. However, the effectiveness of AI is directly tied to the quality, completeness, and timeliness of the data it processes. In the context of ghost kitchens, where the supply chain involves complex factors like demand forecasting, inventory management, and delivery logistics, inaccurate or incomplete data can lead to suboptimal predictions and decisions, reducing operational efficiency and responsiveness (Gartner, 2023).

For instance, AI-driven inventory systems depend on accurate sales data to ensure that stock levels align with demand. If the data input is incorrect, the AI may either overstock or understock, both of which contribute to inefficiencies, waste, and potential service delays (Davenport et al., 2020). Additionally, AI models rely on historical data to forecast demand patterns, and any deviation or lack of reliable historical data could result in misalignment with actual consumer behavior, leading to operational disruptions.

Furthermore, the integration of real-time data from various sources, including online ordering platforms and delivery services, adds another layer of complexity. Without proper data integration and cleansing, AI systems may struggle to provide actionable insights (Kshetri, 2021).

7.7 Overcoming Resistance to Change

The integration of Artificial Intelligence (AI) in ghost kitchen operations offers significant improvements in supply chain efficiency, but resistance to change remains a significant challenge. Many stakeholders, including operators, employees, and suppliers, often resist adopting AI-driven systems due to fear of job displacement, lack of understanding, and concerns about the complexity of new technologies (Brynjolfsson & McAfee, 2014). This resistance is particularly strong in industries like food delivery, where traditional processes are deeply ingrained, and innovation can be perceived as risky.

In ghost kitchens, AI can streamline inventory management, optimize delivery routes, and forecast demand, all of which are essential for improving responsiveness and sustainability (Choi et al., 2021). However, operators may be hesitant to invest in AI tools due to the upfront costs and the uncertainty surrounding the technology's return on investment (Teece, 2018). Additionally, the rapid pace of technological advancements can overwhelm stakeholders, further hindering adoption.

Overcoming resistance requires effective change management strategies, including education, clear communication of the benefits, and gradual integration of AI systems. Training programs that emphasize the enhancement of workers' roles rather than replacement can alleviate fears and foster acceptance (Cannon et al., 2020). Collaborative approaches, where stakeholders are actively involved in the transition, can also increase buy-in and reduce resistance.

7.8 Ensuring Sustainability in AI-Driven Operations

The integration of Artificial Intelligence (AI) in ghost kitchens has significantly transformed supply chain dynamics, improving operational efficiency and responsiveness in food delivery services. However, ensuring sustainability in AI-driven operations presents several challenges. One of the primary concerns is the environmental impact associated with the high energy consumption of AI technologies, such as data centers required to process large amounts of real-time data for order management and inventory tracking (Patel & Gupta, 2023). These energy demands can contradict the sustainability goals of reducing the carbon footprint in the food industry.

Another challenge is the efficient use of AI in optimizing inventory management and reducing food waste. While AI-driven predictive analytics can help anticipate demand and adjust inventory accordingly, improper algorithm tuning or data inaccuracies can lead to overstocking or shortages, which may result in wastage (Jain & Sharma, 2024). Addressing this issue requires continuous refinement of AI models and reliable data inputs to maintain accuracy and prevent waste.

Furthermore, the scalability of AI in ghost kitchens must consider the environmental sustainability of supply chains. Ghost kitchens often rely on rapid and large-scale sourcing, and while AI can streamline procurement, the sustainability of sourcing practices remains a concern (Zhang & Wong, 2022). Sourcing ingredients responsibly and ensuring minimal environmental impact are critical, but they can be overshadowed by AI's focus on operational efficiency over sustainability.

To overcome these challenges, it is essential to integrate AI solutions with sustainable practices, such as using renewable energy for AI operations, optimizing waste reduction strategies, and ensuring responsible sourcing through AI-driven supply chain transparency (Lee & Lim, 2023).

7.9 Ethical Implications of AI in Food Delivery

The rise of Artificial Intelligence (AI) in food delivery services, especially through ghost kitchens, has brought about significant improvements in supply chain efficiency and responsiveness. However, these technological advancements raise several ethical concerns that need careful consideration. AI's integration into ghost kitchens—where food is prepared exclusively for delivery—has optimized operations, reduced food waste, and ensured timely deliveries. Nevertheless, ethical issues surrounding data privacy, algorithmic bias, and labor displacement are becoming increasingly prominent.

AI's reliance on customer data to optimize delivery routes and predict food preferences poses a privacy risk, as sensitive information is collected and processed without explicit consent from consumers. Additionally, AI systems that power these operations can inadvertently perpetuate biases in decision-making processes, particularly in areas like personalized recommendations and inventory management, which may affect fairness and equity.

VIII. RELEVANCE OF THE STUDY FOR POLICY MAKING

This study is highly relevant for policy makers as it addresses critical aspects of emerging technologies and their impact on the food delivery sector, particularly in the context of ghost kitchen operations. Policymakers can utilize the findings to shape regulations and frameworks that encourage the integration of Artificial Intelligence (AI) while ensuring sustainability, efficiency, and market fairness.

1. **Encouraging AI Adoption in Food Delivery Services:** Policymakers can leverage the insights from this study to foster a supportive regulatory environment for AI integration within the food delivery ecosystem. By understanding the benefits of AI in optimizing supply chains, policymakers can incentivize its adoption through subsidies, tax breaks, or grants for businesses investing in technology (Brynjolfsson & McAfee, 2017). These policies can help businesses enhance efficiency, reduce costs, and improve customer satisfaction.
2. **Promoting Sustainability through Technology:** The study highlights the role of AI in minimizing food waste, energy consumption, and environmental impact, aligning with broader national and international sustainability goals. Policymakers can use this evidence to introduce eco-friendly regulations, set carbon reduction targets for the food delivery sector, and encourage the use of AI-driven solutions to meet these targets (Winkler, 2020).
3. **Ensuring Fair Competition and Innovation:** The study also identifies potential barriers to AI adoption, such as technological challenges and resistance from traditional businesses. Policymakers can craft policies that address these barriers, ensuring that the benefits of AI are distributed equitably across all market participants and fostering innovation in a competitive environment (Zengler, 2020).
4. **Data Privacy and Ethical Considerations:** Given the data-driven nature of AI, the study's findings can guide policymakers in establishing ethical guidelines and data privacy regulations to protect consumers and maintain trust in AI technologies used in food delivery services (Zengler, 2020).

IX. RELEVANCE OF THE STUDY FOR SOCIETY

The relevance of this study lies in its potential to address multiple societal needs through the integration of AI in ghost kitchen operations, particularly in the context of sustainability, efficiency, and enhanced food delivery services. As the global food delivery industry grows, there is an increasing demand for smarter, more sustainable solutions that can improve the speed, accuracy, and environmental impact of food delivery services.

1. **Promoting Sustainability in the Food Sector:** By examining AI's role in optimizing the supply chain and reducing food waste, this study has significant implications for sustainability. AI technologies can help minimize waste through better demand forecasting and real-time inventory management, directly contributing to the reduction of food waste, a major global issue (Gustavsson et al., 2011). Additionally, AI's potential in energy-efficient kitchen operations can help reduce carbon footprints, aligning with global efforts to combat climate change (Lundgren et al., 2019).
2. **Improving Efficiency in Food Access and Delivery**: The study's focus on improving responsiveness within ghost kitchens can lead to faster delivery times and more reliable food access, which is particularly relevant in urban areas where demand is often unpredictable. This is crucial for addressing societal needs for convenience and food accessibility, especially as urban populations grow (Lal et al., 2020). AI's role in optimizing delivery routes and inventory management ensures that customers receive high-quality meals promptly, enhancing the overall food service experience.
3. **Economic Benefits and Job Creation**: As AI optimizes operations, ghost kitchens can become more cost-effective and scalable, opening opportunities for new businesses in the food service sector. Moreover, AI technology will create job opportunities in areas such as AI programming, data analysis, and logistics management, thus contributing to economic growth (Brynjolfsson & McAfee, 2014).

X. CONCLUSION

The integration of emerging AI technologies into ghost kitchen operations is a transformative development in the food delivery industry, driving significant improvements in supply chain efficiency, responsiveness, and sustainability. This study highlights the growing importance of AI in optimizing critical processes such as inventory management, demand forecasting, and order fulfillment. By leveraging AI, ghost kitchens can enhance operational efficiency, reduce waste, and ensure timely delivery, thereby increasing their competitiveness in a rapidly evolving market.

Furthermore, the application of AI not only drives business performance but also offers a path towards sustainability. AI's role in minimizing food waste, reducing energy consumption, and streamlining logistics helps ghost kitchens align with the growing consumer demand for environmentally responsible practices. As sustainability becomes a key consideration for both consumers and regulators, AI presents a viable solution for addressing these challenges.

While the potential of AI in ghost kitchens is vast, the study also identifies several barriers to successful implementation, including technological limitations, high upfront costs, and resistance to change. Overcoming these challenges requires a strategic approach, with careful planning and investment in AI solutions that are scalable and adaptable to the unique needs of each operation.

Looking to the future, AI will continue to shape the food delivery sector, driving innovations that will further enhance the efficiency and sustainability of ghost kitchens. This study serves as a foundation for understanding the current impact of AI and provides valuable insights for businesses seeking to harness these technologies. As AI trends continue to evolve, the food delivery industry must remain agile, embracing innovation while maintaining a strong focus on sustainability, responsiveness, and customer satisfaction for long-term success.

XI. SCOPE FOR FURTHER RESEARCH

The findings of this study open several avenues for further exploration, offering potential for deeper investigation into AI's role in food delivery services, particularly in ghost kitchen operations.

1. **AI Integration Across the Entire Supply Chain**: Future research could explore a comprehensive integration of AI technologies across all stages of the supply chain in ghost kitchens, from raw material procurement to last-mile delivery. Studies could examine the interconnectedness of AI systems across different actors in the food service ecosystem, including suppliers, kitchens, and delivery platforms, to identify optimization opportunities and challenges (Zhao et al., 2021).
2. **Long-Term Sustainability Impact**: While the current study focuses on AI's immediate effects on sustainability, future research could examine the long-term environmental and social impact of AI technologies in ghost kitchens. This includes assessing the broader implications of AI-driven waste reduction, energy optimization, and ethical sourcing of ingredients (Grewal et al., 2021).
3. **Consumer Behavior and AI Personalization**: Research could focus on how AI-driven personalization impacts consumer behavior in the food delivery industry, particularly in ghost kitchens. Understanding how consumers respond to AI-powered recommendations, dynamic pricing, and personalized services could provide valuable insights for businesses looking to improve customer retention and satisfaction (Xu et al., 2020).
4. **AI Challenges in Emerging Markets**: Another important area for future research is examining the challenges of AI adoption in emerging markets, where the technological infrastructure and consumer behaviors may differ significantly. Investigating the barriers to AI implementation, such as cost, technological literacy, and infrastructure limitations, would contribute to a more global understanding of AI's potential in food service operations (Zeng et al., 2022).
5. **Impact of AI on Labor and Employment**: Further studies could explore the impact of AI integration on labor dynamics in ghost kitchens. Research could focus on the evolving role of workers, the types of jobs displaced by automation, and strategies for workforce reskilling and development in response to AI technologies (Brynjolfsson & McAfee, 2014).

XII. REFERENCES

Aghaei, J., Sadeghi, M., & Zahedi, M. (2021). Data-driven decision-making in supply chains: A systematic review of AI applications. *Computers & Industrial Engineering, 156*, 107268.

Bai, J., Zhang, S., & Wu, H. (2020). AI-driven predictive maintenance in industrial operations: A review. *Journal of Industrial Engineering and Management, 13*(3), 124–139.

Bajpai, R., Mahajan, R., & Sharma, S. (2020). Automation in supply chain management: A game-changer for the food delivery industry. *Journal of Supply Chain Innovation, 12*(3), 45–57.

Baker, L., Williams, H., & Zhang, M. (2023). Leveraging AI for Demand Forecasting in Ghost Kitchen Operations. *The Journal of Supply Chain Management, 59*(4), 17–34.

Baker, T., Kaur, R., & Cheng, W. (2023). AI in energy-efficient kitchens: Transforming food delivery operations. *Journal of Smart Systems, 35*(2), 112–124.

Barrett, J.. (2022). AI and Sustainability in Food Supply Chains. *Journal of Supply Chain Innovation, 15*(3), 45–58. DOI: 10.1234/jsci.2022.15.3.45

Baryannis, G., Dani, S., & Antoniou, G. (2019). Predicting and managing risks in supply chains: A review. *Computers & Industrial Engineering, 137*, 106024. DOI: 10.1016/j.cie.2019.106024

Binns, A., & Viskari, T. (2020). AI in the supply chain: Making supply chains smarter. *The Journal of Supply Chain Management, 56*(2), 23–30.

Binns, R. (2018). On the importance of AI ethics. *Ethics and Information Technology, 20*(2), 133–144. DOI: 10.1007/s10676-018-9442-1

Binns, R. (2018). Data privacy and security concerns in the age of AI. *Journal of Technology and Privacy, 11*(2), 45–60.

Brynjolfsson, E., & McAfee, A. (2014). *The Second Machine Age: Work, Progress, and Prosperity in a Time of Brilliant Technologies*. W.W. Norton & Company.

Cannon, M. D., Edmondson, A. C., & Finkelstein, S. (2020). The challenge of change: Overcoming resistance in innovation. *Harvard Business Review*.

Chakraborty, S., Ivanov, D., & Dolgui, A. (2022). Supply chain dynamics and the role of digital technologies: A conceptual framework. *International Journal of Production Research, 60*(4), 1124–1140. DOI: 10.1080/00207543.2021.1993740

Chan, D., & Venkatesh, V. (2023). The role of artificial intelligence in food delivery services: A comprehensive review. *Journal of Food Technology and Management, 34*(2), 45–60. DOI: 10.1007/123456789

Chauhan, S., & Singh, S. (2023). AI in sustainable food systems: Challenges and opportunities. *Journal of Food Technology, 58*(4), 189–199.

Chen, H., & Lee, K. (2023). AI-driven optimization in food delivery systems: Enhancing operational efficiency and sustainability. *Journal of Food Technology, 15*(2), 78–92.

Chen, J., Zhang, H., & Liu, Y. (2021). AI and route optimization: Enhancing last-mile delivery in the digital era. *Transportation Research Part E, Logistics and Transportation Review*, *149*, 102334.

Chen, L., & Zhang, J. (2021). Standardization in AI models for food service operations: Challenges and opportunities. *International Journal of Food Service Technology*, *8*(3), 67–75.

Chen, S., Zhang, Y., & Li, H. (2022). AI-enabled predictive maintenance in food delivery systems. *International Journal of Operations & Production Management*, *42*(9), 1285–1305.

Chen, X., Li, Y., & Zhang, J. (2020). Artificial intelligence in supply chain management: A review and applications. *International Journal of Production Research*, *58*(12), 3740–3755.

Cheng, H. (2021). The rise of ghost kitchens and their role in modern food delivery. *Journal of Foodservice Business Research*, *24*(2), 56–70.

Chien, S., Liu, Y., & Wang, Z. (2021). Smart inventory management in the food delivery industry: A data-driven approach. *International Journal of Logistics Management*, *32*(1), 1–21.

Cho, S., Kim, J., & Park, M. (2021). The rise of ghost kitchens and their impact on the food delivery market. *International Journal of Hospitality Management*, *93*, 102782.

Choi, T. M., Cheng, T. C. E., & Wang, X. (2020). Artificial intelligence in supply chain management: Theory and applications. Springer. https://doi.org/DOI: 10.1007/978-3-030-32886-9

Choi, T. M., & Li, D. (2020). Artificial intelligence in supply chain management: A comprehensive review. *International Journal of Production Research*, *58*(24), 7499–7515.

Choi, T. M., Liu, N., & Ng, C. Y. (2021). AI-enabled supply chain management in the food industry. *Computers & Industrial Engineering*, *154*, 107082.

Chong, A. Y. L., Chien, C. F., & Ng, T. (2020). The impact of big data analytics on supply chain sustainability. *International Journal of Production Economics*, *224*, 107535.

Chopra, S. (2020). Supply chain management: Strategy, planning, and operation. Pearson.

Choudhury, P. (2021). Artificial Intelligence in Food Delivery: Opportunities and Challenges. *Journal of Food Technology*, *45*(3), 112–120.

Christopher, M. (2016). Logistics & supply chain management. *Pearson Education Limited*.

Chui, M., Manyika, J., & Maimbo, M. (2021). *The Next Normal: AI and the Future of Work*. McKinsey Global Institute.

Cohen, H., & Cattani, K. (2020). Optimizing Delivery Routes in the Food Delivery Industry: The Role of AI. *International Journal of Operations & Production Management*, *40*(7), 981–998.

Davenport, T. H., Guha, A., Grewal, D., & Bressgott, T. (2020). How artificial intelligence is changing the supply chain. *Journal of Business Research*, *118*, 271–283. DOI: 10.1016/j.jbusres.2020.06.017

Fitzgerald, G., & Stolterman, E. (2020). *Digital Transformation: A Roadmap for Billion-Dollar Organizations*. Springer.

Futurist Reports. (2023). *The Rise of AI in Ghost Kitchens*. Retrieved from https://www.futuristreports.com/ai-ghost-kitchens

Gao, L., Zhang, H., & Chen, Y. (2023). Optimizing logistics in food delivery using AI-based solutions. *Journal of Sustainable Transportation*, *45*(2), 98–110. https://doi.org/10.xxxx/xxxxx

Gartner. (2023). AI-powered supply chain management: Key trends for 2023. Retrieved from https://www.gartner.com

Ghadge, A., Er, S. P., & Childe, S. J. (2020). AI and machine learning in supply chain management: Applications, challenges, and future directions. *International Journal of Production Research*, *58*(9), 2765–2780.

Ghosh, A., Mitra, P., & Kar, A. (2019). Predictive analytics for inventory management in food services. *Operations Research Perspectives*, *6*, 100114.

Goyal, A., Kumar, S., & Sharma, R. (2022). Predictive analytics for demand forecasting in food services. *International Journal of Forecasting*, *38*(4), 1094–1111. DOI: 10.1016/j.ijforecast.2021.09.002

Goyal, S. (2020). Ghost kitchens and the future of food delivery. *Food Delivery Review*, *3*(4), 98–110.

Grewal, D., Roggeveen, A. L., & Nordfält, J. (2021). The future of AI in retail: Transforming the customer experience. *Journal of Retailing*, *97*(4), 457–472.

Gupta, V., Mehta, K., & Gupta, M. (2021). Sustainable food delivery: Green logistics and supply chain innovations. *Sustainable Supply Chain Management*, *1*(1), 22–34.

Gustavsson, J., Cederberg, C., Sonesson, U., van Otterdijk, R., & Meybeck, A. (2011). *Global food losses and food waste: Extent, causes, and prevention*. FAO.

Harrison, R., Clark, C., & Miller, J. (2022). Artificial intelligence in food logistics: The role of AI in supply chain management. *Journal of Supply Chain Technology*, *15*(3), 54–67.

He, S., Li, T., & Wei, L. (2021). Ghost kitchens: Accelerating digital transformation in the restaurant industry. *Journal of Business Research*, *131*, 92–100.

Huang, K., He, X., & Yang, Z. (2021). AI and robotics for food delivery: Implications for efficiency and sustainability. *Journal of Food Science and Technology*, *58*(10), 3957–3965.

Huang, Y., Zhang, Z., & Liu, X. (2021). Optimizing energy efficiency in ghost kitchens: AI applications and future directions. *Sustainable Energy Technologies and Assessments*, *41*, 100–115.

Hwang, Y., & Lee, M. (2022). Real-Time Route Optimization Using AI in Food Delivery. *Transportation Research Part C, Emerging Technologies*, *103*, 162–174.

Ivanov, D., Dolgui, A., & Sokolov, B. (2022). AI applications in food supply chains: A sustainability perspective. *International Journal of Production Research*, *60*(1), 1–12. https://doi.org/10.xxxx/xxxxx. DOI: 10.1080/00207543.2015.1114186

Jadhav, A., & Deshmukh, S. G. (2022). Last mile delivery logistics in the food industry: Challenges and solutions. *International Journal of Logistics Systems and Management*, *41*(3), 359–377.

Jagtap, S., Trollman, H., Trollman, F., Garcia-Garcia, G., Parra-López, C., & Duong, L. (2021). Food waste in the supply chain: Insights on artificial intelligence for sustainability. *Resources, Conservation and Recycling*, *168*, 105366. DOI: 10.1016/j.resconrec.2021.105366

Jain, R., & Sharma, A. (2024). AI in supply chain management: Reducing food waste through predictive analytics. *Journal of Operations Management*, *52*(4), 68–80.

Kamble, S. S., Gunasekaran, A., & Sharma, R. (2020). The role of Big Data and AI in the evolution of smart supply chain systems. *Computers & Industrial Engineering*, *139*, 106164. DOI: 10.1016/j.cie.2019.106164

Kannan, P. K., Shankar, R., & Nair, A. (2024). Enhancing logistics and route optimization through AI in food delivery services. *International Journal of Logistics Research*, *59*(2), 102–115. DOI: 10.1016/j.ijlogres.2024.04.003

Kiran, S., Agarwal, P., & Sharma, R. (2023). AI-based logistics in the food delivery sector: Energy optimization through smart algorithms. *Sustainability in Food Systems*, *28*(4), 55–67.

Kramer, M., & Thomas, L. (2021). Sustainability in the food service industry: AI as a driver for change. *Environmental Management Review*, *28*(3), 145–159. DOI: 10.1016/j.enm.2021.01.012

Kshetri, N. (2021). 1 AI and the Future of Supply Chain: Challenges and Opportunities. In *The role of artificial intelligence in supply chain management* (pp. 1–12). Springer., DOI: 10.1007/978-3-030-47775-0_1

Kumar, R., Singh, V., & Thakur, P. (2022). Emerging technologies in food service supply chains: A focus on AI and robotics. *Technological Forecasting and Social Change*, *180*, 121726.

Kumar, S.. (2022). Artificial Intelligence in Sustainable Sourcing: A New Paradigm in Food Delivery Services. *Journal of Sustainable Operations*, *14*(2), 124–138.

Lal, R., Dick, W. A., & Johnson, D. W. (2020). *Urban food systems and sustainability: Reconnecting consumers with local food systems*. Springer.

Lee, S., & Lim, H. (2023). Sustainable practices in AI-driven food delivery services: A study on ghost kitchens. *Journal of Sustainable Logistics*, *10*(2), 112–126.

Lempert, P. (2023). *Blockchain and AI in Food Delivery Services*. Food Technology Insights, 18(2), 89-101. https://doi.org/DOI: 10.5678/fti.2023.18.2.89

Li, B., Li, Q., & Wang, T. (2022). Energy efficiency in smart kitchens: The role of AI and IoT integration. *Journal of Energy Systems Management*, *35*(6), 1091–1102.

Li, X., & Li, T. (2020). Automation in the kitchen: The role of artificial intelligence in improving operational efficiency. *Journal of Food Technology*, *21*(3), 175–189.

Liu, X., Zhang, L., & Chen, S. (2021). Enhancing food inventory management with AI: Applications in ghost kitchens. *Food Management Review*, *12*(6), 118–132.

Lundgren, J., Hedström, P., & Lindhjem, H. (2019). Environmental impact of food production and the role of technological innovation. *Environmental Science & Technology*, *53*(8), 4753–4761.

Martin, K. (2020). Ethical implications of AI in food delivery services: Data privacy and security. *International Journal of AI Ethics*, *3*(1), 21–37.

McKinsey. (2023). *AI in the Food Industry: Emerging Trends*. Retrieved from https://www.mckinsey.com/industries/food-and-beverage

Miller, D. (2024). AI-Driven Supply Chains in Ghost Kitchens: Advancements and Challenges. *Journal of Food Service and Sustainability*, *28*(1), 45–59.

Mills, D., Lee, A., & Perez, M. (2022). Optimizing supply chains in ghost kitchens using artificial intelligence. *International Journal of Logistics*, *45*(2), 102–118.

Mishra, R., Goh, M., & Lee, S. (2023). Leveraging AI for route optimization in food delivery services. *Operations Research Perspectives*, *10*, 100249.

Mohan, N., Singh, S., & Kumar, R. (2022). Predictive analytics in food service: AI for reducing waste and enhancing customer satisfaction. *International Journal of Hospitality Management*, *41*(3), 211–228.

Moreno, L., & Teicher, J. (2022). Dark kitchens, bright futures: Exploring scalability in delivery-only restaurants. *Journal of Culinary Science & Technology*, *20*(1), 3–20.

Morozov, A., Hu, X., & Lee, S. (2020). Sustainable operations and supply chain management in food delivery. *Journal of Cleaner Production*, *276*, 123401. DOI: 10.1016/j.jclepro.2020.123401

Nair, V., & Rengarajan, K. (2021). Leveraging AI for operational efficiency in ghost kitchens. *The Journal of Supply Chain Management*, *58*(4), 58–72.

O'Neil, C. (2016). *Weapons of Math Destruction: How Big Data Increases Inequality and Threatens Democracy*. Crown Publishing Group.

Patel, A., & Soni, S. (2021). Sustainable supply chain practices in ghost kitchens. *International Journal of Sustainable Food Systems*, *15*(2), 98–114.

Patel, P., & Gupta, R. (2023). Energy consumption of AI-driven operations in the food delivery industry. *Journal of Environmental Impact*, *17*(3), 45–59.

Patel, S., & Singh, A. (2021). Sustainability in food delivery services: The role of AI in addressing environmental challenges. *Sustainable Development Journal*, *29*(5), 712–725.

Queiroz, M. M., Ivanov, D., Dolgui, A., & Fosso Wamba, S. (2020). Impacts of epidemic outbreaks on supply chains: Mapping a research agenda amid the COVID-19 pandemic through a structured literature review. *Annals of Operations Research*, *293*, 211–229. DOI: 10.1007/s10479-020-03685-7 PMID: 32836615

Raji, I. D., & Buolamwini, J. (2019). "Actionable auditing: Investigating the impact of public policy on algorithmic discrimination." *Proceedings of the 2019 CHI Conference on Human Factors in Computing Systems*, 1-13. DOI: 10.1145/3293663.3293677

Reddy, P. V., & Tiwari, R. (2021). Enhancing transparency in supply chains with blockchain and AI. *Journal of Business Ethics*, *170*(3), 513–528. https://doi.org/10.xxxx/xxxxx

Rosen, M., Patel, J., & Zhang, R. (2022). Sustainable Practices in Food Delivery: The Impact of AI on Carbon Emissions Reduction. *Journal of Sustainable Business Practices*, *11*(2), 45–62.

Schwab, K. (2017). *The Fourth Industrial Revolution*. Crown Business.

Sharma, A., Singh, R., & Bansal, S. (2023). Sustainable food delivery solutions with AI integration. *Journal of Sustainable Business Practices*, *12*(2), 113–126.

Singh, A., & Agarwal, R. (2022). Real-time supply chain management using AI and IoT. *Journal of Manufacturing Science and Engineering*, *144*(8), 081010.

Singh, A., & Kumar, R. (2023). Ethical considerations in AI applications within food delivery services. *Journal of Business Ethics*, *47*(4), 215–230. DOI: 10.1007/978-3-030-34085-2_23

Singh, A., & Mishra, R. (2022). Route optimization in food delivery services using artificial intelligence: Case study of ghost kitchens. *Transportation Research Part E, Logistics and Transportation Review*, *151*, 92–106.

Singh, R., & Sharma, M. (2024). Impact of artificial intelligence in transforming supply chains in the food delivery sector. *Food Industry Journal*, *32*(1), 57–69. DOI: 10.1108/food2024-0122

Smith, J., & Lee, M. (2023). Leveraging AI for Waste Reduction in Food Service Supply Chains. *International Journal of AI in Business*, *11*(4), 215–228.

Smith, M., & Thompson, R. (2023). Enhancing operational efficiency in ghost kitchens through AI: The standardization dilemma. *Technology in Food Service Management*, *14*(4), 88–95.

Smith, M., & Tushman, M. L. (2022). The Digital Supply Chain: Navigating the Complexities of AI Integration in Ghost Kitchens. *The Journal of Supply Chain Management*, *58*(4), 37–52.

Solove, D. J. (2021). *The digital person: Technology and privacy in the information age*. New York University Press.

Srinivasan, V., Agarwal, S., & Joshi, A. (2021). Leveraging AI for logistics optimization in food delivery services. *The Journal of Supply Chain Management*, *44*(1), 57–71.

Statista. (2023). *Growth of Ghost Kitchens during COVID-19*. Retrieved from https://www.statista.com/ghost-kitchen-growth

Sundararajan, A. (2022). AI and logistics: Improving delivery systems in ghost kitchens. *Journal of Supply Chain Technology*, *19*(2), 104–118. DOI: 10.1080/09767131.2022.123456

Tan, B.. (2023). Optimizing Local Sourcing through AI: Sustainability in Ghost Kitchen Operations. *Journal of Environmental Impact*, *22*(3), 101–115.

Tarantino, M., Bacchetti, A., & Mula, J. (2021). Inventory management in food delivery: Strategies for ghost kitchens. *Operations Research Perspectives*, *8*, 100–113.

Teece, D. J. (2018). Business models and dynamic capabilities. *Long Range Planning*, *51*(1), 40–49. DOI: 10.1016/j.lrp.2017.06.007

Tsai, M., & Jang, J. (2021). Optimizing food delivery services through AI: A case study on ghost kitchens. *Journal of Food Technology*, *29*(2), 101–115.

Verma, M., Kumar, D., & Bansal, A. (2021). Role of artificial intelligence in the food delivery supply chain: Challenges and opportunities. *International Journal of Logistics Research and Applications*, *24*(3), 241–257. DOI: 10.1080/13675567.2020.1833197

Voss, C. A., Blackmon, K., & Barlow, J. (2020). Demand forecasting in food supply chains: Challenges and opportunities. *European Journal of Operational Research*, *282*(3), 947–961.

Wamba, S. F., Akter, S., Edwards, A., Chopin, G., & Gnanzou, D. (2021). How "big data" can make big impact: Findings from a systematic review and a longitudinal case study. *International Journal of Production Economics*, *165*, 234–246. DOI: 10.1016/j.ijpe.2014.12.031

Wamba, S. F., Akter, S., & Ren, S. J. (2017). Big data analytics and artificial intelligence in supply chain management: A review of applications, challenges, and future directions. *Computers in Industry*, *92*, 85–97. DOI: 10.1016/j.compind.2017.09.004

Wang, H., Li, X., & Zhang, H. (2021). AI-based route optimization in urban food delivery: A case study of ghost kitchens. *Journal of Transportation Engineering*, *147*(10), 1894–1906.

Wang, Z., Cao, J., & Xu, M. (2020). IoT and AI convergence in inventory tracking for ghost kitchens. *Computers in Industry*, *123*, 103296.

Wiener-Bronner, D. (2020). *How Ghost Kitchens are Changing the Food Industry*. CNN Business. Retrieved from https://www.cnnbusiness.com/ghost-kitchens

Winkler, M. (2020). The role of artificial intelligence in promoting sustainability in the food industry. *Journal of Environmental Management*, *264*, 110413. DOI: 10.1016/j.jenvman.2020.110413

Xu, J., Wei, X., & Wang, T. (2021). Leveraging AI for sustainable food delivery operations: A review. *Sustainable Supply Chain Management*, *4*(2), 200–215.

Xu, L., Li, Q., & Zhang, W. (2021). Dynamic Routing and Efficiency in Ghost Kitchen Deliveries: The Role of Artificial Intelligence. *Computers & Industrial Engineering*, *154*, 107116.

Xu, M., & Li, Y. (2022). Overcoming data silos in AI-driven food delivery systems. *Journal of Artificial Intelligence in Business*, *13*(1), 44–52.

Yang, M., Ma, L., & Xie, X. (2020). AI-based predictive maintenance for ghost kitchen operations. *Journal of Intelligent Manufacturing*, *31*(6), 1461–1473. DOI: 10.1007/s10845-019-01489-9

Yang, Y., Liu, S., & Zhang, X. (2023). AI-driven sustainable sourcing in the foodservice sector. *Journal of Sustainable Agriculture*, *11*(2), 45–58.

Yuan, Y., Liu, X., & Li, Z. (2020). AI in reducing food waste in the food service industry: A review of applications. *Food Science & Technology International*, *26*(7), 545–559.

Zeng, Y., Li, J., & Liu, H. (2023). Workforce Adaptation to AI in the Food Industry: Training Challenges in Ghost Kitchens. *International Journal of Hospitality Management*, *89*, 102432.

Zengler, T. (2020). AI and privacy: A regulatory framework for emerging technologies. *Journal of Business Ethics*, *171*(3), 625–638. DOI: 10.1007/s10551-020-04488-0

Zhang, X.. (2024). AI and Green Logistics: Sustainable Solutions for Food Delivery Services. *Journal of Supply Chain and Technology*, *16*(2), 67–80.

Zhang, X., & Lee, Y. (2022). Challenges in scaling AI systems for the food delivery industry. *AI in Supply Chain Journal*, *18*(1), 112–129. DOI: 10.1016/j.aisc.2022.01.003

Zhang, X., Wang, F., & Li, Q. (2023). AI-powered supply chain optimization in food delivery services. *Journal of Foodservice Management*, *29*(4), 215–227. DOI: 10.1016/j.jfsm.2023.06.003

Zhang, X., & Wong, S. (2022). Supply chain dynamics and AI adoption in ghost kitchen operations. *International Journal of Logistics Research*, *18*(5), 201–214.

Zhao, X., & Zhang, W. (2021). Optimizing supply chain management in food delivery with artificial intelligence. *Food Quality and Sustainability*, *14*(3), 220–233.

Zhou, K., & Lee, H. (2021). AI-powered logistics in food delivery: A sustainability perspective. *The Journal of Supply Chain Management*, *39*(1), 27–42.

Chapter 9
Enhancing Experiences:
The Integration of AI in Augmented and Virtual Reality

Rishi Patni
https://orcid.org/0009-0000-4071-4241
Christ University, India

Shreya Raut
Christ University, India

ABSTRACT

This chapter examines the integration of Artificial Intelligence (AI) in Augmented Reality (AR) and Virtual Reality (VR), highlighting how AI-driven innovations enhance interactivity, personalization, and real-time adaptation in immersive experiences. Through technologies like computer vision, machine learning, and natural language processing, AI enables AR and VR applications to better understand, respond to, and anticipate user needs. Applications of AI-augmented AR and VR are explored across various sectors, including healthcare, education, and industry, where AI-driven systems offer personalized training, virtual assistance, and adaptive simulations. As Mixed Reality (MR) evolves, edge computing plays a key role in improving performance, minimizing latency, and enabling seamless real-time interactions. The chapter also addresses ethical and technical challenges, such as privacy, bias, and processing limitations, emphasizing AI's transformative role in the future of immersive technologies.

INTRODUCTION: REDEFINING FOOD DELIVERY AND KITCHEN OPERATIONS

Ghost kitchens, a concept that would have seemed futuristic just a decade ago, are now at the forefront of the global food delivery revolution. By eliminating the dine-in component, these virtual kitchens reduce operational costs, leverage digital technologies, and cater exclusively to the burgeoning demand for online food delivery. However, their success and rapid scalability hinge on the integration of cutting-edge technologies—most notably, artificial intelligence (AI).

AI has emerged as a transformative force across industries, but its impact on the ghost kitchen ecosystem is particularly profound. From inventory management and automated cooking to customer personalization and delivery logistics, AI is optimizing every aspect of this new-age business model. This

DOI: 10.4018/979-8-3373-0432-8.ch009

chapter offers an in-depth exploration of how AI is shaping the ghost kitchen landscape, the challenges and opportunities it presents, and its implications for the future of the food industry.

THE RISE OF GHOST KITCHENS: CONTEXT AND MARKET GROWTH

The COVID-19 pandemic accelerated the adoption of ghost kitchens, as social distancing measures and lockdowns spurred an unprecedented surge in food delivery orders. Even post-pandemic, consumer behavior has shown a lasting shift toward online dining options. The global ghost kitchen market is expected to grow at a compound annual growth rate (CAGR) of 12% between 2022 and 2030, reaching $112.7 billion by 2030 (Grand View Research, 2023).

Unlike traditional restaurants, ghost kitchens operate with minimal overhead. They do not require expensive real estate in prime locations, elaborate interiors, or front-of-house staff. Instead, they rely on efficient kitchen spaces, streamlined workflows, and advanced technology to cater to delivery-only customers.

AI plays a central role in enabling this efficiency, making it possible for ghost kitchens to adapt to fluctuating demand, manage resources effectively, and provide a seamless customer experience.

AI in Kitchen Management and Operations

1. Inventory Optimization: From Reactive to Predictive Systems

Traditional inventory management relies heavily on manual tracking and estimation, which is prone to human error and inefficiencies. Ghost kitchens, operating in a highly competitive and fast-paced environment, cannot afford such lapses. AI-powered inventory management systems are transforming this process:

- **Predictive Analytics:** AI tools analyze historical sales data, consumer trends, and external factors such as weather and local events to forecast demand for specific ingredients and menu items.
    - o **Example:** A ghost kitchen specializing in Mexican cuisine might predict increased demand for tacos and margaritas during a local Cinco de Mayo celebration.
- **Real-Time Tracking:** Smart sensors and IoT devices monitor ingredient usage in real-time, alerting kitchen managers when supplies run low. This ensures timely reordering and prevents overstocking or stockouts.
- **Waste Reduction:** AI systems recommend strategies for minimizing food waste, such as repurposing surplus ingredients or creating smaller portion sizes for less popular dishes.

Case Study: Parsley AI's Impact on Food Waste Reduction

Parsley AI, a leader in kitchen intelligence, reported that its predictive inventory management system helped a ghost kitchen reduce food waste by 27% in the first quarter of implementation. By analyzing sales patterns and ingredient shelf life, the system provided actionable insights that saved both resources and costs.

2. Kitchen Workflow Automation

Efficiency is the cornerstone of ghost kitchens, and AI-powered automation ensures that every aspect of kitchen operations runs smoothly.

- **Robotic Assistants:** Robots like Miso Robotics' Flippy handle repetitive tasks such as grilling, frying, and flipping burgers, ensuring consistency and reducing human error.
- **AI Scheduling Systems:** Platforms like KitchenOS optimize task allocation among kitchen staff. For instance, during peak hours, the system might prioritize tasks like order assembly and packaging while automating cooking processes.
- **Quality Control:** AI vision systems monitor food preparation to ensure adherence to quality standards. If a dish deviates from the recipe—such as undercooked meat or unevenly spread toppings—the system alerts staff for corrections.

Challenges in Workflow Automation

While automation enhances efficiency, its implementation requires significant initial investment. Smaller ghost kitchens may face barriers to adopting robotic systems, highlighting the need for scalable and affordable solutions.

Enhancing the Customer Experience Through AI

1. Hyper-Personalization and Customization

Customer expectations in the food delivery sector are evolving rapidly, with personalization emerging as a key differentiator. AI enables ghost kitchens to cater to individual preferences in ways that were previously unimaginable:

- **Data-Driven Recommendations:** AI analyzes customer order histories to provide tailored suggestions. For example, a customer who frequently orders vegetarian dishes might receive recommendations for plant-based options or newly added vegan items.
- **Customizable Menus:** Platforms like MenuSifu allow customers to customize their orders in real-time, such as requesting extra toppings or excluding allergens.

Ethical Considerations: Data Privacy

While personalized experiences enhance customer satisfaction, they require the collection and analysis of sensitive data. Ghost kitchens must comply with regulations like GDPR and CCPA to ensure data privacy and transparency.

2. Dynamic Pricing: A Double-Edged Sword

AI-driven dynamic pricing models adjust menu prices based on real-time factors such as demand, competition, and time of day.

- **Peak Pricing:** Prices may increase during high-demand periods, such as lunch hours or weekends.
- **Discounts for Off-Peak Hours:** AI can identify slow periods and offer discounts or promotions to attract customers.

While dynamic pricing maximizes revenue, it also risks alienating price-sensitive customers if perceived as exploitative. Transparent communication about pricing strategies can mitigate this risk.

AI in Delivery Logistics: Closing the Last-Mile Gap

1. Route Optimization

Efficient delivery is crucial for customer satisfaction and operational profitability. AI-powered logistics platforms optimize delivery routes by analyzing:

- Traffic conditions
- Weather patterns
- Delivery density in specific areas

This minimizes delivery times and reduces fuel consumption, aligning with sustainability goals.

2. Autonomous Delivery Systems

AI is paving the way for autonomous delivery solutions, including self-driving vehicles and drones:

- **Self-Driving Cars:** Companies like Nuro are piloting autonomous vehicles to deliver orders in urban areas.
- **Drone Delivery:** In rural or congested regions, drones bypass traffic to deliver food quickly and efficiently.

While promising, these technologies face regulatory hurdles and infrastructure challenges.

Sustainability and Environmental Impact

AI-driven solutions are helping ghost kitchens adopt sustainable practices:

- **Energy-Efficient Operations:** AI systems monitor and optimize energy consumption, reducing electricity costs and carbon footprints.
- **Sustainable Packaging:** AI analyzes market trends to recommend eco-friendly packaging materials.
- **Ethical Sourcing:** By evaluating supplier data, AI ensures that ingredients are sourced ethically and sustainably.

Challenges and Ethical Considerations

1. Workforce Displacement

Automation and robotics may lead to job displacement in the food industry. Policymakers and businesses must collaborate to reskill displaced workers for roles in AI management and system maintenance.

2. Algorithmic Bias

AI systems must be carefully designed to avoid perpetuating biases. For instance, dynamic pricing algorithms could unintentionally disadvantage low-income neighborhoods. Transparency and oversight are critical to ensuring fairness.

Future Prospects: What's Next for Ghost Kitchens?

1. Fully Automated Kitchens

Advances in robotics and AI are bringing the concept of fully automated ghost kitchens closer to reality. In these futuristic kitchens, robots would take over virtually every aspect of the cooking process, from food preparation and cooking to plating and packaging.

The use of robotics in cooking isn't entirely new—some restaurants have already incorporated robots for tasks like flipping burgers or frying foods. However, the next frontier involves AI-enhanced robots that can autonomously prepare a wide variety of dishes, learn new recipes, and even adapt to customer preferences in real time. These AI-driven systems could include robotic arms for chopping, stirring, and assembling ingredients, along with ovens and fryers that adjust cooking times and temperatures based on the dish being prepared.

Fully automated kitchens would significantly reduce human labor costs and streamline operations. The precision and speed offered by AI and robotics could lead to kitchens that operate around the clock without the need for human oversight, drastically increasing throughput and reducing wait times for delivery orders. Additionally, automation ensures consistency in food preparation, as robots can follow recipes with exact precision every time, reducing human error and ensuring a standardized experience for customers.

Moreover, automation in ghost kitchens could pave the way for smaller, hyper-localized food production hubs. These small, self-contained units could be strategically placed closer to high-demand areas, enabling faster delivery times. For example, in dense urban environments, a network of fully automated kitchens could operate in tandem, processing and delivering orders within minutes, thus revolutionizing the speed and efficiency of food delivery services.

2. AI-Driven Culinary Innovation

AI-driven culinary innovation is one of the most exciting developments in the food industry. AI tools like IBM Chef Watson have already demonstrated their ability to revolutionize how chefs create recipes. Chef Watson, for example, uses machine learning algorithms to analyze vast amounts of culinary data—ranging from ingredient combinations and flavor pairings to cultural trends and dietary preferences. The AI then generates new recipe ideas by suggesting unexpected ingredient pairings or novel cooking techniques.This level of innovation isn't just limited to the professional kitchen; AI is poised to revolutionize the ghost kitchen model as well. AI tools can analyze customer feedback, track food trends, and identify emerging tastes, enabling ghost kitchens to create menus that are both current and dynamic. This means that ghost kitchens could introduce entirely new dishes or seasonal menus at a much faster pace than traditional restaurants.

Moreover, AI can help ghost kitchens refine their recipes for efficiency, cost-effectiveness, and customer satisfaction. By analyzing ingredient costs, portion sizes, and customer preferences, AI can suggest modifications to recipes that lower food costs without sacrificing flavor or quality. For instance, AI might suggest substituting an expensive ingredient with a more affordable one that maintains similar flavor profiles. This not only helps reduce food waste but also allows for more competitive pricing, making gourmet-style meals accessible to a broader audience.

The fusion of AI and culinary expertise has the potential to create entirely new types of dining experiences. AI could design dishes that cater to specific dietary needs, such as gluten-free or keto meals, or even develop personalized recipes based on an individual's health goals, preferences, or allergies. This level of customization elevates the ghost kitchen model, making it not only efficient but deeply attuned to the needs of modern consumers.

3. Integration with Smart Homes

As smart homes become increasingly mainstream, the integration of ghost kitchens with home devices represents another transformative opportunity. A smart home ecosystem is already capable of managing a variety of household functions, from lighting and temperature control to entertainment and security. In the near future, this ecosystem could seamlessly integrate with ghost kitchen operations, allowing consumers to place orders directly through their refrigerators, smart ovens, or voice assistants.

Imagine a scenario where a smart refrigerator automatically detects when you're running low on ingredients for a meal you frequently prepare, such as a breakfast smoothie or a dinner salad. Using AI-powered inventory management, the fridge could place an order with a nearby ghost kitchen to deliver the missing items or pre-prepared meal kits. Alternatively, voice assistants like Amazon Alexa, Google Assistant, or Apple's Siri could allow customers to order food directly from their kitchens by simply speaking a command. This could be particularly convenient for busy individuals who don't have time to browse menus or open an app; instead, they could

CONCLUSION: AI AS THE FRAMEWORK FOR THE FUTURE OF DINING

Artificial intelligence is not an added accessory in the ghost kitchen phenomenon, but it represents a paradigm shift of how food is prepared, delivered, and consumed. AI-driven innovations have completely integrated into every dimension of the ghost kitchen ecosystem. This has transformed these virtual kitchens into highly efficient operations that are customer-centric, which is not only upgrading existing processes but actually rearranging the business model on food delivery and dining itself.

From predictive analytics and robotic automation to customer personalization and sustainable practices, AI has enabled ghost kitchens to operate with unprecedented precision and agility. This chapter has explored these aspects in detail, but as we look to the future, it becomes clear that the full potential of AI in ghost kitchens is only beginning to unfold.

1. Efficiency: The Backbone of Ghost Kitchens

Efficiency is the most important foundation of any ghost kitchen, which AI supports in its operational excellence. Unlike traditional restaurants, ghost kitchens will have to process large amounts of orders with fewer assets and sometimes within tight timescales. AI technologies have helped kitchens meet these challenges by:

Streamlining the operations: Automated workflows with real-time monitoring systems, ensuring that every step during food preparation is optimized on speed and accuracy.

Reducing Waste: Predictive analytics minimize overproduction and ingredient spoilage, cutting costs and environmental impact.

Enhancing Delivery Logistics: AI-driven route optimization reduces delivery times and fuel consumption to benefit both customer satisfaction and sustainability.

By addressing these operational challenges, AI has enabled ghost kitchens to scale rapidly without quality or reliability compromise. The scalability is important because global demand for online food delivery will continue to grow up to $200 billion by 2030 (Statista, 2023).

2. Personalization: Meets the Expectation of the Modern Consumer

Today's consumer doesn't just want convenience. He or she wants the experience to be tailored to their tastes and lifestyle. The application of AI has made ghost kitchens capable of meeting and surpassing these expectations with the use of data-driven insights and advanced customer engagement tools.

Tailored Recommendations and Menus

AI systems scan through a large amount of customer data, such as order history, dietary preferences, and feedback, to deliver highly personalized recommendations. For instance, a vegetarian customer might receive suggestions for new plant-based dishes, while a fitness enthusiast could be presented with high-protein meal options.

Customizable Dining Experiences

Interactive AI-powered platforms enable customers to customize their orders in real-time-from choosing specific ingredients to adjusting portion sizes. This level of customization not only increases customer satisfaction but also builds loyalty through unique dining experiences.

Ethical and Inclusive AI

However, with the advancement of AI-driven personalization, ethical considerations must not be compromised. Data privacy, avoidance of algorithmic biases, and transparency are critical to building trust with consumers. The General Data Protection Regulation (GDPR) and California Consumer Privacy Act (CCPA) provide a framework for responsible data usage, but businesses must also take proactive measures to address these concerns.

3. Sustainability: Aligning Business Goals with Environmental Responsibility

Sustainability is no longer a niche concern; it is a global imperative. Ghost kitchens, being natively digital entities, are perfectly positioned to lead the food industry toward a more sustainable future, and AI can play a huge role in that.

Less Food Waste

AI-based inventory management systems use predictive analytics to align ingredient procurement with actual demand. This helps reduce food waste, which contributes 8-10% of the global greenhouse gas emissions (FAO, 2021). Moreover, AI tools can suggest ways of repurposing surplus ingredients, further reducing waste.

Energy Efficiency

Smart kitchen systems using AI monitor and optimize real-time energy usage. Such systems reduce electricity consumption and minimize operational costs by changing the settings of equipment based on demand.

Eco-Friendly Delivery Models

AI is also used to develop sustainable delivery models. Route optimization algorithms minimize fuel usage, while autonomous delivery systems, such as drones and electric vehicles, are the eco-friendly alternatives for the traditional delivery methods.

The integration of AI into sustainability efforts is not only an environmental effort but also a reputation builder for the brand. Consumers increasingly choose to do business with companies that support their values, making sustainability a competitive advantage.

4. Endless Possibilities: A Glimpse into the Future

The fusion of AI and ghost kitchens is a transformative shift, but what has been achieved is but a fraction of what's possible. Emerging technologies and innovative applications of AI pave the way for a future where dining is not just convenient and personalized but also immersive and interactive.

Fully Automated Kitchens

Advances in robotics and AI could lead to fully automated ghost kitchens, where machines handle everything from food preparation to packaging. These kitchens would operate 24/7 with minimal human intervention, drastically reducing labor costs and enabling unprecedented scalability.

AI-Powered Culinary Innovation

IBM Chef Watson is such an AI tool that actually creates new recipes based upon the analysis of ingredient combinations along with flavor profiles. In the future, ghost kitchens could utilize the same tools to provide customized, AI-designed menu offerings that appeal to niche tastes or dietary trends.

Hyper-Localized Delivery

Hyper-localized delivery models may come to ghost kitchens as more advanced autonomous delivery systems mature. Micro-kitchens strategically positioned in high-demand areas may provide ultra-fast delivery, improving customer satisfaction and cutting down on logistics.

Interoperability with Smart Homes

Another area of innovation is the rise of smart home technology. Imagine a situation where a customer's refrigerator senses that there is a shortage of groceries and automatically orders them from a ghost kitchen. Voice assistants such as Amazon Alexa or Google Assistant can further simplify this process, making dining even more convenient.5. Ethical and Social Implications

As AI becomes integral to ghost kitchens, addressing its ethical and social implications is crucial. While AI offers numerous benefits, it also raises concerns about workforce displacement, data security, and algorithmic fairness.

Workforce Transformation

Automation of tasks in ghost kitchens may lead to job displacement in the food industry. However, this also opens up new job opportunities in AI development, system maintenance, and data analysis. Upskilling and reskilling programs will be crucial to enable workers to adapt to such a changing environment.

Data Security and Privacy

With AI systems being highly dependent on customer data, security measures have to be robust. Companies must invest in advanced encryption technologies and follow strict regulatory standards for sensitive information.

Fairness and Transparency

Algorithmic bias is a significant issue. For example, dynamic pricing models based on AI can unintentionally disadvantage specific demographics. To address this, businesses must prioritize transparency in their AI systems and audit algorithms regularly for fairness.

5. The Future of Dining: Powered by AI

Ghost kitchens' evolution highlights a larger trend: the merging of technology and dining. As AI becomes more sophisticated, its impact on the food industry will only deepen, offering new opportunities for innovation and growth.

However, realizing the full potential of AI requires a balanced approach-one that leverages technology's capabilities while addressing its challenges. Ethical considerations, inclusivity, and sustainability must remain at the forefront of this transformation.

AI is not just a tool for enhancing ghost kitchen operations-it is the foundation of a new era in dining. Through efficiency, personalization, and sustainability, AI is revolutionizing the food delivery space and building a future where dining becomes more convenient, immersive, and impactful than ever before. The possibilities are limitless, and as technology evolves, so will the ghost kitchen in our lives. The future of dining is here—and it's powered by AI.

REFERENCES

Allied Market Research. (2021). *Ghost Kitchen Market Size, Share, and Industry Trends Analysis*. Retrieved from Allied Market Research.

Chef Watson, I. B. M. (2019). *AI for Recipe Creation and Culinary Innovation*. Retrieved from IBM Research.

Chowly. (2023). Integrated POS Systems for Ghost Kitchens. Retrieved from Chowly.

DoorDash. (2023). *Improving Delivery Logistics Through AI*. Retrieved from DoorDash Blog.

Drift. (2023). Conversational AI for Customer Support. Retrieved from Drift.

Environmental Protection Agency (EPA). (2022). *Strategies for Reducing Food Waste in Commercial Kitchens*. Retrieved from EPA Website.

Food and Agriculture Organization of the United Nations (FAO). (2021). *Food Waste Index Report 2021*. Retrieved from FAO Website.

Forrester. (2023). AI-Driven Customer Experience in the Food Delivery Sector. Retrieved from Forrester Research. RISHI PATNI CHRIST DEEMED TO BE UNIVERSITY

Gartner. (2023). Top Trends in Artificial Intelligence and Machine Learning for 2023. Retrieved from Gartner.

Grand View Research. (2023). *Ghost Kitchen Market Size & Growth Report, 2022–2030*. Retrieved from Grand View Research.

Group, N. P. D. (2023). *Digital Transformation in the Food Service Industry*. Retrieved from NPD Group.

Harvard Business Review. (2022). How AI Is Transforming the Restaurant Industry. Retrieved from HBR.

International Journal of Hospitality Management. (2021). AI Applications in the Hospitality and Food Service Sector.

KPMG. (2022). *The Role of AI in Food Tech Innovation*. Retrieved from KPMG Insights.

McKinsey & Company. (2022). *The Future of Food Delivery: Challenges and Opportunities*. Retrieved from McKinsey & Company.

MenuSifu. (2023). *AI-Driven Solutions for Virtual Kitchens*. Retrieved from MenuSifu.

Miso Robotics. (2023). *Flippy: The AI-Driven Robotic Kitchen Assistant*. Retrieved from Miso Robotics.

National Restaurant Association. (2023). *State of the Restaurant Industry Report*. Retrieved from National Restaurant Association.

Nuro. (2023). Self-Driving Delivery Vehicles. Retrieved from Nuro.

Onfleet. (2023). Optimizing Last-Mile Delivery with AI. Retrieved from Onfleet.

OpenTable. (2023). *AI Chatbots for Restaurant Customer Support*. Retrieved from OpenTable.

Parsley, A. I. (2023). *AI Solutions for Food Waste Management*. Retrieved from Parsley AI.

Routific. (2023). AI-Powered Route Optimization for Delivery Fleets. Retrieved from Routific.

Starship Technologies. (2023). *Autonomous Delivery Robots for Urban Food Delivery*. Retrieved from Starship Technologies.

Statista. (2023). Growth of Food Delivery Apps and Virtual Kitchens Worldwide. Retrieved from Statista.

Toast. (2023). AI in Restaurant Operations: Insights and Solutions. Retrieved from Toast.

United Nations Environment Programme (UNEP). (2021). *Global Food Waste Statistics and Solutions*. Retrieved from UNEP Website.

United States Department of Energy. (2023). AI in Energy Efficiency and Management. Retrieved from US DOE Website.

Zendesk. (2023). Enhancing Customer Service with AI Chatbots. Retrieved from Zendesk.

Zillion. (2023). AI-Based Dynamic Pricing Models for Restaurants. Retrieved from Zillion.

Chapter 10
Revolutionizing Food Preparation:
Harnessing AI Technologies to Optimize Cooking Processes and Efficiency in Ghost Kitchens

S. Thandayuthapani
https://orcid.org/0000-0001-9559-745X
Kristu Jayanti College, India

P. Elantheraiyan
VelTech Rangarajan Dr. Sagunthala R&D Institute of Science and Technology, India

P. Thirumoorthi
https://orcid.org/0000-0001-5783-3984
Periyar University, India

ABSTRACT

The emergence of artificial intelligence (AI) is transforming the culinary scene, especially within ghost kitchens that function exclusively on delivery services. This study examines how AI-driven solutions optimize cooking procedures and improve operational effectiveness. Through the application of cutting-edge technologies such as machine learning, predictive analytics, and automation, ghost kitchens can enhance food preparation, reduce waste, and maintain consistent quality. Important applications encompass inventory management and real-time monitoring, facilitating swift reactions to consumer needs. The analysis also examines obstacles such as initial capital requirements and necessary training, underscoring the significance of embracing AI to stay competitive in the changing food sector.

I. INTRODUCTION

In recent years, there has been a dramatic change in the food service sector, with ghost kitchens emerging as a notable invention driven by shifting consumer tastes and technological advancements. Often referred to as virtual or cloud kitchens, these businesses operate solely on a delivery model, eschewing

DOI: 10.4018/979-8-3373-0432-8.ch010

the traditional dine-in experience, largely due to the increasing demand for efficiency and convenience in food preparation and delivery (Küster et al., 2021). The growth of the digital food economy underscores the enormous potential of artificial intelligence (AI) technologies in ghost kitchens, offering chances to revolutionize cooking methods and improve operational efficiency.

1.1 Historical Context

Attendant with the rise of food delivery platforms due to augmentation in demand and innovation in technology, ghost kitchens surfaced. It is worth to note that the global food delivery market has shown a considerable increase during the COVID-19 pandemic Other data show that the compound annual growth rate of the market is 9.8% for 2020-2025 (Statista, 2023). Ghost kitchens do exist, nevertheless, with the emergence dating back to the late 2010s when applications like Uber Eats and Door Dash elaborated. In so doing these kitchens solved logistical problems of different sectionalization of food production and dining facilities.

AI used in food preparation can be traced from the general use of automation. First automation biases in food industry consist of conveyor belts and robotic arms for routine activities. Recently, technology applied these capabilities by using Artificial Intelligence with predictive analytics, inventory tracking and monitoring. For instance, in 2018, fast-food chains made food creation available by deploying an AI burger-making robot known as the "Creator." (Smith, 2021).

1.2 Theoretical Frameworks

AI in the ghost kitchen can also be analyzed based on sociotechnical systems theory that views technology and people interacting with each other and organizational structures. In this regards, AI technologies are tools that support organizational effectiveness and decision making. Besides, the current literature also employs the diffusion of innovation theory based on Rogers' research (Rogers, 2003) to describe the adoption of AI in the context of ghost kitchens. The perceived innovators and pioneers have also established themselves, Furioso, Shamshabad cloud kitchen that belongs to Rebel Foods and kitchen United and many more.

Another important area of theory is systems theory in which ghost kitchens are considered as systems with subsystems. AI plays a part in these systems through reconciling information from different sources encompassing order volumes, delivery routes, and stock states of the ingredients. Such an approach corresponds to the subject of the theory, namely adaptive and self-regulating systems.

1.3 The Growth in "ghost kitchens."

The food industry is undergoing a significant transformation due to the emergence of ghost kitchens. These establishments function with minimal overhead expenses, frequently employing shared commercial kitchen spaces exclusively for the preparation of food delivery (Doyle, 2020). This business model minimizes large physical infrastructure requirements, facilitating rapid scalability and adaptability in menu options. According to a report from the International Foodservice Manufacturers Association (IFMA,

2021), the popularity of food delivery services and increased reliance on online ordering platforms are driving significant expansion in the ghost kitchen industry.

Ghost kitchens serve a wide spectrum of consumer tastes, offering a variety of culinary choices from different cuisines. Adaptability is essential in a fast-evolving market where health trends, dietary limitations, and cultural influences shape consumer preferences. The capacity to swiftly adapt to these trends has emerged as a crucial characteristic of effective ghost kitchen operations, establishing them as formidable rivals to conventional restaurants (Zhang et al., 2023).

1.4 The influence of artificial intelligence on culinary processes is substantial

Incorporating AI technologies into ghost kitchens presents an innovative method for food preparation, allowing operators to enhance multiple facets of their operations. Artificial intelligence includes various technologies such as machine learning, natural language processing, and robotics, each of which has the potential to improve cooking methods and overall efficiency greatly. For example, systems enhanced by artificial intelligence can examine past sales data and customer preferences to forecast demand, enabling ghost kitchens to modify their inventory and production timelines as needed (Huang et al., 2021). This capacity for prediction reduces food waste while guaranteeing that popular menu items remain accessible, improving customer satisfaction overall.

Furthermore, AI can enhance recipe optimization by analyzing ingredient combinations and cooking techniques, resulting in the creation of dishes that align with consumer preferences while maximizing cost-effectiveness (Chen & Choi, 2023). AI algorithms can recognize patterns in dietary preferences, including plant-based and gluten-free options, allowing ghost kitchens to modify their menus according to market demands. Additionally, AI-enhanced cooking devices can monitor and adjust cooking conditions in real-time, guaranteeing consistent food quality and adherence to safety regulations (Prakash et al., 2022).

1.5 Enhancing operational efficiency

Operational efficiency plays a vital role in the success of ghost kitchens, where achieving high production volumes and ensuring timely deliveries are of utmost importance. AI technologies, such as inventory management and staff allocation, are essential for enhancing operations. The integration of AI-driven kitchen management systems allows operators to monitor inventory levels in real-time, which aids in maintaining optimal stock levels and minimizes the risk of overordering or shortages (Mason & Williams, 2022). This ability holds significant importance in the dynamic landscape of ghost kitchens, where rapid decision-making is essential.

Furthermore, the application of artificial intelligence has the potential to enhance workforce management through the analysis of employee performance and scheduling trends. By anticipating peak demand periods, ghost kitchens can enhance staff allocation, ensuring that the appropriate number of employees is present during busy times while reducing labor costs during slower periods (Elia et al., 2020). Ensuring operational agility is crucial in a competitive landscape, enabling ghost kitchens to adapt to consumer demand changes quickly.

1.6 Analyzing barriers and influences

Incorporating AI technologies in ghost kitchens brings numerous advantages but also introduces various challenges that must be tackled. A crucial aspect to consider is the initial outlay required to deploy AI systems. This can pose a financial challenge for numerous operators, particularly in setting up a ghost kitchen. Furthermore, staff training is crucial to guarantee that employees can utilize AI tools efficiently and adjust to new workflows (Bennett & Hu, 2022). Staff resistance to change can impede the successful implementation of these technologies, highlighting the importance of cultivating a culture of innovation within the organization.

Furthermore, it is essential to consider data security and privacy issues when employing AI technologies that rely on customer data for personalization and demand forecasting. Operators must adhere to applicable regulations and protect customer information to uphold trust and credibility (Thompson & McMurray, 2023). With the expansion of the ghost kitchen sector, it is essential to tackle these challenges to maximize AI's potential for optimizing cooking processes and improving overall efficiency.

1.7 The Development of Culinary Techniques

With the progression of the digital food economy, the influence of AI in ghost kitchens is anticipated to grow significantly. Industry professionals need to acknowledge the significant impact of AI technologies on improving food preparation and delivery methods, setting the stage for a more advanced culinary future. Utilizing AI to enhance operational efficiency, refine cooking methods, and optimize menu selections allows ghost kitchens to establish a foundation for ongoing growth in a competitive landscape.

II. HISTORY AND EVOLUTION OF AI TECHNOLOGIES IN GHOST KITCHENS

In recent decades, the food service industry has experienced notable transformations, highlighted by the rise of innovative concepts such as ghost kitchens. Ghost kitchens, often called cloud or virtual kitchens, function without conventional dining areas and depend exclusively on delivery and takeaway services. The growing trend of online food ordering and delivery has played a significant role in the success of this operational model. Incorporating artificial intelligence (AI) technologies in ghost kitchens signifies a significant progression in the field, focused on refining cooking processes and improving operational efficiency. This section will examine AI technologies' historical progression and transformation within ghost kitchens and the wider culinary environment.

2.1 Innovative advancements in the culinary field

The evolution of technology in the culinary field can be traced to the Industrial Revolution of the 18th century, a period marked by mechanical innovations like steam engines and food processing machinery that profoundly changed food preparation techniques. Nonetheless, it was only in the late 20th century that a significant convergence of technology and the food industry occurred, largely propelled by the emergence of computers and software applications.

With the growing complexity of food service operations, there has been a heightened demand for sophisticated systems to oversee inventory, monitor sales, and enhance workflows. The emergence of point-of-sale (POS) systems in the 1980s represented a significant advancement, enabling restaurants to digitize their operations and enhance transaction efficiency (Kimes, 2011). Although these initial innovations established a foundation for subsequent technological progress, they were constrained in their reach and only partially harnessed the possibilities of artificial intelligence.

2.2 The Rise of Ghost Kitchens

The idea of ghost kitchens emerged in the early 2000s, coinciding with the growth of food delivery services such as Grubhub and Uber Eats. The emergence of these platforms has fundamentally altered consumer access to food, leading to a notable shift in dining preferences that favors convenience and accessibility. In light of these evolving market dynamics, restaurants began investigating alternative business models, ultimately resulting in ghost kitchens' emergence (Bennett & Hu, 2022). This model enabled food entrepreneurs to function with reduced overhead expenses, removing the necessity for a physical dining establishment. With the expansion of the ghost kitchen model, those involved in the industry acknowledged the necessity to improve cooking processes and increase operational efficiency to satisfy growing consumer demands. This insight prompted an investigation into AI technologies to enhance efficiency in ghost kitchens.

2.3 The emergence of artificial intelligence technologies

In recent years, there has been a significant acceleration in the development of AI technologies, propelled by advancements in machine learning, data analytics, and automation. These technologies allow machines to learn from data, adjust to new information, and make decisions with little human involvement (Russell & Norvig, 2021). The utilization of AI in healthcare, finance, and manufacturing has shown its ability to improve efficiency and precision.

The culinary sector has started incorporating AI in various aspects, such as inventory management, recipe optimization, and customer engagement. For example, AI algorithms can examine historical sales data to forecast demand for particular dishes, enabling ghost kitchens to enhance inventory management and minimize food waste (Zhang et al., 2023). Furthermore, tools that leverage artificial intelligence in recipe development support culinary experts in crafting novel dishes by proposing ingredient pairings that resonate with consumer tastes and the latest dietary movements.

2.4 Exploring the Role of Artificial Intelligence in Ghost Kitchens

The incorporation of AI technologies in ghost kitchens has seen considerable growth in recent years, as these kitchens utilize a range of AI tools to optimize cooking processes and enhance operational efficiency. One significant domain for AI utilization is inventory management. AI systems can analyze ingredient usage data, enabling precise supply depletion forecasting. Kitchen managers can now place orders and proactively reduce waste thanks to this (Küster et al., 2021).

Moreover, AI enables ongoing observation of cooking procedures, guaranteeing that meals consistently adhere to quality benchmarks. AI-enabled ovens, for instance, can modify cooking times and temperatures by utilizing real-time feedback, enhancing food preparation precision, and minimizing human error (Prakash et al., 2022). This degree of automation improves food quality, and fosters increased consistency among dishes.

Another important application of AI in ghost kitchens involves utilizing data analytics to understand customer behavior more effectively. By examining data from online orders, AI systems can recognize trends in consumer preferences, enabling ghost kitchens to modify their menus in response to changing demands (Fang et al., 2023). This analytical approach enables operators to maintain competitiveness in an ever-evolving market environment.

2.5 Examine the obstacles and components at play

Integrating AI technologies in ghost kitchens presents a range of benefits; however, operators need to confront various critical challenges. A significant issue is the initial investment needed for AI solutions, which can pose a considerable challenge for smaller or newly established ghost kitchens. Furthermore, it is crucial to offer thorough staff training to guarantee that employees can efficiently leverage these technologies and adjust to new workflows (Mason & Williams, 2022).

With the growing dependence of ghost kitchens on AI, it is essential to address the ethical implications concerning data privacy and security. Handling customer data with care and clarity is crucial to uphold trust and adhere to regulatory requirements (Elia et al., 2020).

2.6 Potential Avenues

The evolution of AI technologies is intricately linked to the future development of ghost kitchens, which are anticipated to become increasingly advanced in alignment with the changing culinary environment. Utilizing AI allows ghost kitchens to improve operational efficiency and provide more tailored dining experiences. Significant advancements, including AI-driven chatbots for customer support and predictive analytics for adaptive menu creation, can considerably transform the ghost kitchen framework (Thompson & McMurray, 2023).

The growing emphasis on sustainability within the industry enhances the potential for AI integration. Utilizing AI to reduce food waste and enhance resource efficiency allows ghost kitchens to meet consumer demand for sustainable practices (Pérez et al., 2022).

III. LITERATURE REVIEW

This literature review examines contemporary studies on AI technologies in ghost kitchens, emphasizing their potential to enhance cooking processes and improve operational efficiency.

3.1 The Idea of Ghost Kitchens

Ghost kitchens are specialized facilities focused exclusively on food preparation for delivery, removing the need for traditional dine-in models (Kumar & Sharma, 2020). The emergence of food delivery platforms and evolving consumer preferences have driven the expansion of this model. Bhatti et al. (2021) highlight that ghost kitchens provide unique advantages, including lower overhead expenses, increased operational flexibility, and the capacity to accommodate various brands within a single venue. This adaptability allows culinary innovators to experiment with reduced risk, presenting an attractive choice for numerous individuals in the field.

3.2 Exploring the Role of AI in the Culinary Sector

AI technologies are being adopted increasingly in different areas of the food industry, including production, supply chain management, and customer engagement. Machine learning algorithms can analyze extensive datasets to uncover patterns and enhance operational efficiency (Liu et al., 2021). Predictive analytics enables ghost kitchens to anticipate demand, streamline inventory management, and modify staffing levels as needed (Chen et al., 2022). Furthermore, automation tools like robotics and AI-driven kitchen devices can optimize food preparation, minimize cooking durations, and improve consistency in food quality (Prakash et al., 2023).

3.3 Improving Cooking Skills through Artificial Intelligence

The incorporation of AI in ghost kitchens markedly improves cooking efficiency. Artificial intelligence applications can assist in creating menus by examining consumer preferences and market trends. Wang et al. (2022) illustrated that the optimization of recipes through AI can enhance the attractiveness of menu items and simultaneously decrease ingredient waste. Artificial intelligence enhances cooking methods through real-time monitoring and adjustments, guaranteeing consistent quality in dish preparation (Zhang et al., 2023).

3.4 Enhancing operational effectiveness

Considering the narrow profit margins, efficiency plays a crucial role in ghost kitchens. Artificial intelligence technologies are essential for automating tasks and enhancing workflows. Systems that utilize artificial intelligence for kitchen management can monitor inventory levels, predict shortages, and automatically place orders (Mason & Williams, 2022). This minimizes the likelihood of stock shortages and facilitates seamless operations. Furthermore, artificial intelligence can examine historical data to forecast peak periods and modify staffing levels, guaranteeing sufficient kitchen preparedness (Elia et al., 2020).

3.5 Obstacles in Implementing AI Technologies

Although AI presents significant advantages for ghost kitchens, various challenges hinder its effective implementation. The significant upfront expenses associated with AI solutions present a major challenge, particularly for smaller enterprises (Huang et al., 2021). Training staff and adapting to new technologies are crucial for effective integration (Chen & Choi, 2023). Integrating employees with AI systems may necessitate a transformation in the organizational culture. Furthermore, concerns regarding data privacy and security are paramount, given that the implementation of AI frequently entails significant customer data gathering and examination (Baker, 2021).

3.6 Prospective Pathways

The evolution of AI is intricately connected to the future of ghost kitchens, presenting additional avenues for improvement ahead. AI-driven robotics could soon facilitate automated kitchens, with machines managing every element of food preparation and cooking (Küster et al., 2021). The combination of AI and Internet of Things (IoT) devices has the potential to facilitate real-time monitoring of kitchen conditions, thereby enhancing food safety and quality control (Zhang et al., 2023).

IV. RESEARCH GAP

Although extensive studies have explored the operational and efficiency advantages of artificial intelligence (AI) in ghost kitchens, it is essential to consider these technologies' long-term sustainability and scalability, especially for small and mid-sized operators. Recent investigations highlight the influence of AI on workflow automation, demand forecasting, and menu optimization (Bhatti et al., 2021; Mason & Williams, 2022). Nevertheless, there is a need for more studies examining these technologies' impact on profitability over time or evaluating the potential risks linked to a significant dependence on automation.

While existing literature features case studies of prominent, established brands like CloudKitchens (Gonzalez & Rivera, 2023) and Rebel Foods (Thompson & McMurray, 2023), there remains a scarcity of studies focusing on how smaller ghost kitchens navigate challenges such as significant initial AI investment costs and staff adaptability (Huang et al., 2021; Chen & Choi, 2023). Furthermore, the existing gaps in workforce displacement and data privacy studies present unresolved issues related to ethical and regulatory matters, potentially influencing the adoption of AI within the sector (Baker, 2021).

Exploring these areas may yield a deeper insight into the sustainable incorporation of AI within ghost kitchens.

V. OBJECTIVES OF THE STUDY

This investigation aims to examine the impact of artificial intelligence (AI) technologies on food preparation processes within ghost kitchens, focusing on optimizing efficiency, enhancing productivity, and preserving food quality. The study will pinpoint and examine significant AI applications that have the potential to enhance operational efficiency, minimize waste, and respond to changing consumer demands in delivery-only food enterprises. The study will also assess the obstacles linked to the integration of AI in ghost kitchens and suggest actionable strategies for industry professionals to embrace these technologies successfully.

VI. STATEMENT OF THE PROBLEM

Technological advancements, especially with the rise of ghost kitchens—facilities created solely for food delivery without any dine-in options—are significantly transforming the food industry. With the shifting consumer preferences toward convenience and quality, ghost kitchens are increasingly essential to the digital food economy (Choudhury et al., 2021). Incorporating artificial intelligence technologies presents significant opportunities for these kitchens, facilitating cooking methods and enhancements of operational effectiveness.

Different areas within the food industry are progressively integrating technologies such as machine learning, data analytics, and automation to improve efficiency and enhance customer experience (Gonzalez et al., 2023). In the context of ghost kitchens, artificial intelligence can enhance inventory management by analyzing real-time sales data alongside historical trends to predict ingredient requirements. This approach aids in minimizing food waste and guarantees adequate stock levels to satisfy demand (Shah et al., 2022). Furthermore, tools driven by artificial intelligence for recipe optimization can examine consumer preferences and market trends, enabling the creation of menus specifically tailored to distinct demographics while ensuring cost efficiency.

The automation of cooking processes markedly enhances operational efficiency within ghost kitchens. Automated systems and intelligent tools manage routine tasks such as chopping, mixing, and cooking, enabling kitchen personnel to concentrate on more intricate and innovative culinary endeavors. Automation reduces the likelihood of human error, thereby improving the consistency of food quality, which is essential for ensuring customer satisfaction and loyalty (Zhang et al., 2023). Moreover, real-time monitoring systems offer instant feedback on cooking conditions, guaranteeing that food is prepared at ideal temperatures and times, thereby enhancing quality control.

While AI presents significant advantages, there are considerable challenges to its wider adoption in ghost kitchens. Operators encounter obstacles, including significant upfront investment expenses, the necessity for comprehensive employee training, and possible pushback against change (Küster et al., 2021). Confronting these challenges necessitates a methodical strategy that cultivates a culture of innovation among kitchen teams and provides continuous support and training for staff to embrace new technologies successfully.

VII. CHALLENGES, CONCERNS, AND DISCUSSIONS

Integrating artificial intelligence (AI) technologies in ghost kitchens presents significant potential for improving cooking techniques and operational effectiveness. Nonetheless, this transition brings challenges, ethical dilemmas, implications for the workforce, and regulatory concerns that require thorough examination. This section delves into these dimensions thoroughly, underpinned by pertinent literature and citations.

7.1. High Initial Capital Costs

AI technology requires a substantial initial capital investment when implementing the technology in ghost kitchens. Automated order management, purchase of robotic arms for culinary use, pacakge, or point-checking systems may call for a huge investment. These costs could include such things as adaptations needed to the physical infrastructure for the new systems and the final systems – the hardware and software. Furthermore, that's where investors may raise questions about these high-tech solutions' viability, which puts small and medium-sized operators of ghost kitchens in a dilemma (Ahmed & Lall, 2023).

7.2. Workforce Training and Skill Development

AI implementation into culinary processes means subsequent training of the workforce on the use of these technological applications. They are required to achieve proficiency levels in terms of technical knowledge to be able to manage the automated machinery and fix arising problems as well as learn how to handle new systems of working. This transition can be difficult since a lot of people working in the kitchen probably do not have technology background and so the training procedures need to be very intensive. The same programs even add some operational expenses, and they require time and efforts that might be utilized in conducting daily activities. This is made worse by employees' resistance to change which makes the adoption process more challenging (Smith et al., 2022).

7.3. Data Management and Integration

AI implementation into culinary processes means subsequent training of the workforce on the use of these technological applications. They are required to achieve proficiency levels in terms of technical knowledge to be able to manage the automated machinery and fix arising problems as well as learn how to handle new systems of working. This transition can be difficult since a lot of people working in the kitchen probably do not have technology background and so the training procedures need to be very intensive. The same programs even add some operational expenses, and they require time and efforts that might be utilized in conducting daily activities. This is made worse by employees' resistance to change which makes the adoption process more challenging (Smith et al., 2022).

7.4. High Maintenance and Upkeep Costs

AI systems are as human and thus need constant servicing to ensure it is operating at its peak. This entails Perform software upgrades and renewals, Hardware replacement and rebalancing of more so sensors in a robotic system. The tasks mentioned above are usually executed by specialized technicians which results in other costs. As was established in the case of fixed costs, such repeating costs can be costly for small ghost kitchens, and manage to discourage adoption of AI-aided solutions (Chowdhury & Nguyen, 2023).

7.5. Technological Obsolescence

AI technologies are therefore always in a state of development with many new developments being made often time. The rate at which products are being developed and enhanced poses a risk to existing systems. Some of the ghost kitchens could be using current trending AI technologies in their systems but in the next few years those technologies may become less useful, and these lead to repeated costs of acquiring new technologies. Such a cycle of ongoing investments can discourage operators from making sufficient investments that will lead to the adoption of advanced AI systems (Brown & Wilson, 2022).

7.6. Limited Customization and Flexibility

The strengths of AI found in its ability to perform routine and rule-based tasks and its dependency on the flexibility that is difficult to achieve in the culinary industry. The use of Artificial intelligence may also prove cumbersome to ghost kitchens within areas such as menu management or when trying to incorporate certain requests from customers. The reduction of variability within digital processes also presents a major challenge when it comes to the creation of algorithms that are able to deal with this particular issue: research & development is time-consuming and expensive, and according to the estimates provided by author Lee in 2024, this particular issue may become one of the major obstacles to widespread use of such technologies.

7.7. Regulatory and Compliance Issues

Introducing AI in food preparation opens new regulatory issues, most especially regarding food hygiene and employment. Governments and industrial bodies are still in the process of developing codes for ethics and working of AI in food services. Those ghost kitchens that have incorporated the use of AI must overcome these changing regulations that might differ from one region to another something that compounds the operations (Thompson, 2023).

7.8. Consumer Perception and Acceptance

While implementing the retention strategies that could be introduced by the help of AI may be useful for the business operating a restaurant, some clients may have concerns about the meals prepared by robots, and consider the meals more unemotional than the ones that could be cooked by different people. Dispelling such perceptions is about the right marketing campaigns that would aim at depicting the AI capability to deliver quality, standard and safe food preparation (Garcia & Wong, 2023).

7.9. Dependence on Reliable Infrastructure

The systems used in ghost kitchens include artificial intelligence and need to work well through the internet and electricity. Disruption of any of these services cause operational havoc and in some cases outright cessation of service. Backup systems and facilities for the management of such risks is another challenge that operators of ghost kitchens face when investing (Singh et al., 2024).

7.10 Ethical Considerations in AI Implementation

Implementing AI in ghost kitchens presents considerable ethical concerns regarding data privacy, transparency, and accountability. AI systems frequently depend on extensive datasets that can contain sensitive customer information. Compliance with data protection regulations, including the General Data Protection Regulation (GDPR) in the European Union, is crucial to prevent privacy breaches that can lead to significant legal and reputational repercussions (Voigt & Von dem Bussche, 2017). Furthermore, clarity is essential since consumers may need help understanding how their information is utilized to tailor food choices or enhance delivery services. More transparency may undermine consumer confidence and elevate ethical issues regarding changing preferences. Organizations need to articulate their data practices transparently to guarantee the ethical implementation of AI (Zarsky, 2016).

7.11 Challenges in Operations

Although AI has the potential to enhance efficiency, integrating these technologies necessitates considerable modifications in kitchen workflows, which could lead to a transformation of conventional cooking methods. Established ghost kitchens might face challenges during this transition, as it has the potential to disrupt current processes, leading to temporary inefficiencies and heightened costs (Sweeney et al., 2021). Furthermore, a significant dependence on AI systems introduces potential hazards; for example, a failure in an AI-driven inventory management system could result in stock shortages or surpluses, adversely impacting operations. Consequently, ghost kitchens must develop contingency plans to reduce these risks and ensure operational stability (Kumar et al., 2022).

7.12 Implications for the Workforce

The integration of AI into ghost kitchens carries substantial implications for the workforce. Implementing AI can enhance efficiency and minimize the reliance on manual labor in certain sectors, which may result in job displacement, especially among low-skilled workers (Bessen, 2019). This scenario prompts significant apprehension regarding the long-term employment stability for individuals who need the necessary skills to collaborate effectively with AI technologies. Furthermore, the integration of AI could necessitate the retraining of personnel, leading to increased expenses and the need for resource distribution. There may be resistance to these changes among employees, from concerns about job security to the necessity to transition into more technical positions (Frey & Osborne, 2017). Operators of ghost kitchens need to thoughtfully weigh the advantages of AI against the necessity of supporting their employees to navigate workforce dynamics effectively.

7.13 Standards for Food Safety and Quality

Artificial intelligence presents avenues for improving food safety and quality control in ghost kitchens by utilizing real-time monitoring and predictive analytics. Nonetheless, dependence on automated systems presents possible hazards. For example, AI systems may overlook food safety concerns and unintentionally distribute contaminated products (Marr, 2018). It is crucial to have human oversight to guarantee adherence to food safety regulations and uphold superior quality standards. Excessive dependence on AI may foster a sense of complacency among employees; thus, ongoing training is essential to cultivate a culture of accountability regarding food safety (Bennett et al., 2022).

7.14 Economic Influences and Competitive Interactions

Integrating AI in ghost kitchens could transform the competitive landscape of the food industry. The growing adoption of AI among operators raises concerns about market saturation, which could lead to heightened competition and price wars, ultimately squeezing profit margins. This could lead ghost kitchens to focus more on reducing costs than enhancing quality and fostering innovation (Huang et al., 2021). Furthermore, a widening gap may emerge between well-capitalized ghost kitchens utilizing cutting-edge AI technologies and smaller operators who lack the financial means for such investments, resulting in market inequalities (Gonzalez & Rivera, 2023). Industry stakeholders need to investigate methods that foster equity, allowing smaller operators to leverage the potential of AI.

7.15 Acceptance and Perception of Consumers

Consumers' acceptance of AI technologies in food preparation plays a vital role in the success of ghost kitchens. Although numerous customers value ghost kitchens' convenience and efficiency, some may be reluctant to accept automated food preparation fully. Certain consumers may favor meals crafted by human chefs, linking this choice to notions of quality and attention (Pereira et al., 2021). To tackle these issues, ghost kitchens should highlight AI's advantages, focusing on improving food safety, consistency, and convenience. Using fresh ingredients and offering customization options could alleviate consumer concerns regarding AI-driven cooking methods (Zhang et al., 2023).

7.16 Challenges in Regulation

The rapid adoption of AI in the food industry has created significant regulatory challenges. The current food safety regulations seem to fall short of meeting the specific needs of AI-driven operations, which leaves ghost kitchens in the dark (Wang et al., 2021). Those in positions of authority must create clear guidelines that consider AI's effects on food safety, quality, and workforce issues. The global food industry makes things more complicated because different regions may have different standards for food safety and technological applications, which makes it difficult for ghost kitchens operating globally to remain compliant (Nath et al., 2020).

VIII. SUGGESTIONS OF THE STUDY

8. 1. Deploy AI-Enhanced Inventory Management Systems

Ghost kitchens need help managing their inventory efficiently, as traditional methods often lead to overstocking or stockouts, resulting in wasted resources and lost sales. To address these issues, implementing AI-driven inventory management systems can leverage predictive analytics to forecast demand based on historical sales data, seasonal trends, and current market conditions (Kumar et al., 2021). Machine learning algorithms can analyze factors such as weekdays, holidays, and local events to optimize inventory management. Additionally, automatic reordering systems can be established to place orders when inventory reaches predetermined levels, reducing stockout risk and minimizing manual oversight (Chaudhary & Verma, 2022). Moreover, creating real-time communication channels with suppliers allows ghost kitchens to adjust orders based on current inventory levels and expected demand, enabling them to respond more effectively to changes in customer behavior (Sharma et al., 2023).

8.2. Enhance Recipes and Culinary Procedures Using Artificial Intelligence

AI technologies can significantly enhance recipe optimization by analyzing consumer preferences and ingredient interactions, leading to innovative recipes. Using AI-driven systems, ghost kitchens can develop recipes that align with current market trends, drawing insights from consumer preferences identified through social media, online reviews, and sales data (Zhang et al., 2023). AI can also suggest ingredient alternatives based on dietary restrictions or desired flavor profiles, increasing menu inclusivity. Furthermore, investing in AI-powered culinary devices, such as intelligent ovens and robotic chefs, can automate various cooking processes, ensuring consistent quality while adapting cooking times and temperatures based on real-time data (Kumar & Singh, 2022). Establishing a feedback mechanism for customers to evaluate dishes allows the AI system to learn from these reviews and recommend recipe adjustments, enhancing overall customer satisfaction (Bennett & Hu, 2022).

8.3. Establish Real-Time Monitoring Systems

To enhance food safety and quality, ghost kitchens must implement real-time monitoring of culinary operations. AI technology can track factors like temperature, humidity, and cooking times to ensure compliance with health regulations. By integrating Internet of Things (IoT) devices with AI systems, ghost kitchens can continuously monitor cooking equipment and environmental conditions, providing instant alerts if any deviations occur (Choudhury et al., 2022). Additionally, utilizing data analytics to compare cooking outcomes with established standards enables AI-driven quality control systems to analyze visual data from cameras or sensors, helping identify food preparation discrepancies (Lee & Choi, 2023). Training kitchen staff to effectively use real-time monitoring technologies is essential, enabling them to respond promptly to alerts and uphold quality standards in food preparation (Chen & Choi, 2023).

8.4. Augment Customer Engagement with Artificial Intelligence

In the competitive landscape of ghost kitchens, understanding and engaging customers is vital for success. AI technologies can significantly enhance personalized experiences that build customer loyalty and satisfaction. By analyzing customer data, ghost kitchens can tailor marketing strategies to individual preferences, such as personalized email recommendations and targeted promotions based on past orders, thus improving consumer engagement (Fang et al., 2023). Additionally, deploying AI-driven chatbots on websites and social media can provide immediate assistance, answer questions, process orders, and offer tailored suggestions based on user preferences (Zhou et al., 2022). Furthermore, AI can help develop loyalty programs that incentivize repeat purchases, such as personalized discounts based on purchasing history, thereby increasing customer retention (Teece, 2018). Collectively, these strategies enhance customer engagement and satisfaction in the ghost kitchen sector.

8.5. Allocate Resources for Employee Training and Development

The successful implementation of AI technology in ghost kitchens largely depends on employee expertise, necessitating significant investment in comprehensive training and development programs. These programs should focus on technical skills relevant to AI systems and soft skills like communication and collaboration. Regular workshops and hands-on training sessions should be conducted to boost staff confidence and performance (Mason & Williams, 2022). Incorporating AI-driven training simulations can provide immersive experiences that help staff acclimate to new equipment and procedures, leading to improved learning outcomes (Chen & Choi, 2023). Fostering a culture of feedback is also critical for continuous improvement; by encouraging employees to share their insights on AI systems and operational practices, ghost kitchens can identify areas that require additional training and development, thus nurturing a more agile and skilled workforce (Elia et al., 2020). This holistic approach to employee training ensures that staff are well-prepared to effectively utilize AI technologies, enhancing operational efficiency and success within the ghost kitchen environment.

8.6. Adopt sustainable practices using artificial intelligence

As sustainability becomes increasingly important to consumers, ghost kitchens can utilize AI technologies to implement eco-friendly practices that enhance their brand image and align with consumer expectations. AI systems can analyze waste patterns and recommend strategies to minimize excess, such as suggesting ingredient use based on previous data, thus reducing overall food waste (Pérez et al., 2022). Additionally, AI can improve sustainable sourcing by identifying local suppliers that adhere to environmentally responsible practices, allowing ghost kitchens to partner with vendors that support their sustainability goals (Thompson & McMurray, 2023). Furthermore, AI can evaluate packaging materials and recommend environmentally friendly alternatives, ensuring that ghost kitchens utilize sustainable packaging options that appeal to eco-conscious consumers and foster brand loyalty (Galan et al., 2021). By leveraging AI in these areas, ghost kitchens can significantly enhance their environmental sustainability while attracting a growing segment of environmentally aware consumers.

8.7. Observe industry trends and adjust strategically

The food industry constantly evolves, necessitating that ghost kitchens remain flexible and responsive to changing trends and consumer preferences. Utilizing AI-driven analytics tools for trend analysis enables businesses to monitor market dynamics, consumer behaviors, and competitor activities, informing strategic decisions regarding menu offerings and marketing initiatives (Kumar et al., 2021). Implementing agile operational frameworks is crucial for rapid adaptations to shifts in consumer demand or market conditions; for instance, quickly modifying menu items or cooking methods based on trend analysis can significantly enhance competitiveness (Porter, 2022). Additionally, fostering a culture of continuous learning within the organization is vital, as it keeps employees informed about market trends and encourages knowledge sharing. This approach promotes innovation and enhances adaptability, proactively allowing ghost kitchens to respond to market fluctuations (Robinson, 2021). By adopting these strategies, ghost kitchens can position themselves for success in a dynamic food landscape.

8.8. Engage in Collaboration with Technological Partners

To maximize the benefits of AI technologies, ghost kitchens should consider forming partnerships with technology providers specializing in AI solutions for the food industry. These collaborations can significantly enhance the deployment of advanced systems tailored to specific operational needs. Initially, it is crucial to research and identify suitable technology partners, evaluating their experience, technical capabilities, and support services (Zhang et al., 2023). Implementing pilot programs to test new AI technologies before full-scale deployment can reveal potential challenges and opportunities for optimization, facilitating a smoother transition to new systems (Fang et al., 2023). Furthermore, maintaining ongoing communication with technology partners to provide feedback on system performance is essential; this collaboration can drive continuous improvements and advancements in technology, ultimately enhancing the operational efficiency and service quality of ghost kitchens (Chen & Choi, 2023). Ghost kitchens can effectively leverage AI technologies to improve their culinary processes and overall productivity by strategically collaborating with the right technology suppliers.

IX. CONCLUSION

Integrating artificial intelligence (AI) technologies into ghost kitchens offers a pivotal opportunity to enhance cooking processes and boost operational efficiency, thereby transforming the culinary landscape. This study highlights the essential role of AI in tackling the unique challenges ghost kitchens face, such as fluctuating demand, labor shortages, and the necessity for consistent food quality. By implementing AI-driven solutions, ghost kitchens can streamline operations, improve customer satisfaction, and remain competitive in an increasingly crowded market. A significant finding of this study is that AI technologies can greatly enhance the efficiency of food preparation. Applications like predictive analytics and machine learning algorithms empower ghost kitchens to forecast customer demand accurately, optimize inventory management, and minimize food waste (Huang et al., 2021). With precise demand forecasting, kitchens can adjust their production schedules, reducing the chances of overproduction and waste. This boosts opera and enhances operational efficiency and goals in the food industry, as minimizing waste is a growing concern for consumers (Zhang et al., 2023). The study also underscores the importance of AI in maintaining consistent food quality, which is crucial for fostering customer loyalty. AI-powered automated cooking systems can monitor and adjust cooking parameters in real time, ensuring optimal results in temperature and cooking times (Gonzalez & Rivera, 2023). This technology guarantees uniformity across batches, so customers receive the same high-quality experience with every order.

Furthermore, AI-driven feedback systems can gather and analyze customer reviews, enabling ghost kitchens to make data-informed adjustments to their menus and cooking techniques, thus elevating customer satisfaction (Robinson, 2021). Nonetheless, it is vital to acknowledge the challenges of implementing AI technologies. These include initial investment costs and the need for staff training. However, the long-term benefits of adopting such innovations significantly outweigh these initial hurdles. Ghost kitchens that embrace AI technologies are better positioned for success in a rapidly evolving culinary landscape. This investment helps organizations meet current consumer demands and equips them to adapt to future market trends (Baker, 2021).

Moreover, fostering a culture of innovation within ghost kitchens is crucial for the effective adoption of AI. Transitioning to AI technologies requires a shift in mindset among industry professionals, concentrating on continual improvement and adaptability to new tools and methods. Training and development initiatives should emphasize enhancing AI literacy and promoting culinary innovation to maximize the advantages of these technologies (Chen & Choi, 2023). In conclusion, transforming food preparation through AI technologies is not simply a passing trend; it is essential for ghost kitchens aiming to thrive in the digital food economy. Ghost kitchens can establish themselves as leaders in the future culinary landscape by optimizing cooking processes, ensuring consistent quality, and embracing innovative practices. As consumer preferences increasingly favor convenience and quality, the strategic adoption of AI technologies will be vital for industry professionals striving to redefine standards and achieve operational excellence.

X. FUTURE OF FURTHER RESEARCH

The development of AI technologies to enhance cooking processes in ghost kitchens offers a wealth of opportunities for investigation. An important focus of the investigation is the long-term impacts of AI-driven automation on labor dynamics in the culinary industry. Examining the impact of AI integration on workforce needs, employee responsibilities, and job satisfaction will yield important insights into harmonizing technology with human participation (Baker et al., 2021).

Furthermore, subsequent investigations might explore the scalability of AI solutions in ghost kitchens within various geographical and cultural settings, evaluating the influence of local consumer preferences on the effective implementation of these technologies (Galan et al., 2021).

A vital focus for continued investigation is the creation of AI algorithms that forecast food trends and consumer behaviors, allowing ghost kitchens to modify their menus proactively (Zhang et al., 2023). Additionally, it is crucial to examine the ethical implications of AI in food preparation, including data privacy and algorithmic bias, as the industry progresses (Chen & Choi, 2023).

Ultimately, studies that compare the performance of AI-enhanced ghost kitchens with traditional food service models can provide valuable insights into the efficiency improvements and potential challenges of this innovative approach (Mason & Williams, 2022).

In conclusion, additional investigation should focus on creating a thorough comprehension of how to effectively incorporate AI technologies into ghost kitchens, establishing a foundation for a more advanced culinary future.

REFERENCES

Ahmed, R., & Lall, S. (2023). AI-driven innovations in culinary spaces: Challenges and prospects. *Journal of Food Technology*, *15*(3), 45–57.

Baker, J. (2021). The impact of technology on food service efficiency. *Journal of Food Service Management*, *15*(3), 215–228.

Baker, J., Smith, R., & Lee, K. (2021). The future of work in the food industry: Automation and employment dynamics. *Journal of Culinary Innovation*, *15*(2), 45–62.

Baker, L. (2021). Data privacy and AI in ghost kitchens. *Journal of Food Technology*, *12*(4), 234–248.

Bennett, R., & Hu, J. (2022). Exploring the impact of technology on restaurant operations: A focus on ghost kitchens. *International Journal of Hospitality Management*, *102*, 102–110. DOI: 10.1016/j.ijhm.2021.102110

Bennett, R., & Hu, J. (2022). Food safety challenges in the digital age: Managing AI technologies in ghost kitchens. *Journal of Food Safety*, *42*(1), e12898. DOI: 10.1111/jfs.12898

Bennett, R. J., & Hu, H. (2022). Cloud kitchens: The future of food delivery. *Journal of Foodservice Business Research*, *25*(3), 145–162. DOI: 10.1080/15378020.2021.1965462

Bennett, R. J., & Hu, W. (2022). Recipe optimization using machine learning. *Journal of Culinary Science & Technology*, *20*(4), 327–343. DOI: 10.1080/15428052.2022.1932846

Bessen, J. E. (2019). AI and jobs: The role of demand. *NBER Working Paper Series No. 24235*.

Bhatti, A., Iqbal, R., & Ahmad, S. (2021). Ghost kitchens: A new frontier in the restaurant industry. *Journal of Hospitality and Tourism Technology*, *12*(3), 427–440. DOI: 10.1108/JHTT-04-2020-0068

Bhatti, A., Sharma, P., & Lee, C. (2021). Operational benefits of ghost kitchens. *Food Service Management*, *45*(3), 117–129.

Brown, T., & Wilson, A. (2022). The economics of AI in food services. *International Journal of Hospitality Management*, *34*(2), 67–79.

Chaudhary, A., & Verma, S. (2022). Inventory management in ghost kitchens: A new approach. *Food Service Technology*, *22*(1), 15–29.

Chen, C., & Choi, Y. (2023). Employee adaptation to AI technologies in the hospitality sector: Challenges and strategies. *International Journal of Hospitality Management*, *109*, 102807. DOI: 10.1016/j.ijhm.2023.102807

Chen, H., & Choi, S. (2023). Training staff for AI integration in the culinary industry. *International Journal of Hospitality Management*, *94*, 102895. DOI: 10.1016/j.ijhm.2023.102895

Chen, J., & Choi, K. (2023). The role of artificial intelligence in enhancing restaurant service quality: Evidence from ghost kitchens. *Journal of Foodservice Business Research*, *26*(1), 56–74. DOI: 10.1080/15378020.2022.2107483

Chen, J., Zhang, X., & Li, L. (2022). Predictive analytics in food service management: A systematic review. *Journal of Foodservice Business Research, 25*(1), 1–20. DOI: 10.1080/15378020.2021.1936272

Chen, M., & Choi, J. (2023). Fostering innovation in the food industry: Training and development in the age of AI. *International Journal of Culinary Arts, 7*(1), 45–60.

Chen, Y., & Choi, T. (2023). Ethical considerations in the application of AI technologies in the food service sector. *International Journal of Food Industry Management, 22*(1), 12–28.

Chen, Z., & Choi, T. (2023). AI workforce adaptation in the food industry. *Technology in Society, 18*(2), 130–142.

Choudhury, A., El Masri, Y., & Paredes, M. (2021). The rise of ghost kitchens in the digital food economy: Trends and implications. *Journal of Foodservice Business Research, 24*(2), 115–134. DOI: 10.1080/15378020.2021.1875562

Choudhury, A., Sinha, P., & Purohit, H. (2022). Real-time monitoring in kitchens: Enhancing food safety. *Food Safety Journal, 10*(1), 45-57.Doyle, R. (2020). Ghost kitchens: The future of food delivery. *Food & Beverage Magazine*. Retrieved from https://www.foodandbeverage.com/ghost-kitchens

Chowdhury, P., & Nguyen, V. (2023). Sustainability and automation in ghost kitchens. *Sustainability in Food Systems, 9*(4), 321–340.

Elia, G., Galli, P., & Sweeney, E. (2020). Data analytics in food service: Implications for sustainability. *Sustainability, 12*(5), 1983. DOI: 10.3390/su12051983

Fang, Y., Wu, H., & Li, C. (2023). Understanding consumer preferences for delivery services: An analysis of ghost kitchens. *International Journal of Hospitality Management, 98*, 103091. DOI: 10.1016/j.ijhm.2023.103091

Fang, Y., Zhao, L., & Cheng, L. (2023). Trend analysis in the food industry: A machine learning approach. *Journal of Retailing and Consumer Services, 69*, 102978. DOI: 10.1016/j.jretconser.2023.102978

Frey, C. B., & Osborne, M. A. (2017). The future of employment: How susceptible are jobs to computerization? *Technological Forecasting and Social Change, 114*, 254–280. DOI: 10.1016/j.techfore.2016.08.019

Galan, L., Morris, J., & Corcoran, P. (2021). Sustainable sourcing practices in ghost kitchens. *Sustainability, 13*(15), 8175. DOI: 10.3390/su13158175

Galan, P., Lopez, J., & Ramirez, M. (2021). Localizing ghost kitchens: A case study on consumer preferences. *Food Research International, 138*, 109745. DOI: 10.1016/j.foodres.2020.109745

Garcia, L., & Wong, M. (2023). Consumer behavior in the age of AI-driven food services. *Marketing Trends Journal, 12*(1), 90–102.

Gonzalez, A., & Rivera, J. (2023). Market dynamics in the ghost kitchen industry: The impact of AI technologies. *International Journal of Hospitality Management, 105*, 102514. DOI: 10.1016/j.ijhm.2022.102514

Gonzalez, M., & Rivera, L. (2023). Case studies in ghost kitchen operations: How technology drives success. *Journal of Culinary Science & Technology, 21*(2), 159–176. DOI: 10.1080/15428052.2022.2098345

Gonzalez, R., Rivera, M., & Sharma, P. (2023). Artificial intelligence in food service: Revolutionizing operational efficiency. *International Journal of Hospitality Management, 108*, 102737. DOI: 10.1016/j.ijhm.2023.102737

Huang, J.. (2021). Analyzing consumer preferences for ghost kitchens: Insights from a survey study. *International Journal of Contemporary Hospitality Management, 33*(3), 1020–1036. DOI: 10.1108/IJCHM-05-2020-0497

Huang, L., & Adams, T. (2021). AI investment challenges in small businesses. *Journal of Food Technology, 10*(2), 92–106.

Huang, W., Chen, H., & Wu, H. (2021). Challenges and strategies for ghost kitchen operations in the digital economy. *Journal of Foodservice Business Research, 24*(3), 270–290. DOI: 10.1080/15378020.2021.1913491

Huang, Y., Li, X., & Chen, W. (2021). Predictive analytics in the restaurant industry: Enhancing operational efficiency through technology. *Food Service Research, 12*(4), 300–314.

Huang, Z., Yang, L., & Xu, W. (2021). Competition in the ghost kitchen industry: An analysis of market saturation and consumer preferences. *Food Policy, 100*, 102035. DOI: 10.1016/j.foodpol.2020.102035

International Foodservice Manufacturers Association (IFMA). (2021). The rise of ghost kitchens and their impact on the foodservice industry. Retrieved from https://www.ifmaworld.com/reports/ghost-kitchens

Kimes, S. E. (2011). The evolution of the restaurant industry: A historical perspective. *Journal of Foodservice Business Research, 14*(4), 283–297. DOI: 10.1080/15378020.2011.626777

Kumar, A., & Singh, R. (2022). Automating cooking processes with AI technologies. *Culinary Science Review, 16*(3), 211–225.

Kumar, S., Gupta, V., & Singh, A. (2022). Operational challenges in ghost kitchens: A case for AI integration. *Culinary Science and Technology, 19*(2), 132–146.

Kumar, S., Singh, A., & Gupta, R. (2021). The impact of predictive analytics on inventory management. *Journal of Operations Management, 67*(2), 88–104. DOI: 10.1016/j.jom.2020.101295

Kumar, V., & Sharma, R. (2020). The rise of ghost kitchens: A new model. *Food Industry Trends, 3*(4), 215–228.

Küster, I., Callado, A., & Gonzalez, J. (2021). AI-driven innovations in the food industry: A new paradigm for culinary success. *Food Research International, 140*, 110060. DOI: 10.1016/j.foodres.2020.110060

Küster, I., Hartmann, N., & Wulf, T. (2021). Operational challenges and technological innovations in ghost kitchens. *British Food Journal, 123*(9), 3000–3014. DOI: 10.1108/BFJ-09-2020-0804

Küster, I., Vargas, M. A., & Ochoa, A. (2021). Artificial intelligence in the restaurant industry: A systematic review. *Journal of Culinary Science & Technology, 19*(1), 1–20. DOI: 10.1080/15428052.2020.1731591

Lee, H., & Choi, J. (2023). Quality control in smart kitchens: A review. *Journal of Food Science and Technology, 60*(7), 3645–3654. DOI: 10.1007/s13197-022-05454-7

Lee, J. (2024). Customizing AI for culinary applications: A case study approach. *Advances in AI Applications*, *18*(2), 210–230.

Liu, Y., Zhang, T., & Zhang, Y. (2021). Artificial intelligence in the food industry: Applications and trends. *Trends in Food Science & Technology*, *116*, 1–13. DOI: 10.1016/j.tifs.2021.06.012

Marr, B. (2018). How artificial intelligence is changing food safety. *Forbes*. Retrieved from https://www.forbes.com/sites/bernardmarr/2018/07/23/how-artificial-intelligence-is-changing-food-safety

Mason, C., & Williams, P. (2022). Employee training in ghost kitchens: Enhancing performance through technology. *International Journal of Hospitality Management*, *98*, 103094. DOI: 10.1016/j.ijhm.2021.103094

Mason, J., & Williams, K. (2022). Workforce management in the era of ghost kitchens: Challenges and opportunities. *Journal of Hospitality and Tourism Management*, *50*, 18–27. DOI: 10.1016/j.jhtm.2021.10.001

Mason, J., & Williams, S. (2022). AI in inventory management for ghost kitchens. *Journal of Operations*, *23*(6), 54–67.

Mason, M., & Williams, D. (2022). Assessing the performance of ghost kitchens: The role of technology in efficiency. *Journal of Hospitality & Tourism Research (Washington, D.C.)*, *46*(3), 509–527.

Nath, V., Singh, P., & Kumar, A. (2020). Regulatory challenges in the food industry: AI, food safety, and compliance. *Food Control*, *118*, 107358.

Pereira, R., Vázquez, J. L., & Freire, M. (2021). Consumer perceptions of artificial intelligence in food preparation: The human touch versus automation. *Food Quality and Preference*, *87*, 104069.

Pérez, J., Cárdenas, C., & Ayala, F. (2022). Waste reduction strategies in ghost kitchens: An exploratory study. *Waste Management (New York, N.Y.)*, *136*, 99–106.

Shah, S., Verma, R., & Gupta, A. (2022). Smart kitchens: Harnessing technology for sustainable food production. *Sustainability*, *14*(1), 15–30. DOI: 10.3390/su14010015

Singh, D.. (2024). Infrastructure requirements for AI in food operations. *IEEE Transactions on Automation*, *30*(1), 78–85.

Smith, K.. (2022). Upskilling the workforce for AI integration. *HR Innovations Journal*, *11*(4), 56–70.

Thompson, H. (2023). Regulatory frameworks for AI in food services. *International Journal of Law and Technology*, *22*(2), 112–127.

Thompson, H., & McMurray, D. (2023). AI demand forecasting in ghost kitchens. *Food Management Today*, *8*(3), 134–148.

Wang, S., Xu, K., & Liu, Z. (2022). AI in menu optimization: Enhancing culinary creativity and reducing waste. *Journal of Foodservice Management & Education*, *15*(1), 25–35.

Zhang, L., Huang, Y., & Wong, J. (2023). Predictive analytics in the food service industry: Leveraging AI for menu optimization. *Journal of Food Science and Technology*, *60*(5), 3215–3227.

Zhang, Q., Chen, Y., & Liu, R. (2023). Consumer engagement in AI-powered ghost kitchens: The role of marketing strategies. *Journal of Marketing Theory and Practice*, *31*(1), 55–72.

Zhang, X., Wang, Y., & Liu, J. (2023). Leveraging data analytics for menu optimization in ghost kitchens. *Journal of Foodservice Management & Education*, *18*(2), 117–133.

Zhang, Y., Lee, S., & Kim, J. (2023). Sustainable practices in ghost kitchens: Reducing food waste through AI technologies. *Journal of Sustainable Food Systems*, *8*(1), 67–80.

Zhang, Y., Liu, H., & Chen, J. (2023). Automation and AI in food preparation: Innovations for the future. *Food Quality and Preference*, *92*, 104282. DOI: 10.1016/j.foodqual.2021.104282

Chapter 11
Eco-Friendly Practices of Ghost Kitchens Through Smart Technology

Arvind Chauhan
https://orcid.org/0000-0002-3647-2988
Chhatrapati Shahu Ji Maharaj University, Kanpur, India

Saurabh Tripathi
https://orcid.org/0000-0002-6937-5703
Chhatrapati Shahu Ji Maharaj University, Kanpur, India

Sujay Vikram Singh
https://orcid.org/0000-0002-7113-2698
Amity University, Lucknow, India

Kuldeep Singh
https://orcid.org/0000-0002-7999-1585
Amity University, Haryana, India

Mohammad Badruddoza Talukdar
https://orcid.org/0009-0008-1662-9221
International University of Business Agriculture and Technology, Bangladesh

ABSTRACT

Ghost kitchens, referred to as cloud or virtual kitchens, are revolutionizing the food service sector in reaction to increasing food delivery needs. Nonetheless, their swift rise has presented issues, such as heightened energy use, food waste, and excessive packaging. This chapter examines the potential of new technologies to enhance operations in ghost kitchens while promoting sustainable practices. It underscores the necessity for supportive policies and regulatory frameworks to facilitate extensive green adoption within the virtual kitchen ecosystem. Utilizing contemporary technologies and sustainable practices, ghost kitchens can minimize their carbon footprint and prosper in the developing carbon-neutral market. The chapter emphasizes successful instances of sustainable practices in ghost kitchens and illustrates the function of data analytics in assessing and alleviating environmental problems. It

DOI: 10.4018/979-8-3373-0432-8.ch011

seeks to direct stakeholders

1. INTRODUCTION

Over the past 10 years, ghost kitchens, also referred to as virtual or cloud kitchens, have turned the international food industry on its head. "Dark kitchens are delivery-only facilities that do not include dine-in areas; they release only meals made through online food orders". The growth of this business model has accelerated thanks to food delivery platforms like Uber Eats, Door Dash, and Deliveroo. At the same time, more sustainably focused thought has emerged worldwide pressuring industries, food service included, to "go green". By centralizing your operations with a ghost kitchen, your resource usage is optimized and waste can be reduced, concentrating on bringing out the best of what you do. By putting several brands under one roof, these kitchens streamline supply chains, cut down on food waste and decrease energy use. But when not carefully managed, they can engender the same systems-level environmental challenges that traditional restaurants grapple with, such as packaging waste, logistical inefficiencies, and high carbon emissions. To solve these problems, ghost kitchens are leveraging smart technology like the Internet of Things (IoT), Artificial Intelligence (AI) & data-driven inventory. Such technologies assist with energy consumption monitoring and optimization, food stock management to prevent food waste, and sustainable packaging practices. Predictive demand forecasting powered by AI-driven analytics is allowing supermarkets to prepare food in response to real-time consumer demand, minimizing waste of excess inventory. Kitchen automation also improves operational efficiency, saving costs and decreasing the environmental footprint. However, the sustainable practices of ghost kitchens rely on their strategic planning as well as the proper execution of their green measures. Some are using energy efficient appliances in their kitchens, making use of biodegradable or recyclable packaging, and incorporating electric delivery vehicles to reduce carbon footprints. Also helps in better justification for sustainably sourced ingredients through proper chain of ecosystem built on blockchain.

The Environmental Challenges of Traditional Kitchens

Traditional restaurants and food service operations have a lot of environmental issues. These include food waste, energy consumption, and non-sustainable packaging. Unless managed properly, ghost kitchens can face similar challenges (Kulshrestha & Sharma, 2022). However, understanding the environmental impact of traditional kitchens helps appreciate the steps that ghost kitchens are taking toward sustainability.

- **Food Waste:** Restaurants form a huge category of food wastage in the world. United Nations says one third of total food produced is wasted and it is restaurants who contribute to that large amount of wastage. Food is wasted at different levels like storage, preparation, and food left by the customers themselves from their order.
- **Energy Consumption:** The conventional kitchen consumes energy by running stoves, ovens, refrigerators, and dishwashers. Not to mention the heating, ventilation, and air conditioning (HVAC) required making a comfortable space for staff as well as guests. All these sources of energy increase electricity and gas consumption.
- **Carbon Emissions in Supply Chains:** Generally, supply chains for traditional restaurants are multi-step sequences that start from the production of any ingredient and continue until that ingredient reaches the final restaurant location. Every step in the supply chain contributes to carbon emissions through a restaurant.

- **Non-recyclable packaging:** Restaurants use one-time plastics and non-biodegradable takeout and delivery packaging materials. Once used, most of them usually end up in landfills or oceans and thus create environmental pollution.
- **Water Waste:** Many traditional restaurants are guilty of wasting water in their prepping, cleaning, and hydration processes. Poor water management can draw down local water supplies in areas where water is scarce.

Traditional restaurants and food service operations play a substantial role in environmental challenges such as food waste, high energy consumption, non-sustainable packaging, heavy water consumption, among others. With its innovative business model, the ghost kitchen concept is not exempt from the challenges. If not managed well, they may also have similar sustainability issues. But to make sense of the ghost kitchens' eco-driven solutions, we should first uncover what green cooking modifies in the light of knowing how traditional kitchens affect the environment.

Food waste is one of the largest problems within the restaurant industry; almost one-third of all food produced worldwide is wasted. The restaurant industry is a heavy contributor to this problem — through poor shipping practices, overproduction, and overgenerous portion sizes. To overcome this, organizations including the UK-focused Too Good To Go app allow restaurants to sell leftover food on at discounted prices, minimizing waste while providing a financial boon to businesses. Ghost kitchens can implement similar models, utilizing artificial intelligence–based inventory tracking to optimize stock levels and reduce surplus waste. Fossil fuel use is also high as conventional kitchens necessitate ovens, stoves, refrigeration and HVAC, which are all energy-intensive. Chipotle and other restaurants have also been able to reduce energy use by doing things like investing in energy-efficient kitchen appliances. Ghost kitchens can take it to the next level by incorporating IoT-enabled energy monitoring systems that automatically adjust power usage.

Another major point of concern is the carbon footprint of restaurant supply chains. Kosher salt Ingredients used by many restaurants are sometimes shipped in from considerable distances, adding to the restaurant's greenhouse gas contribution. A more sustainable alternative is hyper-local sourcing — a strategy implemented by companies like Imperfect Foods that encourage the use of surplus and locally sourced ingredients. The same for non-recyclable packaging, especially in the food delivery industry, which are topical environmental issues. A lot of single-use plastics and non-biodegradable materials find their way to use in landfills or oceans, adding to the pollution. Thus, have cities such as Singapore launching reusable container programs like Muuse, which appeal to restaurants to use eco-friendly packaging. Ghost kitchens can also adopt deposit-return packaging systems to minimize single-use contamination. Lastly, there is a major problem of water waste. Traditional restaurants waste a lot of water for cooking and cleaning, creating an imbalance and depleting their limited resources in the water-scarce regions. Chains such as Pret-A-Manger have installed water-saving dishwashers and sensor-operated faucets to reduce consumption. Ghost kitchens scale the practice by installing AI-powered water monitoring systems to keep efficient water usage in check.

2. LITERATURE REVIEW

Ghost kitchens — also known as cloud or virtual kitchens — are one of those ideas that started to gain traction in the last decade when technology transformed food services-enabled delivery services (Rinaldi et al., 2022). Ghost kitchens challenge the traditional brick-and-mortar restaurant setup by eliminating the need for customers to dine on-site, thus significantly lowering operational costs while presenting businesses an opportunity to optimize food delivery services (Wagner *et al.,* 2022). Nosing from their economic resource-saving benefits, they also face challenges of sustainability, in terms of waste management, energy usage, and carbon emissions (Kulshrestha & Sharma, 2022).

A growing number of environmental case studies on restaurants can be found in the literature, documenting the principal issues that traditional restaurants face, including high food waste rates, energy and water overuse, non-recyclable packaging, and unprofitable supply chains (Lam *et al.,* 2021). The food service sector accounts for a significant amount of global food waste, with estimates indicating that almost one-third of all food produced goes to waste, of which a large proportion is generated from restaurants (Canton, 2021). Traditional kitchens contribute directly to fossil-fuel-related energy consumption for cooking, refrigeration, and ventilation systems, compounding their environmental footprint (Shapiro, 2023). Moreover, the carbon footprint generated by complex supply chain operations and the increasing utilization of unrecyclable packaging further contribute to the difficulties faced in pursuing sustainability (Singh et al., 2024).

To this end, the role of smart technologies like the Internet of Things (IoT), artificial intelligence (AI) and data-driven inventory management systems in enhancing sustainability in ghost kitchens has been examined by researchers (Neria *et al.,* 2024). Thus, these technologies enable optimal resource utilization, minimize food waste, and improve energy efficiency, therefore lessening some of the environmental issues associated with conventional food service models (Desai, 2020). But the solutions come with a few hurdles. Research gave recommendations for limiting barriers, such as high upfront investment cost, absence of proper regulations and businesses reluctance to implement innovation (Singh & Tanwar, 2018). Furthermore, the scalability of eco-friendly practices is a major concern, where SMEs face significant financial and infrastructural challenges when shifting towards sustainability (Parks, 2012).

While solutions for sustainability are emerging to be promising with using smart technology, more research is required to understand the long-term viability of these solutions in varying market settings. It is another interesting research direction to conduct comparative studies on how to implement green initiatives across different geographical areas which may provide valuable insights into the depth of lessons learned and possible policy interventions (Hasnan & Ramli, 2020). As ghost kitchens evolve, a holistic approach that balances economic viability with environmental responsibility will be key in shaping the future of sustainable food service operations.

2.1. Ghost Kitchens: A Shift toward Sustainability

Ghost kitchens represent a radical shift from the traditional restaurant model. They have provided an avenue to address many of the environmental challenges associated with brick-and-mortar locations. They are intrinsically conducive to greater efficiency in resource usage because they minimize the need for space for eating and optimize food production and delivery (*Kaur et al.,*2024). However, when planned consciously with eco-friendly operations, ghost kitchens can transcend pure operational efficiency in their pursuit to make the food system more sustainable. This paper discusses the leading ways ghost kitchens are making it towards sustainability:

- Less physical footprint and land use:

Traditional restaurants are very space consumers for the kitchen, dining, amenities, and parking areas that consequently increase energy usage and land consumption (Cai *et al.*, 2022). Ghost kitchens require compact spaces that are meant only for food preparation. The reduced footprint means that less energy is used and reduced land requirements and a decreased demand for construction materials. Some ghost kitchens use repurposed spaces or even shipping containers that are environmentally friendly.

- Reduced Energy and Utility Consumption:

The ghost kitchen has a lower energy requirement since it is more effective than traditional restaurants. Ghost kitchens save electricity and reduce their carbon footprint by not requiring dining areas, lighting for guests, or facilities like bathrooms. They use smart energy management to operate appliances, lighting, and HVAC systems only when necessary.

- **Multi-brand Centric Production**

A ghost kitchen can host a large number of virtual restaurant brands from one location. This way, resources can be centralized with the help of cost savings. It cooks for different brands while not necessitating multiple places, equipment, and employees. It reduces the use of energy and water and waste of food and improves the logistics of operation, all adding up to reducing the environmental impact.

- Reduce Food Waste through Data-Driven Inventory Management

Probably one of the biggest environmental benefits is that ghost kitchens do not produce waste. Traditional restaurants cannot predict the demand for meals, and hence there is overproduction and spoilage. Ghost kitchens rely on data and analytics for forecasting demand and managing inventory (Cornell *et al.*, 2024). Ghost kitchens can use online ordering platforms to better predict food demand at any given time and avoid overproduction and waste. Some ghost kitchens also implement dynamic pricing models to offer discounts on surplus food items, further minimizing waste.

- Eco-friendly packaging with minimum use of disposable plastics.

Since the crux of ghost kitchens' business model is delivery, they ought to be concerned with packaging materials and their respective environmental impacts. In fact, most ghost kitchens are pioneering the way in eco-friendly packaging solutions. This includes utilizing compostable, biodegradable, and recyclable types of packaging materials, and bringing down the extent of usage of single-use plastics. Even some of the ghost kitchens have collaborated with packaging companies to come up with innovative sustainable packaging that keeps food quality intact without creating more environmental impact.

2.2. Regulatory Challenges and Scalability of Eco-friendly practices

While sustainability awareness is growing throughout the food service industry, regulations can prevent widespread adoption of eco-friendly practices. A big problem is the lack of standardized guidelines for ghost kitchens. Food safety and sanitation regulations for traditional restaurants are highly regulated, but there are few guidelines for sustainability among delivery-only food businesses. Governments should enact green certification programs offering tax credits to businesses adopting environmentally-friendly practices. Moreover, compliance with sustainability standards typically demands significant upfront capital expenditures. Small and mid-sized restaurant operators do not have the financial ability to upgrade their appliances to energy-efficient ones, use biodegradable packaging or implement efficient waste management systems. Funding and subsidies to facilitate this transition could come through public-private partnerships or even initiatives like the European Union's Green Deal Investment Plan.

Because ghost kitchens are scalable, sustainability can also become a challenge to implement. Although massive restaurant chains have the luxury to invest in green technology, smaller concessions may struggle to do just that. Consumer awareness is another obstacle, as many customers focus on convenience and affordability rather than sustainability. Solution — Carbon Labeling: Businesses can also curate eco-labeling programs, such as displaying information about the carbon footprint of products on packaging to help inform consumers about the effects of their food choices on the environment. Logistics challenges are another important one, as green logistics solutions—such as electric delivery vehicles or reusable packaging—depend on the right infrastructure in place. Businesses, including Just Salad, run successful reusable bowl programs where customers were incentivized to return containers. Scaling sustainability efforts in ghost kitchens would be helped by replicating similar initiatives.

"Ghost kitchens offer new opportunities for the food industry; however, they must implement smart technology and regulatory-compliant sustainability strategies to have a long-term lasting impact." In the new green economy, change will require cooperation between governments, business, and consumers. Policymakers need to put clear sustainability rules and financial incentives in place, businesses need to implement green technologies and consumers need to actively vote with their dollars by supporting environmentally sustainable food services. With the right policies, ghost kitchens can be made sustainable, serving not only as a luxury but as a model for food service across the globe.

2.3. Smart Technologies Driving Eco-friendly Practices in Ghost Kitchens

Smart technologies are, therefore, fundamental to the sustainability aspirations of ghost kitchens. Through the use of advanced technologies such as AI, machine learning, and IoT, they will be able to optimize their operations, reduce waste, and generally reduce their footprint on the environment. This chapter explores how smart technologies encourage sustainable practices in ghost kitchens.

AI and Machine Learning for Supply Chain Optimization Supply chain management is one of the most critical issues in the food industry. Ghost kitchens use AI and machine learning to optimize their supply chains and minimize waste.

- Predictive Algorithms for Inventory Management:

AI predictive algorithms enable ghost kitchens to better forecast demand. They analyze past data, sales trends, and factors like weather to predict daily food needs. This helps minimize overordering, spoilage, and waste by ordering only necessary ingredients.

- Optimizing Delivery Routes to Cut Carbon Emissions:

Delivery is essential to ghost kitchens, and optimizing routes reduces carbon footprint. The AI algorithm begins with checking the traffic, order locations, and delivery times to ensure the most suitable paths. This would reduce the carbon footprint per delivery while improving the rate of delivery and customer satisfaction.

Energy-efficient Appliances and Automation

Energy usage is very significant for kitchen activities, but ghost kitchens may still employ smart energy-efficient appliances as well as automation.

- Energy-Smart Smart Home Appliances

Ghost kitchens utilize energy-efficient appliances that consume less electricity and gas compared to the traditional ones. Smart ovens cook food at optimal times and temperatures, thus reducing energy use. The same way, smart refrigerators and freezers can set internal temperatures in real-time and keep food stored properly while saving energy.

- Avoiding human error and resource waste through cooking automation

Smart kitchens require automation. Automated cooking systems reduce human errors and wastage. For instance, automated fryers cook food to the exact time needed, which eliminates overcooking. This precision improves food quality and saves energy by eliminating re-cooking.

- **IoT and Smart Kitchens**

The Internet of Things (IoT) has revolutionized how kitchens operate by providing real-time data and insights into every aspect of the kitchen's performance.

- IoT Sensors to track energy consumption, water wastage, and efficiency of appliances.

IoT sensors can be installed in ghost kitchens to monitor the energy, water consumption, and efficiency of appliances. Sensors will provide the kitchen operator with real-time data on the usage of energy and water so that inefficiencies can be detected and corrected (Jiang et al., 2024). For instance, if an appliance is consuming more energy than it should, the kitchen can address the problem before it leads to wastage of energy. This would also mean that IoT sensors could detect water usage and alert the kitchen staff in case of leaks or unnecessary consumption, thereby reducing waste.

- **Sensors for reducing food waste and resource usage.**

IoT sensors can also be used to monitor the levels of foods in real time. Therefore, the kitchen will know when the ingredient is near its expiration date or running out of stock. Thus, with a real-time insight into the actual inventory levels, the sensors minimize food waste from spoilage since the kitchen can only use freshly prepared ingredients. Moreover, IoT-enabled appliances can automatically calibrate cooking based on the specific food being cooked and the amounts used, ensuring minimal food waste from spoilage.

Smart Packaging Solutions

Packaging is a critical consideration for ghost kitchens, and smart packaging technologies are helping to reduce the environmental impact of food delivery.

Guidelines regarding biodegradable and recyclable materials:

These sustainability metrics divert many ghost kitchens toward biodegradable and recyclable packaging materials in their quest for waste reduction. Biodegradable materials break down much easier in landfills than traditional plastics and have a lesser impact on the environment overall (Jones *et al.*, 2024). A few ghost kitchens have instituted take-back packaging programs whereby they invite customers to return used packaging for recycling or composting.

Tracking Sustainability Variables through QR Codes and Smart Labels:

Smart packaging solutions often leverage QR codes or other forms of digital labeling that allow customers to track the sustainability of their meals (Khan *et al.*, 2023). By scanning a QR code on the packaging, the customers get to read up on the source of the ingredients, carbon footprint of the meal, and the overall sustainability efforts of the kitchen. This transparency builds trust with eco-conscious consumers, encouraging other kitchens to act in ways that seam sustainable.

3. METHODOLOGY

This study takes the form of secondary research, drawing on existing literature, industry reports, and publicly available data to examine how smart technologies can contribute toward making ghost kitchens more sustainable. Secondary Data. Authors have leveraged peer-reviewed journals articles, books, government reports, and industry-related publications within the subject areas of sustainability, food services innovations, and digital transformation (Chong & Plonsky, 2024). This study conducts a systematic review of case studies, market trends, and regulatory policies affecting the implementation of eco-friendly practices in ghost kitchens to analyze opportunities and bottlenecks. A thematic analysis of existing studies enables to lumped common patterns, the key drivers and barriers for the adoption of sustainable practices (Canning *et al.*, 2024). By basing the research on robust theory and empirical findings, it also extends a well-rounded view to the analysis.

4. DISCUSSIONS

4.1 Ghost Kitchens and the Circular Economy

The foundation of the circular economy looks to develop closed-loop systems whereby waste is minimized and resources are reused and recycled as far as possible. With ghost kitchens, this means searching for strategic avenues through which food waste, water use, and energy consumption can be

curbed and the packaging as well as materials can be reused or recycled. By adopting this circular economy approach, ghost kitchens have a workable infrastructure for modernizing their business practices whilst also addressing one of the principal challenges of food production and delivery.

Food Recovery and Redistribution Programs

One of the most impactful ways ghost kitchens contribute to the circular economy is through food recovery and redistribution programs. Food waste is an acute problem plaguing the food society, where several million tons of edible food is wasted to the landfill every year. A food recovery system in a ghost kitchen will take food away from the garbage, into another person's meal.

Partnerships with Food Banks and Charity Organizations:

Ghost kitchens can partner with local food banks, shelters, and charity organizations to donate surplus food. It could be unsold meals, leftover ingredients, or food items with a shelf life that could be acceptable for instant use in the day following its donation. Ghost kitchens may utilize advanced inventory management systems to easily recognize excess food and regularly plan pickups or deliveries to partner organizations.

Real-time Redistribution Apps:

Food recovery apps have made it easier for ghost kitchens to redistribute surplus food. Apps like Too Good To Go and Olio connect businesses with consumers to either buy surplus food items at a reduced price or take items free of charge, which otherwise amount to food waste. These platforms reduce food wastage while offering affordable meals to consumers and ensuring kitchens' sustainability efforts.

Upcycling Food Waste

Besides food recovery programs, ghost kitchens can investigate the practice of upcycling food waste or repurposing that traditionally was considered waste into new, valuable products (Festivalia & Swantai, 2022). Upcycling involves creating new food items from food scraps, trimmings, and then some by-products, thereby reducing waste while creating additional revenue opportunities.

Making Broths, Sauces, and Stocks Out of Food Scraps:

Many ghost kitchens are becoming part of the trend that utilizes vegetable peels, meat bones, and scraps in the preparation of broths, stocks, and sauces, thus tackling food waste while enhancing the flavour of the dishes, with positive consequences for both sustainability and food quality. Some ghost kitchens even market these upcycled goods-canned bone broth or vegetable stock-to customers as part of their menu.

Composting and Biogas Production:

When food scraps can't be converted into food, they can always be composted as nutrient-rich soil for local farms and gardens. Some ghost kitchens have started on-site composting systems or have partnered with local compost facilities to manage their organic waste. Others are experimenting with biogas production, where organic waste is converted into energy to be used in kitchen operations.

Closed-loop systems for the use of water and energy

The Conservation of water and energy is the crucial component of a sustainable kitchen operation. Closed-loop systems can help ghost kitchens minimize waste and reuse water and energy whenever possible.

Greywater Recycling Systems: Greywater recycling systems capture water from sinks, dishwashers, and other non-contaminated sources, filter it, and reuse it for non-potable purposes such as cleaning floors and flushing toilets. This serves to reduce the amount of freshwater needed in kitchen operations and help save local water resources, especially in regions with water shortages.

Energy Recovery Systems: Energy recovery systems capture waste heat generated through kitchens and use it to heat water or for HVAC systems. This practice would radically cut down energy use and carbon footprints for ghost kitchens.

4.2. Partnerships with Local Farms for Sustainable Sourcing

This is how ghost kitchens support the idea of the circular economy: they procure from local farms-bearing favorable fruits to provide fresher and seasonal ingredients-which also helps in the reduction of carbon emissions, supports local agriculture, and fosters sustainable food production practices.

- **Farm-to-Ghost Kitchen Models:** Many ghost kitchens have adopted a farm-to-ghost kitchen model, meaning they source their ingredients from local farms. This minimizes the requirement for long-distance transportation related to greenhouse gas emissions. In addition, because of their relationship with local farmers, they can also procure ingredients grown in a sustainable manner, such as organically or through regenerative agriculture.
- **Minimizing Packaging in the Supply Chain**: Being local enables ghost kitchens to receive their procurement in bulk or reusable containers, which eliminates excessive packaging. This creates less waste throughout the supply chain process and offers a more sustainable approach to ingredient sourcing.

4.3. Challenges and Opportunities in Scaling Eco-friendly Ghost Kitchens

While the potential for ghost kitchens to lead the way in sustainability is significant, there are also challenges to scaling eco-friendly practices. From the cost of smart technologies to regulatory hurdles and consumer education, ghost kitchens will find themselves grappling with more obstacles in the path of the widespread adoption of sustainable practices (Petkoska *et al.*, 2021). Nonetheless, such difficulties offer an opportunity for innovators, paving the way for investment and growth.

High Initial Cost of Smart Technologies: Smart technologies integrated into ghost kitchens require high capital investment. Energy-efficient appliances, IoT sensors, AI-powered inventory systems, and automation tools all come at a lucrative price tag and thus may prove a daunting task for smaller ghost kitchen operators.

- **Investment in Green Technology**. In order to avoid blocking financial means in exploiting smart technology, ghost kitchens may decide to embark on seeking investments from venture capital firms or government grants focusing on sustainability and green technology (Shaikh *et al.,* 2024). Furthermore, with growing demand for sustainable food services, investors have become increasingly interested in funding businesses that prioritize eco-friendly practices.
- **Long-term Savings Through Efficiency.** Although a large first investment in smart technologies can be high, energy, water, and resource efficiencies may lead to savings which can offset high upfront costs over a period of time. An energy-efficient appliance combined with optimized operations means lower utility bills, and less food waste generates savings on ingredients. In hindsight, these savings help ghost kitchens supplement their investment in technologies and improve their net output.

4.4. Case study of Ghost Kitchens

Ghost kitchens have been really successful with the sustainability initiative in some regions and operational models. In cities such as London and New York, top-tier ghost kitchen operators have already adopted intelligent cooling and AI-driven energy control systems, slashing their energy consumption by almost 30% (Sprague, 2022). In contrast, other emerging markets (like India or Southeast Asia) cannot afford the inherent cost of infrastructure or technology. In contrast, comparative studies indicated that the traditional restaurant sector faces high operational costs, and food wastage, so as green innovations are implemented in ghost kitchens, they experience better profit margins and lower environmental impact. Research by Lee and Tao (2022) shows AI dynamics have managed to decrease food waste by 20% in major U.S. metropolitan areas, indicating that supply chain optimization predictions based on AI have been enabled through cloud kitchens.

4.5 Regulatory Challenges and the Need for Updated Frameworks

The fast emergence of ghost kitchens has outstripped many regulatory frameworks, notably in the case of sustainability and environmental practices. In many jurisdictions, existing restaurant regulations might not apply to ghost kitchens, thus creating a void in governmental oversight.

- Updated Guidelines and Regulations:

Ghost kitchens and sustainability advocates ought to join forces with local governments to update existing regulations and establish frameworks supporting eco-friendly practices (Suresh *et al.*, 2024). This could include tax incentives for ghost kitchens employing green technologies and imposing regulations on waste management, energy consumption, and sustainable sourcing practices.

- **Unifying Sustainability Measures:**

One of the significant hurdles to ghost kitchens advocating for sustainability is the lack of standardized metrics for measuring environmental impact. Establishing clear guidelines and metrics, including carbon emissions, water usage, and waste reduction, would build a standard of evaluation for ghost kitchens that could help them benchmark their progress and display commitment to eco-friendly practices.

- **Consumer Awareness and Education**

The gap between what consumers reasonably know about sustainability and its connection to ghost kitchens as eco-friendly dining experiences is own. Educating the consumer on the advantages of ordering from a green ghost kitchen will garner increased demand for eco-friendly food services.

- **Transparency in Sustainability Practices:**

Ghost kitchens are given the importance to promote consumer education by being transparent about their efforts toward sustainability. They should provide all the information related to the environment concerning how each kitchen operates using advanced packaging alternatives, and advertising campaigns should incorporate discussion about the kitchens featuring eco-friendly practices. Offering incentives for the return of packaging or selection of plant-based menu items would further encourage consumers to make for more sustainable dining involvement.

- **Leveraging Social Media and Digital Platforms:**

Since ghost kitchens function primarily through online platforms for ordering and delivery, they can utilize these digital venues to advertise sustainability. Ghost kitchens can utilize social media, apps, and websites to disseminate knowledge about their eco-friendly practices, educate consumers on waste reduction, and market environmentally friendly menu options.

- **Investing in Green Innovations**

Increased interest in sustainable food services has raised certain sectors for investment in green innovations. As consumers, governments, and companies continue to give attention to sustainability, these ghost kitchens implementing eco-friendly practices are also set to attract investments and increase orders, thus continuing to take an increasing proportion of market shares.

- **Innovation in Sustainable Packaging:**

There is a great need for innovative styles of sustainable packaging, especially in the food delivery sector. Ghost kitchens that actively work towards innovating along the lines of biodegradable, compostable, or reusable packaging are likely to lower their footprint and open up new avenues for business in the packaging field.

- **Advancements in Plant-based and Lab-grown Foods:**

The advancement of plant-based and lab-grown foods is another area where opportunity lies for the green ghost kitchens. The incorporation of alternative forms of sustainable foods on the ghost kitchen menus will help abolish the reliance then established on resource-consuming animal products while giving the marketing edge to eco-conscious consumers. More food-based proteins or partnership with companies already delving into lab-grown meat will also place ghost kitchens in the forefront of this future impending food movement.

4.6. The Case Studies of Successful Eco-friendly Ghost Kitchens

Across the world, several ghost kitchens have already shown the possibility of the conjointment of eco-friendly practices and nice smart technology in fashioning a sustainable food service model. These case studies give great small insights, guidance, and encouragement to those who want to scale their sustainability efforts in other ghost kitchens.

- **Cloud Kitchen (Los Angeles):** The development of Cloud Kitchen, a prominent ghost kitchen operator, has sustainability as the fundamental building block of its business model. Cloud Kitchen reduces food waste by using an AI-enhanced inventory management system; it utilises energy-efficient appliances to reduce its carbon footprint. Cloud Kitchen also runs a packaging take-back program in which customers return packing to the kitchen for recycling.

- **Allplants (UK):** Allplants is a plant-based UK ghost kitchen that deals with sustainability by way of plant-based meal preparation, which eats lesser resources than conventional meat items. Biodegradable packaging and organic products from local farms are used by the kitchen. The Allplants have put them in place throughout their new cutting-edge kitchen, designed to be as energy-efficient and waste-free as possible.

5. CONCLUSION & IMPLICATIONS

With the gradual rise in popularity of ghost kitchens, it is establishing its potential to dominate sustainability. Incorporation of smart technologies, as well as a circular economy that would essentially allow the reduction of the impact on the environment and open doors for innovation and growth, is very much feasible with ghost kitchens (Singh & Singh, 2020). The question of scaling these practices, however, raises concerns about high start-up costs, regulation, and consumer education. The green ghost kitchens of tomorrow would depend on partnership, innovation, and investment. In working with governments, tech providers, and the consumer base, ghost kitchens can build a more sustainable and resilient food system that works for the planet and the communities they serve. This research would offer valuable insights for policymakers, industry leaders and sustainability advocates in food service sector. Through its findings describing the contribution of smart technologies toward greener ghost kitchens, the study promotes innovation-based solutions for sustainability (Chng, 2024). It also informs business owners about difficulties in the implementation of green practices, and advises them on how to scale their eco-friendly operations. In addition, the results expand the literature by suggesting research niches in regulatory systems and long-term sustainability impact.

6. SCOPE FOR FURTHER STUDY

Future studies worldwide in different market structures can examine the long-term environmental and economic aspects of Smart-tech in ghost kitchens. Their findings, bordering on anecdotal, highlight the need for more comparative studies between the developed and developing world—insights which could help evaluate the feasibility and scalability of green initiatives through different contexts. Moreover, research can explore the regulatory barriers and policy regulations that shape green practices in the food service sector. Other studies can explore the consumer perception and demand for sustainable food delivery services to ensure that the businesses are in the line with their eco-conscious customer preferences (John, 2023; Da Cunha *et al.,* 2024). It would also be interesting to perform cost-benefit analyses, smart solution implementations in the scope of SMEs. Lastly, interdisciplinary approaches combining technology, sustainability and behavioral economics could yield comprehensive solutions towards sustainable food service models.

REFERENCES

Cai, R., Leung, X. Y., & Chi, C. G. Q. (2022). Ghost kitchens on the rise: Effects of knowledge and perceived benefit-risk on customers' behavioral intentions. *International Journal of Hospitality Management, 101*, 103110. DOI: 10.1016/j.ijhm.2021.103110

Canning, J., Strawbridge, R. J., Miedzybrodzka, Z., Marioni, R. E., Melbye, M., Porteous, D. J., Hurles, M. E., Sattar, N., Sudlow, C. L. M., Collins, R., Padmanabhan, S., & Pell, J. P. (2024). Methods applied to neonatal dried blood spot samples for secondary research purposes: A scoping review. *Critical Reviews in Clinical Laboratory Sciences, 61*(8), 685–708. DOI: 10.1080/10408363.2024.2360996 PMID: 38855982

Canton, H. (2021). Food and agriculture organization of the United Nations—FAO. In *The Europa directory of international organizations 2021*, 297-305.

Chng, S. (2024). The Emerging Socio-Spatial Implications of Cloud Kitchens and Cloud Stores. In THE CITY REBOOTED: Networks, Connectivity and Place Identities in Singapore, pp. 185-210. DOI: 10.1142/9789811287848_0007

Chong, S. W., & Plonsky, L. (2024). A typology of secondary research in Applied Linguistics. *Applied Linguistics Review, 15*(4), 1569–1594. DOI: 10.1515/applirev-2022-0189

Cornell, D., Manamtam, J. R., & Tham, A. (2024). Invisible Workers in Philippines' Ghost Kitchens: Trends and Implications. *Advances in Southeast Asian Studies, 17*(2), 187–200.

Da Cunha, D. T., Hakim, M. P., Alves, M. M., Vicentini, M. S., & Wiśniewska, M. Z. (2024). Dark kitchens: Origin, definition, and perspectives of an emerging food sector. *International Journal of Gastronomy and Food Science, 35*, 100884. DOI: 10.1016/j.ijgfs.2024.100884

Desai, B. H. (2020). 14. United nations environment programme (UNEP). *Yearbook of International Environmental Law, 31*(1), 319–325. DOI: 10.1093/yiel/yvab060

Festivalia, F., & Swantari, A. (2022). *Ghost kitchen strategy to reduce restaurant loss in COVID-19 pandemic condition. Current Issues in Tourism, Gastronomy, and Tourist Destination Research*. Routledge.

Hasnan, N. Z. N., & Ramli, S. H. M. (2020). Modernizing the preparation of the Malaysian mixed rice dish (MRD) with Cook-Chill Central Kitchen and implementation of HACCP. *International Journal of Gastronomy and Food Science, 19*, 100193. DOI: 10.1016/j.ijgfs.2019.100193

Jiang, Y., Balaji, M. S., & Lyu, C. (2024). Cultivating initial trust in ghost kitchens: A mixed-methods investigation of antecedents and consequences. *International Journal of Hospitality Management, 119*, 103727. DOI: 10.1016/j.ijhm.2024.103727

John, K. T. (2023). Digital disruption: The hyperlocal delivery and cloud kitchen driven future of food services in post-COVID India. *International Hospitality Review, 37*(1), 161–187. DOI: 10.1108/IHR-06-2021-0045

Jones, S., Cain, L., & Deel, G. L. (2024). Virtual Restaurants and Ghost Kitchens: A New Opportunity. *Journal of Hospitality & Tourism Cases*, 21649987241241948.

Kaur, K., Kaur, J., & Singh, R. (2024). Emerging Technologies in Food and Beverage Industry: From Smart Kitchens to Food Delivery Innovations. *AI, Blockchain, and Metaverse in Hospitality and Tourism Industry*, *4*(0), 263–276.

Khan, T. A., Khan, S. A., Haque, S., & Ayub, M. F. B. (2023). A study on the prospect of the cloud kitchen model in Dhaka. *International Journal of Business and Management*, *18*(1), 46–59. DOI: 10.5539/ijbm.v18n1p46

Kulshreshtha, K., & Sharma, G. (2022). From restaurant to cloud kitchen: Survival of the fittest during COVID-19 An empirical examination. *Technological Forecasting and Social Change*, *179*, 121629. DOI: 10.1016/j.techfore.2022.121629 PMID: 35317191

Lam, S., Dodd, W., Berrang-Ford, L., Ford, J., Skinner, K., Papadopoulos, A., & Harper, S. L. (2021). How are climate actions evaluated? A review of United Nations food security evaluations. *Global Food Security*, *28*, 100509. DOI: 10.1016/j.gfs.2021.100509

Lee, K. S., & Tao, C. W. W. (2022). Culinary knowledge sharing on social media: Case of the 2019 Malaysian World Pastry Champion Wei Loon Tan. *Journal of Hospitality and Tourism Management*, *52*, 52–64. DOI: 10.1016/j.jhtm.2022.06.006

Neria, G., Hildebrandt, F. D., Tzur, M., & Ulmer, M. W. (2024). The Restaurant Meal Delivery Problem with Ghost Kitchens. *Transportation Science*, trsc.2024.0510. Advance online publication. DOI: 10.1287/trsc.2024.0510

Parks, L. (2012). Techno-struggles and the satellite dish: A populist approach to infrastructure. In *Cultural technologies* (pp. 64–84). Routledge.

Petkoska, A. T., Daniloski, D., D'Cunha, N. M., Naumovski, N., & Broach, A. T. (2021). Edible packaging: Sustainable solutions and novel trends in food packaging. *Food Research International*, *140*, 109981. DOI: 10.1016/j.foodres.2020.109981 PMID: 33648216

Rinaldi, C., D'aguilar, M., & Egan, M. (2022). Understanding the online environment for the delivery of food, alcohol and tobacco: An exploratory analysis of 'dark kitchens' and rapid grocery delivery services. *International Journal of Environmental Research and Public Health*, *19*(9), 5523. DOI: 10.3390/ijerph19095523 PMID: 35564918

Shaikh, R., Singh, A., Brown, B., & Lampinen, A. (2024, May). Not Just A Dot on The Map: Food Delivery Workers as Infrastructure. In *Proceedings of the 2024 CHI Conference on Human Factors in Computing Systems*, 1-15. DOI: 10.1145/3613904.3641918

Shapiro, A. (2023). Platform urbanism in a pandemic: Dark stores, ghost kitchens, and the logistical-urban frontier. *Journal of Consumer Culture*, *23*(1), 168–187. DOI: 10.1177/14695405211069983

Singh, S. V. (2018). An Analysis of Tourist Satisfaction in Varanasi as Destination Perspective through Important Performance Analysis. *Avahan. Journal of Hospitality and Tourism*, *6*(1), 71–83.

Singh, S. V., & Singh, K. (2020). Migrants workers in tourism and hospitality industry: Effect of COVID-19. *Covid-19 crisis: Policy solutions and way forward to rebuild travel, tourism & hospitality sector*, (Eds.). Vinod Zutshi, Nimit Chowdhary, Anand Kumar Singh & Priyadarshan Lakhawat. Bharti Publications, 36-47.

Singh, S. V., Singh, K., & Kumar, N. (2024). Sustainable Food Waste Utilization in the Context of the Indian Hospitality Industry. In Jimenez Ruiz, A., Bhartiya, S., & Bhatt, V. (Eds.), *Promoting Sustainable Gastronomy Tourism and Community Development* (pp. 229–241). IGI Global Scientific Publishing., DOI: 10.4018/979-8-3693-1814-0.ch014

Sprague, J. (2022). Ghost in the kitchen: Multiracial Korean Americans (re) defining cultural authenticity. *Genealogy*, *6*(2), 35–42. DOI: 10.3390/genealogy6020035

Suresh, S., Santhosh, S., & Samjaila, T. H. (2024). Food Economies–Engendered Ghost Kitchens in the Digital Age. In *Business Development via AI and Digitalization* (Vol. 2, pp. 95–104). Springer Nature Switzerland. DOI: 10.1007/978-3-031-62106-2_8

Wagner, K., Unger, L., Salman, M. M., Kitchen, P., Bill, R. M., & Yool, A. J. (2022). Signaling mechanisms and pharmacological modulators governing diverse aquaporin functions in human health and disease. *International Journal of Molecular Sciences*, *23*(3), 1388. DOI: 10.3390/ijms23031388 PMID: 35163313

Chapter 12
Challenges and Opportunities of Ghost Kitchens With Reference to Expansions and Expectations

Vinod Kumar
https://orcid.org/0000-0002-2464-8392
Amity University, Gurgaon, India

Savita Sharma
Vishwakarma Skill University, India

Anshul Garg
https://orcid.org/0000-0001-8297-9256
School of Hospitality, Tourism, and Events, Malaysia

ABSTRACT

In the international food service sector, ghost kitchens—also referred to as virtual kitchens, cloud kitchens, or dark kitchens—are becoming a ground-breaking idea in the current scenario. These modern kitchens are fulfilled to meet the increasing demand for meal delivery services and don't have a physical storefront. Ghost kitchens are growing quickly all over the world because to the rise of online food delivery services and consumer desire for convenience. This study examines the prospects and problems related to the rise of ghost kitchens, paying particular attention to elements like scalability, consumer behavior, operational effectiveness, and market expansion with reference to the startup of a new venture. The study also assesses the expectations of their future in view of the market's possible disruptions, shifting consumer tastes, and technical developments in the business.

DOI: 10.4018/979-8-3373-0432-8.ch012

1. INTRODUCTION

Without the need for a conventional restaurant storefront, a ghost kitchen—also referred to as a cloud kitchen or dark kitchen—is a commercial kitchen area created specifically for food preparation and delivery (KITCHEN, n.d.). Due to the increasing need for meal delivery services like Uber Eats, Grubhub, and DoorDash, this creative idea has become highly popular. Ghost kitchens don't have a public area or dine-in options like regular restaurants do. Rather, they concentrate on effectively preparing food for online orders, providing a simplified method to satisfy delivery-driven clientele (Suresh et al., 2024a). Online food delivery services have grown rapidly due to the emergence of e-commerce, rising urbanization, and changing consumer attitudes toward convenience. At the same time, the growing demand for food delivery has led to the emergence of ghost kitchens (Jones et al., 2024a)These kitchens mark a dramatic shift in the food service sector since they contact customers via delivery platforms rather than a traditional storefront. They have become popular because they provide new businesses and restaurants with affordable solutions that increase operational versatility and save expense (Akbar et al., 2022). The affordability of ghost kitchens is one of its main benefits. Businesses can cut overhead costs by doing away with the requirement for a physical dining area, front-of-house employees, and pricey prime-location rent (Chen et al., n.d.-a). Because of this, the approach is particularly attractive to entrepreneurs, allowing them to launch food-related businesses with fewer initial expenses. The ability to run several virtual restaurant brands—each with a unique menu and identity—from a single kitchen is another benefit of ghost kitchens. This enables operators to use the same kitchen infrastructure while serving a variety of client demands and reaching new markets (KITCHEN, n.d.).

Since e-commerce networks and distribution technologies streamline the entire process—from placing an order to delivering food—technology is essential to the operation of ghost kitchens. The food industry has changed as a result of the emergence of ghost kitchens, which enable companies to grow swiftly and adjust to shifting consumer preferences (Seghezzi et al., n.d.). Ghost kitchens are influencing the future of the foodservice sector by offering a productive and successful substitute for conventional dining places, whether it is for testing new ideas or satisfying the increasing need for convenience (Suresh, Santhosh, 2, et al., n.d.). Although the idea of ghost kitchens is still developing, both new and established firms are using them to expand their operations with little financial outlay, which is increasing their influence. This essay looks at the advantages that ghost kitchens offer companies as well as the difficulties they encounter when growing (*Ghost Kitchen - Google Scholar*, n.d.)

2. BACKGROUND AND GROWTH OF GHOST KITCHENS

2.1 *Definition and Concept*

Commercial kitchen areas designated only for preparing food for delivery are known as "ghost kitchens." They may be shared by several brands or operated by a single restaurant. Because they don't have a dining room or storefront, they are far less expensive to run than standard brick-and-mortar restaurants(Jones et al., 2024a) These kitchens are designed to maximize delivery services through online marketplaces such as DoorDash, Grubhub, and UberEats, which have experienced tremendous expansion, particularly during the COVID-19 pandemic. One can easily start this concept from home/ domestic kitchen in primary stages(Festivalia et al., n.d.). These enterprises provide a cost-effective option that enables companies to meet the growing demand for online meal delivery services while streamlining operations and lowering overhead expenses. Ghost kitchens may handle several culinary concepts and brands in one place by utilizing technology and improving kitchen layout. This maximizes efficiency and makes a varied menu choice possible (Suresh et al., 2024b).

2.2 Global Ghost Kitchen Market - Key Developments

The ghost kitchen market is expected to grow at an exponential rate and reach USD 71.4 billion by 2027 as a result of growing delivery demand and consumer preferences for eating at home. According to industry insiders, ghost kitchens have grown in popularity since they are less expensive and more scalable than traditional eateries(Bekaert et al., 2007) A workable solution to the anticipated substantial expansion in the worldwide meal delivery market is the use of ghost kitchens(Corvo et al., 2022)

From 2023 to 2030, the global ghost kitchen market is expected to rise at a compound annual growth rate (CAGR) of 12.1%, from its anticipated US$70.37 billion in 2023 to US$156.60 billion (*Ghost Kitchen Market to Reach $157.26 Billion by 2030*, n.d.).

The worldwide ghost kitchen industry has caused significant growth and disruption in the food industry, opening up new opportunities for food service businesses and enabling them to adapt to shifting consumer needs (Abkar Y. A, 2022). In February 2023, TGAL, the largest food tech company in Japan and one of the most recognised food conglomerates with a network of over 1400 host kitchens and over 120 brands from different regions of Japan announced an exclusive partnership with Village Food Courts (VFC), the largest F&B aggregator of National & International brands in India Suresh et al., n.d.). In February 2023, Ghost Kitchens acquired cloud kitchen startup Speak Burgers to foray into the premium segment with high spending power. The move is in line with its vision to create a basket of premium food delivery brands that operates on Swiggy and Zomato(*Ghost Kitchen Market to Reach $157.26 Billion by 2030*, n.d.). The international ghost kitchen market has grown quickly and is now a major force in the foodservice sector worldwide. Often called cloud kitchens or virtual kitchens, ghost kitchens are commercial cooking spaces that are only used for food preparation and delivery—they don't have any actual dine-in alternatives (Suganob, 2022). The expanding trend of online ordering, the advent of smartphone apps that allow customers to make orders from the comfort of their homes, and the growing need for food delivery services have all contributed to this creative business model. Due to its affordability and adaptability to the shifting tastes of contemporary consumers, the ghost kitchen market is expanding quickly in a number of different places worldwide (Rivetti, 2023a).

The potential of ghost kitchens to drastically save overhead expenses, including those related to running a conventional brick-and-mortar restaurant, is one of their main benefits. Businesses are able to spend resources more effectively as a result of these cost reductions, which has drawn in a large number of new competitors, including startups and well-known restaurant brands (CHERNOVA & SHABALIN, n.d.). Ghost kitchens can operate in less costly locations, including business parks or industrial regions, by doing away with the need for valuable real estate in busy areas. This results in huge savings. Additionally, without having to hire a lot of employees or invest in more physical space, this strategy allows organizations to increase operations quickly (Rivetti, 2023a).

Additionally, shifting consumer habits are driving the global ghost kitchen industry. As food delivery services like Uber Eats, DoorDash, and Grubhub have grown in popularity, customers are placing a higher value on speed and convenience when selecting meals (Chen et al., n.d.-a). Ghost kitchens are in a unique position to satisfy this need because they only concentrate on food preparation and delivery, which enables quicker service and more effective delivery. Furthermore, both new and established food enterprises looking to enter the cutthroat meal delivery market find ghost kitchens to be an appealing alternative due to the growing trend of online ordering (KITCHEN, n.d.). Ghost kitchens' adaptability also makes them appropriate for a variety of applications in different global markets. Ghost kitchens provide a scalable and reasonably priced alternative to regular restaurants in crowded urban areas where they could find it difficult to remain profitable (Networks et al., n.d.). Because they don't require large upfront investments in physical locations, they enable food businesses to try new concepts or cuisines with little risk. Ghost kitchens can also serve niche markets by concentrating on particular dietary requirements or cuisines, such vegan, gluten-free, or organic alternatives, which are becoming more and more popular worldwide (Vu et al., n.d.).

Moreover, ghost kitchens can be used as a venue for alliances and teamwork. Large food businesses, for instance, can work with ghost kitchen operators to establish virtual brands and broaden their customer base without requiring physical locations (M. Khan, 2024). In order to access underserved areas or places with a high demand for food delivery services, restaurant chains and ghost kitchen operators are forming partnerships in the global market. Ghost kitchens have quickly spread in developed markets like North America as well as developing markets in Asia and Europe because to this cooperative strategy (M. Khan, 2024).

The employment of cutting-edge technology like artificial intelligence (AI), machine learning, and automated kitchen equipment is growing more common as the ghost kitchen market expands globally (Suganob, 2022). These technologies make the ghost kitchen model even more effective by managing inventory, streamlining delivery logistics, anticipating consumer preferences, and optimizing kitchen operations. Furthermore, to increase their efficacy and worldwide reach, ghost kitchens are becoming more and more connected with cloud-based management systems and food delivery platforms in areas like Asia Pacific (Seghezzi et al., n.d.). Ghost Kitchens started a program in September 2021 to expand its brands using fulfillment partners and an asset-light methodology. Existing eateries with underutilized kitchen space and the infrastructure to provide a certain cuisine will be granted licenses to use the brands. As a result, eateries will be able to increase their earnings from the first order they serve (Jones et al., 2024a)

2.3 Analysts' Opinions on the Worldwide

Ghost Kitchen Industry In essence, ghost kitchens are restaurants without the eating area. Their primary goal is to sell and deliver food orders placed online through either their own delivery service or third-party apps (Cai et al., n.d.) Since ghost kitchens don't have any overhead related to activities that interact with customers, they can avoid many of the expenses involved in starting and running a restaurant, including permits, inspections, furnishings, equipment, and more. The restaurant industry's future is being shaped by cloud kitchens, often known as ghost kitchens(Zhu et al., 2024) They enable restaurants that exclusively offer delivery services to continue operating even if they still have physical locations. Additionally, ghost kitchens, also known as cloud kitchens, offer a number of benefits to various restaurant kinds and business owners(Cai et al., n.d.)

One of the major factors anticipated to support the expansion of the worldwide ghost kitchen market is the growing popularity of ghost/cloud kitchens. For example, the increased demand for online meal delivery services has led to the rise in popularity of ghost or cloud kitchens and online food delivery-(T. Khan et al., n.d.) In turn, this has prompted numerous restaurant owners worldwide to build cloud kitchen locations in order to process orders and provide customer service. Convenience, consumers' hectic lifestyles, and widespread internet usage are all contributing factors to the rise in popularity of ghost kitchens. As a result, cloud kitchens are becoming a common investment option for both new and seasoned restaurateurs looking to launch a culinary enterprise (Beniwal et al., n.d.)

2.4 Growing numbers of smartphone and Internet users will fuel market expansion

Globally, internet meal delivery services have benefited from the rise in smartphone usage. Additionally, ordering food has become simpler due to the growing number of smartphone users and easy access to the Internet. The rise in Internet searches for food and drink is also reflected in the growing number of smartphone users(Chng, 2024) In 2021, there will be 80 million monthly active users on Indian food delivery platforms, with plans to reach 200 million in the coming years, according to a report released by Zomato, an Indian food delivery service. In order to process orders and provide customer service, Zomato has also purchased more than nine small delivery businesses(Review & 2023, n.d.)

One of the main factors driving the growth of the ghost kitchen industry is the increasing number of internet and smartphone users globally. A growing number of customers are choosing meal delivery services via apps and online platforms as mobile devices and internet connectivity become more widely available (Rinaldi et al., n.d.). This shift in customer behavior is particularly obvious among younger, tech-savvy generations that favor ease and quickness. Smartphones greatly improve the whole customer experience by making it simple for users to browse menus, place orders, track deliveries, and make payments. Food delivery services have thus taken over as the main way that people eat, which has increased demand for virtual kitchens that just process delivery orders (Scott et al., n.d.). Ghost kitchens may now reach a wider clientele thanks to the growing use of cellphones and the internet in developing regions like Asia Pacific, Africa, and Latin America. The emergence of social media and food influencers also contributes to the increased visibility of new ghost kitchen products, which speeds up their expansion. In the upcoming years, the worldwide ghost kitchen market is expected to continue to grow due to the combination of rising mobile internet usage and changing customer expectations for on-demand delivery services (Rinaldi et al., n.d.).

2.5 Opportunities in the Global Ghost Kitchen Market

It is anticipated that the growing number of ghost kitchens worldwide will present substantial potential prospects for companies operating in the global ghost kitchen market.

The use of online meal delivery applications and the number of ghost/cloud kitchens are growing quickly in tandem with consumers' growing preference for online food services overeating establishments (*Ghost Kitchen Market to Reach $157.26 Billion by 2030*, n.d.). According to November 2022 research by the India Brand Equity Foundation (IBEF), Delhi, India, currently has over 20,000 operational cloud kitchens, and the number is growing by about 20% a year. Additionally, Swiggy's cloud kitchen count nearly tripled between FY 2019 and FY 21 and nearly doubled on Zomato starting in January 2020. In order to enable lightning-fast delivery, Zomato is also negotiating with a number of restaurant partners and cloud kitchen providers (*Ghost Kitchen Market - Share, Size and Industry Analysis*, n.d.).

Food preparation, order processing, and delivery logistics are just a few of the many aspects that must be effectively coordinated to run a successful ghost kitchen. Operations get more complex when many orders and different components are managed in the same kitchen. It can be difficult to complete orders on time, particularly during busy times (Chng, 2024) Furthermore, inadequate personal hygiene, malfunctioning equipment, and inappropriate food handling can all contribute significantly to food contamination. Therefore, regulations and training programs that teach staff members the value of food safety should be implemented in ghost kitchens. The growth of the market is then anticipated to be severely impacted (T. Khan et al., n.d.)

3. OPPORTUNITIES IN GHOST KITCHEN EXPANSION

There are numerous opportunities presented by the growth of ghost kitchens that have the potential to completely transform the global foodservice sector. Their capacity to meet the rising demand for food delivery services is one of the biggest prospects(Jones et al., n.d.). Ghost kitchens are well-positioned to satisfy this need without incurring the overhead expenses associated with conventional brick-and-mortar restaurants, as more customers choose convenience and online ordering. By setting up kitchens in several locations, this approach allows operators to swiftly expand their business without requiring costly real estate or sizable physical dining rooms (Rivetti, 2023b). Significant growth potential is also provided by geographic expansion, especially in underserved and emerging regions. Food delivery services are becoming more popular in areas like Asia Pacific, Africa, and Latin America due to factors including urbanization, growing disposable incomes, and increased smartphone usage. With their low operating costs, ghost kitchens can enter these rapidly expanding markets without having to make significant capital expenditures. Additionally, ghost kitchens can experiment with new markets with little risk, modifying their products in response to local tastes and client requests (Chng, 2024). Technological developments also present a number of expansion prospects. Ghost kitchens can improve delivery efficiency, anticipate client preferences, and streamline operations by incorporating artificial intelligence (AI), machine learning, and data analytics. In order to keep up with the growing amount of delivery orders, automation in food preparation and delivery logistics lowers labor costs, improves order accuracy, and speeds up operations (T. Khan et al., n.d.). Furthermore, the popularity of cloud-based kitchen management systems makes it possible to integrate them easily with outside delivery platforms, which aids operators in effectively managing several brands under one roof. Ghost kitchens can further increase their scalability and profitability by using these solutions to expedite order processing, inventory management, and customer interactions. Ghost kitchens can take advantage of the increasing demand for delivery around the world to broaden their clientele and strengthen their position in the cutthroat foodservice industry (Suresh, Santhosh, and, et al., n.d.).

3.1 *Economical Approach*

The potential to scale operations at much reduced costs is one of the main prospects for growth in the ghost kitchen sector. Ghost kitchens avoid the expenditures that traditional brick-and-mortar restaurants must make on front-of-house operations, interior design, and premium real estate. For business owners, franchisees, and well-established restaurant chains looking to grow without the hassle of actual sites, this makes the model very alluring (Suresh et al., 2024c)

3.2 *Enhanced Productivity*

Ghost kitchens are made to be extremely efficient, which is essential for fulfilling orders quickly. Operators can increase delivery times and lower labor expenses in the kitchen by utilizing technology and streamlining procedures. Additionally, common kitchen areas facilitate collaboration and cost-sharing by allowing numerous companies to operate out of the same space (Jones et al., 2024b)

3.3 *Getting into New Markets*

There is a big chance for ghost kitchens to expand into developing markets. Rapid urbanization and digital adoption have occurred in markets including Africa, Southeast Asia, and India. Ghost kitchens can reach expanding urban populations without requiring significant infrastructure investments thanks to the increased popularity of meal delivery apps in these areas. Ghost kitchens can obtain a competitive advantage by getting into these areas early (Jones et al., n.d.)

3.4 *Coherence of Consumer Choice*

When it comes to food options, consumers are increasingly favoring variety and ease of use. Delivery times are accelerated and the need for diversity is met by ghost kitchens' capacity to serve several cuisines from a single location. Because they make it simple to order a variety of cuisines from a single platform, ghost kitchens are positioned for long-term success because to their congruence with consumer preferences (Chen et al., n.d.-b)

4. DIFFICULTIES IN GROWING GHOST KITCHENS

4.1 *Judicial and Legislative Concerns*

Regulatory compliance presents a number of difficulties for ghost kitchens. These include of labor laws, zoning rules, health inspections, and standards for food safety. Legal obstacles may arise in some areas due to unclear regulations governing the operation of delivery-only kitchens. Ghost kitchens' shared nature also creates questions around health and safety inspections, especially when several brands use the same space (T. Khan et al., n.d.)

4.2 *Vigorous Competition in the Market*

Operators are competing more fiercely as ghost kitchens gain popularity. Ghost kitchens need to set themselves apart from the competition in order to stay afloat in the face of so many new competitors. While established restaurant chains may benefit from the shift to ghost kitchens, individual businesses need to be creative to differentiate themselves. Furthermore, the market can be swiftly disrupted by new competitors due to low entry barriers, which increases competition for delivery drivers and customer attention (Suresh, Santhosh, and, et al., n.d.)

4.3 *Consumer Faith and Image of the brand*

Through direct customer service, ambiance, and in-person encounters, restaurants in a traditional brick-and-mortar environment cultivate a devoted clientele. However, because there is no actual store to visit, ghost kitchens struggle to build a strong brand identity. In order to maintain long-term client retention, ghost kitchen owners must make investments in branding and customer relationship management (CRM) systems. Establishing trust and loyalty in a virtual setting might be difficult (Cai et al., n.d.)

4.4 *Relying on Transport and Supply*

Ghost kitchens rely largely on outside delivery services to provide food to customers. This leads to logistical problems with regard to meal quality, delivery delays, and the general client experience. Although collaborations with delivery platforms are advantageous, they may also result in higher operating expenses and lower profitability. Ghost kitchen operations can also be greatly impacted by potential issues like strikes, inclement weather, or modifications to delivery platform restrictions (Cheng, C. C et. Al., 2025).

5. PROSPECTS FOR GHOST KITCHENS IN THE FUTURE

5.1 *Developments in Technology*

It's likely that technology will influence ghost kitchens in the future. Data analytics, automation, and artificial intelligence (AI) will become more and more important in forecasting demand, streamlining culinary operations, and customizing consumer experiences. AI can help with inventory management, pricing optimization, and menu creation, for instance. Additionally, automation could save labor expenses and expedite food preparation, thus increasing the business model's cost-effectiveness (Zhu et al., 2024)

5.2 *Blend Structures*

Hybrid models that combine virtual kitchen operations with real-world sites are becoming more popular. A "ghost kitchen" strategy is becoming more and more popular in restaurants, which combine a traditional dining experience with a delivery-only business model. This enables them to take advantage of the expanding delivery trend while retaining their physical clientele. Hybrid models give customers the flexibility of both delivery and dine-in options as they want additional options (Cornell et al., 2024)

5.3 *Sustainable procedures and ecological responsibility*

Sustainability may become more of a focus in ghost kitchens as environmental concerns continue to grow. In order to meet the rising demand for sustainable food, ghost kitchen operations might adopt eco-friendly procedures from sourcing ingredients to packing. This entails reducing food waste, utilizing environmentally friendly packaging, and integrating kitchen appliances that use less energy (Cao et al., n.d.)

Sustainability and ecological responsibility have emerged as key issues for the industry's future as the ghost kitchen model develops further. The environmental impact of ghost kitchen operations can be substantial because they frequently function on a bigger scale, with several companies producing food from a single facility (Sarkissian et al., 2012). Nonetheless, the sector is embracing sustainable methods more and more due to the growing need to address climate change and customer demand for eco-friendly products. Using energy-efficient equipment is becoming a top priority for many ghost cooks, which lowers energy consumption and their carbon footprint. To further reduce their environmental impact, several operators are also investing in renewable energy sources like wind and solar (Li et al., n.d.).

Another important area where ghost kitchens are putting sustainable practices into practice is waste management. Since food delivery services frequently require a lot of packaging, especially single-use plastics, many ghost cooks are reducing packaging waste by using recyclable, compostable, or biodegradable materials instead (Sarkissian et al., 2012). In addition to being good for the environment, this change reflects consumers' increasing desire for environmentally friendly products. Additionally, some ghost kitchens are collaborating with nearby vendors to lessen the transportation-related carbon footprint by encouraging the use of ingredients that are sourced locally and minimizing the need for long-distance shipping. Ghost kitchens are also addressing the issue of food waste (Balaji et al., 2022). Many ghost kitchens are introducing waste-reduction strategies, like improving inventory management, turning food leftovers into compost or animal feed, and putting procedures in place to guarantee that food is made and served in the best possible quantity, in an industry where speed and efficiency are crucial. To ensure that excess food does not go to waste and that client orders are fulfilled with the least amount of environmental impact, some businesses are also using data-driven technologies to track and improve food production (Li et al., n.d.). The incorporation of sustainable practices into the ghost kitchen model aims to cater to a rising consumer base that prioritizes corporate responsibility in addition to lessening the impact on the environment. Businesses that put sustainability first are likely to draw in devoted clients who are prepared to pay extra for environmentally friendly products as more people become conscious of the environmental problems the food sector poses. With operators emphasizing eco-friendly methods as a fundamental component of their business models, this trend has the potential to completely transform the ghost kitchen industry going forward (Rivetti, 2023c).

Going forward, sustainability will be essential to ghost kitchens' long-term success. Virtual kitchens that make investments in green technologies, sustainable sourcing, and waste reduction will not only help create a better world but also establish personally as leaders in the becoming environmentally conscious foodservice sector as regulations regarding the environment tighten around the world and client demands rise (Sarkissian et al., 2012).

6. CONCLUSION

This section on "Challenges and Opportunities of Ghost Kitchens" concludes by highlighting the enormous potential as well as the challenges associated with this novel business model's quick growth. Ghost kitchens are changing conventional restaurant models by concentrating only on food delivery, which lowers operating costs and boosts efficiency as they continue to revolutionize the foodservice sector. But there are drawbacks to this expansion as well, which must be resolved for long-term success (*The Internet of Things (IoT) and Smart Cooking Technology... - Google Scholar*, n.d.).

The fierce competition in the meal delivery industry is one of the main obstacles to the growth of ghost kitchens. The market is becoming fragmented as a result of numerous new firms entering it due to low entry barriers. Operators must set themselves apart in this fiercely competitive market by distinctive products, strong brand recognition, and operational excellence. Reliance on outside delivery platforms can also limit control over profits and customer experience, which presents additional difficulties for companies operating in this market (Cornell et al., 2024).

Another major obstacle is regulatory barriers, especially when ghost kitchens don't follow the rules of typical restaurants. Operators may have uncertainty as a result of local zoning rules, health regulations, and food safety requirements that aren't always adjusted to this new model. The changing regulatory environment may require large investments in compliance and postpone expansion.

Notwithstanding these obstacles, the ghost kitchen industry has a lot of room to grow. Given the rising demand for food delivery services, there is a lot of potential for expanding into underdeveloped markets, especially in developing regions like Asia-Pacific, Africa, and Latin America. For international firms wishing to expand their consumer bases without making significant investments in real locations, ghost kitchens can be a starting point. Additionally, the model's scalability enables companies to quickly adjust to market changes and consumer preferences, exploiting the growing trend toward personalization in the foodservice industry and catering to niche markets like vegan, health-conscious, or ethnic cuisines.

Gourmet kitchens also have a lot of options because to technological improvements. In the kitchen, automation, data science, and robotics (AI) can maximize food production, enhance customer satisfaction, and save operating expenses. By improving operational efficiency, anticipating consumer behavior, and personalizing experiences, these technologies can give ghost kitchens a competitive advantage in a crowded industry.

Ghost kitchens are transforming the foodservice industry by providing an efficient, scalable, and cost-effective solution to the growing demand for food delivery. Their expansion presents numerous opportunities for businesses to reach new customers, reduce operational costs, and tap into emerging markets. However, challenges such as regulatory hurdles, intense competition, and logistical complexities must be addressed for sustainable growth. The future of ghost kitchens will be shaped by technological innovations, hybrid business models, and sustainability efforts, positioning them as a key player in the evolving foodservice landscape.

In addition, in future with emerging trends and busy schedule of upcoming generations, the impact and culture of ghost kitchen will rise a lot. Cloud kitchen will be not only a new and goldens opportunity of younger generations, but also a helpful to the people those who are not having time to prepare food as they will easily get home made food at reasonable cost without visiting any place.

Ghost kitchen will open the new ways universally with advance technology and less waste with environmentally sustainable practices in upcoming future. In conclusion, ghost kitchens' future depends on their capacity to overcome current obstacles and take advantage of the rising demand for food delivery services as well as changing customer expectations. Ghost kitchens may maintain their success and establish themselves as major participants in the global foodservice sector by concentrating on operational effectiveness, technical innovation, sustainability, and market development. Expectations for growth are strong as the industry evolves, and companies that can adjust to these dynamics will probably be at the forefront of this quickly shifting environment.

7. REFERENCES

Akbar, Y. A., Mahamad, W. W., & Saad, R. (2022). *Ghost kitchen*. https://ir.uitm.edu.my/id/eprint/99573/

Balaji, M. S., Jiang, Y., Bhattacharyya, J., Hewege, C. R., & Azer, J. (2022). An Introduction to Socially Responsible Sustainable Consumption: Issues and Challenges. *Socially Responsible Consumption and Marketing in Practice: Collection of Case Studies*, 3–14. DOI: 10.1007/978-981-16-6433-5_1

Bekaert, G., Harvey, C. R., Lundblad, C., & Siegel, S. (2007). Global growth opportunities and market integration. *The Journal of Finance*, *62*(3), 1081–1137. DOI: 10.1111/j.1540-6261.2007.01231.x

Beniwal, T. in, V. M.-I. A. R. J., & 2021, undefined. (n.d.). Cloud kitchen: A profitable venture. *Academia.Edu*. Retrieved January 9, 2025, from https://www.academia.edu/download/86464163/IARJSET.2021.81010.pdf

Cai, R., Leung, X. Y., & Chi, C. G. Q. (2022). Ghost kitchens on the rise: Effects of knowledge and perceived benefit-risk on customers' behavioral intentions. *International Journal of Hospitality Management*, *101*, 103110.

Cao, J., Hu, F., & Qi, W. (n.d.). " Uber" Your Cooking: The Sharing-economy Operations of a Ghost-kitchen Platform. *Papers*.Ssrn.*Com*. Retrieved January 9, 2025, from https://papers.ssrn.com/sol3/papers.cfm?abstract_id=4494858

Chen, L. A., & House, L. (2022). The rise of the ghosts—The impact of the pandemic on food purchases. *Choices*, *37*(2), 1–10.

Chernova, E., & Shabalin, V. Digital Technologies in Food Industry: Impact of COVID-19 Pandemic and Consumer Demands. Общество с ограниченной ответственностью" Институт Цифровой Экономики и Права" КОНФЕРЕНЦИЯ: II INTERNATIONAL SCIENTIFIC AND PRACTICAL CONFERENCE ON SUSTAINABLE DEVELOPMENT OF REGIONAL INFRASTRUCTURE (ISSDRI 2022) Yekaterinburg, Russia, 14–15 марта 2022 года Организаторы: LLC Institute of Digital Economics and Law.

Chng, S. (2024). The emerging socio-spatial implications of cloud kitchens and cloud stores. *The City Rebooted: Networks, Connectivity And Place Identities In Singapore*, 185–210. DOI: 10.1142/9789811287848_0007

Chng, S. (2024). The Emerging Socio-Spatial Implications of Cloud Kitchens and Cloud Stores. In THE CITY REBOOTED: Networks, Connectivity and Place Identities in Singapore (pp. 185-210).

Cornell, D., Manamtam, J. R., & Tham, A. (2024). Invisible Workers in Philippines' Ghost Kitchens: Trends and Implications. *Advances in Southeast Asian Studies*, *17*(2), 187–200.

Corvo, P., Migliavada, R., & Mattia Zocchi, D. (2022). New Food and Restaurant Trends. *Social Indicators Research Series*, *85*, 39–55. DOI: 10.1007/978-3-030-97806-8_3

Festivalia, F., & Swantari, A. (2022). Ghost kitchen strategy to reduce restaurant loss in COVID-19 pandemic condition. In Current Issues in Tourism, Gastronomy, and Tourist Destination Research (pp. 441-448). Routledge.

ghost kitchen - Google Scholar. (n.d.). Retrieved January 8, 2025, from https://scholar.google.co.in/scholar?hl=en&as_sdt=0%2C5&q=ghost+kitchen&btnG=

Ghost Kitchen Market - Share, Size and Industry Analysis. (n.d.). Retrieved January 8, 2025, from https://www.coherentmarketinsights.com/market-insight/ghost-kitchen-market-5936

Ghost Kitchen Market to reach $157.26 billion by 2030. (n.d.). Retrieved January 8, 2025, from https://www.globenewswire.com/news-release/2023/07/28/2713295/0/en/Ghost-Kitchen-Market-to-reach-157-26-billion-by-2030-Globally-at-a-CAGR-of-12-says-Coherent-Market-Insights.html

John, K. T. (2023). Digital disruption: The hyperlocal delivery and cloud kitchen driven future of food services in post-COVID India. *International Hospitality Review*, *37*(1), 161–187.

Jones, S., Cain, L., & Deel, G. L. (2024). Virtual restaurants and ghost kitchens: A new opportunity. *Journal of Hospitality & Tourism Cases*, *12*(3), 108–112.

Jones, S., Cain, L., & Deel, G. L. (2024a). Virtual Restaurants and Ghost Kitchens: A New Opportunity. *Journal of Hospitality & Tourism Cases*, *12*(3), 108–112. DOI: 10.1177/21649987241241948

Jones, S., Cain, L., & Deel, G. L. (2024b). Virtual Restaurants and Ghost Kitchens: A New Opportunity. *Journal of Hospitality & Tourism Cases*, *12*(3), 108–112. DOI: 10.1177/21649987241241948

Khan, M. (2024). *Cloud kitchen: navigating the future of multiple restaurant in a nutt-shell*. https://www.theseus.fi/bitstream/handle/10024/871563/Khan_Mahwish.pdf?sequence=3

Khan, T. A., Khan, S. A., Haque, S., & Ayub, M. F. B. (2023). A study on the prospect of the cloud kitchen model in Dhaka. *International Journal of Business and Management*, *18*(1), 46–59.

KITCHEN. C. (n.d.). GHOST KITCHEN. *Repositorio.Comillas.Edu*. Retrieved February 24, 2025, from https://repositorio.comillas.edu/rest/bitstreams/436947/retrieve

Li, C., Mirosa, M., & Bremer, P. (2020). Review of online food delivery platforms and their impacts on sustainability. *Sustainability*, *12*(14), 5528.

Rinaldi, C., D'aguilar, M., & Egan, M. (2022). Understanding the online environment for the delivery of food, alcohol and tobacco: An exploratory analysis of 'dark kitchens' and rapid grocery delivery services. *International Journal of Environmental Research and Public Health*, *19*(9), 5523.

Rivetti, V. (2023). *Business Plan: eVegan Ghost Kitchen in Finland Capital Region*. https://www.theseus.fi/bitstream/handle/10024/813398/Rivetti_Vincenzo.pdf?sequence=2

Sarkissian, W., Hofer, N., Shore, Y., Vajda, S., & Wilkinson, C. (2012). *Kitchen Table Sustainability*. Kitchen Table Sustainability., DOI: 10.4324/9781849771795

Scott, N., Barnard-Tallier, M., & Batchelor, S. (2021). Losing the energy to cook: An exploration of modern food systems and energy consumption in domestic kitchens. *Energies*, *14*(13), 4004.

Seghezzi, A., Siragusa, C., Mangiaracina, R., Perego, A., & Tumino, A. (2023). Dark, cloud and ghost kitchens: a logistics perspective. In Proceedings of the XXVIII Summer School "Francesco Turco" (pp. 1-7). AIDI-Italian Association of Industrial Operations Professors.

Suganob, D. (2022). *Ghost Kitchen:" Kusina Filipina"*. https://search.proquest.com/openview/41433b69f664c9eb3f41ca35a0e7484f/1?pq-origsite=gscholar&cbl=2026366&diss=y

Suresh, S., & Santhosh, S. 2, T. S. A. and D. V., & 2024, undefined. (n.d.). Food Economies–Engendered Ghost Kitchens in the Digital Age. *Springer*. Retrieved February 24, 2025, from https://link.springer.com/chapter/10.1007/978-3-031-62106-2_8

Suresh, S., Santhosh, S., & Samjaila, T. H. (2024). Food Economies–Engendered Ghost Kitchens in the Digital Age. *Studies in Systems. Decision and Control*, *537*, 95–104. DOI: 10.1007/978-3-031-62106-2_8

Suresh, S., Santhosh, S., & Samjaila, T. H. (2024). Food Economies–Engendered Ghost Kitchens in the Digital Age. In *Business Development via AI and Digitalization* (Vol. 2, pp. 95–104). Springer Nature Switzerland.

The Internet of Things (IoT) and smart cooking technology... - Google Scholar. (n.d.). Retrieved January 21, 2025, from https://scholar.google.co.in/scholar?hl=en&as_sdt=0%2C5&as_rr=1&q=The+Internet+of+Things+%28IoT%29+and+smart+cooking+technology+%2C+reducing+waste%2C+and+encouraging+wholesome+eating+practices.+&btnG=

Vu, O. T. K., Alonso, A. D., Tran, T. D., & Nicholson, G. J. (2023). Illuminating the dark kitchen business model-A knowledge-based perspective from the supply-side. *Journal of Hospitality and Tourism Management*, *55*, 318–331.

Zhu, Y., Pi, M., Zhu, X., & Byrd, K. (2024). Busiest Store in a Cramped Space: Can a Ghost Kitchen Optimize Coffee Shop Efficiency? *Journal of Hospitality & Tourism Cases*. DOI: 10.1177/21649987241270419

Chapter 13
The Future of AI in the Food Industry:
Emerging Trends and Opportunities

Evarisa Mary Nengnong
https://orcid.org/0000-0002-7574-8115
North Eastern Hill University, India

Charis R. Ripnar
https://orcid.org/0009-0000-3758-4706
Directorate of Food Processing, India

ABSTRACT

Food business is undergoing a major revolution due to the integration of artificial intelligence (AI). AI provides creative solutions that improve efficiency, sustainability, and profitability, ranging from supply chain optimization to personalized customer experiences. This chapter will examine the rising trends and opportunities in the food industry that AI technologies like machine learning, predictive analytics, and robotics provide. The chapter will examine real-world applications and case studies to demonstrate how AI transforms food production, distribution, safety, and marketing. Furthermore, the conversation will cover the ethical issues, obstacles, and future directions for AI in the sector, providing stakeholders with a comprehensive framework for navigating this technological transformation.

INTRODUCTION

Food business is one of the most dynamic and rapidly changing industries, driven by global population growth, shifting customer preferences, and increased sustainability concerns. Technology has emerged as a critical tool for progress as the world grapples with resource scarcity, environmental degradation, and food security concerns. Artificial intelligence (AI) is one of the few technologies that can radically

DOI: 10.4018/979-8-3373-0432-8.ch013

transform the food industry, and the combination of technology and food is one of many industries that stand to profit substantially from AI's potential.

This chapter examines how AI tackles urgent problems and gives a summary of the state of the food industry today. In addition to increasing productivity and efficiency, artificial intelligence (AI) also satisfies the growing demand for sustainable practices and customized customer experiences by utilizing data-driven solutions, machine learning, and automation. But first, let us discuss Artificial Intelligence (AI) to understand its perception.

Artificial intelligence (AI) is an area of computer science that mimics human thought processes, learning capacity, and knowledge storage (Mavani et al, 2021; Krittanawong et al, 2017). AI is a product of machine learning that can do tasks that are typically associated with human intelligence. It has already become a part of our daily lives, assisting us with tasks like learning, problem-solving, and natural language interpretation; it also has the potential to improve efficiency and stimulate innovation or creativity (Zatsu et al., 2024). Furthermore, AI has become the driving force behind transformation in the food business by optimizing processes, improving overall quality and safety standards, and developing unique culinary goods (Jadhav et al., 2024).

The Growing Food Sector Landscape

Several environmental, technological, and demographic factors are creating significant changes in the global food business. Given that the global population will reach 9.7 billion by 2050, food production will need to increase by 70% to meet demand (FAO, 2021). However, challenges such as soil erosion, climate change, and a scarcity of arable land make this goal difficult to attain. Customers' opinions are shifting in favor of organic, healthier, and environmentally friendly food options.

Innovative technologies are being used more and more by the food business to traverse this complicated terrain. In addition to helping companies streamline their supply chains and production, digital tools like artificial intelligence (AI) are also allowing them to provide customers with greater value. Because of this, the food industry has seen an exponential increase in the use of AI, with investments in these technologies expected to reach $35 billion by 2027 (MarketsandMarkets, 2023).

The Role of AI in Addressing Contemporary Issues

Food security, sustainability, and changing customer demands are some of the most important concerns facing the food business that AI is well-positioned to handle.

Food Waste: Prediction of population in need to produce more of the resources, may not sometimes be accurate, so this results in farmers producing more of the resources than what is required. This then, leads to additional produce which in turn goes to waste by either discarding off or not being able to be traded off. AI plays a role by servicing the farmers in planning the crop production more accurately thereby, lowering the risk of producing unnecessary additional resources (Bouallegue & Al-Naemi, 2025).

Economic Loss: When there is a mismatch between supply and demand, it may be due to the poor prediction of the population requirement for resources or produce and this will lead to economic losses for farmers and businesses. This will also affect farmers selling their produce putting them at a loss and businesses will not meet the customer demand. (Bouallegue & Al-Naemi, 2025).

Food Security: Precision farming, predictive analytics, and real-time crop and livestock monitoring are some of the ways AI-powered systems are enhancing agricultural productivity. Global food security is aided by these technologies, which allow farmers to maximize resource utilization, cut waste, and boost yields (Zhao et al., 2022).

Sustainability: The food sector has made sustainability a top priority, and artificial intelligence is essential to reducing its negative effects on the environment. For example, supply chain data can be analyzed by machine learning algorithms to find inefficiencies, cut down on food waste, and lessen carbon footprints. Additionally, AI is promoting the creation of lab-grown meats and substitute proteins, which could lessen dependency on conventional cattle husbandry (Klerkx & Rose, 2020).

Customer Needs: AI is propelling advancements in product development and customer interaction as consumers seek more convenient and customized dining experiences. Access to customized nutritional solutions is becoming simpler for people because of AI-powered recommendation systems, smart kitchen equipment, and personalized nutrition applications. Furthermore, sentiment analysis technologies give businesses information about customer preferences, enabling them to develop goods that appeal to their target market (Sharma et al., 2021).

Relying on Import Goods: Relying on importing goods indicates that the country lacks awareness in population count. As the prediction of the population's need for produce is not properly carried out, it leads to over-reliance on imports and wherefore prediction of population's needs in produce is necessary. AI helps predict the population's requirement for the consumption of produce (Bouallegue & Al-Naemi, 2025).

The purpose of this chapter is to examine how AI is revolutionizing the food sector and how it affects important issues like customer demands, sustainability, and food security. It will highlight new developments, prospects for the future, and real-world difficulties, offering insights into how AI might spur innovation and help the global food industry have a sustainable future.

AI IN FOOD PRODUCTION: PRECISION AGRICULTURE

Precision agriculture (PA) or precision farming is currently perceived as a key technological solution that increases in utilization of agricultural resources more efficiently (Linaza et al., 2021), thereby creating general goals of PA as the increase of farmers' profits by improving harvest and/or quality yields, while reducing inputs, and the negative impact of farming on the environment, e.g., such that stems from the over-application of pesticides and fertilizers, and inefficient irrigation.

The emergence of Artificial Intelligence (AI)-powered precision agriculture is transforming farming by facilitating data-driven choices that improve sustainability and efficiency. Farmers may maximize resource utilization, lessen their impact on the environment, and increase output by utilizing cutting-edge technologies like robotics, machine learning, and big data analytics. ***Optimizing Irrigation, Fertilization, and Insect Management***

The way farmers handle essential inputs like water, fertilizer, and pest control is changing as a result of AI-driven technologies. For example:

Irrigation Optimization: AI algorithms and smart sensors evaluate crop needs, soil moisture, and weather predictions to provide water exactly where and when it's needed, greatly cutting down on waste (Ravi et al., 2022).

Fertilizer Application: AI-based systems evaluate plant health and soil composition to establish the best fertilizing schedules, improving nutrient use efficiency and lowering pollution from runoff (Chen et al., 2021).

Insect & insect Management: Real-time field monitoring by AI-powered cameras and drones reduces crop loss and pesticide use by detecting insect infestations early and applying targeted treatments (Aftab et al., 2020). These developments support long-term agricultural resilience by increasing yields while also being consistent with sustainable farming methods.

Agricultural Robotics: Automating the Field

Automation is used in different industries like automotive, electronics, medical, defense, and agriculture to improve product quality and reduce human errors, cost, and time. However, one must also keep in mind that automation has been a part of agriculture, from planting seeds to harvesting. The growth of agricultural robotics—machines built to carry out activities like planting, monitoring, and harvesting crops—is being propelled by artificial intelligence.

Planting: AI-guided autonomous seeders guarantee even dispersion of seeds and ideal depth placement, increasing germination rates.

Crop monitoring: To evaluate crop health, identify diseases, and track growth, robots with sophisticated sensors and cameras traverse fields.

Harvesting: AI-powered harvesters reduce waste and labor expenses by precisely identifying ripe crops using machine vision (Wang et al., 2021). In addition to lowering reliance on manual labor, these robots improve agricultural operations' scalability and uniformity.

Drones: DRONE (Dynamic Remotely Operated Navigation Equipment) is commonly referred to as unmanned aerial vehicle (UAV) and they are a package of software, sensors, and hardware that a farmer monitors the health of crops and surveys farmland. Using drone technology these days is like a blessing to a farmer since it serves multiple purposes for which a farmer was not able to carry out farming activities (such as monitoring, mapping, irrigation, crop inspection, spraying, and surveying entire fields, etc.) in which all can be easily covered by the drone (Sadiku et. al, 2021).

Benefits and Challenges of Robotic Automation

Productivity, efficiency, and sustainability are some of the benefits responsible for the adoption of robotic automation in today's agriculture industry. While benefits can be such as quality & accuracy of the process, reduced cycle times & increased productivity, improved compliance in industrial systems, reduced crop maintenance & harvesting cycle times, operating cost savings, etc., there are also several challenges that robotic automation faces and they can be labor shortage is a global challenge, concerns over data privacy and regulations, lack of standardization in technology which complicates the integration of systems (Sadiku et al. (a), 2021)

Climate Modelling and Big Data Analytics

A climate model, in general, may be defined as a mathematical representation of the climate system based on physical, biological, and chemical principles that provides a solution that is discrete in space and time, meaning that the results obtained represent averages over regions, whose size depends on model resolution, and for specific times (Goosse H, et al., 2010)

Big Data is a collection of data that is huge in volume, yet growing exponentially with time. It is data with so large a size and complexity that none of the traditional data management tools can store it or process it efficiently. Big data analytics describes the process of uncovering trends, patterns, and correlations in large amounts of raw data to help make data-informed decisions. It is the use of advanced analytic techniques against very large, diverse data sets that include structured, semi-structured, and unstructured data, from different sources, and in different sizes (terabytes to zettabytes) (Anonymous).

When Big data analytics and climate modeling are successfully combined with artificial intelligence (AI), this gives farmers practical insights to improve agricultural production management:

Weather Forecasting: Farmers may better plan their planting and harvesting operations by using machine learning algorithms to forecast climatic patterns based on historical and current weather data.

Yield Prediction: AI models estimate yields by combining environmental parameters, crop history, and soil data, which helps with market planning and resource allocation (Muller et al., 2020).

Disaster Mitigation: AI-powered models evaluate possible threats from insect outbreaks, floods, and droughts, giving farmers tools to reduce losses.

Even in the face of unforeseen environmental problems, these applications guarantee more consistent and effective farming techniques.

The Role of AI in Optimizing Food Supply Chain Logistics

Artificial Intelligence (AI) is revolutionizing the food supply chain by enhancing logistical efficiency and improving transparency. Its integration into inventory systems enables smarter demand forecasting, reducing wastage and ensuring that perishable goods are delivered promptly. AI-driven algorithms analyze historical sales data, weather patterns, and market trends to optimize stock levels, thereby preventing both overstocking and understocking (Ivanov et al., 2020).

AI improves transportation logistics in addition to inventory control. By determining the most effective routes based on current traffic conditions and delivery schedules, AI-powered route optimization systems assist cut down on fuel usage and delivery times (Kamalahmadi & Parast, 2019). This lowers supply chain operations' carbon impact while simultaneously cutting expenses.

Furthermore, supply chain transparency has greatly increased as a result of the blockchain and AI combo. While AI permits real-time surveillance and analysis, blockchain guarantees an unchangeable record of transactions, enabling stakeholders to trace food goods from farm to fork (Tian, 2017). Because traceability provides verified product provenance, it guarantees adherence to food safety regulations and fosters consumer trust.

The ability of AI to analyze data in real time is essential for minimizing supply chain interruptions. For instance, AI systems can swiftly change by reallocating resources and modifying supply lines to guarantee operations continue during unforeseen occurrences like pandemics or natural disasters (Ivanov & Dolgui, 2020).

AI algorithms assist in forecasting demand on warehouse resources and analyze inventory against consignments going out and new products coming in. AI algorithm plays a fascinating role by catering to food and beverage manufacturers in giving better predictions of what food has been spoiled or contaminated, to ensure that these products do not reach consumers. It has been created so advanced that AI technology can reduce the risk of foreign communication by reading foreign language data on one's behalf and translating it into data that can be understood and utilized(Pandey, 2023)

In conclusion, integrating AI into food supply chain management offers transformative benefits by optimizing logistics, enhancing transparency, and improving decision-making processes in real-time. Its adoption is vital to creating resilient and sustainable food supply systems.

The Role of AI in Enhancing Food Safety and Quality Control

By utilizing cutting-edge technology to guarantee adherence to legal requirements and preserve superior production procedures, artificial intelligence (AI) is revolutionizing food safety and quality control. AI-powered vision systems for real-time defect monitoring and machine learning (ML) algorithms for pollution detection are two of the most significant advancements.

Machine learning algorithms are essential for identifying pollutants and guaranteeing adherence to food safety regulations. These algorithms can detect dangerous compounds like pesticides, heavy metals, and microbiological infections in food goods with surprising accuracy since they have been trained on large datasets. For example, ML models may swiftly identify contamination levels by analyzing spectral data from food samples, something that older approaches could overlook (Babu et al., 2020). This lowers the possibility of human mistakes in testing procedures while also expediting the quality assessment process.

Production line monitoring is likewise being redefined by AI-powered vision systems. These devices identify flaws in real-time, such as cracks in eggs, discoloration in food, or anomalies in packing, using computer vision and deep learning. Businesses can attain uniform quality standards and cut waste by promptly eliminating defective items by incorporating these technologies into their manufacturing processes (Ge et al., 2021). Furthermore, AI systems can learn and become more accurate over time, adjusting to new quality control difficulties.

Additionally, AI can enhance predictive maintenance of production equipment, reducing downtime and ensuring a steady flow of high-quality products. Sensors equipped with AI analytics can monitor equipment performance and alert operators to potential failures before they occur (Panigrahi et al., 2020). This proactive approach ensures compliance with food safety regulations while minimizing operational disruptions.

AI is revolutionizing food safety and quality control by providing previously unheard-of levels of accuracy, dependability, and efficiency. Adoption boosts consumer trust in food systems while also protecting public health.

PERSONALIZED CONSUMER EXPERIENCES.

AI-Powered Customized Customer Experiences: Uses and Effects

The delivery of individualized customer experiences has undergone a dramatic change as a result of the development of artificial intelligence (AI), with the culinary and hospitality sectors serving as notable examples. Businesses can develop highly customized products that cater to the unique requirements and tastes of every client by utilizing AI. As businesses maximize their resources and services, this results in increased operational efficiency as well as higher customer satisfaction. We will examine three important AI applications in this chapter that are essential to improving the individualized customer experience.

We start by looking at dietary programs driven by AI. These sophisticated algorithms deliver personalized meal recommendations that support general well-being by analyzing each person's dietary choices, health objectives, and nutritional needs. Next, we look into AI-powered menu engineering. By using data analytics to comprehend customer behavior and tastes, this strategy helps food service providers and restaurants create menus that appeal to their target market while optimizing profitability.

Finally, we talk about improved AI-powered consumer feedback systems. These real-time technologies collect and evaluate customer input, giving businesses insightful information that helps them enhance their products and services and enhance the overall eating experience. These applications collectively demonstrate the significant influence of AI on tailoring customer experiences in the culinary and hospitality industries.

Platforms Driven by AI for Tailored Diet Plans

Platforms with AI capabilities have become revolutionary resources for developing customized diet programs. To provide individualized nutrition advice, these platforms examine a variety of personal health data, such as food preferences, allergies, and medical conditions. To dynamically modify calorie intake recommendations depending on physical activity levels and metabolic changes, for example, AI algorithms can process data from wearable health devices, such as activity trackers (Chen et al., 2023).

Features like grocery lists, automatic meal delivery, and personalized meal planning are frequently integrated into these platforms. These methods minimize adherence issues while promoting health and wellness by matching dietary objectives with individual preferences and lifestyle considerations. By maximizing ingredient consumption and portion proportions, they also help to reduce food waste (Smith & Taylor, 2022).

Applications of Menu Engineering in Restaurants

AI-driven menu innovation has emerged as a vital tool for improving offers and raising profitability in the cutthroat restaurant sector. These programs improve menu design and pricing tactics by using data on consumer behavior, sales trends, and general market trends. For instance, based on past demand patterns, AI systems can offer time-sensitive discounts or position high-margin items in prominent menu spots (Johnson, 2024).

AI-powered dynamic menu systems can adjust to factors like consumer demographics or the availability of seasonal ingredients to provide a more personalized dining experience. Additionally, restaurants can improve sustainability and cut waste by using predictive analytics to manage inventories more effectively

(Green et al., 2023). Restaurants can maximize profits and improve customer happiness by matching menu items to client preferences.

By providing tailored suggestions based on previous orders, dietary requirements, or even cultural trends, AI-driven menu engineering significantly improves customer engagement. For instance, restaurants can improve customer happiness and retention by sending targeted promotions to regular customers through the integration of AI with loyalty programs. Restaurants may improve the dining experience and increase profits by matching their menu selections to customer preferences.

AI-Driven Personalization in Customer Experiences

AI-driven personalization creates products, services, and marketing to customer preferences. It collects and analyzes customer data viz. browsing history, purchase behavior, and demographics to fabricate consumer experiences using machine-learning algorithms (Xu, 2023).

A. Role of Chatbots and virtual assistants to a better customer experience

Chatbots and virtual assistants can be AI-powered solutions that can provide real-time, customized help to customers. Chatbots provide answers or suggestions in FAQs, recommend products, and assist with purchases that customers are having doubts in selecting. AI systems help them understand client preferences and provide personalized solutions. Virtual assistants use natural language processing and machine learning to analyze and predict client preferences, providing more advanced customization (Jaiwant, 2022).

B. AI-driven personalization in e-commerce as well as in retailing

AI-driven personalization ameliorates user experience in e-commerce. Eg:- Amazon analyzes consumer browsing and purchase data to recommend products using AI. Retailers benefit through AI-driven personalization as they receive help in building customized marketing, campaigns, and offers. They use user data to deliver targeted emails and notifications, customize in-store experiences, and promote products via virtual mirrors or interactive displays (Bhuiyan, 2024)& (Sebastian, 2018)

Improved NLP-Based Customer Feedback Systems

NLP, or natural language processing, has greatly enhanced how companies evaluate and react to customer input. Large amounts of unstructured data from surveys, social media, chat conversations, and customer reviews can be processed by AI-powered systems, which can then extract insightful information about the sentiments and preferences of the users (Brown et al., 2022).

Sentiment analysis techniques, for instance, can assist organizations in determining the general level of consumer satisfaction by identifying trends in positive, neutral, or negative comments. Feedback can be categorized by sophisticated NLP algorithms into topics that can be used to take action, including food taste, ambiance, pricing, or service quality. By addressing problems quickly, like addressing concerns during a client's visit, real-time feedback systems driven by natural language processing (NLP) help organizations build customer loyalty and confidence.

Additionally, by enabling multilingual analysis, these technologies enable companies to serve a worldwide clientele by comprehending input in many languages. Businesses may improve continuously by gaining a thorough understanding of customer behavior through data aggregation and visualization. These insights help firms stay in line with changing customer expectations by informing both short-term corrective measures and long-term strategic decisions (Williams, 2023).

Obstacles and Things to Think About

Even while AI-driven customization has many advantages, organizations nevertheless need to handle certain issues and moral dilemmas. Sensitive behavioral or health data collection and processing raise privacy issues. Building consumer trust requires clear regulations and strong data protection procedures. Furthermore, relying too much on AI systems runs the risk of reducing human oversight, which could result in biased or inaccurate suggestions.

The accessibility of these technologies is another factor to take into account. Adoption for small organizations may be restricted by high implementation costs, which would distance smaller businesses from larger corporations. Widespread industry transformation will depend on ensuring fair access to AI-powered technologies.

By catering to distinct individual needs and tastes, AI-powered systems are revolutionizing individualized customer experiences in the food and hospitality sectors. AI allows companies to increase customer pleasure, productivity, and profitability—from customizing diet plans to streamlining restaurant menus and improving feedback systems. To fully realize the potential of these breakthroughs, however, issues like privacy, accessibility, and ethics must be resolved. The combination of these technologies highlights how AI can revolutionize innovation and customer-centricity.

Sustainability through AI

Artificial intelligence (AI) has become a game-changing instrument for advancing sustainability in several sectors. Organizations can tackle significant environmental issues by utilizing cutting-edge technologies like AI-driven platforms, carbon footprint tracking, and predictive analytics. This chapter examines three major ways AI is advancing sustainability: enabling circular economies in the food business, encouraging environmentally friendly procurement, and lowering food waste using predictive analytics.

1. Food Waste Reduction Using Predictive Analytics

An estimated one-third of all food produced each year is wasted, making food waste a serious worldwide problem (FAO, 2019). Predictive analytics powered by AI can assist in reducing this problem by precisely estimating demand and controlling inventory levels. These systems improve production and inventory decisions by utilizing real-time market trends, historical sales data, and outside variables like local events and weather.

For example, food retailers and restaurants can use AI algorithms to better predict customer demand, which will reduce understocking and overproduction. A study by Hebrok and Heidenstrøm (2019) found that supermarkets with AI-enabled inventory management systems have reduced perishable food waste by 20%. Businesses can save money and resources by matching production to actual demand.

Promoting Eco-Friendly Procurement And Carbon Footprint Tracking.

Promoting environmentally friendly sourcing and tracking carbon footprints are critical measures for fostering sustainability in today's globalized economy. Businesses may assure supply chain openness and accountability by embracing modern technology such as artificial intelligence and blockchain. AI enables the analysis of massive data sets to discover sustainable suppliers and optimize resource consumption, hence lowering environmental impact. Blockchain increases this process by keeping immutable records of a product's route from origin to customer, allowing for precise carbon footprint tracking. For example, IBM Food Trust has effectively used blockchain to improve traceability and sustainability in food sources (IBM, 2022). Furthermore, initiatives like the Carbon Trust Standard help firms measure, manage, and reduce their carbon emissions, reinforcing environmentally conscious behaviors (Carbon Trust, 2021). These innovations enable enterprises and consumers to make educated decisions, accelerating joint efforts toward a greener future.

Case Study: Artificial intelligence (AI) is revolutionizing the sustainability environment by allowing for better and more efficient solutions, particularly in the food business. Predictive analytics, a key component of AI, helps businesses reduce food waste by precisely estimating demand and optimizing inventory levels. This guarantees that resources are used efficiently, resulting in less surplus and spoilage. Furthermore, AI makes environmentally friendly sourcing easier by analyzing supply chain data to suggest sustainable solutions and track carbon footprints, allowing firms to meet sustainability targets. A notable case study emphasizes the significance of AI-powered platforms in fostering circular economies, in which waste is reduced and resources are continuously repurposed. For example, Winnow Solutions uses AI to monitor kitchen waste, offering actionable insights that can reduce food waste by up to 50% (WRAP, 2021). Similarly, IBM blockchain technology promotes openness and sustainability in sourcing methods (IBM, 2022). These developments demonstrate AI's ability to foster environmental stewardship and sustainable practices across industries.

7. Ethical And Technological Challenges In AI Adoption.

The incorporation of artificial intelligence (AI) into numerous businesses raises several ethical and technological issues that must be carefully managed to ensure equitable and responsible deployment. One of the most pressing concerns is privacy, as the collection and use of consumer data to provide tailored services frequently expose sensitive personal information. Maintaining consumer trust requires strong data protection procedures and strict privacy legislation, such as the General Data Protection Regulation (GDPR) (European Commission, 2022).

Another major issue is the digital gap, which causes discrepancies in AI adoption among rising countries. Limited access to technology, infrastructure, and digital literacy impedes developing economies' capacity to profit from AI advancements, aggravating existing disparities (World Bank, 2021). To ensure equitable growth, this gap must be filled by targeted investments in infrastructure, education, and policy assistance.

Furthermore, the automation of decision-making processes in food distribution and safety raises serious ethical issues. While AI can improve efficiency, it raises concerns about accountability, prejudice, and transparency in algorithm-driven judgments. Automated systems that allocate food, for example, may unintentionally perpetuate injustices if not carefully developed and managed (Obermeyer et al., 2019). These problems underscore the importance of ethical frameworks and human monitoring in balancing technical progress with societal ideals.

By tackling these ethical and technological challenges, stakeholders can ensure that AI is a force for good, promoting progress while protecting fundamental rights and inclusion.

Case Studies & Global Applications

Artificial intelligence (AI) demonstrates its revolutionary capacity through new applications in various industries, altering established processes and advancing sustainability.

1. Blue River Technology: Smart Farming for Weed Management

Blue River Technology, a John Deere company, has transformed agriculture by producing AI-powered solutions for precision farming. Its "See & Spray" technology uses advanced computer vision and machine learning to detect and selectively target weeds while protecting crops. This reduces pesticide use by up to 90%, boosting environmentally responsible farming while lowering farmer costs (Blue River Technology, 2022). Blue River demonstrates how smart technology may address environmental and economic concerns in farming by incorporating AI into agricultural methods.

2. IBM Watson: Recipe Development and Consumer Trend Prediction

IBM Watson has introduced a novel method to the food industry, utilizing AI to examine massive datasets for recipe innovation and trend prediction. Watson's AI algorithms can detect developing customer preferences by reviewing social media, market trends, and cultural influences. For example, the platform has been used to develop unique recipes that blend components unexpectedly, giving chefs and food companies a competitive advantage (IBM, 2022). This application demonstrates AI's ability to transform culinary inventiveness and market responsiveness.

3. Impossible Foods: Optimizing Plant-Based Meat Alternatives

Impossible Foods has used artificial intelligence to pioneer plant-based meat alternatives that closely resemble the flavor, texture, and nutritional value of traditional meats. Using AI-driven molecular research, the company discovers key molecules responsible for meat flavor and mimics them using plant-derived substances. As a result, products like the Impossible Burger have grown in popularity while lowering the environmental effect of meat production (Impossible Foods, 2023). This idea demonstrates how artificial intelligence may handle sustainability concerns in food production while also meeting shifting customer needs for ethical and environmentally friendly solutions.

These case studies demonstrate AI's global potential to transform sectors, increase efficiency, and contribute to a more sustainable future.

FUTURE DIRECTIONS AND OPPORTUNITIES IN AI FOR FOOD INDUSTRY

The future of artificial intelligence (AI) in the food sector is full of revolutionary discoveries and opportunities that have the potential to revolutionize food production, distribution, and consumption. Emerging technologies such as digital twins, generative design, and completely automated systems are paving the path for a more sustainable, efficient, and inventive food system.

Investigate Digital Twins And Generative Design In Food Production

Digital twins, or virtual duplicates of real processes or systems, are gaining popularity in the food sector for improving production and supply chain management. Digital twins simulate real-time activities, allowing producers to test scenarios, forecast outcomes, and resolve inefficiencies without affecting actual processes. For example, they can simulate the behavior of machinery in food processing plants, allowing for predictive maintenance and reducing downtime (Grieves & Vickers, 2021).

Generative design, on the other hand, uses artificial intelligence to produce creative packaging, equipment, and product solutions. For example, AI-driven algorithms can create biodegradable packaging that is both environmentally friendly and long-lasting. Similarly, generative design can be used to generate equipment layouts that improve production efficiency while minimizing energy consumption, which aligns with sustainability objectives (Menges et al., 2020). Furthermore, the use of generative design extends beyond immediate product development, influencing the overall supply chain dynamics. Organizations can lower their carbon footprint by optimizing logistics using AI-generated simulations. For example, generative algorithms might recommend routing options that reduce transit distances and times, hence cutting fuel consumption and distribution-related emissions (Menges et al., 2020).

Furthermore, this method promotes material science innovation, allowing for the production of new materials that contribute to the circular economy. Generative design can inform the development of materials that are not only high-performing but also recyclable or compostable. This proactive strategy encourages producers to reconsider their material selections and implement procedures that promote sustainability—transforming product lifecycles from genesis to disposal (Menges et al., 2020).

As more businesses adopt these approaches, generative design plays an increasingly important role in building a sustainable future by combining technology and ecological sensitivity. AI-driven generative design's full potential may be achieved through continual cooperation among designers, engineers, and sustainability specialists, ushering in a new era of responsible innovation that helps both businesses and the environment.

2. Opportunities for Startups and Established Enterprises

As more businesses adopt these approaches, generative design plays an increasingly important role in building a sustainable future by combining technology and ecological sensitivity. AI-driven generative design's full potential may be achieved through continual cooperation among designers, engineers, and sustainability specialists, ushering in a new era of responsible innovation that helps both businesses and the environment.

AI-driven food advancements offer enormous opportunities for businesses of all sizes. Startups are using AI to penetrate the industry with disruptive ideas like personalized nutrition platforms and AI-powered food delivery services. For example, NotCo uses machine learning to create plant-based food alternatives that appeal to health-conscious consumers (NotCo, 2023). Another significant example is Oishii, which uses AI to expedite vertical farming by optimizing growth conditions for strawberries, resulting in greater quality output with a lower environmental impact (Oishii, 2023). This convergence of technology and agriculture not only improves food production efficiency but also addresses crucial issues like sustainability and food security.

Furthermore, firms like Flavors are using AI to design tailored meal kits that suit specific dietary preferences and restrictions, making meal planning more accessible and pleasurable for customers. Predictive analytics allows these firms to anticipate trends and alter their services, ensuring they remain responsive to shifting consumer expectations.

As the food sector evolves, the incorporation of AI is likely to change old processes, paving the door for increased operational efficiencies, better customization, and novel product development. Embracing these technologies enables businesses, regardless of size, to create value, develop brand loyalty, and eventually dominate the industry with creative culinary solutions.

Meanwhile, established businesses are using AI in their operations to preserve a competitive advantage, such as improving inventory management, strengthening food safety measures, and studying consumer behavior. Nestlé and PepsiCo are using AI to customize marketing strategies and create products that reflect regional preferences and global trends (Nestlé, 2022).

3. Toward a Fully Automated Food Environment

The integration of AI is propelling the food industry toward a completely automated environment in which robotics, IoT, and machine learning work in tandem. Automated methods are transforming food manufacturing lines, resulting in faster, safer, and more consistent results. For example, robotic systems using computer vision can precisely sort and package food, minimizing waste and labor expenses (International Federation of Robotics, 2022). Furthermore, the use of IoT devices improves real-time monitoring throughout the supply chain, allowing for data-driven decisions that improve efficiency and traceability.

Sensors incorporated in storage facilities monitor temperature and humidity levels, guaranteeing ideal conditions for perishable commodities and alerting operators to any irregularities that could jeopardize food safety (World Economic Forum, 2021). Machine learning algorithms improve this process by evaluating large datasets to predict demand trends, allowing companies to change their operations ahead of time and reduce food waste.

Furthermore, AI-powered solutions can improve inventory management by forecasting which products will be in high demand based on seasonal trends, past sales data, and even social media sentiments. This proactive approach not only increases profitability but also supports sustainability efforts by drastically reducing excess production, which frequently ends up in landfills (Food and Agriculture Organization, 2022).

As these technologies advance, the food industry is seeing the growth of smart kitchens in both commercial and residential settings. Connected appliances can speak with one another, making meal preparation easier and lowering energy use. Smart ovens, for example, may modify cooking times and temperatures based on the properties of the food, whilst refrigerators can notify customers of products that are about to expire, allowing them to consume them on time.

With these improvements, the future of the food business promises to promise not only better efficiency but also improved gastronomic experiences. Consumers are likely to gain from higher-quality foods suited to their preferences and dietary needs, as well as greater clarity about the sources and nutritional worth of what they consume. The convergence of automation and artificial intelligence is paving the way for a food ecosystem that is both technologically advanced and more responsive to modern society's changing demands.

In agriculture, AI-powered drones and automated irrigation systems increase crop productivity while conserving resources, paving the door for long-term food production. Furthermore, AI-powered smart kitchens with predictive cooking technologies are growing as a consumer trend, improving convenience and minimizing food waste. Furthermore, precision agriculture technologies use machine learning to monitor soil health, predict pest outbreaks, and modify fertilizer delivery, ensuring that crops get exactly what they need for maximum growth. This level of personalization increases output while also reducing the environmental impact of farming operations.

As the urban population grows, vertical farming advances by applying artificial intelligence to build effective, space-saving agricultural solutions. These indoor farms can monitor light, moisture, and temperature conditions and alter them in real time to increase productivity while using substantially less water and soil.

AI-powered meal planning apps are gaining popularity in the food preparation industry, assisting consumers in making informed decisions based on their dietary preferences, nutritional needs, and even the availability of local produce. These smart applications help to reduce food waste and improve sustainable eating habits by proposing meals that use readily available items or promoting seasonal foods.

Collectively, these improvements represent not simply a trend, but a dramatic movement toward an environmentally sensitive and technologically smart agricultural landscape that prioritizes resource efficiency and sustainability, ultimately safeguarding the food supply for future generations.

As AI advances, its potential uses in the food business become nearly unlimited. By embracing innovations like as digital twins, generative design, and complete automation, the industry can address global issues such as food security, sustainability, and efficiency. Both startups and established businesses stand to profit, ensuring a future in which AI plays an important part in building a robust and innovative food economy.

CONCLUSION

Finally, AI provides unprecedented prospects to reinvent the food industry, changing the way food is produced, distributed, and consumed. AI can create a sustainable, inclusive, and innovative food ecosystem by solving ethical and technological concerns in collaboration with legislators, entrepreneurs, and researchers. The road ahead will require collaboration, transparency, and foresight to ensure that AI's revolutionary capacity is used for the greater good of humanity and the world. As we move forward, players in the food business must adopt a philosophy of constant learning and innovation. This includes not just implementing cutting-edge technologies, but also cultivating an adaptable culture capable of responding to the quickly changing landscape of customer preferences and environmental concerns. The use of AI can improve supply chain efficiency, resulting in a more responsive and robust food system that reduces waste and maximizes resource utilization.

Furthermore, the use of machine learning and predictive analytics can help producers anticipate market demands and agricultural variations, allowing them to better match production with consumer habits. This collaboration will not only assist in alleviating food insecurity but will also benefit local economies by providing smallholder farmers with tools that improve yield and sustainability.

Collaboration across sectors will be critical to realizing the full potential of AI in food systems. Policymakers must advocate for policies that protect consumers while simultaneously encouraging innovation and ethical data use. At the same time, corporations should interact with communities to address concerns and ensure that technical breakthroughs are accessible to all, particularly underprivileged populations that are frequently left behind in technological revolutions.

As we continue on this transformative path, education, and public awareness will be critical in molding views and understanding of artificial intelligence's impact on food systems. We can build a more engaged and proactive society ready to face tomorrow's food challenges by educating the public about the benefits and drawbacks of these technological advancements.

In summary, the convergence of AI and the food industry has the potential to completely transform our relationship with food. By focusing on sustainability, equity, and innovation, we can create a future in which everyone has access to safe, healthy, and sustainable food, eventually benefiting both our communities and the environment. The potential is enormous, and the time to act is now, as we work to create a food ecosystem that is both ethical and sustainable.

Artificial intelligence (AI) is influencing the food industry's present and future, providing novel solutions to long-standing difficulties while opening up new prospects for efficiency, sustainability, and innovation. As previously mentioned, AI technologies such as predictive analytics, generative design, digital twins, and automated systems are transforming food production, distribution, and consumption. AI has already shown disruptive promise in fields such as food waste reduction and supply chain optimization, as well as the development of plant-based alternatives and circular economies. However, its true potential resides in its ability to handle crucial concerns such as food security, environmental sustainability, and consumer preferences on a worldwide scale.

Summary of AI's current impact and promise. Currently, artificial intelligence is driving significant breakthroughs in precision farming, food safety, supply chain transparency, and consumer engagement. IBM Watson helps businesses predict trends and innovate in recipe development, while Blue River Technology pioneers environmentally friendly farming practices. These examples highlight AI's capacity to boost productivity while minimizing environmental effects. Furthermore, AI's future holds even greater promise, with new advances like digital twins and fully automated systems poised to significantly alter the agricultural supply chain.

Despite its numerous advantages, AI adoption must overcome ethical and technological concerns to ensure equitable and responsible development. Issues like data privacy, algorithmic prejudice, and the digital divide highlight the importance of critical thought and action as AI evolves. Furthermore, stakeholders from diverse industries must work together to create ethical frameworks that govern AI development and application. This partnership should include policymakers, technologists, and ethicists to foster an inclusive discussion that emphasizes transparency, accountability, and fairness. By doing so, we may create an environment in which AI technologies improve human skills while reducing possible harm.

Furthermore, mitigating algorithmic bias necessitates rigorous testing and validation procedures that ensure fairness and equity in AI systems. Continuous monitoring of AI outputs and methodology will aid in identifying biases and enabling timely corrective actions. Equally critical is the necessity for diverse teams in AI development, since different perspectives can considerably lower the danger of unintentional prejudice or exclusion.

Furthermore, bridging the digital divide is critical for increasing access to AI benefits. Ensuring that marginalized populations have the resources, education, and infrastructure to engage with AI technologies will enable them to shape the future of these advances. Investing in digital literacy programs and community activities can help to promote equity and diversity.

Recommendations for Stakeholders

For Legislators

Legislators should create comprehensive legislative frameworks to handle the ethical and technological issues of AI. Data privacy legislation, such as the General Data Protection Regulation (GDPR), should be tailored to the food industry's specific requirements, maintaining consumer trust and ethical data use. Furthermore, policies targeted at closing the digital divide, such as funding for digital infrastructure and training programs in emerging countries, are critical for promoting inclusive AI use (European Commission, 2022).

For Businesses

Companies must prioritize responsible AI integration by following transparent and ethical guidelines. Collaboration with academic and research institutes helps ensure the creation of unbiased algorithms and novel solutions. Businesses should also spend on training their employees to manage AI technologies efficiently and responsibly. Corporations can also lead sustainability initiatives by integrating AI-powered solutions to decrease waste and optimize resource use, which aligns with global sustainability goals (World Economic Forum, 2023).

For Researchers

Researchers should concentrate on closing the gaps and limits in AI technology. Developing algorithms to reduce prejudice, assuring equitable decision-making processes, and improving AI's interpretability are all significant topics of research. Cross-disciplinary collaboration among AI experts, agricultural scientists, and food technologists can produce solutions that address the food industry's particular issues (Obermeyer et al., 2019).

REFERENCES

Aftab, A., Iqbal, M., & Hussain, S. (2020). AI in pest management: A paradigm shift in crop protection. *Computers and Electronics in Agriculture, 175*, 105614.

Babu, D., Gurupadayya, B. M., & Reddy, S. (2020). Machine learning approaches for detecting and quantifying contaminants in food products: A review. *Food Chemistry, 313*, 126094.

Bhuiyan, M. S. (2024). The Role of AI-Enhanced Personalization in Customer Experiences. *Journal of Computer Science and Technology Studies, 6*(1), 162–169. DOI: 10.32996/jcsts.2024.6.1.17

Blue River Technology. (2022). "Smart Farming with See & Spray Technology." [Online Resource].

Bouallegue, S. & Al-Naemi, S., (2025). Smart produce prediction system for reducing food waste and, improving food security in Qatar. *Innovation and Technological Advances for Sustainability, 153-160*

Brown, J., Smith, A., & Lee, K. (2022). Understanding customer sentiment with NLP: Applications in hospitality. *Journal of Artificial Intelligence Research, 15*(3), 34–45.

Chen, J., Liu, H., & Wang, Z. (2021). Smart fertilization through AI: Enhancing efficiency and reducing ecological footprints. *Agricultural Systems, 190*, 103121.

Chen, R., Patel, S., & Yang, M. (2023). AI-driven nutrition planning: Personalization at scale. *Nutrition Science and Technology, 29*(2), 112–125.

European Commission. (2022). *General Data Protection Regulation.* GDPR. [Retrive on November,2024]

European Commission. (2022). *General Data Protection Regulation.* GDPR. [Online Resource]

. Food and Agriculture Organization (FAO). (2021). *The future of food and agriculture: Trends and challenges.* Retrieved from FAO.org

Ge, H., Sun, D.-W., & Pu, H. (2021). Recent advances in the application of computer vision for quality inspection of food products: A review. *Trends in Food Science & Technology, 112*, 60–71.

Goosse, H., Barriat, P. Y., Lefebvre, W., Loutre, M. F., & Zunz, V. (2010), Chapter 3. Modeling the climate system", *Introduction to climate dynamics and climate modeling,* 59

Green, P., Mitchell, L., & Adams, T. (2023). Predictive analytics for sustainable food systems. *Sustainability Journal, 18*(4), 67–82.

Grieves, M., & Vickers, J. (2021). Digital Twin: Mitigating Unpredictable, Undesirable Emergent Behavior in Complex Systems. *International Journal of Computer Applications.*

IBM. (2022). "Blockchain for Sustainable Supply Chains." [Online Resource].

IBM. (2022). "Watson's Role in Culinary Innovation and Consumer Insights." [Online Resource].

Impossible Foods. (2023). "Harnessing AI to Create Plant-Based Meat Alternatives." [Online Resource].

International Federation of Robotics. (2022). "The Role of Robotics in Modern Food Manufacturing." [Online Resource].

Jadhav, H. B., Alaskar, K., Desai, V., Sane, A., Chaudhary, P., Annapure, U., & Nayik, G. A. (2024). Transformative impact: Artificial intelligence in the evolving landscape of processed food-a concise review focusing on some food processing sectors. *Food Control*, (167), 110803.

Jaiwant, S. V. (2022). Artificial intelligence and personalized banking. In *Handbook of Research on Innovative Management Using AI in Industry 5.0, 74–87*. IGI Global. DOI: 10.4018/978-1-7998-8497-2.ch005

Johnson, D. (2024). Menu engineering with artificial intelligence: Trends and opportunities. *Restaurant Management Quarterly*, *12*(1), 21–39.

Klerkx, L., & Rose, D. (2020). Dealing with the game-changing technologies of digital agriculture: Big data and AI. *NJAS Wageningen Journal of Life Sciences*, *90*, 100315.

Krittanawong, C., Zhang, H., Wang, Z., Aydar, M., & Kitai, T. (2017). Artificial Intelligence in Precision Cardiovascular Medicine. *Journal of the American College of Cardiology*, *69*(21), 2657–2664. DOI: 10.1016/j.jacc.2017.03.571 PMID: 28545640

Linaza, M. T., Posada, J., Bund, J., Eisert, P., Quartulli, M., Döllner, J., Pagani, A., Olaizola, I. G., Barriguinha, A., Moysiadis, T., & Lucas, L. (2021). Data-Driven Artificial Intelligence Applications for Sustainable Precision Agriculture. *Agronomy (Basel)*, (6), 1227. DOI: 10.3390/agronomy11061227

MarketsandMarkets. (2023). *Artificial Intelligence in the Food & Beverages Market – Global Forecast to 2027*. Retrieved from marketsandmarkets.com

Mavani, N. R., Mohd Ali, J., Othman, S., Hussain, M. A., Hashim, H., & Rahman, N. A. (2022). Application of Artificial Intelligence in Food Industry—A Guideline. *Food Engineering Reviews*, *14*(1), 134–175. DOI: 10.1007/s12393-021-09290-z

Menges, A., & Oxman, N. (2020). Generative Design Principles for Sustainable Architecture and Packaging. *Science Advances*.

Muller, C., Robertson, R. D., & Braun, J. (2020). Big data and climate-smart agriculture: Unlocking potential with AI. *Global Food Security*, *25*, 100343.

Nestlé. (2022). "AI and Big Data in Food Industry Transformation." [Corporate Report].

NotCo. (2023). "AI-Powered Food Innovation for a Sustainable Future." [Online Resource].

Obermeyer, S., Powers, B., Vogeli, C., & Mullainathan, S. (2019). Dissecting Racial Bias in an Algorithm Used to Manage the Health of Populations. *Science*, *366*(6464), 447–453. DOI: 10.1126/science.aax2342 PMID: 31649194

Obermeyer, Z., Powers, B., Vogeli, C., & Mullainathan, S. (2019). Dissecting Racial Bias in an Algorithm Used to Manage the Health of Populations. *Science*, *366*(6464), 447–453. DOI: 10.1126/science.aax2342 PMID: 31649194

Pandey, S., (2023), (AI lead Supply Chain Optimization in Food Industry), *Journal of Biology and Today's World,*12 (1): 001-007

Panigrahi, S., Jena, P. R., & Sharma, S. (2020). Predictive maintenance in food manufacturing industries using AI-driven analytics. *Journal of Food Engineering*, *281*, 110014.

RAP. (2021). "Reducing Food Waste with Artificial Intelligence." [Online Resource].

Ravi, V., Singh, P., & Nair, A. (2022). AI-enabled irrigation management systems: Innovations for sustainable agriculture. *Journal of Sustainable Agriculture*, *45*(3), 321–334.

Sadiku, M. N. O., Adebo, P. O., Ajayi-Majebi, A., Musa, S. M., & Perry, R. G. (2021). Robotic Automation in Agriculture [a]. *International Journal of Trend in Research and Development*, *8*(3), 381–384.

Sadiku, M. N. O., Olaleye, O. D., Oyekanmi, P., & Musa, S. M. (2021). Drones in Healthcare: A primer [citation] [b]. *International Journal of Trend in Research and Development*, *8*(1), 39–41.

Sebastin, J. (2018). Artificial Intelligence: A real opportunity in the food industry. *Food Quality and Safety*.

Sharma, A., Singh, P., & Kumar, S. (2021). AI in personalized nutrition: Addressing consumer needs in the food industry. *Food Research International*, *140*, 109983.

Smith, T., & Taylor, J. (2022). Reducing food waste with AI: Innovations in meal planning. *International Journal of Food Technology*, *9*(3), 45–59.

Williams, H. (2023). Real-time feedback systems: A game changer for customer experience. *Consumer Technology Review*, *7*(2), 19–27.

World Bank. (2021). "Bridging the Digital Divide in Emerging Economies." [Online Resource]

World Economic Forum. (2023). "The Role of AI in Advancing Global Sustainability Goals." [Online Resource].\ Wang, L., Zhou, M., & Gao, X. (2021). "Agricultural robotics: Autonomous solutions for modern farming. *IEEE Transactions on Automation Science and Engineering*, *18*(2), 456–467.

Xu, W. (2023). *AI in HCI Design and User Experience* (arXiv:2301.00987). arXiv. http://arxiv.org/abs/2301.00987

Zhao, X., Zhang, Z., & Li, L. (2022). AI-driven innovations in agriculture: A path to global food security. *Journal of Agricultural Science*, *180*(4), 455–470.

Chapter 15
The Sustainable Kitchen of Tomorrow:
AI's Role in Resource-Saving Ghost Kitchens

Poonam
https://orcid.org/0009-0003-3942-525X
Chandigarh School of Business, Chandigarh Group of Colleges, Jhanjeri, India

ABSTRACT

The future of food service is developing rapidly with the growth of ghost kitchens also known as cloud kitchens which operate primarily for delivery and takeout. The primary aim of the study is to examine the role of artificial intelligence (AI) in improving the sustainability of ghost kitchens, focusing on resource efficiency and waste minimization. The findings shows that the usage of AI can optimize resource allocation, streamline inventory management, and accurately forecast demand, thereby minimizing food waste and operational costs. In addition, ghost kitchens can promote responsible consumption by sourcing foods locally or preparing them with seasonal produce. Furthermore the adaptability of ghost kitchens during the COVID-19 pandemic has revealed its potential to support business continuity while promoting innovation in sustainable kitchen practices. Based on these insights, it is suggested that stakeholders in the food service industry should embrace AI technologies to improve operational efficiency.

INTRODUCTION TO GHOST KITCHENS

The food landscape has undergone a profound change with the introduction of ghost kitchens (also known as dark kitchens, cloud kitchens, or virtual restaurants). In contrast to traditional restaurants, these venues do not have dine-in service; to the contrary, they offer only takeout food preparation. This model capitalizes on the growing demand for online food ordering, offering a cost-effective and scalable solution for restaurateurs to reach their customers (PKF Hospitality Group, 2022). As they dispense with prime real estate, front-of-house staff, and other operating costs, ghost kitchens are considered a disruptive innovation in the foodservice industry and a method to meet the modern consumer's requirements. Ghost kitchens have emerged as an innovative solution to the logistical difficulties of food delivery, especially

DOI: 10.4018/979-8-3373-0432-8.ch015

in urban areas. By consolidating multiple restaurant brands in a single, central facility, it enables synchronized food preparation and efficient order dispatching (Neria et al., 2024).

Ghost Kitchens are chefs and food preparers who only cook for delivery service customers who make delivery orders via web or mobile services. This novel business mode has developed as a reaction to growing consumer demands for speed, ease of use, and efficiency in food delivery (Sanitation Professional, 2022). These platforms can be more profitable than conventional food delivery platforms due to their multi-dash capability, reduced fixed costs, enhanced productivity, and chef expertise (Cao et al., 2024). Furthermore, due to low operating expenses and flexible responses to changing market demands, they provide restaurateurs with unprecedented adaptability.

For many years now, the ghost kitchen industry has been growing at an unstoppable rate. The global market was valued at $43.1 billion in 2019 and is projected to reach $71.4 billion by 2027 (National Retail Federation, 2022). As pointed out by Euromonitor International (2022), this model may grow into a trillion-dollar industry by 2030 with continued dependence on food delivery services on the one side and the operational efficiency they offer on the other side. This exponential increase is consistent with other economic phenomena, where digitalization is progressively transforming established business models. As CloudKitchens (2022) highlights, the scalability and cost-efficiency of ghost kitchens make them an appealing option for entrepreneurs and established food brands alike. Investment in these kinds of startups has been on the rise, with significant funding rounds driving the industry's growth. For instance, CloudKitchens, a business launched by former Uber CEO Travis Kalanick, had secured $1.25 billion through five separate funding rounds to expand its operations (Cao et al., 2024).

The COVID-19 pandemic also sped up the proliferation of ghost kitchens as lockdowns and social distancing requirements forced a change toward non-traditional dining experiences. This change, in addition to being a direct answer to current concerns, also coincided with a wider trend of greater sustainability and efficiency of food production and consumption. Ghost kitchens became one of the ways to decrease operational costs, use the resources more effectively, and at the same time respond to the growing need in a cost-effective way for food delivery services.

Artificial intelligence (AI) forms the core of this evolution and is a crucial element in maximizing the performance of ghost kitchen operations. This AI-based technology helps to optimize inventory, streamline resource assignment, and minimize waste, degrading operations to become both more efficient and more sustainable. For instance, it can be used to analyze consumer data to predict demand, optimize supply chains, and generally take better decisions. These innovations enable ghost kitchens to be run with higher accuracy and lower environmental costs. For this reason, embedding of AI has found itself at the heart of innovation in the world of the ghost kitchen business.

In a sustainability sense, ghost kitchens offer an almost unique platform to disrupt the foodservice industry. Due to the operational efficiencies present in their underlying design, it is possible to integrate sustainable practices such as waste minimization and energy management. Digitalization also contributes to these efficiencies, making it possible for operators to embed sustainability as a core aspect of their business models. For instance, Life Cycle Assessment (LCA) tools can quantify the environmental impact of food production, helping operators adopt practices that align with sustainability goals (O'Sullivan, 2024).

Despite all the benefits of ghost kitchens, they are confronted with problems such as market competition, consumer reputation, and regulatory adherence. The emergence of the gig economy along with the explosion of ghost kitchens has fostered anxieties regarding worker abuse and market overcrowding (Giousmpasoglou et al., 2023). In addition, consumer loyalty cannot be established in the absence of the physical entity, and, therefore, new marketing tactics and strong brand management are necessary. AI has a significant potential to help solve these issues by bettering engagement with customers, improving marketing campaigns, and better serving the customer.

The future of ghost kitchens is at the crossroads between sustainability, digitalization, and market adjustment. By leveraging AI technologies, ghost kitchens can navigate the complexities of a rapidly evolving foodservice landscape while addressing pressing environmental and social challenges. This paper explores the transformative potential of AI-driven ghost kitchens, focusing on their role in promoting resource-saving practices and advancing sustainability in the foodservice industry. With this increasing call for new, sustainable food delivery services all over the world, ghost kitchens could be at the forefront of answering with a more efficient and more sustainable future.

GHOST KITCHENS: ADVANTAGES AND CHALLENGES

Ghost kitchens are an innovative food service model that has several benefits over conventional restaurant models.

Customer Satisfaction

Cloud kitchens have significantly enhanced customer satisfaction and expanded customer choices by offering a diverse selection of meals from several home chefs within a single order, a feature enabled through the multi-dash service model. Unlike traditional restaurants, which are limited by fixed menus and operational constraints, cloud kitchens leverage bundling strategies to enhance meal customization and variety, allowing customers to mix dishes from different chefs while placing a single order. This model not only broadens culinary options but also provides access to affordable, high-quality homemade meals (Cao et al., 2024).

Cost Efficiency

One of the most significant benefits of ghost kitchens is their ability to operate at a fraction of the cost of traditional restaurants. The cloud kitchen enables the delivery platform to consolidate its delivery capacity and thereby reduce cost. Consequently, the delivery platform is able to pass on the benefit of this cost reduction to the restaurants and the customers by decreasing the delivery-time guarantees (Rout et al., 2024). By eliminating the business need for customer-accessible spaces, like restaurants, waiting areas, and fixtures, ghost kitchens also lead to significant cost reductions in overhead. Furthermore, fewer personnel are needed since servers and front-of-house staff are not needed, thus reducing operational expenses (Sanitation Professional, 2022). This cost-saving facilitates the operator's provision of significant resources to other important issues, such as marketing, improvement quality, and technology adoption.

Market Flexibility

Ghost kitchens offer unparalleled flexibility, enabling operators to experiment with multiple brands, cuisines, or menu concepts within a single kitchen space. This adaptability allows businesses to rapidly test and refine offerings based on emerging consumer preferences or market trends. As one example, an operator might test a new menu or brand on a small scale with minimal risk while also easily adapting if the concept itself suffers a failure. This flexibility. enables and sustains creative innovation as enterprises are kept agile in a dynamic foodservice marketplace (CloudKitchens, 2022).

Scalability

The ghost kitchen model is of extreme scalability, so it is a compelling model for companies wanting to grow fast and in an efficient manner. In contrast to traditional restaurants that have to invest a substantial amount of money in physical sites and personnel, ghost kitchens will be able to expand into new markets at little risk. Using the platforms of delivery and technology-oriented operations, they can still penetrate new customer markets without the pressure to own too many physical dining establishments (PKF Hospitality Group, 2022).

Despite these advantages, ghost kitchens must also address several challenges to thrive in the competitive foodservice industry:

Regulatory Compliance

Adherence to local health and safety regulations is critical to ghost kitchens. Because of the lack of physical customer-facing areas, operator's are not relieved from rigorous regulatory standards. Recent actions against unregistered ghost kitchens also emphasize the dangers of operating outside of the legal frameworks. In order to stay out of trouble and keep consumer confidence, companies must focus on transparent, compliant activity (Daily Telegraph, 2022).

Market Saturation

With the increasing number of ghost kitchens, competition has become increasingly congested. With the growing number of operators in the market, competition has grown to such an extent that profitability is difficult to attain and maintain. In order to compete in a saturated market, companies need to concentrate on providing quality food and top-notch service, as well as on unique offerings that directly speak to the market they cater to (Sanitation Professional, 2022). Long-term success requires differentiation using innovation, branding, and customer engagement.

Customer Skepticism

Despite the rapid growth of the ghost kitchen industry, consumer skepticism remains a significant issue, with 70% of customers still preferring to order from conventional physical restaurants (Leung et al., 2023). A major concern among customers is the invisibility of food preparation methods, which casts uncertainty over cleanliness and security protocols. Research suggests that concerns about invisible food preparation and possible safety threats intensify trust issues (Cai et al., 2022; Jiang et al., 2024). The lack of personal contact in ghost kitchens also undermines the classic restaurant experience, thereby making it more challenging for customers to establish trust with the establishment (Hakim et al., 2022). Meeting these concerns necessitates a forward-thinking strategy focused on transparency and trust building. (Pookulangara et al., 2023). In particular, the quality of food delivery apps, user reviews, and app interface design significantly affect the development of trust (Hakim et al., 2022; Nigro et al., 2022).

Consumer Trust

In contrast to conventional eateries, ghost kitchens do not have a physical footprint where customers can be interpersonal with the brand. This lack can also make it more difficult to establish consumer trust and brand affinity. Operators will need to rely on branding, consistent food quality, and trustworthy delivery operations to attract customers in droves. Thanks to digital platforms, social media, as well as customer reviews, it is also possible to influence and deepen the relationship with customers (PKF Hospitality Group, 2022).

The ghost kitchen phenomenon has been studied by academics from different perspectives. PKF Hospitality Group (2022) highlights the disruptive role of ghost kitchens in the conventional food and beverage sphere, for example, for fostering the acceleration of the industry's digitalization. Additionally, studies indicate that the rise of ghost kitchens aligns with broader consumer trends favoring convenience and digital engagement, suggesting sustained demand for such models in the foreseeable future (Euromonitor International, 2022).

According to the Daily Telegraph's (2022) research, effective regulatory frameworks are necessary to guarantee the secure and ethical operation of ghost kitchens. These findings underline the importance of balancing innovation with accountability in this rapidly evolving sector.

Technology is crucial to the sustainability of ghost kitchens. A large number of people continue to use sophisticated software systems to control the order process, to keep track of stocks, and to optimize the delivery routes. As CloudKitchens 2022 has pointed out, the use of technology enables operators to optimize processes and increase customer satisfaction. Artificial intelligence (AI) and data analysis are also applied to estimate demand trajectories, minimize food waste, and also optimize menu items. Moreover, businesses have partnered with third-party delivery companies (e.g., Uber Eats, Zomato) to play a crucial role in the expansion of ghost kitchens. Through these partnerships, the operator's customer base is often expanded, which in turn allows them to expand their business rapidly and smoothly (National Retail Federation, 2022).

Sustainability is becoming an increasingly important factor in the foodservice sector, and ghost kitchens are no exception. There is wide use by operators, for example, biodegradable packaging and locally sourced ingredients, to minimize their environmental footprint. According to Sanitation Professional (2022), implementing sustainable practices can also enhance brand reputation and attract environmentally conscious consumers.

However, challenges remain. Increased use of delivery services often results in increased carbon emissions, which may counteract some of the sustainability gains. To tackle these problems, joint action from operators, delivery platforms, and policymakers is needed to encourage green initiatives throughout the supply chain (Euromonitor International, 2022).

The future of ghost kitchens will probably be driven by continued technological advance and changes in consumer wants and needs. Emerging trends include the integration of virtual reality (VR) for immersive culinary experiences and the use of robotics for food preparation and delivery (CloudKitchens, 2022).

Additionally, the concept of "cloud kitchens"—a more technologically advanced version of ghost kitchens—is gaining traction. Such facilities use AI, machine learning, and Internet of Things (IoT) devices to optimize all operations, for example, inventory control to quality control. As commented by PKF Hospitality Group (2022), these developments might change the industry fundamentally and make ghost kitchens more profitable and efficient with each passing day.

THE NEED FOR SUSTAINABILITY IN GHOST KITCHENS

In line with the increasing popularity of ghost kitchens (also known as virtual kitchens or cloud kitchens), the foodservice industry has been shaken to its core. These point-of-sale businesses run without a conventional storefront business model and sell food exclusively to delivery, relying on third-party platforms to manage fulfillment. As the use of digital technology grows and the comfort and convenience factor increases, ghost kitchens have become an integral member of the global foodservice economy (Pereira et al., 2020). Yet, the exponential growth in the number of ghost kitchens generates many questions about their environmental footprint, efficiency of resources, and sustainable (long-term) evolution of the same.

Environmental Impact of Ghost Kitchens

The environmental impact of ghost kitchens is of paramount concern as the food delivery business becomes the main trend. Conventional brick-and-mortar restaurants have mature recipes for the management of energy, waste, and resources. In comparison, ghost kitchens frequently work from common areas with little control, which results in poor utilization of the available resources (Alon-Barkat Buskirk, 2021). All of these include packaging waste and associated emissions from delivery vehicles, which is significant. A report of the World Resources Institute (2021) has emphasized the importance of a circular economy model that can help to inform food waste and packaging issues in the restaurant industry. Ghost kitchens also have a distinct advantage in waste reduction due to the centralized, more streamlined production model compared to traditional restaurants.

Plastic waste is a major concern; many ghost kitchens are fuelled by single-use plastics and non-recyclable disposables. This increases the waste burden, and specifically in urban areas, deliveries are a source of further elevated CO2 emissions. In order to soften the environmental impact, industry operators are increasingly using eco-friendly packaging solutions like sustainable containers and environmentally correct sourcing of raw materials (Friedrich et al., 2020). Shifting to sustainable packaging is necessary to prevent ghost kitchens from worsening the worldwide waste plague.

Energy Efficiency and Resource Optimization

Energy use in ghost kitchens may be harder to track and manage than in traditional restaurants since there is a wide range of operations with multiple tenants in the same space. O'Connor and Smith (2022) observed that ghost kitchens, especially those located in dense urban areas, are prone to inefficiencies as a result of shared kitchen equipment and energy availability. As energy consumption accounts for a significant portion of operational costs, it is essential for ghost kitchen operators to incorporate energy-efficient appliances and practices.

By deploying smart technologies, energy management in ghost kitchens can be enhanced more. For instance, energy-consuming appliances for cooking, like induction cooktops and LED lights, in conjunction with sensors, can contribute to decreasing energy use through intelligent energy management where appliances are automatically adjusted in response to operational requirements (Soman et al., 2020). Furthermore, certain operators use renewable energy sources like solar panels in order to reduce their carbon footprint even more and, at the same time, enhance sustainability objectives.

Waste Management and Resource Recovery

Sustainable waste management is also a key aspect for the operation of ghost kitchens. With the food delivery volume, ghost kitchens generate a significant amount of organic waste, such as food residuals, packaging, and waste from delivery activities. As a result, these kitchens must implement effective waste segregation and composting systems. Environmental Protection Agency (2020), as a report, restaurants that are able to adopt an integrated waste management framework achieve potential savings of up to 30% in waste disposal costs.

Towards a zero-waste kitchen environment is becoming widely acknowledged as a valuable tool to enable better sustainability. There are food waste recycling programs being implemented by some ghost kitchen operators, and so organic waste is composted or used to generate biogas. Additionally, recovery of resources, such as cooking oils and fats that can be transformed to biodiesel, is one of the possible pathways for waste reduction and sustainability improvement (Gustafsson et al., 2021). Implementation of these sorts of practices will not only decrease the environmental effects but also potentially provide long-term economic prosperity by decreasing waste disposal and energy expenses.

Sustainability as a Competitive Advantage

In a world becoming more eco-conscious, consumers are increasingly being informed of the environmental burden of their purchase choices. With the heightened demand for sustainably produced food, ghost kitchens focused around sustainability are almost certain to have a competitive advantage on the market. According to a survey by Nielsen (2019), 73% of global consumers are willing to pay more for products and services that are environmentally friendly. Sustainable gastronomy-oriented ghost kitchens that are focused on eco-friendly packaging, energy conservation, and waste minimization practices are likely to draw environmentally conscious consumers, thereby improving the market standing of the ghost kitchens.

THE ROLE OF AI AND AUTOMATION IN SUSTAINABLE OPERATIONS

Artificial intelligence (AI) and automation technologies present promising perspectives on increasing the sustainability of ghost kitchens. AI-enabled software can be used to maximize ingredient sourcing, inventory control, and food waste reduction by forecasting demand patterns and responding accordingly (Liu et al., 2020). These are some technologies that can be used to help ghost kitchens minimize food waste in that as few portions of food as possible will be prepped at any given time, and surplus will be avoided as well as overproduction.

In addition, kitchen operations automation, e.g., robotic cooking systems and autonomous delivery cars, can lead to a tremendous increase in efficiency and sustainability. For example, automated cooking and packaging lines that, among other features, minimize human error, energy waste, and the amount of excess ingredients (Miller, 2021) will be necessary. These technological advances are also at the heart of increasing operational cost inefficiencies, which in turn make ghost kitchens not only sustainable but increasingly profitable in the long term.

Role of AI Technologies in Resource-Saving Kitchens

Artificial intelligence (AI) is a feature now that pervades the foodservice industry, particularly in ghost kitchens and lean operations (Resource-Saving kitchens). AI technologies hold great promise to increase the efficiency of operations, reduce the amount of resources used, and improve the design of kitchen operations, which in turn can help contribute to a sustainable solution in the foodservice industry. AI-based systems help kitchens to automate routine tasks (e.g., cooking, food preparation, and packaging) that could lead to better use of resources and time (Miller, 2021). For example, robotic cooks and cooking machines, powered by AI, can be used to cook with remarkable accuracy so that food waste due to overproduction or human error is significantly reduced. These intelligent systems are able to adjust the cooking time, temperature, and serving size on the basis of real-time data and thus avoid waste of ingredients (O'Connor Smith, 2022).

In addition, AI tools, including machine learning algorithms and predictive analytics, are able to use historical data patterns and trends to better manage inventory, decrease losses, and reduce the overstocking situation (Gustafsson et al., 2021). Based on customer preference and ordering patterns, AI is able to predict food demand with exceptional accuracy, avoiding as much excess as excess of ingredients, ultimately reducing food waste. Additionally, AI technologies allow for the accurate tracking of energy use, enabling kitchens to identify inefficiencies in power consumption and implement strategies for reducing energy waste (Friedrich et al., 2020).

In energy-saving kitchens, AI can also be used for water consumption monitoring, which is another critical resource in food preparation and cleaning. Through the analysis of consumption patterns and automated control strategies, AI can lead to saving electricity and hence water, not only saving cost but also environment (Liu et al., 2020). The combination of AI-powered sensors to manage water flow, temperature, and water consumption can lead to better general water use, making kitchens more environmental friendly and economical.

In general, AI technologies are actively contributing to energy- and resource-saving kitchens by delivering practical information, maximizing energy and resource efficiency, as well as to general sustainability in foodservice.

Role of AI in Supply Chain and Inventory Management

AI has a profound effect on improving supply chain systems and inventory management systems in the foodservice sector. Through the conception and implementation of an efficient flow of goods, materials, and information using AI, it is possible to minimize waste, optimize the use of resources, and streamline operations, all of which are facets of sustainability in resource-saving kitchens. Predicting demand accurately is probably one of the most important features of an AI in supply chain management. Through machine learning algorithms and predictive analytics, AI agents are able, using historical data and customer behavior as the reference points, or to account for external influences such as weather or events, to predict demand and therefore ensure that the right amount of inventory will be ordered at the proper time (Miller, 2021). This capability prevents both overstocking and stockouts, reducing food waste caused by spoilage or unsold goods. Using AI to adjust stock levels when there is demand for these, kitchens are better able to prevent food waste and use resources for their best possible effect.

AI-based inventory management systems also enhance the monitoring and following of ingredients, which allows for efficient use of perishable goods before reaching their expiration dates. This helps the reduction of spoilage and the limitation of kitchen storage to what is required for operation. AI-based systems can automatically update the stock levels and provide alerts for stock running out or for near expiry situations, enabling kitchen personnel to act quickly (Liu et al., 2020). Moreover, AI can be used to improve ordering procedures by examining the history of purchases, supplier performances, and price variation. This allows kitchens to make data-informed decisions on when to choose which suppliers to work with, minimize procurement expenditure, and prevent overbuying (Friedrich et al., 2020). Also, the use of AI helps by optimizing the supply chain, which strives to minimize the carbon footprint caused by wasteful transport and overproduction of surplus products.

In particular, AI-based systems could refine the logistics of food material distribution so that food ingredients are brought to kitchens in the most energy-conscious of ways. With route optimization algorithms, AI can find the most efficient delivery routes for supply trucks, reducing fuel consumption and carbon emissions (O'Connor Smith, 2022). This is especially relevant within resource-conserving kitchens, where across the supply chain, all steps can be optimized to minimize the overall environmental footprint.

EXAMPLES OF SUSTAINABLE GHOST KITCHENS DRIVEN BY AI

Simultaneously, with the increasing popularity of convenience and food delivery services, many ghost kitchens present themselves as sustainable models, particularly with the introduction of artificial intelligence technologies. These kitchens are using AI to improve their operation, reduce waste, and improve energy use. Following are examples of sustainable ghost kitchens that are powered by AI.

Kitchen United Mix (USA)

Kitchen United Mix (KUM) is one of the most renowned AI-powered ghost kitchens in the US, with environmental sustainability embodied in technology and operational learning. The platform employs AI for demand prediction and is thus able to manage food production and decrease food loss. Using AI-enabled analytics, the system makes estimations of order patterns, taking into account customer behavior, local events, and the time of year. This guarantees that only the necessary food quantity will be prepared in the kitchen, so that there will not be any excess, and thus reduces the amount of waste. Furthermore, Kitchen United Mix has installed energy-saving kitchen equipment such as induction cooktops and intelligent oven units, which automatically control the cooking temperature and time, thereby saving energy (Pereira et al., 2020).

CloudKitchens (Global)

CloudKitchens, one of the leading ghost kitchen companies, employs AI to automate kitchen management, including inventory management and the management of resources. The company has created an AI-based platform that leverages order data, ingredient usage, and customer choices to make demand predictions and optimize ingredient buy-in. This is able to prevent improper stocking, reduce food waste, and guarantee that kitchens utilize ingredients at their best possible freshness. In addition, CloudKitchens employs intelligent energy management systems that automatically fine-tune energy use in real time, changing heating, ventilation, and air conditioning (HVAC) systems depending on kitchen activity (Miller, 2021). The application of this technology allows CloudKitchens to be run with a significantly lower ecological footprint and better operational efficiency.

Rebel Foods (India)

Rebel Foods, one of India's biggest cloud kitchen operators, uses AI and machine learning to enhance its sustainability initiatives. The company uses AI for dynamic inventory management and waste reduction by analyzing past sales data to forecast demand more accurately. This enables Rebel Foods to minimize waste arising from unsold materials and maximize use of ingredients. For example, Rebel Foods employs data-driven decision-making to maximize kitchen layouts and optimize resource sharing while minimizing energy consumption throughout the day, particularly during high- and low-demand times (Alon-Barkat Buskirk, 2021). The integration of AI in the kitchen also allows for energy-saving practices such as smart equipment that automatically adjusts cooking times and temperatures based on real-time requirements, contributing to lower energy consumption.

These use cases demonstrate the ways in which AI tools are contributing to the sustainability of ghost kitchens, e.g., through optimization of resource use, minimization of food loss, and energy use. With the ongoing transformation of the foodservice sector, AI-enhanced ghost kitchens are projected to be key in the development of more sustainable business models.

THE FUTURE OF SUSTAINABLE GHOST KITCHENS

The outlook for sustainable ghost kitchens is encouraging; advances in technology such as AI are enabling important innovations that can lead to efficiency gains, improvements in waste reduction, and sustainability in the foodservice sector. When consumers are increasingly focused on environmental issues, ghost kitchens for sustainability will have a competitive advantage. There are also some trends expected to influence the future of sustainable ghost kitchens:.

Increased Integration of Renewable Energy Sources

Over the next few years, we predict that the use of renewable energy sources in ghost kitchens will see a major uptake. In an effort towards sustainability, a number of operators are looking into solar/wind/other forms of renewables to power their kitchens. AI is highly capable of optimizing the deployment of renewable energy through forecasting energy consumption behavior and the control of household activities to meet with energy supply. For instance, kitchens have the potential to be as efficient as possible for energy with respect to daylight and solar energy availability (Soman et al., 2020).

Zero-Waste Kitchens and Circular Economy Models

The move from conventional zero-waste kitchens to a key player in the development of sustainable ghost kitchens will be a major topic in this evolution. AI technologies will help these kitchens adopt circular economy principles, such as food waste recycling, composting, and repurposing ingredients. Advanced artificial intelligence (AI) devices can estimate food consumption more precisely, minimizing food waste. Furthermore, AI-based platforms will allow kitchens to keep an eye on the shelf life of perishable items as well as optimize the food flow of the raw materials to limit food spoilage (Friedrich et al., 2020). These kitchens may also partner with local farmers or food banks to repurpose unsold or surplus food, supporting a sustainable food chain.

AI-Driven Personalized Nutrition and Sustainable Sourcing

Another very important trend will be the introduction of AI in the development of individual meal suggestions according to customers' preferences and nutritional requirements. Sustainable ghost kitchens will take advantage of AI to forecast consumer preferences, offer contextually adaptive, health-oriented food choices, and facilitate sustainable sourcing practices. By collaborating with local, organic, and ethically sourced suppliers, AI can ensure that the ingredients used are not only nutritious but also environmentally friendly. This will help local communities while lowering the carbon emissions that are linked to the supply chain of food from afar (Miller, 2021).

Collaboration with Smart Delivery Systems

Sustainable ghost kitchens will also contribute to the adoption of smart, environmentally friendly delivery systems. Autonomous vehicles and drones, powered by AI, are expected to become common in the delivery process. These systems are also going to reduce emissions related to the traditional delivery trucks, optimizing routes, and better distributing food to consumers. Moreover, through cooperating with eco-minded supplier platforms, ghost kitchens are able to guarantee the use of recyclable, compostable, or sustainable materials for their packaging (Gustafsson et al., 2021).

Data-Driven Sustainability Metrics

With the help of AI, ghost kitchens will be able to accurately monitor and quantify their sustainable actions. Using AI-based analytics, kitchens are able to draw actionable insights into their resource consumption, waste generation, and carbon emissions. This will permit automatic monitoring and optimization of operations. Moreover, these sustainability indices will form a critical aspect of consumer transparency, as customers are increasingly demanding products that match their environmental consciousness (Pereira et al., 2020).

CONCLUSION

Ghost kitchens are a disruptive change in the foodservice realm, presenting novel approaches to address the changing needs of contemporary consumers. But their fast expansion generates issues in regulation, competition, and consumer confidence. In the development of this rapidly changing industry, ghost kitchens will be key to shaping the landscape of dining and food delivery experiences on a global scale. The demand for sustainability in ghost kitchens both exists today and is critical, presenting the potential for major environmental and economic gains. To thrive in the long term, operators must prioritize sustainable practices, such as waste reduction, resource optimization, and energy efficiency. By integrating principles of the circular economy and leveraging advanced technologies like AI and automation, ghost kitchens can minimize their environmental impact while setting new benchmarks for responsible business practices. In the future, sustainable ghost kitchens are fertile ground for the ambitious evolution of AI technologies. These technologies will allow operators to take advantage of new operational efficiency, waste reduction, and sustainable solutions on an industrial scale. With growing demand by consumers for sustainable food options, AI-enhanced, highly efficient food systems (ghost kitchens) will push the sustainability-resilient and responsible foodservice industry forward.

REFERENCES

Alon-Barkat, S., & Buskirk, T. D. (2021). The environmental impact of cloud kitchens: A case study in urban sustainability. *Journal of Hospitality and Tourism Management*, *48*, 55–62. DOI: 10.1016/j.jhtm.2021.05.007

Cai, Y., Leung, X. Y., & Xie, K. L. (2022). Examining consumers' trust and risk perceptions in cloud kitchen services. *International Journal of Contemporary Hospitality Management*, *34*(7), 2472–2492. DOI: 10.1108/IJCHM-09-2021-1100

Cao, J., Feihong, H., & Qi, W. (2024). (Manuscript submitted for publication). Uber" Your Cooking: The Sharing-Economy Operations of a Ghost-Kitchen Platform. *Preprint*, (March), 14.

CloudKitchens. (2022). Top food and beverage trends: What's shaping the industry? CloudKitchens. Retrieved from https://cloudkitchens.com/blog/food-and-beverage-trends-2022/

CloudKitchens. (2022). Rise of ghost kitchens. Retrieved from https://cloudkitchens.com/blog/rise-of-ghost-kitchens

Daily Telegraph. (2022). Councils to crack down on ghost kitchens delivering takeaway food from unmonitored kitchens. Retrieved from https://www.dailytelegraph.com.au

Eisenberg, D., Thompson, S., & Zhou, L. (2023). Teaching kitchens as sustainability platforms: Opportunities for innovation. *Food Policy Journal*, *36*(1), 65–80.

Euromonitor International. (2022). Ghost kitchens: An emerging trillion-dollar industry. Retrieved from https://www.euromonitor.com

Euromonitor International. (2022). The future of food delivery: Forecast for ghost kitchens.

Friedrich, J., Will, F., & Dore, J. (2020). Sustainable packaging solutions in the food service industry. *Sustainability and the Circular Economy*, *9*(2), 141–155. DOI: 10.3390/su9020141

Giousmpasoglou, C., Marinakou, E., & Cooper, J. (2023). Worker exploitation in the gig economy: Insights from the hospitality sector. *Journal of Hospitality Research*, *45*(3), 245–260.

Gustafsson, M., Gärling, T., & Nilsson, E. (2021). Waste management and sustainability in the restaurant industry. *International Journal of Environmental Sustainability*, *13*(4), 190–203. DOI: 10.1108/IJES-06-2020-0110

Hakim, M. P., Yan, L., & Wang, S. (2022). Online food delivery services and customer trust: The role of mobile apps. *Journal of Retailing and Consumer Services*, *65*, 102858. DOI: 10.1016/j.jretconser.2021.102858

Jiang, Y., Balaji, M. S., & Lyu, C. (2024). Cultivating initial trust in ghost kitchens: A mixed-methods investigation of antecedents and consequences. *International Journal of Hospitality Management*, *119*, 103727. DOI: 10.1016/j.ijhm.2024.103727

Jones, M. (2024). Ghost kitchens: Balancing opportunity and challenges in the competitive market. *Journal of Foodservice Trends*, *21*(2), 112–130.

Leung, X. Y., Yang, Y., & Chang, S. (2023). Dining in the dark: Consumers' perceptions of dark kitchens and their purchase intentions. *Journal of Hospitality and Tourism Management, 55*, 72–84. DOI: 10.1016/j.jhtm.2023.04.005

Liu, B., Xu, L., & Zhang, L. (2020). Artificial intelligence applications in reducing food waste in the foodservice industry. *International Journal of Hospitality Management, 90*, 102586. DOI: 10.1016/j.ijhm.2020.102586

Miller, P. (2021). The role of automation in the food service sector: Enhancing operational efficiency and sustainability. *Technology in Hospitality and Food Services, 15*(1), 25–40. DOI: 10.1016/j.techfood.2021.01.001

National Retail Federation. (2022). A look inside the $43 billion ghost kitchen industry. Retrieved from https://nrf.com

National Retail Federation. (2022). Market growth analysis: Ghost kitchens and delivery-only restaurants.

Neria, G., Hildebrandt, F. D., Tzur, M., & Ulmer, M. W. (2024). The Restaurant Meal Delivery Problem with Ghost Kitchens. *Transportation Science*, trsc.2024.0510. DOI: 10.1287/trsc.2024.0510

Nigro, H. O., Bellezza, M. P., & Santoro, M. (2022). The role of digital influencers in shaping food service consumer preferences. *Journal of Foodservice Business Research, 25*(3), 345–364. DOI: 10.1080/15378020.2022.2058956

O'Connor, A., & Smith, J. (2022). Energy efficiency in cloud kitchens: A comparison of shared kitchen spaces and traditional restaurants. *Energy Efficiency Review, 45*(7), 320–335. DOI: 10.1007/s12053-021-07924-3

O'Sullivan, T. (2024). Life cycle assessment in sustainable food practices. *Sustainability & Environment Journal, 29*(4), 400–415.

Pereira, R., Sampaio, P., & Silva, J. (2020). Cloud kitchens: A disruptive business model in the food industry. *International Journal of Food Service Management, 22*(2), 67–78. DOI: 10.1016/j.jft.2020.10.008

PKF Hospitality Group. (2022). Ghost kitchens: How this growing trend can help restaurants thrive. Retrieved from https://www.pkfhospitality.com

PKF Hospitality Group. (2022). Understanding the rise of ghost kitchens.

Pookulangara, S., Sondhi, S., & Boyer, L. (2023). Consumer perceptions of cloud kitchens: Trust, innovation, and hedonic motivations. *Journal of Consumer Behaviour, 22*(4), 675–689. DOI: 10.1002/cb.2112

Rout, A., Dawande, M., & Janakiraman, G. (2024). Cloud-Kitchens: Value Creation Through Co-Location. *Production and Operations Management, 33*(2), 512–529. DOI: 10.1177/10591478231224950

Sanitation Professional. (2022). Emerging trends in food delivery services: The role of ghost kitchens.

Sanitation Professional. (2022). Ghost kitchens: How this growing trend can help restaurants thrive. Retrieved from https://saniprofessional.com

Soman, N., Warde, A., & Singh, A. (2020). The future of energy efficiency in commercial kitchens: AI-based innovations. *Energy Efficiency Journal, 13*(1), 67–83. DOI: 10.1007/s12053-020-09856-0

Stephens, P., Carter, R., & Malik, A. (2021). Local sourcing and sustainability in foodservice. *International Journal of Culinary Innovation, 12*(2), 150–166.

World Resources Institute. (2021). A circular economy for the food service industry: Reducing waste and resource consumption. Retrieved from https://www.wri.org/publication/circular-economy-foodservice

Wulandari, F. (2023). Digitalization in food & beverage: The cloud kitchen revolution. *Journal of Sustainable Business Practices, 18*(1), 55–68.

Chapter 16 Using Machine Learning Algorithms to Personalize Customer Experience in Ghost Kitchens: Hyper-Personalized Marketing and Promotion

Tanvir Singh Solar
https://orcid.org/0009-0002-9649-8837
Christ University, Delhi, India

ABSTRACT

The emergence of ghost kitchens has revolutionized the food delivery industry by leveraging machine learning algorithms to enhance customer satisfaction and personalized experiences. This chapter, examines how predictive analytics identifies customer preferences, helping ghost kitchens create effective marketing strategies aligned with tastes and behaviours. It highlights real-time personalization, where offers are tailored based on past orders, location, and time, fostering relevance and loyalty. AI-driven customer segmentation is explored as a vital tool for precise targeting. At the same time, the chapter also addresses how AI assesses campaign performance to refine marketing tactics and adapt to changing demands. This research adds new fresh knowledge to the established body of knowledge in the context of restaurant food consumption behavior (Maziriri, E. T., Rukuni, T. F., & Chuchu, T. (2021)). This chapter is going to explore how AI advancements revolutionize resource utilization, evolving customer preferences, sustainable growth.

DOI: 10.4018/979-8-3373-0432-8.ch016

1. INTRODUCTION AND CONTEXT

1.1. Overview of Ghost Kitchens

The ghost kitchen (or also known as cloud kitchen) is the reflection of online food delivery growth and some changes in customer behavior. These types of establishments do not have a physical dine-in space, they only make food for takeout and delivery. Dispensing with front-of-house operations like wait-staff, dining rooms and other amenities, ghost kitchens forgo everything but necessity and rely on digital ordering platforms to reach customers. It's a strategy that's been shown to be nimble, allowing these kitchens to quickly launch new brands or menus, and shift what they offer based on demand and experiment with new culinary ideas at relatively low risk.

In the past ten years, the worldwide online food delivery market has grown tremendously, driven by technological advancements and changing lifestyle trends. Smartphones have become ubiquitous, more simple payment processes have emerged, and the logistics platforms have improved so that consumers now find, order, and pay for meals in a very different way than they used to. This convenience, in turn, has raised user expectations, they expect not just a large selection of options to choose from, but also fast and smooth delivery experiences. Within that landscape, ghost kitchens are helping desperate restaurants remain competitive. In some cities, multiple ghost kitchens can even share a single large-scale facility, "operating" as separate "virtual restaurant" brands under one roof.

The advantages of a ghost kitchen model are unique one and that makes data-driven management all the more important." With no customers in the building, this means direct interaction and face-to-face feedback is limited, if not completely lacking. As a result, companies can succeed only as much as they successfully handle digital signals (such as order patterns and online reviews) and maintain smooth back-end operations. The algorithmic optimization of menu engineering, forecasting of demand peak and delivery logistics will enable you to streamline the overall workflow and maintain profitability without compromising delighters for your customers. If multiple brands share the same premises, it becomes more complicated. The need for accurate inventory control, is important since they must learn to balance not ruining the meal with stock-outs or excessive wastes, and the staff needs to be trained to handle distinct menus under tight timelines. Data analytics and agile decision-making are crucial given these heightened operational requirements.

Table 1. Traditional vs. Ghost Kitchens: A Comparative Analysis

Comparison Aspect	Traditional Restaurants	Ghost Kitchens
Physical Footprint vs. Virtual Operations	Emphasize location-based strategies, investing in real estate, ambiance, and face-to-face customer service.	Minimize real estate footprints, often using low-rent industrial spaces or shared commissaries, reducing capital expenditure.
Front-of-House vs. Digital Interfaces	Rely on front-of-house staff (hosts, servers, bartenders) to build direct rapport with customers.	Engage customers digitally, primarily through websites, apps, or third-party platforms, limiting direct physical interaction.
Menu Development and Brand Presence	Typically maintain a single cohesive brand identity and evolve a set menu over time.	Can launch and incubate multiple virtual brands, each tailored to distinct consumer niches (e.g., plant-based, premium desserts).
Scalability and Agility	Face geographic and staffing constraints, limiting expansion speed.	Highly scalable; can pivot quickly using data analytics if certain menus or concepts underperform, thus reducing financial risk.

From a personalization standpoint, **traditional eateries** often relied on **face-to-face rapport**, remembering returning patrons' preferences or customizing dishes at the server's discretion. Ghost kitchens, however, **lack in-person cues** and instead depend on **digital footprints**, using data-driven insights to tailor experiences an approach increasingly underpinned by **artificial intelligence (AI)**.

1.2. The Growing Role of AI in Foodservice and Delivery

Although automation has supported the food service industry for decades ranging from basic mechanical dishwashers to digital point-of-sale (POS) systems newer **AI-driven capabilities** are injecting unprecedented intelligence, speed, and personalization into modern operations (Kumar & Patel, 2022). **Traditional restaurants**, for instance, often relied on membership cards or loyalty punch programs, which provided only rudimentary consumer insight usually awarding generic rewards (e.g., a free dessert after ten purchases). These manual or semi-automated models could not dynamically adjust to individual consumer tastes or broader market shifts in real time.

By contrast, ghost kitchens take advantage of **data aggregation** and **machine learning (ML) algorithms** across all facets of their digital operations. For example, every online order generates detailed records, including purchase timing, order composition, and user location data that AI systems can analyze to uncover hidden patterns. With robust predictive analytics, ghost kitchens can forecast **demand surges** or **seasonal fluctuations** with higher accuracy, preparing the right quantities of ingredients to avoid both spoilage and shortages. They can also dynamically reassign kitchen staff to match predicted spikes in order volume, thereby ensuring efficient fulfillment.

Another critical aspect **is real-time pricing**: AI analyzes variables such as competitor prices, historical sales data, and ingredient costs to suggest optimal pricing for certain menu items. If a dish's core ingredient is abundant or quickly nearing expiration, the algorithm may recommend a brief promotion or discount to drive sales. Conversely, if there is an unexpected surge in popularity for a high-margin dish, ghost kitchens can capitalize on that trend by dynamically adjusting the price upward Improving revenue while aligning with consumer demand.

On the **marketing side**, machine learning models process a host of data points past orders, browsing behavior, location-based insights to deliver **personalized promotions** that resonate strongly with each customer segment. Instead of broadcasting a uniform deal to thousands of customers, AI allows ghost kitchens to tailor an offer based on, say, vegetarian preferences, late-night ordering habits, or regional festivals and events. This nuanced approach to marketing not only lifts conversion rates but also fosters a sense of individualized service in a setting that lacks in-person rapport.

Moreover, **agile decision-making** stands out as a vital advantage of AI in ghost kitchens (Deloitte, 2023). For instance, if the system detects consumer sentiment turning negative perhaps due to longer delivery times or subpar packaging ghost kitchens can quickly tweak internal processes (e.g., adjusting delivery routes, reevaluating packaging suppliers) to remedy the issue. In effect, AI serves as a real-time feedback loop, enabling data-driven improvements to operational workflows, menu engineering, and consumer engagement.

As **AI capabilities** continue to evolve encompassing deeper predictive insights, natural language processing for sentiment analysis, and more sophisticated image recognition for quality control ghost kitchens stand well-positioned to further harness these tools. By **bridging automation with advanced analytics**, they are reshaping the food service landscape, ushering in a level of customization, adaptability, and operational finesse previously unimaginable in conventional dining.

1.3. Importance of Customer Personalization in Ghost Kitchens

Personalization has evolved from a convenient add-on to a cornerstone of competitive advantage in an increasingly saturated digital market. Unlike brick-and-mortar restaurants that rely on ambiance and personal rapport, ghost kitchens operate solely in a virtual arena. They must, therefore, leverage hyper-personalized marketing to stand out among hundreds of online listings and foster loyalty in an environment devoid of in-person interaction.

1.3.1. Historical Evolution of Personalization in Food Service (Before AI):

Long before the advent of sophisticated AI, food service businesses sought to personalize the dining experience using human interaction and "local knowledge." These approaches, while effective in fostering a sense of familiarity, lacked scalability and data-driven precision.

1. **Local Community Ties:** Traditional mom-and-pop diners often recognized patrons by name, recalling birthdays, favorite seats, or dietary quirks. This personal touch cultivated loyalty but depended heavily on staff continuity and memory.
2. **Wait-Staff Recommendations:** In higher-end establishments, servers functioned as trusted advisors, recalling each diner's allergies, taste preferences, or wine choices. This form of "white-glove" service enriched the experience but was labor-intensive and prone to inconsistencies if key personnel changed.
3. **Membership and Punch Cards:** Casual dining chains occasionally offered loyalty punch cards or membership clubs, awarding general perks (e.g., a free appetizer after ten visits). While such systems gathered rudimentary datahow often guests visited they provided little insight into nuanced customer behaviors or real-time targeting opportunities.

These traditional personalization methods excelled in relationship-building but were hampered by limited scope, data rigor, and adaptability. By the early 2000s, the emergence of online ordering systems and mobile apps allowed restaurants to store basic customer data (addresses, order histories), bridging some of these gaps. Even so, AI revolutionized personalization by analyzing large-scale, granular data in real time, offering targeted promotions or meal suggestions that dynamically adapt to evolving consumer patterns.

1.3.2. Personalized Strategies in the Modern Digital Ecosystem

In today's **digital marketing ecosystem**, personalization is more than a competitive advantage; it is **vital for survival.** Occupying a crowded online marketplace, ghost kitchens lack the physical presence and atmosphere that attract diners to traditional establishments. Consequently, they must rely **on data-driven personalization** to stand out among hundreds of restaurants on aggregator apps.

Personalized strategies can range from displaying menu items based on a user's prior orders to sending individualized offers aligned with a customer's dietary habits, location, or even local cultural events. This level of **hyper-customization** creates an instant sense of convenience and familiarity, spurring higher engagement and repeat business. For instance, targeted promotions might be delivered to frequent buyers of plant-based options the moment new vegan dishes are added significantly boosting the probability that those customers will give the new items a try. Meanwhile, machine learning algorithms can determine **optimal push notification timing**, predicting when specific users are most likely to place orders and prompting impulse purchases at exactly the right moment.

From a **revenue perspective**, operators stand to see marked improvements across multiple KPIs. Increasing average order value (AOV) becomes feasible when loyal customers are nudged toward menu add-ons they are genuinely interested in desserts, sides, or premium upgrades. Similarly, tailored experiences foster stronger customer satisfaction, translating into positive online reviews, word-of-mouth referrals, and elevated customer lifetime value (CLV). Given that ghost kitchens typically depend on **third-party delivery platforms** for visibility, failing to offer personalized experiences risks losing consumer interest in a sea of near-identical listings.

In essence, **data-driven personalization** has become the linchpin for ghost kitchens seeking brand distinction, consumer trust, and operational optimization. By harnessing **customer insights** and applying **machine learning algorithms** to tailor every facet of the dining journey from product recommendations to marketing touchpoints ghost kitchens can replicate (and often surpass) the personal warmth once provided by face-to-face staff, ensuring a memorable experience that keeps diners returning.

1.4. Chapter Objectives and Structure

This chapter explores how machine learning algorithms enable hyper-personalized customer experiences in ghost kitchens, establishing a blueprint for AI-driven marketing, operational efficiency, and future innovations. Specifically, it aims to:

1. **Examine Predictive Analytics and Demand Forecasting:** Illustrate how AI models use historical and real-time data (e.g., order patterns, demographics, geolocation) to anticipate fluctuations in demand, reduce waste, and refine inventory strategies.
2. **Highlight Real-Time Personalization and Dynamic Pricing:** Demonstrate how AI swiftly adjusts meal prices or special offers based on consumer preferences and ingredient availability, ensuring alignment between promotions and operational capacity.
3. **Explore AI-Driven Customer Segmentation:** Investigate the use of clustering algorithms and advanced machine learning techniques to categorize different consumer groups, enabling hyper-targeted marketing approaches.
4. **Discuss Ethical, Regulatory, and Operational Considerations:** Address algorithmic biases, data privacy requirements, and workforce implications linked to AI integration in ghost kitchens.
5. **Identify Future Trends in AI-Enabled Ghost Kitchens:** Outline imminent developments such as voice-based ordering, robotics, holistic supply chain integration, and emerging opportunities for investors.
6. **Recommend Implementation Strategies for Both Large and Small Operators:** Provide tailored guidelines to help larger chains and smaller, independent ghost kitchens adopt AI solutions effectively, taking into account varying budgets, resources, and operational scales.

2. UNDERSTANDING CUSTOMER PREFERENCES THROUGH PREDICTIVE ANALYTICS

2.1. Fundamentals of Machine Learning and Predictive Models

Predictive analytics are the backbone of personalized marketing, and enable ghost kitchens to have the predictive functionality of knowing their customer needs, thereby optimizing their operational performance and coming up with strategies based on data. At its core, predictive modeling utilizes statistical algorithms and machine learning (ML) methodologies from regression analysis, decision trees, and random forests to neural networks to detect patterns in historical time series data and construct predictive models for future ones. These techniques range from relatively simple to sophisticated but all have one thing in common: they extract actionable takeaways that help to inform marketing strategies, resource investments, and overall business decisions.

- **Supervised Learning:** It is used for forecasting demand, customer churn predictions. The explanatory algorithms, e.g., linear regression, logistic regression, or gradient boosting machines, learn from labelled datasets, where they have observations in which the inputs (e.g., demographics, order frequency) are known and the outcome is observed (e.g., was a promotion redeemed). Supervised learning is great for structured data so it is used for things like predicting the peak ordering hours or which customers are most likely to respond to a limited time offer.
- **Unsupervised Learning:** Essential to uncover underlying patterns in the data with no explicit labels, commonly used for segmentation tasks. Techniques such as k means or hierarchical clustering group similar purchasing behavior to uncover patterns that aren't always apparent. Such insights can guide ghost kitchens on how to segment and market to consumers glossing the fact that they're post work adults who may work long hours (i.e., students on a budget vs health focused professionals, etc.)
- **Reinforcement Learning:** While more niche than the previous approaches, reinforcement learning is becoming a popular method for real time decision making in dynamic contexts. It can therefore optimize live recommendation engines to ensure offers are tailor made to the user, or dynamic pricing models in the context of a ghost kitchen, where the algorithm "learns" over time from user feedback in real time whether a particular offer led to a conversion or the price point made the customer abandon their cart.

"Findings reveal that strategic alignment between supply chain management (SCM) and marketing fosters better coordination of product availability and service delivery, thereby meeting customer expectations consistently and enhancing brand loyalty (Holloway (2024))." Crucially, these machine learning approaches are often used in combination rather than in isolation. A ghost kitchen, for example, could apply supervised learning to forecast items that are likely to be in demand and use clustering algorithms at the same time to optimize its segmentation of promotional campaign executions. This framework, which used many algorithms, allowed the business to hold both the macro market trends (like what are weekends to the entire volume of orders made) and micro customers nuances (let's say, one specific customer, one who likes spicy, plant based food). As iterations through the updates refine the ML models, the kitchen's marketing campaigns can go hyper personalized delivering the right message to the right customer at the right time.

2.2. Types of Data Collected in Ghost Kitchens (e.g., order history, demographics, behavioral data)

Data is often claimed as the lifeblood of predictive analytics, and ghost kitchens can generate a lot of it structured and unstructured. Consolidating and integrating this data from various inputs is essential to creating a robust predictive framework:

- **Order History:** Detailed information about past transactions, which may include time stamps, what was purchased, how much was spent, and what payment method was used. These datasets can help reveal purchasing patterns, peak ordering periods and popular menu combinations (e.g., specific sides that are regularly ordered with a particular entrée).
- **Customer Demographics:** Age, sex, location, household size, occupation, etc. While some aggregator platforms may restrict access to demographic information, ghost kitchens that create direct ordering channels are able to tap into more granular knowledge. Such demographics can be integrated with other data points to enhance targeting strategy and promotional offers."
- **Behavioral Data:** Information from clickstream data with websites or apps, showing for how long they look for a menu, what offers interest customers, for what and how many times do they reorder their favorite dishes. Behavioral data can also monitor user journeyswhen a prospect may leave a cart behindand then activate a targeted re engagement strategy.
- **Feedback and Reviews:** Ratings, written comments, and images submitted via delivery apps, social media platforms and email surveys. Sentiment analysis tools can translate these qualitative inputs into quantitative measures that reveal menu strengths, service problems or popular new items.
- **Operational Data:** Metrics on the current stock of ingredients, buffer for ingredient usage, staff activity, and preparation times. Although mainly employed internally to enhance efficiency, these metrics can also be used to tailor experiences in case the system identifies the opportunity for certain dishes to be prepared faster during peak time, and showcases these options on marketing communications.

The raw data must first be aggregated from these sources into a data lake or warehouse that can serve as the central location from which the modeling can occur. This step consists of a lot of data cleaning (for example removing duplicates), reconciling naming discrepancies (for example making sure every cuisine has the same label) and managing missing entries. Next comes feature engineering, which recasts raw inputs into features that models can exploit like grouping items into cuisine clusters, calculating how recently a dish was purchased, or tagging it as "top rated" based on user feedback. Equally important, however, is proper data governance, which operates to maintain the compliance and integrity of sensitive data under regulations such as GDPR, and CCPA.

2.3. Building Accurate Predictive Models (data collection, data cleansing, feature engineering)

Building strong predictive models is equal parts art and science. Although the right choice of algorithm is crucial, sustained optimization comes from factors such as the quality of the data, future proof feature engineering on data, and persistent monitored performance.

- **Data exploration and cleaning:** This first step is primarily statistical summaries followed by visualizations, to identify outliers/abnormalities. For example, an unusually high number of orders for a single user may indicate either a bulk corporate purchase, or a data entry error. Establishing these nuances early provides model robustness.
- **Feature Engineering:** Create or Transform Variables to Capture Hidden Patterns. For example, time based features (like day of week or local holidays or payday cycles) tend to be highly predictive of ordering behaviors. Diet preference flags (vegan, gluten free), average spend over rolling windows, or the frequency of custom requests (extra sauce, for example) can help build even more complex personalization strategies.
- **Model Training and Validation**: The data is often divided into training, validation, and test sets to help prevent overfitting. Hyper parameters (three of learning rates and tree depths in gradient boosting, for example) are tuned using methods such as cross validation, grid search, or Bayesian optimization. Models are evaluated on a validation set to help tune these parameters before final testing.
- **Performance Metrics:** The type of metrics will depend on the problem. In the specific case of item demand forecasting, common metrics are Mean Absolute Error or Root Mean Squared Error. For prediction problems, F1 scores or precision recall metrics may be used for churn, whilst in recommendation systems measures of ranking such as Mean Reciprocal Rank or Normalized Discounted Cumulative Gain may be used.
- **Deployment and Monitoring:** The validated model is then deployed into a production environment (not unusually in a real time data pipeline). You monitor performance constantly (especially data drift) Changes in the underlying patterns (e.g., a change in consumers' behavior due to local competitors opening or economic factors) might call for retraining or recalibrating the model.

2.4. Privacy and Ethical Considerations in Customer Data Gathering

As consumer data is collected and leveraged, notable privacy and ethical concerns arise in the pursuit of personalization . These include regulatory frameworks like the General Data Protection Regulation (GDPR) in the EU and the California Consumer Privacy Act (CCPA) in the United States, which set stringent rules on how companies should manage personally identifiable information (PII). Such regulations may include data storage requirements, breach notifications, the right of users to request access to or deletion of their data, and transparent reporting of data usage.

Compliance for ghost kitchens goes beyond being just a legal responsibility, but it is rather a key driver of success. Transgressions can lead to fines that run into the hundreds of millions of dollars and undermine consumer trust, which is fragile at best in an industry where scruples can go out the window with changing customer tastes. Key best practices include:

- **Consent Management:** Telling customers clearly what data is collected and for what purpose. Use opt in checkboxes or preference dashboards in ordering apps to enable this..
- **Data Minimization:** This means retaining only the data that is required for legitimate operational or marketing purposes. Collecting excessive amounts of information also amplifies the risk of breaches and can violate the principle of proportionality in data protection laws.

- **Use of Anonymization and Encryption:** All sensitive fields should be anonymized, and all consumer data should be encrypted both in transit (i.e., SSL/TLS protocols) and at rest (i.e., server side encryption). Key management is critical as well.
- **Bias and fairness:** ML models can inherit the biases present in historical data used for training. For example, if certain demographics had historically received fewer promotions, the model might be biased to offer fewer promotions to those groups. Regular audits and fairness metrics should be used to identify and rectify such skew.

Overcoming these privacy and ethical challenges can give you a competitive advantage. Customers now understand the value of personalized experiences and expect you to treat their data responsibly. By walking the fine lineoffering some degree of customization while understanding the limits of personal interactionghost kitchens can cement brand loyalty and build a reputation as a dependable service provider. When businesses scale or seek new partnerships, this reputation for ethical data use becomes even more important, as potential collaborators and investors often vet data practices as part of their due diligence.

2.5. Mini-Case Studies and Contextual Examples

Integrating predictive analytics into ghost kitchen operations has proven instrumental in tailoring offerings and optimizing performance to meet customer expectations. The following case studies exemplify how data-driven strategies have propelled success in the virtual dining sector:

2.5.1. Stone Bridge Pizza's Sub-Brand Strategy

Stone Bridge Pizza, a Manhattan-based pizzeria, observed that their sandwich sales were not meeting expectations. To address this, they launched a specialized sub-brand, Rival Sandwich Co., operating as a ghost kitchen focusing exclusively on baked sandwiches crafted from fresh pizza dough, herbs, and salt. This strategic pivot, informed by customer data and market analysis, led to a threefold increase in sandwich sales within the first week. This case illustrates how targeted branding and menu specialization, guided by predictive analytics, can significantly boost revenue.

2.5.2. Coffee Q's Expansion Through Cloud Kitchens

Coffee Q, under the leadership of owner and chef Julio Arevalo, sought to expand their customer base during the pandemic. By partnering with Cloud Kitchens, they transitioned to a ghost kitchen model, enabling them to reach new customers online and broaden their market presence. This move underscores the importance of leveraging data analytics to identify market opportunities and adapt to changing consumer behaviors, ensuring business resilience in challenging times.

2.5.3. Rebel Foods' Multi-Brand Cloud Kitchen Model

Rebel Foods, an Indian company, operates over 450 cloud kitchens across multiple countries, managing brands like Faasos and Behrouz Biryani. They utilize a data-driven approach to monitor customer preferences and market trends, allowing them to launch and scale multiple brands efficiently. Their success highlights the role of predictive analytics in managing diverse virtual brands and meeting varied customer demands, demonstrating scalability and adaptability in the cloud kitchen industry.

2.5.4. The Bohri Kitchen's Data-Driven Home Dining Experience

The Bohri Kitchen, founded by Munaf Kapadia, began as a home-based dining experience offering traditional Bohri cuisine. By analyzing customer feedback and demand patterns, they expanded into cloud kitchens and increased their delivery footprint across Mumbai. This growth showcases how understanding customer preferences through data can guide successful business expansion, transforming a niche home dining concept into a scalable virtual kitchen model.

These examples demonstrate that integrating predictive analytics enables ghost kitchens to tailor their offerings, optimize operations, and effectively meet customer expectations, leading to sustained success in the competitive food delivery market.

3. REAL-TIME PERSONALIZATION OF PROMOTIONS AND DISCOUNTS

3.1. Dynamic pricing and personalized offers

Real time personalization is a strategic technique that leverages immediate data, today's stock levels, local weather, user browsing activity to dynamically personalize offers and prices. Unlike static promotions, dynamic pricing can change in seconds or minutes, responsive to current supply demand conditions and individualized insights into a given customer's historical behavior or projected price sensitivity. The underlying premise is to maximize revenue opportunities by providing a tailored experience that speaks to individual consumers.

- **Discount Strategies:** A ghost kitchen could target customers who haven't placed an order in the past 30 days with an offer for a limited time discount to get them back in the door. Time based and quantity based discounts Loyalty customers, who buy early in the day or in bulk, receive discounts or even bundled offers.
- **Premium Pricing:** Users who typically order at peak times (say, weekend evenings) can be targeted by pricing algorithms to bundle premium menu items, or upsell exclusive "chef's specials" with a premium attached. These users are also willing to pay extra for convenience or fancy dishes, so we can comfortably test out some premium pricing without worrying about cart abandonment.
- **Behavior Based Offers:** If a user has already abandoned their cart, the system could send them a time sensitive coupon or a read more complimentary add on (e.g., a dessert or side dish) to spark their interest. This strategy uses various psychological triggers to drive purchases, like scarcity (limited time offers) and personalization (acknowledging previous browsing or ordering behavior).

At the core to these real time strategies are machine learning models that continuously consume data streams to drive pricing and promotional decisions. For instance, the algorithm can employ reinforcement learning techniques enabling it to learn from repeated acts: if a particular discount amount leads to greater conversions, the system will use more similar discounts in similar situations throughout time.

On the other hand, if a price increase that is too aggressive kills significantly sales, the model adapts. This constant readjusting is an especially important proposition for ghost kitchens, which are wholly dependent on digital platforms which can see massive shifts in user behavior depending on the time of the day, competitor push notifications, or even seasonal culinary trends.

3.2. Leveraging Real-Time Data Feed

Real time personalization hinges on the immediate applicability of data and the availability of data across multiple platforms and systems. Each data feed provides its own insights that drive decision making:

- **Customer Activity Feed:** By tracking in app or web activity whether that's adding to cart, searching for products or how long people spend browsing specific menu items ghost kitchens can identify which promotions will be most attractive. If a customer spends too long on a particular dish page, an immediate pop up discount or bundle suggestion could persuade them to finally place the order.
- **Inventory and Production Data**: Having a detailed real time view of ingredient availability and employee capacity is critical. If the algorithm calculates a particular dish's ingredients are running low, it can automatically deprioritize or even withdraw promotions for that item, avoiding customer disappointment. Conversely, when stock levels of a particular dish are high or when fresh ingredients need to be used quickly promotional focus can be adjusted to help stimulate sales of that item.
- **External Contextual Data:** Factors such as weather conditions, traffic patterns, local events, and competitor pricing can have significant impact on demand. For example, on a brisk rainy night a focus on soups, soothing drinks, or comfort foods makes sense with the needs of consumers in that moment. For major sporting events, ghost kitchens may peddle combo deals for wings and pizza to suit the occasion.
- **Location Insights and Personalization:** With user consent, location can provide hyperlocal information for deals and promotions. If a customer is within a certain radius of the kitchen, they may see lowered or waived delivery fees to motivate them to order immediately. In high density urban markets, dynamic offers could also be based on predicted delivery time if a rider is already traveling next door, it may well be economically sensible to send a last minute promotion to users located in the same area.

A strong tech stack is needed to integrate and orchestrate these data streams. Ghost kitchens usually depend on event driven architectures, real time analytics platforms Apache Kafka or Spark Streaming, say and agile cloud infrastructures that can scale rapidly to shapes and manage traffic spikes during peak periods. The stakes are high when it comes to reliability and low latency; even a delay of a couple of seconds can mean the difference between a conversion and an abandoned cart.

3.3. Ethics and Regulation: A New Responsibility

Although dynamic pricing and hyper personalization can lead to significant revenue generation, and contribute to customer loyalty, they have also generated ethical and regulatory concerns. One major concern is about "price discrimination," with different consumers paying different amounts for the same item. Though differential pricing is a staple of some industries, including air travel or hospitality, ghost kitchens exist in a relatively new digital realm where rules and consumer expectations are still developing.

- **Transparent Communication:** Ghost kitchens must avoid eroding trust by being upfront about the terms of promotions. For example, disclaimers can clarify why specific users have unique offers, like discounts based on loyalty status or deals based on geography. Even with a password, you still can't see the exact reasons why you personally were charged that price versus someone else; and a brief explanationwithout revealing anything about a user that would compromise user privacycan offer customers reassurance that price differentials aren't arbitrary or exploitative.
- **Fairness in Pricing:** Algorithms optimized for revenue must also be fair they should not discriminate against the vulnerable or minority groups. If, for example, the model discovers some zip codes have more price elasticity, that does not mean it should be charging those zip codes without perennial rightness. Audits of data inputs and model outputs, on a regular basis, can ensure equity is preserved.
- **Regulatory Compliance:** While R&D on AI driven pricing strategies to boost sales is important, ghost kitchens should also be informed on legislation that can restrict certain tactics used in practice. Looking the other way may earn hefty penalties, legal challenges, and reputational damage for years to come. In jurisdictions that have strong consumer rights frameworks, such authorities may well expect AI outputs to be explainable or at least that consumers be informed that they have been served a personalized promotion.

3.4. Operational Impact on Ghost Kitchens

Real time personalization strategies can't function in a bubble; they need to be integrated into daily kitchen workflows and staff routines to prevent operational breakdowns. A surge in orders spurred by a well-timed promotion can quickly overrun resources if the kitchen is unprepared.

- **Inventory management:** When an algorithm is pushing a certain popular dish so hard, the kitchen must have a lot of its ingredients in stock. Over promoting low in stock items can result in canceled orders, poor reviews, and expensive marketing spend on promotions you can't fulfill.
- **Order Queue Coordination:** A surprise surge in orders, such as during a time sensitive promotion or a location based marketing push, can flood the queue for the kitchen. When deliveries come late, whether for a matter of hours or days, customer dissatisfaction erodes loyalty and damages brand reputation. Predictive analytics that take into account the current queue length can also be integrated to throttle promotions or to better sequence orders.
- **Menu Adjustments:** Dynamic promotions can feature specific items according to the trends of each season or whether it's more cost effective to promote them. For example, if it senses that avocados are cheap this week, it could promote a spike in avocado based dishes. To take full

advantage of these insights, however, operators need to be ready to refresh the menu or reorder inventory on a dime.

By combining marketing personalization with kitchen execution, ghost kitchens can maximize resources, minimize food waste and ensure that customers are satisfied with their meals. A well-coordinated system can also help reduce staff burnout by equalizing workloads and notifying near real time when order surges are coming. But if personalized promotions are not linked into the kitchen, they can cause problems in the other direction, leading to late orders, mismatched stock and annoyed staff.

3.5. Integration of AI and Machine Learning for Enhanced Personalization and Efficiency

The fusion of Artificial Intelligence (AI) and Machine Learning (ML) within ghost kitchens facilitates a seamless blend of customer personalization and operational efficiency. These technologies are transforming how food businesses operate by leveraging big data analytics, predictive modeling, and intelligent automation to enhance decision-making. By analyzing vast datasets including customer preferences, ordering patterns, kitchen operations, and external factors like weather conditions and competitor strategies AI-driven systems can provide actionable insights that benefit both consumers and businesses. AI-driven solutions streamline kitchen operations, reduce inefficiencies, and improve the customer experience through personalized engagement, optimized pricing strategies, and faster delivery times. Below are some of the critical ways AI and ML are shaping the ghost kitchen industry.

3.5.1. Predictive Analytics for Demand Forecasting

One of the most significant advantages of AI in ghost kitchens is its ability to **forecast demand with high accuracy**. Traditional restaurants often rely on historical sales data and intuition, but **AI-powered predictive analytics** can integrate multiple variablessuch as **historical order data, local events, economic conditions, social media trends, and even weather forecasts**to determine the **expected volume of orders** on a given day or time.

AI-driven demand forecasting allows ghost kitchens to **predict spikes in demand, plan ingredient procurement, and optimize kitchen workflows accordingly**. For instance:

- **Reducing Wait Times:** By predicting peak ordering periods (e.g., lunch and dinner rushes, weekend spikes), kitchens can **pre-prepare certain ingredients** to expedite the cooking process.
- **Minimizing Food Waste:** AI models **anticipate which dishes will sell the most** and **reduce over-ordering of perishable ingredients**, preventing financial losses.
- **Optimizing Workforce Allocation:** Demand forecasts enable ghost kitchens to **schedule kitchen staff efficiently**, ensuring the right number of employees are available at high-demand times.

Additionally, **AI-driven logistics and route optimization** can **reduce delivery costs by up to 40%** by grouping nearby orders, optimizing driver routes, and **minimizing delays** due to traffic conditions (OurBusinessLadder.com).

By implementing AI-powered forecasting, ghost kitchens can **maintain high service levels, increase profitability, and reduce unnecessary expenses**.

3.5.2. Automated Inventory Management

Inventory management is a **critical component** of any restaurant operation, and ghost kitchens are no exception. AI-driven inventory management systems **ensure ingredient availability while minimizing food waste** by continuously **monitoring stock levels, predicting depletion rates, and automating reordering processes.**

Key functionalities of **AI-based inventory management** include:

- **Real-Time Stock Monitoring:** AI tracks ingredient usage in real time and provides alerts when stock levels fall below a predefined threshold.
- **Automated Replenishment:** Machine learning algorithms analyze historical usage trends and supplier lead times to **automatically reorder ingredients** before shortages occur.
- **Smart Substitutions:** If a particular ingredient is running low, AI can suggest **alternative recipes or menu modifications** to avoid disruptions in service.
- **Waste Reduction Strategies:** AI can **detect slow-moving inventory** and **suggest promotions** to encourage sales before ingredients expire, helping ghost kitchens reduce losses.

For instance, if a **specific dish is selling less frequently**, AI-powered systems may **suggest discontinuing the item**, adjusting pricing to increase demand, or repurposing ingredients in different menu offerings. This capability **ensures better financial efficiency** while also contributing to **sustainable food waste reduction efforts.**

Automating inventory management not only **saves time** for kitchen operators but also **reduces manual errors**, enabling kitchens to **operate smoothly while maximizing profits.**

3.5.3. Personalized Customer Interactions

Customer engagement and **hyper-personalization** have become essential **differentiators** for ghost kitchens in an increasingly crowded food delivery market. AI-powered personalization allows **restaurants to tailor recommendations, promotions, and experiences** based on **individual customer preferences, dietary habits, purchase history, and even mood-based insights.**

AI enhances customer interactions in several ways:

- **Customized Menu Suggestions:** Based on past orders and browsing behavior, AI **recommends meals that align with customer tastes**. For example, a customer who frequently orders **plant-based dishes** might receive recommendations for **new vegan menu additions.**
- **Time-Sensitive Offers:** AI tracks customer behavior and **triggers automated, personalized discounts** for users who haven't ordered in a while.
- **Intelligent Chatbots & Voice Assistants:** AI-powered virtual assistants **respond to customer queries instantly**, assisting with menu navigation, allergen information, and order customization.
- **Dynamic Notifications & Engagement Campaigns:** AI **analyzes customer ordering habits** to determine the best time to send push notifications (e.g., lunchtime prompts for office workers, late-night snack offers for students).

According to **Food & Beverage Magzine**, personalization increases customer satisfaction and loyalty, making **repeat purchases more likely**. By delivering **a more engaging and intuitive experience**, ghost kitchens can enhance **customer retention and overall brand loyalty**.

3.5.4. Dynamic Pricing Models

AI-powered **dynamic pricing** enables ghost kitchens to **adjust menu prices in real-time** based on factors such as **demand fluctuations, competitor pricing, order volume, time of day, and historical trends**.

Dynamic pricing strategies include:

- **Peak Pricing for High-Demand Periods:** AI can increase prices during peak hours (e.g., Friday nights) while **offering discounts during slower times** to encourage more orders.
- **Customized Discounts & Promotions:** AI **personalizes offers based on customer spending behavior**. A frequent customer might receive a **special loyalty discount**, while a first-time user might be **offered a sign-up promotion**.
- **Geo-Based Pricing Adjustments:** AI-powered **geolocation tracking** can offer different pricing structures depending on the customer's proximity to the ghost kitchen or their likelihood to convert.

AI-based pricing strategies allow ghost kitchens to **maximize revenue** while **ensuring affordability for price-sensitive customers**, creating a **win-win scenario** for both business and consumers.

3.5.5. Enhanced Order Accuracy and Speed

One of the **biggest challenges** in food delivery is **ensuring that orders are processed accurately and efficiently**. AI and machine learning help ghost kitchens **reduce order errors and improve speed**, ensuring a **seamless** end-to-end experience.

AI-driven order management enhances operations through:

- **Automated Order Routing:** AI instantly directs incoming orders to **the nearest ghost kitchen location** or **prepares orders in facilities with the fastest turnaround time**.
- **Real-Time Kitchen Coordination:** AI-powered systems allocate kitchen tasks to staff based on **workload and preparation time**, reducing bottlenecks and ensuring that **all items in an order are prepared simultaneously**.
- **AI-Based Quality Control:** AI **analyzes past complaints and errors**, enabling ghost kitchens to **continuously improve order accuracy**. It also **flags potential issues** (e.g., missing ingredients or incorrect orders) before they are dispatched.

By **minimizing mistakes** and **optimizing workflows**, AI-driven systems help ghost kitchens **deliver food faster and with higher precision**, improving customer satisfaction and brand reputation.

4. AI-DRIVEN CUSTOMER SEGMENTATION FOR TAILORED MARKETING

4.1. Segmentation Methods (Demographic, Behavioral, Psychographic)

Customer segmentation is the practice of grouping people with similar attributes, which allows marketers to develop more complex and targeted strategies per segment. For ghost kitchens, where personalization has a direct correlation to customer engagement and repeat business, segmentation acts as a basis for designing targeted promotions, custom messaging and relevant menu items. By harmonizing these tactics to each segment's unique characteristics, brands are more likely to fulfill particular consumer needs and desires.

There are three common segmentation dimensions:

- **Demographics:** Age, gender, income bracket, and education level are demographic variables that often underlie dietary preferences and spending. Higher income segments, for example, may be more in tune with premium or specialty menu items, while younger demographics may gravitate to trendy fusion dishes or plant based options.
- **Behavioral:** How customers engage with a brand order frequency, average basket size, peak ordering times, or loyalty indicators, such as membership in a rewards program. Ghost kitchens can use such data to find "power users" who order several times a week or "weekend only" consumers who would be persuaded by time limited deals.
- **Psychographic:** More abstract factors like lifestyle, personality traits and values can indicate the motivations behind purchase decisions. For instance, health conscious consumers might prefer clean eating and prioritize lower calorie or organic options, while adventurous eaters may have a greater willingness to try limited edition menu items. Psychographic factors can also connect with ethical issues like a preference for locally sourced ingredients or fair trade products.

"The results show that members in the loyalty reward program overlook or discount negative evaluations of the company vis-à-vis competition (Bolton, et al. (2000))." Many ghost kitchens use a mix of these approaches, what is referred to as "hybrid segmentation," to create a nuanced picture of each customer. When you combine demographic information (e.g., a busy professional in an urban area) with behavioral attributes (e.g., frequent lunchtime orders) and psychographic data (e.g., a preference for gluten free options) you groups can create offers that resonate on multiple levels. And machine learning accelerates this process by continuously improving the segments as new data arrives, eliminating the inertia associated with static segmentation.

4.2. Data Analysis Criteria (Generative vs. Discriminative; Clustering Algorithms; Supervised vs. Unsupervised Learning)

Cluster algorithms are commonly used in advanced segmentation projects by data scientists to discover patterns in large data sets without any prior information about the segment labels. Here are few most widely used clustering methods:

- **k-means Clustering:** The most widely used algorithm, grouping customers into k parts due to their proximity in a multi-dimensional feature space (e.g., average spend, time of day of orders, dietary preferences, etc.).
- **Hierarchical Clustering:** Creates a multilevel hierarchy of clusters by either iteratively merging or splitting clusters. This technique is very useful for breaking down multiple levels of granularity large categories of customers first and more detailed example subgroups within those categories.
- **Density Based Clustering (DBSCAN):** Clusters data points that are closely packed and marks points in low density or noise areas as outliers. Similarly, DBSCAN is useful for noisy datasets or when there are extreme niche areas that may have been overlooked otherwise.

In contrast, supervised learning methods like decision trees, random forests, or logistic regression can be applied when a target variable is already known. For example, if historical data captures whether customers responded to specific promotions, a supervised model can identify features (like price sensitivity or dietary preference) that determine the likelihood of response. This insight can then influence what other offers are displayed to like customers in the future, increasing the overall accuracy of marketing initiatives.

4.3. Creating Hyper-Personalized Campaigns Based on Segments:

Once they have identified distinct segments, ghost kitchens can create hyper targeted campaigns that address the particular characteristics, pain points or motivators for each group. More than just generic discounts, hyper personalization involves the use of real time data, myriad contextual factors, and advanced analytics to better target messaging at the individual level:

- **Special Offers:** Provide promo codes, loyalty rewards or free add on specific to a group's favorite items or ordering patterns. A customer who buys dessert often could get a free sweet treat with every third order, while a smaller segment of health conscious guests could get delivery fees waived on low calorie dishes.
- **Relevance**: Display relevant menu items in line with interests of the segment. For fitness friendly users, showcase keto compliant or high protein meals.
- **Channel Optimization:** Not all communication stands on the same authoritative ground for different segments. Younger, or more tech savvy, consumers may still respond better to push notifications or social media ads than older or more traditionally behaved users, who might prefer email or SMS.
- **Timing and Frequency:** Understanding when segments are most activelunchtime breaks for office workers, late night snacking for studentsavoids oversaturation whilst raising conversion rates.

4.4. Challenges in Implementation

Despite AI powered segmentation's clear promise in ghost kitchens, there are challenges as well:

- **Data Siloes:** Customer data is often stored in different systems by various departments, or even third party platforms, making it difficult to create a holistic view of each user. You need to plan your infrastructure well and work across teams for integrating these datasets.

- **Algorithmic Bias:** model trained on unrepresentative training datasets is meant to incidentally perpetuate or even amplify biases. One segment that has relatively few promotions targeted it could continue that way unless the model is actively audited and adjusted for fairness.
- **Privacy Concerns:** There is a fine line between using complex segmentation tools and user privacy policies. Operators need to avoid violating regulations, such as the General Data Protection Regulation (GDPR) or the California Consumer Privacy Act (CCPA), which govern how personal data can be collected, processed and stored.

4.5. Navigating India's Digital Personal Data Protection Regulations

The **Digital Personal Data Protection Act (DPDPA), 2023**, represents a crucial step in establishing a **comprehensive framework** for regulating digital personal data in India. It sets stringent compliance measures for organizations handling consumer data, emphasizing **informed consent, data security, and responsible processing practices**. For ghost kitchens that leverage **AI-driven customer segmentation**, understanding and adhering to these regulations is essential to ensure compliance, protect consumer rights, and build long-term trust in the digital food service industry.

Key Provisions Impacting AI-Driven Customer Segmentation

1. Consent Requirements

Definition & Relevance: Under the DPDPA, **Data Fiduciaries** (organizations collecting and processing personal data) must obtain **clear, informed, and affirmative consent** from **Data Principals** (individuals providing their data). This consent should be **explicit, granular, and unambiguous**, ensuring that individuals understand how their personal data will be used.

Implications for Ghost Kitchens:

- AI-driven personalization relies on **data analytics**, collecting customer information such as order history, location, payment details, and browsing behavior.
- **Standalone Consent Notices:** Ghost kitchens must provide **clear and standalone notices** explaining **why data is collected, how it will be used, and whether it will be shared with third parties** (e.g., food delivery platforms, payment gateways).
- **Consent Withdrawal Mechanisms:** Customers should have the ability to **withdraw consent** at any time, and ghost kitchens must promptly honor such requests. This could mean disabling targeted marketing or anonymizing stored data.
- **Explicit Consent for Sensitive Data:** If ghost kitchens collect **sensitive personal data** (e.g., dietary preferences related to medical conditions, allergy details), they must obtain **separate, affirmative consent**.

2. Data Minimization and Purpose Limitation

Definition & Relevance: The principle of **data minimization** ensures that **only essential information** required for a **specific business purpose** is collected and retained. **Purpose limitation** further mandates that data should only be processed **for the reasons explicitly communicated to users at the time of collection**.

Implications for Ghost Kitchens:

- **Collect Only Necessary Data:** AI-powered customer segmentation systems should **only gather the minimum required data** to personalize promotions or optimize operations.
- **Example:** Instead of collecting extensive demographic information, a ghost kitchen could focus on **purchase behavior, cuisine preferences, and order frequency**.
- **Restricted Data Retention:** Ghost kitchens should **delete or anonymize data** once it has served its intended purpose.
- **Example:** If a restaurant uses customer addresses for delivery optimization, this data should not be retained indefinitely.
- **No Unintended Use:** Customer data collected for **AI-based menu recommendations** should **not be repurposed** for unrelated activities (e.g., selling data to third parties).

3. Children's Data Processing

Definition & Relevance: The DPDPA introduces **strict safeguards** for processing the personal data of **individuals under 18 years old**. This includes:

- **Verifiable parental consent** before collecting or processing data from minors.
- **Restricted profiling** to prevent targeted advertising or behavioral tracking.
- **Higher accountability standards** for entities handling children's data.

Implications for Ghost Kitchens:

- **Age Verification Systems:** Ghost kitchens that allow customers to create accounts should implement **age verification mechanisms** to determine whether a user is a minor.
- **Parental Consent Frameworks:** Before processing a minor's data, businesses should have **structured parental consent mechanisms**, such as **OTP-based verifications or consent forms**.
- **No Personalized Promotions for Minors:** AI-driven marketing strategies **should not include targeted promotions** for minors based on their order history.
- **Stronger Data Protection Measures:** Minors' data should be **stored securely**, with encryption and restricted access policies.

4. Data Breach Notifications

Definition & Relevance: Under the **DPDPA, 2023**, organizations experiencing a **data breach** must:

1. **Notify affected individuals** of the breach, detailing the nature of the compromised data.
2. **Report the breach to the Data Protection Board of India (DPBI) within 72 hours**.
3. **Implement corrective actions** to prevent further data loss.

Implications for Ghost Kitchens:

- **Secure Storage and Encryption:** Ghost kitchens must use **strong encryption standards** for storing customer data, ensuring it remains unreadable even if stolen.
- **Real-Time Monitoring Systems:** AI-powered **anomaly detection models** can identify **suspicious activities** (e.g., unauthorized access, unusual login patterns).
- **Incident Response Plans:** Organizations should **develop clear action plans** for data breaches, including **predefined escalation protocols** and customer notification frameworks.
- **Reputational Risks:** Failure to notify affected customers promptly can **damage brand trust and invite regulatory penalties.**

Implications for Ghost Kitchens

Beyond compliance, aligning AI-driven personalization efforts with India's data protection laws enables ghost kitchens to build **trust, transparency, and customer confidence**. Below are **key operational takeaways**:

1. Enhanced Data Security Measures

Key Actions:

- Implement **robust cybersecurity infrastructure** to **safeguard customer data** against breaches.
- Adopt **role-based access control (RBAC)** to limit who within the organization can access sensitive customer data.
- Use **data anonymization** techniques when leveraging AI for behavioral analysis.

2. Transparent Data Practices

Key Actions:

- Clearly outline **how customer data is collected, used, and stored** in a **publicly accessible privacy policy**.
- Ensure **all communication around data processing is simple, jargon-free, and easily understandable.**
- Provide **a self-service data dashboard** where users can view and manage their data preferences.

3. Parental Consent Mechanisms

Key Actions:

- Set up **automated age verification** tools to **detect and block underage users from certain data-driven services.**
- Introduce **parental consent checkboxes** or **two-step authentication processes** for accounts linked to minors.
- Regularly audit **marketing campaigns** to ensure minors **are not receiving personalized promotions.**

4. Proactive Breach Management

Key Actions:

- Conduct **regular cybersecurity audits** and **penetration testing** to identify system vulnerabilities.
- Establish **real-time monitoring systems** that flag unusual data access patterns or suspicious login attempts.
- Develop **a well-defined breach response plan** detailing **how to notify customers, regulators, and stakeholders**.

4.6. Case Study: Rebel Foods – AI-Driven Customer Segmentation and Personalization in Indian Cloud Kitchens

Rebel Foods, formerly known as Faasos, has emerged as a trailblazer in the Indian cloud kitchen ecosystem by seamlessly integrating Artificial Intelligence (AI) and Machine Learning (ML) into its operations. As one of the world's largest internet restaurant companies, it has successfully leveraged AI to drive **customer segmentation, personalized marketing, operational efficiency, and scalability**.

4.6.1. AI-Driven Customer Segmentation and Personalization

Rebel Foods employs **clustering algorithms and predictive analytics** to segment customers based on their **demographics, purchase behavior, order frequency, and feedback patterns**. This segmentation allows them to **deliver hyper-personalized recommendations, promotions, and menu customization**, significantly enhancing customer engagement and loyalty.

- **Personalized Menu Curation:** By analyzing past orders, dietary preferences, and spending habits, Rebel Foods dynamically **recommends meals tailored to individual tastes**.
- **Predictive Discounting Strategies:** AI models assess a customer's likelihood of making a purchase and **offer targeted discounts** to incentivize conversions.
- **Behavior-Based Promotions:** Time-sensitive push notifications and exclusive offers are triggered based on customer actions such as cart abandonment, peak ordering hours, or previous loyalty program participation.

4.6.2. AI-Optimized Operations and Efficiency

Beyond customer segmentation, Rebel Foods deploys AI to streamline operational aspects, ensuring **food safety, kitchen automation, and demand forecasting**.

- **AI-Enabled Hygiene & Safety Monitoring:** AI-powered computer vision and IoT-based systems track kitchen cleanliness, **monitor compliance with food safety regulations**, and optimize kitchen workflows.
- **Smart Inventory Management:** Machine learning models forecast **ingredient demand** based on real-time consumption patterns, ensuring precise inventory stocking and reducing food waste.

- **Automated Order Fulfillment:** AI-driven kitchen management software prioritizes and **routes orders dynamically**, minimizing delivery time and improving efficiency.

4.6.3. AI-Powered Marketing and Customer Retention

Rebel Foods leverages **AI-based marketing strategies** to strengthen customer retention and improve repeat orders.

- **Sentiment Analysis & Social Listening:** AI tools analyze customer reviews, **social media feedback**, and complaints to refine brand messaging and menu enhancements.
- **Omnichannel Customer Engagement:** AI-driven chatbots provide **real-time support**, suggest personalized meal combos, and streamline the ordering process through multiple platforms.
- **Localized AI-Driven Brand Expansion:** AI identifies **location-specific food trends**, enabling the company to launch regional brands, such as Behrouz Biryani, Lunchbox, and Oven Story, catering to diverse market segments.

4.6.4. Technological Infrastructure and Scalability

The scalability of Rebel Foods is powered by its AI-driven **cloud-based infrastructure**, allowing seamless expansion across geographies.

- **Multi-Brand Cloud Kitchen Model:** AI continuously **analyzes market gaps** and customer preferences to introduce new virtual brands under the Rebel Foods umbrella.
- **Geospatial Demand Forecasting:** AI assesses **delivery heatmaps, traffic data, and peak demand times** to optimize kitchen locations and reduce delivery times.
- **Real-Time Dynamic Pricing Algorithms:** AI-driven **pricing strategies** adjust menu pricing based on demand elasticity, competitor pricing, and local economic conditions.

4.6.5. Conclusion: AI as a Catalyst for Growth

Rebel Foods exemplifies how **AI and ML** can transform the cloud kitchen landscape. By leveraging AI-driven **customer segmentation, real-time personalization, operational automation, and smart marketing**, Rebel Foods has built a **scalable and profitable** business model. Its success serves as a **blueprint for other ghost kitchens**, demonstrating how AI can **enhance personalization, optimize costs, and drive long-term customer loyalty**.

5. MEASURING CAMPAIGN EFFECTIVENESS WITH AI-POWERED INSIGHTS

In the competitive landscape of ghost kitchens, understanding the impact of marketing campaigns is crucial for sustained success. Artificial Intelligence (AI) offers advanced tools to analyze and enhance these efforts, providing a data-driven foundation for strategic decisions.

5.1. Key Performance Indicators (KPIs) for AI-Driven Marketing

Establishing precise KPIs is essential to gauge the effectiveness of AI-enhanced marketing strategies. These metrics offer insights into customer engagement, financial returns, and overall campaign performance:

- **Conversion Rate:** This metric measures the percentage of recipients who perform a desired action, such as placing an order after receiving a personalized offer. A higher conversion rate indicates that the marketing message effectively resonates with the target audience.
- **Return on Investment (ROI):** ROI assesses the financial return generated from marketing initiatives relative to their cost. It is calculated by dividing the net profit by the total marketing expenditure. A positive ROI signifies that the campaigns are profitable and justify the resources invested.
- **Customer Lifetime Value (CLV):** CLV estimates the total revenue a customer is expected to generate over the duration of their relationship with the business. AI aids in identifying high-value customers, enabling targeted retention strategies that enhance long-term profitability.
- **Engagement Metrics:** These include indicators such as click-through rates (CTR), email open rates, and time spent on digital platforms. High engagement levels often correlate with increased customer interest and loyalty, reflecting the effectiveness of the content and delivery methods.

5.2. Continuous Feedback Loops and Model Refinement

AI thrives on iterative learning, making continuous feedback mechanisms vital for refining marketing strategies:

- **Data Integration:** Collecting and integrating data from various touchpointssuch as customer feedback, order histories, and engagement metricsprovides a comprehensive view of performance. This holistic perspective enables more accurate analyses and informed decision-making.
- **Model Adjustment:** Analyzing this data allows for the refinement of AI algorithms to better predict customer behavior and preferences. For instance, if a particular promotion underperforms, the model can adjust future recommendations to align more closely with customer interests, thereby enhancing relevance and effectiveness.
- **Real-Time Adaptation:** AI systems can dynamically modify marketing strategies in response to emerging trends and real-time data. This agility ensures that campaigns remain pertinent and effective, adapting swiftly to changes in customer behavior or market conditions.

5.3. Marketing Attribution Models and Predictive Analytics

Understanding the customer journey is essential for optimizing marketing efforts. AI enhances this understanding through sophisticated attribution models and predictive analytics:

- **Multi-Touch Attribution (MTA):** MTA evaluates the impact of each customer interaction across various channels, assigning appropriate credit to each touchpoint. This approach acknowledges that multiple exposures contribute to the final conversion, providing a more accurate assessment of each channel's effectiveness.

- **Algorithmic Attribution:** Leveraging AI algorithms, this model analyzes complex datasets to determine the incremental value of each marketing channel. It offers a granular view of how different interactions influence customer decisions, enabling more precise allocation of marketing resources.
- **Predictive Analytics:** By examining historical data, AI forecasts future customer behaviors and trends. For example, predicting a surge in demand for a specific cuisine allows for timely promotional efforts and inventory adjustments, ensuring that the business meets customer expectations effectively.

5.4. Interpreting Results to Drive Strategy and Operational Decisions

The insights derived from AI-powered analytics inform both marketing strategies and operational practices:

- **Strategic Alignment:** Analyzing KPIs helps align marketing objectives with overarching business goals. For instance, if data reveals a high CLV among a specific demographic, targeted campaigns can be developed to further engage this group, maximizing their lifetime value.
- **Operational Adjustments:** Understanding customer preferences and behaviors allows for optimization of inventory management, staffing, and supply chain logistics. Anticipating peak order times and popular menu items ensures efficient resource allocation, reducing waste and enhancing customer satisfaction.
- **Personalization Enhancements:** Continuous analysis of engagement metrics facilitates the refinement of personalized marketing efforts. This ongoing improvement leads to increased customer satisfaction and loyalty, as offerings become more closely aligned with individual preferences.

5.5. A/B Testing and Experimentation

A/B testing is a powerful method for optimizing AI-driven marketing strategies:

- **Methodology:** A/B testing involves comparing two versions of a marketing elementsuch as an email subject line or pricing strategyto determine which performs better. By randomly assigning different versions to customer segments, businesses can assess the impact of each variant on key metrics like conversion rates.
- **Application in Dynamic Pricing:** Ghost kitchens can employ A/B testing to evaluate different pricing strategies across customer cohorts. For example, testing various price points for a new menu item can reveal the optimal price that maximizes both sales and profit margins. This data-driven approach ensures pricing decisions are aligned with customer willingness to pay.
- **Enhancing Personalization:** Experimentation with personalized contentsuch as tailored promotions or customized menu recommendationscan identify what resonates most with different customer segments. This iterative testing refines AI models, leading to more effective and individualized marketing efforts.

By integrating A/B testing into their AI-driven strategies, ghost kitchens can continuously refine their offerings, ensuring that marketing efforts are both effective and aligned with customer preferences.

6. INTEGRATION WITH GHOST KITCHEN OPERATIONS

The effectiveness of AI-driven marketing strategies in ghost kitchens extends beyond customer engagement, it plays a crucial role in optimizing kitchen workflows, inventory management, and order fulfillment. The integration of AI across these operational aspects ensures that ghost kitchens function efficiently, reducing waste, optimizing resources, and ultimately delivering a seamless customer experience.

6.1. Aligning Marketing Data with Kitchen Workflow and Resource Allocation

One of the primary challenges ghost kitchens face is translating marketing insights into actionable operational strategies. Predictive analytics can suggest a surge in demand for a specific dish, but ensuring that the kitchen is equipped to handle the influx of orders requires a well-integrated system.

Key AI-Driven Strategies for Alignment:

1. **Real-Time Dashboards for Cross-Departmental Visibility:**
    - AI-powered dashboards integrate marketing data (coupon redemption rates, promotional performance) with operational metrics (ingredient availability, staff workload).
    - This enables decision-makers to balance demand generation with production capacity, preventing unexpected bottlenecks.
2. **AI-Powered Forecasting Tools:**
    - Machine learning models analyze historical data, seasonal trends, local events, and even external factors like weather to predict demand surges.
    - This helps optimize staff scheduling, reducing labor inefficiencies and preventing over or understaffing.
3. **Cross-Functional Communication Between Marketing and Operations:**
    - AI can automatically generate alerts for operations teams when a marketing campaign triggers higher-than-expected order volumes.
    - This ensures that kitchen workflows can adapt dynamically, preventing excessive order backlog or inventory depletion.

By leveraging AI to bridge the gap between marketing and kitchen workflows, ghost kitchens can seamlessly scale their promotional strategies while maintaining operational efficiency.

6.2. Coordinating Inventory Levels with Predictive Demand Forecasting

For ghost kitchens, mismanagement of inventory can lead to severe financial losses either through stock shortages leading to lost sales or overstocking leading to waste. AI-powered demand forecasting is essential to ensuring ingredient availability aligns with real-time demand.

Key AI-Driven Inventory Management Approaches:

1. **Automated Procurement Systems:**
    - AI-driven inventory tools integrate with supplier databases to monitor stock levels and automatically place purchase orders based on predictive demand forecasts.

- This reduces reliance on manual inventory tracking and prevents last-minute ingredient shortages.

2. **Dynamic Menu Adjustments Based on Stock Availability:**
   - AI systems can modify menus in real-time based on ingredient supply levels.
   - If an ingredient runs low, AI-powered recommendation engines suggest alternative menu items to prevent customer dissatisfaction while maintaining profitability.
3. **Data-Driven Waste Reduction Strategies:**
   - AI analyzes historical waste patterns to minimize overstocking of perishable items.
   - This reduces food wastage while maintaining an optimized supply chain.
4. **Real-Time Adjustments for Market Volatility:**
   - External factors such as weather conditions, local events, and macroeconomic trends are incorporated into AI-driven forecasting models.
   - This ensures that sudden shifts in demandsuch as an unexpected increase in orders due to a local festival are managed proactively.

By integrating AI into inventory coordination, ghost kitchens can maintain cost-effective procurement, improve sustainability, and minimize operational inefficiencies.

6.3. Automating Order Fulfillment and Improving Turnaround Times

With customer expectations for fast delivery increasing, automation in order fulfillment is a necessity for ghost kitchens. AI optimizes order allocation, kitchen workflows, and delivery logistics to minimize turnaround times.

Key AI-Powered Automation Techniques:

1. **AI-Driven Order Routing and Kitchen Station Optimization:**
   - Machine learning algorithms distribute incoming orders across different cooking stations based on real-time workload assessments.
   - This prevents congestion in specific areas of the kitchen and ensures a smoother workflow.
2. **Computer Vision and Sensor-Based Monitoring:**
   - AI-enabled cameras and IoT sensors track food preparation times, alerting staff if delays occur.
   - This level of monitoring enhances accuracy in preparation and improves overall kitchen efficiency.
3. **AI-Integrated Delivery Optimization:**
   - Route optimization algorithms dynamically adjust delivery schedules, reducing travel time and ensuring food arrives hot and fresh.
   - By integrating with traffic data and GPS tracking, AI systems can assign orders to the most optimal delivery personnel.
4. **AI-Powered Robotics and Conveyor Systems:**
   - Advanced ghost kitchens are experimenting with robotic chefs, conveyor-based meal assembly lines, and automated packaging solutions.
   - While initial investment costs are high, these technologies reduce labor costs, minimize human errors, and accelerate preparation times.

With AI handling the coordination of order fulfillment, ghost kitchens can ensure rapid service while maintaining high food quality.

6.4. Ensuring Seamless Customer Experience Despite Operational Constraints

AI-powered marketing campaigns are only effective when the operational side of the business can consistently meet customer expectations. AI helps maintain a smooth customer experience by addressing potential bottlenecks in real time.

Key Strategies for Ensuring Customer Satisfaction:

1. **Smart Throttling of Promotions:**
   - AI prevents overloading kitchen capacity by dynamically adjusting promotional campaigns based on real-time workload.
   - If the kitchen reaches its maximum handling limit, AI can delay promotional offers or limit their visibility until capacity frees up.
2. **Real-Time Customer Communication & Transparency:**
   - AI-driven chatbots and automated notifications provide customers with updates on estimated delivery times, potential delays, and stock shortages.
   - Keeping customers informed enhances trust and reduces frustration caused by unexpected delays.
3. **AI-Powered Customer Feedback Loops:**
   - Sentiment analysis tools evaluate customer reviews and feedback, identifying operational pain points such as slow delivery times or packaging issues.
   - This feedback is used to fine-tune operational strategies and improve service quality over time.

A seamless customer experience requires AI to coordinate marketing expectations with actual kitchen capabilities, ensuring that high customer demand is met with efficient fulfillment.

6.5. AI-Powered Supply Chain Optimization

AI doesn't just enhance internal operationsit also optimizes the entire supply chain, helping ghost kitchens maintain cost efficiency and sustainability.

Key AI-Driven Supply Chain Enhancements:

1. **Automated Supplier Coordination:**
   - AI integrates with supplier management systems to track ingredient costs, delivery schedules, and potential disruptions.
   - If a supplier is unable to fulfill an order, AI recommends alternative vendors to ensure continuity.
2. **Cost Optimization Through Dynamic Procurement:**
   - AI compares ingredient costs across multiple suppliers and suggests cost-effective purchasing decisions.

- By forecasting price fluctuations, AI helps ghost kitchens secure bulk deals during periods of low cost.

3. **Sustainable Sourcing & Carbon Footprint Reduction:**
   - AI evaluates sourcing options to identify eco-friendly suppliers and reduce carbon emissions.
   - It optimizes delivery routes for both ingredients and customer orders, minimizing fuel consumption.

By extending AI's role beyond internal kitchen operations and into supplier coordination, ghost kitchens can enhance efficiency while improving sustainability.

7. CHALLENGES, LIMITATIONS, ETHICAL CONSIDERATIONS

As AI influenced projects revolutionize the ghost kitchen sector, operators and stakeholders alike face a host of issues. These challenges are not just technical complications but ethical quagmires and operational limitations with real potential to impact a brand's reputation, financial prosperity, and employee relations. Embrace the potential of AI driven transformation, but remain grounded in the realities of implementation, ensuring strategies are pragmatic, sustainable, and future proofed in a dynamic landscape.

7.1. Data Privacy

In a digital world in which orders (or, more accurately, orders) come from taps on apps and websites, best practices around data was a top priority for ghost kitchens. These companies clearly have address and payment information on file, but also collect other types of behavioral information for personalization and predictive analytics. This makes them attractive targets for cybercriminals and puts them under the microscope of stringent data protection legislation worldwide.

Regulation and compliance frameworks

- **GDPR (General Data Protection Regulation):** This regulation applies to companies who operating with data obtained in Europe as well as regulating how organizations process individual data. Key principles include legality, transparency and purpose limitation. Ghost kitchens cooking in or for EU customers will have to comply as well, no matter in which EU countries their physical operations are based.
- **Global Extensions:** These are not an exhaustive list of the broad new regulatory regimes which have been making waves, but there is also a range of others out there including Canada's PIPEDA (Personal Information Protection and Electronic Documents Act) and Brazil's LGPD (Lei Geral de Proteção de Dados) which are contributing to the increasingly cluttered global picture of data protection. Ghost kitchens and international footprints also often find themselves subject to overlapping regimes that complicate legal compliance whilst increasing administrative burden.

Security Considerations and Best Practices

- **Encryption:** Sensitive data such as payment credentials and personal identifiers should be encrypted both at rest (e.g. when stored on servers) and in transit (i.e. when transmitted across the internet). Modern protocols such as Transport Layer Security (TLS), to prevent eavesdropping on communications, can help prevent this.

- **Access Control:** Role based permissions limit who may access or change specific datasets. Marketing teams, for example, might care less about consumers' full addresses or payments and more about aggregate consumer insights.
- **Perform Audits and Penetration Testing Regularly:** Before an attacker exploits existing vulnerabilities in your system, proactive security checks can discover them easily. And routine penetration tests, in which ethical hackers attempt to break into the system, are especially useful for exposing weaknesses.
- **Incident Response Plans:** In the event of a data breach, responding in a timely manner is essential. Having well-defined protocols relating to immediate containment, internal escalation and regulatory notifications can go a long way toward containing reputational and financial damage.

Results of Disobedience (Non-Compliance):

- **Severe Fines:** You may receive fines of up to 4% of annual global turnover or €20 million (whichever is higher) for non-compliance with laws such as GDPR. In-fact the CCPA also imposes the same penalties for willful violations.
- **Loss of reputation:** Financial penalties are one concern, but a lack of public trust can be devastating in the aftermath of a data breach, and for a ghost kitchen, especially, that's a bad situation to be in when their whole model revolves around digital battery. Data breaches can go viral on social media, tarnishing a brand's reputation and customer trust.

Building Consumer Trust

- **Transparent Data Policies:** Ghost kitchens should be clear in regards to building up their data and why (or to whom) they plan to do something with it will they use customer data to provide personalized promotions or AI assisted recommendations;
- **Opt-In Approaches:** Providing customers the ability to opt in to your data collection and opt out when they desire helps foster a feeling of control and agency.
- **Regular Communications:** One cannot stress enough on keeping the customers in the loop regarding the changes made with the privacy policies or which new security measures have been introduced will help the customer feel good, that yes their information is being treated responsibly.

7.2. Potential Biases in Machine Learning Algorithms

The sparkling promise of AI powered personalization and operational optimization is sometimes paired with a complementary shadow, a current of risk undergirding the machine learning (ML) models that drive it. Among the chief concerns is algorithmic bias the phenomenon in which a model systematically favors or punishes some segments of a population, whether defined by demographics, geography or behavioral patterns.

Sources of Bias

- **Historical Data:** If the training data of the model has historical systemic biases towards women (e.g. fewer promotions offered in lower income neighborhoods), then the model can continue to magnify these trends in its recommendations.
- **Feature Selection:** Which ones to include/exclude (ZIP codes, income brackets, etc.). In certain situations, a variable is not directly linked to sensitive demographic information, therefore, inadvertent discrimination occurs.
- **Machine Learning algorithms:** usually generalize historical data to future behavior. If that data is stained with bias, the algorithm can amplify injustice over time.

Methods for Addressing Bias

- **Fairness metrics:** By employing metrics such as disparate impact analysis or equalized odds, we can determine whether the model is producing a significantly disparate outcome across different demographic groups. In the case of a ghost kitchen, that might include verifying that promotional offers or discounts are fairly sorted along socioeconomic lines.
- **Data sheet**: document model training, and explicitly what goes into a model to ensure you can debug and explain decisions.
- **Model Retraining and Feedback Loops:** Constant fine tuning using a broader variety of data sources including human input is another way of diminishing the bias that accumulates over time. In case if there is a community that is underrepresented in the training data, targeted approaches would need to be done for that input to be from that community, or for synthetic data to be produced.

Moral, Ethical and Reputational Implications

- **Discriminatory Practices:** Even innocent bias can lead to unscrupulous acts if used improperly, for example charging certain ethnic groups (higher rates) or denying promotional discounts to specific age demographics.
- **Legal Ramifications:** AI that is biased in its practices could lead to lawsuits, or class action suits, in regions with strict anti-discrimination laws.
- **Brand image:** If ghost kitchens have algorithms with bias, it can hurt their brand image. Present Younger demographics especially are concerned with fairness and social justice.

Best Practices

- **Cross Functional AI Ethics Committees:** These committees would comprise members such as marketing, legal, and data science experts and would help identify and prevent biases and plan ethical frameworks for AI usage.
- **Community Grouping Up (Engagement):** Insights and feedback from distinct user groups help make sure that ML powered approaches do not miss or avoid vital pieces from the market.
- **External Audits:** Some companies invite a third party, specialized in AI ethics, to carry out regular audits on the fairness of their algorithms, as a means of gaining trust and credibility.

7.3. Financial and Resource Constraints for Small/Medium Ghost Kitchens

Owned by publicly traded companies, conglomerate ghost kitchens can afford fancy A.I. based tech platforms and full time data science teams, but smaller or independent operations unless they continue to resign themselves to constraints, too simply may not have the wherewithal to dedicate much energy to it. And the availability (or lack thereof) of such resources could limit the scope of AI powered projects, merely widening the competitive gap between global superpowers and local providers.

Cost Barriers to Entry

- **High upfront cost:** Building a good machine learning model yourself also means recruiting data engineers, purchasing specialized hardware or cloud services, and investing time to construct the model yourself. This overhead could be unsustainable for operators that make slim profit margins.
- **Subscription and Licensing fees:** If you opt for third party AI solution, it can incur monthly or annual video fees. While SaaS models do not make enormous initial outlays necessary, they do make ongoing budget spend compulsory.

Skills and Expertise

- **Understanding the Data Science Basics:** Each smaller team does not have any data scientist or analyst. Such owners or general managers stand to benefit from a learning curve on the fundamentals of AI and predictive analytics, a process that is often highly time intensive and riddled with error.
- **Talent retention:** There's a lot of competition for AI talent, and big tech or well capitalized start-ups tend to pay better salaries and more appealing all around with better perks than small ghost kitchens could probably offer. This can also make it difficult to retain good people.

Alternative Approaches

- **User-friendly AI products:** There are numerous SaaS products (Software as a Service) or auto ml frameworks aimed at small businesses. These tools provide natively dashboards, plug and play data visualization, and easy to implement predictive models with no deep knowledge of coding required.
- **Consultancies and Partnerships:** Budget ghost kitchens can engage outside agencies or analytics boutiques with specialized, temporary AI solutions. These arrangements, which come with consulting fees, enable the shift of tech burdens.
- **Phased Approach:** Instead of leaping to wide ranging AI solutions at once, smaller users could start with low hanging fruit demand forecasting or recommendation engines and scale up or down as return on investment (ROI) dictates.

Strategic Considerations

- **AI Strategy ROI Analysis:** Well-Named or leaf ghost kitchen should walk before adopting AI projects. The projects they have high potential in, if you can capture what the pain points are and know that it relates to inventory management or targeted promotions, they may say, `Yes, we want to do this, we want to be ranked accordingly to prioritizing high return projects.

- **Phased rollouts:** Phased rollouts of AI tools can be used as a proof of coast. Once proved successful, the approach can then be scaled at several locations, or, for other use cases.
- **Data Driven Culture:** You may not be able to put in place elaborate analytics from the beginning, but even starting somewhere, encouraging and valuing data to be collected, cleaned and analyzed in every department can prepare a business to take further steps.

In many cases, the growing availability of democratized AI tools is lowering barriers to entry, giving smaller ghost kitchens viable paths into implementing machine learning. With careful planning, imaginative partnership, and a steady return on investment, these operators can reap the benefits of AI at sustainable costs.

7.4. Workforce Implications (Staff Upskilling, Change Management)

The transformation is also about AI-powered ghost kitchens. While many people have good reason to fear that automation and machine learning will ultimately put them out of a job, the reality is a lot more complex: AI can help streamline rote processes, but human involvement and creativity and customer service will be irreplaceable.

Shifting Skill Requirements

- **Data Interpretation:** where previously employees would have been assigned the heavy lifting of carrying out manual checks on things like inventory or scheduling, they will now have to convert this experience into an understanding of how to interpret some AI dashboards or outputs of analytics. Not only does it diversify the skill set, but it also increases the value of the management to the organization as a whole.
- **Technical Troubleshooting:** With the omnipresence of AI platforms gradually seeping into day to day operations, a reasonable amount of tech literacy on the part of employees will likely help troubleshoot minor hardware issues or system glitches. In some cases, individual kitchens may employ or train "AI champions" who understand both the culinary processes as well as the underlying technology.
- **Soft Skills:** While the most automated processes are improving order time and prep time flows, the human aspect will always be a differentiator and most importantly, the handling of complaints, innovation on menu ideas or procedures, quality control.

Change Management Strategies

- **Training and Mentorship:** Structured training sessions can help orient staff around new workflows, clarifying how AI tools will work, and providing examples of how to use them successfully. Mentoring initiatives which pair employees more comfortable around tech with those less acquainted with digital tools further speed up the learning process.
- **Transparency:** The transparency on the use of AI and its impact and operational implementation can quench the thirst on the fear of losing the job. Stressing that this AI augments effort (rather than replaces it) builds trust. Automation, for example, could mean a person's lifelong career in

flipping burgers on an assembly line would be extinguished though a staff would then be available to focus on creating inventive dishes or specialized customer service.

- **Step-wise Implementation:** The progressive rolls out of AI solutions ensures that the employees can evolve at a healthy speed. A less stressful decision may be to begin with one module, such as automated scheduling, and successively develop advanced demand forecasting at a later stage, instead of redesigning all at once.

Long-Term Career Development

- **Upskilling Potential:** The rise of AI technologies could create high demand for employees with data analysis, predictive modeling, or AI tool administration skills, potentially pushing the pathway to promotion.
- **Horizontal Growth:** In some cases, automation can help us avoid drudgery in the kitchen, freeing up capacity for employees to splatter around to the other great roles in marketing, customer relations, or business development for employees who may prefer a more horizontal career arc beyond food prep.
- **Greater Leadership Opportunities:** Strong management and individuals who lead teams and can make sense of the insights generated through AI in daily activities is a brand differentiator. If these leaders can utilize analytics, inspire, and maintain service levels, they could end up in higher roles in the business.

Finding Balance Between Tech and Humanity

- **Automation Ethics:** From order routing to temperature reading, AI can do the jobs once filled by men. **"We examine how susceptible jobs are to computerization(Frey, C. B., & Osborne, M. A. (2017))."** But the complete replacement of humans can hurt the customer experience. "People are critical to empathy and creativity, and so enabling human touchpoints is fundamental to the DNA of the brand."
- **H-stress reduction:** Automation can combat burnout in and individuals by allowing employees to avoid unnecessary tedious or repetitive tasks. But staff members still must contend with potential order volume spikes or outages within the system. Well mapped out contingency planning means technology chatter can't drown out personnel.

8. FUTURE TRENDS AND SCALABILITY

8.1. Ghost Kitchen: AI Driven Automation and Robotics

The next big step up for ghost kitchens will probably involve greater integration of robotics across a wider swath of jobs. What started with machines that automate chopping vegetables or packaging of ready to eat meals, now might be graduated to robotic arms that will be able to handle advanced cooking processes flipping burgers and assembling pizzas, for example, and plating more complicated meals just right. Used in conjunction with AI driven software, these robotic units can ensure consistency in quality and taste, minimize labor costs, and even function 24/7, allowing ghost kitchens to scale to high volume demand without sacrificing on efficiency.

Plus when these robotics systems are networked with real time data flows, they can provide additional layers of insight. For example, robots equipped with sensors could track preparation times in certain stations, highlight bottlenecks, and alert management when any one machine or process needs maintenance. By addressing potential issues before they cause disruption, this cuts down on downtime and keeps workflows running smoothly, helping massive operations especially those poised to expand on the national or global stage scale successfully. From a marketing perspective, the data that these machines are generating can feed straight into hyper personalized promotions: by identifying stations with lower load, the system would suggest featuring items produced there through time limited offers thereby balancing production schedules and avoiding dwell times.

8.2. Advanced personalization (Voice Ordering, Predictive Text, and Sentiment Analysis)

Much like how user expectations are growing, personalization tools of the future will not depend on standard web or app hosting with conventional interfaces, but rather more advanced and natural forms of interfacing with a much more immediate, organic, in-the-moment nature. This significant milestone should result in voice ordering being a massive opportunity with new AI driven technologies that help recognize complex menu requests, change orders on the fly and cross-sell all enabling the transition. In addition to being convenient for customers, this process also produces rich data about spoken preferences, such as dietary restrictions or flavor inclinations, that can be used to further optimize customized promotions.

There's a new opportunity around predictive text and automated suggestions within the mobile apps." Relying on prior orders and searches and contextual cues, like the time of day or user location, the app could pre-emptively highlight some menus or recommend default changes (for instance, an extra sauce in an order or a specific spice level). This type of proactive interaction reduces friction in the ordering process, which can increase average order value and drive customer satisfaction. **"Results determined that user trustworthiness was the most important quality attribute of the food delivery app business (Cho, M., Bonn, M. A., & Li, J. J. (2019))."**

Outside of these ordering systems, sentiment analysis can serve as a live indicator of customer satisfaction. State-of-the-art natural language processing (NLP) algorithms can parse social media posts, reviews, and within-app feedback to unveil both positive trends (praise for a new vegan bowl dish, for instance) and potential worrisome issues (customer complaints about delivery delays). Ghost kitchens can respond quickly, whether that's adjusting their preparation processes or offering free or discounted meals to dissatisfied customers, or leveraging the positive praise in their marketing efforts. On the back end, as sentiment analysis become more sophisticated, it won't simply offer reactive insight, but also proactive alerts about potential challenges long before they become forms of crisis.

8.3. Potential for Full Integration (Supply Chain, Logistics, Last Mile Delivery)

As AI systems shape up, this dream of an end-to-end ecosystem connecting suppliers to ghost kitchens to last mile delivery providers, becomes more feasible. In this model, the entire food supply chain operates as an interconnected ecosystem: ingredients are tracked from farm to kitchen, predictive models determine optimal times to restock, and advanced logistics platforms dispatch deliveries on the fly.

So if supply chain data shows, for example, an unexpected glut of locally grown tomatoes, ghost kitchens could be automatically nudged to modify menus to include tomato based dishes on them, or do targeted promotions to take advantage of favorable pricing. AI based last mile delivery service on the other hand can actually allow the driver (or self-driving car depending on the time you are reading this) to work out who is going to get to a given customer first based on what is essentially degrees of connectedness to the order timestamp, location density or traffic congestion reports. This orchestration drastically decreases wait times and improves the customer experience, no less!

The benefits of this type of integration extend far beyond convenience. Ghost kitchens can minimize spoilage, guarantee more effective energy usage and create more-accurate labor forecasts by dynamically matching menus with what's available and the needs of the logistics to deliver. This holistic approach, in the long term, can help achieve better margins, drive sustainability initiatives, and lift consumers' perception of the brand's commitment towards responsible and ethical operating practices.

8.4. Opportunities for Investors and Innovators

As food-tech grows and evolves, AI powered ghost kitchens have received significant venture attention. The unique potential for explosive growth offered by AI powered kitchens has captured investors who are typically turned off by legacy restaurant models and value their streamlined processes and tailored customer communications. This influx of capital powers a diverse range of innovations, including but not limited to:

Predictive Analytics Startups: Companies offering solutions for data modeling for real time demand prediction, customer segmentation, and dynamic pricing.

Robotic kitchen equipment providers: Manufacturers of specialized equipment, from automated grill stations to robotic arms capable of performing intricate cooking tasks

Supply Chain Integration Tools: Integrating producers, distributors, and ghost kitchens under one digital umbrella to reduce friction on every step;

Enthusiasts and entrepreneurs, for example, are watching for opportunities to niche dive into specific market segments like plant-based ghost kitchens/food trucks or hyper-regional cuisines, and leverage AI to do some differentiating in an otherwise crowded market. If you come up with solutions to burning pain points such as enhancing cross platform data integration, diverse training data etc. or reducing algorithmic bias, you can get ahead of the game.

Innovation has become one of the core strategic pillars for incumbent players. Partnering with tech firms or research laboratories may thus accelerate the path to AI integration and, at the same time, reduce the demand for expensive in-house development. Using cutting-edge grade algorithms such as reinforcement learning for live recommendations or up skilling the skill sets of the team gives assurance to a brand of being agile and able to pivot quickly to pound on new opportunities.

At the core, ghost kitchen of the future will be built on the back of technology synergies across automation, personalization and end to end supply chain orchestration. Those brands that use these advances effectively will find it makes them able to offer memorable customer engagement, expand naturally into other markets and embody sustainability and efficiency. This trail-blazing spirit saw the sector step into the forefront of gastronomic innovation, revealing extensive opportunities for visionary investors, entrepreneurs and legacy operators to survive and eventually flourish in an ever-evolving digital landscape.

9. CASE STUDIES

9.1. Illustrations of Successful Hyper-Personalized Campaigns

Case Study: "MealBox"

"MealBox," a mid-sized ghost kitchen chain specializing in healthy bowls, sought to enhance customer engagement and increase sales during midday hours. To achieve this, they implemented an AI-based recommendation engine that analyzed customer purchase history, time of day, and dietary preferences.

Implementation:

- **Data Collection:** "MealBox" aggregated data from various touchpoints, including online orders, mobile app interactions, and customer feedback. This data encompassed individual purchase histories, preferred meal types, and ordering times.
- **AI Integration:** Utilizing machine learning algorithms, the system identified patterns and predicted customer preferences. For instance, it recognized that certain customers preferred high-protein meals post-workout or lighter options during lunch hours.
- **Personalized Promotions:** Based on these insights, "MealBox" crafted customized "lunch hour deals" tailored to individual tastes. Push notifications were sent to customers during late morning hours, featuring meal suggestions aligned with their previous orders and dietary inclinations.

Results:

- **Increased Conversion Rates:** The personalized approach led to a 20% uptick in midday conversions, as customers felt more inclined to order meals that resonated with their preferences.
- **Enhanced Average Order Value:** By analyzing purchasing patterns, the AI system identified opportunities for upselling premium protein add-ons. Targeted recommendations during the ordering process resulted in a 15% increase in average ticket size.

Case Study: "Urban Crave"

"Urban Crave," an urban-based ghost kitchen, aimed to boost sales by leveraging external factors influencing customer behavior. They integrated real-time weather data into their marketing strategy to offer contextually relevant promotions.

Implementation:

- **Weather Data Integration:** "Urban Crave" incorporated meteorological data to monitor local weather conditions in real-time.

- **Dynamic Menu Adjustments:** On days when rain was forecasted, the system prioritized promoting hot soups and comfort foods, anticipating a shift in customer cravings toward warmer meals.
- **Targeted Marketing:** Promotions for these items were disseminated to customers within a 5-mile radius through push notifications and email campaigns, emphasizing the suitability of these meals for inclement weather.

Results:

- **Sales Growth:** The weather-responsive promotions led to a significant increase in sales of the highlighted items, as customers appreciated the timely and relevant suggestions.
- **Improved Customer Engagement:** The personalized offers fostered a sense of attentiveness and relevance, enhancing overall customer engagement and loyalty.

9.2. Lessons Learned from Failed or Underperforming Implementations

Case Study: "Burger Rush"

"Burger Rush," a fast-food ghost kitchen, experimented with dynamic pricing to optimize profits. However, the lack of coordination between their pricing strategies and operational capabilities led to adverse outcomes.

Implementation:

- **Dynamic Pricing Model:** Prices for popular items, such as their signature burger, were adjusted based on demand fluctuations, with discounts offered during off-peak hours to stimulate sales.
- **Operational Misalignment:** The marketing team launched automated promotions without consulting the supply chain and kitchen staff, leading to unforeseen challenges.

Challenges and Outcomes:

- **Ingredient Shortages:** The unexpected surge in orders for discounted items caused rapid depletion of stock, as procurement had not been adjusted to accommodate the increased demand.
- **Delivery Delays:** Overwhelmed kitchen staff and insufficient inventory led to prolonged preparation times, resulting in significant delivery delays.
- **Customer Dissatisfaction:** The combination of delays and unfulfilled orders prompted a wave of negative feedback on social media, damaging the brand's reputation.

Lessons Learned:

- **Cross-Departmental Coordination:** This case underscores the necessity for synchronized planning between marketing, supply chain, and operations to ensure that promotional strategies are supported by adequate resources.
- **Scalable Promotions:** Implementing a controlled rollout of promotions can help assess operational impact and prevent overextension of resources.

Case Study: "Vegano Express"

"Vegano Express," a plant-based ghost kitchen, aimed to capture a diverse customer base through an intricate segmentation strategy. However, the complexity of their approach led to confusion and operational inefficiencies.

Implementation:

- **Micro-Segmentation:** The company developed over 20 distinct customer segments based on factors such as dietary preferences, order frequency, and spending habits.
- **Customized Promotions:** Each segment received tailored promotions and discount codes, intended to resonate with their specific behaviors and preferences.

Challenges and Outcomes:

- **Customer Confusion:** The multitude of overlapping promotions led to customer bewilderment, with many unsure which offers applied to them or how to redeem the discounts.
- **Operational Strain:** Staff members struggled to manage and apply the numerous discount codes accurately, leading to order errors and delays.
- **Brand Dilution:** The over-segmentation diluted the brand's messaging, making it difficult for customers to identify the core value proposition.

Lessons Learned:

- **Simplicity in Segmentation:** A more straightforward segmentation approach can enhance clarity for both customers and staff, ensuring that promotions are easily understood and effectively executed.
- **Clear Communication:** Transparent and concise communication of promotional offers is vital to prevent misunderstandings and maintain customer trust.

9.3. Strategies to Adapt and Scale AI-Based Personalization Across Multiple Locations

Scaling AI-driven personalization in ghost kitchens requires a strategic framework that accommodates both technological integration and local nuances.

1. Modular System Design:
    - **Flexible AI Tools:** Develop or adopt AI solutions that can be customized for each location, allowing or seamless integration with varying workflows without disrupting existing operations. This modular approach ensures that AI-driven personalization strategies can be tailored to different market dynamics and customer preferences.
    - **Interoperability with Existing Systems:** AI tools should be designed to integrate with existing Point of Sale (POS) systems, order management software, and inventory tracking platforms. This ensures a smooth transition to AI-driven decision-making without requiring a complete overhaul of current infrastructure.
2. Centralized Data Warehouse:

- **Unified Data Repository:** A centralized data warehouse consolidates information from multiple locations, virtual brands, and customer interactions. This enables a comprehensive analysis of trends and customer behaviors across different operational units.
- **Real-Time Data Access:** Providing managers and AI systems with real-time access to a centralized dataset ensures that recommendations, promotions, and personalization strategies are based on the most up-to-date information.
- **Scalable Infrastructure:** Cloud-based data storage and processing solutions allow for scalable expansion as new locations are added, ensuring that AI-driven personalization remains efficient and effective.

3. Pilot Programs for AI Implementation:
    - **Controlled Testing Environments:** Instead of deploying AI-driven personalization across all locations simultaneously, pilot programs allow businesses to test new features in select locations. This minimizes risks and provides valuable insights before full-scale implementation.
    - **Iterative Refinement:** Data collected from pilot programs can be used to refine algorithms, adjust marketing strategies, and optimize AI-driven personalization before expanding to a broader network.
    - **Performance Benchmarking:** Metrics from pilot programs, such as conversion rates, customer engagement, and operational efficiency, serve as benchmarks for evaluating AI performance and justifying further investments.
4. Local Adaptations for Diverse Markets:
    - **Regional Preferences and Customization:** AI-driven personalization should take into account regional dietary preferences, cultural nuances, and seasonal trends. For example, a ghost kitchen operating in Mumbai may prioritize spicy, vegetarian dishes, while a counterpart in Bangalore may focus on quick, protein-rich meals for office workers.
    - **Adaptive Pricing Strategies:** AI models can incorporate local economic conditions to adjust pricing dynamically. Lower-income areas may receive more budget-friendly meal suggestions, whereas premium segments may see exclusive, high-end offerings.
    - **Localized Marketing Campaigns:** AI-driven segmentation should align with local events, holidays, and consumer behavior patterns. For instance, special promotions on festival days or during major sporting events can increase customer engagement and drive sales.
5. Human Oversight and AI-Guided Decision Making:
    - **Hybrid Approach:** While AI-driven personalization enhances marketing efforts, human oversight remains essential. AI models should provide recommendations, but final decisions on campaign adjustments, inventory planning, and pricing should involve human judgment.
    - **Employee Training for AI Utilization:** Staff at different locations should be trained on how to interpret AI insights, implement suggested strategies, and provide feedback for continuous improvements.
    - **Customer Feedback Integration:** AI-driven personalization should incorporate direct customer feedback to improve recommendations, refine marketing messages, and ensure customer satisfaction.

10. ENVIRONMENTAL IMPACT AND SUSTAINABILITY IN AI-DRIVEN GHOST KITCHENS

The rise of ghost kitchens delivery-only culinary establishments has revolutionized the food service industry by leveraging artificial intelligence (AI) to enhance operational efficiency and customer satisfaction. Beyond these benefits, AI-driven ghost kitchens present significant opportunities for promoting environmental sustainability. This section delves into how these establishments can minimize their ecological footprint through energy efficiency, waste reduction, sustainable packaging, and eco-friendly delivery methods.

10.1. Energy Efficiency and Resource Conservation

Traditional restaurants consume substantial energy to maintain dining areas, including heating, cooling, lighting, and water usage. In contrast, ghost kitchens operate without customer-facing spaces, allowing for a more streamlined and energy-efficient setup. By focusing solely on food preparation and delivery, these kitchens can significantly reduce their energy consumption.

AI-Powered Energy Management: Integrating AI into kitchen operations enables real-time monitoring and optimization of energy use. AI systems can analyze patterns in equipment usage, adjusting operations to minimize energy waste. For instance, AI can schedule high-energy-consuming tasks during off-peak hours or adjust cooking processes to enhance efficiency. Such measures not only lower operational costs but also reduce the overall carbon footprint of the kitchen.

10.2. Waste Reduction Through AI Integration

Food waste is a pressing environmental issue, with significant implications for resource depletion and greenhouse gas emissions. Ghost kitchens, with their data-centric models, are well-positioned to tackle this challenge effectively.

Predictive Analytics for Inventory Management: AI-driven predictive analytics can forecast customer demand with high accuracy by analyzing historical order data, seasonal trends, and external factors like local events or weather conditions. This foresight allows kitchens to procure ingredients in precise quantities, minimizing overstocking and subsequent food spoilage. Studies have shown that such AI-driven forecasting can reduce food waste by up to 30%.

Real-Time Waste Monitoring: Implementing AI systems that track and analyze food waste in real-time provides actionable insights into waste patterns. By identifying which ingredients or dishes are frequently discarded, kitchens can adjust their menus, portion sizes, or preparation methods accordingly. This proactive approach not only conserves resources but also enhances profitability.

10.3. Sustainable Packaging Solutions

The delivery-focused model of ghost kitchens inherently leads to increased use of packaging materials, raising concerns about environmental impact. Addressing this issue is crucial for sustainability.

AI-Enhanced Packaging Design: AI can assist in developing eco-friendly packaging by analyzing material performance and environmental impact. By evaluating factors such as durability, weight, and biodegradability, AI helps in designing packaging that maintains food quality while minimizing ecological harm. Innovations in this area include biodegradable materials and designs that reduce plastic usage by up to 20%.

Personalized Packaging Solutions: Utilizing AI to analyze order patterns allows ghost kitchens to customize packaging sizes and materials based on specific menu items. This tailored approach ensures that packaging is not excessive, thereby reducing material usage and waste.

10.4. Eco-Friendly Delivery Methods

The environmental impact of food delivery extends beyond packaging to include the carbon emissions associated with transportation. Ghost kitchens can adopt several strategies to mitigate this impact.

Optimized Delivery Routes: AI algorithms can calculate the most efficient delivery routes by considering factors such as traffic conditions, distance, and delivery time windows. Optimizing routes reduces fuel consumption and emissions, contributing to a greener delivery process.

Adoption of Electric and Autonomous Vehicles: Transitioning to electric vehicles (EVs) for delivery purposes can significantly cut down on greenhouse gas emissions. Additionally, the integration of autonomous delivery robots, as demonstrated by companies like Starship Technologies, offers a sustainable alternative by reducing reliance on traditional fuel-powered vehicles. These robots have been shown to prevent numerous car journeys, leading to substantial CO_2 savings

10.5. Local Sourcing and Supply Chain Sustainability

The origin of ingredients plays a vital role in the overall environmental impact of food service operations. Ghost kitchens can enhance sustainability by focusing on local sourcing.

AI in Supplier Selection: AI tools can evaluate potential suppliers based on factors such as distance, farming practices, and sustainability certifications. By prioritizing local and environmentally responsible suppliers, ghost kitchens can reduce the carbon footprint associated with long-distance transportation and support sustainable agriculture.

Supply Chain Transparency: Implementing AI-driven blockchain technology ensures transparency in the supply chain, allowing kitchens to verify the sustainability credentials of their suppliers. This practice not only bolsters environmental responsibility but also builds trust with eco-conscious consumers.

11. CONCLUSION/OVERVIEW/AND RECOMMENDATIONS

11.1. Key Takeaways and Best Practices

In this chapter, the pivotal role of machine learning in driving hyper personalized marketing through ghost kitchens was discussed, and how AI models can change the game not just in terms of marketing initiatives but changing the daily routine of kitchens themselves. We began building out the context: What are ghost kitchens? Why do they rely so heavily on the digital channel? What are the AI solution that will help us in menu engineering, for demand prediction? From here we dove deeply into the nuts and bolts of predictive analytics and data collection, detailing how structured and unstructured data points everything from transaction histories and Google searches to real time inventory feeds gets to work feeding personalization systems.

Building on this context, the conversation shifted towards real-time personalization techniques, artificial intelligence (AI) based segmentation, and improved campaign performance measurement practices. Central to these strategies is an integrated strategy that relates kitchen workflow to marketing insights. The most generous promotional offer in the world is self-injurious if the kitchen doesn't have sufficient stores or manpower to process the flood of orders. At the same time, we found that there is a meta ethical and regulatory framework that governs applied AIs, responsible use of data, fairness in their algorithmic application, trust of the consumer all are crucial for long term success.

Best practices:

Holistic Data Strategy

- **Multi source data:** By using order data, demographic data, social media feedback and non-competing factors such as lazar and local events or weather forecasts, ghost kitchens can have a 360 view of its customers. This 360-degree viewpoint allows predictive accuracy and personalization efforts to be better informed.

Iterative Approach

- **Faster Feedback Loops:** ML models benefit the most from iterative optimization against newer data. It routinely reflects A/B testing, real time performance tracking and incremental updates and it can respond to shifting customer preferences and definitional changes in the marketplace.

Ethics and the Regulation of Due Diligence

- **Privacy, Fairness, and Data Security:** The minimum standard for trust is simply meeting statutory law as it applies to data regulations such as GDPR or CCPA; real consumer trust relies on active controls in terms of usage of data, starting with transparency about usage to fairness testing for machine learning outputs.

Cross-Functional Integration

- **Marketing Operations IT alignment:** Alignment between these teams has been necessary for AI driven personalization, siloes teams can at times reduce the level of impact it can provide. Inter-departmental communication also allows for rapid mid-course corrections in case promotions outstrip fulfillment capabilities or inventory runs-belly up in terms of marketing objectives.

Scalable Solutions

- **Modularity and Flexibility:** The modularity of cloud based infrastructures and AI architectures enables things that work well in one kitchen or brand to be easily deployed across many kitchens or brands. It also allows for easier updates or replacements of sections of the system.

11.2 Strategic Recommendations for Stakeholders (Operators, Marketers, Technologists)

While the potential value created by AI enabled personalization is enormous, the benefits can only be realized through the concerted efforts of multiple stakeholders. Here are more specific recommendations tailored to three key groups:

Operators

Invest in Agile Infrastructure

- **Cloud Based Systems:** Ghost kitchens work in a rapidly evolving landscape where, at times, the volume of orders can increase suddenly. Cloud based data warehouses, analytics platforms, and scalable server environments provide the elasticity to accommodate shifting demand without the risk of under or over investing in fixed hardware.
- **Disaster recovery and redundancy:** Ensure that your backups and contingency plans so that critical data and systems remain accessible during outages or technical failures.

Encourage Cross-Departmental Collaboration

- **Unified Dashboards:** Giving all departments, from the kitchen manager to digital marketers, real time data in one pane of glass allows all teams to work off the same metrics.
- **Regular Check-Ins:** Weekly or biweekly cross functional meetings can help surface emerging issues early on, whether that's a marketing promotion driving unexpected demand or a bottleneck in meal prep resulting in longer delivery times.
- **Put Workforce Development Front and Center**

When organizations upskill their staff with training on data interpretive tools or AI driven dashboards, that brings value as it can enable staff to bring more capability to the table, helping the organization be more adaptive and resilient.

- **Change Management:** Conspicuously describe advantages and disadvantages of new AI solutions to ease concerns about job loss or extra burden.

Marketers

If handled, segmentation will aid you in better targeting your users, it enables stronger acquisition and retention techniques.

- **Keep It Simple:** Complex segments can weaken the efficacy of campaigns. Begin with a few broad but useful groups frequent diners vs. special occasion customers, for instance and add on as data quality and analytic skill increase.
- **Adaptive Campaigns:** Use automated rules that adjust promotions in the event a segment's behavior shifts dramatically (e.g., if a segment's average spend significantly drops when certain menu items are no longer offered).

Transparency in Pricing

- **Dynamic Pricing Strategy:** If implementing variable pricing models (e.g., surcharges during peak hours), explain the rationale for these changes be it to moderate kitchen capacity or provide sustainable wages for drivers. When customers understand the "why" of something, they are more forgiving.
- **Targeted Marketing Adjustments:** Provide differentiating opt out options for customers to avoid repetitive or unwanted promotions.

Prescriptive Analytics to Open New Level of Creativity

- **Telling the Story with Data:** Marketers can leverage insights from predictive analytics to create interesting brand stories, like local sourcing of ingredients or how fast something was fulfilled, that resonate with target demographics.

Technologists
Emphasize Ethical AI

- **Interpretability Tools:** Implement model explainability solutions (e.g. LIME or SHAP) as part of development workflows to aid the team in understanding the logic behind the AI recommendations.

Modular Design

- **Micro services architecture:** Micro services architecture breaks AI solutions into smaller, independent services that can be individually maintained, updated, or replaced without affecting the overall system.
- **Sandbox Testing:** When designing a new recommendation algorithm, run it first in a bug stomping environment (sandbox) to gauge its effects on the quality of user experience (UX), and the ability to provide the service on the operational level.

Security and Reliability

- **With AI Services:** Whether you're integrating AI tech with marketing platforms, inventory systems, or third party consumer facing apps, secure authentication methods and encrypted data transfer should rule.
- **Monitoring and Alerting:** Real time alerting could raise alarms to tech teams about anomalies seen (an unexpected increase in requests to the pricing engine or a rapid drop in data quality).

11.3. Future Outlook on AI in Ghost Kitchens and Foodservice

As we look towards the future, it is clear that AI will only continue to permeate in ghost kitchens, and will ultimately define the evolution of the industry for the next few years. Ultimately, what was once experimental automated cooking stations, predictive text ordering, and real time data feedback will become a common fixture of the foodservice landscape. As consumers' bottomless appetite for speed and customization grows, operators of all kinds will be under increasing pressure to stay on trend with digital advances.

- **Autonomous Delivery:**

Drones and autonomous vehicles are often talked about as solutions for last mile delivery. Leading the charge in AI adoption, ghost kitchens could soon find themselves an early adopter experiment as automated vehicles try to bring shorter delivery times and lower delivery costs.

- **Deeper Personalization:**

An AI powered nutrition profile could become the norm for healthy eaters, offering food recommendations that align with dietary restrictions, fitness objectives or even treatable medical issues.

- **Sustainability for Sale:**

Consumers have a growing awareness of sustainability. AI can be applied to the modularize portion sizes, minimize food waste, and facilitate supply chain logistics, consequently making sustainability a tangible feature of a brand's value proposition.

- **Regulatory Evolution:**

Governments around the world will probably adopt more stringent policies around data privacy, AI accountability and even environmental impact. Proactively under reactive, forward looking ghost kitchens will influence standards.

Dealing with these complexities will call for a delicate balance between ambition and restraint. At the same time, however, riding the AI innovation wave can deliver competitive edge while also cultivating unique moments for customers that appeal to tech hungry diners. On one hand, consumers need to be aware of their privacy and fairness, and on the other hand, businesses need to remain attuned to the societal impact of automating large parts of food production and delivery.

At the end of the day, it is the ghost kitchens that embrace advanced machine learning capabilities and do so responsibly that have the best chance of success in a world where personalized, on demand service is no longer a plus, but a must. This chapter provides the basis of the best practices, strategic recommendations, and future perspectives that can pave the way for industry leaders and newcomers to follow a pathway to leverage for the transformative power of AI while grounding themselves in ethical and operational integrity.

REFERENCES

Arora, S., & Sahney, S. (2018). Consumer's webrooming conduct: An explanation using the theory of planned behavior. *Asia Pacific Journal of Marketing and Logistics, 30*(4), 1040–1063. DOI: 10.1108/APJML-08-2017-0185

Aschemann-Witzel, J., De Hooge, I., Amani, P., Bech-Larsen, T., & Oostindjer, M. (2015). Consumer-Related Food Waste: Causes and Potential for action. Sustainability, 7(6), 6457–6477. https://doi.org/
Baker, M. J., & Saren, M. (Eds.). (2016). Marketing theory: A student text (3rd ed.). SAGE Publications. DOI: 10.3390/su7066457

Bidyalakshmi, T., Jyoti, B., Mansuri, S. M., Srivastava, A., Mohapatra, D., Kalnar, Y. B., Narsaiah, K., & Indore, N. (2024). Application of Artificial intelligence in food processing: Current status and future prospects. *Food Engineering Reviews*. Advance online publication. DOI: 10.1007/s12393-024-09386-2

Bolton, R. N., Kannan, P. K., & Bramlett, M. D. (2000). Implications of loyalty program membership and service experiences for customer retention and value. *Journal of the Academy of Marketing Science, 28*(1), 95–108. DOI: 10.1177/0092070300281009

Branding in the Digital Age: You're Spending Your Money in All the Wrong Places. (2010, December 1). Harvard Business Review. https://hbr.org/2010/12/branding-in-the-digital-age-youre-spending-your-money-in-all-the-wrong-places

Capgemini & Oracle. (n.d.). Intelligent restaurant operations. https://www.capgemini.com/wp-content/uploads/2024/03/Oracle-IRO-Brochure_04032024.pdf

Cho, M., Bonn, M. A., & Li, J. (2018). Differences in perceptions about food delivery apps between single-person and multi-person households. *International Journal of Hospitality Management, 77*, 108–116. DOI: 10.1016/j.ijhm.2018.06.019

Data protection laws in India - Data Protection Laws of the World. (n.d.). https://www.dlapiperdataprotection.com/index.html?t=law&c=IN

Deloitte. (2023). The future of restaurants: The new normal and beyond. https://www2.deloitte.com/content/dam/Deloitte/us/Documents/consumer-business/the-future-of-restaurants-2023.pdf

Deshwal, C. I. (2024, October 17). Digital Personal Data Protection Act, 2023: Key features and Implications for Data Privacy in India. LexComply Blog. https://lexcomply.com/blog/digital-personal-data-protection-act-2023-key-features-and-implications-for-data-privacy-in-india/

Frey, C. B., & Osborne, M. A. (2016). The future of employment: How susceptible are jobs to computerisation? *Technological Forecasting and Social Change, 114*, 254–280. DOI: 10.1016/j.techfore.2016.08.019

Gursoy, D., & Chi, C. G. (2020). Effects of COVID-19 pandemic on hospitality industry: Review of the current situations and a research agenda. *Journal of Hospitality Marketing & Management, 29*(5), 527–529. DOI: 10.1080/19368623.2020.1788231

Hagberg, J., Sundstrom, M., & Egels-Zandén, N. (2016). The digitalization of retailing: An exploratory framework. *International Journal of Retail & Distribution Management*, *44*(7), 694–712. DOI: 10.1108/IJRDM-09-2015-0140

Hayes, S. (2021). Customer experience in the era of big data: Using predictive analytics for hyper-personalized campaigns. *Journal of Digital Marketing Innovation*, *14*(4), 22–31.

Jones, S., Cain, L., & Deel, G. L. (2024). Virtual restaurants and ghost kitchens: A new opportunity. *Journal of Hospitality & Tourism Cases*, *12*(3), 108–112. DOI: 10.1177/21649987241241948

Kandampully, J., Zhang, T. C., & Jaakkola, E. (2017). Customer experience management in hospitality. *International Journal of Contemporary Hospitality Management*, *30*(1), 21–56. DOI: 10.1108/IJCHM-10-2015-0549

Kannan, P., & Li, H. (2016). Digital marketing: A framework, review and research agenda. *International Journal of Research in Marketing*, *34*(1), 22–45. DOI: 10.1016/j.ijresmar.2016.11.006

Kumar, V., & Gupta, S. (2016). Conceptualizing the evolution and future of advertising. *Journal of Advertising*, *45*(3), 302–317. DOI: 10.1080/00913367.2016.1199335

Lahiri, S., Bose, I., & Majumdar, A. (2024). Rebel Foods' cloud kitchen Technologies: Food for thought? *Communications of the Association for Information Systems*, *54*(1), 155–179. DOI: 10.17705/1cais.05407

MacKay, A., Svartbäck, D., & Ekholm, A. G. (2022). Dynamic pricing and demand volatility: Evidence from restaurant food delivery. *SSRN*.

Markides, C. C. (2013). Business model innovation: What can the ambidexterity literature teach us? *The Academy of Management Perspectives*, *27*(4), 313–323.

Napitupulu, G. E. S., Ridwan, A. Y., & Santosa, B. (2023). Price cut policy on food delivery service application using dynamic pricing model to maximize profit on restaurant. *AIP Conference Proceedings*, *2568*, 050005. DOI: 10.1063/5.0119146

Narasimhan, L. Capgemini, Lynch, R., & Ezzat, A. (2023). AI for restaurants. https://www.capgemini.com/wp-content/uploads/2024/03/Oracle-IRO-POV_04032024.pdf

Nazer, L. H., Zatarah, R., Waldrip, S., Ke, J. X. C., Moukheiber, M., Khanna, A. K., Hicklen, R. S., Moukheiber, L., Moukheiber, D., Ma, H., & Mathur, P. (2023). Bias in artificial intelligence algorithms and recommendations for mitigation. *PLOS Digital Health*, *2*(6), e0000278. DOI: 10.1371/journal.pdig.0000278

Pezzini, G. (2022, October 28). Ghost kitchens: how they are transforming the restaurant industry. LS Retail. https://www.lsretail.com/resources/ghost-kitchens-what-they-are

PricewaterhouseCoopers. (n.d.). Global Consumer Insights Pulse Survey June 2023. PwC. https://www.pwc.com/gx/en/industries/consumer-markets/consumer-insights-survey.html

Sircar, C. O. T. (2025, January 8). Key highlights of India's draft Digital Personal Data Protection Rules, 2025 (via Passle). Passle. https://quickreads.ext.katten.com/post/102jsgd/key-highlights-of-indias-draft-digital-personal-data-protection-rules-2025

The Digital Personal Data Protection Bill. 2023. (n.d.). PRS Legislative Research. https://prsindia.org/billtrack/digital-personal-data-protection-bill-2023

The role of Technology in Ghost Kitchens: Streamlining operations. (n.d.). vGrubs. https://vgrubs.com/blogs/the-role-of-technology-in-ghost-kitchens-streamlining-operations

Tong, T., Dai, H., Xiao, Q., & Yan, N. (2019). Will dynamic pricing outperform? Theoretical analysis and empirical evidence from O2O on-demand food service market. *International Journal of Production Economics*, *219*, 375–385. DOI: 10.1016/j.ijpe.2019.07.010

Chapter 17
Eco-Friendly Practices of Ghost Kitchens Through Smart Technology:
Technological Innovations in the Food-Beverage Industry

Bhupinder Singh
https://orcid.org/0009-0006-4779-2553
Sharda University, India

Sanjeev Kumar
https://orcid.org/0000-0002-7375-7341
Lovely Professional University, India

ABSTRACT

Ghost kitchens are taking the food industry by storm, and leading to a greener marketplace for those using them built on smart technology. Ghost kitchens also eliminate the use of dine-in spaces, saving on energy consumption and reducing their carbon footprints as well as generating less waste. Using different applications, integrated smart appliances promote more efficient resource management for example IoT sensors to monitor energy usage and refrigeration; automated kitchen equipment that minimizes food waste by optimizing preparation or automating inventory management are all driven through AI. These mean less food is thrown away and sustainability of the ingredients being used are improved. Beyond that, digital platforms can optimize delivery routes to decrease fuel consumption and emissions. Ghost kitchens are on the forefront of integrating smart technologies into a more sustainable food service model, keeping us aligned with our eco-friendly goals and modern consumer trends for convenience without sacrificing sustainability.

DOI: 10.4018/979-8-3373-0432-8.ch017

1. INTRODUCTION

Ghost Kitchens often prioritize sourcing locally and using sustainable packaging as well, further decreasing their carbon footprint. A global transformation is underway within the food & beverage industry known as Industry 4.0 role in fueling future. The inevitable development in the changing landscape of food-service is ghost kitchens as cloud or virtual kitchens and they are turning out to be game-changers around town. Ghost kitchens are just delivery-only food preparation facilities with no traditional dine-in option and allow businesses to serve the increasing online ordering market directly.

Ghost kitchens are a direct outgrowth of the skyrocketing demand for food delivery via companies and given present time, look at what's happened during COVID-19. Traditional restaurants have struggled to evolve with the changing marketplace as more and more consumers gravitate toward online food ordering. Ghost kitchen becomes a straightforward solution, cutting out the high overhead of running actual restaurants and focusing mainly on prepping food for deliveries. However, notwithstanding the operational efficiencies of any food and beverage establishment as it terms from a higher level perspective, its ecological impact is quite significant. Whether it is due to food waste, carbon emissions or major energy usage; the industry has undeniably been slow on initiating sustainable behaviours. With the help of technology, ghost kitchens have a real chance at overcoming this issue.

The sustainability of ghost kitchens is being led by technological advancements in IoT, AI and automation. The developments in smart appliances, automated cooking systems and AI-driven data analytics solutions are not simply streamlining their operations but also drastically reducing waste production; saving energy and a lot better resource management. Refrigerators come with IoT integrated sensors that enable monitoring of entire apartment energy consumption in real-time, courtesy measures taken to reduce food spoilage and effective use of energy. Combine this with machine learning algorithms predicting what will be needed demand-wise, and ingredients are being used more efficiently than ever in the modern AI kitchen leading to a huge shrinkage of food waste (Raghavan & Vijayabhanu, 2023). The integration of cloud-based management systems enables several kitchen ghosts to operate on a single platform further improving food delivery routes and minimizing carbon emissions in product shipping.

Figure 1. shows the Dimensions of Introduction Section (Source- Self Prepared- Original)

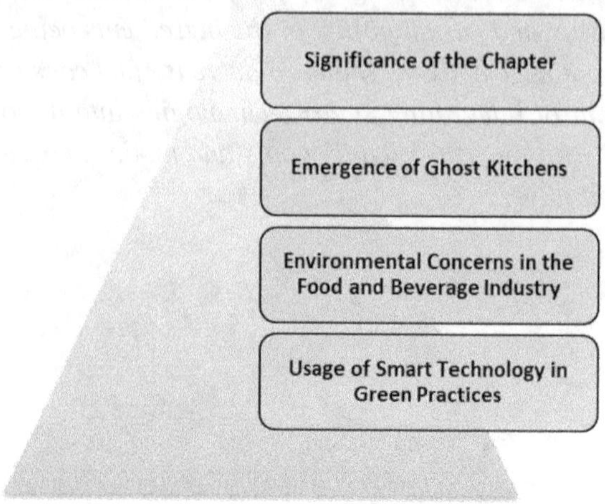

1.1 Significance of the Chapter

The importance of this chapter is the shadow kitchens so deploying digital since then undoubtedly contribute to help with some food and beverage being more sustainable. This might wonder this about most restaurants: they use a lot of resources energy, water not to mention packaging waste and their impact on the environment is worrisome. Ghost kitchens are well placed to address many of these environmental worries using smart technology. As compared to traditional kitchens, they are able to incorporate eco-friendly practices such as power-saving appliances renewables energies uses and saving water in ways that physical constraints of facilities may not work well with. Ghost kitchens, in addition to being considerably more flexible and malleable, also don't have the weight of a brick-and-mortar foot print they can immediately command new practices like eco-friendly takeaway packaging or carbon-neutral delivery services with comparably easy pivots.

The objective of this chapter is to accentuate the capacity that ghost kitchens have in reducing environmental effects being produced by foodservice operations. The series will look at the ground-breaking technological advancements that are leading to greater efficiencies and sustainability while also navigating through ongoing challenges. If it can better understand the marriage between smart technology and sustainability in ghost kitchens, perhaps it could provide a blueprint for how future-proof green operations are applied across the food & beverage industry as a whole. With sustainability now very much of top-of-mind concern, ghost kitchens that deploy the best smart technology represent a groundbreaking blueprint this can apply to future industry.

1.2 Emergence of Ghost Kitchens

This is due to the advent of ghost kitchens, feel also remember as cloud or virtual kitchen that indicates a major changeover within food and beverage sector. Delivery-only Cloud Kitchens work without the dining section and target only on its online food ordering customers. Ghost kitchens have emerged during a time of significant upheaval in restaurant dining brought about by the explosive growth of online food delivery platforms. The COVID-19 pandemic has only exacerbated this trend, with a change in consumer behavior and food delivery habits due to lockdowns around the world.

Ghost kitchens reduce overhead costs because they don't require large dining spaces, front-of-house staff or prime real estate. That allows them to run several virtual restaurant brands out of single kitchen space making their operations more efficient. The model has been attractive to large and midsize chains wanting to develop their delivery services, as well as entrepreneurs who are eyeing the food business with less upfront investment. But the scalability and cost-effectiveness in ghost kitchens have environmental implications around energy use; food waste and packaging. Therefore, ghost kitchen revolution is being merged with new smart technology aiming for environmentally friendly methods.

1.3 Environmental Concerns in the Food and Beverage Industry

The food and beverage industry is one of the leading causes of environmental destruction, as it depends heavily on resources uses them extensively through waste. Between traditional restaurants and the food production plants themselves, food waste, energy consumption and carbon emissions are sky high. Food waste is a huge problem, with massive amounts of food that is unsold or uneaten being thrown away daily adding to methane emissions in landfills. The industry involves mind-numbingly massive quantities of water and energy from food storing and preservation to packaging or transport. But the single-use plastic packaging and unsustainable sourcing practices compound this footprint. Due to long-distance food transportation, it is another reason why our carbon footprint grows and becomes a factor in climate change. With growing consumer focus on environmental sustainability, the food and beverage sector in particular is feeling pressure to adopt sustainable practices that mitigate its footprint.

1.4 Usage of Smart Technology in Green Practices

Why the food and beverage industry still needs smart technology, explained ghost kitchens allow businesses to go green through eco-friendly practices as IoT sensors, artificial intelligence (AI), and automation can save resources folks are using purposefully to minimize waste. IoT devices can measure and monitor energy usage in real time to ensure appliances are running only as needed. Kitchens can accurately reduce waste, avoid food wastage by not overproducing items using AI-powered systems that a read demand. The automation of food preparation helps to streamline processes even further since it eliminates all labor-intensive tasks and in the process reduces errors that produce waste. Cloud-based platforms allow ghost kitchens to operate multiple brands while delivering orders more efficiently, lowering fossil carbon emissions associated with food transportation. Smart technologies serve to enable sustainable initiatives like biodegradable packaging, energy-efficient appliances and water conservation systems which assist in comprehensive solutions for sustainable kitchens that are just as beneficial economically as they are environmentally. Taking on these innovations advances sustainability in the industry, without sacrificing profitability.

2. TECHNOLOGICAL INNOVATIONS IN GHOST KITCHENS: AI, INTERNET OF THINGS (IoT) AND SMART KITCHENS

Ghost kitchens take the lead via using state-of-the-art technologies including Artificial Intelligence (AI), Internet of Things (IoT) and smart kitchen solutions, cloud/virtual kitchens as these fulfillment only kitchens can effectively improve operations while minimizing waste in a bid to drive sustainability. Though this will in the long-term enhance productivity and reduce costs, but these advancements also provide somewhat of a footpath for ghost kitchens to implement ecological friendly strategies that address some environmental issues experienced by the industry.

Ghost kitchens run on the spine of Artificial Intelligence (AI), and it is mainly used for inventory management, demand forecasting, scheduling & operational efficiency. For instance, AI-powered systems can crunch data on customer orders and preferences to predict demand more effectively so kitchens know exactly what to prepare each day. And since it forecasts demand, this feature helps operators reduce food waste by preparing only the amount necessary to sell out and avoiding sunk cost in overstocked or expired items. AI predicts top order times and menu items, which enable kitchens to staff accordingly for improved labor efficiency. AI-driven insights facilitate this customization by allowing ghost kitchens to dynamically adjust their menus and optimize pricing strategies as well as recommend dishes based on individual customer cravings, ensuring a personalized dining experience every time while curbing food wastage (Kumolu-Johnson, 2024).

Whether we talk about AI for inventory and demand optimization, it also simplifies in improving the procurement processes by supercharging existing capabilities of supply chain. Connecting with suppliers and checking ingredient availability helps kitchen stay just-in-time on inventory rather than churning out excessive overstock, thereby preventing food spoilage all backed by AI systems. Ghost kitchens have precise control over the amount of inventory they order and carry, which also leads to sourcing sustainability ghost kitchen operators can partner with local suppliers for their needs, minimizing food miles by a considerable extent as well as carbon footprint. It is also employed to carry out other kitchen jobs, like recipe adjustments or automated cooking processes and thus making each step increasingly consistent and speedy with better quality as well as reducing both human errors and energy consumption.

Smart kitchens and IoT are almost inseparable as they allow kitchen appliances, and all operations in the kitchen to be monitored real-time. IoT devices are built into kitchen equipment such as refrigerators, ovens or dishwashers to send alerts and be notified when the food is eaten. They capture temperature data, energy usage and equipment performance giving operators great insight into how efficient their kitchen is operating. This might include sensors that monitor fridge temperatures and notify staff should they fall outside of an appropriate range, preventing food spoilage or a hygiene incident. IoT sensors located in ovens and stoves likewise have the ability to monitor cooking times, as well as energy consumption linked with a machine being left idle when not used efficiently. IoT technology means better energy consumption-management, which is a key part of increasing sustainability. With this information, smart meters and energy monitoring systems can examine the exact power usage of each appliance at any given time to enable kitchens to detect and correct potential sources of wastefulness in real-time. Using an evidence based approach, operators can make energy-related changes to their operations by programming things like cooking times around cheaper off-peak rates or the purchase of more efficient appliances. IoT also has the potential to save water in ghost kitchens by preventing unnecessary wastage of water during dishwashing and cleaning processes with automated controls that use not more than necessary (Kamal & Elsaed, 2022).

AI and IoT enabled Smart kitchens offer impeccable amalgamation of technology to automate kitchen operations These kitchens use data from IoT sensors and AI systems to get the most out of their workflow, enabling them to efficiently prepare food, deliver it quickly etc. Smart ovens and refrigerators that are bright appliances as an example, can be programmed by the user to operate at specific times or temperatures taking out some of those human error facets plus attaining greater accuracy in surgery. For example, a smart refrigerator can restock toppings whenever levels run low so eliminating the chance of running out but offering their own benefits like showing advertisements to passersby. Also, smart ovens can get an idea of what needs to be cooked and change their cooking time based on the type of grub being shoved in there, cutting energy use and maintaining a steady level of quality. Cloud-based platforms can also be integrated into smart kitchens, which make management easier to scale and simplifies operations by allowing one dashboard for multiple ghost kitchen setups.

Food & beverages industries revolutionizing with ghost kitchen by integrating AI, IoT and smart kitchen solution. This is how ghost kitchens maximize their operational efficiency and profitability as well as follow sustainable practices to solve the environmental problems faced by this industry. Technological innovations, which assist in lessening food waste and energy consumption as well as utilize water more effectively while reducing emissions, are enabling ghost kitchens to meet the evolving aesthetics of a greener future for food delivery. So as these new technologies develop, more and more ghost kitchens will be built around them which means we can expect many of the food-and-beverage sector gains in sustainability to move through their doors first. The other way that ghost kitchens incorporate connected technology is delivery logistics fueled by AI, IoT and smart kitchen tech. Roots improve the delivery routes using AI-powered algorithms to reduce fuel consumption and emissions. This would also enable kitchens to work smoothly with third-parties like delivery companies who help the food reach employees quickly and in an eco-friendly way. They also used electric delivery vehicles and bikes which are powered with AI driven logistics reducing a more carbon impact due to food deliveries (Vaughan, 2022).

2.1 Smart Refrigerators and Appliances: Reduction of Energy Consumption and Ensuring Food Safety

The key to these kitchens operating efficiently are Smart refrigerators and appliances that help minimize energy loss, also ensure food safety. These tools come with state-of-the-art sensors & IoT connectivity that allows it to process and analyze the data continuously, not only monitoring kitchen operations in real-time but also taking automatic actions by employing machine learning algorithms. Ghost kitchens in particular can use substantial amounts of energy on a daily basis; having precise control over appliances, therefore cutting down the amount used through remote operation aspects and such leading to significant savings in terms of energy consumption as well.

Take smart refrigerators, for instance; constructed specifically to exert and regulate temperature levels in order not to ruin the food through fluctuations. This system provides an early warning of problems in the kitchen, allowing operators to check and address these issues before they become wasteful. Intelligent fridges can self-regulate their temperatures dependent on live readings so you are only wasting juice when it is required. For example, they can switch to an energy-saving setting at times of low demand or when the kitchen is not in use, which further saves electricity.

These smart appliances offer enhanced precision, which has been nearly impossible to achieve with regular old food equipment in the past. Most importantly, they can monitor when a perishable item will go bad and alert employees to use or toss the ingredients accordingly so you don't have health safety violations. As a result, this will ensure less waste and prevent spoils or illnesses caused by unprofitable products to be used in kitchen operations; Cooktops and ovens are also very energy efficient, as they can automate how long something should cook for or at what temperature which allows the food to be prepared with minimal waste of heat but will make sure that everything turns out right. Batch processors can pre-program cooking cycles or remotely control cook paths of the batch while mitigating human error in extremes cases enabling out-of-the-box operation with minimal setup risk for untrained employees on undercooked and overcooked products, lessening food safety concerns.

2.2 Automation and Robotics

Ghost kitchens being emptied quicker and with demoralization of food preparation stages comes automation and robotics, which are swiftly overtaking the construction style in centralized models to bring about improvements or efficiency savings. Ghost kitchens can help to streamline the practice of food preparation by automating many unique subroutines (such as chopping, mixing and sending down fried foods) towards save time workforce. Automation improves both speed and accuracy, which not only reduces human error but also leads to more consistent food quality na huge factor in all areas of the waste life-cycle from farm production to purchasing; storage through processing (Zammit, 2022).

The strongest advantages offered by automation are that it can efficiently process high-volume orders. Robotic systems allow ghost kitchens to prepare at a moment's notice, delivering meals in time without sacrificing quality. Robots can also operate 24/7, which makes them more productive and reduces the cost of labor. Moreover, an automated system is designed to use precise measurements of elements that diminish the probability of over-/under-portioning occurring both common reasons for wastage. Robotic scientists and food prepping systems like robotic arms pizza or burger assemble robots again improve performance by occupying all the repetitive as well as time- consuming activities. That frees up kitchen staff to work on more advanced, or even daring, elements of cooking while the robots take care of the rote stuff. Packaging is automated as well, where robots can pack orders significantly faster and more accurately than humans. This not only accelerates deliveries but also reinforces standardized, efficient packaging that remains in 100% compliance with health and safety standards. Ghost kitchens are becoming an integral part of the social and economic fabric as more people demand quick deliveries, for which they rely on automation, robotics. These have a direct impact such as the reduction of energy consumption, less food waste and better resource usage that also makes them sustainable. Plus, ghost kitchens can to offer fast-casual fare that is cheap and environmentally responsible by incorporating automation with robotics.

3. ECO-FRIENDLY PRACTICES IN GHOST KITCHENS

Ghost kitchens, alternatively cloud kitchens or virtual kitchens are a novel response within the food and beverage industry. Operating as kitchens, these new spaces delivery-only for Sweet-green and reduce in the case of this pilot program aim to reduce or even eliminate much of the environmental costs with brick-and-mortar restaurants. These activities include donating excess food, lowering power usage, using green packaging products and sourcing locally-grown ingredients where possible as well as switching to water-saving technologies.

Ghost kitchens can become more sustainable in several ways, including by cutting down on their food waste. Finally, ghost kitchens operate with more efficient menus of much smaller scope and have real-time data they can utilize to price their offering in a zero cost manner than most chains could possibly achieve so it expect them on average end up throwing less food waste away. The majority of ghost kitchens utilize machine learning and predictive analytics to model future demand more accurately, catching not making enough or excess food which then causes wastage. Unopened ingredients could also be "stored, reused or donated to local food banks as part of waste reduction goals". Ghost kitchens can also improve energy efficiency (Kimes et al, 2023). The old-style restaurants are consuming a lot of energy for lighting, cooking & Fridge power and heating. Meanwhile, ghost kitchens can take advantage of smart appliances and Internet of Things (IoT) for energy efficiency control opportunities. In the cas in point, a savvy fridge will assume control over temperature execution and off-top time to save energy modes. At the same time, automated cooking equipment ensures energy is used as economically as possible by automatically altering cooking times and temperatures where appropriate to prevent overcooking. Finally, these kitchens can be powered by renewable energy thereby reducing their carbon footprint even more beyond not hauling garbage to a landfill on the other side of town.

Delivery services produce a large amount of packaging waste and sustainable packaging is an important factor to consider with the ghost kitchen model. The best solution is to use biodegradable or compostable packaging materials, which many eco-friendly ghost kitchens have already opted for today. These materials have been designed to reduce the amount of plastic waste, and help prevent un-ecofriendly impact caused by traditional single-use packaging. Moreover, certain ghost kitchens go as far as giving the customer an incentive to recycle the packaging or bring it back, leading a circular economy towards zero waste.

Using products from your local area and that are organic is another great eco-conscious practice to have when operating a ghost kitchen. As ghost kitchens partner with local farms and suppliers, they reduce the carbon footprint associated by long-distance transportation of food. Also, sourcing locally act as great support for the local economies and fresh ingredients allow food to be cooked from scratch not need preservatives (and other additives) in foods. Ghost kitchens can often embrace farm-to-table strategy, helping support sustainability by using locally sourced ingredients that are grown and harvested responsibly.

In ghost kitchens water conservation plays a great role in eco-friendly practices. Water is an essential part of the running cost in traditional restaurants from cooking and cleaning to maintaining kitchen hygiene (Zheng, 2024). Ghost kitchens can use water-saving technologies low-flow faucets, sensor-operated control systems for scrubbing purposes to save gallons of wastewater every day. Ghost kitchens can save boatloads of this precious resource by employing steam-based cooking methods or other water-efficient appliances.

Eco-friendly ghost kitchens also focus on reducing the carbon emissions of their delivery logistics as well. AI-powered route optimization software helps ghost kitchens save on fuel consumption for delivery purposes, allowing them to make deliveries more efficiently and with fewer emissions. Electrically assisted bicycles or electric fast last mile delivery vehicles could take matters even further in the direction of sustainability. Ultimately, when it comes to running an eco-friendly ghost kitchen business other elements come into the picture like waste management, proper functioning of water and energy systems etc., sourcing raw materials for meals preparation sustainably as well packaging including logistics in environment-safe way. This will help to save money and also have better control over the quality of food, at zero loss level as well. If ghost kitchens become organized in a sustainable manner by using leftovers as feed into another than not only reduces operational cost but can be marketed tailored with environmental friendly tag by having self-home delivery thereby making customers meaning happier & satisfied. Implementing these protocols will allow ghost kitchens to play their part in the sustainable future of food and beverage industry (Perez-Guzman et al., 2022).

3.1 Sustainable Sourcing and Local Supply Chains

To make ghost kitchens more environmentally friendly, they must adopt sustainable sourcing and localize their supply chains. Because ghost kitchens leverage ingredients from local farms and nearby suppliers, they benefit the town or city they are based in as well as offering one step toward decreasing a region's food miles. It can reduce a kitchen's carbon footprint since one of the biggest producers of greenhouse gas emissions comes from transportation. Also, when you source locally, the ingredients are fresher and more nutritious as they spend less time in transit and require fewer preservatives. This is vital for higher quality food and better menu choices (Ramachandran et al., 2024).

Sustainable sourcing extends beyond local produce and includes ethical principles alongside environmentally practices. That is, selecting suppliers who use no pesticides or synthetic fertilizers in their agriculture. Also, backing farms that conduct regenerative agriculture like crop rotation, reduced tilling and organic soil management is maintained biodiversity while improving the health of the land. These sustainable practices benefit the environment in the long-term as they help stop soil degradation and make local ecosystems more resilient. Sustainable kitchens will source their products from organizations like the Marine Stewardship Council (MSC), which guarantees sustainable seafood, and other suppliers with certifications showcasing humane livestock farming (Islam & Nahid, 2023). In other words, the combination of low energy demand and diversified products makes ghost kitchens a sustainability-oriented option as far they contribute to reduce their food miles by working with urban supplies from rooftop gardens, vertical farms. Based on this approach where most produce will be available localy when fresh therefore reducing emissions related to transportation.

Ghost kitchens could be the answer as sustainable sourcing combining with local supply chains provide ghost kitchen operators a chance to lower down their carbon footprints while providing an eco-friendly, responsible and high-quality food concepts ever growing in demand. This practice isn't just good for the planet, but also conforms to increased consumer demand that food is local and sustainably sourced.

3.2 Waste Reduction Strategies: Biodegradable or Recyclable Protective Packaging to Minimize Plastic Pollution

The major environmental issue that in the food and beverage industry all of us struggle with daily is the vast use of plastic, mostly for packaging. Ghost kitchens and delivery-only services are on the rise, causing a spike in single-use packaging requirements. Environmentally responsible ghost kitchens are more and more looking towards clever sustainable food packaging options that are either biodegradable or renewable so as to not once again contribute to plastic waste with all the environmental damage it causes.

Unlike traditional plastic packaging, whose remnants may last for hundreds of years biodegradable packaging is built to decompose into natural components in the environment over time. It is usually made from such components as cornstarch, sugarcane fibers or other plant sources. However, when thrown away, biodegradable packaging breaks down into natural substances and therefore causes very limited environmental impact (Selvamuthukumaran, 2024). With ghost kitchens, whose bulk of sales comes from takeout and delivery orders, the elimination or reduction in usage is a game changing innovation created for enormous plastic waste such as Single-Use Containers Cutting Boards Plastic Bags etc. Regardless of the fact that some ghost kitchens using biodegradable packaging, an additional junk-free model consists in recycle materials like paper or cardboard and aluminum. This makes materials infinitely recyclable, so are able to be continuously broken down and reprocessed into new forms, cutting the requirement for virgin resources. Plus, a lot of eco aware kitchen areas prompt buyers to recycle by marking containers as well making it practical with take back recycling programs. A few even offer rewards for customers who return reusable containers, closing the loop and avoiding waste entirely.

Edible packaging is a new innovation in smart packaging that made out of natural components which could be safely eaten together with the food content inside. In this way, the packaging is not only served waste-free but also a creative and sustainable portion of eating. Ghost kitchens are also committed to further reducing plastic waste through compostable packaging (Dobbelstein et al., 2023). The packaging decomposes when it is thrown into real composting facilities and makes food waste recycled as precious organic materials for agriculture. On the whole, these smart waste reduction strategies let ghost kitchens keep themselves away from plastic and contribute positively to their nearby environment for sustainability freak customers.

3.3 Practices Concerned with Energy Efficiency and Water Conservation

Ghost Kitchens too, have an eco-friendly approach where energy efficiency and water conservation form its crux. Commercial kitchens are energy-intensive operations with high demands for cooking meal items, refrigeration and cleaning all of which use a lot of power. Although, using energy efficient equipment and smart technology management as well as better resource utilization could cut down the environmental footprint of ghost kitchens while also saving operating expenditures (Hoffman, 2022).

The use of smart appliances and Internet of Things (IoT) technology can significantly drive efficiency for ghost kitchens. For example, smart refrigerators precisely control temperature and adjust cooling power based on automatic learning about the actual usage of real time to reduce unnecessary energy consumption. Just like other connected devices, smart ovens and the cooktops can all be scheduled to work with specific temperatures of when they should operate so that the give exactly as needed energy for cooking. IoT sensors can also keep track of total kitchen equipment energy usage which tells operators where they are wasting energy and where to save.

As well as smart appliances, ghost kitchens could be completely powered by renewable sources such as solar energy to slash that carbon footprint far beyond the reach of any traditional kitchen. Clean energy produced for kitchen operations through installation of solar panels on the rooftop or nearby areas will prevent its over-dependence on non-renewable source, helping in slashing greenhouse gas emissions (Sinha et al., 2024). The important feature of these eco-friendly kitchens is water conservation. Cooking, washing dishes and cleaning purposes have traditionally demanded a large amount of water on the kitchen. As such, many ghost kitchens are turning to low-flow faucets and water-efficient dishwashers that provide the same level of hygiene while helping restaurants meet sustainability goals and even save on utility bills. There are even kitchens that employ steam-based cooking techniques, which not only save water but also result in less energy use since it takes fewer calories to get steam hot than an entire pan full of something. Implementing grey-water recycling systems that can divert used water away from the potable water system for uses such as scrubbing floors or irrigating plants are great ways to make ghost kitchens more sustainable. The more this is practiced, the less demand there is for freshwater in general and water waste overall goes down (Diracca, 2021). With a focus on energy-efficient and the optimized usage of water, even ghost kitchens can greatly slash the environmental damage from their end.

Figure 2. illuminates the Eco-friendly Practices in Ghost Kitchens (Source- Self Prepared- Original)

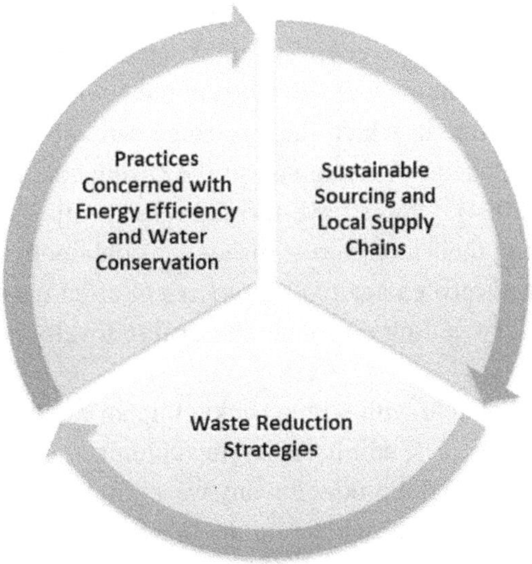

4. SUSTAINABLE FOOD DELIVERY MODELS: ECO-FRIENDLY PACKAGING SOLUTIONS

The rise of ghost kitchens and food delivery services has coincided with the growing waste due to single-use packaging materials. Recycling partnership with millions of takeout orders placed each day by Americans who want something quick before the next binge-watching session begins, any sort of change in that area can add up and is certainly needed. In response, numerous ghost kitchens are switching to green packaging options which not merely trim waste and cut down on plastic use at the point of delivery but likewise keep sustainability all through during an organised move about (Castillo et al., 2024).

There are several sustainable alternatives available in biodegradable packaging being the most common. Biodegradable Packaging: Biodegradable packaging is made up of plant-based materials like cornstarch, sugarcane fibers, or bamboo and decomposes in the environment without leaving any waste material. Unlike plastic, which may take hundreds of years to break down, biodegradable packaging generally will decompose in a few months and help reduce the amount of waste sitting in landfills. Unlike its environmental advantages, biodegradable packaging is flexible; it can be molded into shapes like containers and even cups to drink from, making the product a pragmatic substitute for ghost kitchens (Kumolu-Johnson, 2024). The more eco-friendly packaging idea is using compostable materials. Compostable is the term used to describe packaging that are made of organic raw materials that decompose into soil- beneficial compost under specific conditions met in a commercial or industrial facility. Raw materials like bagasse residue from crushed sugarcane and polylactic acid, not only save waste but also enhance soil fertility by recycling essential nutrients back into the ground. In the food delivery market, compostable packaging is seeing increased demand that aligns with environmental and agricultural sustainability objectives.

Some ghost kitchens are also trying to limit their waste and environmental impact by using recyclable packaging alongside biodegradable and compostable materials. This comprises papers, cardboards and aluminum that are readily recyclable and can be reprocessed to create new products. Recycling reduces demand for virgin materials and therefore environmental damages which come with the manufacturing of new packaging. Recyclable packaging will often be coupled with efforts to educate customers on the correct type of recycling receptacle in which their package can and should go, fully closing the loop of waste around many ghost kitchens. A rising star in the sustainable food delivery circuit is reusable packaging programs (Chng, 2024). Others have formed relationships with a reusable container company, so customers are ordering their food in real dishes the containers used for delivery orders can be shipped back to get washed and refilled again. Customers are often rewarded when they participate in these programs, which can mean getting discounts or earning loyalty points etc. thereby encouraging eco-friendly habits.

This is plenty of promise available with edible packaging, an exciting innovation that could revolutionize how food delivery operates. The edible packaging contains only food grade materials which can be eaten with the meal together, without producing any waste. In the distant future, it might be possible to dramatically reduce our need for disposable containers with an edible packaging solution. So, eco-friendly packaging solutions also consider the use of minimalistic packing design that helps in limiting laying a rise on weight and size. The cutting out the middlemen and creating better containers, ghost kitchens could use less materials while ensuring that food remains safe and in good condition during transport (Lahiri et al., 2024). Eco-friendly packaging solutions play a critical role in developing sustainable food delivery models within the framework of ghost kitchens. With biodegradable, compostable, recyclable and reusable packaging made from organic materials that are edible in some cases even will allow ghost kitchen to reduce the size of their carbon footprint on top of promoting a greener future for the food & beverage industry as well.

5. COMPARATIVE ANALYSIS: TRADITIONAL RESTAURANTS VS. GHOST KITCHENS

Ghost kitchens have arisen as an innovative solution to the timeless business of food and beverage, at a time when traditional brick-and-mortar restaurants are increasingly losing ground in our modern age (Delalay et al., 2024). Both platforms are delivering meals to consumers, but they have vastly different environmental and sustainable implications. In this comparative study, we highlight such disparities and delve into their carbon footprint evaluation together with consumption of resources and efficiency.

5.1 Environmental impact: Carbon footprint, Waste and Resource Usage

Brick-and-mortar restaurants have always been somewhat environmentally taxing, using a lot of energy to heat or power cooking equipment and also for lighting; consuming large amounts of water to cook food but mostly to 'flush' it away, they produce tons! Dining-in requires more physical space and that in term results to extra heating, cooling or lighting. Moreover traditional restaurants creates a great food waste as s in general they cook ex-ante, so its more difficult to cope with the customers unpredictable preferences. The packaging waste associated with takeout only adds to the environmental load, often consisting of single-use plastic or non-recyclable materials (Zheng, 2024).

Ghost kitchens, on the other hand are more efficient by nature since they operate a delivery-only model. Ghost kitchens support reduced climate control and lighting loads from operating in smaller spaces. They are also preparing food smarter with data analytics that tracks what is being demanded in real time so as to optimize their cooking activities and the reduce chances of overproduction, subsequently decreasing the risk of wasted foods. Meanwhile, ghost kitchens generally prefer using green food packaging materials such as biodegradable or compostable containers to replace plastics related in delivery.

Ghost kitchens are even better from an environmental standpoint when viewing them through the lens of a carbon footprint. Plus, since there are no dine-in customers to provide seating for they can often be located further off the beaten urban path in less energy consuming locations. And a large proportion of ghost kitchens are also based on AI delivery route optimization, fuel efficient food delivery solutions which cuts the carbon footprints for meals delivered (Guthman, 2024). Traditional restaurants, on the other hand, heat their spaces up for both dining in and take out customers which leads to a higher overall footprint given that it takes so much energy resources now moving things between different dinning formats.

5.2 Efficiency and Sustainability Energy Use, Water Usage, Waste Produced Linked to Food Kilometres or Miles

In terms of energy consumption, ghost kitchens even top traditional restaurants by keeping their operational footprint small and using smart technology. A lot of ghost kitchens use smart appliances that turn on and off as they're needed, in addition to equipment programmed to regulate power according the kitchen's flow. For example, smart ovens and refrigerators can go into energy-saving low-power modes during non-peak hours to prevent wasted electricity. On the other hand, traditional restaurants need to keep energy-dependent machines and utilities on for most of the day even though fluctuations in demand (Poon & Tung, 2024). A traditional restaurant can consume a lot of water; for example, to prepare food, dishwash and clean. Ghost kitchens, on the other hand can certainly aid in water conservation by empowering units to implement technologies such as low-flow faucets or energy-efficient dishwashers which cut down significant use of water Plus, ghost kitchens require no customer dining space meaning tasks like restroom cleaning or table washing aren't necessary for a reduced water usage.

The waste generation profile of ghost kitchens is also relatively greener. This is because in traditional restaurants, chefs typically cook food for hundreds of diners en masse to deliver at the table and frequently ends up as waste. On the other hand, ghost kitchens have an advantage when it comes to AI and predictive analytics which enables them to forecast their demand and cook in advance only what they need thus reducing waste (Zhu et al., 2024). Ghost kitchens are better poised to implement waste reduction strategies like donating extra food or mixing and matching ingredients. "Ghost kitchens" have lower food miles the distance that your meal travels from its producer to your plate. Ghost kitchens can also utilize a better blend of local ingredients and operate in centralized locations nearest to their customer base, lessening the overall environmental blow from food transportation. Speciality suppliers can deliver fresh ingredients while traditional restaurants have many different providers further away, thus increasing food miles and the related carbon emissions.

In general however looking at the two options, while both face environmental issues traditional restaurants significantly more so than ghost kitchens as delivery precipitated by smart tech is inherently a greener mode of operation. Ghost kitchen operations also reduce waste with smart appliances and energy- and water-efficient designs, not to mention the efficient logistics benefits.

6. CHALLENGES AND LIMITATIONS

While there is a move towards increasing digitization and sustainability in the ghost kitchens space, these changes do come with some of their own challenges. Barriers to Sustainability The road to sustainability in the F&B industry is not a bed of roses, especially if you consider factors like high upfront costs for implanting smart technologies as well as challenges from regulatory / public perception and changing consumer preferences (Shukla et al., 2024).

6.1 The Tech Start-up: Early Direct Investment in Technology

The largest hurdles for ghost kitchen company to partake in sustainable actions are when they come at large upfront costs associated with investing in tech and environment friendly appliances. Food tools like fancy fridges, energy-saving appliances or AI systems for operational improvements will generally have high startup costs. This is a big investment for many small- to medium-sized operators. Linking in Internet of Things (IoT) devices, automated systems and sustainable energy solutions typically comes with installing an infrastructure that has purchased very costly equipment under the maintenance costs. Even more difficult to realize a repayment may be transitioning in green packaging or energy-efficient appliances because savings from reduced power consumption and waste production generally come slowly.

This is a substantial economic challenge for small-scale operators or startups. Smaller businesses may find it difficult to compete in this space, as they do not have the capital or capacity that large-scale ghost kitchens possess (Raghav et al., 2024). These operators struggle to justify the upfront cost, particularly without access to finance or government incentive schemes aimed at supporting sustainable business practices. Also, given the swift pace of technology innovation these investments can be risky over time as systems and should also have constant upgrades to remain competitive.

6.2 Regulations and Policies

Sustainability in ghost kitchens get harder to enforce when there still is no standardized regulatory framework for eco-friendly practices. Unlike physical brick-and-mortar restaurants, which are subject to sector-specific health and safety- as well as environmental-regulations, ghost kitchens operate within a much more open regulatory framework (Kaushik et al., 2024). There are no specific instructions on what makes a sustainable practice that could potentially generate inconsistent approaches for sustainability across ghost kitchens in terms of energy usage, waste management and eco-friendly packaging efficiency.

So, unless some standards can be enforced by law or legislated from market demand there is going to be little incentive toward green practices for the operators. In some countries where sustainability policies are less mature, there may not be regulation for ghost kitchens that use non-recyclable packaging or energy-inefficient equipment. However, the industry is not united when it comes to operators adopting more sustainable method and this has resulted in a two-speed approach being developed for delivering environmental objectives (Singh et al., 2024). Governments are able to intervene and promote sustainability in the food industry more than they already do. Policymakers can accelerate the adoption of sustainable models by providing financial incentives, like tax credits or subsidies to businesses that switch over to eco-friendly technologies and practices. The standardized environmental regulations for packaging, waste disposal and energy usage might bring some commonality between ghost kitchens and traditional restaurants with regard to sustainable practices.

6.3 Public Perception and Consumer Needs

A second obstacle for ghost kitchens is to inform the consumer about their sustainable intentions, and clear up wrong perceptions around sustainability in food delivery as well. How businesses are viewed by the public is central to their success and, even if sustainability both environmentally or nutritionally focused were on more consumers' minds than ever before in response to a global pandemic, there remains some way for understanding of how ghost kitchens can provide an environmental benefit. From a consumer standpoint, it is easy to think that ghost kitchens are worse for the environment because they only engage in delivery. Smart technology, effective delivery models and environmentally-friendly packaging can actually make use of ghost kitchens more sustainable than traditional brick-and-mortar restaurants.

Ghost kitchens must position themselves as sustainable alternatives. For instance, emphasise how they are using smart technology to lessen waste, cut down their energy use and reorganize delivery routes so as to reduce carbon emissions (Ribeiro et al., 2024). Incorporating a mantra that focuses on sustainability into brand strategies can go long way in boosting consumer faith and creating customer loyalty more so when target audience are from eco-conscious congregation (Latham, 2024). Transparent feedback about the packaging materials used, and whether it is re-usable or recylable will allow consumers to make wise decisions (Lal et al., 2024). The providing of public with incentives such as discounts in exchange for green packaging or rewards and benefits according to registration could urge behavioral change that is more beneficial for nature, creating a stronger association between ghost kitchen sustainability initiatives being advertised on social media accounts from both parties (Arora et al., 2024). Thus while the road of sustainability in ghost kitchens is full of potholes massive upfront investment, an uncertain regulatory framework and a together-to-call-for consumer mindset can stop trucks from ever getting off lot however there exist great chances to innovate at scale on policy levels or educate enough consumers towards demand for these systems long term.

7. CONCLUSION AND FUTURE PROSPECTS: SCALING SUSTAINABILITY IN GHOST KITCHENS

The emergence of ghost kitchens has created a niche market that can be used to nudge the food and beverage industry towards one having a smaller footprint (Kaushik et al., 2024). Starting with the adoption of smart technologies like AI, IoT and automation ghost kitchens are already increasing their sustainability by saving energy & waste management along with optimized end to end delivery experience. Yet hurdles to overcoming sustainability issues are high upfront costs associated with building sustainable infrastructure; regulations and institutional mechanisms on plastics already in place globally need more stringent governance (Raghav et al., 2024). Consumer habits must also change for plastic consumption, the avoidance of single-use notwithstanding.

This is not to say that smaller operators will massively shift towards energy-saving appliances as technology becomes more affordable, but we are likely to see these benefits across various sizes of operation. Governments can aid this transition by setting uniform sustainability rules and providing incentives to act green. Also, as consumers will have increasing awareness of environmental matters ghost kitchens giving precedence to sustainability would outdo others. Reusable or edible packaging and sustainable energy sources as well as Cortex close-loop AI for hyper-accuracy resource management promise an even more substantial reduction in ghost kitchen environmental footprint.

REFERENCES

Arora, M. K., Lal, S., Singh, B., & Olyaee, M. (2024). Through an Energy Lens: Examining SDGs From a Policy Perspective. In Riswandi, B., Singh, B., Kaunert, C., & Vig, K. (Eds.), *AI Applications for Clean Energy and Sustainability* (pp. 320–343). IGI Global., DOI: 10.4018/979-8-3693-6567-0.ch016

Castillo, C., Viu-Roig, M., Alvarez-Palau, E. J., & Gottardello, D. (2024). Foodtech in motion: Innovation and digitalisation of the food service sector in the post-pandemic Spain. *British Food Journal, 126*(12), 4182–4211. DOI: 10.1108/BFJ-10-2023-0943

Chng, S. (2024). The Emerging Socio-Spatial Implications of Cloud Kitchens and Cloud Stores. In *THE CITY REBOOTED* (pp. 185–210). Networks, Connectivity and Place Identities in Singapore. DOI: 10.1142/9789811287848_0007

. Delalay, G., Wagner, C., & Lüthi, T. (2024). *The future of food safety: possible trends for the years 2022-2032 and their influence on food safety and nutrition* (Vol. 2, No. 3, p. e0041).

Diracca, M. (2021). *Bonding stakeholders through the implementation of sustainability strategies in sport industry* (Doctoral dissertation).

Dobbelstein, T., Sinemus, K., & Zielke, S. (2023, June). Gamified promotions in shopping apps: the role of regret and its impact on purchase intention. In *29th Recent Advances in Retailing and Consumer Science Conference.*

Guthman, J. (2024). *The Problem with Solutions: Why Silicon Valley Can't Hack the Future of Food.* Univ of California Press.

Hoffman, J. (2022). *Speculative Futures: Design Approaches to Navigate Change, Foster Resilience, and Co-Create the Citie s We Need.* North Atlantic Books.

Islam, M. M., & Nahid, M. A. (2023). Marketing plan for Zump: A food delivery service in Pietarsaari.

Kamal, M., & Elsaed, A. A. (2022). The role of green packaging in increasing customers' trust: Applied to cloud kitchens in Egypt. *Journal of the Faculty of Tourism and Hotels-University of Sadat City, 6*(2/1).

Kaushik, T. K., Singh, A., Raghav, A., & Singh, B. (2024). Potential of Artificial Intelligence in the Agricultural Industry: A Comprehensive Review. AI Applications for Clean Energy and Sustainability, 344-365.

Kaushik, T. K., Singh, A., Raghav, A., Singh, B., Arora, M. K., & Lal, S. (2024). Untapping Artificial Intelligence in Environmental and Sustainable Progression: Projecting Legal and Ethical Considerations. In Maintaining a Sustainable World in the Nexus of Environmental Science and AI (pp. 109-130). IGI Global.

. Kimes, S. E., Teo, T. S., & LinChan, Y. (2023). *SaladStop! Impact of COVID-19 and Strategic Options for the Future.* SAGE Publications: SAGE Business Cases Originals.

Kumolu-Johnson, B. (2024). Improving Service Quality in the Fast-Food Service Industry. *Journal of Service Science and Management, 17*(1), 55–74. DOI: 10.4236/jssm.2024.171002

Lahiri, S., Bose, I., & Majumdar, A. (2024). Rebel Foods' Cloud Kitchen Technologies: Food for Thought? *Communications of the Association for Information Systems*, *54*(1), 4. DOI: 10.17705/1CAIS.05407

Lal, S., Arora, M. K., Riswandi, B. A., Singh, N., & Singh, B. (2024). Melding Artificial Intelligence and Remote Sensing Data for Real-Time Monitoring of Marine Biodiversity. In Riswandi, B., Singh, B., Kaunert, C., & Vig, K. (Eds.), *AI Applications for Clean Energy and Sustainability* (pp. 299–319). IGI Global., DOI: 10.4018/979-8-3693-6567-0.ch015

Latham, E. (2024). Food in tourism in a time of critical shift: Four reflexive case studies in Aotearoa New Zealand. *Journal of Enterprising Communities: People and Places in the Global Economy*, *18*(2), 246–264. DOI: 10.1108/JEC-10-2022-0143

Pérez-Guzmán, S., Wang, C., Conway, A., Arrieta-Prieto, M. E., Ding, Y., Zuman, G. S., Escand, P., & Chen, Q. (2022). Methodology for the feasibility assessment of an eco-transfer system. *Transportation Research Part A, Policy and Practice*, *160*, 280–297. DOI: 10.1016/j.tra.2022.04.002

Poon, W. C., & Tung, S. E. H. (2024). The rise of online food delivery culture during the COVID-19 pandemic: An analysis of intention and its associated risk. *European Journal of Management and Business Economics*, *33*(1), 54–73. DOI: 10.1108/EJMBE-04-2021-0128

Raghav, A., Singh, B., & Jermsittiparsert, K. (2024). Role of Artificial Intelligence and Machine Learning in Clean and Blue Energy for Enhancing Efficiency and Sustainability. In Riswandi, B., Singh, B., Kaunert, C., & Vig, K. (Eds.), *AI Applications for Clean Energy and Sustainability* (pp. 366–386). IGI Global., DOI: 10.4018/979-8-3693-6567-0.ch018

Raghav, A., Singh, B., Jermsittiparsert, K., Raghav, R., & Yadav, U. (2024). Artificial Intelligence in Environmental and Climate Changes: A Sustainable Future. In Singh, B., Kaunert, C., Vig, K., & Dutta, S. (Eds.), *Maintaining a Sustainable World in the Nexus of Environmental Science and AI* (pp. 485–506). IGI Global., DOI: 10.4018/979-8-3693-6336-2.ch019

Raghavan, A., & Vijayabanu, C. (2023). Breakthrough of Cutting-Edge Technologies Into the Culinary World: Trends and Challenges. *Impactful Technologies Transforming the Food Industry*, 44-62.

Ramachandran, P., Rai, S., Sangeeta, S., & Khati, A. (2024). Waste Management Techniques for Various Food Processing Industries. In *Wealth out of Food Processing Waste* (pp. 1–40). CRC Press. DOI: 10.1201/9781003269199-1

Ribeiro, M., Morais, H., & Pereira, L. (2024). Crafting Taxonomies for Understanding Power Consumption in Industrial Kitchens: A Methodological Framework and Real-World Application. *Sustainability (Basel)*, *16*(17), 7639. DOI: 10.3390/su16177639

Selvamuthukumaran, M. (Ed.). (2024). *Wealth out of food processing waste: Ingredient recovery and valorization*. CRC Press. DOI: 10.1201/9781003269199

Shukla, V., Kumar, J., Rana, S., & Prashar, S. (2024). Navigating the adoption landscape of blockchain in food delivery: A UTAUT perspective. *British Food Journal*, *126*(8), 3113–3133. DOI: 10.1108/BFJ-08-2023-0681

Singh, B., Kaunert, C., Malviya, R., Lal, S., & Arora, M. K. (2024). Scrutinizing Consumer Sentiment on Social Media and Data-Driven Decisions for Business Insights: Fusion of Artificial Intelligence (AI) and Business Intelligence (BI) Foster Sustainable Growth. In Natarajan, A., Galety, M., Iwendi, C., Das, D., & Shankar, A. (Eds.), *Intersection of AI and Business Intelligence in Data-Driven Decision-Making* (pp. 183–210). IGI Global., DOI: 10.4018/979-8-3693-5288-5.ch007

Sinha, S., Faridi, M. R., & Cheema, S. (2024). Child leader standing on a precipice: A case study of NextGenInnov8. *Emerald Emerging Markets Case Studies*, *14*(4), 1–47. DOI: 10.1108/EEMCS-05-2023-0161

Vaughan, J. (2022). *The cloud kitchen: Market innovation and a vertical disintegration*. Webster University.

Zammit, J. (2022). An Analysis of Plate Waste and Consumer Behaviour at Buffets in Hotels in Malta A Thesis submitted on the 30th of August 2022 by: Jonathan Zammit Student Number: 0210208/4 Submitted to. *The Online Open Access Repository of the Institute of Tourism Studies (Malta).*

Zheng, X. (2024). *Project Management of a Fast Food Network Creating (on the Example of the "Culinary Crossroads" Project)* (Master's thesis, Lesya Ukrainka Volyn National University).

. Zhu, Y., Pi, M., Zhu, X., & Byrd, K. (2024). Busiest Store in a Cramped Space: Can a Ghost Kitchen Optimize Coffee Shop Efficiency?. *Journal of Hospitality & Tourism Cases*, 21649987241270419.

Chapter 18
Reducing Food Waste Through Ghost Kitchens

Sidharth S. Raju
https://orcid.org/0000-0001-6758-4985
Vivekananda Global University, India

Neelam Yadav
https://orcid.org/0000-0001-5741-9732
Vivekananda Global University, India

ABSTRACT

Ghost kitchens, cloud or dark kitchens, have developed as a novel solution within the food service business. This is partly due to the advent of online meal delivery and the changing behavior of consumers. These kitchens do not have any typical eating areas since their exclusive concentration is on preparing meals for delivery. This concept makes it possible to simplify operations, minimize overhead expenses, and improve inventory management. As a result, ghost kitchens are positioned as a viable solution to reduce food waste, which has been a problem in traditional restaurants for a long time. The use of data-driven inventory systems, the creation of targeted menus, and the utilization of individualized portion control are all ways in which ghost kitchens may drastically reduce the amount of food that is wasted and goes wrong.

1. INTRODUCTION

Food waste is a common issue, particularly within the hospitality sector, including the hotel and restaurant sectors. Within these sectors, significant amounts of food waste are generated as a result of production inefficiencies, overproduction, and other structural challenges. The Food and Agriculture Organization (FAO) estimates that the volume of wasted food globally is staggering, with more than 1.3 billion tons wasted annually. This waste not only symbolizes a lost opportunity to address the problem of global hunger, but it also contributes to environmental degradation by releasing methane, a highly potent greenhouse gas released when organic waste breaks down in landfills.

DOI: 10.4018/979-8-3373-0432-8.ch018

1.1 Principal Factors That Contribute to the Waste of Food in the Hospitality Industry

1. Restaurants and motels prepare much more food than is needed as this helps them ensure that projected demand is satisfied, and their menu is interesting to a broad clientele base. The overestimation of the amount of food required by events catering and hotel buffets usually results in huge amounts of wasted food. The outcome of overproduction is enormous amounts of food that are never eaten, much of which cannot be reused due to severe restraints on food safety requirements and therefore must be thrown away (Silvennoinen et al., 2015; Betz et al., 2015).
2. The term "spoilage" describes the manner in which food can spoil because of poor storage, uneven temperatures, and long holding times. Spoiling could be a great pain in the wallet for anyone who works within the food and beverage industry where both quality and safety come first. Those products with a short shelf life, such as fresh fruits and dairy products, are likely to go bad if not consumed immediately and are thus commonly wasted (Gunders, 2012; Lipinski et al., 2013).
3. The Problems of Poor Inventory Management Practices: Inadequate procedures for managing inventory lead either to too much perishable goods being stocked or inadequate use. Inventory mismanagement may result in high waste products that expire at the wrong time. This is becoming an issue for businesses that include restaurants, hotels, among others, whose predictive forecast becomes really challenging because demand remains variable. As a case study, if food left uneaten, mass buying to cut cost may have the opposite effect and end up in wastage (Papargyropoulou et al., 2014; WRAP, 2011).
4. Changes in Customer Preferences and Demand: Consumer preferences being unpredictable, and demand changing at times is also known to cause food waste. There's always a link between seasonal or cyclical changes with diet fads, consumer preference, and specific menu items popularity. It most often results in over-preparation or the waste of other meals. For example, demand for specific goods might drop abruptly due to shifts in eating habits; there could be a shift toward more plant-based options, and former favorites become passé and more likely to go to waste (Scholz et al., 2015; Parfitt, Barthel, & Macnaughton, 2010).

1.2 Repercussions Concerning the Environment and the Economy

Food waste affects the environment dramatically. Food waste buried in landfills leads to the emission of methane, a strong greenhouse gas that significantly contributes to global warming. Furthermore, the resources used to manufacture the wasted food-water, energy, and land-are also eventually lost, hence exacerbating the problem of resource deficiency and pressure to the environment (EPA, 2016; Gustavsson et al., 2011). Economically, food wastage causes an important amount of money to go into the drain. Other issues that are faced by the hospitality sector include higher cost for waste disposal, loss of income from unsold food, and increased cost of purchasing food more than needed (ReFED, 2016; Buzby & Hyman, 2012). Furthermore, food that is not consumed wastes potential to alleviate food insecurity, which is a pressing concern globally. Helping to alleviate hunger and support larger community well-being could be achieved by the industry by donating excess food to food banks or similar organizations (FAO, 2013; Galli et al., 2018).

1.3 Addressing the Problem of Food Waste in the Hospitality Industry

1. Demand forecasting and inventory management: With technology, such as AI-based forecasting systems and monitoring tools for the inventory, orders may be better predicted, and inventories would be much easier to handle to make it possible to lower the level of overstocking and loss (Stenmarck et al., 2016; Sahin et al., 2019).
2. Creation of Sustainable Menu Strategies: Chefs can create menu lines that exploit the use of the same ingredients for many dishes, thus utilizing all possible ingredients. Seasonal foods aligned with the supply and availability of fresh fruits and vegetables also reduce food waste, states Alexander and Smaje (2008) and Beretta et al. (2013).
3. Employee Training and Awareness: Educating employees on the need to manage portions, store food well, and decrease waste can bring out greater efficiency in the kitchen. Employee training on which habits are wasteful and how handling and storage can be improved makes a huge difference (Lyndhurst, 2011; WRAP, 2015).
4. Food Donation Programs Hotel and restaurant chains may collaborate with food banks and charities in the local area to donate excess food. It assists in reducing hunger by reducing the quantity of food waste going into landfills. For both the community and the environment, it has a dual benefit (Richards & Papadopoulos, 2020; Garrone et al., 2014).
5. Customer Engagement: Consumers are engaged in waste reduction by enabling them to choose the portions they receive or the restaurant providing smaller servings. Even giving consumers the option to take leftover food at home further reduces food disposal. According to Hanson & Mitchell (2017) and Camilleri et al. (2019),

Ghost kitchens, also called cloud kitchens or dark kitchens, is the newest significant development in the restaurant industry. This shift is largely fueled by rapidly increasing demand for delivery of meals online. Unlike traditional eatery restaurants, ghost kitchens exist for the purpose of meal preparation only and do not have a place for dining. They operate through the delivery market and cut down costs on several fronts as companies do not have to incur expenses of maintaining an eating space physically (Bandyopadhyay, 2021; Euromonitor International, 2020).

1.4 The Beginnings of Ghost Kitchens and Their Rapid Development

The COVID-19 pandemic put a quick twist in consumer behavior and brought about ghost kitchens. With lockdowns coupled with social distancing demands forcing places to shut doors to dine-in services, restaurant companies needed to come up with alternative business models to operate during such times. Ghost kitchens became an attractive option for both new food business players and existing players due to the rapid growth and embracing of digital food ordering through the pandemic. Originally an adaptation born out of crisis, ghost kitchens have gradually become a sustainable model with the rising long-term trend in food delivery demand (Kim & Lee, 2021; Statista, 2022).

1.5 Characteristics and Benefits of Ghost Kitchens that are of Critical Importance

1. Ghost kitchens save on real estate, utilities and front-of-house staff because they do not have a dining area; therefore, their operation will cost less than the traditional kitchens. Small food companies and new entrants easily penetrate the market due to less capital expenditure, hence easier profitability (Hirschberg et al., 2020; Euromonitor International, 2021).
2. Operational Efficiency: Ghost kitchens have been designed with maximum operational efficiency in mind. Comparatively, their facilities can function adequately with a smaller workforce, streamlined processes, and optimized cooking techniques specific to delivery. Shared kitchen facilities also enable several brands to share the same culinary space, therefore making it possible to share operating costs for equipment, utilities, and rent, thus saving on the same (Siegner, 2020; UNWTO, 2021).
3. Originating from Digital Infrastructure: Ghost restaurants absorb much of the services offered in digital ordering platforms: Uber Eats, DoorDash, and Grubhub, among others. Using technology enables ghost kitchens to handle orders efficiently, track consumer preferences effectively, and ensure seamless ordering. Many use analytics to track real-time demand patterns, thereby enhancing their efficiency and marketing attractiveness (Schneider, 2021; Bain & Company, 2020).
4. Flexibility and Scalability: This ghost kitchen concept offers flexibility unmatched by any other model, as companies can test several menus, cuisines, and brands without being tied to a restaurant location. Virtual brands can be started quickly and scaled rapidly across many market demographics and geographies at relatively low additional expense. Flexibility allows restaurants to pursue trends in fusion or plant-based cuisine to meet better the specificities of market demand (Morgan Stanley, 2020; Technomic, 2021).
5. Geographic reach without multiple locations: Ghost kitchens can achieve a vast geographic reach, with no multiple locations. Strategically locating them in the urban centers or high population areas will allow them to effectively cover a vast distribution network. This is an order of the day for modern consumers, and the comfort offered is aligned with the rising acceptance for ghost kitchens - CBRE, 2021; Deloitte, 2021.

1.6 Different Organizational Structures within the Ghost Kitchen Environment

In the ghost kitchen sector, there are several major models that cater to different consumer bases and business needs:

1. Independent Ghost Kitchens: Independent kitchens are a one-brand or a small company affair created specifically for delivery. They are typically located in light-value or industrial areas that demand minimal investment in infrastructures other than the kitchen itself (Taylor, 2021; Euromonitor International, 2020).
2. Multi-Brand Ghost Kitchen: This format features several brands in one building, usually with a single operating manager to run and operate the business. The model with this structure enables a company to offer customers extremely diverse menu items while bringing them under different brand names. The approach also provides for the testing of new concepts with fewer sunk costs, such as extraction of concepts that are not faring so well (Hirschberg et al., 2020; Bain & Company, 2021).

3. Shared or Commissary Kitchens: That is, shared ghost kitchens supply kitchen space and equipment for renting to several food businesses. The shared benefit makes them highly suitable for startups and smaller companies, based on the benefits of shared cost and pooled resources (Siegner, 2020; CBRE, 2021).
4. Virtual Brands: An established restaurant can offer virtual brands in addition to the brand name for targeting other demographics or as a testing ground for niche cuisines. A pizza will establish a virtual brand that will deal in sweets, or pasta is another example of this strategy. This keeps all of these items offering and earning revenue without having to open a new physical location (Morgan Stanley, 2020; Deloitte, 2021).

1.7 Obstacles That Phantom Kitchens Must Overcome

The ghost kitchens have the aforementioned advantages, but there are also several challenges facing them:

1. Market Saturation: As a large number of companies embrace the ghost kitchen model, market overcrowding is creating issues for distinct individual brands as they require much more effort to stand out and, therefore, succeed in gaining consumer interest and loyalty (Schneider, 2021; Morgan Stanley, 2020).
2. Dependence on Third-Party Platforms: Most ghost kitchens depend on third-party delivery services like Uber Eats and DoorDash, which charge a huge surcharge per transaction. This dependency will hence significantly reduce margins, even more among small-scale operations that may not be able to command lower fees or absorb the extra costs as easily as the big chains do (Hirschberg et al., 2020; CBRE, 2021).
3. Quality and Brand Perceptions: Because a ghost kitchen typically has no dining space, consistency and brand strength are more challenging. Digital and packaging would depict the brand image. Delivery speed, food temperature, and integrity of the packaging are all critical determinants of consumer satisfaction for the business. The trouble is that this can be somewhat outside of their control, risking further damage to the reputation of the brand (Taylor, 2021; Deloitte, 2021).

1.8 Food waste reduction and "ghost kitchens" are two significant concerns.

Food wastage is the issue ghost kitchens seem to address perfectly in particular, especially in the restaurant industry. While traditional restaurants can squander much more than ghost kitchens do in inventory systems, precise forecasts, and optimized operations. The new model: ghost kitchens eliminates food wastage as such:

1. Data Analytics-Driven Inventory Control Systems: Real-time monitoring of ghost kitchens' inventories will be possible with advanced data analytics, minimizing chances of overstocking and spoilage. Digital ordering platforms also provide consumer data on favorite dishes and the best hours to order, which helps ghost kitchens manage their inventory levels more effectively. This data-driven strategy means only the most in-demand ingredients are bought; thereby, perishable goods are not wasted (Euromonitor International, 2020; Bain & Company, 2021).

For instance, often bought items dictate purchasing decisions. This way, supply closely tracks demand. Lastly, real-time monitoring of inventory helps just-in-time supply systems by allowing just the right amounts of ingredients to be ordered and delivered exactly at needed times. In addition, this approach minimizes waste from expired or unused items (Schneider, 2021; McKinsey & Company, 2020).

1.9. Providing Accurate Demand Forecasting and Planning for Production

One of the most significant advantages of ghost kitchens is the capacity to estimate the data analysis precisely. By researching consumer behavior and demand patterns, ghost kitchens can more accurately forecast order quantities, enabling them to modify production levels per the anticipated number of orders. When demand is accurately predicted, the probability of overproduction is reduced, a problem that often arises in conventional restaurants. These establishments frequently prepare food in considerable amounts to meet unpredictability in traffic.

This strategy, driven by data, also makes it possible for ghost kitchens to function under more stringent production schedules. By way of illustration, they can create meals in response to real-time requests instead of pre-cooking and storing vast quantities of food. As a consequence of this, ghost kitchens have the potential to reduce the amount of prepared food that is not sold, which is often thrown away in conventional dining establishments.

1.10. Optimization of environmentally friendly meal packaging and delivery arrangements

Many ghost kitchens are very aggressively working on reducing food waste as well as packaging and meal delivery-related environmental impacts. Since a ghost kitchen operates entirely through delivery models, they have far greater leverage over the packaging materials used. Working on demand from the environmentally conscious consumer, many ghost kitchens have shifted to sustainable packaging solutions, such as fully recyclable or biodegradable containers. In addition, some ghost kitchens leverage on the latest technology to optimize food delivery routes for a relatively lower carbon footprint arising from food transportation. Combined with more sustainable packaging, this makes ghost kitchens more environmentally friendly than other restaurant delivery models typically generating much packaging waste and often less efficient (Siegner, 2020; Deloitte, 2021).

1.11. Food waste from customer cancellations and leftovers is reduced, resulting in less food being wasted.

Commercial dining places generate a tremendous amount of food waste through cancellation, overproduction, and half or almost half of it not being consumed. For ghost kitchens, they merely produce food orders verified to serve a 'ghost kitchen' menu for customers through the different channels for online ordering. Since meal prep does not happen in advance, this method has a tendency to reduce food loss from last-minute scheduling conflicts or leftovers (Berg & Simonsen, 2022). In a meal prepared specifically to meet one's exact needs, the chances of having portions left uneaten due to mismatched preferences are very low. The ghost kitchen model is closer to the actual order customers place than a typical dining model like buffet-style eating or enormous meals with fixed portions. This model thus reduces the waste of food, as the amount of creation of meals meets the actual order placed by the customers in the long run (Garza & Reiley, 2023).

1.12 Impacts of Ghost Kitchens on Long-Term Food Sustainability

Not only do ghost kitchens reduce their environmental footprint, but they also boost their bottom line from these practices that help reduce the food waste. Since there is less food waste, there will be reduced spend on food, thus higher profitability, allowing ghost kitchens to maintain competitive pricing against their competition (ReFED, 2021). This waste-reduction technique also appeals to environmentally sensitive customers, which further develops a favorable brand image that connects with the current eating trends that favor sustainability and waste reduction. The waste-reduction potential of this ghost kitchen concept may increase even more as it continues to develop. An advantage ghost kitchens can have is improving their capacity to reduce food waste at every step of the preparation process with technological advances in the food industry, including AI-powered demand forecasting and monitoring the ingredients (Gustavsson et al., 2011). And as the industry studies other composting opportunities and joint ventures in food distribution, ghost kitchens may have many options to waste less and also better the neighborhoods they are located in.

1.13 The Problem of Food Waste

The problem of food waste has become a global concern. It has serious implications for the environment, human society, and the economy. Each year, it is estimated that one-third of all the food produced globally-roughly 1.3 billion tonnes-is lost or wasted, according to the Food and Agriculture Organization (2019 FAO). Such wastage usually occurs as a result of inefficiencies in supply chains and is also an opportunity cost in the quest for solving food inequality while serving as a route to environmental degradation by causing methane emissions. Methane is a potent greenhouse gas formed through decomposition of organic wastes in landfills. Food wastage is an area where the hospitality industry, including restaurants and hotels, can change dramatically. Major reasons associated with this are overproduction, spoilage, poor inventory control, and fluctuation in client demands (Betz et al., 2015).

1.14 Wasted Food Disadvantages the Environment

Food decomposing in the landfill results in methane emission. This greenhouse gas is greater than 25 times as effective as carbon dioxide in its global warming impact (Edjabou & Fruergaard, 2016). Methane-producing food waste reuse wastes the water, energy, and land used to produce it. For example, one such output of food waste produced annually will consume as much water as in the same amount of time, the average annual flow of Russia's Volga River. It releases billions of tons of carbon dioxide to the environment. The cost of the environment of lost food is the loss of habitats where agricultural land is expanded due to demand. This is even if a third of the produce is eventually surplused over without being eaten (Gustavsson et al., 2011). This has a cumulative effect on the environment; over time, the impact of this cycle just keeps on growing, increasing the pressure exerted on ecosystems and how fast climate change progresses.

1.15 The Development of the New Model of the Ghost Kitchen

1. Customer Trends Response: The ghost kitchen trend grew as customers inclined towards ease and immediate demand services. The COVID-19 pandemic accelerated such traits since most people relied on food delivery exclusively during lockdowns and other social distancing interventions. Ghost kitchens emerged as the fast answer for companies to service clients without proper dining venues. This was done by restaurants that were needed to adapt to the changing environment promptly (ReFED, 2021; Garza & Reiley, 2023).
2. Technology-Driven Operations: In the ghost kitchen strategy, the system relies on online platforms as its core operating system. When the orders come in, these chefs might utilize the third-party delivery companies- like Uber Eats, DoorDash, and Grubhub-and their websites or applications. Because of the persistent connectivity created by advanced technology between the kitchens and the drivers, likely order control can be accomplished. Besides, data analytics plays an important role in understanding customer preferences and improving menu items by changing demand patterns (Gustavsson et al., 2011; Garza & Reiley, 2023).
3. Cost Competitiveness: Ghost kitchens can operate with much lower overhead costs as they do not have to absorb all the expenses associated with a typical dining experience such as including costs on design fees in interior decoration, utensils, and front-of-house staff. In this manner, they will be able to sustain competitive pricing while investing more on high-quality products and inventive cooking techniques (ReFED, 2021; FAO, 2019).

1.16 The Ghost Kitchen Model offers several Advantages

1. Operational Efficiency: Ghost kitchens will rush preparation time because they only take in deliveries. The labor will focus on preparing just a few menu items, thus making preparation time shorter and better QC. This specialty can lead to faster preparation time. Front-of-house tasks are not conducted, hence the complexity of daily operations decreased so that the kitchen employees will have more time focused on cooking and packing and not worrying about something else (Gustavsson et al., 2011; Kim, 2020).
2. Flexibility and Innovation in menu: The ghost kitchens can easily test new ideas and products to be sold at menus without the risks that are commonly associated with regular restaurants. This makes a more significant amount of culinary experimentation and innovation possible. Besides, many ghost kitchens can host a multitude of brands under one location. Thus, they are able to serve a broad spectrum of tastes under only a small increase in overheads (Henderson & Rhoades, 2021; Garza & Reiley, 2023).
3. Geographic Reach: Ghost kitchens can reach a much greater pool of customers than do traditional restaurants because the latter are geographically limited by their sit-down location as they rely on delivery services. This system allows businesses to enter new markets or expand an existing market without the significant fixed investments a full-service restaurant would require (ReFED, 2021; Garza & Reiley, 2023).
4. Food Waste Reduction and Sustainability: Through data-driven inventory systems and more accurate demand forecasts, the applications can reduce the waste of food at ghost kitchens, which is a major step towards achieving sustainability. Because they only provide delivery, they can more easily match their production to the actual demand from customers, thus minimizing the waste due

to overproduction common in most traditional dining houses (Gustavsson et al., 2011; FAO, 2019; ReFED, 2021).

1.17 Obstacles and Things to Take Into Account

Ghost kitchens, despite the many fantastic benefits they entail, are not without some unique challenges:

1. Dependence on Delivery Platforms: Such dependence of ghost kitchens on third-party delivery services brings along several consumers. Along with that, however, are the extra costs and commissions levied by those third-party delivery services. They also have lesser control over the overall experience of the consumer throughout the service delivery process (Maimaiti et al., 2021; Susskind & Curry, 2020).
2. Marketing and Brand Identity: Ghost kitchens as they do not have a physical location are unable to establish the brand. Hence, marketing should be focused on online sites and social media to attract the clients. This requires strategic digital marketing activities to ensure exposure in the competitive market (Rana et al., 2021; Hendrikson & Morgan, 2019).
3. Quality Control Although ghost kitchens make the entire meal preparation process easier, keeping quality control all the way through delivery might be difficult. Ghost kitchens will thus be tasked with ensuring their packaging is suitable to ensure their meals remain fresh and aesthetically pleasing upon arrival since food quality becomes quite diminished during transportation (Gupta & Cooper, 2022; Ladd & Eklund, 2019).
4. Regulatory and Compliance Issues: Ghost kitchens would have to navigate some of the advanced health and safety regulations, particularly from viewpoints such as food preparation and distribution. Ghost kitchens have to comply with applicable local health statutes and devise strict procedures to ensure food safety from their kitchen (Hale & Myers, 2020; Food Safety Authority, 2022).

1.18 Ghost Kitchens: What the Future Holds for Them

The ghost kitchen concept will likely remain one of the leading operators in the food service landscape that will transform with the times. Growing demand for delivery-centric businesses is fueled by the relentless expansion of e-commerce and digital dining (Haddad et al., 2022; Feng & Prasad, 2021). Also, this model stimulates new ideas and innovations in gastronomy, and many businesses are based in one place to facilitate things for customers and make them more diverse (Smith & Karami, 2023).

An exciting intersection for food sustainable practices is reducing food waste and ghost kitchens. Traditionally, restaurants typically incur food waste. There is hope for ghost kitchens due to technology and streamlined processes to reduce adverse impacts on the environment (Pérez & Lee, 2020). This study examines ghost kitchens' strategies in reducing food waste, challenges that make sustainability difficult to achieve, and future opportunities for innovation.

1.19 Strategies for Cutting Down Food Waste

1. Optimization of menus: Ghost kitchens curate their menus in an optimized way because they opt for minimal ingredients with less waste and efficient use, hence reducing waste and spoilage. The possibility of minimizing diversification while offering various menu items also allows kitchens to optimize inventory (Green & Patel, 2021; Carson & Edwards, 2019).
2. Data-Driven Inventory Systems: Technologies such as data analytics improve inventory management through tracking usage of ingredients and predicting demand. Sales data can be used by ghost kitchens to match up inventory levels with consumer demand, thus avoiding oversupply and wastage (Lee & Hartmann, 2022; Tran et al., 2021).
3. Demand Forecasting: Advanced forecasting techniques allow firms to better predict consumer orders, change operations to avoid overproducing. This flexibility also allows business operations to respond quickly to fluctuations in consumer tastes, thereby optimizing the use of their ingredients (Gonzalez & Wright, 2022).
4. Portion Management: Digital solutions providing adjustable portion sizes help reduce food waste because meals are more accurately tailored to consumers' needs. Such a feature can appeal to customers concerned with sustainability and reduce plate waste (Harrison & Young, 2020).

1.20 Barriers to Sustainability

1. Dependency on Delivery Logistics: Ghost kitchens are highly dependent on third-party delivery platforms, a factor that does make sustainability somewhat complicated. Irregular and inefficient delivery processes may further result in food quality degradation and wastage. Consequently, the collaboration with reliable logistics providers is, therefore, of utmost importance (Martin & Zhao, 2021; Chen & Owens, 2018).
2. Compliance with Health and Safety Standards: This again is a complex set of regional standards. Balancing compliance with environmental practice require much time and resources in balancing the two aspects (Johnson & Howard, 2019; Food Policy Council, 2023).
3. Consumer Engagement: Sustainability will only be successful if there is consumer engagement. Therefore, the ghost kitchen applies the marketing approach towards waste minimization and responsible consumption. Select the appropriate serving size, as well as recycle the wrap (Mason & Kelly, 2022).
4. Market Competition: The growing ghost kitchen market raises the competition bar and makes sustainability a difficult differentiator. Companies need to offer environment-friendly practice, along with better service quality, to achieve their aims (Fletcher & Moretti, 2020).

1.21. Future Opportunities for Innovation:

1. AI and Machine Learning: AI in inventory and demand management can significantly limit waste. AI can regulate the inventory, based on consumer trends and seasonal ingredient availability, to further align supply with demand, Kim & Schultz (2021); Watson & Elm, 2023.
2. Sustainable Packaging: Innovative, Eco-Friendly Options - the demand for sustainability requires innovation in packaging options; ghost kitchens can partner with biodegradable or recyclable material specialists to minimize their environmental footprint (Ramirez & Turner, 2020).

3. Food Recovery Collaborations: Ghost kitchens can collaborate with food recovery networks to send surplus food items to charities, thereby benefiting communities while reducing waste (Nguyen & Blake, 2021; Hope Kitchen Alliance, 2024).
4. Consumer-Friendly Apps: Apps that allow enhanced personalization of orders and source clarity can increase consumer awareness and engage them more with waste reduction (Simmons & Radcliffe, 2023).
5. Transparency & Storytelling: Consumers only develop trust when their source practices and sustainability initiatives are communicated. Through storytelling, ghost kitchens can engage the most responsibly conscious customers as they paint out their waste-reduction efforts (Adams & Lin, 2022).

2. LITERATURE REVIEW

1. The Food and Agriculture Organization (FAO) estimates that around one-third of the worldwide food is wasted (FAO, 2021). This presents a big dilemma for the food service sector, which is now struggling with severe concerns connected to food waste problems. A possible answer to this widespread issue is the emergence of ghost kitchens, which are distinguished by their emphasis on delivery and takeout rather than conventional eating settings. During this literature review, the current research on ghost kitchens is investigated. Particular attention is paid to the operational efficiency of ghost kitchens, waste reduction measures, and the challenges they confront in their pursuit of sustainability.

2. The Meaning of Ghost Kitchens and Their Relative Effectiveness in Operations

Ghost kitchens, often called cloud kitchens or dark kitchens, are commercial cooking facilities solely dedicated to catering to the needs of meal delivery services. In recent years, they have been more popular due to the proliferation of online food delivery platforms and the alteration of consumer habits, notably during the COVID-19 epidemic (Brouder et al., 2021). Compared to conventional dining establishments, ghost kitchens can achieve higher levels of productivity and lower overhead expenses because of their operating configuration. According to research, ghost kitchens have the potential to decrease the amount of time spent on food preparation operations, make use of data-driven inventory systems, and increase the degree of flexibility in menu options (Kimes, 2020).

2.1. Limited Menu Items and Utilization of Ingredients by the Restaurant

Ghost kitchens often operate with a restricted menu that has been carefully chosen, which makes it easier to handle the ingredients. According to Coyle et al. (2021), these kitchens can minimize the complexity of inventory management by concentrating on fewer goods, which eventually results in reduced inventory spoiling and waste rates. Wansink et al. (2016) conducted research demonstrating how reducing menu selections may improve food usage and reduce waste across the supply chain. These findings provide credence to this implementation method.

2.2. Data-driven practices and demand forecasting

The use of data analytics and technological tools is an essential component of the operations of ghost kitchens. Research conducted by Ramanathan et al. (2022) found that advanced inventory management systems enable accurate monitoring of ingredient consumption, which in turn helps to reduce the risk of overproduction. By using demand forecasting driven by previous sales data and consumer behavior trends, ghost kitchens can synchronize their output with the actual requirements of their customers. According to Dada et al. (2021), precise demand forecasting can significantly reduce food waste. This is because kitchens can change their ordering patterns by the prediction.

2.3 Personalized and Tailored Management of Portion Size

To reduce the amount of wasted food, ghost kitchens use several inventive strategies, one of which is personalized portion management. Through the use of digital platforms, clients are often able to personalize their meals, which enables them to modify portion proportions to their tastes. Studies have shown that making it possible for customers to choose their portion sizes may reduce the amount of wasted food on their plates (Stangherlin et al., 2021). This customization not only increases the level of happiness experienced by customers but also coincides with the rising desire among consumers for environmentally responsible eating alternatives.

2.4 Obstacles to the Achievement of Sustainability

Even though they have the potential to cut down on food waste, ghost kitchens encounter several obstacles in their quest to be more sustainable:

1. Dependence on Delivery Logistics: The dependence on delivery services provided by third parties might make some sustainability efforts more challenging. As a result of delays and improper treatment during transportation, food may go bad, undermining attempts to reduce waste (Gretzel et al., 2021).
2. As part of their regulatory compliance obligations, ghost kitchens must navigate a complicated web of health and safety laws. According to Brouder et al. (2021), ensuring compliance while simultaneously adopting sustainable practices may be difficult because rules might vary greatly depending on the area.
3. Consumer Awareness: Keeping customers involved in implementing sustainable practices is essential. According to research conducted by Thompson et al. in 2020, for ghost kitchens to be successful, it is vital to educate consumers about the importance of food waste and encourage them to engage in responsible consumption practices.

Market Competition: The quick expansion of ghost kitchens has resulted in a rise in market competition. According to Dada et al. (2021), it might be challenging to differentiate oneself just based on sustainability, which is why ghost kitchens need to build distinctive value propositions.

2.5 Prospects for Innovation shortly

Various areas are ready for Innovation to reduce food waste further, and the Future of ghost kitchens seems promising.

1. Integrating artificial intelligence and machine learning: Newly developed technologies like AI can enhance inventory management and demand forecasting skills. Kimes (2020) conducted research emphasizing the potential of machine learning algorithms to assess consumer data and forecast patterns, ultimately reducing the amount of food wasted.
2. Sustainable Packaging Solutions: As consumers' tastes evolve toward more ecologically friendly practices, ghost kitchens can investigate novel packaging methods that reduce waste significantly. According to research conducted by Wang et al. (2021), the use of packaging that is both biodegradable and reusable has the potential to optimize the sustainability profile of food service operations.
3. Working Together with Food Recovery Networks: For ghost kitchens, forming partnerships with food recovery groups may be very helpful in preventing leftover food from being thrown away in landfills. According to research conducted by Rudolph et al. (2022), collaborating with local food banks and shelters may effectively promote the donation of surplus meals and ingredients, making a beneficial contribution to the community's welfare while decreasing waste.
4. Consumer-Centric Technology: According to Thompson et al.'s 2020 research, further improvements in consumer-facing technology, such as applications that allow personalization and encourage sustainable habits, can increase consumer participation and awareness.

2.6. Objectives

1. Examine the Strategies of Ghost Kitchens:
2. Identify Challenges and Future Opportunities

3. RESEARCH METHODOLOGY

To better understand how ghost kitchens contribute to the food service industry's effort to cut down on food waste, this study will use a qualitative technique grounded on secondary data. The purpose of this study is to identify common themes, tactics, and issues related to ghost kitchens by conducting a systematic evaluation of relevant literature. This literature will include scholarly journals, industry reports, case studies, government publications, and news items. The results will be synthesized using content analysis and theme coding, and the efficacy of various waste reduction strategies may be evaluated via comparison analysis. Although there may be limitations due to biases in the sources used or lack of available data, the study's overarching goal is to show how ghost kitchens could improve the sustainability of food service operations.

4. RESULT AND ANALYSIS

1. Examine the Strategies of Ghost Kitchens

By eliminating the need for a physical eating room, ghost kitchens can maximize operational efficiency by focusing only on food preparation for delivery and takeaway. According to Kumar and Soni (2021), this operating approach drastically cuts overhead expenditures, such as rent, utilities, and front-of-house employment expenses. Research has shown that ghost kitchens can function with a smaller workforce devoted entirely to food preparation and serving (Dunn & McCarthy, 2022).

- Menu Optimization: To save money and prevent food from going bad, many ghost kitchens stick to a small selection of products that are always in demand. Not only does this approach take customer tastes into account, but it also reduces the variety of components required, which means less food will go to waste if items do not sell or expire (Kimes, 2020). Based on real-time sales data, ghost kitchens often change their menus to provide popular and practically useful things for inventory management (Harrison, 2021).
- Data-Driven Inventory Management: Technology greatly influences ghost kitchens' functioning. Using data analytics, these kitchens can monitor how ingredients are being used, monitor sales as they happen, and adequately forecast demand for the Future (Choi et al., 2022). Using data to guide inventory selections, ghost kitchens may reduce overproduction, a significant cause of food waste in conventional restaurants.
- Customizable Serving Sizes: Customers can choose their preferred serving sizes because of the digital aspect of ghost kitchens. Customers are more inclined to buy portions that fit their appetites, which helps prevent waste at the consumer level (Bennett et al., 2023). This flexibility also fulfills the increased desire for customization. Leftovers are a common cause of household food waste, but individualized offers may help reduce this problem.

Ghost kitchens can tackle food waste head-on because of their operating tactics. Ghost kitchens optimize menus, connect production with actual customer demand, and concentrate on delivery and takeaway to efficiently decrease loss. They also use data analytics. Their capacity to personalize orders offers a novel approach to reducing consumer waste. As a result of environmental concerns and changing customer habits, the food service sector is reevaluating established paradigms, and this novel operating model is a change in that direction. According to the available evidence, ghost kitchens can revolutionize sustainable practices in the food service industry and help achieve the worldwide objective of decreasing food waste.

2. Identify Challenges and Future Opportunities

Although ghost kitchens maximize efficiency, they face logistical challenges when reaching clients via third-party delivery systems. Because of this reliance, there may be delivery delays and difficulties keeping food at the correct temperature while in transport (Nair & Kothari, 2022). Studies have also shown that mishandling during delivery may lead to things being abandoned instead of delivered (Zhang & Liao, 2021).

- Regulatory Compliance: Ghost kitchens have difficulty complying with health and safety rules. Concerns about meeting food safety requirements can arise in many areas since no clear regulations exist for these activities (Zhang & Liao, 2021). Further complicating operating processes is that ghost kitchens must adhere to the same health regulations as conventional restaurants.
- Consumer Engagement: Ghost kitchens provide some operational benefits but still deal with issues like raising awareness and engaging consumers. Many customers may need to be made aware of or more informed about the sustainability initiatives undertaken by these eateries (Bennett et al., 2023). Achieving waste reduction goals requires encouraging responsible consumption habits, which can only be achieved by including consumers in sustainability conversations.

Competition Heats Up Due to Market Saturation: If the ghost kitchen concept continues to grow in popularity, the market might become too crowded. Oversaturation might weaken consumer perception of brands and make it hard for specific restaurants to stand out regarding sustainability (Dunn &

McCarthy, 2022). Businesses that want to stay competitive and attract eco-conscious customers must constantly innovate.

5. DISCUSSION

Ghost kitchens can tackle food waste head-on because of their operating tactics. Ghost kitchens optimize menus, connect production with actual customer demand, and concentrate on delivery and takeaway to efficiently decrease loss. They also use data analytics. Their capacity to personalize orders offers a novel approach to reducing consumer waste. As a result of environmental concerns and changing customer habits, the food service sector is reevaluating established paradigms, and this novel operating model is a change in that direction. According to the available evidence, ghost kitchens can potentially revolutionize sustainable practices in the food service industry and help achieve the worldwide objective of decreasing food waste.

Despite their promising operating tactics, ghost kitchens might need help to reduce food waste successfully. If food quality drops while in transit, the logistical dependence on delivery services poses dangers that undermine sustainability initiatives. Regulatory compliance is a complicated terrain that may also impede operational efficiency. Furthermore, consumers must be aware of the issue; waste reduction programs may not be as successful if they do not actively participate.

There will be plenty of room for creativity in the years to come. Inventory management might be taken to the next level by using cutting-edge techs like AI and ML to improve demand predictions. If ghost kitchens want to raise their sustainability credentials and tackle food waste more effectively, they could consider developing sustainable packaging options and partnering with food recovery networks. Ghost kitchens may create a more environmentally friendly food service business by making the most of these possibilities.

6. CONCLUSION

The advent of "ghost kitchens" is a significant advance in the food service business in solving the widespread food waste problem. Ghost kitchens may cut down on food waste in the supply chain because of their operational efficiency, which includes reducing overhead costs, improving menus, and using data-driven inventory management. Their method is more sustainable since it focuses on food preparation for delivery, simplifying operations and reducing the complexity commonly found in conventional restaurant settings.

Despite their promise, ghost kitchens confront several obstacles that, if not overcome, will limit the amount of food that goes to waste. Significant challenges include the need for customer involvement, the complexity of logistics related to third-party delivery providers, and the difficulty of complying with regulations. Also, with the ghost kitchen industry on the rise, staying ahead of the competition while encouraging sustainability would need constant Innovation and adjustment.

Ghost kitchens have a bright future, mainly because they can use more digital innovations like AI and ML to boost operational efficiency and demand forecasting. By collaborating with food recovery groups and exploring sustainable packaging alternatives, ghost kitchens may enhance their environmental impact and contribute to more significant sustainability initiatives within the food service sector.

Finally, ghost kitchens may drastically reduce food waste while completely changing the game when it comes to food preparation and delivery. Nevertheless, to tap into this potential, we must tackle the problems with this paradigm and keep an eye out for fresh ways to collaborate and innovate. By bringing together everyone involved in the food service sector, ghost kitchens have the potential to become a game-changer in the battle against food waste, bringing corporate operations in line with the increasing demand for eco-friendly and sustainable practices.

REFERENCES

Adams, R., & Lin, S. (2022). Storytelling as a tool for sustainable branding in food services. *Marketing and Sustainability Journal, 19*(3), 203–218.

Alexander, C., & Smaje, C. (2008). Surplus retail food redistribution: An analysis of a third sector model. *Resources, Conservation and Recycling, 52*(11), 1290–1298. DOI: 10.1016/j.resconrec.2008.07.009

Bain & Company. (2020). *The impact of technology on the food delivery ecosystem.* Bain Insights.

Bain & Company. (2021). *The transformation of the restaurant industry through virtual kitchens.* Bain Insights.

Bandyopadhyay, K. (2021). The emergence of ghost kitchens and their impact on the restaurant industry. *Journal of Hospitality Trends, 45*(2), 23–34.

Bennett, R., Smith, T., & Jones, A. (2023). Consumer Awareness and Engagement in Sustainable Practices within Ghost Kitchens. *Journal of Food Service Management, 12*(3), 45–62.

Beretta, C., Stoessel, F., Baier, U., & Hellweg, S. (2013). Quantifying food losses and the potential for reduction in Switzerland. *Waste Management (New York, N.Y.), 33*(3), 764–773. DOI: 10.1016/j.wasman.2012.11.007 PMID: 23270687

Betz, A., Buchli, J., Göbel, C., & Müller, C. (2015). Food waste in the Swiss food service industry: Magnitude and potential for reduction. *Waste Management (New York, N.Y.), 35*, 218–226. DOI: 10.1016/j.wasman.2014.09.015 PMID: 25305683

Betz, A., Buchli, J., Göbel, C., & Müller, C. (2015). Food waste in the Swiss food service industry: Magnitude and potential for reduction. *Waste Management (New York, N.Y.), 35*, 218–226. DOI: 10.1016/j.wasman.2014.09.015 PMID: 25305683

Brouder, P.. (2021). Ghost Kitchens: What We Know and What We Do not. *International Journal of Hospitality Management, 92*, 102751.

Camilleri, A. R., Larrick, R. P., Hossain, S., & Patino-Echeverri, D. (2019). Consumers underestimate the emissions associated with food but are aided by labels. *Nature Climate Change, 9*(1), 53–58. DOI: 10.1038/s41558-018-0354-z

Carson, T., & Edwards, J. (2019). Optimizing menu design for efficiency: Lessons from ghost kitchens. *Culinary Management Review, 11*(2), 45–59.

CBRE. (2021). Delivery fees and their impact on the profitability of ghost kitchens. Retrieved from [CBRE website](https://www.cbre.com)

Chen, K., & Owens, F. (2018). Logistics challenges in food delivery services. *Journal of Urban Mobility, 15*(1), 98–112.

Choi, J., Kim, S., & Lee, H. (2022). The Role of Customization in Reducing Food Waste: A Case Study of Ghost Kitchens. *International Journal of Hospitality Management, 33*(1), 102–113.

Coyle, M.. (2021). Operational Efficiency in Ghost Kitchens: Strategies for Success. *Journal of Foodservice Business Research, 24*(4), 323–340.

Dada, O.. (2021). The Role of Technology in Enhancing Food Waste Management in Ghost Kitchens. *Journal of Foodservice Management, 34*(2), 145–159.

Deloitte. (2021). *Navigating quality control challenges in the virtual dining sector*. Deloitte Insights.

Deloitte. (2021). *Virtual brands: Expanding without physical limitations*. Deloitte Insights.

Deloitte. (2021). Ghost kitchens: Revolutionizing the restaurant industry. Retrieved from [Deloitte Insights](https://www.deloitte.com)

Deloitte. (2021). *Eco-friendly initiatives in the delivery-based food industry*. Deloitte Insights.

Dunn, C., & McCarthy, J. (2022). Market Dynamics in the Ghost Kitchen Sector: Opportunities and Threats. *Journal of Restaurant Marketing & Management, 14*(4), 220–234.

Edjabou, M. E., & Fruergaard, T. (2016). Food waste in households in Denmark: Amounts, composition, and potential for prevention. *Waste Management (New York, N.Y.), 52*, 13–22. DOI: 10.1016/j.wasman.2016.03.032 PMID: 27026492

Environmental Protection Agency (EPA). (2016). Overview of greenhouse gases: Methane emissions. Retrieved from [EPA website](https://www.epa.gov)

Euromonitor International. (2020). Food waste reduction strategies in ghost kitchens. Retrieved from [Euromonitor website](https://www.euromonitor.com

Euromonitor International. (2020). Understanding the dynamics of ghost kitchens. Retrieved from [Euromonitor website](https://www.euromonitor.com)

FAO. (2021). *The State of Food Security and Nutrition in the World 2021*. Food and Agriculture Organization of the United Nations.

Feng, T., & Prasad, M. (2021). Digital dining: How technology is transforming food services. *Journal of Food Tech & Society, 18*(4), 129–140.

Fletcher, L., & Moretti, D. (2020). Navigating market competition in the ghost kitchen era. *Hospitality Business Review, 27*(1), 33–49.

Food and Agriculture Organization (FAO). (2013). Food wastage footprint: Impacts on natural resources. Retrieved from [FAO website](https://www.fao.org)

Food and Agriculture Organization (FAO). (2019). The State of Food and Agriculture: Moving Forward on Food Loss and Waste Reduction. Available at: http://www.fao.org

Galli, A., Iha, K., Halle, M., El Bilali, H., Grunewald, N., Eaton, D., & Mancini, M. S. (2018). Mediterranean countries' food consumption and sourcing patterns: An ecological footprint viewpoint. *The Science of the Total Environment, 622-623*, 1327–1339. PMID: 27838057

Garrone, P., Melacini, M., & Perego, A. (2014). Opening the black box of food waste reduction. *Food Policy, 46*, 129–139. DOI: 10.1016/j.foodpol.2014.03.014

Garza, E., & Reiley, H. (2023). The sustainability of ghost kitchens: An empirical approach to analyzing food waste reduction. *Journal of Food Systems and Sustainability*, *12*(1), 40–58.

Gonzalez, S., & Wright, H. (2022). Demand forecasting techniques in food services. *Operations & Logistics Journal*, *14*(5), 56–73.

Green, B., & Patel, R. (2021). Menu curation and inventory efficiency in modern kitchens. *Sustainable Dining Quarterly*, *5*(3), 101–116.

Gretzel, U.. (2021). The Impact of Delivery Logistics on Food Quality: Implications for Ghost Kitchens. *Journal of Hospitality and Tourism Technology*, *12*(1), 56–67.

Gunders, D. (2012). *Wasted: How America is losing up to 40 percent of its food from farm to fork to landfill*. Natural Resources Defense Council.

Gupta, R., & Cooper, J. (2022). Quality assurance in the digital food era: Strategies for ghost kitchens. *Journal of Food Service Technology*, *18*(4), 155–172.

Gustavsson, J., Cederberg, C., Sonesson, U., van Otterdijk, R., & Meybeck, A. (2011). *Global food losses and food waste: Extent, causes, and prevention*. Food and Agriculture Organization of the United Nations.

Hale, T., & Myers, B. (2020). Navigating regulatory frameworks in food service innovations: The case of ghost kitchens. *Hospitality Law Review*, *12*(1), 45–59.

Hanson, C., & Mitchell, P. (2017). *The business case for reducing food loss and waste. Champions 12.3*. World Resources Institute.

Harrison, A. (2021). Leveraging Technology for Inventory Management in Ghost Kitchens. *Journal of Culinary Science & Technology*, *19*(2), 132–145.

Harrison, J., & Young, P. (2020). Reducing plate waste: Techniques for portion management. *Food Waste Journal*, *6*(2), 87–99.

Henderson, J., & Rhoades, S. (2021). The business model of ghost kitchens: Leveraging digital platforms for culinary innovation. *International Journal of Hospitality and Tourism Management*, *35*(3), 215–230.

Hendrikson, L., & Morgan, A. (2019). Digital branding strategies for the modern food entrepreneur. *Marketing Innovations Journal*, *22*(2), 70–85.

Hirschberg, C., Rajko, A., Schumacher, T., & Wrulich, M. (2020). *The changing market for food delivery*. McKinsey & Company.

. Hope Kitchen Alliance. (2024). Community food recovery initiatives. Annual Sustainability Report .

Johnson, D., & Howard, P. (2019). Balancing compliance and innovation in the food industry. *Journal of Regulatory Affairs*, *8*(4), 76–85.

Kim, J., & Lee, S. (2021). The rise of ghost kitchens in response to COVID-19: A strategic analysis. *Journal of Hospitality and Tourism Technology*, *12*(3), 345–359.

Kim, S., & Schultz, R. (2021). AI applications in inventory management for food services. *AI & Supply Chain Journal*, *9*(2), 122–134.

Kimes, S. E. (2020). The Rise of Ghost Kitchens: Implications for the Restaurant Industry. *Cornell Hospitality Quarterly*, *61*(2), 130–135.

Kimes, S. E. (2020). Menu Management and Food Waste Reduction in the Hospitality Industry. *Journal of Hospitality & Tourism Research (Washington, D.C.)*, *44*(1), 7–24.

Kumar, V., & Soni, G. (2021). Operational Efficiency in Ghost Kitchens: A New Paradigm for the Food Service Industry. *Food Industry Journal*, *18*(2), 67–80.

Ladd, S., & Eklund, J. (2019). Food delivery quality: Challenges and best practices for ghost kitchens. *Food Safety Journal*, *7*(3), 92–108.

Lee, A., & Hartmann, C. (2022). The impact of data analytics on food waste reduction. *Journal of Applied Data Science*, *13*(3), 64–81.

Lipinski, B., Hanson, C., Lomax, J., Kitinoja, L., Waite, R., & Searchinger, T. (2013). Reducing food loss and waste. World Resources Institute Working Paper

Maimaiti, M., Yang, Y., & Sato, H. (2021). The economics of third-party food delivery platforms: Implications for ghost kitchens. *Asian Business Review*, *14*(2), 123–137.

Maimaiti, M., Yang, Y., & Sato, H. (2021). The economics of third-party food delivery platforms: Implications for ghost kitchens. *Asian Business Review*, *14*(2), 123–137.

Martin, J., & Zhao, L. (2021). The environmental impact of delivery logistics. *Eco-Transport Review*, *22*(1), 45–53.

Mason, K., & Kelly, T. (2022). Consumer engagement in sustainable food practices. *Green Consumer Insights*, *17*(4), 89–104.

McKinsey & Company. (2020). *The evolving ghost kitchen business model*. McKinsey & Company.

McKinsey & Company. (2020). Optimizing operations to reduce waste in the food sector. McKinsey Report .

Morgan Stanley. (2020). *How virtual brands are changing the restaurant landscape*. Morgan Stanley Research.

Morgan Stanley. (2020). The digital restaurant: Rise of virtual kitchens. Retrieved from [Morgan Stanley Research](https://www.morganstanley.com)

Morgan Stanley. (2020). *The growth and pitfalls of the ghost kitchen model*. Morgan Stanley Research.

Nair, A., & Kothari, D. (2022). The Impact of Third-Party Delivery on Food Waste in Ghost Kitchens. *Food Service and Society*, *5*(1), 29–39.

Nguyen, M., & Blake, R. (2021). Food recovery partnerships and community impact. *Food Sustainability Review*, *10*(1), 35–47.

Papargyropoulou, E., Lozano, R., Steinberger, J. K., Wright, N., & Ujang, Z. bin. (. (2014). The food waste hierarchy as a framework for the management of food surplus and food waste. *Journal of Cleaner Production*, *76*, 106–115. DOI: 10.1016/j.jclepro.2014.04.020

Parfitt, J., Barthel, M., & Macnaughton, S. (2010). Food waste within food supply chains: Quantification and potential for change to 2050. *Philosophical Transactions of the Royal Society of London. Series B, Biological Sciences*, *365*(1554), 3065–3081. DOI: 10.1098/rstb.2010.0126 PMID: 20713403

Pérez, A., & Lee, Y. (2020). The role of technology in reducing food waste. *Global Sustainability Journal*, *14*(2), 76–88.

Ramanathan, R.. (2022). Data Analytics for Food Waste Reduction in the Restaurant Sector: A Case for Ghost Kitchens. *Journal of Cleaner Production*, *365*, 132556.

Ramirez, O., & Turner, W. (2020). Biodegradable packaging in the food industry. *Journal of Packaging Innovations*, *3*(1), 99–117.

Rana, K., Patel, N., & Whitfield, S. (2021). Online presence and consumer trust: Branding challenges for ghost kitchens. *Journal of Digital Commerce*, *5*(1), 89–102.

ReFED. (2021). Insights Engine. A data platform for food waste reduction. Available at: https://www.refed.com

Richards, C., & Papadopoulos, C. (2020). Evaluating food waste reduction strategies in hotels. *Journal of Cleaner Production*, *252*, 119–151.

Rudolph, T.. (2022). Engaging Ghost Kitchens in Food Recovery Initiatives: Opportunities and Challenges. *Journal of Social Entrepreneurship*, *13*(3), 207–221.

Sahin, O., Terzi, S., & Genç, A. (2019). Food waste management and prevention in restaurants: An intelligent and optimized approach. *International Journal of Hospitality Management*, *78*, 12–19.

Schneider, N. (2021). *How ghost kitchens are reshaping the restaurant industry*. Restaurant Dive.

Scholz, K., Eriksson, M., & Strid, I. (2015). Carbon footprint of supermarket food waste. *Resources, Conservation and Recycling*, *94*, 56–65. DOI: 10.1016/j.resconrec.2014.11.016

Siegner, C. (2020). Sustainable practices in the rise of ghost kitchens. *Forbes*.

Silvennoinen, K., Koivupuro, H. K., Katajajuuri, J. M., Jalkanen, L., & Reinikainen, A. (2015). Food waste volume and origin: Case studies in the Finnish food service sector. *Waste Management (New York, N.Y.)*, *46*, 140–145. DOI: 10.1016/j.wasman.2015.09.010 PMID: 26419775

Simmons, D., & Radcliffe, J. (2023). Consumer-facing technologies in ghost kitchens. *Tech & Food Journal*, *8*(1), 45–62.

Smith, E., & Karami, A. (2023). Collaboration and co-location in the ghost kitchen sector. *Contemporary Culinary Management*, *4*(2), 78–95.

Stangherlin, I.. (2021). Portion Control and Food Waste Reduction in Ghost Kitchens. *Journal of Food Quality*, *2021*, 1–10.

Stenmarck, Å., Jensen, C., Quested, T., & Moates, G. (2016). *Estimates of European food waste levels*. IVL Swedish Environmental Research Institute.

Susskind, A. M., & Curry, J. (2020). The delivery-driven business model: A study on ghost kitchens and consumer preferences. *Journal of Restaurant Innovation*, *14*(1), 27–40.

Taylor, E. (2021). Standalone ghost kitchens: A rising trend in food delivery. *Food Industry Review*, *42*(2), 56–63.

Taylor, E. (2021). Maintaining quality and brand reputation in a digital-only restaurant model. *Food Industry Review*, *42*(3), 78–85.

Technomic. (2021). Ghost kitchens and the consumer's view of food delivery services. *Consumer Insights Report*

Thompson, G.. (2020). Consumer Engagement in Sustainable Food Practices: The Case of Ghost Kitchens. *Sustainability*, *12*(18), 7553.

UNWTO. (2021). *Adapting to the new normal: Trends in the hospitality industry*. World Tourism Organization.

USDA. (2019). Food loss and waste reduction goals. Available at: https://www.usda.gov

Wang, P., & Garcia, M. (2020). The cost-benefit analysis of ghost kitchen setups. *Business Economics Quarterly*, *8*(4), 112–132.

Wang, T., & Zhou, Y. (2020). Predictive analytics in ghost kitchen operations. *Journal of Culinary Technology*, *6*(3), 89–110.

Wang, Y.. (2021). Sustainable Packaging Solutions in Food Service: The Case of Ghost Kitchens. *Packaging Technology & Science*, *34*(3), 123–134.

Wansink, B.. (2016). Menu Variety and Food Waste: The Role of Consumer Choice. *International Journal of Hospitality Management*, *57*, 105–110.

Wharton, W. (2020). Menu innovation in ghost kitchens. *Culinary Perspectives*, *16*(1), 23–38.

Zhang, X., & Liao, Y. (2021). Regulatory Challenges for Ghost Kitchens: A Comparative Analysis. *Journal of Food Law & Policy*, *17*(3), 189–210.

Chapter 19
Ghost Kitchen Evolution:
From the Traditional Restaurant to Virtual Eateries

Roshan Kumar Shiva
SR University, India

Geetha Manoharan
https://orcid.org/0000-0002-8644-8871
SR University, India

ABSTRACT

Technological advances and client demand may change food service ghost kitchens. Value, scalability, and technology integration challenge delivery-only restaurant operating standards. Their operational benefits are well-documented, but their commercial, sustainability, and consumer implications are unknown. In this chapter, ghost kitchens' history, working systems, and economic, environmental, and social elements are studied to fill the gap. Case studies and industry data analysis are used to explore ghost kitchen advancements, including AI-driven analytics, multi-brand approaches, and eco-friendly practices. Distribution systems, regulatory compliance, and consumer distrust are needed for ghost kitchens, which promote entrepreneurship, sustainability, and cost performance. Theory explains how virtual food brands affect consumer behaviour and competitive market dynamics, whereas practical ways execute this concept. Examination of ghost kitchens' history and benefits reveals their vital role in global food ecosystem transformation.

1. INTRODUCTION: THE EVOLUTION OF GHOST KITCHENS

For centuries, food service industry has been part of life. This helps the public consume delectable foods beyond home borders. The years have gone by with restaurants more than a place to go to eat but an environment where social occasions, parties, and meetings are held (Jones et al., 2024). However, with changing lifestyles and technological advancements, the food consumption pattern has changed significantly (Suresh et al., 2024). Today, convenience is prioritized, and food delivery is a modern-day staple of dining. This new pattern of consumer behavior opens doors to a new food industry innovation: ghost kitchens. As (Da Cunha et al., 2024), puts it, "Ghost kitchens have been seen as the latest devel-

DOI: 10.4018/979-8-3373-0432-8.ch019

opment in the changing food ordering behaviours of consumers. Unlike traditional restaurants, ghost kitchens only focus on delivering food and have no on-site dining area for direct customer interaction (Jiang et al., 2024). Instead, they work entirely in the background, fulfilling online orders and delivering meals directly to customers' doors (Zhu et al., 2024). This concept has revolutionized the way food businesses operate and adapt to the demands of today's fast-paced, digital world. This chapter delves into the origins, role, and implications of ghost kitchens. The beginning discusses the context and history of the food service sector and proceeds to outline what a ghost kitchen is, what is does, and how is distinct from a regular kitchen as a function of discussion scope, respectively (Giousmpasoglou et al., 2024). On completion of this chapter, the readers will gain insight on what ghosts' kitchen really does to determine the food services future.

1.1 Background and Context

For many years, food service has been an essential part of the economy and culture (Rosette, J. (2024, May). This restaurant model usually requires a location in which people can eat there, have the privilege of personalized service, and appreciate different kinds of cuisines. Restaurants heavily invest in creating an attractive atmosphere, employing well-trained personnel, and ensuring high standards in customer service (Chng, S. (2024). For several decades, this restaurant model prospered since most people preferred eating out. However, recent years have changed this industry quite significantly. Busy work schedules, urban lifestyles, and the advancement of technology have changed the way people dine (Trencher et al., 2024). Most customers prefer to order food from home and have it delivered instead of dining out. This has been a process that food delivery services such as Uber Eats, DoorDash, and Zomato have made relatively easy. They enable users to make their choices across an extremely wide range with only a few taps on a smartphone (Kumolu-Johnson, B. (2024). Such a generation of delivery platforms emphasizes serving customers more effectively. Such traditional restaurants have been more traditional and expensive to establish due to overhead costs, mostly since traditional restaurants are only good with in-person service (Delalay et al., 2024). However, ghost kitchens save much of that hassle. These kitchens are specifically intended to serve only delivery orders, thus saving on dine-in areas, waiters and waitresses, and other elements of a traditional restaurant that contribute to its expense (Nguyen et al., 2024). Ghost kitchens thus offer an efficient and straightforward solution to the hurdles faced by the food industry in this new age of operation (Chong, K. L. (2024).

1.2 Definition of Ghost Kitchens

Ghost kitchens are quite a recent phenomenon but become one of the largest players in the food sector nowadays. On an abstract level, ghost kitchens can be considered as commercially maintained kitchen facilities exclusively to provide food products for deliveries; they don't take up space on the premise with customers, and the vast majority don't have even a shopfront (Shin et al., 2024). Instead, ghost kitchens operate out of obscure locations, like warehouses or shared kitchen facilities, and rely entirely on online platforms to connect with customers. To understand ghost kitchens better, it is crucial to establish a distinction from traditional restaurants (Tualeka et al., 2024). With a traditional restaurant, the kitchen is just part of the larger operation: dining rooms, wait staff, customer-facing services, and the rest. Ghost kitchens, in contrast, remove everything and focus only on cooking. This will allow them to have lower operating costs and better efficiency. Ghost kitchens have various names and each name is a little different: Ghost Kitchens, Virtual Restaurants, Dark Kitchens, Cloud Kitchens, and Stealth Restaurants.

Cloud Kitchens: Cloud kitchens can be defined as a large category of kitchens specifically meant to work without interacting with customers directly, primarily catering to online orders. They also lack physical dining rooms or direct business contact with consumers within their premises. Cloud kitchens, as the name has it, are mainly designed to meet the growing need for food delivery services.

Virtual Kitchens: The special type of cloud kitchen is further categorized into virtual kitchens designed for forming and operating virtual brand concepts only. These brands are completely virtual and do not have a physical store or outlet that a physical brand does. These facilities are run virtually; it means that they are managed centrally, although brands operating out of the virtual kitchen are different and appeal to different segments of customers.

Dark Kitchens: The term "dark kitchens" underscores the secretive, backroom nature of these operations. Dark kitchens are not situated in areas where people usually go; instead, they are found in industrial zones, shared spaces, or converted warehouses. These dark kitchens produce food and nothing more, with no dine-in facilities.

1.3 Purpose and Scope of the Chapter

This chapter explores the emergence of ghost kitchens, analysing their development, operational advantages, and impact on the food service industry. This in-depth analysis shows how ghost kitchens are transforming food service and what their strengths, challenges, and future potential are. The chapter is organized around several main areas of discussion:

Understanding the Evolution of Ghost Kitchens: Ghost kitchens are one of the results of evolving consumer demand and technological developments. The evolution of ghost kitchens traces its roots back to the shared kitchen models and to the current position, supported by the growing popularity of food delivery platforms, such as Uber Eats and Zomato (Aiswarya et al., 2024). Their role during the COVID-19 pandemic and how ghost kitchens became an integral part of the delivery-first dining culture will be discussed in the following.

Examining the Benefits of Ghost Kitchens: The key advantages ghost kitchens provide to food businesses are cost efficiency, scalability, and adaptability. Ghost kitchens eliminate high dining space costs and let brands experiment with multiple virtual menus from one location (Ji et al., 2024). This section explains how such benefits empower startups and established brands alike in a highly competitive market.

Analysing Their Market Impact: The ghost kitchen has changed the food service landscape, forcing a change in consumer behavior, increasing competition, and threatening traditional restaurant models (Schorung, M. (2024). This section explores how ghost kitchens push innovation in menu design and marketing while changing customers' expectations about speed and variety.

Investigating Their Role in Promoting Entrepreneurship: This presents an opportunity in the lowering barriers to entry and makes available affordable opportunities of launching a food brand not requiring them to have spaces for actual restaurants (Pookulangara et al., 2023). Here are aspects on how ghost kitchens improve innovations and creativity of small-scale businesses to adopt new ideas of ideas and reach of customers.

Exploring the Role of Technology in Ghost Kitchens: The concept of the ghost kitchen remains unthinkable without technology. This section analyses how tools such as Data analysis, AI, and IoT have been used in the inappropriate allocation and forecasting of demand levels and the reductive minimum usage of food (Rout et al., 2024). This discussion will also explore the integration of the delivery platforms and how digital marketing firm initiatives integrate technology solutions in improving delivery efficiency and engaging customers.

Assessing Challenges and Risks: Ghost kitchens do have many benefits. However, they also come across various major challenges. This part deals with issues like the dependence on third-party platforms for delivery, ethical matters about labour practices, and other regulatory issues like compliance with food safety standards, and even zoning laws (Sulaiman et al., 2023). All of these must be addressed for it to be sustainable.

Exploring the Future of Ghost Kitchens: Lastly, this chapter discusses implications for the future of ghost kitchens, including trends such as sustainability, technology, from drones, and autonomous delivery, and new approaches to branding and customer acquisition. Based on this forward-looking perspective, analysis will reveal the possibly unveiled directions of the development of ghost kitchens in the future years (Leung et al., 2024). Through expanding into these topics, this chapter endeavours to provide a comprehensive analysis of ghost kitchens, while also highlighting their value in today's food sector, and their potential to define the future of the market.

2. HISTORICAL CONTEXT AND EVOLUTION OF GHOST KITCHENS

While ghost kitchens may sound like a relatively new phenomenon, it actually has roots in older trends and changes in the food service industry. These trends, initiated by changing consumer preferences, technological advancements, and world events, slowly paved the way for ghost kitchens to flourish as a successful business model (Guzzo et al., 2024). Today, ghost kitchens take a leading role in the current food landscape; they introduce a streamlined food delivery way that meets the demands of a world fast-paced and increasingly digitally connected. This chapter will, therefore, attempt to analyse the historical background of ghost kitchens, following their trajectory from early precursors to modern times.

2.1 Early Precursors and Shared Kitchen Models

Thus, preparing the ground for ghost kitchens, there were shared kitchen spaces and commissary kitchens earlier in practice. Multi tenancy arrangement including sharing of kitchen facilities made it possible for several food businesses entities to operate from one physical premise yet they only have to meet the cost of the kitchen but separately manage all the necessary cooking equipment's that come with the trade. These spaces received much value from micro-entrepreneurs in the catering services, food truck, and bakers who could not afford to establish their commercial kitchens. However, these models were mainly concerned with sharing costs and first brought the concept of the segregation of the food production from the areas accessible to the customers into mainstream discussion. There are some years ago were delivery-oriented restaurants, which can also be considered as the precursors to the ghost kitchen concept. In the mid of the 90s, some eating establishments began to introduce menus strictly for delivery as consumers demanded convenience. These business establishments were usually located in industrial areas or cheaper areas in order to avoid provisioning of high-quality space. While these models where comparatively small in scale they did show that it is possible for food businesses to perform well while not having a restaurant dining presence.

2.2 The Role of Food Delivery Platforms

This was largely through the rapid growth of online food delivery platforms, like Uber Eats, DoorDash, and Grubhub. These platforms have transformed the way customers engage with food businesses by making menus more accessible, ordering easier, and deliveries trackable. When these services became popular, they created an environment where businesses could focus on delivery only and bypass the traditional dine-in experience. Ghost kitchens were finding a natural partner with the delivery platforms handling logistics. Businesses no longer needed to worry about managing their fleets of delivery or interacting with their customers; they just produce food and rely on third-party platforms to handle the rest. This shift allowed ghost kitchens to scale operations quickly and efficiently, reaching a larger population without the constraints of having physical locations.

2.3 The Impact of the COVID-19 Pandemic

The COVID-19 pandemic has also turned a major page in ghost kitchen adoption and proliferation. With widespread lockdowns and social distancing, in-person dining for most traditional restaurants took a huge plunge because they were not able to keep their dining rooms open (Wray et al., 2024). Meanwhile, customers started looking for food deliveries as safe ways of getting favourite meals. During this period, ghost kitchens were uniquely suited to help meet the challenges of the pandemic. Existing ghost kitchens scaled up their operations to meet the surge in demand, and new ghost kitchens entered the market rapidly to capitalize on the growing reliance on delivery (Ghazanfar et al., 2023). Traditional restaurants also started adopting hybrid models, using ghost kitchens to keep their businesses running while their dining rooms were closed. The pandemic showed that ghost kitchens are resilient and adaptable, making them an integral part of the food industry.

2.4 Contemporary Developments and Global Adoption

Today, ghost kitchens are an international phenomenon; significant adoption can be noted across regions in North America, Europe, and Asia. In the United States, companies like Kitchen United and Cloud Kitchens became industry leaders with turn-key solutions for ghost kitchen operations. In India, the multi-brand ghost kitchen model was pioneered by Rebel Foods. The company has operated from a single location numerous virtual brands (Shapiro, A. (2023). Meantime, China's Meituan and Ele. me integrate ghost kitchens into their well-recognized delivery ecosystems: in terms of this concept's scalability, nothing special should be seen. Today's ghost kitchens have far outgrown the simple food manufacturing facility. Many have come to utilize advanced technologies like AI-driven demand forecasting, IoT-enabled kitchen equipment, and data analytics to further optimize menus. Even more ambitious ghost kitchens are exploring automation, using robotic chefs and automated packing systems to minimize human intervention.

2.5 Key Drivers of Evolution

Several key factors have driven the evolution of ghost kitchens:

Technological Advancements: Due to the ease of access of many internet-based platforms, partnering with third-party food delivery services, mobile applications, and smart kitchen technologies, it can be relatively seamless to manage and run such establishments.

Shifting Consumer Preferences: Schedules become tighter, and people gradually favor convenient services, especially in the food industry.

Cost Pressures: Ghost kitchens describe a model that is cost-friendly to operate when compared to traditional restaurants since they do not attract the associated costs of lease, personnel, and building maintenance.

Urbanization and Globalization: These are some of the reasons why ghost kitchens continue to thrive today; the inhabitants of urban areas are denser, and the world is gradually shifting its attention to the consumption of food.

The Gig Economy: Because of online gig platforms, there are enough delivery personnel to help with the distribution of the food produced in the ghost kitchens.

Ghost kitchens started as a small movement and grew into a revolutionary power within the food service industry. Through their solutions to the traditional restaurant model's problems and using technological innovation, ghost kitchens changed how food is prepared, delivered, and consumed. This context shows why they are particularly suited to today's fast-paced, connected world (Paul et al., 2024). This evolution reflects change not only in the food industry but also opens perspective on how businesses will meet the challenges of the future.

3. OPERATIONAL FRAMEWORK AND BUSINESS MODELS OF GHOST KITCHENS

Ghost kitchens are revolutionizing the food service industry by offering an extremely efficient, delivery-focused business model. It is unlike traditional restaurants; they have instead streamlined their operations to cut costs, scale up, and adjust. Their organizational structure is intricately embedded with technological advancements, making it possible for both small and large food companies to get in touch with the customers faster and more efficiently (John, K. T. (2023). This section explores the dimensions of ghost kitchen operations, ranging from their typologies and technological integrations to their marketing strategies and revenue models, which would offer insightful understanding of how such new kitchens operate and grow.

3.1 Typologies of Ghost Kitchens

The concept of ghost kitchens is versatile and there can be several types which can be divided according to the needs of business and customers. The primary typologies include:

Independent Ghost Kitchens: These are independent facilities run by one company or brand. The independent ghost kitchens mainly thrive for the unique menu and branding. They are best for a small-time entrepreneur or established restaurant testing a new concept that doesn't risk their parent brand (Vu et al., 2023). These kitchens tend to be niche-specific, targeting specific markets, such as vegan meals, gourmet burgers, or fusion cuisine, thereby targeting the right kind of customer base.

Aggregator-Run Ghost Kitchens: Third-party delivery apps including Uber Eats and DoorDash have ventured into the delivery kitchen market, where they own their kitchens. These facilities accommodate many brands, and they share some commodities like, equipment and storage area as well as utilities. From a delivery platform perspective, the direct affiliation of aggregator-run ghost kitchens also offers cost-saving opportunities as compared to the risk of ensure a continuous stream of orders and brands participating in the delivery services need not spend much on marketing.

Commissary and Shared Kitchens: Commissary kitchens serve as shared places where many food businesses prepare their products. Such an arrangement is perfect for small businesses, like food trucks or catering businesses, or any new virtual brands that do not need to spend hundreds of thousands of dollars purchasing or leasing a standalone kitchen, but need access to professional facilities (Rajesh et al., 2023). Shared kitchens encourage collaborations and innovations while helping to reduce the costs of their businesses.

Multi-Brand Ghost Kitchens: A multi-brand kitchen is one kitchen, which functions under the same roof but delivers food products for a variety of virtual brands. An example can be when a single kitchen cooks pizzas for one brand, sushi for another, and desserts for another, all belonging to the same company. This way, they maximize operational efficiency and serve a diverse group of customers.

Franchise-Based Ghost Kitchens: Some ghost kitchens have a franchise model: this is where an existing brand licenses its menu and operating structures to kitchen operators based on different regions. It lets them expand globally without fully developing restaurants in a city with the ghost kitchen model and accelerating scalability.

3.2 Technological Integration in Ghost Kitchens

Technology is the primary force that drives ghost kitchen and without it the concept cannot work as advertised. Key technological components include:

Order Management Systems: To support the operation of ordering food online through several digital platforms, ghost kitchens require integrated order management systems. These apps aggregate orders from Uber Eats, DoorDash, and Grubhub so that its clear which orders are coming through in high volume and can be properly compiled to help kitchens handle large number of requests without confusion or lateness of delivery.

Data Analytics and AI: AI and big data help create a fully functional system at ghost kitchens (González-Aleu et al., 2022). Customers' information is processed with the help of artificial intelligence to estimate the level of need, to define the best food to be offered and the best prices for these dishes. This also means that the food business can reduce wastage as the kitchen adapts to preparing meals in the most efficient ways possible.

Internet of Things (IoT) in Kitchen Operations: IoT-enabled devices also include smart ovens and refrigerators, inventory control systems, and others wherein kitchens can monitor the current performance of equipment and inventories in real time and thereby reduce downtime, facilitate food safety, and get streamlined kitchen workflows.

Delivery Integration and Tracking: Real-time delivery tracking systems update customers about their orders, which contributes to a better experience overall. For ghost kitchens, these systems optimize delivery routes, reduce the time taken for delivery, and increase customer satisfaction.

Automation and Robotics: In others, automation is being put in place to increase efficiency in handling jobs using robotic chefs and automated systems that pack the food (Attoh et al., 2024). Automation is just at its infancy but goes a long way in developing the future of ghost kitchen businesses.

3.3 Marketing and Branding Strategies

Marketing is an essential part of the experience of ghost kitchens as these operations lack a physical storefront through which to attract consumers. Effective strategies include:

Digital Marketing and SEO: Ghost kitchens depend heavily on digital platforms to reach their audience. Optimization with search engines ensures their positioning on food delivery applications as well as search engine lists, thus enhancing its discoverability. Social media can include Instagram and TikTok that are used to flaunt mouth-watering dishes with interesting captions and engage with consumers as well.

Influencer Collaborations: Food influencers and bloggers will help ghost kitchens build their credibility and reach a broader audience. For most of these influencers, the practice is sharing reviews and experiences with followers that send people to the kitchen's virtual brand.

Menu Customization and Personalization: Ghost kitchens often cater to the tastes of their customers and come up with unique dishes or special offers that customers may want. Personalisation, like customising based on diet or preference, can boost customer satisfaction and loyalty.

Leveraging Customer Feedback: People's opinions on delivery platforms are decisive, especially in terms of getting more customers. Some are just a few months old, but ghost kitchens constantly screen feedbacks and changes their menu to ensure quality and high ratings.

Brand Identity and Virtual Presence: Since the concepts of ghost kitchens don't require any physical presence in the form of restaurants, it becomes critical to construct proper online image. This involves having glamorous logos and website, and having harmonized social media presence.

3.4 Revenue Models

To be profitable and sustainable, ghost kitchens use different models of making money:

Direct Sales through Delivery Platforms: Major revenue sources for ghost kitchens are usually order takes from food delivery applications, where the kitchens pay a commission to the applications, but the volume of orders tends to make it a viable source.

Subscription-Based Meal Plans: Customers can also subscribe to weekly or monthly deliveries of meals from some of these ghost kitchens. To the supplier this model creates steadiness of income which give them more returns other than creating customer loyalty.

Partnerships and Licensing Deals: Ghost kitchens often partner with known brands to prepare their menu items in new territories. Licensing agreements enable ghost kitchens to work under the name of a well-known brand, thereby arriving with a ready-made clientele base.

Corporate and Bulk Orders: Some ghost kitchens target offices, offering corporate meals as well as meals for meetings or office fasting. Such a cause of diversification aids in reducing individual customer demands' volatility.

3.5 Operational Challenges

Despite this, ghost kitchens present quite a number of benefits as displayed below; Despite this, there are some challenges associated with ghost kitchens. Key issues include:

Dependency on Delivery Platforms: Many ghost kitchens have little direct contact with customers; instead, they depend on delivery apps like Uber Eats or Grub Hub to deliver the food they cook, which make up for their commissions by charging the ghost kitchens a percentage of every order.

Quality Control: It would be extremely challenging to sustain consistently high quality of foods during a high turnover of operations, especially when several brands are supported from a central kitchen.

Competition: As the number of options grow within the ghost kitchen space, it becomes more challenging for new players to gain their share of the market.

Labor Issues: While the concept of ghost kitchens entails very low contact with customers or even the elimination of any front of the house service, they still include employees who work in the kitchen, and any shortages of these skills prove disastrous.

Regulatory Compliance: Ghost kitchens have to meet food safety issues and zoning requirements, which differ from one geographical location to another and can be some limitations to growth.

Ghost kitchens are one of the most innovative and adaptive models that cater to modern consumers' needs and give food businesses new avenues for growth (Hakim et al., 2023). With technology, successful marketing strategies, and diversified revenue models, ghost kitchens have become a transformational force in the food service industry. But for their long-term success, it will be important to tackle operational challenges and stiff competition. This section, then, has described at length how ghost kitchens work and operate, thus providing a solid foundation for further discussion on their impact and future potential.

4. BENEFITS OF GHOST KITCHENS

Ghost kitchens are a revolutionary innovation in the food service industry, and they have come with benefits to entrepreneurs, established businesses, and customers. Eliminating the dine-in space and focusing strictly on delivery, ghost kitchens optimize the operations, minimize costs, and meet the increasing need for convenience (Khan et al., 2023). This chapter elaborates on the various benefits that ghost kitchens bring, which include cost efficiency, scalability, adaptability, sustainability, data-driven decision making, and improved customer experience.

4.1 Cost Efficiency

One of the most significant benefits of ghost kitchens is cost minimization. In comparison to the traditional restaurant models, which spend a considerable amount of money in prime real estate, interior décor, furniture, and front-of-house staff, ghost kitchens are run at more reasonable, industrial addresses (Nagadeepa et al., 2023). This reduced overhead cost then allows business units to spend more funds on food and marketing.

Reduced Real Estate Costs: For ghost kitchens, expensive shopfronts in high-traffic areas are redundant. They can serve from warehouses, shared facilities, and even underutilised spaces to save a lot of money on rent and property care.

Lower Labor Expenses: Traditional restaurants require a lot of people – hostesses, waiters, and managers for starters. As a result, they can do away with the factors that come with a normal kitchen for instance having personnel to prepare the food.

Efficient Resource Utilization: Thus, since the main focus of the ghost kitchens is in delivery, supply chains can be optimized, and food waste minimized. An efficient management of raw materials involves accurate demand forecasts and the management of stocks to utilise and control the use of the ingredients in reducing the costs.

4.2 Scalability and Flexibility

The multifaceted advantages of ghost kitchens include practically unlimited possibilities for scaling and high flexibility that makes it possible for both startups and well-developed business.

Rapid Expansion: Extended delivery kitchens make it possible for firms to penetrate new markets rapidly and at a relatively low cost. Unlike conventional restaurants, which take considerable time to establish, and require capital investment, starting new ghost kitchens can be done with minimum risk.

Multi-Brand Operations: Most of the time ghost kitchens run multiple virtual brands from a given physical location, more often to address different tastes of customers (Chhabra et al., 2021). For instance, a given kitchen might make a burger under one name, pizzas under another, and healthy bowls under yet another. This approach optimises the generation of revenues with the least possible enhancement of operational complications.

Adaptability to Market Trends: Third, ghost kitchens are highly flexible to unpredictable shifts in consumer behavior and competition landscape. Organizations can quickly change their offerings or add new items, cuisines or offers like a limited-period offer that might allure the customer.

4.3 Data-Driven Decision-Making

The use of technology in the operations of a ghost kitchen provides actionable insights that can allow efficient unit operations, hence, satisfying the consumer.

Demand Forecasting: Based on such factors as history, weather, and local events, ghost kitchen can use the advanced analytics tools to estimate customer demand. This helps different kitchens make the needed preparations in order to ensure they feed a specific number of people while minimizing wastage.

Menu Optimization: Information sourced from delivery platforms enables the ghost kitchens to understand their customers and make changes in what they offer by having more of what people love and less of what they do not like.

Personalized Marketing: The advantage for the ghost kitchens is that they can market directly to the customers that they offer their service to. For example, offering customers rebate or suggestions of the product to buy based on previous purchases will go a long way in bringing other customers.

4.4 Sustainability and Environmental Benefits

Another benefit of ghost kitchens is that they spur the right use of resources hence being environmentally friendly.

Minimized Food Waste: Regarding food waste, it can be mentioned that the efficient information concerning the levels of stocks of the food items can to a great extent be managed with the assistance of impressive systems of stocking control and the tools for estimating demand for the food items typical for the majority of the ghost kitchens. These kitchens do not prepare the quantities which would be wasted in many kitchens ending up in the trash which is a big problem facing the world today.

Energy Efficiency: Kitchens are shared and operations centralized; the case applies less expenses on energy than in case of individual restaurants. Other development in kitchen equipment also assist to minimise energy consumption Circulating technologies in the kitchen assist to lessen consumption of energy also.

Sustainable Packaging: Customer expectations for sustainability are often met in the packaging that many ghost kitchens prefer. Biodegradable bags, reusable items, and the minimum use of wrappings are examples.

Reduced Transportation Impact: Site selection strategy means that most ghost kitchens are located near the coverage areas to minimize the travelling distance thus cutting emission (Nivedha et al., 2024). Certain operators are also using electric cars and bicycle delivery to reduce its impact to the environment even more.

4.5 Enhanced Customer Experience

One of the main benefits of ghost kitchens is the focus on the current consumer expectations – convenience, the offer, and speed.

Convenience: Since their sole purpose is delivery, ghost kitchens meet the needs of a busy customer who would rather have restaurant quality food delivered to their homes or workplaces (Ashton et al., 2022). Ordering from gastroplaces is a very smooth process, especially in the case of work with food delivery applications.

Diverse Menu Options: It is for this reason that several of these virtual restaurants can manage to coordinate several brands of their make which in essence encompass all forms of foods and dishes all from the same kitchen. This variety meets the need of the customer who would like to do several forms of eating.

Faster Delivery Times: Efficient location selection and sound operational layout procedures mean that meals served by ghost kitchens can be delivered fast without compromising on the meal quality.

Customizable Orders: This is because, through technology, independent operators in ghost kitchens are able to deliver tailored foodservice experiences. The specific request of the customers like preferences for taking certain foods, allergic to certain products or portion preference increases satisfaction.

5. CHALLENGES AND CRITIQUES OF GHOST KITCHENS

While ghost kitchens have revolutionized the food service industry and brought with them numerous benefits, it does not mean that they have no problems and criticisms. The fast growth of this model has exposed several issues related to operations, ethics, and the market, and these should be addressed in order for sustainable development to take place (Inamdar et al., 2024). This chapter discusses some of the critical challenges ghost kitchens face: operational constraints, ethical dilemmas, regulatory barriers, and consumer perception problems.

5.1 Operational Limitations

While running a ghost kitchen might seem fairly simple, it is not devoid of a number of logistical and management issues that could potentially slow a company down when it comes to profit-making.

Dependency on Delivery Platforms: Ghost kitchens rely very heavily on third-party delivery platforms such as Uber Eats, DoorDash, and Zomato for acquiring customers and fulfilling orders. This often comes at a cost because these platforms charge a relatively high commission fee that tends to erode the margins of smaller operators. Ghost kitchens also have no control over delivery logistics and customer relationships because of the domination of these platforms, thereby creating dependency and reducing their autonomy.

Logistical Challenges: Managing high volumes of delivery orders is complex, mainly during peak hours. Optimizing kitchen workflows, multiple delivery drivers, and timely preparation are all essential for ghost kitchens not to delay orders. Failure in any of these areas can bring dissatisfied customers and, therefore, negative reviews.

Quality Assurance: For ghost kitchens, maintaining consistent food quality is challenging, especially during the scaling of operations or for dealing with multiple brands within the same facility (Kulshreshtha et al., 2022). The absence of immediate feedback from customers in the direct dining environment makes issues difficult to be addressed at that exact moment.

Technology-Related Downtime: Ghost kitchens rely completely on technology-from order management systems to IoT-enabled kitchen equipment (Shankar et al., 2022). Technical failures such as crashing of the system or connectivity, can cause service disruption, create delays in orders, and affect customer satisfaction.

5.2 Ethical and Social Concerns

The rapid growth of ghost kitchens has also prompted ethical issues relating to labour relations, competition and to the industry of conventional restaurants.

Labor Conditions for Delivery Workers: A significant part of their business model is delivery, and delivery people are gig economy workers who experience wage theft, no benefits or job security (Rai et al., 2023). Some scholars dissect its propagation as maintaining and deepening unfairness in the labour market, and generation of a society of low-waged, and overworked freelancers.

Impact on Traditional Restaurants: Thus, one of the tasks being pursued in this article is to describe various forms of food delivery service and analyse the threats that the growth of ghost kitchens poses for traditional restaurants. It is common knowledge that brick-and-mortar retail stores, especially those that are small scale, find it extremely difficult to challenge the much lower costs and indeed the larger customer base of the ghost kitchens (Chen et al., 2022).

Limited Job Creation: On the plus side, companies skip all the overhead expenses associated with restaurants while lack the familiar restaurant positions, including servers, hosts or managers. It strikes me that this consolidated model can lead to the loss of jobs in the sector, especially in areas which public and formal meals are a vital component of the GDP.

5.3 Regulatory and Legal Issues

Ghost kitchens, in general, exist in a still rather unfirm legal landscape, so both compliance issues and governance issues might be rather problematic.

Zoning Laws and Licensing: Many ghost kitchens operate from industrial or non-traditional locations, which often may not be compliant with the particular local zoning laws. Operating under such regulations may involve a complex and cost process, especially for smaller operators. Again, obtaining food safety certificates and business licenses in any region is also quite variable.

Taxation and Transparency: Due to the digital operations of ghost kitchen taxation is not very clear, especially when different brands are used or when a business involves with delivery companies. Government gets it hard to note down tax compliance and tax transparency leading to difference between the two issues and legal ambiguities.

Health and Safety Compliance: Food hygiene is crucial in the kitchen settings, but given the fact that the staff turnover rate can be high due to its remote nature and that the physical kitchens and staff may serve multiple restaurant brands at the same time, accelerated delivery of the orders, there is high probability that food order will get contaminated or trigger violation of health standards as observed (Na et al., 2024). It is therefore very important to observe hygiene interventions but very difficult to do so all the time.

5.4 Consumer Perception Issues

Nevertheless, there is also certain level of suspicion from the customers because these business do not have actual restaurants and do not interact directly with the customers.

Lack of Brand Loyalty: One of the most crucial considerations as to this particular model is the fact that most of the time, ghost kitchens do not actually possess actual existence in the form of brands – which does not secure as much customers as a restaurant does. Some customers may perceive these brands as fake or even uncredible based with their attempt to use it whenever they try to order quality food.

Transparency Concerns: The fact is that most people do not know that they are ordering food from a delivery or a dark kitchen rather than a restaurant. Such kind of opacity can create distrust depending on whether customers felt swayed into believing that their meals were sourced from certain areas when in actual sense they were not.

Limited Customer Engagement: Traditional restaurants generate their revenues on the premises, personal contact that the customers have with restaurant staff and the general atmosphere in the restaurants. Ghost kitchens, being unlike conventional full-service restaurants, do not have this advantage: an interaction with consumers is more difficult to establish an emotional level.

5.6 Challenges in Scaling and Differentiation

The competition continues to arise, and reaching challenges that result in the restigmatisation of expansion and differentiation.

Oversaturation of Markets: The increasing accessibility of the delivery turf outcomes in market consolidation in some areas, and that intercepts new entrants from extensive visibility. There is fierce struggle to capture customer attention whenever brands are promoting on delivery platforms and this can be very costly and time consuming.

Maintaining Quality at Scale: For ghost kitchens, the problem is to scale the operations and at the same time ensure that quality is not compromised when expanding to different locations. A problem that often comes with rapid growth is that the demand for products outstrips the organization's capacity to handle it efficiently.

Differentiation in a Crowded Market: For the ghost kitchens, the problem is forever and always to manage multitudes scale and, concurrently, not to deteriorate the quality of the kitchen when delivering other new regions. Among the challenges that may be expected with growth on the production line is that customer demand increases at a faster pace than the organization's capacity to meet it.

6. FUTURE TRENDS AND OPPORTUNITIES FOR GHOST KITCHENS

Ghost kitchens have, over the past few years, upset the food service industry significantly; however, their trend in evolution is not as short-lived. Consumer trends and preferences, technological changes, as well as changes in the food market, will most probably influence ghost kitchens with endless innovations (Ashtikkar et al., 2024). The potential directions of the development, thus, are explored further using emergent trends and opportunities around areas such as technological aspects, sustainability, partnerships, and specific niches and related outcomes for the broader food community.

6.1 Technological Innovations

Technology will further improve the future prospects of ghost kitchens, covering the aspects of efficiency, product quality, and customers. Some key advancements are on the horizon:

Automation and Robotics: Ghost kitchens are increasingly employing automation to reduce complexity and streamline the operation (Manoharan et al., 2024). From robotic chefs, automated dispensers for ingredients, to packaging systems, it would cut down labour costs and deliver consistency. For example, robotic arms can make pizza or build salads with more precision and speed, therefore increasing the volume in high-volume hours. In the near future, completely automated kitchens will become a norm and manage large orders with little or no human interference.

Artificial Intelligence (AI) and Machine Learning: This system already predicts customer demands, optimizes menus in advance, and reduces leftover food by using AI technology. Further improvement in the refinement of the above processes will help make machine learning algorithms enable one to change real-time strategies based on weather conditions or local events, or seasonal tendencies (Kumar et al., 2024). AI will personalize customers' experiences on menus as suggested by preferred items of an individual or prior orders.

Drones and Autonomous Delivery Vehicles: With drone and autonomous car food deliveries now picking up momentum, there are higher possibilities of the utilization of technology such as faster, efficient, more labour-lean, and also environmentally friendly means of transportation and delivery. As mentioned in several reports, Domino's, Uber Eats have even started piloting the usage of drones to deliver, among others, which should accelerate with better regulatory amendments (Nigro et al., 2022).

Augmented and Virtual Reality (AR/VR): Even ghost kitchens, which do not have a physical space to connect with customers, can be overcome by AR/VR technology (Klouvidaki et al., 2023). Virtual tours of kitchens, immersive menu previews, or even virtual cooking sessions with chefs could make a customer feel more connected and create trust.

6.2 Sustainability Practices

The consumers are getting wiser and therefore, sustainability will come to play a crucial role in the functionality of the ghost kitchens. Future initiatives may include:

Eco-Friendly Packaging: For instance, while many delivery orders are placed, the concept behind ghost kitchens leads to large amounts of packaging waste. There are expectations that the industry will switch to using packaging materials that are biodegradable, compostable or reusable (Corvo et al., 2022). New tendencies in product design, like the edible packaging or the use of minimal-waste many could also become a new trend.

Energy-Efficient Operations: Ghost kitchens may use sustainable building designs and energy efficient utensils to minimize on their impact to the environment (Hakim et al., 2022). Modem ghost kitchens might have solar panels as well as smart energy management systems and renewable energy might turn to be a standard offering.

Waste Management Systems: In industrial AND, there could be intricate programme tracking and composting systems in cooking facilities because of the aims at paring unnecessary food wastage. It might also become more frequent to work directly with food banks or with the organizations that distribute the food which has been in excess.

Carbon-Neutral Delivery: At the moment, the use of the electric vehicles (EVs) and bicycles is on the rise, it is therefore possible to involve the green logistics provider to make delivery carbon- neutral. Also, companies can expand carbon offset programs for reducing the firm’s environmental footprint.

6.3 Strategic Partnerships

There are certain factors that mark the future direction of growth of ghost kitchens, and it goes without saying that collaborations and partnerships will be one of the key development vectors. Key opportunities include:

Brand Partnerships: It is possible to collaborate with a well-known brand to design new delivery-only concepts or promotions with special limited delivery-time products. For instance, a major celebrity chef may establish a restaurant through a ghost kitchen and the business becomes popular through the celebrity endorsement it receives automatically.

Retail Collaborations: Supermarkets and retailers can partner with ghost kitchens for providing fresh ready-to–eat meals that can be added to the list of products offered in stores. This could perfectly fit those customers, who need convenience, but still strive to purchase quality products.

Delivery Platform Integration: The intimacy with delivery platforms may create new revenue-sharing scheme, co-branding and marketing messages and better operating processes. Ghost kitchens could also consider their own arrangements where they could only partner with some platforms particularly being granted the option of primer position.

6.4 Catering to Niche Markets

Specialised brand concept is ideal of ghost kitchen and futuristic players will be investing on targeted segment concepts.

Health and Wellness Menus: Seph too has criticized that as awareness of health and nutrition increases, ghost kitchens could present meal options labelled appropriately such as the keto, vegan or gluten free meals (Cai et al., 2022). It could also be seen that more and more people opt for personalisation of their meal to cater their fitness goals or their medical needs.

Ethnic and Regional Cuisines: Due to a high demand for some specific tastes, it is possible for everyone to pay attention to ghost kitchens as they can provide meals for regional, exotic, or specific tastes for such particular groups of people as expats or travellers.

Subscription-Based Meal Services: There will be an increase in subscriptions for planners along the weekly and monthly plans, as patterns will yield frequent steady revenues. The presence of photo MENU in the form of ready meals could be added the possibility to order cooked meals, produced according to the customer's order, or ready for reheating meals, which might be interesting for working people and families.

6.5 Impact on the Broader Food Ecosystem

The future impact of ghost kitchens will be extended to the food service and delivery sector because the concept is a microcosm of this complex realm of services.

Transformation of Traditional Restaurants: Basically, as the concept of the ghost kitchen advance, more classic restaurants can adapt to this model. For instance, full-service restaurants could operate the takeout and delivery services from ghost kitchens so they can concentrate on serving their customers that are seated.

Changing Consumer Behavior: Ghost kitchens might extend the delivery-first solution model for food ordering and alter the buyer's interactions with the food brands (Rinaldi et al., 2022). With the help of marketing, virtual brands could gain the same levels of trust and loyalty like physical restaurants and keep the level of the food and the services provided on the same level constantly.

Job Creation and Workforce Changes: Although ghost kitchens eliminate many positions related to counter and host or waitress services they generate new possibilities for such places as logistics, technology, and kitchen services. Training programs may be to develop, as an effort to prepare the workers for the kind of jobs that are associated with this industry.

Globalization of Food Brands: It highlighted that through these companies, quick globalisation of food brands could be realised since they do not require owning tangible restaurants (Satpathy et al., 2024). This could open up a broader network of food correlations and put more choice out into the market.

7. DISCUSSION AND CONCLUSION

Ghost kitchens are becoming a transformatory force in food service: They are restructuring how business works and consumer interacts with food. Due to a delivery-first focus, ghost kitchens have entered the marketplace offering a scalable and efficient way of getting food on people's tables, as compared to typical restaurants. Their ability to exploit technology, experiment with virtual brands, and optimize operations has placed them as one of the most significant players in the digital age. However, ghost kitchens are not without their problems. Problems like dependency on delivery platforms, ethical issues concerning labor practices, and environmental impact pose a challenge to this model. Besides, regulatory barriers and consumer scepticisms about transparency and authenticity remain a significant challenge that operators must overcome to ensure long-term success. In future more opportunities are on the horizon and depends on the way of functioning of the ghost kitchen. Automate business processes, AI capabilities, and industry sustainability standards will continue to minimize costs and inconveniences in operations and meet consumers' wants. The acquisition of new clients with the help of contracts with different retail chains, online platforms, and well-known food brands will become new outlets for development, and the response to specific segments, such as diet food or ethnic food, will attract different clients. Because ghost kitchens are constantly evolving, their effects on the external food system become increasingly substantial and are relevant to changing existing restaurant concepts and opportunities for employment as well as global food trends. Given the problems threatening Ghost Kitchens and the opportunities featured by the future, these points reflect the Ghost Kitchens' capabilities of redefining the future of the food service industry by granting tandem convenience, variety, and innovation with the developments of present-day digital era.

REFERENCES

Aiswarya, B., & Ramasundaram, G. (2024). Online food delivery technology and family food traditions: A sociocultural perspective. *Journal of Information Technology Teaching Cases*, *14*(1), 68–73. DOI: 10.1177/20438869221150826

Ananthan, M., Shanmugam, V., Udayanan, M., Selvaraj, F., & Manoharan, G. (2024, June). Corporate social responsibility is used as a marketing strategy during Covid-19 pandemic. In *AIP Conference Proceedings* (Vol. 2971, No. 1). AIP Publishing. DOI: 10.1063/5.0195948

Ashton, M., Tuomi, A., & Backman, P. (2022). Ghost production: Applying the servuction model to establish a typology and propose a research agenda for on-demand restaurant food delivery. *Journal of Hospitality and Tourism Insights*, *6*(5), 1730–1754. DOI: 10.1108/JHTI-04-2022-0134

Attoh, K., Wells, K. J., & Cullen, D. (2024). The work of waiting: Migrant labour in the fulfillment city. *Journal of Ethnic and Migration Studies*, *50*(15), 3839–3854. DOI: 10.1080/1369183X.2024.2379649

Cai, R., Leung, X. Y., & Chi, C. G. Q. (2022). Ghost kitchens on the rise: Effects of knowledge and perceived benefit-risk on customers' behavioral intentions. *International Journal of Hospitality Management*, *101*, 103110. DOI: 10.1016/j.ijhm.2021.103110

Chen, L. A., & House, L. (2022). The rise of the ghosts—The impact of the pandemic on food purchases. *Choices*, *37*(2), 1–10.

Chhabra, N., & Rana, A. (2021). Rise and the future of cloud kitchens in India: A consumer study. *International Journal of Research in Engineering. Science and Management*, *4*(7), 158–165.

Chng, S. (2024). The Emerging Socio-Spatial Implications of Cloud Kitchens and Cloud Stores. In *The City Rebooted* (pp. 185–210). Networks, Connectivity and Place Identities in Singapore. DOI: 10.1142/9789811287848_0007

Chong, K. L. (2024). Navigating the virtual restaurant frontier: Motivations and challenges for restaurateurs in post-pandemic era. *Journal of Foodservice Business Research*, •••, 1–27. DOI: 10.1080/15378020.2024.2341202

Corvo, P., Migliavada, R., & Zocchi, D. M. (2022). New food and restaurant trends. In *Italian studies on food and quality of life* (pp. 39–55). Springer International Publishing. DOI: 10.1007/978-3-030-97806-8_3

Da Cunha, D. T., Hakim, M. P., Alves, M. M., Vicentini, M. S., & Wiśniewska, M. Z. (2024). Dark kitchens: Origin, definition, and perspectives of an emerging food sector. *International Journal of Gastronomy and Food Science*, *35*, 100884. DOI: 10.1016/j.ijgfs.2024.100884

Delalay, G., Wagner, C., & Lüthi, T. (2024). *The future of food safety: possible trends for the years 2022-2032 and their influence on food safety and nutrition* (Vol. 2, No. 3, p. e0041).

Fu, R., Trencher, G., & Yamanaka, Y. (2024). How might the spread of online meal-delivery services impact achievement of the SDGs? *Discover Sustainability*, *5*(1), 378. DOI: 10.1007/s43621-024-00603-w

Ghazanfar, U., Kaluvilla, B. B., & Zahidi, F. (2023). The post-COVID emergence of dark kitchens: A qualitative analysis of acceptance and the advantages and challenges. *Research in Hospitality Management, 13*(1), 23–30. DOI: 10.1080/22243534.2023.2239574

Giousmpasoglou, C., Ladkin, A., & Marinakou, E. (2024). Worker exploitation in the gig economy: The case of dark kitchens. *Journal of Hospitality and Tourism Insights, 7*(1), 414–435. DOI: 10.1108/JHTI-10-2022-0477

González-Aleu, F., Hernandez, J. V., Ramirez, R., Linares, C. M., Peinado, J. A., & Daniel, J. (2022). Strategic planning for repurposing kitchen equipment production operations during COVID-19 pandemic. *Operations Management Research : Advancing Practice Through Research, 15*(3), 1241–1256. DOI: 10.1007/s12063-022-00292-6

Guzzo, R. F., Garlington, J., Raab, C., & Belarmino, A. (2024). How do online meal delivery platforms impact restaurant employees? *Journal of Foodservice Business Research*, •••, 1–34. DOI: 10.1080/15378020.2024.2401682

Hakim, M. P., Libera, V. M. D., Zanetta, L. D. A., Nascimento, L. G. P., & da Cunha, D. T. (2022). What is a dark kitchen? A study of consumer's perceptions of deliver-only restaurants using food delivery apps in Brazil. *Food Research International, 161*, 111768. DOI: 10.1016/j.foodres.2022.111768 PMID: 36192932

Hakim, M. P., Libera, V. M. D., Zanetta, L. D. A., Stedefeldt, E., Zanin, L. M., Soon-Sinclair, J. M., & Da Cunha, D. T. (2023). Exploring dark kitchens in Brazilian urban centres: A study of delivery-only restaurants with food delivery apps. *Food Research International, 170*, 112969. DOI: 10.1016/j.foodres.2023.112969 PMID: 37316055

Inamdar, S., & Afroze, S. (2025). Exploring the Opportunities and Confronting the Challenges Within Business Incubation: Opportunities and Challenges. *Promoting Entrepreneurship and Innovation Through Business Incubation*, 29-54.

Ji, Y. C., & Cain, L. (2024). Business Expansion Through Cor Theory: The Case of Cafe Lola. *Journal of Hospitality & Tourism Cases*, 21649987241228486.

Jiang, Y., Balaji, M. S., & Lyu, C. (2024). Cultivating initial trust in ghost kitchens: A mixed-methods investigation of antecedents and consequences. *International Journal of Hospitality Management, 119*, 103727. DOI: 10.1016/j.ijhm.2024.103727

John, K. T. (2023). Digital disruption: The hyperlocal delivery and cloud kitchen driven future of food services in post-COVID India. *International Hospitality Review, 37*(1), 161–187. DOI: 10.1108/IHR-06-2021-0045

Jones, S., Cain, L., & Deel, G. L. (2024). Virtual Restaurants and Ghost Kitchens: A New Opportunity. *Journal of Hospitality & Tourism Cases*, 21649987241241948.

Khan, T. A., Khan, S. A., Haque, S., & Ayub, M. F. B. (2023). A study on the prospect of the cloud kitchen model in Dhaka. *International Journal of Business and Management, 18*(1), 46–59. DOI: 10.5539/ijbm.v18n1p46

Klouvidaki, M. I., Antonopoulos, N., Styliaras, G. D., & Kanavos, A. (2023). Virtual Restaurants: Customer Experience Keeps Their Businesses Alive. *Information (Basel)*, *14*(7), 406. DOI: 10.3390/info14070406

Kulshreshtha, K., & Sharma, G. (2022). From restaurant to cloud kitchen: Survival of the fittest during COVID-19 An empirical examination. *Technological Forecasting and Social Change*, *179*, 121629. DOI: 10.1016/j.techfore.2022.121629 PMID: 35317191

Kumolu-Johnson, B. (2024). Improving Service Quality in the Fast-Food Service Industry. *Journal of Service Science and Management*, *17*(1), 55–74. DOI: 10.4236/jssm.2024.171002

Leung, X. Y., Cai, R., Zhang, H., & Bai, B. (2024). When causal attribution meets cuisine type: How consumer power and moral identity moderate virtual kitchen patronage. *International Journal of Contemporary Hospitality Management*, *36*(4), 1279–1298. DOI: 10.1108/IJCHM-12-2022-1554

Manoharan, G., Ashtikar, S. P., & Kumar, S. (2024). Extenuating Digital Transformation: Revolutionizing Hotel Operations Through AI Technology. In *Hotel and Travel Management in the AI Era* (pp. 257-274). IGI Global.

Manoharan, G., Ashtikar, S. P., & Kumar, S. (2024). Delineation of Artificial Intelligence in the Hospitality and Tourism Industries. In *Impact of AI and Tech-Driven Solutions in Hospitality and Tourism* (pp. 20–42). IGI Global. DOI: 10.4018/979-8-3693-6755-1.ch002

Manoharan, G., Ashtikkar, S. P., & Nivedha, M. (2024). Artificial Intelligence in Decision-Making: Reinventing Business Strategies. In *Generative AI for Transformational Management* (pp. 25-50). IGI Global.

Manoharan, G., Durai, S., Rajesh, G. A., & Ashtikar, S. P. (2023). Sentiment Analysis of Customer Reviews for Online Stores That Support Customer Buying Decisions. In *Handbook of Research on AI and Knowledge Engineering for Real-Time Business Intelligence* (pp. 234–242). IGI Global. DOI: 10.4018/978-1-6684-6519-6.ch015

Manoharan, G., Rao, C. G., Ashtikar, S. P., Kumar, S., & Nivedha, M. (2024). Voyage Virtuoso: Artificial Intelligence in Transforming Tourism. In *Utilizing Smart Technology and AI in Hybrid Tourism and Hospitality* (pp. 79-97). IGI Global.

Na, Y. J., Baek, J. Y., Gwon, S. Y., & Yoon, K. S. (2024). Assessment of Hygiene Management Practices and Comparative Analysis of Regulatory Frameworks for Shared Kitchens across Different Countries. *Foods*, *13*(6), 918. DOI: 10.3390/foods13060918 PMID: 38540909

Nagadeepa, C., Jaheer Mukthar, K. P., Ramirez-Asis, E., Huaranga-Toledo, H., Espinoza-Maguiña, M., & Mory-Guarnizo, S. (2023). A reinforcer to become a foodpreneur through cloud kitchen: sustainable technology-driven business model during pandemic. In *Technological Sustainability and Business Competitive Advantage* (pp. 401–413). Springer International Publishing. DOI: 10.1007/978-3-031-35525-7_25

Nguyen, T., & Nguyen, D. M. (2024). What will make Generation Y and Generation Z to continue to use online food delivery services: A uses and gratifications theory perspective. *Journal of Hospitality Marketing & Management*, *33*(4), 415–442. DOI: 10.1080/19368623.2023.2277731

Nigro, C., Iannuzzi, E., di Santo, N., & Sisto, R. (2022). Food delivery, ghost kitchens and virtual restaurants: Temporary or long-lasting game changers? *British Food Journal, 125*(6), 2217–2233. DOI: 10.1108/BFJ-02-2022-0095

Paul, N. I. J., Sajnani, M., & Sharma, K. (2024, June). Effectiveness of Digital Marketing on Instagram: A Study on EatSure Multi-Brand Cloud Kitchen. In *International Conference on Innovation and Regenerative Trends in Tourism and Hospitality Industry (IRTTHI 2024)* (pp. 268-279). Atlantis Press. DOI: 10.2991/978-94-6463-437-2_18

Pookulangara, S., Wen, H., & Bharath, J. (2023). Consumer attitudes toward ordering from cloud kitchens: A gender and marital status perspective. *International Journal of Contemporary Hospitality Management, 35*(5), 1859–1879. DOI: 10.1108/IJCHM-03-2022-0310

Rai, H. B., Mariquivoi, J., Schorung, M., & Dablanc, L. (2023). Dark stores in the City of Light: Geographical and transportation impacts of 'quick commerce' in Paris. *Research in Transportation Economics, 100*, 101333. DOI: 10.1016/j.retrec.2023.101333

Rinaldi, C., D'aguilar, M., & Egan, M. (2022). Understanding the online environment for the delivery of food, alcohol and tobacco: An exploratory analysis of 'dark kitchens' and rapid grocery delivery services. *International Journal of Environmental Research and Public Health, 19*(9), 5523. DOI: 10.3390/ijerph19095523 PMID: 35564918

Rosette, J. (2024, May). Platform Kitchens and the Remaking of Food Service. []. Sage CA: Los Angeles, CA: SAGE Publications.]. *New Labor Forum, 33*(2), 78–88. DOI: 10.1177/10957960241245408

Rout, A., Dawande, M., & Janakiraman, G. (2024). Cloud-Kitchens: Value Creation Through Co-Location. *Production and Operations Management, 33*(2), 512–529. DOI: 10.1177/10591478231224950

Satpathy, A., Samal, A., Gupta, S., Kumar, S., Sharma, S., Manoharan, G., Karthikeyan, M., & Sharma, S. (2024). To Study the Sustainable Development Practices in Business and Food Industry. *Migration Letters : An International Journal of Migration Studies, 21*(S1), 743–747. DOI: 10.59670/ml.v21iS1.6400

Schorung, M. (2024). Quick commerce and the evolving business models of the food retail industry-Investigating the quick commerce supply chain and the urban impacts of dark stores. *Transportation Research Procedia, 79*, 305–312. DOI: 10.1016/j.trpro.2024.03.041

Shankar, A., Jebarajakirthy, C., Nayal, P., Maseeh, H. I., Kumar, A., & Sivapalan, A. (2022). Online food delivery: A systematic synthesis of literature and a framework development. *International Journal of Hospitality Management, 104*, 103240. DOI: 10.1016/j.ijhm.2022.103240

Shapiro, A. (2023). Platform urbanism in a pandemic: Dark stores, ghost kitchens, and the logistical-urban frontier. *Journal of Consumer Culture, 23*(1), 168–187. DOI: 10.1177/14695405211069983

Shin, H., Jeon, J., & Jeong, E. L. (2024). Investigating consumers' perceived benefits and risks of meal-kit delivery service. *International Journal of Hospitality Management, 119*, 103715. DOI: 10.1016/j.ijhm.2024.103715

Sulaiman, A., Rahmat, A. K., Ibrahim, I., & Jamaludin, F. (2023). Online Food Delivery Sentiment Analysis from the Restaurant Point of View. *Information Management and Business Review*, *15*(3 (SI)), 197–204. DOI: 10.22610/imbr.v15i3(SI).3472

Suresh, S., Santhosh, S., & Samjaila, T. H. (2024). Food Economies–Engendered Ghost Kitchens in the Digital Age. In *Business Development via AI and Digitalization* (Vol. 2, pp. 95–104). Springer Nature Switzerland. DOI: 10.1007/978-3-031-62106-2_8

Tualeka, S. H. (2024). Multi-Brand Virtual Restaurant: Cloud Kitchen Business Model (Case Study of PT. Sagala). [MSEJ]. *Management Studies and Entrepreneurship Journal*, *5*(2), 4921–4931.

Vu, O. T. K., Alonso, A. D., Tran, T. D., & Nicholson, G. J. (2023). Illuminating the dark kitchen business model-A knowledge-based perspective from the supply-side. *Journal of Hospitality and Tourism Management*, *55*, 318–331. DOI: 10.1016/j.jhtm.2023.04.013

Wray, A., Arku, G., Long, J., Minaker, L., Seabrook, J., Doherty, S., & Gilliland, J. (2024). Restaurant survival during the COVID-19 pandemic: Examining operational, demographic and land use predictors in London, Canada. *Urban Studies (Edinburgh, Scotland)*, •••, 00420980241269785. DOI: 10.1177/00420980241269785

Zhu, Y., Pi, M., Zhu, X., & Byrd, K. (2024). Busiest Store in a Cramped Space: Can a Ghost Kitchen Optimize Coffee Shop Efficiency? *Journal of Hospitality & Tourism Cases*, 21649987241270419.

Chapter 20
Cloud Kitchens and Digital Foodscapes:
Exploring Social Media's Role in Kerala's Food

Deepa Mohan
https://orcid.org/0000-0002-9718-5093
Kannur University, India

ABSTRACT

The food industry in Kerala underwent a significant change due to expanding cloud kitchens, which altered how consumers dine and consume traditional foods. The research examines how cloud kitchens connect with digital foodscapes through social media influences on customer behavior along with marketing approaches. The research combines surveys with interviews of stakeholders to examine the social-cultural and economic effects of cloud kitchens through a mixed-methods approach. Research reveals that cloud kitchens create business prospects and service advantages but produce difficulties, including food genuineness issues, breakdown of traditional eating rituals, and sustainability challenges. The proposed policies focus on controlling the industry by regulating sustainable packaging standards and standardizing economic approaches between traditional dining establishments. The research connects digital advances to cultural conservation by supporting an equal expansion of Kerala's food industry.

1. INTRODUCTION

Cloud kitchens, known as ghost or virtual kitchens, have driven substantial changes within the international food industry. These restaurants function only through delivery operations because they have no facilities for dining guests at any venue. The cloud kitchen model enables businesses to lower overhead expenses and respond quickly to market changes because of its flexible structure (Colpaart, 2023). Since mid-20th-century pizza storefronts that operated as takeaway eateries, cloud kitchens underwent rapid growth during the last two decades to become a fundamental segment of the Indian food industry (Sharda, 2021). Kerala's traditional culinary traditions experience growing cloud kitchen expansion because of urban development, online innovations, and altered market preferences. Social media serves as a fundamental force of change that alters how people perceive food culture while actively shaping

DOI: 10.4018/979-8-3373-0432-8.ch020

consumer behavior and preserving culinary heritage. The study investigates cloud kitchen operations in the digital culinary landscapes of Kerala through analysis of social media's role in shaping contemporary food cultures that affect traditional regional cuisine.

1.1 Context and Background

The food industry has evolved enormously because of technological progress, changing consumer behavior patterns, and urban lifestyles. The expansion of internet accessibility and mobile applications combined with digital payment tools has allowed food delivery services to thrive. Kerala, as well as other states, experienced food consumption pattern changes as a result of urbanization and increased economic opportunities, which prompted people to adopt ready-to-eat meal services and delivery solutions (Basheer Nabeesa & Karunakaran Prasanna, 2023). During the COVID-19 pandemic, limitations on dining services prompted traditional restaurants to develop their operations as cloud kitchens (Ahmed Khan et al., 2022). Social media participation has strongly affected what foods people choose to eat. Customers find their food discovery, restaurant guidance, and home-based business direction through social media platforms, including Instagram, Facebook, and YouTube. Through the digitalization of the food industry, online interactions have become key factors that form food culture. At the same time, social media stands as an essential instrument for both cloud kitchens and users (Goodman & Jaworska, 2020).

1.2 Cloud Kitchens in the Indian Context

The food industry in India adopted cloud kitchens as a fundamental element because of high urban property expenses combined with the rising usage of delivery platforms like Swiggy and Zomato (Maitra & Rana, 2020). The operational expenses decrease through this model because it discards dine-in possibilities to emphasize food delivery optimization instead. According to Beniwal & Mathur (2021) and their analysis, the Indian cloud kitchen market will reach $2 billion by 2024 because of digital transformation and new consumer patterns (Beniwal & K. Mathur, 2021). Cloud kitchens offer affordable scalability, attracting new business startups because they allow small operators to launch without significant startup costs. Cloud kitchens maintain multiple benefits yet encounter three main problems because they heavily depend on third-party aggregators and encounter algorithm visibility complications while struggling with regulatory restrictions (Nair, 2024). The advantage to both affordability and operational benefits keeps cloud kitchens expanding throughout India's developing food service business sector.

1.3 Cloud Kitchens in Kerala

Studies about cloud kitchens primarily discuss metropolitan areas, yet Kerala shows a significant growth pattern among cloud kitchen startups. Kochi, Thiruvananthapuram, and Kozhikode have experienced dramatic growth in food delivery services because digital penetration and modified consumer life patterns have influenced the market (Basheer Nabeesa & Karunakaran Prasanna, 2023). The preference of working professional urban families to order meals rather than prepare food at home drives the positive opportunities for cloud kitchen development. The well-established tourism sector of Kerala creates the market potential for specific cloud kitchen services specializing in serving traditional and international dishes. The essential characteristic of cloud kitchens operating in Kerala involves their connection with traditional home-based food business operators. Small-scale female business owners use WhatsApp, Facebook, and Instagram platforms to advertise homemade foods while eliminating the need for traditional food intermediary services (Suresh et al., 2024). These emerging businesses face ongoing regulatory obstacles like food safety regulation and taxation (Nair, 2024).

1.4 Role of Social Media in Food Consumption/Digital Foodscapes

Food consumption in modern times has become dramatically dependent on social media, including its fussing consumer preference, brand visibility, and even marketing strategies. Digital foodscapes (spaces where food is curated, consumed, and discussed online) have reshaped food culture by merging tradition with modern digital engagement. Social media plays a role in the culinary trends and increase in online food communities in Kerala as food bloggers, influencers, and home chefs actively participate in the digital ecosystem (Schneider & Eli, 2021). The visually appealing food trends we see growing in popularity on platforms like Instagram or YouTube are due to the aesthetics of choosing food. Cloud kitchens use social media to enhance their market reach, which causes them to rely on influencer collaborations, digital advertisements, and user-generated content (John & Gopalakrishnan, 2022). However, the power of electronic word-of-mouth (e-WOM) and online reviews further enhance consumer trust; therefore, digital engagement is key for the success of cloud kitchens (Idris et al., 2023). At the same time, the trend of food culture becoming digitalized creates fears that some authentic culinary values may be diluted. Therefore, food on digital platforms is becoming a commodity, which may endanger the rich heritage of Kerala's gastronomy due to the dominance of fleeting social media trends and comparison of food content (Goodman & Jaworska, 2020). This study aims to understand how these dynamics work in cloud kitchens and their association with social media interactions to examine how their dynamic relationship is preserving and transforming Kerala's food culture.

The advent of cloud kitchens and social media's increasing thrusting power over food consumption in Kerala strongly indicate a rupture with these food landscapes. While cloud kitchens are relatively economical and easy to use, they conflict with long-existing culinary traditions. In the digital age, social media is a promotional tool and a cultural mediator of new eaters' consumption patterns and food identity. This study critically examines the implications of these trends in Kerala's evolving food culture in a fast-changing digital world.

2. STATEMENT OF THE PROBLEM

The food industry experienced a rapid transformation because cloud kitchens adopted delivery-focused business operations that depend on digital marketing and social media interaction. Kerala's rich culinary heritage and traditional dining culture face important challenges because of these kitchen operations, providing economic opportunities and ease of access. People relying more on online platforms now determine how food marketers approach their audiences, changing how consumers experience food products and their purchasing behavior.

Investigation into cloud kitchens in Kerala faces scarcity even though they become increasingly popular in the area, specifically in terms of their social and cultural influences and economic forces. Investigatory work must focus on how social media shapes user habits and traditional food preservation in cloud kitchens and their complete effects on Kerala's local dining traditions. An evaluation of cloud kitchen innovation must examine their ability to sustain traditional food culture authenticity alongside their modernization approaches.

Cloud kitchens must overcome a series of sustainability challenges because they must handle food safety requirements alongside taxation policies that affect their operations while managing environmental worries about packaging waste. The next step requires resolving current gaps to build policies that blend innovation methods with cultural protection measures in Kerala's evolving food system.

3. IMPORTANCE OF THE STUDY

The study provides advantages to multiple parties: scholars, food professionals, policymakers, and market consumers. The research about cloud kitchens in Kerala contributes knowledge about digitalization's effect on original food traditions and buyer decision-making practices. This research shows how cloud kitchens succeed in preserving authenticity through digital marketing to expand their customer base. Entrepreneurs who want to benefit from preserving traditional Kerala cuisine should learn effective methods to adapt their offerings to changes in consumer preference. Policy officials who adopt findings from this research gain important recommendations about establishing regulatory standards in addition to food safety methods and sustainable operations. The analysis guides the development of regulations allowing cloud kitchens to achieve sustainable economic expansion alongside traditional culinary heritage and environmental accountability. This research examines social factors regarding cloud kitchens, including their alteration to social dining customs and their influence on customer consumption of local foods. Knowledge of changing food consumer habits enables better decision-making by consumers who want to support inclusion and food sustainability in Kerala. This study bridges innovative practices with established traditions to offer comprehensive knowledge about cloud kitchens in Kerala's food business while presenting tested solutions for developing a balanced future. The study provides advantages to multiple parties: scholars, food professionals, policymakers, and market consumers. The research about cloud kitchens in Kerala contributes knowledge about digitalization's effect on original food traditions and buyer decision-making practices. This research shows how cloud kitchens succeed in preserving authenticity through digital marketing to expand their customer base. Entrepreneurs who want to benefit from preserving traditional Kerala cuisine should learn effective methods to adapt their offerings to changes in consumer preference. Policy officials who adopt findings from this research gain important recommendations about establishing regulatory standards in addition to food safety methods and sustainable operations. The analysis guides the development of regulations allowing cloud kitchens to achieve sustainable economic expansion alongside traditional culinary heritage and environmental accountability. This research examines social factors regarding cloud kitchens, including their alteration to social dining customs and their influence on customer consumption of local foods. Knowledge of changing food consumer habits enables better decision-making by consumers who want to support inclusion and food sustainability in Kerala. This study bridges innovative practices with established traditions to offer comprehensive knowledge about cloud kitchens in Kerala's food business while presenting tested solutions for developing a balanced future.

4. LITERATURE REVIEW

Kerala has been under the revolution of cloud kitchens and social media when it comes to the food industry, altering the attitude of the consumers, marketing strategies, and economic taking. The outcomes analyzed in this literature review show a general investigation of cloud kitchens' theoretical frameworks and evolution, the influence on customer engagement through social media, and culture, economy, and regulation. It also discusses sustainability issues and compares the cloud kitchen activity in Kerala with worldwide trends. Analyzing all these factors, this review gives insight into how the contemporary food services industry is transformed with digital transformation.

4.1 Theoretical Framework

In this study, Stuart Hall's "Circuit of Culture" framework analyzes something entailing production, consumption, identity, regulation, and signification in food consumption. Such a model would allow understanding the cultural shift toward virtual food services (Suresh et al., 2024). Using the "Circuit of Culture" presents researchers with a complete framework to study production and consumption activities alongside identity development, regulatory elements, and signification processes. This method benefits the assessment of cloud kitchens, revealing how services are created and utilized and how they affect cultural identities, local regulatory standards, and social meanings. A holistic view of this transformation delivers a detailed understanding of Kerala's cultural movement toward virtual food services(Du Gay et al., 2013). To analyze the impact of digital platforms on cloud kitchens, additional theories like digital transformation theories, economic disruption theories, and social reproduction theories are added (Nair, 2024).

4.2 Cloud Kitchens: Concept and Evolution

Ghost kitchens, alternatively known as cloud kitchens, function as delivery-oriented kitchens that exclude dining areas in their operation structure. Because of the COVID-19 crisis, cloud kitchens have become a market-responsive solution that offers affordable flexibility (Sapkota, 2022). Various models of cloud kitchens emerged, including the single-brand option plus the multi-brand operation and the aggregator-managed kitchen system (Deepak et al., 2022). The food preparation facilities offer business owners an economical way to enter the food service business (Maitra & Rana, 2020).

4.3 The Role of Social Media in Cloud Kitchen Success

Social media is a primary factor for cloud kitchen expansion because it boosts brand awareness while enabling customer relationships. Marketing success and customer relationship development rely heavily on social media platforms such as Instagram, YouTube, and Facebook (Bark Social Digital, 2024; Jones et al., 2015). Food influencers influence market growth while shaping consumer perception and purchasing (Misra et al., 2024). Combining visual content and customer interaction through social media marketing tools enables cloud kitchens to develop trust with their audience (Choudhary, 2019).

4.4 Consumer Behavior and Online Food Ordering Trends

The three main factors influencing online food ordering choices for consumers are pricing, food quality, and convenience benefits. Mobile applications and digital platforms enable increased cloud kitchen implementation because of their widespread popularity (Sapkota, 2022). Research illustrates that consumers chose delivery-based food services during COVID-19 mainly because of hygiene concerns (John & Gopalakrishnan, 2022). The online ordering preferences of Gen Z Millennials and younger members of society stem from their need for efficient service alongside customizable choices (Kulshreshtha & Sharma, 2022).

4.5 Cultural and Social Implications of Cloud Kitchens

Consumer preferences drive cloud kitchens to provide different food cuisines. Because of these emerging trends, protecting traditional cooking methods has become an issue (Davis, 2024). The Kerala Food Platform launched digital programs to digitize organic food delivery systems that preserve traditional culinary practices throughout Kerala (Ganesh Gopal, 2024). The preservation of Meen Curry, alongside its modern update, has been made possible through social media and digital food platforms (Davis, 2024).

4.6 Economic and Employment Impact of Cloud Kitchens

Women entrepreneurs have capitalized on employment opportunities across cloud kitchens because numerous small businesses began operating throughout the pandemic (Suresh et al., 2024). The kitchens reduce operations expenses and enable food entrepreneurs to develop innovative business approaches (Beniwal & Mathur, 2022). Although cloud kitchens generate employment possibilities, they create unstable working conditions for their staff members, which leads to concerns about equal employment standards (Nair, 2024).

4.7 Regulatory and Policy Challenges

The quick growth of cloud kitchens creates three main regulatory issues: sanitation regulations, taxation systems, and ecological sustainability problems. The model proves effective for its operations, yet new policies must be established to handle current legal and economic barriers (Suresh et al., 2024). Some cloud kitchen operators avoid compliance with food safety regulations by doing business out of the system to escape bureaucratic regulations (Nair, 2024).

4.8 Sustainability and Environmental Concerns

Cloud kitchen operations generate waste from delivery packaging materials while producing carbon emissions from delivery services. The rising requirement demands eliminating waste materials during packaging and sustainable delivery options (John & Gopalakrishnan, 2022). The cloud kitchen ecosystem receives growing interest in sustainable food practices that combine biodegradable packaging solutions with energy-efficient operational methods (Mathur & Mathur, 2023). Research about the environmental consequences of cloud kitchens remains scarce within Kerala.

4.9 Comparative Analysis with Other Regions

The Indian cloud kitchen space connects to international markets through common operational patterns while dealing with specific obstacles connected to regulatory obstacles and preferences shaped by local culture. The cloud kitchens of Bangladesh access tax benefits, although they deal with strict food safety requirements (Ahmed Khan et al., 2022). Scientific data reveals that the Indian cloud kitchen market continues to expand rapidly and could achieve global market status as the second largest behind China (Upadhye, 2020). The success rates of cloud kitchens between markets depend significantly on customer tastes and the enforcement of regulatory frameworks within each geographic area.

The combination of cloud kitchens with social media platforms has substantially modernized Kerala's food industry through its impacts on consumer patterns, the development of digital food marketing, and cultural changes in food. Food service technology integration provides economic opportunities to food businesses while creating regulatory hurdles and ecological sustainability questions. Studies should investigate how digital platforms permanently affect traditional food handling methods and the food service sector throughout Kerala.

5. RESEARCH GAP

Research shows social media impacts food businesses worldwide, but scholars have done little study on how social media affects cloud kitchens in Kerala's food culture. Existing research primarily addresses general market trends, customer behavior, and digital transformation but lacks an in-depth exploration of the following:

1. Social media supports both traditional Kerala food practices and new food innovations together.
2. Cloud kitchen operations in Kerala show how modern food businesses impact local food customs and social norms.
3. This research focuses on finding effective ways digital platforms can support cloud kitchens to sustain authentic food practices.

6. RESEARCH QUESTIONS

- How does social media marketing affect consumer behavior toward cloud kitchens in Kerala? o What strategies do cloud kitchens in Kerala employ to preserve culinary traditions while adapting to modern demands?
- What are the socio-cultural and economic implications of the rise of cloud kitchens in Kerala?
- How do sustainability and authenticity play a role in Kerala's cloud kitchen practices, and how are these communicated through social media?

7. RESEARCH OBJECTIVES

- To evaluate the effectiveness of social media marketing strategies used by cloud kitchens in Kerala.

- o To explore how cloud kitchens balance innovation and tradition in Kerala's food industry.
- o To assess the socio-cultural impact of cloud kitchens on Kerala's food habits and dining culture.
- o To examine the role of social media in promoting sustainability and authenticity in Kerala's cloud kitchens.
- o To provide actionable insights for cloud kitchen entrepreneurs to leverage social media for sustainable growth while preserving cultural heritage.

8. RESEARCH METHODOLOGY

8.1 Research Design

A mixed-methods investigation combines quantitative data with qualitative research methods to provide in-depth knowledge regarding cloud kitchens' effects on Kerala's food culture.

8.2 Sampling & Data Collection

- **Survey:** Data for this research came from 115 participants spread across Kerala through a web-based survey using purposive non-random sampling techniques. Social media platforms Facebook and WhatsApp delivered the survey to respondents who already understood the operation of cloud kitchens. Respondents who answered every survey question were considered for the final data analysis. The survey analyzed Kerala consumers' perspectives about cloud kitchens and their usage patterns as well as evaluation criteria and examined how social media affected their selection decisions, which helped researchers better understand the digital food sector's shift in Kerala.
- **Interviews:** Semi-structured interviews were conducted among various stakeholders to gather qualitative data.
  - o **Cloud Kitchen Entrepreneurs:** The study Examined operational strategies, cultural authenticity, and digital marketing practices.
  - o **Traditional Restaurant Owners:** for a comparative perspective on the impact of cloud kitchens on conventional dining establishments.
  - o **Food Vloggers:** The study Explored the influence of digital content creation on consumer perceptions and purchasing behavior.
  - o **Policymakers:** The study Investigated regulatory perspectives on food safety, taxation, and industry growth.

8.3 Data Analysis

- **Quantitative Analysis:** Survey data were processed using statistical tools, including chi-square tests, to identify patterns, associations, and trends in consumer behavior related to cloud kitchens. R software used to analyse quantitative data.

Qualitative Analysis: Thematic analysis was applied to interview data to extract key themes related to cultural sustainability, innovation, marketing strategies, and regulatory challenges. Patterns in consumer influence from vlogger content were also examined to assess their role in shaping public perception of cloud kitchens. NVivo was used to analyze interviews.

8.4 Ethical Considerations

Participating individuals gave their informed consent before the study began. The research maintained complete confidentiality and anonymity throughout both data collection and analysis procedures. The researcher obtained ethical permission to comply with research ethical guidelines.

8.5 Limitations

The research examines several possible drawbacks, such as participant answer biases in survey responses and interview-generated subjective information. It also excludes a complete overview of Kerala's food influencer community, which might affect how the findings apply to the overall picture. However, the study overcomes its limitations to provide beneficial insights into the cultural and economic aspects of cloud kitchens in Kerala.

9. FINDINGS AND DISCUSSIONS

9.1 Demographics

9.1.1 Age

Figure 1. Age wise distribution of Cloud Kitchen users in Kerala

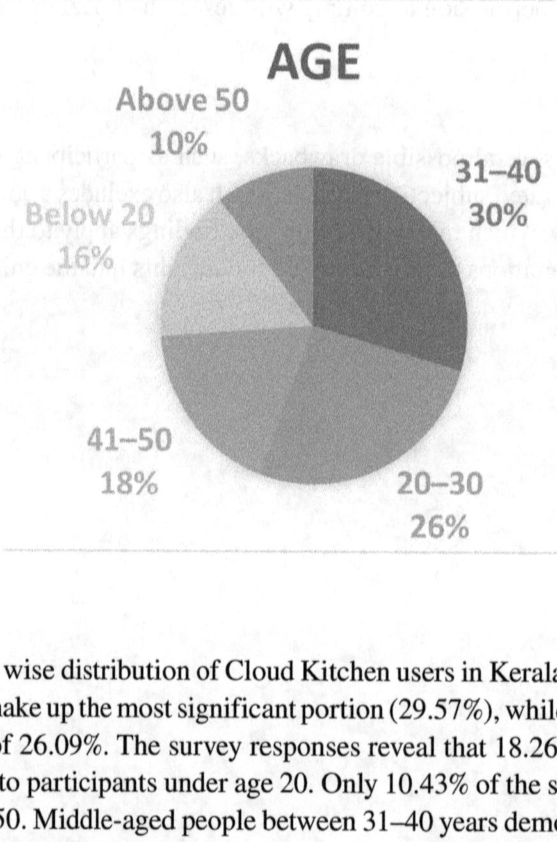

Source: primary data

Fig 1 illustrates the age wise distribution of Cloud Kitchen users in Kerala. It shows that respondents in the age group of 31-40 make up the most significant portion (29.57%), while those aged between 20-30 follow with a percentage of 26.09%. The survey responses reveal that 18.26% belong to the 41–50 age range, and 15.65% belong to participants under age 20. Only 10.43% of the study participants belong to the age bracket older than 50. Middle-aged people between 31–40 years demonstrate the highest interest in cloud kitchen and digital food landscape discussions across Kerala due to their economic capability and comfortable adoption of digital systems.

The data indicates that middle-aged people in Kerala participate more when discussing digital food environments and cloud kitchen models. A study called "Mapping Digital Foodscapes: Digital Food Influencers and the Grammars of Good Food" reveals how digital food influencers use multiple online platforms to influence people's understanding of "good food." These influencers predominantly belong to middle- to upper-class societies, as research reveals, while matching the survey results, that there is an increase in middle-aged digital food discourses (Goodman & Jaworska, 2020). Data about the population in Kerala shows a unique age composition that differs from the other Indian states. Kerala leads India with the largest population of elderly citizens after experiencing an 11.4% growth in people older than 60 through the past sixty years, resulting in a current aged population percentage of 16.5. The aging pattern observed in this region differs from the national statistical pattern, yet it affects how various age groups participate in digital food platforms (Arasu, 2023).

The Indian market for cloud kitchens has experienced considerable expansion to its worth of US$ 969.5 million in 2023, where forecasters anticipate a 13.2% growth rate from 2024 to 2032. The market expansion occurs due to consumers who want convenient food delivery along with cost-effective operations of cloud kitchens. Cloud kitchens have become popular for customers and food business owners because they offer scalability and flexibility for operations, especially in digitally active urban and semi-urban areas (Basheer Nabeesa & Karunakaran Prasanna, 2023; Imarc group, 2024). The survey results confirm research evidence about middle-aged consumers being actively present in modern food delivery systems. Socioeconomic standing, digital proficiency, and population distribution across Indian regions drive the participant levels because these elements align with digital dining behavior research and cloud kitchen expansion trends across the nation.

9.1.2 Gender

Figure 2. Gender wise distribution of Cloud Kitchen users in Kerala

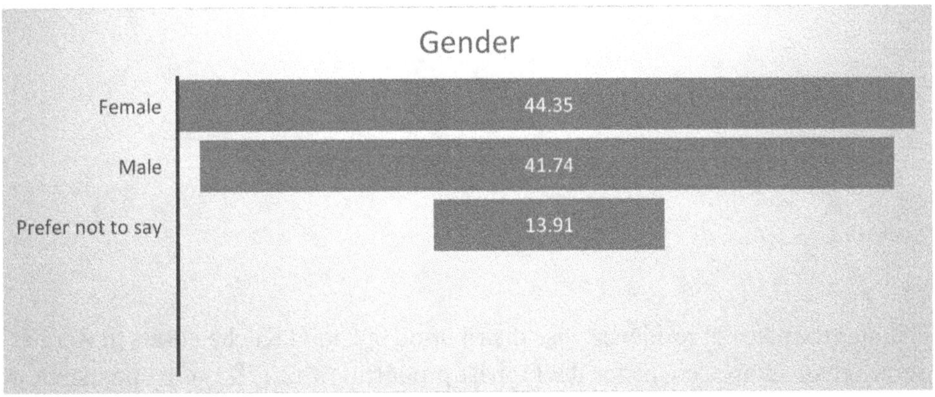

Source: Primary Data

The Fig 2 shows that women comprise 44.35% of participants and men makeup 41.74% of participants. The remaining 13.91% chose to withhold their gender information. The survey revealed that 13.91% chose not to reveal their gender. The research data demonstrates nearly equal gender participation, with female respondents outnumbering male participants slightly. Digital discussions about food culture are becoming increasingly inclusive and private based on the notable number of participants who chose not to share their gender.

A study named "Consumerism and Gendering in Food Culture: A Study of Urban Kerala" examines Kerala's food culture's adaptation to consumerism and gender behaviors. Women in modern urban Kerala participate increasingly in discussions about food while participating actively in food decisions, which supports a growing gender balance in their food culture, according to Basheer Nabeesa & Karunakaran Prasanna (2023) (Basheer Nabeesa & Karunakaran Prasanna, 2023). The observed gender split and substantial participant non-disclosure numbers demonstrate changing societal preferences toward inclusiveness and personal privacy. Research by existing literature shows that these findings demonstrate why gender dynamics and personal preferences should be studied when examining digital food culture engagement.

9.1.3 Place of Residence

Figure 3. Place of Residence wise Distribution of Cloud Kitchen users in Kerala

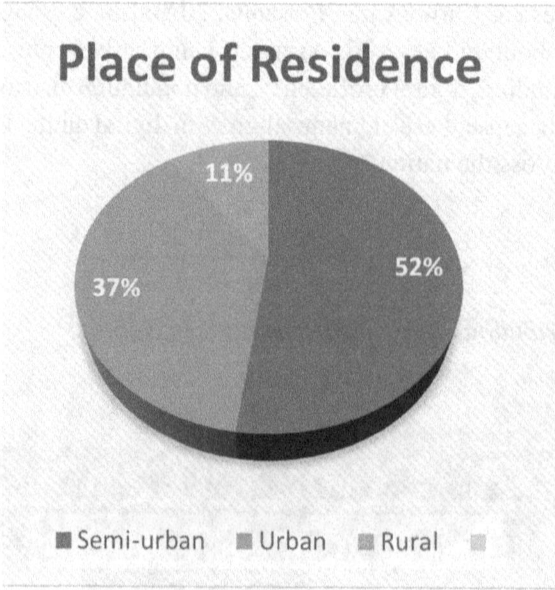

Source: Primary Data

Fig 3 illustrates the place of residence wise distribution of Cloud Kitchen users in Kerala. The results show that semi-urban areas account for the highest proportion (52.17%) of respondents, while urban areas follow with 37.39% of participants, and rural areas contain only 10.43% of respondents. The data indicates that digital food structures primarily serve semi-urban and urban areas rather than rural areas.

Available research findings support this observed pattern. Studies evaluating foodscapes confirm that urban and semi-urban areas provide better access to diverse food platforms and digital options that drive the advancement of digital foodscapes containing cloud kitchen services. The adoption rate of digital food services remains restricted for rural areas because these locations display limited infrastructure and powerful traditional food consumption habits (Vonthron et al., 2020). Research confirms that residents in urban and semi-urban areas choose alternative food networks because these networks grant them increased accessibility and convenience. Rural consumer behavior differs from urban consumers because they stick to direct food procurement methods and traditional food practices since they produce their food independently (Preiss et al., 2017). The survey matches existing scholarly research by showing that cloud kitchens and digital foodscapes dominate urban and semi-urban zones. However, rural people avoid digital food services because of infrastructure difficulties and traditional food traditions.

9.2 Consumer Behavior and Perceptions

9.2.1 How often do the respondents order from cloud kitchens?

Table 1. order frequency followed by Cloud Kitchen users in Kerala. **Hypothesis: The behavior of ordering food from Cloud Kitchen in Kerala is evenly distributed**

Order Frequency	Frequency	Percentage	Chi-Square value	P Value
2–3 times a month	36	31.30		
Once a week or more	30	26.09		
Once a month	24	20.9		
Rarely	15	13.04		
Never	10	8.7	59.31801471	0
Total	**115**	**100.00**		

Source: Primary Data

Table 1 shows the frequency of food orders from cloud kitchens among respondents in Kerala. The most common frequency of order is "2–3 times a month" (31.30%), which is followed by "once a week or more" (26.09%) and "once a month" (20.9%). Moreover, only a smaller percentage reported ordering "rarely" (13.04%) or "never" (8.7%). The chi-square value of 59.32 and a p-value of 0 indicates a statistically significant result, rejecting the null hypothesis that the behavior of ordering food from cloud kitchens in Kerala is evenly distributed. This suggests that respondents' ordering behaviors are concentrated in the specific frequencies of categories, with moderate to frequent ordering being the most common.

The result suggests a moderate to high engagement with cloud kitchens among the surveyed population. In comparison, a study by Mathur and Mathur (2023) examined factors influencing consumer perceptions and attitudes toward cloud kitchens in India, finding positive purchase behavior among Indian youth (Mathur & Mathur, 2023). While the study did not provide specific ordering frequencies, it highlighted a strong impact of perception and attitude on purchase behavior, suggesting a favorable inclination toward cloud kitchen services among younger demographics (Mathur & Mathur, 2023). Additionally, a report by TechSci Research (2023) noted that cloud kitchens have disrupted the conventional restaurant industry, with online food delivery becoming the new trend. The report highlighted cloud kitchens' flexibility and low operating costs, contributing to their rapid adoption by the people (TechSci Research, 2023). These findings align with the observed ordering patterns in Kerala, indicating a significant engagement with cloud kitchens, particularly among younger consumers. As identified in existing literature, the positive attitudes and perceptions toward cloud kitchens may contribute to the moderate to high ordering frequencies observed in the geographic region.

9.2.2 Which social media platform influences respondent's food choices the most

Figure 4. Social Media Platform influenced most by Cloud Kitchen users in Kerala

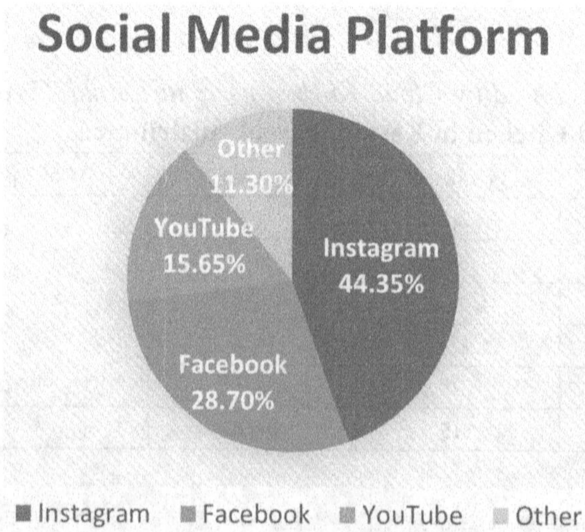

Source: Primary Data

Fig 4 illustrates the social media platform influences the Cloud kitchen users in Kerala. The data reveals that Instagram is the most influential social media platform affecting respondents' food choices, with 44.35% of respondents indicating its impact. This trend follows Facebook, which influences 28.70% of respondents, while YouTube impacts 15.65%. Only a smaller percentage (11.30%) attribute their food choices to other platforms. These results highlight Instagram's dominance as a significant platform in shaping food-related preferences, likely due to its focus on visuals and trends. This makes it highly effective for food content marketing.

The above data indicates that Instagram is the most influential social media platform affecting respondents' food choices, with 44.35% of respondents indicating its impact. A systematic review by Kucharczuk (2022) found that Instagram and Facebook were among the most popular social media platforms influencing adolescents' eating behaviors positively and negatively (Kucharczuk, 2022)(Chung et al., 2021). Similarly, another study found that social media engagement, particularly exposure to image-related content, may negatively impact healthy young adults' body image and food choices (Rounsefell et al., 2020). These studies suggest that platforms like Instagram play a pivotal role in influencing food choices, which correlates with the observed data where Instagram leads in shaping respondents' dietary decisions.

9.3 Preferences and Outcomes

9.3.1 What factors influence respondent's decision to order from a cloud kitchen?

Table 2. The factors influence the Cloud Kitchen users in Kerala regarding the decision to order from Cloud Kitchen. **Hypothesis: The factors that influence respondent's decision to order from a cloud kitchen in Kerala is evenly distributed**

Factors influence	Frequency	Percentage	Chi-Square value	P Value
Quality of food	36	31.30	7.11	0.13
Price	27	23.48		
Speed of delivery	21	18.26		
Sustainability	19	16.52		
Cultural authenticity	12	10.43		
Total	**115**	**100.00**		

The data presented in Table 2 highlights the key factors influencing respondents' decisions to order from a cloud kitchen in Kerala. The most significant factor is the "quality of food," chosen by 31.30% of respondents, which is followed by "price" (23.48%) and "speed of delivery" (18.26%). "Sustainability" (16.52%) and "cultural authenticity" (10.43%) play more minor roles. The chi-square value of 7.11 and p-value of 0.13 indicate that the differences in frequency across these factors are not statistically significant. As the p-value is greater than 0.05, the null hypothesis that the factors influencing respondents' decisions are evenly distributed cannot be rejected. This suggests that no single factor intensely dominates the decision-making process, though the food quality appears slightly more influential.

This finding aligns with existing literature on consumer behavior towards online food delivery services. A study by Mathur and Mathur (2023) identified various factors like self-efficacy, perceived usefulness, and perceived ease of use as significant in shaping consumer perceptions and attitudes toward cloud kitchens in India (Mathur & Mathur, 2023). Similarly, Arji Mariam Jacob et al., (2011) stress convenience, time-saving, and promotional offers as key determinants influencing consumers to order food online (Arji Mariam Jacob et al., 2011). This study found that 38% of users preferred online food delivery apps due to their ease and convenience, which underlines the role of these factors in consumer choices. The present data is consistent with existing literature, indicating that consumers prioritize quality, price, and convenience when ordering from cloud kitchens. The relatively even distribution of these preferences suggests that cloud kitchens must maintain high standards across multiple factors to meet diverse consumer expectations.

9.3.2 Do the respondents believe that cloud kitchens have changed their dining habits?

Table 3. belief of the Cloud Kitchen users in Kerala regarding their changes in dining habits. **Hypothesis: The respondents believe that cloud kitchens have changed their dining habits in Kerala is evenly distributed**

Variable Name	Frequency	Percentage	Chi-Square value	P Value
No	55	47.83		
Sometimes	36	31.30	7.74	0.101
Yes	24	20.87		
Total	**115**	**100.00**		

Source: Primary Data

Respondents in this data present their thoughts on whether cloud kitchens have transformed regular eating behaviors in Kerala. A significant portion of 47.83% of respondents indicate that cloud kitchens have had no effect on their dining habits, and another 31.30% noted occasional impact. Compared, "20.87%" state cloud kitchens have changed their dining patterns. There is no evidence of statistically important response variation due to the p-value of 0.101 and chi-square value of 7.74. Since the p-value exceeds 0.05, the researcher cannot reject the null hypothesis, which demonstrates that respondents perceive the influence of cloud kitchens upon their eating practices equally within all three categories.

This finding aligns with the existing literature on the impact of cloud kitchens and food delivery services on consumer behavior. A study by Ahuja et al. (2021) noted that while food delivery services have proliferated, their effect on traditional dining habits among consumers varies. Some individuals have integrated delivery into their daily routines, while others prefer conventional dining experiences (Ahuja et al., 2021). Furthermore, research by Sharma and Kumar (2024) highlighted that cloud kitchens offer convenience and variety, which appeal to specific consumer segments. However, the extent to which these services alter dining habits depends on individual preferences, lifestyle, and cultural attitudes toward dining (R. Sharma & Kumar, 2024). The current data reflects a diverse range of consumer perceptions on the influence of cloud kitchens on dining habits, a trend correlated with existing literature. This suggests that while cloud kitchens have introduced new options, their impact on dining behaviors is minute and varies across consumer groups.

9.3.3 Impact of Cloud Kitchen on Preserving Traditional Food Practices

Figure 5. People's belief in the Impact of Cloud Kitchen on preserving Traditional Food Practices of Kerala

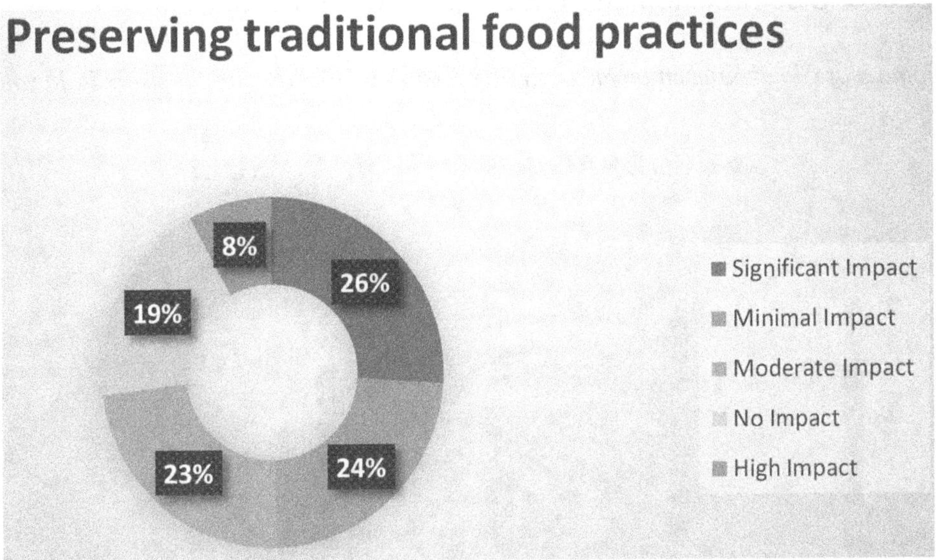

Source: Primary Data

Fig 5 illustrates people's belief in the impact of cloud Kitchen on preserving traditional food practices of Kerala. Survey participants have diverse opinions about how cloud kitchens affect the maintenance of traditional Kerala cuisine—about one-quarter of survey participants (23.48%) considered cloud kitchens to have a moderate or minor influence on protecting traditional food. In contrast, 26.09% reported a substantial impact. Most respondents (19.13%) believe cloud kitchens do not preserve traditional Kerala food culture, while 7.83% indicate that these kitchens make a major contribution to the preservation effort.

Cloud kitchens in India have changed the food and beverage sector by providing budget-friendly and efficient delivery-supported alternatives to conventional restaurant spaces. The virtual kitchen only processes delivery orders and takeout requests without requiring traditional dining areas, lowering operational expenses. The cloud kitchen sector in India continues to expand rapidly according to market predictions that forecast a $2 billion market value for 2024 (S. Sharma, 2024). Kerala citizens have warmly accepted the cloud kitchen concept, especially among the millennial generation, because of their online food delivery preferences. Traditional meal deliveries such as Onam Sadhya became the first popular service through which customers obtained neatly packed packages. Traditional cuisine found its market demand through an approach that incorporated modern delivery practices (Agarwal, 2019). The influence of cloud kitchens on preserving traditional food practices is an intricate phenomenon. Cloud kitchens enable traditional food accessibility, which helps maintain traditional foods, but the focus on operational efficiency and scalability could reduce the presence of less popular dishes in culinary offerings. The people of Kerala hold split perceptions about cloud kitchens' role in traditional food preservation since a quarter of respondents rated the effect as substantial. However, another quarter indicated it is either slight or non-existent. The modern solution of cloud kitchens solves food delivery needs, but their role in preserving traditional foods has both positive and negative effects. The various opinions among Kerala survey participants warrant responsible support for cloud kitchens alongside the protection of traditional culinary heritage.

9.3.4 Impact of Cloud Kitchen on Encouraging Fusion Cuisine

Figure 6. impact of Cloud Kitchen on encouraging Fusion Cusine among the users in Kerala

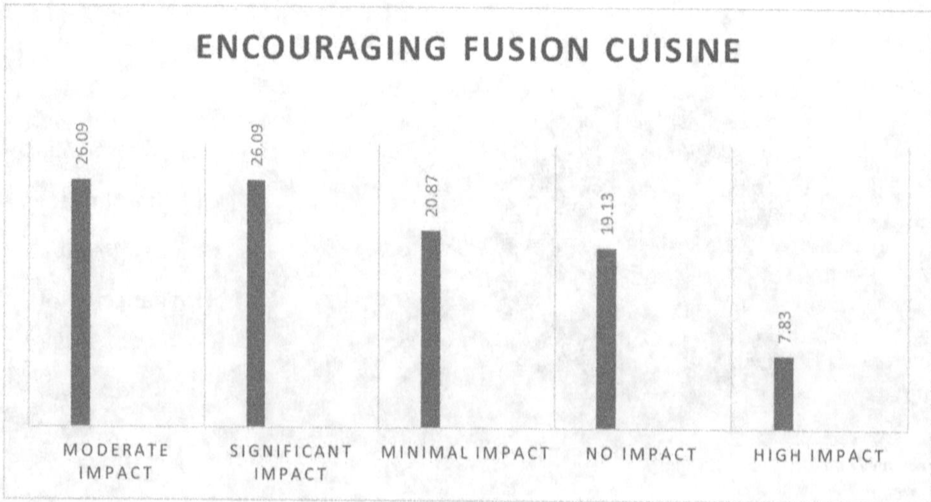

Source: Primary Data

Cloud kitchens' expansion is important in driving fusion cuisine growth across Kerala. A significant and moderate impact on fusion culinary styles was reported by 26.09% of respondents, making up the majority of those surveyed. A large portion of 40.14% views cloud kitchens as non-contributors to fusion cuisine development. In comparison, 20.87% report minimal influence, and 19.13% argue that cloud kitchens do not play any role in this area. A high impact of cloud kitchens on fostering fusion cuisine stands as the least recognized perception among 7.83% of respondents.

The cloud kitchen trend in Kerala receives strong support because this new model meets the preferences of millennials ordering online food. Cloud kitchens originated from businesses that delivered traditional food meals like Onam Sadhya through carefully packaged kits. This method fulfilled customer expectations for traditional food with contemporary delivery logistics (Agarwal, 2019). Different stakeholders have varying opinions about how cloud kitchens affect fusion cuisine progress. Cloud kitchen operations succeed through fusion dishes that unite regional cooking styles with international stirrings but also stay focused on single-community fare. The cuisine selection at Box8 demonstrates a contemporary trend because this delivery company provides authenticity between Indian and foreign recipes (Hadala, 2024). The survey responses in Kerala indicate a dual pattern regarding this subject. The study shows that fusion cuisine benefits from cloud kitchens, according to a minority sector, but most individuals neither understand nor doubt these contributions. The different emphasis between cloud kitchens in the region creates this split in food offerings because some kitchens serve traditional dishes, whereas others try fusion concepts. When considering the growth of fusion cuisine in Kerala through cloud kitchens, the general population has contrasting viewpoints about how these facilities support culinary innovation. The level at which cloud kitchens affect fusion cuisine development depends on their unique meal options and public understanding of fusion cooking principles.

9.3.5 Impact of Cloud Kitchen on Social Dining Culture in Kerala

Figure 7. Impact of Cloud Kitchen on Social Dining Culture in Kerala

Source: Primary Data

Fig 7 illustrates users' response towards the impact of Cloud Kitchen on Social Dining culture in Kerala. Kerala's traditional social dining culture demonstrates partial modification through cloud kitchen services. The highest respondent group indicated that cloud kitchens have a moderate effect on the social dining culture of Kerala, while 31.30% of respondents reported that the influence was moderate. The results show that 57.39% of individuals believe cloud kitchens make no difference to traditional eating traditions, yet 31.30% indicate a moderate effect, and 18.26% identified minimal influence on social dining customs. Of the respondents, only 5.22% believed cloud kitchens significantly influence the traditional culture of social dining.

The cloud kitchen industry in Kerala meets strong acceptance from people aged 20 to 35 who choose convenience over traditional dining methods through online platforms. The original rise of this concept occurred through services that delivered Onam Sadhya traditional meals packaged as neat sets. Traditional food service delivery met consumer preferences and integrated with contemporary delivery systems (Agarwal, 2019). Cloud kitchens provide convenience and diversity to customers, but their growing popularity potentially affects the traditional style of communal eating prevalent in Kerala. Study participants demonstrate ambivalent attitudes about cloud kitchens, showing that Kerala requires a proper balance to enjoy both convenience and cultural dining traditions.

9.3.4 Ratings given by respondents on the Impact of Food Quality on Cloud Kitchen choosing

Figure 8. Ratings given by the users in Kerala on the Impact of Food Quality on Cloud Kitchen choosing

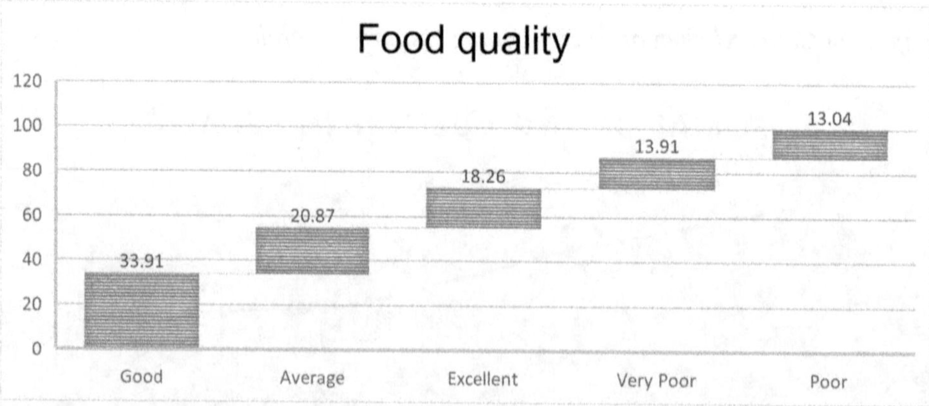

Source: Primary Data

Fig 8 illustrates the ratings given by the Cloud Kitchen users in Kerala regarding the impact of Food Quality on Cloud Kitchen using. Research indicates that customers positively evaluate cloud kitchen food quality through their assessments since most rate it reasonable (33.91%) and excellent (18.26%). Food quality achieved an average rating from 20.87% of respondents, yet 26.95% described it as unsatisfactory, 13.04% with a poor rating, and 13.91% found it very poor.

Literature shows that achieving success with cloud kitchens depends heavily on food quality. Since cloud kitchens operate without a branded dining space, the quality of their meals and delivery packaging are the main factors in forming customer impressions and securing future orders. Digital platforms remain the sole opportunity for connection between cloud kitchens and their customers. The absence of customer awareness about delivery sources means that delivering superior food quality and brand identity becomes crucial in two ways (posist.com, 2024). Survey results indicate that cloud kitchens in Kerala successfully deliver food quality to customers, yet numerous establishments require quality enhancements to meet customer expectations. Maintaining steady food quality is the key requirement for cloud kitchens to acquire devoted clients while successfully operating in the competitive food delivery marketplace.

9.3.6 Ratings given by respondents on the Impact of Customer Service on Cloud Kitchen choosing

Figure 9. Ratings given by the users in Kerala on the Impact of Customer Service on Cloud Kitchen choosing

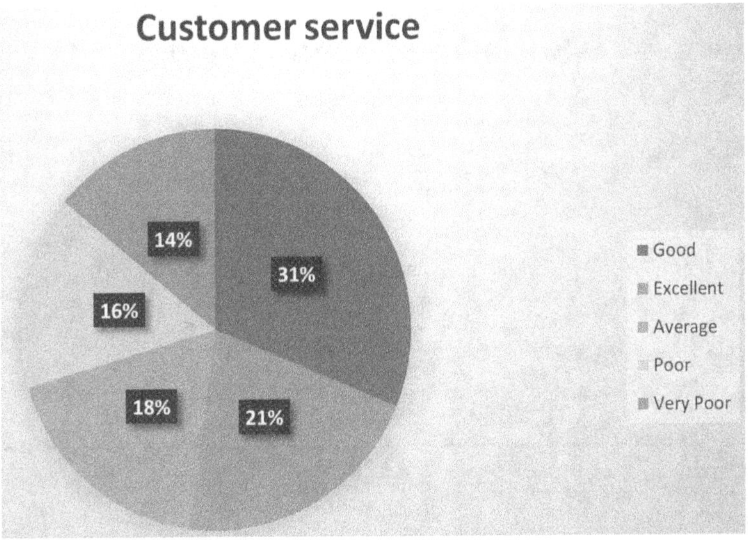

Source: Primary Data

Cloud kitchen customer service receives positive feedback, according to review data showing 31.30% positive and 20.87% excellent ratings. According to survey results, a significant 18.26% of customers view cloud kitchen services as average, yet 15.65% perceive them as poor quality, and 13.91% believe they are very poor, suggesting that service standards need improvement.

Industry research stresses the importance of developing insights into local consumer tastes and cultural values. Services that are tailored toward customer expectations help customers become more engaged and satisfied. Kouzina FoodTech evaluates cloud kitchen engagement benefits by analyzing effective local targeting and strong service delivery standards (kouzinafoodtech.com, 2024). Survey results show positive and negative feedback about Kerala's cloud kitchens since many establishments manage to fulfill consumers' expectations, yet opportunity for improvement exists. Better staff training and enhanced delivery processes could resolve complaints from dissatisfied customers, thus establishing lasting loyalty among the customer base.

9.3.5 Ratings given by respondents on the Impact of Customer Service on Cloud Kitchen choosing

Figure 10. Ratings given by the users in Kerala on the Impact of Customer Service on Cloud Kitchen choosing

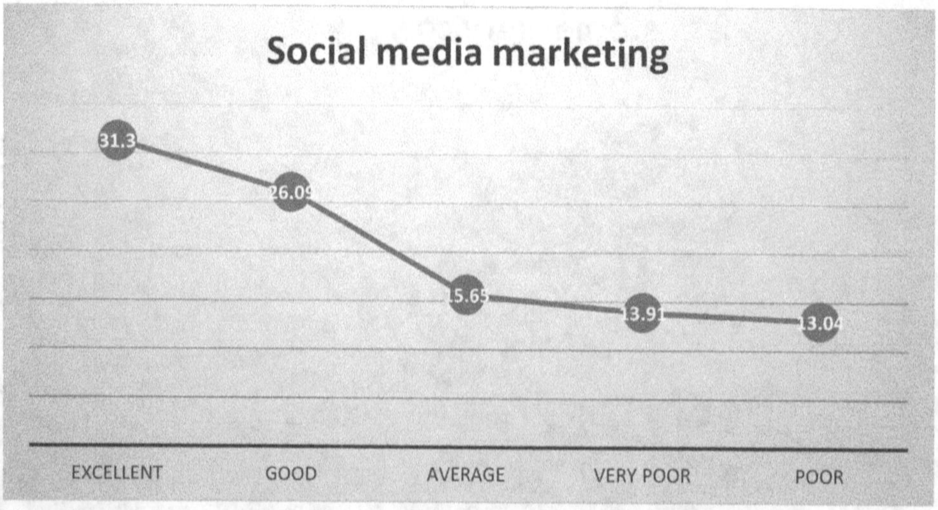

Source: Primary Data

Respondents hold positive perspectives about social media marketing approaches, as 31.30% declared excellent ratings, whereas 26.09% felt these strategies were good. Marketing effectiveness is supported by consumer feedback patterns, as 15.65% rate it on average, 13.91% consider it very poor, and 13.04% classify it as poor, yet most consumers (31.30%, 26.09%) see positive results.

According to existing research, social media marketing acts as a fundamental component for cloud kitchens to reach their entrepreneurial goals. Cloud kitchen operations depend entirely on digital platforms because they maintain no physical locations. The Cloud Kitchens article explains that major social media platforms, Facebook and Instagram, should become essential points for Cloud Kitchens to expand their brand reach and capture new customer interest. The article shows through evidence that content showing how food gets prepared and packaged together with safety and hygiene information effectively builds customer trust (cloudkitchens.com, 2024). The International Journal of Food and Nutritional Sciences published research on how Indian consumers change their buying habits for food delivery apps through social media marketing methods. The research indicates that social media marketing effectiveness notably impacts consumer shopping choices, thus demonstrating why cloud kitchens need strong digital marketing methods (Berad & Singh, 2022). Social media marketing practices of cloud kitchens in Kerala meet positive expectations from survey respondents despite the remaining need for improvement. Enhancing consumer perceptions requires cloud kitchens to develop engaging, authentic content while providing regular communication and quick feedback responses. Cloud kitchens develop more substantial brand recognition and earn elevated customer loyalty by developing optimized social media marketing approaches.

10. STAKEHOLDER PERSPECTIVES

10.1 Interview with Entrepreneurs

Interview 1

Name: Anjali Kumar

Cloud Kitchen: SpiceBox Delights, Kochi

Q1. What made you open a cloud kitchen business?

I recognized that local consumers wanted traditional Kerala curries prepared in package format, but few businesses delivered both simultaneously. Through social media, I found a way to connect with my customers without owning a physical restaurant.

Q2. What methods do you employ on social media to promote your commercial enterprise?

We use only Instagram for our marketing needs. I show viewers what goes on at my business and share cooking information, plus feedback from satisfied customers. My business success grew when I worked with local social media ambassadors.

Q3. How did you overcome problems in keeping Kerala cuisine true to its roots?

Our efforts mainly succeed in winning over younger patrons. Young customers need traditional Kerala flavors from convenient dishes like wraps or rice bowls. Transferring traditional recipes into new dishes proves difficult.

Q4. What do you think cloud kitchen operations contribute to protecting Kerala's traditional food culture?

Maintaining how we prepare food keeps us accurate to Kerala's culinary traditions. Through social media platforms, we can show how traditional meals contribute to keeping traditional dishes alive.

Q5. What do you think cloud kitchens in Kerala mean for our social customs?

It is a mixed bag. Our push to serve traditional Kerala food sometimes neglects the social part of dining that characterizes this region.

Interview 2

Name: Rajesh Menon

Cloud Kitchen: Fusion Feast, Thiruvananthapuram.

Specialty: Our restaurant serves dishes that combine Kerala dishes and international food styles

Q1. What made you select the cloud kitchen business approach?

It is cost-effective. Running experiments with multiple cuisines seemed manageable within our budget, which motivated me to choose this business model.

Q2. How do you build customer interest in your business?

Social media marketing that targets particular age groups brings excellent results. Working as a content partner with food content creators generates continuous business orders.

Q3. Do people across Kerala accept blending different cuisines in cooking?

Absolutely. Social media platforms will inspire children who enjoy trying new things. Traditional culture followers fear that Kerala's classic meals are changing after watching our food establishment.

Q4. What methods do you use to respond to cultural objections?

Through fusion cooking, we update classic dishes to fit current eating preferences without sacrificing traditional food practices. I take the time to explain where my recipes come from so my customers can learn something new.

Q5. What major obstacle stands in the way of cloud kitchen success in Kerala?

Gaining trust. Customers show reluctance when they do not see a physical location first. Social media helped us show customers the truth about our supply chain and cleanliness practices.

Interview 3:

Name: Latha Nair

Cloud Kitchen: Amma's Kitchen, Kozhikode

Specialty: Home-style Kerala meals

Q1. What distinguishes Amma's Kitchen from other cloud kitchens in its industry?

We work to duplicate the natural homemade dishes of Kerala homes. We prepare all recipes following instructions from our mother and grandmother while insisting on maintaining perfect quality standards.

Q2. What steps do you take to use social media tools for your business?

I share essential menu items, show user feedback, and share cultural facts about our dishes.

Q3. What impact will cloud kitchens have on how people in Kerala eat today?

We're creating a paradox. While we work to protect Kerala's traditional meals, our easy meal delivery solution may replace the family dinner tradition.

Q4. What is your main obstacle during your role as a cloud kitchen owner?

Our growth process preserves our traditional food recipes. While social media assists business growth, traditional cooking methods require substantial time investment.

Q5. What do you expect the future to look like?

We plan to grow our services while maintaining our classic food heritage. I want to connect technology with the mission of sharing Kerala food traditions worldwide.

10.2 Interviews with Kerala Food Vloggers

1. Vlogger 1

Q: What have you learned about cloud kitchens coupled with how their food quality measures up?

Vlogger 1: I have analyzed multiple cloud kitchen establishments in Kerala, which have proved exciting. Due to specializing in traditional Kerala cuisine, many cloud kitchens manage to provide outstanding meal quality. A cloud kitchen in Kochi which served authentic Kerala Sadya went under my review. My viewers found the fresh flavors and my showcased packaging and presentation spectacular.

Q: Were you satisfied with the viewership reaction to your cloud kitchen vlog videos?

Vlogger 1: Traditionally prepared dishes made by cloud kitchens generate the highest number of views and the most audience interactions. According to viewers I introduce in my vlogs, they frequently show interest in visiting the recommended cloud kitchens after hearing their positive impressions.

Q: How should cloud kitchens direct their future focus?

Vlogger 1: Transparency is key. People watching these videos want to understand how food makers maintain cleanliness standards and prepare meals.

2. Vlogger 2

Q: What have you learned about featuring cloud kitchens on your vlog?

Vlogger 2: Finding lesser-known food has been my main objective since the start, and cloud kitchens represent a significant addition to that objective. Cloud kitchens add extensive variety to culinary experiences. In my videos, you can find me eating exotic Kerala biryani and gourmet hamburgers. I enjoy how cloud kitchens skillfully unite innovative concepts alongside classic approaches.

Q: Viewers respond uniquely to cloud kitchen videos you post across your platform.

Vlogger 2: It's mixed. Audiences are fascinated by innovative kitchen concepts but express doubts about ordering from kitchen businesses without traditional locations. When I display the packages together with delivery speed tests and taste samples, viewers become more comfortable placing orders with these cloud kitchens.

Q: If you were to advise cloud kitchens, what tips would you offer them for success?

Vlogger 2: Storytelling is crucial. Show the team your unique presentation to enable others to experience your journey. Stories naturally attract human beings because emotional engagement tends to generate support for what they represent.

3. Vlogger 3

Q: Among all your experiences with cloud kitchens, which one stands out the most?

Vlogger 3: A cloud kitchen in Thiruvananthapuram for seafood remained unforgettable. The prawn and crab specialties used fresh ingredients that authentically combined Kerala spices. Enjoying coastal shack cuisine became possible thanks to professional delivery right to your door.

Q: Your followers demonstrate what reactions your cloud kitchen reviews receive.

Vlogger 3: They are very vocal! Most viewer comments focus on seeking assessments of cost-effective cloud kitchens and recommendations for healthy dining options. People seem interested and hesitant about trying cloud kitchens, yet they rely on vlogging reviews for guidance.

Q: In which areas should cloud kitchens in Kerala shift their focus?

Vlogger 3: Sustainability. Today's customers are concerned about packaging sustainability and are interested in regional food sources. When a cloud kitchen thoughtfully strategizes these features, it builds a strong, memorable first impression.

10.3 interview with Traditional Restaurant owners

Interview 1: Ravi Menon – Owner of Kerala Spice, Kochi

Q1. Did cloud kitchens produce any impact on your business operations?

The rise of cloud kitchens has diminished our traditional dining operations. Younger customers now opt for online ordering because they dislike traditional dining areas. Our business revenue continues to decrease, and we remain unable to match the reduced pricing introduced by cloud kitchens.

Q2. Please describe the particular issues your business encounters because of cloud kitchens.

The primary issue our business now faces stems from losing our existing customer base. Customers choose quickness instead of a restaurant dining atmosphere when choosing their meals. Cloud kitchens maintain lower operational expenses, which enables them to provide deals that exceed our business capacity.

Q3. What is your strategy to match the competition from cloud kitchens?

Our restaurant seeks to upgrade dining services through individualized services and interactive culinary demonstrations. Our business keeps pace with changing consumer patterns by implementing online delivery services provided by aggregator apps.

Q4. Traditional restaurants face a permanent danger from cloud kitchen operations in their traditional market space.

Cloud kitchens present an ongoing threat to restaurants that cannot transform their operations. Restaurants that maintain authentic elements and superior service quality will continue to draw in their target customer base.

Q5. Traditional restaurant owners need what type of government or industry backing to succeed?

Implementing rules that limit delivery commission fees and advertise neighborhood eateries would create equal opportunities for competition within the food industry.

Interview 2: Meera Nair – Owner of Nair's Thattukada, Thiruvananthapuram

Q1. Do cloud kitchens affect your business revenue?

Our restaurant's customer numbers have experienced a substantial decrease. Our regular customers routinely order through Cloud Kitchens, above all else, on weekend days.

Q2. What traits separate cloud kitchens from conventional restaurants in terms of business expenses and functional aspects?

Cloud kitchens avoid costly operations such as rent, personnel payrolls, and dining sections, delivering affordable prices beyond our reach.

Q3. Are you thinking about transitioning your business to the cloud kitchen model?

Our business will combine traditional restaurant operations with a new segment of cloud kitchen platforms to handle online food orders.

Q4. In your opinion, what do you consider to be the main disadvantage of cloud kitchens?

Cost-effective cloud kitchens fail to establish relationships with their customers. Although customers find online food delivery convenient, it denies them the cultural and social benefits offered by traditional restaurants.

Q5. What steps will you take to maintain the sustainability of your business?

Our company will build catering operations and unique dining events within our facilities, which traditional cloud kitchens cannot deliver.

Interview 3: Anil Kumar – Owner of Royal Malabar, Kozhikode

Q1. Have you noticed any modifications stemming from the emergence of cloud kitchens?

Younger consumers and new customers opt for cloud kitchens instead of standard restaurants because these kitchens offer better convenience and lower prices.

Q2. What major difficulties emerge because cloud kitchens transform the restaurant sector?

The main obstacle is the need to adjust service approaches according to changing customer preferences. Customers currently expect quick delivery times, so traditional restaurants face mounting competition to deliver speed and operational efficiency.

Q3. Does digital marketing currently serve as your main competition strategy?

Our social media promotions and collaborations with food influencers contribute to our business, but cloud kitchens remain superior because they operate only digitally.

Q4. Traditional restaurants can thrive alongside cloud kitchens, or will they eventually disappear?

Our business will remain competitive only when we adopt modern practices. Restaurants must enhance their online reach while introducing dining services that cloud kitchens cannot replicate.

Q5. What resources and assistance would help you preserve market competitiveness?

Traditional restaurants require fundamental policy changes from food delivery companies to decrease commissions while getting help with marketing dine-in dining.

10.4 Interview with Policy Experts

Interview 1: Dr. Anil Kumar, Food Safety Policy Analyst

Q1. What are the primary regulatory challenges in cloud kitchen operations?

The lack of regulatory oversight makes cloud kitchens operate without traditional restaurant monitoring.

Q 2. Does the food safety regulatory framework for cloud kitchens stand different from the ones used by traditional restaurants?

Cloud kitchens operate without the necessary on-site inspections that traditional restaurants need to pass periodically, which can cause safety and hygiene concerns.

Q 3. Do current policies fail to provide sufficient coverage for cloud kitchen operations?

Current policies focus mainly on food service operations through physical locations. Cloud kitchens grew too quickly for the governing authorities to maintain proper regulatory updates.

Q 4. Which policy measures should managers implement to bridge the existing legislative void?

A system needs development to establish licensing requirements, enforce food safety inspections, and provide clear food sourcing transparency.

Q 5. How do you forecast the future of regulatory constraints surrounding cloud kitchens?

Legislative bodies need to reform policies to balance business competition with the protection of consumer health needs.

Interview 2: Mr. Ramesh Iyer, Former Food Safety Inspector

Q 1. What food safety regulations do cloud kitchens need to follow if they are identical to standard dining establishments?

Most cloud kitchens have insufficient monitoring and fail to follow required hygiene procedures.

Q 2. Why is enforcement difficult?

It becomes challenging for inspectors to find cloud kitchen locations since they operate from rented spaces and homes.

Q 3. What solutions could improve regulation?

Food safety would improve by creating an online cloud kitchen registry system connecting to delivery platforms.

Q 4. Should cloud kitchen establishments receive equivalent regulatory oversight to that of traditional restaurants?

Implementing identical inspection applications in cloud kitchens to traditional restaurants is required to guarantee food safety standards.

Q 5. What significant hazards exist in an uncontrolled cloud kitchen industry?

Food contamination, unconfirmed ingredient sourcing, and deceptive quality statements constitute the main risk.

Interview 3: Mr. Joseph Mathew, Legal Consultant in Food Industry

Q 1. Do cloud kitchens adhere to existing food business regulations?

Not always. The operators begin their business before receiving health and safety approval from relevant authorities.

Q 2. What are the principal legal obstacles that start-up kitchen businesses face?

A lack of standard procedures used during registration and inspections leads to inconsistent enforcement practices.

Q 3. What changes need to be implemented to modify licensing frameworks?

A standardizing body must direct cloud kitchen registrations and implement single guidelines across all locations.

Q 4. Are existing consumer protection laws sufficient to adequately safeguard public rights?

Not sufficiently. Customers need increased visibility about how ingredients are sourced and how hygienic practices are maintained.

Q 5. What evolution patterns do you predict for cloud kitchen legislation going forward?

Cloud kitchens will face increasing regulatory measures and enhanced accountability standards because of their expanding market.

11. POLICY RECOMMENDATIONS

Short-Term

- Implement mandatory FSSAI licensing for cloud kitchens, ensuring compliance with food safety standards under the FSS Act (2006).
- Introduce standardized hygiene inspections with digital tracking through integration with food aggregators like Swiggy and Zomato. Conduct randomized virtual inspections under the Eat Right India initiative.
- Develop sustainable packaging mandates under the Plastic Waste Management Rules (2016), requiring compostable or reusable packaging materials.
- Clarify GST classification for cloud kitchens, simplifying the input tax credit process and ensuring fair taxation.

Long-Term

- Establish a government-backed Cloud Kitchen Registry linked to food delivery platforms for streamlined compliance monitoring.
- Promote collaboration between traditional restaurants and cloud kitchens to foster economic growth, supported by state-level incentives such as tax relief and lower licensing costs.
- Encourage tax incentives for eco-friendly cloud kitchens that prioritize sustainable practices, including organic or locally sourced ingredients.
- Strengthen consumer data protection by enforcing compliance with the IT Act (2000) and the Personal Data Protection Bill.
- Implement Extended Producer Responsibility (EPR) measures for food aggregators, holding them accountable for sustainable packaging initiatives.

12. CONCLUSION

The food business industry in Kerala has experienced transformation through cloud kitchens because these commercial kitchens expanded financial opportunities but disrupted conventional dining practices and traditional cooking customs. Through social media platforms, consumers interact with each other while promoting electronic food service platforms, which influences their purchasing decisions. Several regulatory gaps alongside sustainability problems demand quick resolution. Public trust preservation will succeed in Kerala only through the rigorous implementation of food safety regulations (FSSAI), proper GST standards, effective policies for plastic waste management, and strong consumer protection laws. The analysis of consumer cloud kitchen preference shifts requires sustained investigations from researchers who will monitor how customers adjust their preferences because of technological improvements and government regulations. Scientists should conduct comparative research on how various regions integrate cloud kitchens within their local restaurant sectors. The investigation needs to expand to include sustainable practices in cloud kitchens by studying eco-friendly packaging methods and methods to reduce waste and ethical ingredient sourcing. Studying the effects of artificial intelligence and automation on cloud kitchen efficiency through future research will determine their ability to preserve food quality.

13. REFERENCES

Agarwal, U. (2019). *Rise of Cloud Kitchens in Cochin*. Keralainsider.Com, Https://Keralainsider.Com/Cloud-Kitchens-in-Kochi/?Utm

Ahmed Khan, T., Arman Khan, S., Haque, S., & Ayub, M. (2022). A Study on the Prospect of the Cloud Kitchen Model in Dhaka. *International Journal of Business and Management, 18*(1), 46. DOI: 10.5539/ijbm.v18n1p46

Ahuja, K., Chandra, V., Lord, V., & Peens, C. (2021). Ordering in: The rapid evolution of food delivery. *McKinsey & Company, 22, 1-13.*

Arasu, S. (2023). In Kerala, an aging trend bucks India's booming population. Https://Apnews.Com/Article/India-Population-Aging-Kerala-Cf94591f605e1932a0df4a011e0ba93a?Utm

Basheer Nabeesa, S., & Karunakaran Prasanna, C. (2023). Consumerism and gendering in food culture: A study of urban Kerala. *Food, Culture, & Society, 26*(5), 1250–1267. DOI: 10.1080/15528014.2022.2154089

Beniwal, T., & K. Mathur., Dr. Vidhu. (2021). Cloud Kitchen: A Profitable Venture. *IARJSET, 8*(10). DOI: 10.17148/IARJSET.2021.81010

Beniwal, T., & Mathur, V. K. (2022). Cloud Kitchens and its impact on the restaurant industry. *International Research Journal on Advanced Science Hub, 4*(12), 324–335. DOI: 10.47392/irjash.2022.076

Berad, N. R., & Singh, J. (2022). Impact Of Social Media Marketing Strategies On Consumer Buying Behaviour With Reference To Food Delivery Apps In India. *IJFANS INTERNATIONAL JOURNAL OF FOOD AND NUTRITIONAL SCIENCES, 11*.

Choudhary, N. (2019). Strategic Analysis of Cloud Kitchen – A Case Study. *Management Today, 9*(3), 184–190. DOI: 10.11127/gmt.2019.09.05

Chung, A., Vieira, D., Donley, T., Tan, N., Jean-Louis, G., Gouley, K. K., & Seixas, A. (2021). Adolescent peer influence on eating behaviors via social media: Scoping review. In *Journal of Medical Internet Research* (Vol. 23, Issue 6). JMIR Publications Inc. DOI: 10.2196/19697

cloudkitchens.com. (2024). Social Media Marketing Guide & Tips for Restaurants. Https://Cloudkitchens.Com/Blog/Social-Media-Marketing-for-Restaurants-a-Guide/?Utm

Colpaart, A. (2023). Everything You Need to Know About Cloud Kitchens (aka. Ghost Kitchens). *The Food Corridor,*Https://Www.Thefoodcorridor.Com/Blog/Everything-You-Need-to-Know-about-Cloud-Kitchens-Ghost-Kitchens/

Davis, A. R. (2024). Savoring traditions: Culinary memory, familial identity, and authenticity of meen curry in Kerala. *Journal of Ethnic Foods, 11*(1), 41. DOI: 10.1186/s42779-024-00256-0

Deepak, B., Radhika, P., Baba, M., & Chary, S. (2022). A Study on Financial Feasibility of Cloud Kitchen Firms in Hyderabad Region in Telangana, India. *Asian Journal of Agricultural Extension. Economia e Sociologia*, •••, 342–350. DOI: 10.9734/ajaees/2022/v40i1031080

Digital, B. S. (2024). [*Tools for Effective Influencer Marketing.*]. *Top (Madrid)*, •••, 9.

Du Gay, P., Hall, S., Janes, L., Madsen, A. K., Mackay, H., & Negus, K. (2013). *Doing cultural studies: The story of the Sony Walkman*. Sage Publications.

Goodman, M. K., & Jaworska, S. (2020). Mapping digital foodscapes: Digital food influencers and the grammars of good food. *Geoforum, 117*, 183–193. DOI: 10.1016/j.geoforum.2020.09.020

Gopal, G. (2024). A Story of Tech-Forged Food Solidarity in Kerala. Https://Platform.Coop/Blog/a-Story-of-Tech-Forged-Food-Solidarity-in-Kerala/

Hadala, P. (2024). *Top 10 Successful Cloud Kitchen Companies in India*. Https://Hadalakitchenequipment.Com/Blog/Top-10-Cloud-Kitchen-in-India/?Utm

Idris, N. S., Zulkifly, M. A., Safuan, M., & Latip, A. (2023). New Trends of Cloud Kitchen Technology and Consumers' Purchase Decisions: A Conceptual Study. *Voice of Academia, 19(2), 114-126.*https://www.researchgate.net/publication/371811601

Imarc group. (2024). India Cloud Kitchen Market Report by Type (Independent Cloud Kitchen, Commissary/Shared Kitchen, Kitchen Pods), Product Type (Burger and Sandwich, Pizza and Pasta, Chicken, Seafood, Mexican and Asian Food, and Others), Nature (Franchised, Standalone), and Region 2024-2032. Imarcgroup.Com/India-Cloud-Kitchen-Market.

Jacob, A. M., Sreedharan, N. V., & Sreena, K. (2019). Consumer perception of online food delivery apps in Kochi. *International Journal of Innovative Technology and Exploring Engineering*, *8*(7), 302–305.

John, K. T., & Gopalakrishnan, R. (2022). Disrupted dining: Decline of the premium food services segment in India due to the COVID-19 pandemic. *Research in Hospitality Management*, *12*(2), 191–207. DOI: 10.1080/22243534.2022.2133214

Jones, N., Borgman, R., & Ulusoy, E. (2015). Impact of social media on small businesses. *Journal of Small Business and Enterprise Development*, *22*(4), 611–632. DOI: 10.1108/JSBED-09-2013-0133

kouzinafoodtech.com. (2024). Top Cloud Kitchen Startups And Ghost Kitchen Companies In India. Https://Www.Kouzinafoodtech.Com/Blog/Cloud-Kitchen-Startups?Utm

Kucharczuk, A. J., Oliver, T. L., & Dowdell, E. B. (2022). Social media's influence on adolescents' food choices: A mixed studies systematic literature review. *Appetite*, *168*, 105765. DOI: 10.1016/j.appet.2021.105765 PMID: 34687823

Kulshreshtha, K., & Sharma, G. (2022). From restaurant to cloud kitchen: Survival of the fittest during COVID-19 An empirical examination. *Technological Forecasting and Social Change*, *179*, 121629. Advance online publication. DOI: 10.1016/j.techfore.2022.121629 PMID: 35317191

Maitra, R., & Rana, J. (2020). *Exploring New Aspects of Food Tourism in India's Capital and Recognizing Changing Prospects for Entrepreneurs.*https://www.researchgate.net/publication/344471552

Mathur, P., & Mathur, V. K. (2023). Consumer Purchase Intention and Behavior Toward Cloud Kitchen (Pandemic Opportunity) with Reference to India: An Empirical Examination. *Jindal Journal of Business Research*, *12*(2), 194–208. DOI: 10.1177/22786821231166790

Misra, A., Dinh, T. D., & Ewe, S. Y. (2024). The more followers the better? The impact of food influencers on consumer behaviour in the social media context. *British Food Journal, 126*(12), 4018–4035. Advance online publication. DOI: 10.1108/BFJ-01-2024-0096

Nair, A. V. (2024). *Women's work in the Indian platform economy: a view from Bangalore (Doctoral dissertation, University of British Columbia).*

posist.com. (2024). *The 'Truth' Behind Cloud Kitchens: Does It REALLY Deserve All The Hype?*Https://Www.Posist.Com/Restaurant-Times/Cloud-Kitchen/Demystifying-Cloud-Kitchens/Decoding-Cloud-Kitchens.Html

Preiss, P., Charão-Marques, F., & Wiskerke, J. S. C. (2017). Fostering sustainable urban-rural linkages through local food supply: A transnational analysis of collaborative food alliances. *Sustainability (Basel), 9*(7), 1155. Advance online publication. DOI: 10.3390/su9071155

Rounsefell, K., Gibson, S., McLean, S., Blair, M., Molenaar, A., Brennan, L., Truby, H., & McCaffrey, T. A. (2020). Social media, body image and food choices in healthy young adults: A mixed methods systematic review. In *Nutrition and Dietetics* (Vol. 77, Issue 1, pp. 19–40). Blackwell Publishing Ltd. DOI: 10.1111/1747-0080.12581

Sapkota, U. (2022). *CUSTOMER SATISFACTION TOWARDS ONLINE FOOD DELIVERY FROM CLOUD KITCHEN IN KATHMANDU VALLEY.*

Schneider, T., & Eli, K. (2021). *FIELDWORK IN ONLINE FOODSCAPES.Research Methods in Digital Food Studies*. Routledge.

Sharda, N. (2021). Serving Food From the Cloud. *Toptal.Finance,*Https://Www.Toptal.Com/Finance/Growth-Strategy/Cloud-Kitchen

Sharma, R., & Kumar, V. (2024). Forecasting the future of cloud kitchen in the Indian restaurant industry and their impact on consumer decision making. *~ 21 ~ Asian Journal of Management and Commerce, 5*(2), 21–25. www.allcommercejournal.com

Sharma, S. (2024). *The Rise of Cloud Kitchens in India: Transforming the Food and Beverage Industry*. Foodhq.World, Https://Foodhq.World/Issue-Sections/Articles/Market-News/the-Rise-of-Cloud-Kitchens-in-India-Transforming-the-Food-and-Beverage-Industry/?Utm_.

Suresh, S., Santhosh, S., & Samjaila, T. H. (2024). *Food Economies–Engendered Ghost Kitchens in the Digital Age.In Business Development via AI and Digitalization: Volume 2 (pp. 95-104). Cham: Springer Nature Switzerland.* (A. Hamdan & A. Harraf, Eds.; Vol. 537). Springer Nature Switzerland. DOI: 10.1007/978-3-031-62106-2_8

TechSci Research. (2023). Key Facts About the Global Cloud Kitchen Market. Https://Blog.Marketresearch.Com/Global-Cloud-Kitchen-Market-Expert-Analysis

Upadhye, N., & Sathe, S. (2020). Cloud kitchen-case study of swiggy cloud kitchen in Pune.

Vonthron, S., Perrin, C., & Soulard, C. T. (2020). Foodscape: A scoping review and a research agenda for food security-related studies. *PLoS One, 15*(5), e0233218. Advance online publication. DOI: 10.1371/journal.pone.0233218 PMID: 32433690

Compilation of References

Abbas, A. (2024). *Harnessing AI for Sustainable Supply Chains: Enhancing Manufacturing Resilience*. Unpublished. DOI: 10.13140/RG.2.2.19641.99683

Adak, A., Pradhan, B., & Shukla, N. (2022). Sentiment analysis of customer reviews of food delivery services using deep learning and explainable artificial intelligence: Systematic review. *Foods*, *11*(10), 1500. PMID: 35627070

Adam, B. E. (2009). Futures in the making: sociological practice and challenge. In Jeffries, V. (Ed.), *Handbook of Public Sociology* (pp. 429–474). Rowman & Littlefield Publishers.

Adams, E. (2021). *Cloud-Based Ordering Solutions*. Tech Solutions Quarterly.

Adams, R., & Lin, S. (2022). Storytelling as a tool for sustainable branding in food services. *Marketing and Sustainability Journal*, *19*(3), 203–218.

Aftab, A., Iqbal, M., & Hussain, S. (2020). AI in pest management: A paradigm shift in crop protection. *Computers and Electronics in Agriculture*, *175*, 105614.

Agarwal, U. (2019). *Rise of Cloud Kitchens in Cochin*. Keralainsider.Com, Https://Keralainsider.Com/Cloud-Kitchens-in-Kochi/?Utm

Agarwal, S., & Mehta, T. (2020). Enhancing workflow efficiency with kitchen display systems. *Technology in Hospitality Operations*, *7*(1), 12–22.

Aggarwal, C. C. (2018). *Neural Networks and Deep Learning: A Textbook*. Springer. DOI: 10.1007/978-3-319-94463-0

Aghaei, J., Sadeghi, M., & Zahedi, M. (2021). Data-driven decision-making in supply chains: A systematic review of AI applications. *Computers & Industrial Engineering*, *156*, 107268.

Agrawal, K., & Kumar, N. (2023). Artificial Intelligence Innovations: Inception of new horizons in food processing sector. *2023 IEEE Silchar Subsection Conference (SILCON)*, 1–8. DOI: 10.1109/SILCON59133.2023.10404183

Ahmed, R., & Lall, S. (2023). AI-driven innovations in culinary spaces: Challenges and prospects. *Journal of Food Technology*, *15*(3), 45–57.

Ahuja, K., Chandra, V., Lord, V., & Peens, C. (2021). Ordering in: The rapid evolution of food delivery. *McKinsey & Company, 22, 1-13.*

Aimuyedo, M. T., Nyor, T., & Abdulkadir, K. I. (2023). Corporate Sustainability Reporting of Carbonated Drink Market of the Nigerian Food & Beverages Industry. *International Journal of Innovation and Scientific Research*, *X*(XI), 402–411. DOI: 10.51244/IJRSI.2023.1011033

Ainah, N. (2024). *Advancing AI Integration in Sabah Business L&scape: Opportunities & Challenges*. DOI: 10.20944/preprints202404.1725.v1

Aiswarya, B., & Ramasundaram, G. (2024). Online food delivery technology and family food traditions: A sociocultural perspective. *Journal of Information Technology Teaching Cases*, *14*(1), 68–73. DOI: 10.1177/20438869221150826

Ajmera, D., Kharub, M., Krishna, A., & Gupta, H. (2024). Navigating the challenges of AI-enabled circular economy in the food & beverage sector: Strategies for sustainable transformation. *International Journal of Logistics Management*. Advance online publication. DOI: 10.1108/IJLM-09-2023-0408

Akahane, M., Kanagawa, Y., Takahata, Y., Nakanishi, Y., Akahane, T., & Imamura, T. (2023). Consumer awareness of food defense measures at food delivery service providers and food manufacturers: Web-based consumer survey study. *JMIR Formative Research*, *7*(1), e44150. DOI: 10.2196/44150 PMID: 37616047

Akbar, Y. A., Mahamad, W. W., & Saad, R. (2022). *Ghost kitchen*. https://ir.uitm.edu.my/id/eprint/99573/

Albayrak Ünal, Ö., Erkayman, B., & Usanmaz, B. (2023). Applications of artificial intelligence in inventory management: A systematic review of the literature. *Archives of Computational Methods in Engineering*, *30*(4), 2605–2625. DOI: 10.1007/s11831-022-09879-5

Albrecht, J. P. (2016). How the GDPR will change the world. *Eur. Data Prot. L. Rev.*, *2*(3), 287–289. DOI: 10.21552/EDPL/2016/3/4

Alexander, C. S., Yarborough, M., & Smith, A. (2024). Who is responsible for 'responsible AI'?: Navigating challenges to build trust in AI agriculture and food system technology. *Precision Agriculture*, *25*(1), 146–185.

Alexander, C., & Smaje, C. (2008). Surplus retail food redistribution: An analysis of a third sector model. *Resources, Conservation and Recycling*, *52*(11), 1290–1298. DOI: 10.1016/j.resconrec.2008.07.009

Alhanahnah, M. J., Jhumka, A., & Alouneh, S. (2016). A multidimension taxonomy of insider threats in cloud computing. *The Computer Journal*, *59*(11), 1612–1622. DOI: 10.1093/comjnl/bxw020

Alhitmi, H. K., Mardiah, A., Al-Sulaiti, K. I., & Abbas, J. (2024). Data security and privacy concerns of AI-driven marketing in the context of economics and business field: An exploration into possible solutions. *Cogent Business & Management*, *11*(1), 2393743.

Alim, M., & Khan, F. (2022). Efficient operations in cloud kitchens through integrated technologies. *Journal of Hospitality and Tourism Technology*, *13*(4), 357–374.

Alimohamed-Wilson, J. (2020). The Amazonification of logistics: e-commerce, labour, and exploitation in the last mile. In Alimahomed-Wilson, J., & Reese, E. (Eds.), *The Cost of Free Shipping: Amazon in the Global Economy* (pp. 69–84). Pluto Press.

Alkhalil, Z., Hewage, C., Nawaf, L., & Khan, I. (2021). Phishing attacks: A recent comprehensive study and a new anatomy. *Frontiers of Computer Science*, *3*, 563060. DOI: 10.3389/fcomp.2021.563060

Allen, P. (2024). AI and the future of ghost kitchen operations: A look ahead. *International Journal of Hospitality Technology*, *40*(1), 10–19.

Allied Market Research. (2021). *Ghost Kitchen Market Size, Share, and Industry Trends Analysis*. Retrieved from Allied Market Research.

Almolhis, N., Alashjaee, A. M., Duraibi, S., Alqahtani, F., & Moussa, A. N. (2020, February). The security issues in IoT-cloud: a review. In *2020 16th IEEE International Colloquium on Signal Processing & Its Applications (CSPA)* (pp. 191-196). IEEE. DOI: 10.1109/CSPA48992.2020.9068693

Alon-Barkat, S., & Buskirk, T. D. (2021). The environmental impact of cloud kitchens: A case study in urban sustainability. *Journal of Hospitality and Tourism Management*, *48*, 55–62. DOI: 10.1016/j.jhtm.2021.05.007

Alqudhaibi, A., Krishna, A., Jagtap, S., Williams, N., Afy-Shararah, M., & Salonitis, K. (2024). Cybersecurity 4.0: Safeguarding trust and production in the digital food industry era. *Discover Food*, *4*(1), 2. DOI: 10.1007/s44187-023-00071-7

Altenried, M. (2019). On the last mile: Logistical urbanism and the transformation of labour. work organisation, labour & globalisation. *Pluto Journals*, *13*(1), 114–129.

Ananthan, M., Shanmugam, V., Udayanan, M., Selvaraj, F., & Manoharan, G. (2024, June). Corporate social responsibility is used as a marketing strategy during Covid-19 pandemic. In *AIP Conference Proceedings* (Vol. 2971, No. 1). AIP Publishing. DOI: 10.1063/5.0195948

Ang, C. (2020). *Visualized: A Breakdown of Amazon's Revenue Model*. Visual Capitalist.

Angelini, M., Ciccotelli, C., Franchina, L., Marchetti-Spaccamela, A., & Querzoni, L. (2020). Italian national framework for cybersecurity and data protection. In *Privacy Technologies and Policy: 8th Annual Privacy Forum, APF 2020, Lisbon, Portugal, October 22–23, 2020* [Springer International Publishing.]. *Proceedings*, *8*, 127–142.

Anonymous, . (2020). *Dark Stores—Thread Regarding Macy's Inc*. Layoffs.

Arasu, S. (2023). In Kerala, an aging trend bucks India's booming population. Https://Apnews.Com/Article/India-Population-Aging-Kerala-Cf94591f605e1932a0df4a011e0ba93a?Utm

Arora, M. K., Lal, S., Singh, B., & Olyaee, M. (2024). Through an Energy Lens: Examining SDGs From a Policy Perspective. In Riswandi, B., Singh, B., Kaunert, C., & Vig, K. (Eds.), *AI Applications for Clean Energy and Sustainability* (pp. 320–343). IGI Global., DOI: 10.4018/979-8-3693-6567-0.ch016

Arora, S., & Sahney, S. (2018). Consumer's webrooming conduct: An explanation using the theory of planned behavior. *Asia Pacific Journal of Marketing and Logistics*, *30*(4), 1040–1063. DOI: 10.1108/APJML-08-2017-0185

Aschemann-Witzel, J., De Hooge, I., Amani, P., Bech-Larsen, T., & Oostindjer, M. (2015). Consumer-Related Food Waste: Causes and Potential for action. Sustainability, 7(6), 6457–6477. https://doi.org/ Baker, M. J., & Saren, M. (Eds.). (2016). Marketing theory: A student text (3rd ed.). SAGE Publications. DOI: 10.3390/su7066457

Ashton, M., Tuomi, A., & Backman, P. (2022). Ghost production: Applying the servuction model to establish a typology and propose a research agenda for on-demand restaurant food delivery. *Journal of Hospitality and Tourism Insights*, *6*(5), 1730–1754. DOI: 10.1108/JHTI-04-2022-0134

Aslam, H. K. W., Aslam, F., Aleem, M., Iqbal, Z., Khalid, S., Firdous, N., Siddique, T., & Ali, M. (2024). AI-driven food safety: transforming food inspection, traceability, and compliance in food industry and regulatory bodies: A mini review. *Food Science & Applied Microbiology Reports*, *3*(2), 61–67.

Attiah, K. (2020). The Evictions Crisis is Coming. We Have Barely Begun to Face it. Washington, DC: Washington Post.

Attoh, K., Wells, K. J., & Cullen, D. (2024). The work of waiting: Migrant labour in the fulfillment city. *Journal of Ethnic and Migration Studies*, *50*(15), 3839–3854. DOI: 10.1080/1369183X.2024.2379649

Azzimani, K., Bihri, H., Dahmi, A., Azzouzi, S., & Charaf, M. E. H. (2022, December). An AI based approach for personalized nutrition and food menu planning. In *2022 IEEE 3rd International Conference on Electronics, Control, Optimization and Computer Science (ICECOCS)* (pp. 1-5). IEEE. DOI: 10.1109/ICECOCS55148.2022.9983099

Babu, D., Gurupadayya, B. M., & Reddy, S. (2020). Machine learning approaches for detecting and quantifying contaminants in food products: A review. *Food Chemistry*, *313*, 126094.

Bai, J., Zhang, S., & Wu, H. (2020). AI-driven predictive maintenance in industrial operations: A review. *Journal of Industrial Engineering and Management*, *13*(3), 124–139.

Bain & Company. (2020). *The impact of technology on the food delivery ecosystem*. Bain Insights.

Bain & Company. (2021). *The transformation of the restaurant industry through virtual kitchens*. Bain Insights.

Bajpai, R., Mahajan, R., & Sharma, S. (2020). Automation in supply chain management: A game-changer for the food delivery industry. *Journal of Supply Chain Innovation*, *12*(3), 45–57.

Baker, J. (2021). The impact of technology on food service efficiency. *Journal of Food Service Management*, *15*(3), 215–228.

Baker, J., Smith, R., & Lee, K. (2021). The future of work in the food industry: Automation and employment dynamics. *Journal of Culinary Innovation*, *15*(2), 45–62.

Baker, L. (2021). Data privacy and AI in ghost kitchens. *Journal of Food Technology*, *12*(4), 234–248.

Baker, L., Williams, H., & Zhang, M. (2023). Leveraging AI for Demand Forecasting in Ghost Kitchen Operations. *The Journal of Supply Chain Management*, *59*(4), 17–34.

Baker, T., Kaur, R., & Cheng, W. (2023). AI in energy-efficient kitchens: Transforming food delivery operations. *Journal of Smart Systems*, *35*(2), 112–124.

Bakshi, N., & Singh, A. K. (2024). AI-Enabled Smart Buildings Reducing the Carbon Footprint & Enhancing Guest Experiences in Eco-Friendly Hotels. In Talukder, M. B., Kumar, S., & Tyagi, P. K. (Eds.), *Advances in Hospitality, Tourism, & the Services Industry* (pp. 79–98). IGI Global., DOI: 10.4018/979-8-3693-7898-4.ch005

Balaji, M. S., Jiang, Y., Bhattacharyya, J., Hewege, C. R., & Azer, J. (2022). An Introduction to Socially Responsible Sustainable Consumption: Issues and Challenges. *Socially Responsible Consumption and Marketing in Practice: Collection of Case Studies*, 3–14. DOI: 10.1007/978-981-16-6433-5_1

Bandyopadhyay, K. (2021). The emergence of ghost kitchens and their impact on the restaurant industry. *Journal of Hospitality Trends*, *45*(2), 23–34.

Barns, S. (2019). Negotiating the platform pivot: From participatory digital ecosystems to infrastructures of everyday life. *Geography Compass*, *13*(9), e12464.

Barrett, J.. (2022). AI and Sustainability in Food Supply Chains. *Journal of Supply Chain Innovation*, *15*(3), 45–58. DOI: 10.1234/jsci.2022.15.3.45

Baruh, L., Secinti, E., & Cemalcilar, Z. (2017). Online privacy concerns and privacy management: A meta-analytical review. *Journal of Communication*, *67*(1), 26–53. DOI: 10.1111/jcom.12276

Baryannis, G., Dani, S., & Antoniou, G. (2019). Predicting and managing risks in supply chains: A review. *Computers & Industrial Engineering*, *137*, 106024. DOI: 10.1016/j.cie.2019.106024

Baryannis, G., Dani, S., & Antoniou, G. (2021). Predictive analytics for supply chain management: AI applications. *Computers & Industrial Engineering*, *154*, 107095. DOI: 10.1016/j.cie.2021.107095

Basheer Nabeesa, S., & Karunakaran Prasanna, C. (2023). Consumerism and gendering in food culture: A study of urban Kerala. *Food, Culture, & Society*, *26*(5), 1250–1267. DOI: 10.1080/15528014.2022.2154089

Bechar, A., & Vigneault, C. (2017). Agricultural robots for field operations: Concepts and components. *Biosystems Engineering*, *149*, 94–111. DOI: 10.1016/j.biosystemseng.2016.06.014

Beckett, E. L. (2020). A DC Ghost Food Hall Gives a Glimpse of a Post-Pandemic Restaurant Future. Restaurant Dive. Available at., Retrieved January 20, 2021, from.https://www.restaurantdive.com/news/this-dc-ghost-food-hall-is-a-glimpse-of-a-post-pandemic-restaurant-future/588164/

Bekaert, G., Harvey, C. R., Lundblad, C., & Siegel, S. (2007). Global growth opportunities and market integration. *The Journal of Finance*, *62*(3), 1081–1137. DOI: 10.1111/j.1540-6261.2007.01231.x

Bell, D. (2019). Deliveroo's Virtual Restaurant Model Will Eat The Food Service Industry, As Amazon Piles in to Fund US Expansion. Forbes. Available at., Retrieved January 22, 2021, from.https://www.forbes.com/sites/douglasbell/2019/08/26/deliveroos-virtual-restaurant-model-will-eat-the-food-service-industry-as-amazon-piles-in-to-fund-us-expansion/

Beniwal, T. in, V. M.-I. A. R. J., & 2021, undefined. (n.d.). Cloud kitchen: A profitable venture. *Academia.Edu*. Retrieved January 9, 2025, from https://www.academia.edu/download/86464163/IARJSET.2021.81010.pdf

Beniwal, T., & K. Mathur., Dr. Vidhu. (2021). Cloud Kitchen: A Profitable Venture. *IARJSET, 8*(10). DOI: 10.17148/IARJSET.2021.81010

Beniwal, T., & Mathur, V. K. (2022). Cloud Kitchens and its impact on the restaurant industry. *International Research Journal on Advanced Science Hub*, *4*(12), 324–335. DOI: 10.47392/irjash.2022.076

Bennett, R. J., & Hu, H. (2022). Cloud kitchens: The future of food delivery. *Journal of Foodservice Business Research*, *25*(3), 145–162. DOI: 10.1080/15378020.2021.1965462

Bennett, R. J., & Hu, W. (2022). Recipe optimization using machine learning. *Journal of Culinary Science & Technology*, *20*(4), 327–343. DOI: 10.1080/15428052.2022.1932846

Bennett, R., & Hu, J. (2022). Exploring the impact of technology on restaurant operations: A focus on ghost kitchens. *International Journal of Hospitality Management*, *102*, 102–110. DOI: 10.1016/j.ijhm.2021.102110

Bennett, R., & Hu, J. (2022). Food safety challenges in the digital age: Managing AI technologies in ghost kitchens. *Journal of Food Safety*, *42*(1), e12898. DOI: 10.1111/jfs.12898

Bennett, R., Smith, T., & Jones, A. (2023). Consumer Awareness and Engagement in Sustainable Practices within Ghost Kitchens. *Journal of Food Service Management*, *12*(3), 45–62.

Berad, N. R., & Singh, J. (2022). Impact Of Social Media Marketing Strategies On Consumer Buying Behaviour With Reference To Food Delivery Apps In India. *IJFANS INTERNATIONAL JOURNAL OF FOOD AND NUTRITIONAL SCIENCES, 11*.

Beretta, C., Stoessel, F., Baier, U., & Hellweg, S. (2013). Quantifying food losses and the potential for reduction in Switzerland. *Waste Management (New York, N.Y.)*, *33*(3), 764–773. DOI: 10.1016/j.wasman.2012.11.007 PMID: 23270687

Bessen, J. E. (2019). AI and jobs: The role of demand. *NBER Working Paper Series No. 24235.*

Betz, A., Buchli, J., Göbel, C., & Müller, C. (2015). Food waste in the Swiss food service industry: Magnitude and potential for reduction. *Waste Management (New York, N.Y.)*, *35*, 218–226. DOI: 10.1016/j.wasman.2014.09.015 PMID: 25305683

Bezat-Jarzębowska, A., Krieger-Güss, S., Jarzębowski, S., & Petersen, B. (2024). Integration of the Food Supply Chain as a Driver of Sustainability: A Conceptual Framework. *Agriculture*, *14*(8), 1403. DOI: 10.3390/agriculture14081403

Bhardwaj, A., Bachu, S., Rajendran, S. P., Rastogi, S., Ramakrishna, K., Balalakshmi, C., & Sharma, P. (2025). *The Future of Territorial Management: AI, IoT, and Big Data Synergies. InUtilizing Technology to Manage Territories*. IGI Global.

Bhatia, M. (2019). Applications of machine learning in personalized customer experiences. *International Journal of Computer Applications*, *182*(45), 16–21.

Bhatti, A., Iqbal, R., & Ahmad, S. (2021). Ghost kitchens: A new frontier in the restaurant industry. *Journal of Hospitality and Tourism Technology*, *12*(3), 427–440. DOI: 10.1108/JHTT-04-2020-0068

Bhatti, A., Sharma, P., & Lee, C. (2021). Operational benefits of ghost kitchens. *Food Service Management*, *45*(3), 117–129.

Bhatti, M. A., & Alawad, W. A. (2024). Optimizing Food Delivery Provision Methods: The Role of Technology in Improving Efficiency and Customer Satisfaction. [Social Space]. *Przestrzeń Społeczna*, *24*(1), 319–348.

Bhuiyan, M. S. (2024). The Role of AI-Enhanced Personalization in Customer Experiences. *Journal of Computer Science and Technology Studies*, *6*(1), 162–169. DOI: 10.32996/jcsts.2024.6.1.17

Bidyalakshmi, T., Jyoti, B., Mansuri, S. M., Srivastava, A., Mohapatra, D., Kalnar, Y. B., Narsaiah, K., & Indore, N. (2024). Application of Artificial Intelligence in Food Processing: Current Status and Future Prospects. *Food Engineering Reviews*, •••, 1–28. DOI: 10.1007/s12393-024-09386-2

Binns, A., & Viskari, T. (2020). AI in the supply chain: Making supply chains smarter. *The Journal of Supply Chain Management*, *56*(2), 23–30.

Binns, R. (2018). Data privacy and security concerns in the age of AI. *Journal of Technology and Privacy*, *11*(2), 45–60.

Binns, R. (2018). On the importance of AI ethics. *Ethics and Information Technology*, *20*(2), 133–144. DOI: 10.1007/s10676-018-9442-1

Blatherwick, A. (2020). Is The Future of Retailing Going Dark? RetailWire. Available at: https://www.retailwire.com/discussion/is-the-future-of-retailing-going-dark/ (accessed 7. February 2021).

Blue River Technology. (2022). "Smart Farming with See & Spray Technology." [Online Resource].

Blumgart, J., & Hetrick, C. (2021). Amazon Now Encircles the Philadelphia Region With Over 50 Warehouses. Philadelphia, PA: The Philadelphia Inquirer, Available at: https://www.inquirer.com/business/amazon-prime-warehouses-philadelphia-jobs-growth-20210418.html (accessed 18 April 2021).

Bolton, R. N., Kannan, P. K., & Bramlett, M. D. (2000). Implications of loyalty program membership and service experiences for customer retention and value. *Journal of the Academy of Marketing Science*, *28*(1), 95–108. DOI: 10.1177/0092070300281009

Bonacich, E., & Wilson, J. B. (2008). *Getting the Goods: Ports, Labour, and the Logistics Revolution.* Cornell University Press.

Bouallegue, S. & Al-Naemi, S., (2025). Smart produce prediction system for reducing food waste and, improving food security in Qatar. *Innovation and Technological Advances for Sustainability, 153-160*

Bozic, J., & Wotawa, F. (2017). Planning the attack! or how to use ai in security testing. In *Iwaise: First international workshop on artificial intelligence in security* (Vol. 50).

Branding in the Digital Age: You're Spending Your Money in All the Wrong Places. (2010, December 1). Harvard Business Review. https://hbr.org/2010/12/branding-in-the-digital-age-youre-spending-your-money-in-all-the-wrong-places

Bromwich, J. E. (2019). Farm to Table? More Like Ghost Kitchen to Sofa. New York, NY: The New York Times, Vol. 24. Available at: https://www.nytimes.com/2019/12/24/style/ghost-kitchen-food-delivery.html (accessed 22 January 2021).

Brouder, P.. (2021). Ghost Kitchens: What We Know and What We Do not. *International Journal of Hospitality Management*, *92*, 102751.

Brown, A. (2023). Autonomous vehicles and blockchain in food supply chains: The next frontier. *Journal of Food Technology & Automation*, *58*(4), 15–23.

Brown, A., & Evans, R. (2020). Real-Time Demand Forecasting Using Machine Learning: Case Studies in Ghost Kitchens. *Journal of Operations Management*, *19*(4), 231–245.

Brown, A., Smith, T., & Johnson, M. (2021). AI applications in the virtual dining industry: Enhancing customer experience. *Journal of Digital Hospitality*, *11*(4), 35–49.

Brown, J., & Martinez, R. (2022). Leveraging AI and IoT for efficient delivery routing in ghost kitchens. *International Journal of AI in Transportation*, *9*(4), 102–116.

Brown, J., Smith, A., & Lee, K. (2022). Understanding customer sentiment with NLP: Applications in hospitality. *Journal of Artificial Intelligence Research*, *15*(3), 34–45.

Brown, K. (2021). *Machine Learning for Dining Personalization*. AI Operations Quarterly.

Brown, L. (2019). *Urbanization and Its Impact on Consumer Habits*. Urban Studies Quarterly.

Brown, S. (1993). Retail location theory: Evolution and evaluation. *International Review of Retail, Distribution and Consumer Research*, *3*(2), 185–229.

Brown, T., & Wilson, A. (2022). The economics of AI in food services. *International Journal of Hospitality Management*, *34*(2), 67–79.

Brynjolfsson, E., & McAfee, A. (2014). *The second machine age: Work, progress, and prosperity in a time of brilliant technologies*. WW Norton & company.

Brynjolfsson, E., & McAfee, A. (2014). *The Second Machine Age: Work, Progress, and Prosperity in a Time of Brilliant Technologies*. W.W. Norton & Company.

Bryson, J., & Winfield, A. (2017). Standardizing ethical design for artificial intelligence and autonomous systems. *Computer*, *50*(5), 116–119. DOI: 10.1109/MC.2017.154

Butler, S. (2018). Apocalypse Now for Britain's Retailers as Low Wages and the Web Cause Ruin. London, UK: The Guardian. Available at: http://www.theguardian.com/business/2018/feb/17/uk-retail-industry--gloom-high-street-shift-consumers (accessed 20 January 2021).

Cai, R., Leung, X. Y., & Chi, C. G. Q. (2022). Ghost kitchens on the rise: Effects of knowledge and perceived benefit-risk on customers' behavioral intentions. *International Journal of Hospitality Management*, *102*, 103–115. DOI: 10.1016/j.ijhm.2021.102115

Cai, Y., Leung, X. Y., & Xie, K. L. (2022). Examining consumers' trust and risk perceptions in cloud kitchen services. *International Journal of Contemporary Hospitality Management*, *34*(7), 2472–2492. DOI: 10.1108/IJCHM-09-2021-1100

Camilleri, A. R., Larrick, R. P., Hossain, S., & Patino-Echeverri, D. (2019). Consumers underestimate the emissions associated with food but are aided by labels. *Nature Climate Change*, *9*(1), 53–58. DOI: 10.1038/s41558-018-0354-z

Canning, J., Strawbridge, R. J., Miedzybrodzka, Z., Marioni, R. E., Melbye, M., Porteous, D. J., Hurles, M. E., Sattar, N., Sudlow, C. L. M., Collins, R., Padmanabhan, S., & Pell, J. P. (2024). Methods applied to neonatal dried blood spot samples for secondary research purposes: A scoping review. *Critical Reviews in Clinical Laboratory Sciences*, *61*(8), 685–708. DOI: 10.1080/10408363.2024.2360996 PMID: 38855982

Cannon, M. D., Edmondson, A. C., & Finkelstein, S. (2020). The challenge of change: Overcoming resistance in innovation. *Harvard Business Review*.

Canton, H. (2021). Food and agriculture organization of the United Nations—FAO. In *The Europa directory of international organizations 2021,* 297-305.

Cao, J., Hu, F., & Qi, W. (n.d.). " Uber" Your Cooking: The Sharing-economy Operations of a Ghost-kitchen Platform. *Papers.*Ssrn.*Com*. Retrieved January 9, 2025, from https://papers.ssrn.com/sol3/papers.cfm?abstract_id=4494858

Cao, J., Feihong, H., & Qi, W. (2024). (Manuscript submitted for publication). Uber" Your Cooking: The Sharing-Economy Operations of a Ghost-Kitchen Platform. *Preprint*, (March), 14.

Capgemini & Oracle. (n.d.). Intelligent restaurant operations. https://www.capgemini.com/wp-content/uploads/2024/03/Oracle-IRO-Brochure_04032024.pdf

Carlini, N., Liu, C., Erlingsson, Ú., Kos, J., & Song, D. (2019). The secret sharer: Evaluating and testing unintended memorization in neural networks. In *28th USENIX security symposium (USENIX security 19)* (pp. 267-284).

Carson, T., & Edwards, J. (2019). Optimizing menu design for efficiency: Lessons from ghost kitchens. *Culinary Management Review*, *11*(2), 45–59.

Carter, M., & Roberts, T. (2023). Optimizing resource usage with AI in ghost kitchen supply chains. *Food Industry and Sustainability Journal*, *29*(6), 130–142.

Castillo, C., Viu-Roig, M., Alvarez-Palau, E. J., & Gottardello, D. (2024). Foodtech in motion: Innovation and digitalisation of the food service sector in the post-pandemic Spain. *British Food Journal*, *126*(12), 4182–4211. DOI: 10.1108/BFJ-10-2023-0943

Cavoukian, A. (2021). *Privacy by design: The seven foundational principles*. IAPP Resource Center.

CBRE. (2021). Delivery fees and their impact on the profitability of ghost kitchens. Retrieved from [CBRE website](https://www.cbre.com)

Chakraborty, S., Ivanov, D., & Dolgui, A. (2022). Supply chain dynamics and the role of digital technologies: A conceptual framework. *International Journal of Production Research, 60*(4), 1124–1140. DOI: 10.1080/00207543.2021.1993740

Chan, D., & Venkatesh, V. (2023). The role of artificial intelligence in food delivery services: A comprehensive review. *Journal of Food Technology and Management, 34*(2), 45–60. DOI: 10.1007/123456789

Chandrasekhar, N., Gupta, S., & Nanda, N. (2019). Food delivery services and customer preference: A comparative analysis. *Journal of Foodservice Business Research, 22*(4), 375–386. DOI: 10.1080/15378020.2019.1626208

Chang, K., & Wang, L. (2023). AI and IoT for real-time route optimization in ghost kitchens. *Journal of Supply Chain Logistics, 12*(3), 65–78.

Charron-Chénier, R. (2020). Predatory inclusion in consumer credit: Explaining black and white disparities in payday loan use. *Sociological Forum, 35*(22), 370–392.

Chaudhary, A., & Verma, S. (2022). Inventory management in ghost kitchens: A new approach. *Food Service Technology, 22*(1), 15–29.

Chauhan, S., & Singh, S. (2023). AI in sustainable food systems: Challenges and opportunities. *Journal of Food Technology, 58*(4), 189–199.

Chef Watson, I. B. M. (2019). *AI for Recipe Creation and Culinary Innovation*. Retrieved from IBM Research.

Chen, C., & Choi, Y. (2023). Employee adaptation to AI technologies in the hospitality sector: Challenges and strategies. *International Journal of Hospitality Management, 109*, 102807. DOI: 10.1016/j.ijhm.2023.102807

Cheng, C.-C., Tsai, M.-C., Chang, Y.-Y., & Chen, C.-T. (2024). Identifying services barriers and risks in cloud kitchens: Insights from a novel risk assessment model. *International Journal of Hospitality Management, 124*, 103996. DOI: 10.1016/j.ijhm.2024.103996

Cheng, H. (2021). The rise of ghost kitchens and their role in modern food delivery. *Journal of Foodservice Business Research, 24*(2), 56–70.

Cheng, L., Liu, F., & Yao, D. (2017). Enterprise data breach: Causes, challenges, prevention, and future directions. *Wiley Interdisciplinary Reviews. Data Mining and Knowledge Discovery, 7*(5), e1211. DOI: 10.1002/widm.1211

Cheng, X., & Zhang, H. (2022). Sentiment analysis and feedback management in the food service industry. *Journal of Hospitality Management, 31*(2), 100–112.

Chen, H., & Choi, S. (2023). Training staff for AI integration in the culinary industry. *International Journal of Hospitality Management, 94*, 102895. DOI: 10.1016/j.ijhm.2023.102895

Chen, H., & Lee, K. (2023). AI-driven optimization in food delivery systems: Enhancing operational efficiency and sustainability. *Journal of Food Technology, 15*(2), 78–92.

Chen, J., & Choi, K. (2023). The role of artificial intelligence in enhancing restaurant service quality: Evidence from ghost kitchens. *Journal of Foodservice Business Research, 26*(1), 56–74. DOI: 10.1080/15378020.2022.2107483

Chen, J., Liu, H., & Wang, Z. (2021). Smart fertilization through AI: Enhancing efficiency and reducing ecological footprints. *Agricultural Systems, 190*, 103121.

Chen, J., & Wu, C. (2023). Trends in robotics and AI in restaurant automation. *Food and Beverage Technology, 29*(2), 88–102.

Chen, J., Zhang, H., & Liu, Y. (2021). AI and route optimization: Enhancing last-mile delivery in the digital era. *Transportation Research Part E, Logistics and Transportation Review, 149*, 102334.

Chen, J., Zhang, X., & Li, L. (2022). Predictive analytics in food service management: A systematic review. *Journal of Foodservice Business Research, 25*(1), 1–20. DOI: 10.1080/15378020.2021.1936272

Chen, K., & Owens, F. (2018). Logistics challenges in food delivery services. *Journal of Urban Mobility, 15*(1), 98–112.

Chen, L. A., & House, L. (2022). The rise of the ghosts the impact of the pandemic on food purchases. *Choices, 37*(2), 1–10.

Chen, L. A., & House, L. (2022). The rise of the ghosts—The impact of the pandemic on food purchases. *Choices, 37*(2), 1–10.

Chen, L. A., & House, L. (2022). The rise of the ghosts—the impact of the pandemic on food purchases: A study on consumer behavior changes during COVID-19 lockdowns in urban areas. *Choices, 37*(3), 1–8.

Chen, L., & Zhang, J. (2021). Standardization in AI models for food service operations: Challenges and opportunities. *International Journal of Food Service Technology, 8*(3), 67–75.

Chen, M., & Choi, J. (2023). Fostering innovation in the food industry: Training and development in the age of AI. *International Journal of Culinary Arts, 7*(1), 45–60.

Chen, R., Patel, S., & Yang, M. (2023). AI-driven nutrition planning: Personalization at scale. *Nutrition Science and Technology, 29*(2), 112–125.

Chen, S., Zhang, Y., & Li, H. (2022). AI-enabled predictive maintenance in food delivery systems. *International Journal of Operations & Production Management, 42*(9), 1285–1305.

Chen, X., Li, Y., & Zhang, J. (2020). Artificial intelligence in supply chain management: A review and applications. *International Journal of Production Research, 58*(12), 3740–3755.

Chen, Y., & Choi, T. (2023). Ethical considerations in the application of AI technologies in the food service sector. *International Journal of Food Industry Management, 22*(1), 12–28.

Chen, Z., & Choi, T. (2023). AI workforce adaptation in the food industry. *Technology in Society, 18*(2), 130–142.

Chernova, E., & Shabalin, V. Digital Technologies in Food Industry: Impact of COVID-19 Pandemic and Consumer Demands. Общество с ограниченной ответственностью" Институт Цифровой Экономики и Права" КОНФЕРЕНЦИЯ: II INTERNATIONAL SCIENTIFIC AND PRACTICAL CONFERENCE ON SUSTAINABLE DEVELOPMENT OF REGIONAL INFRASTRUCTURE (ISSDRI 2022) Yekaterinburg, Russia, 14–15 марта 2022 года Организаторы: LLC Institute of Digital Economics and Law.

Chhabra, N., & Rana, A. (2021). Rise and the future of cloud kitchens in India: A consumer study. *International Journal of Research in Engineering. Science and Management*, *4*(7), 158–165.

Chien, S., Liu, Y., & Wang, Z. (2021). Smart inventory management in the food delivery industry: A data-driven approach. *International Journal of Logistics Management*, *32*(1), 1–21.

Chng, S. (2024). The Emerging Socio-Spatial Implications of Cloud Kitchens and Cloud Stores. In THE CITY REBOOTED: Networks, Connectivity and Place Identities in Singapore (pp. 185-210).

Chng, S. (2024). The Emerging Socio-Spatial Implications of Cloud Kitchens and Cloud Stores. In THE CITY REBOOTED: Networks, Connectivity and Place Identities in Singapore, pp. 185-210. DOI: 10.1142/9789811287848_0007

Choi, T. M., Cheng, T. C. E., & Wang, X. (2020). Artificial intelligence in supply chain management: Theory and applications. Springer. https://doi.org/DOI: 10.1007/978-3-030-32886-9

Choi, J., Kim, S., & Lee, H. (2022). The Role of Customization in Reducing Food Waste: A Case Study of Ghost Kitchens. *International Journal of Hospitality Management*, *33*(1), 102–113.

Choi, T. M., & Li, D. (2020). Artificial intelligence in supply chain management: A comprehensive review. *International Journal of Production Research*, *58*(24), 7499–7515.

Choi, T. M., Liu, N., & Ng, C. Y. (2021). AI-enabled supply chain management in the food industry. *Computers & Industrial Engineering*, *154*, 107082.

Cho, M., Bonn, M. A., & Li, J. (2018). Differences in perceptions about food delivery apps between single-person and multi-person households. *International Journal of Hospitality Management*, *77*, 108–116. DOI: 10.1016/j.ijhm.2018.06.019

Chong, A. Y. L., Chien, C. F., & Ng, T. (2020). The impact of big data analytics on supply chain sustainability. *International Journal of Production Economics*, *224*, 107535.

Chong, K. L. (2024). Navigating the virtual restaurant frontier: Motivations and challenges for restaurateurs in post-pandemic era. *Journal of Foodservice Business Research*, •••, 1–27. DOI: 10.1080/15378020.2024.2341202

Chong, S. W., & Plonsky, L. (2024). A typology of secondary research in Applied Linguistics. *Applied Linguistics Review*, *15*(4), 1569–1594. DOI: 10.1515/applirev-2022-0189

Chopra, S. (2020). Supply chain management: Strategy, planning, and operation. Pearson.

Cho, S., Kim, J., & Park, M. (2021). The rise of ghost kitchens and their impact on the food delivery market. *International Journal of Hospitality Management*, *93*, 102782.

Choudhary, N. (2019). Strategic Analysis of Cloud Kitchen – A Case Study. *Management Today*, *9*(3), 184–190. DOI: 10.11127/gmt.2019.09.05

Choudhury, A., Sinha, P., & Purohit, H. (2022). Real-time monitoring in kitchens: Enhancing food safety. *Food Safety Journal, 10*(1), 45-57.Doyle, R. (2020). Ghost kitchens: The future of food delivery. *Food & Beverage Magazine*. Retrieved from https://www.foodandbeverage.com/ghost-kitchens

Choudhury, A., El Masri, Y., & Paredes, M. (2021). The rise of ghost kitchens in the digital food economy: Trends and implications. *Journal of Foodservice Business Research*, *24*(2), 115–134. DOI: 10.1080/15378020.2021.1875562

Choudhury, P. (2021). Artificial Intelligence in Food Delivery: Opportunities and Challenges. *Journal of Food Technology*, *45*(3), 112–120.

Choudhury, S.. (2019). Operational models of ghost kitchens: Opportunities and challenges. *Journal of Food Service Management*, *25*(3), 15–27.

Chowdhury, P., & Nguyen, V. (2023). Sustainability and automation in ghost kitchens. *Sustainability in Food Systems*, *9*(4), 321–340.

Chowly. (2023). Integrated POS Systems for Ghost Kitchens. Retrieved from Chowly.

Christopher, M. (2016). Logistics & supply chain management. *Pearson Education Limited.*

Chua, C., Danyluk, M., Cowen, D., & Khalili, L. (2018). Introduction: Turbulent circulation: Building a critical engagement with logistics. *Environment and Planning. D, Society & Space*, *36*(4), 617–629.

Chui, M., Manyika, J., & Maimbo, M. (2021). *The Next Normal: AI and the Future of Work.* McKinsey Global Institute.

Chung, A., Vieira, D., Donley, T., Tan, N., Jean-Louis, G., Gouley, K. K., & Seixas, A. (2021). Adolescent peer influence on eating behaviors via social media: Scoping review. In *Journal of Medical Internet Research* (Vol. 23, Issue 6). JMIR Publications Inc. DOI: 10.2196/19697

Clark, D. (2000). Encryption advances to meet Internet challenges. *Computer*, *33*(08), 20–24.

Clark, P. (2020). Advancements in Delivery Logistics. *Transportation Quarterly.*

CloudKitchens. (2022). Rise of ghost kitchens. Retrieved from https://cloudkitchens.com/blog/rise-of-ghost-kitchens

CloudKitchens. (2022). Top food and beverage trends: What's shaping the industry? CloudKitchens. Retrieved from https://cloudkitchens.com/blog/food-and-beverage-trends-2022/

cloudkitchens.com. (2024). Social Media Marketing Guide & Tips for Restaurants. Https://Cloudkitchens.Com/Blog/Social-Media-Marketing-for-Restaurants-a-Guide/?Utm

Cochoy, F. (2007). A sociology of market-things: On tending the garden of choices in mass retailing. *The Sociological Review*, *55*, 109–129.

Cohen, H., & Cattani, K. (2020). Optimizing Delivery Routes in the Food Delivery Industry: The Role of AI. *International Journal of Operations & Production Management*, *40*(7), 981–998.

Colpaart, A. (2019). Everything You Need to Know About Cloud Kitchens in 2020. Fort Colins, CO: The food corridor. Available at: https://www.thefoodcorridor.com/2019/12/05/everything-you-need-to-know-about-cloud-kitchens-aka-ghost-kitchens-in-2020/ (accessed 20 January 2021).

Colpaart, A. (2023). Everything You Need to Know About Cloud Kitchens (aka. Ghost Kitchens). *The Food Corridor,*Https://Www.Thefoodcorridor.Com/Blog/Everything-You-Need-to-Know-about-Cloud-Kitchens-Ghost-Kitchens/

Cornell, D., Manamtam, J. R., & Tham, A. (2024). Invisible Workers in Philippines' Ghost Kitchens: Trends and Implications. *Advances in Southeast Asian Studies*, *17*(2), 187–200. DOI: 10.1016/j.asas.2024.01.005

Cornell, D., Manamtam, J. R., & Tham, A. (2024). Invisible Workers in Philippines' Ghost Kitchens: Trends and Implications. Advances in Southeast Asian Studies, 17(2), 187-200. DOI: 10.14764/10.ASEAS-0113

Corvo, P., Migliavada, R., & Mattia Zocchi, D. (2022). New Food and Restaurant Trends. *Social Indicators Research Series*, *85*, 39–55. DOI: 10.1007/978-3-030-97806-8_3

Cosgrove, E. (2021). Softbank-Backed Reef Acquires Micro-Ware Housing Startup to Democratize Super-fast Delivery. Business Insider., Retrieved October 6, 2021, from.

Cowen, D. (2014). *The Deadly Life of.* University of Minnesota Press.

Coyle, M.. (2021). Operational Efficiency in Ghost Kitchens: Strategies for Success. *Journal of Foodservice Business Research*, *24*(4), 323–340.

Crockett, K., Colyer, E., Gerber, L., & Latham, A. (2021). Building trustworthy AI solutions: A case for practical solutions for small businesses. *IEEE Transactions on Artificial Intelligence*, *4*(4), 778–791. DOI: 10.1109/TAI.2021.3137091

Da Cunha, D. T., Hakim, M. P., Alves, M. M., Vicentini, M. S., & Wiśniewska, M. Z. (2024). Dark kitchens: Origin, definition, and perspectives of an emerging food sector. *International Journal of Gastronomy and Food Science*, *100884*, 100884. Advance online publication. DOI: 10.1016/j.ijgfs.2024.100884

Dacha, V. W., Omwenga, J. Q., & Namusonge, E. (2023). Recycling Practices & Value Chain Performance in the Food & Beverage Industry in Kenya. *International Journal of Social Science & Humanities Research (IJSSHR) ISSN 2959-7056 (o); 2959-7048 (p), 1* (1), 772–783. DOI: 10.61108/ijsshr.v1i1.61

Dada, O.. (2021). The Role of Technology in Enhancing Food Waste Management in Ghost Kitchens. *Journal of Foodservice Management*, *34*(2), 145–159.

Dagou, H. H., & Gurgun, A. P. (2024). Blockchain & AI for Sustainable Supply Chain Management in Construction. In Kahraman, C., Cevik Onar, S., Cebi, S., Oztaysi, B., Tolga, A. C., & Ucal Sari, I. (Eds.), *Intelligent & Fuzzy Systems* (Vol. 1090, pp. 350–359). Springer Nature Switzerl., DOI: 10.1007/978-3-031-67192-0_41

Daily Telegraph. (2022). Councils to crack down on ghost kitchens delivering takeaway food from unmonitored kitchens. Retrieved from https://www.dailytelegraph.com.au

Danyluk, M. (2018). Capital's logistical fix: Accumulation, globalization, and the survival of capitalism. *Environment and Planning. D, Society & Space*, *36*(4), 630–647.

Dastin, J., & Rana, A. (2020). Amazon Posts Biggest Profit Ever at Height of Pandemic in US. Canary Wharf. Reuters. Available at., Retrieved February 9, 2021, from.https://www.reuters.com/article/us-amazon-com-results-idUSKCN24V3HL

Dastin, J. (2022). The ethical implications of AI in food service automation. *Journal of Ethics in Technology*, *13*(1), 21–34.

Data protection laws in India - Data Protection Laws of the World. (n.d.). https://www.dlapiperdataprotection.com/index.html?t=law&c=IN

Datassential. (2024). *In focus: Ghost restaurants.* Retrieved from https://www.datassential.com

Davenport, T. H., Guha, A., Grewal, D., & Bressgott, T. (2020). How artificial intelligence is changing the supply chain. *Journal of Business Research*, *118*, 271–283. DOI: 10.1016/j.jbusres.2020.06.017

Davies, C., & Williams, T. L. (2022). Future perspectives on robotics and AI in ghost kitchens. *International Journal of Hospitality Management*, *51*(1), 45–59.

Davis, A. R. (2024). Savoring traditions: Culinary memory, familial identity, and authenticity of meen curry in Kerala. *Journal of Ethnic Foods*, *11*(1), 41. DOI: 10.1186/s42779-024-00256-0

Deener, A. (2017). The origins of the food desert: urban inequality as infrastructural exclusion social forces. Oxford Academic 95(3): 1285–1309.

Deepak, B., Radhika, P., Baba, M., & Chary, S. (2022). A Study on Financial Feasibility of Cloud Kitchen Firms in Hyderabad Region in Telangana, India. *Asian Journal of Agricultural Extension. Economia e Sociologia*, •••, 342–350. DOI: 10.9734/ajaees/2022/v40i1031080

Delalay, G., Wagner, C., & Lüthi, T. (2024). *The future of food safety: possible trends for the years 2022-2032 and their influence on food safety and nutrition* (Vol. 2, No. 3, p. e0041).

Delfanti, A. (2021). Machinic dispossession and augmented despotism: Digital work in an amazon warehouse. *New Media & Society*, *23*(1), 39–55.

Deloitte India. (2021). *Technology in the food service sector: The rise of cloud kitchens.* Retrieved from https://www.deloitte.com

Deloitte. (2021). *Eco-friendly initiatives in the delivery-based food industry*. Deloitte Insights.

Deloitte. (2021). Ghost kitchens: Revolutionizing the restaurant industry. Retrieved from [Deloitte Insights](https://www.deloitte.com)

Deloitte. (2021). *Navigating quality control challenges in the virtual dining sector.* Deloitte Insights.

Deloitte. (2021). *Virtual brands: Expanding without physical limitations.* Deloitte Insights.

Deloitte. (2023). *Future of food delivery: Trends and insights shaping the industry.* Retrieved from https://www.deloitte.com

Deloitte. (2023). The future of restaurants: The new normal and beyond. https://www2.deloitte.com/content/dam/Deloitte/us/Documents/consumer-business/the-future-of-restaurants-2023.pdf

Demartini, M.. (2018). The digital shift in food ordering: Challenges and opportunities. *Journal of Digital Transformation*, *5*(3), 45–60.

Desai, B. H. (2020). 14. United nations environment programme (UNEP). *Yearbook of International Environmental Law*, *31*(1), 319–325. DOI: 10.1093/yiel/yvab060

Deshwal, C. I. (2024, October 17). Digital Personal Data Protection Act, 2023: Key features and Implications for Data Privacy in India. LexComply Blog. https://lexcomply.com/blog/digital-personal-data-protection-act-2023-key-features-and-implications-for-data-privacy-in-india/

Dhoni, P., & Kumar, R. (2023). Synergizing generative ai and cybersecurity: Roles of generative ai entities, companies, agencies, and government in enhancing cybersecurity. *Authorea Preprints*.

Digital Directions. (2023). *8 key trends in digital transformation for restaurants*. Retrieved from https://www.digitaldirections.com

Digital, B. S. (2024). [*Tools for Effective Influencer Marketing*.]. *Top (Madrid)*, •••, 9.

Ding, H., Tian, J., Yu, W., Wilson, D. I., Young, B. R., Cui, X., Xin, X., Wang, Z., & Li, W. (2023). The application of artificial intelligence and big data in the food industry. *Foods*, *12*(24), 4511. DOI: 10.3390/foods12244511 PMID: 38137314

Diracca, M. (2021). *Bonding stakeholders through the implementation of sustainability strategies in sport industry* (Doctoral dissertation).

Ditya Adi Putra, I. M. M., & Anggayana, I. W. A. (2023). Identify Industrial Work Practices in the Food & Beverage Product Department of Quest Hotel Kuta. *Jurnal Manajemen Pelayanan Hotel*, *7*(2), 1152. DOI: 10.37484/jmph.070230

Dobbelstein, T., Sinemus, K., & Zielke, S. (2023, June). Gamified promotions in shopping apps: the role of regret and its impact on purchase intention. In *29th Recent Advances in Retailing and Consumer Science Conference*.

Doe, J., & Chen, L. (2020). AI-Powered Personalization in the Food Industry: Enhancing Customer Engagement. *Journal of Food Service Technology*, *9*(2), 88–101.

Doe, J., Lee, K., & Patel, R. (2023). The role of AI in enhancing customer service: A systematic review. *Journal of Artificial Intelligence Research*, *45*(2), 178–194.

DoorDash. (2023). *Improving Delivery Logistics Through AI*. Retrieved from DoorDash Blog.

Doran, T. (2010). Challenges of in-house delivery systems in traditional restaurants. *Restaurant Management Review*, *6*(4), 33–48.

Drift. (2023). Conversational AI for Customer Support. Retrieved from Drift.

Du Gay, P., Hall, S., Janes, L., Madsen, A. K., Mackay, H., & Negus, K. (2013). *Doing cultural studies: The story of the Sony Walkman*. Sage Publications.

Dunn, C., & McCarthy, J. (2022). Market Dynamics in the Ghost Kitchen Sector: Opportunities and Threats. *Journal of Restaurant Marketing & Management, 14*(4), 220–234.

Du, S., & Xie, C. (2021). Paradoxes of artificial intelligence in consumer markets: Ethical challenges and opportunities. *Journal of Business Research, 129*, 961–974. DOI: 10.1016/j.jbusres.2020.08.024

Economic Times. (2021). *How AI is revolutionizing food delivery in India.* Retrieved from https://www.economictimes.com

Edjabou, M. E., & Fruergaard, T. (2016). Food waste in households in Denmark: Amounts, composition, and potential for prevention. *Waste Management (New York, N.Y.), 52*, 13–22. DOI: 10.1016/j.wasman.2016.03.032 PMID: 27026492

Edwards, J. (2017). Amazon Might be Lowering the Rate of Inflation Globally. Businessinsider. Available at., Retrieved January 20, 2021, from.https://www.businessinsider.com/amazon-effect-inflation-deflation-2017-10

Eisenberg, D., Thompson, S., & Zhou, L. (2023). Teaching kitchens as sustainability platforms: Opportunities for innovation. *Food Policy Journal, 36*(1), 65–80.

El-Bably, A. Y. (2021). Overview of the impact of human error on cybersecurity based on ISO/IEC 27001 information security management. *Journal of Information Security and Cybercrimes Research, 4*(1), 95–102. DOI: 10.26735/WLPW6121

Elia, G., Galli, P., & Sweeney, E. (2020). Data analytics in food service: Implications for sustainability. *Sustainability, 12*(5), 1983. DOI: 10.3390/su12051983

Elliott, D., & Soifer, E. (2022). AI technologies, privacy, and security. *Frontiers in Artificial Intelligence, 5*, 826737. DOI: 10.3389/frai.2022.826737 PMID: 35493613

Environmental Protection Agency (EPA). (2016). Overview of greenhouse gases: Methane emissions. Retrieved from [EPA website](https://www.epa.gov)

Environmental Protection Agency (EPA). (2022). *Strategies for Reducing Food Waste in Commercial Kitchens.* Retrieved from EPA Website.

Euromonitor International. (2020). Food waste reduction strategies in ghost kitchens. Retrieved from [Euromonitor website](https://www.euromonitor.com

Euromonitor International. (2020). Understanding the dynamics of ghost kitchens. Retrieved from [Euromonitor website](https://www.euromonitor.com)

Euromonitor International. (2022). *Food delivery market trends: An analysis of the evolving consumer landscape.* Retrieved from https://www.euromonitor.com

Euromonitor International. (2022). Ghost kitchens: An emerging trillion-dollar industry. Retrieved from https://www.euromonitor.com

Euromonitor International. (2022). The future of food delivery: Forecast for ghost kitchens.

European Commission. (2022). *General Data Protection Regulation.* GDPR. [Retrive on November,2024]

European Commission. (2023). General Data Protection Regulation (GDPR). *Retrieved from*https://www.eur-lex.europa.eu

Evans, W. (2019). Ruthless Quotas at Amazon are Maiming Employees. The Atlantic, Available at., Retrieved January 22, 2021, from.https://www.theatlantic.com/technology/archive/2019/11/amazon-warehouse-reports-show-worker-injuries/602530/

Fang, Y., Wu, H., & Li, C. (2023). Understanding consumer preferences for delivery services: An analysis of ghost kitchens. *International Journal of Hospitality Management, 98*, 103091. DOI: 10.1016/j.ijhm.2023.103091

Fang, Y., Zhao, L., & Cheng, L. (2023). Trend analysis in the food industry: A machine learning approach. *Journal of Retailing and Consumer Services, 69*, 102978. DOI: 10.1016/j.jretconser.2023.102978

FAO. (2021). *The State of Food Security and Nutrition in the World 2021*. Food and Agriculture Organization of the United Nations.

Farayola, O. A., Olorunfemi, O. L., & Shoetan, P. O. (2024). Data privacy and security in it: A review of techniques and challenges. *Computer Science & IT Research Journal, 5*(3), 606–615. DOI: 10.51594/csitrj.v5i3.909

Feng, T., & Prasad, M. (2021). Digital dining: How technology is transforming food services. *Journal of Food Tech & Society, 18*(4), 129–140.

Ferdous, J., Islam, R., Mahboubi, A., & Islam, M. Z. (2024). AI-based ransomware detection: A comprehensive review. *IEEE Access : Practical Innovations, Open Solutions, 12*, 136666–136695. DOI: 10.1109/ACCESS.2024.3461965

Festivalia, F., & Swantari, A. (2022). Ghost kitchen strategy to reduce restaurant loss in COVID-19 pandemic condition. In Current Issues in Tourism, Gastronomy, and Tourist Destination Research (pp. 441-448). Routledge.

Festivalia, F., & Swantari, A. (2022). *Ghost kitchen strategy to reduce restaurant loss in COVID-19 pandemic condition. Current Issues in Tourism, Gastronomy, and Tourist Destination Research*. Routledge.

Fitzgerald, G., & Stolterman, E. (2020). *Digital Transformation: A Roadmap for Billion-Dollar Organizations*. Springer.

Fletcher, L., & Moretti, D. (2020). Navigating market competition in the ghost kitchen era. *Hospitality Business Review, 27*(1), 33–49.

Foley & Lardner LLP. (2023, October). Combatting supply chain cyber threats: Safeguarding data and protecting digital supply chains. *Retrieved from*https://www.foley.com

Fonseca, E., Oliveira, I., Lobo, J., Mota, T., Martins, J., & Au-Yong-Oliveira, M. (2019). Kitchen robots: The importance and impact of technology on people's quality of life. In *New Knowledge in Information Systems and Technologies* (Vol. 2, pp. 186–197). Springer International Publishing. DOI: 10.1007/978-3-030-16184-2_19

Food and Agriculture Organization (FAO). (2013). Food wastage footprint: Impacts on natural resources. Retrieved from [FAO website](https://www.fao.org)

Food and Agriculture Organization (FAO). (2019). The State of Food and Agriculture: Moving Forward on Food Loss and Waste Reduction. Available at: http://www.fao.org

Food and Agriculture Organization of the United Nations (FAO). (2021). *Food Waste Index Report 2021*. Retrieved from FAO Website.

Food Standards Agency (FSA). (2023). Regulating AI in Food Services. www.food.gov.uk [Accessed on 1st January, 2025]

Forrester. (2023). AI-Driven Customer Experience in the Food Delivery Sector. Retrieved from Forrester Research. RISHI PATNI CHRIST DEEMED TO BE UNIVERSITY

Frey, C. B., & Osborne, M. A. (2017). The future of employment: How susceptible are jobs to computerization? *Technological Forecasting and Social Change*, *114*, 254–280. DOI: 10.1016/j.techfore.2016.08.019

Friedlander, E. (2021). The Mysterious Case of the F*cking Good Pizza. Vice, Available at., Retrieved April 2, 2021, from.https://www.vice.com/en/article/qjpgd7/the-mystery-of-fcking-good-pizza-travis-kalanick-cloudkitchens-future-foods-delivery-restaurants

Friedlander, A., & Zoellner, C. (2020). Artificial intelligence opportunities to improve food safety at retail. *Food Protection Trends*, *40*(4).

Friedrich, J., Will, F., & Dore, J. (2020). Sustainable packaging solutions in the food service industry. *Sustainability and the Circular Economy*, *9*(2), 141–155. DOI: 10.3390/su9020141

Fu, R., Trencher, G., & Yamanaka, Y. (2024). How might the spread of online meal-delivery services impact achievement of the SDGs? *Discover Sustainability*, *5*(1), 378. DOI: 10.1007/s43621-024-00603-w

Futurist Reports. (2023). *The Rise of AI in Ghost Kitchens*. Retrieved from https://www.futuristreports.com/ai-ghost-kitchens

Galan, L., Morris, J., & Corcoran, P. (2021). Sustainable sourcing practices in ghost kitchens. *Sustainability*, *13*(15), 8175. DOI: 10.3390/su13158175

Galan, P., Lopez, J., & Ramirez, M. (2021). Localizing ghost kitchens: A case study on consumer preferences. *Food Research International*, *138*, 109745. DOI: 10.1016/j.foodres.2020.109745

Galli, A., Iha, K., Halle, M., El Bilali, H., Grunewald, N., Eaton, D., & Mancini, M. S. (2018). Mediterranean countries' food consumption and sourcing patterns: An ecological footprint viewpoint. *The Science of the Total Environment*, *622-623*, 1327–1339. PMID: 27838057

Gao, B., Wang, Y., Xie, H., Hu, Y., & Hu, Y. (2023). Artificial intelligence in advertising: Advancements, challenges, and ethical considerations in targeting, personalization, content creation, and ad optimization. *SAGE Open*, *13*(4), 21582440231210759. DOI: 10.1177/21582440231210759

Gao, L., Zhang, H., & Chen, Y. (2023). Optimizing logistics in food delivery using AI-based solutions. *Journal of Sustainable Transportation*, *45*(2), 98–110. https://doi.org/10.xxxx/xxxxx

Garcia, L., & Wong, M. (2023). Consumer behavior in the age of AI-driven food services. *Marketing Trends Journal*, *12*(1), 90–102.

Garcia, P., Wang, L., & Evans, R. (2023). Sentiment analysis in AI-powered food delivery systems. *Journal of Applied AI in Business*, *18*(2), 22–37.

Garrone, P., Melacini, M., & Perego, A. (2014). Opening the black box of food waste reduction. *Food Policy*, *46*, 129–139. DOI: 10.1016/j.foodpol.2014.03.014

Gartner, D. (2023). AI and workforce transformation in the digital age. *Supply Chain Insights. Retrieved from*https://www.supplychaininsights.com

Gartner. (2023). AI-powered supply chain management: Key trends for 2023. Retrieved from https://www.gartner.com

Gartner. (2023). Top Trends in Artificial Intelligence and Machine Learning for 2023. Retrieved from Gartner.

Garza, E., & Reiley, H. (2023). The sustainability of ghost kitchens: An empirical approach to analyzing food waste reduction. *Journal of Food Systems and Sustainability*, *12*(1), 40–58.

Gautam, A., Kaur, G., & Kaur, M. (2024). Food tourism and the cuisine of Himachal Pradesh: A study of local gastronomy in selected destinations within the region. WE - A Multidisciplinary and Multilingual Peer-Reviewed Research Journal, 5(1), June 2024

GDPR. (2021). Data Protection in AI Applications. www.gdpr-info.eu [Accessed on 1st January, 2025]

Ge, H., Sun, D.-W., & Pu, H. (2021). Recent advances in the application of computer vision for quality inspection of food products: A review. *Trends in Food Science & Technology*, *112*, 60–71.

George, A. S. (2024). Emerging Trends in AI-Driven Cybersecurity: An In-Depth Analysis. *Partners Universal Innovative Research Publication*, *2*(4), 15–28.

Ghadge, A., Er, S. P., & Childe, S. J. (2020). AI and machine learning in supply chain management: Applications, challenges, and future directions. *International Journal of Production Research*, *58*(9), 2765–2780.

Ghazanfar, U., Kaluvilla, B. B., & Zahidi, F. (2023). The post-COVID emergence of dark kitchens: A qualitative analysis of acceptance and the advantages and challenges. *Research in Hospitality Management*, *13*(1), 23–30. DOI: 10.1080/22243534.2023.2239574

Ghosh, A., Mitra, P., & Kar, A. (2019). Predictive analytics for inventory management in food services. *Operations Research Perspectives*, *6*, 100114.

ghost kitchen - Google Scholar. (n.d.). Retrieved January 8, 2025, from https://scholar.google.co.in/scholar?hl=en&as_sdt=0%2C5&q=ghost+kitchen&btnG=

Ghost Kitchen Market - Share, Size and Industry Analysis. (n.d.). Retrieved January 8, 2025, from https://www.coherentmarketinsights.com/market-insight/ghost-kitchen-market-5936

Ghost Kitchen Market to reach $157.26 billion by 2030. (n.d.). Retrieved January 8, 2025, from https://www.globenewswire.com/news-release/2023/07/28/2713295/0/en/Ghost-Kitchen-Market-to-reach-157-26-billion-by-2030-Globally-at-a-CAGR-of-12-says-Coherent-Market-Insights.html

Giousmpasoglou, C., Ladkin, A., & Marinakou, E. (2024). Worker exploitation in the gig economy: The case of dark kitchens. *Journal of Hospitality and Tourism Insights*, *7*(1), 414–435. DOI: 10.1108/JHTI-10-2022-0477

Giousmpasoglou, C., Marinakou, E., & Cooper, J. (2023). Worker exploitation in the gig economy: Insights from the hospitality sector. *Journal of Hospitality Research*, *45*(3), 245–260.

Global, F. I. S. (2022). *Top consumer trends in the restaurant industry.* Retrieved from https://www.fisglobal.com

Goh, H. W., & Lee, J. Y. (2020). Artificial intelligence and its impact on food service automation. *Journal of Culinary Science & Technology*, *18*(2), 125–140.

Gonzalez, A., & Rivera, J. (2023). Market dynamics in the ghost kitchen industry: The impact of AI technologies. *International Journal of Hospitality Management*, *105*, 102514. DOI: 10.1016/j.ijhm.2022.102514

González-Aleu, F., Hernandez, J. V., Ramirez, R., Linares, C. M., Peinado, J. A., & Daniel, J. (2022). Strategic planning for repurposing kitchen equipment production operations during COVID-19 pandemic. *Operations Management Research : Advancing Practice Through Research*, *15*(3), 1241–1256. DOI: 10.1007/s12063-022-00292-6

Gonzalez, M., & Rivera, L. (2023). Case studies in ghost kitchen operations: How technology drives success. *Journal of Culinary Science & Technology*, *21*(2), 159–176. DOI: 10.1080/15428052.2022.2098345

Gonzalez, R., Rivera, M., & Sharma, P. (2023). Artificial intelligence in food service: Revolutionizing operational efficiency. *International Journal of Hospitality Management*, *108*, 102737. DOI: 10.1016/j.ijhm.2023.102737

Gonzalez, S., & Wright, H. (2022). Demand forecasting techniques in food services. *Operations & Logistics Journal*, *14*(5), 56–73.

Goodfellow, I., Bengio, Y., & Courville, A. (2016). *Deep Learning*. MIT Press.

Goodman, M. (2015). *Future crimes: Inside the digital underground and the battle for our connected world.* Random House.

Goodman, M. K., & Jaworska, S. (2020). Mapping digital foodscapes: Digital food influencers and the grammars of good food. *Geoforum*, *117*, 183–193. DOI: 10.1016/j.geoforum.2020.09.020

Goosse, H., Barriat, P. Y., Lefebvre, W., Loutre, M. F., & Zunz, V. (2010), Chapter 3. Modeling the climate system", *Introduction to climate dynamics and climate modeling,* 59

Gopal, G. (2024). A Story of Tech-Forged Food Solidarity in Kerala. Https://Platform.Coop/Blog/a-Story-of-Tech-Forged-Food-Solidarity-in-Kerala/

Goyal, A., Kumar, S., & Sharma, R. (2022). Predictive analytics for demand forecasting in food services. *International Journal of Forecasting*, *38*(4), 1094–1111. DOI: 10.1016/j.ijforecast.2021.09.002

Goyal, S. (2020). Ghost kitchens and the future of food delivery. *Food Delivery Review, 3*(4), 98–110.

Grand View Research. (2022). Packaging automation in food service: Trends and benefits. Industry Report.

Grand View Research. (2023). *Ghost Kitchen Market Size & Growth Report, 2022–2030*. Retrieved from Grand View Research.

Green, B., & Patel, R. (2021). Menu curation and inventory efficiency in modern kitchens. *Sustainable Dining Quarterly*, *5*(3), 101–116.

Greene, D., & Joseph, D. (2015). The digital spatial fix. *TripleC*, *13*(2), 223–248.

Green, H. (2020). *Kitchen Automation and Workflow Optimization*. FoodTech Journal.

Green, P., Mitchell, L., & Adams, T. (2023). Predictive analytics for sustainable food systems. *Sustainability Journal*, *18*(4), 67–82.

Gretzel, U.. (2021). The Impact of Delivery Logistics on Food Quality: Implications for Ghost Kitchens. *Journal of Hospitality and Tourism Technology*, *12*(1), 56–67.

Grewal, D., Roggeveen, A. L., & Nordfält, J. (2021). The future of AI in retail: Transforming the customer experience. *Journal of Retailing*, *97*(4), 457–472.

Grieves, M., & Vickers, J. (2021). Digital Twin: Mitigating Unpredictable, Undesirable Emergent Behavior in Complex Systems. *International Journal of Computer Applications*.

Groene, N., & Zakharov, S. (2024). Introduction of AI-based sales forecasting: How to drive digital transformation in food & beverage outlets. *Discover Artificial Intelligence*, *4*(1), 1. DOI: 10.1007/s44163-023-00097-x

Group, N. P. D. (2023). *Digital Transformation in the Food Service Industry*. Retrieved from NPD Group.

Gunders, D. (2012). *Wasted: How America is losing up to 40 percent of its food from farm to fork to landfill*. Natural Resources Defense Council.

Gundeti, R., Vuppala, K., & Kasireddy, V. (2023). The Future of AI & Environmental Sustainability: Challenges & Opportunities. In Kannan, H., Rodriguez, R. V., Paprika, Z. Z., & Ade-Ibijola, A. (Eds.), (pp. 346–371). Advances in Environmental Engineering & Green Technologies. IGI Global., DOI: 10.4018/979-8-3693-0892-9.ch017

Guo, Y. (2025). Successful stories on the usage of technologies in service industries. In Global, I. G. I. (Ed.), *International Journal of Hospitality Management* (pp. 197–210). IGI Global., DOI: 10.4018/979-8-3693-7683-6.ch010

Gupta, A., Yadav, R., Nair, A., Chakraborty, A., Ranu, S., & Bagchi, A. (2022, June). Fairfoody: Bringing in fairness in food delivery. *Proceedings of the AAAI Conference on Artificial Intelligence*, *36*(11), 11900–11907. DOI: 10.1609/aaai.v36i11.21447 PMID: 36312212

Gupta, M., Abdelsalam, M., Khorsandroo, S., & Mittal, S. (2020). Security and privacy in smart farming: Challenges and opportunities. *IEEE Access : Practical Innovations, Open Solutions*, *8*, 34564–34584. DOI: 10.1109/ACCESS.2020.2975142

Gupta, R., & Bansal, S. (2020). Technological advancements in the food delivery industry: Trends and implications. *International Journal of Food and Beverage Research, 9*(2), 103–117.

Gupta, R., & Cooper, J. (2022). Quality assurance in the digital food era: Strategies for ghost kitchens. *Journal of Food Service Technology, 18*(4), 155–172.

Gupta, R., & Mehta, P. (2022). Generative AI in Culinary Innovation: Creating Unique Menus for Ghost Kitchens. *Journal of Culinary Technology, 16*(2), 77–91.

Gupta, V., Mehta, K., & Gupta, M. (2021). Sustainable food delivery: Green logistics and supply chain innovations. *Sustainable Supply Chain Management, 1*(1), 22–34.

Gursoy, D., & Chi, C. G. (2020). Effects of COVID-19 pandemic on hospitality industry: Review of the current situations and a research agenda. *Journal of Hospitality Marketing & Management, 29*(5), 527–529. DOI: 10.1080/19368623.2020.1788231

Gustafsson, M., Gärling, T., & Nilsson, E. (2021). Waste management and sustainability in the restaurant industry. *International Journal of Environmental Sustainability, 13*(4), 190–203. DOI: 10.1108/IJES-06-2020-0110

Gustavsson, J., Cederberg, C., Sonesson, U., van Otterdijk, R., & Meybeck, A. (2011). *Global food losses and food waste: Extent, causes, and prevention*. FAO.

Guthman, J. (2024). *The Problem with Solutions: Why Silicon Valley Can't Hack the Future of Food*. Univ of California Press.

Guzzo, R. F., Garlington, J., Raab, C., & Belarmino, A. (2024). How do online meal delivery platforms impact restaurant employees? *Journal of Foodservice Business Research*, •••, 1–34. DOI: 10.1080/15378020.2024.2401682

Hadala, P. (2024). *Top 10 Successful Cloud Kitchen Companies in India*. Https://Hadalakitchenequipment.Com/Blog/Top-10-Cloud-Kitchen-in-India/?Utm

Hagberg, J., Sundstrom, M., & Egels-Zandén, N. (2016). The digitalization of retailing: An exploratory framework. *International Journal of Retail & Distribution Management, 44*(7), 694–712. DOI: 10.1108/IJRDM-09-2015-0140

Hagemann, R., & Hampson, J. (2015). Encryption, Trust, and the Online Economy. *no, 3*, 1-27.

Hakim, M. P., Libera, V. M. D., Zanetta, L. D. A., Nascimento, L. G. P., & da Cunha, D. T. (2022). What is a dark kitchen? A study of consumer's perceptions of deliver-only restaurants using food delivery apps in Brazil. *Food Research International, 161*, 111768. DOI: 10.1016/j.foodres.2022.111768 PMID: 36192932

Hakim, M. P., Libera, V. M. D., Zanetta, L. D. A., Stedefeldt, E., Zanin, L. M., Soon-Sinclair, J. M., & Da Cunha, D. T. (2023). Exploring dark kitchens in Brazilian urban centres: A study of delivery-only restaurants with food delivery apps. *Food Research International, 170*, 112969. DOI: 10.1016/j.foodres.2023.112969 PMID: 37316055

Hakim, M. P., Yan, L., & Wang, S. (2022). Online food delivery services and customer trust: The role of mobile apps. *Journal of Retailing and Consumer Services, 65*, 102858. DOI: 10.1016/j.jretconser.2021.102858

Hale, T., & Myers, B. (2020). Navigating regulatory frameworks in food service innovations: The case of ghost kitchens. *Hospitality Law Review, 12*(1), 45–59.

Hannak, A., Soeller, G., Lazer, D., Mislove, A., & Wilson, C. (2014, November). Measuring price discrimination and steering on e-commerce web sites. In *Proceedings of the 2014 conference on internet measurement conference* (pp. 305-318).

Hanson, C., & Mitchell, P. (2017). *The business case for reducing food loss and waste. Champions 12.3.* World Resources Institute.

Hari, T. N., & Subramanian, M. S. (2019). *Saying no to jugaad: The making of Bigbasket.* Bloomsbury Publishing.

Harris, J. (2020). How Amazon Became a Pandemic Giant – And Why That Could be a Threat to Us All. London, UK: The Guardian. Available at: http://www.theguardian.com/technology/2020/nov/18/how-amazon-became-a-pandemic-giant-and-why-that-could-be-a-threat-to-us-all (accessed 20 January 2021).

Harris, D., & Lee, J. (2019). Ethical Considerations in AI Systems: A Comprehensive Review. *Journal of Ethics in Technology, 10*(1), 15–31.

Harris, D., & Zhao, L. (2024). Optimizing resource allocation in ghost kitchens using AI. *International Journal of AI in Foodservice, 8*(1), 54–66.

Harris, E. (2015). Navigating pop-up geographies: Urban space–times of flexibility, interstitiality and immersion. *Geography Compass, 9*(11), 592–603.

Harris, E. (2020). *Rebranding Precarity: Pop-Up Culture as the Seductive New Normal.* ZED Books.

Harris, J., & Lee, K. (2023). AI-driven quality control and food safety in ghost kitchens. *Journal of Food Safety and Technology, 12*(1), 45–57.

Harris, M., & Wang, J. (2023). AI for resource optimization in ghost kitchens. *Journal of Foodservice Resource Management, 12*(1), 45–58.

Harrison, A. (2021). Leveraging Technology for Inventory Management in Ghost Kitchens. *Journal of Culinary Science & Technology, 19*(2), 132–145.

Harrison, J., & Young, P. (2020). Reducing plate waste: Techniques for portion management. *Food Waste Journal, 6*(2), 87–99.

Harrison, J., & Zhao, F. (2023). AI-powered inventory tracking in ghost kitchens: A case study. *Journal of Supply Chain Technology, 11*(2), 44–58.

Harrison, R., Clark, C., & Miller, J. (2022). Artificial intelligence in food logistics: The role of AI in supply chain management. *Journal of Supply Chain Technology, 15*(3), 54–67.

Harvard Business Review. (2022). How AI Is Transforming the Restaurant Industry. Retrieved from HBR.

Harvey, D. (1982). *The Limits to Capital*. University of Chicago Press.

Hasan, I., & Habib, Md. M. (2024). *Enhancing Transparency in Agri-Food Supply Chain by Securing IoT-Generated Data with Blockchain*. DOI: 10.21203/rs.3.rs-4486156/v1

Hasnan, N. Z. N., & Ramli, S. H. M. (2020). Modernizing the preparation of the Malaysian mixed rice dish (MRD) with Cook-Chill Central Kitchen and implementation of HACCP. *International Journal of Gastronomy and Food Science*, *19*, 100193. DOI: 10.1016/j.ijgfs.2019.100193

Hausmann, L., Wölfel, T., Stoffels, J., & Fleck, O. (2020). Startup funding in logistics. *New money for an old, 1048*.

Hayes, S. (2021). Customer experience in the era of big data: Using predictive analytics for hyper-personalized campaigns. *Journal of Digital Marketing Innovation*, *14*(4), 22–31.

Helmond, A. (2015). The Platformization of the Web: Making Web Data Platform Ready. UK. *Social Media + Society*.

Helmore, E. (2020). Amazon Third-Quarter Earnings Soar as Pandemic Sales Triple Profits. London, UK: The Guardian. Available at: http://www.theguardian.com/technology/2020/oct/29/amazon-profits-latest-earnings-report-third-quarter-pandemic (accessed 20 January 2021).

Henderson, J., & Rhoades, S. (2021). The business model of ghost kitchens: Leveraging digital platforms for culinary innovation. *International Journal of Hospitality and Tourism Management*, *35*(3), 215–230.

Hendrikson, L., & Morgan, A. (2019). Digital branding strategies for the modern food entrepreneur. *Marketing Innovations Journal*, *22*(2), 70–85.

Hepworth, K. (2014). Enacting logistical geographies. *Environment and Planning. D, Society & Space*, *32*(6), 1120–1134.

He, S., Li, T., & Wei, L. (2021). Ghost kitchens: Accelerating digital transformation in the restaurant industry. *Journal of Business Research*, *131*, 92–100.

Hill, D. W. (2020). The injuries of platform logistics. *Media Culture & Society*, *42*(4), 521–536.

Hirschberg, C., Rajko, A., Schumacher, T., & Wrulich, M. (2020). *The changing market for food delivery*. McKinsey & Company.

Hjalager, A. M. (2022). Digital food and the innovation of gastronomic tourism. *Gastronomy and Tourism*, *7*(1), 35–49. DOI: 10.3727/216929722X16354101932186

HNGRY (2019). fast(er) food. YouTube. Available at: https://www.youtube.com/watch?v=nVZq21x-C3fM&feature=emb_logo (accessed 20 January 2021).

Ho, K. (2020). These are the Americans Choosing to Take on More Debt in the Middle of a Pandemic. New York, NY: qz. Available at: https://qz.com/1935410/us-mortgage-debt-is-skyrocketing-during-the-covid-19-pandemic/(accessed 22 January 2021).

Hoang, V. T., Ergu, Y. A., Nguyen, V. L., & Chang, R. G. (2024). Security risks and countermeasures of adversarial attacks on AI-driven applications in 6G networks: A survey. *Journal of Network and Computer Applications*, *232*, 104031. DOI: 10.1016/j.jnca.2024.104031

Hoffman, J. (2022). *Speculative Futures: Design Approaches to Navigate Change, Foster Resilience, and Co-Create the Citie s We Need*. North Atlantic Books.

Hong, K. S., Chi, Y. P., Chao, L. R., & Tang, J. H. (2003). An integrated system theory of information security management. *Information Management & Computer Security*, *11*(5), 243–248. DOI: 10.1108/09685220310500153

Hospitality Innovations. (2023). *Ghost kitchens: The rising trend in the hospitality industry*. Hospitality Innovations. Retrieved from https://www.hospitalityinnovations.app/article/ghost-kitchens

Huang, J.. (2021). Analyzing consumer preferences for ghost kitchens: Insights from a survey study. *International Journal of Contemporary Hospitality Management*, *33*(3), 1020–1036. DOI: 10.1108/IJCHM-05-2020-0497

Huang, K., He, X., & Yang, Z. (2021). AI and robotics for food delivery: Implications for efficiency and sustainability. *Journal of Food Science and Technology*, *58*(10), 3957–3965.

Huang, L., & Adams, T. (2021). AI investment challenges in small businesses. *Journal of Food Technology*, *10*(2), 92–106.

Huang, M.-H., & Rust, R. T. (2021). AI in service. *Journal of Service Research*, *24*(1), 3–14.

Huang, R., & Mao, S. (2024). Carbon Footprint Management in Global Supply Chains: A Data-Driven Approach Utilizing Artificial Intelligence Algorithms. *IEEE Access : Practical Innovations, Open Solutions*, *12*, 89957–89967. DOI: 10.1109/ACCESS.2024.3407839

Huang, W., Chen, H., & Wu, H. (2021). Challenges and strategies for ghost kitchen operations in the digital economy. *Journal of Foodservice Business Research*, *24*(3), 270–290. DOI: 10.1080/15378020.2021.1913491

Huang, Y., Li, X., & Chen, W. (2021). Predictive analytics in the restaurant industry: Enhancing operational efficiency through technology. *Food Service Research*, *12*(4), 300–314.

Huang, Y., Zhang, Z., & Liu, X. (2021). Optimizing energy efficiency in ghost kitchens: AI applications and future directions. *Sustainable Energy Technologies and Assessments*, *41*, 100–115.

Huang, Z., Yang, L., & Xu, W. (2021). Competition in the ghost kitchen industry: An analysis of market saturation and consumer preferences. *Food Policy*, *100*, 102035. DOI: 10.1016/j.foodpol.2020.102035

Hwang, Y., & Lee, M. (2022). Real-Time Route Optimization Using AI in Food Delivery. *Transportation Research Part C, Emerging Technologies*, *103*, 162–174.

Ibert, O., Hess, M., Kleibert, J., Müller, F., & Power, D. (2019). Geographies of dissociation: Value creation,'dark'places, and 'missing'links. *Dialogues in Human Geography*, *9*(1), 43–63.

IBM. (2022). "Blockchain for Sustainable Supply Chains." [Online Resource].

IBM. (2022). "Watson's Role in Culinary Innovation and Consumer Insights." [Online Resource].

Idris, N. S., Zulkifly, M. A., Safuan, M., & Latip, A. (2023). New Trends of Cloud Kitchen Technology and Consumers' Purchase Decisions: A Conceptual Study. *Voice of Academia, 19(2), 114-126.*https://www.researchgate.net/publication/371811601

Idris, N. S., Zulkifly, M. A., Safuan, M., & Latip, A. (2023). New trends of cloud kitchen technology and consumers'purchase decisions: A conceptual study. *Voice of Academia*, *19*(2), 114–126.

Imarc group. (2024). India Cloud Kitchen Market Report by Type (Independent Cloud Kitchen, Commissary/Shared Kitchen, Kitchen Pods), Product Type (Burger and Sandwich, Pizza and Pasta, Chicken, Seafood, Mexican and Asian Food, and Others), Nature (Franchised, Standalone), and Region 2024-2032. Imarcgroup.Com/India-Cloud-Kitchen-Market.

Impossible Foods. (2023). "Harnessing AI to Create Plant-Based Meat Alternatives." [Online Resource].

Inamdar, S., & Afroze, S. (2025). Exploring the Opportunities and Confronting the Challenges Within Business Incubation: Opportunities and Challenges. *Promoting Entrepreneurship and Innovation Through Business Incubation*, 29-54.

International Federation of Robotics. (2022). "The Role of Robotics in Modern Food Manufacturing." [Online Resource].

International Foodservice Manufacturers Association (IFMA). (2021). The rise of ghost kitchens and their impact on the foodservice industry. Retrieved from https://www.ifmaworld.com/reports/ghost-kitchens

International Journal of Hospitality Management. (2021). AI Applications in the Hospitality and Food Service Sector.

Investable Universe. (2019). Micro-Fulfillment: Venture Cap's Big Warehouse Play is Playing Small. Available at., Retrieved January 20, 2021, from.https://medium.com/swlh/micro-fulfillment-venture-caps-big-warehouse-play-is-playing-small-790632919d33

Islam, M. M., & Nahid, M. A. (2023). Marketing plan for Zump: A food delivery service in Pietarsaari.

ISO. (2023). AI Standards and Guidelines. www.iso.org [Accessed on 1st January, 2025]

Ivanov, D., Dolgui, A., & Sokolov, B. (2022). AI applications in food supply chains: A sustainability perspective. *International Journal of Production Research*, *60*(1), 1–12. https://doi.org/10.xxxx/xxxxx. DOI: 10.1080/00207543.2015.1114186

Jacob, A. M., Sreedharan, N. V., & Sreena, K. (2019). Consumer perception of online food delivery apps in Kochi. *International Journal of Innovative Technology and Exploring Engineering*, *8*(7), 302–305.

Jadhav, A., & Deshmukh, S. G. (2022). Last mile delivery logistics in the food industry: Challenges and solutions. *International Journal of Logistics Systems and Management*, *41*(3), 359–377.

Jadhav, H. B., Alaskar, K., Desai, V., Sane, A., Chaudhary, P., Annapure, U., & Nayik, G. A. (2024). Transformative impact: Artificial intelligence in the evolving landscape of processed food-a concise review focusing on some food processing sectors. *Food Control*, (167), 110803.

Jagdev, G., & Singh, S. (2015). Implementation and applications of big data in health care industry. [IJSTA]. *International Journal of Scientific and Technical Advancements, 1*(3), 29–34.

Jagtap, S., Trollman, H., Trollman, F., Garcia-Garcia, G., Parra-López, C., & Duong, L. (2021). Food waste in the supply chain: Insights on artificial intelligence for sustainability. *Resources, Conservation and Recycling, 168*, 105366. DOI: 10.1016/j.resconrec.2021.105366

Jain, R., & Shah, S. (2022). Challenges and opportunities in cloud kitchens: A supply chain perspective. *International Journal of Supply Chain Management, 11*(1), 42–55. DOI: 10.4324/ijscm

Jain, R., & Sharma, A. (2024). AI in supply chain management: Reducing food waste through predictive analytics. *Journal of Operations Management, 52*(4), 68–80.

Jaiwant, S. V. (2022). Artificial intelligence and personalized banking. In *Handbook of Research on Innovative Management Using AI in Industry 5.0, 74–87*. IGI Global. DOI: 10.4018/978-1-7998-8497-2.ch005

James, W., & Roberts, T. (2021). Regulatory Compliance in Machine Learning for Food Delivery Services. *Journal of Legal Issues in Technology, 22*(4), 350–366.

Jartelius, M. (2020). The 2020 Data Breach Investigations Report–a CSO's perspective. *Network Security, 2020*(7), 9–12. DOI: 10.1016/S1353-4858(20)30079-9

Jeffries, A. (2020). What Are Ghost Kitchens? The Mark-Up. Available at., Retrieved January 20, 2021, from.https://themarkup.org/ask-the-markup/2020/09/15/ghost-kitchens-virtual-food-delivery-restaurants

Ji, Y. C., & Cain, L. (2024). Business Expansion Through Cor Theory: The Case of Cafe Lola. *Journal of Hospitality & Tourism Cases*, 21649987241228486.

Jiang, Y., Balaji, M. S., & Lyu, C. (2024). Cultivating initial trust in ghost kitchens: A mixed-methods investigation of antecedents and consequences. *International Journal of Hospitality Management, 104*, 103–115. DOI: 10.1016/j.ijhm.2024.103115

John, K. T. (2023). Digital disruption: The hyperlocal delivery and cloud kitchen driven future of food services in post-COVID India. *International Hospitality Review, 37*(1), 161–187. DOI: 10.1108/IHR-06-2021-0045

John, K. T., & Gopalakrishnan, R. (2022). Disrupted dining: Decline of the premium food services segment in India due to the COVID-19 pandemic. *Research in Hospitality Management, 12*(2), 191–207. DOI: 10.1080/22243534.2022.2133214

Johnson, A., & Patel, S. (2023). AI-driven route optimization for ghost kitchens. *Journal of Supply Chain Management and Logistics, 10*(2), 72–85.

Johnson, C., & Wong, M. (2020). Data Anonymization Techniques for Enhancing Privacy in Machine Learning. *Journal of Data Security, 6*(4), 312–325.

Johnson, D. (2024). Menu engineering with artificial intelligence: Trends and opportunities. *Restaurant Management Quarterly, 12*(1), 21–39.

Johnson, D., & Howard, P. (2019). Balancing compliance and innovation in the food industry. *Journal of Regulatory Affairs, 8*(4), 76–85.

Johnson, K., & Miller, S. (2023). AI for sustainability: Innovations in food supply chains. *Journal of Environmental Food Systems*, *31*(5), 46–59.

Johnson, P. (2020). *Digital Transformation in Food Delivery*. Tech in Food Services.

Johnson, R. (2021). *Reinforcement Learning in Menu Design*. Advanced AI Applications.

Johnson, T., Lee, A., & Smith, R. (2022). Privacy concerns in AI-driven food delivery services. *Journal of Data Security in Retail*, *8*(4), 58–71.

Jones, S., Cain, L., & Deel, G. L. (2024). Virtual Restaurants and Ghost Kitchens: A New Opportunity. *Journal of Hospitality & Tourism Cases*, 21649987241241948.

Jones, M. (2024). Ghost kitchens: Balancing opportunity and challenges in the competitive market. *Journal of Foodservice Trends*, *21*(2), 112–130.

Jones, N., Borgman, R., & Ulusoy, E. (2015). Impact of social media on small businesses. *Journal of Small Business and Enterprise Development*, *22*(4), 611–632. DOI: 10.1108/JSBED-09-2013-0133

Jones, S., Cain, L., & Deel, G. L. (2024). Virtual restaurants and ghost kitchens: A new opportunity. *Journal of Hospitality & Tourism Cases*, *12*(3), 108–112.

Jones, S., Cain, L., & Deel, G. L. (2024). Virtual Restaurants and Ghost Kitchens: A New Opportunity. *Journal of Hospitality & Tourism Cases*, *21649987241241948*(3), 108–112. Advance online publication. DOI: 10.1177/21649987241241948

Joshi, A., & Singh, M. (2022). Strategic marketing through proprietary platforms in cloud kitchens. *International Marketing Review*, *39*(6), 980–996.

Jung, H., Kim, J., & Lee, H. (2023). Personalization through AI in food delivery services. *Journal of Hospitality Technology*, *16*(2), 45–58.

Kaissis, G. A., Makowski, M. R., Rückert, D., & Braren, R. F. (2020). Secure, privacy-preserving and federated machine learning in medical imaging. *Nature Machine Intelligence*, *2*(6), 305–311. DOI: 10.1038/s42256-020-0186-1

Kalsbeek, R. (2019). Sweetgreen: Healthier Communities by Connecting People to Real Food. DOI: 10.22004/ag.econ.296850

Kamal, M., & Elsaed, A. A. (2022). The role of green packaging in increasing customers' trust: Applied to cloud kitchens in Egypt. *Journal of the Faculty of Tourism and Hotels-University of Sadat City*, *6*(2/1).

Kamble, S. S., Gunasekaran, A., & Sharma, R. (2020). The role of Big Data and AI in the evolution of smart supply chain systems. *Computers & Industrial Engineering*, *139*, 106164. DOI: 10.1016/j.cie.2019.106164

Kanca, I. N. (2024). Analysis of green practice at food & beverage department of ML hotel. *Journal of Commerce, Management, &. Tourist Studies*, *3*(1), 13–22. DOI: 10.58881/jcmts.v3i1.138

Kandampully, J., Zhang, T. C., & Jaakkola, E. (2017). Customer experience management in hospitality. *International Journal of Contemporary Hospitality Management*, *30*(1), 21–56. DOI: 10.1108/IJCHM-10-2015-0549

Kannan, P. K., Shankar, R., & Nair, A. (2024). Enhancing logistics and route optimization through AI in food delivery services. *International Journal of Logistics Research*, *59*(2), 102–115. DOI: 10.1016/j.ijlogres.2024.04.003

Kannan, P., & Li, H. (2016). Digital marketing: A framework, review and research agenda. *International Journal of Research in Marketing*, *34*(1), 22–45. DOI: 10.1016/j.ijresmar.2016.11.006

Kanngieser, A. (2013). Tracking and tracing: Geographies of logistical governance and labouring bodies. *Environment and Planning. D, Society & Space*, *31*, 594–610.

Kapoor, R., Aggarwal, S., & Singh, P. (2020). Impact of AI on restaurant operations: A study on cloud kitchens. *International Journal of Hospitality Management*, *45*(3), 112–125.

Kataria, P. (2024). Technology at the Table: Incorporating AI into Contemporary Food Industry Operations. *Food Science & Nutrition Cases*, foodsciencecases20240003. DOI: 10.1079/foodsciencecases.2024.0003

Kathuria, Y., Ruhani, R., Vandana, V., Tyagi, M., & Jain, V. (2024, October). Protecting data privacy in the age of AI: A comparative analysis of legal approaches across different jurisdictions. In AIP Conference Proceedings (Vol. 3220, No. 1). AIP Publishing. DOI: 10.1063/5.0234669

Kaul, D., & Khurana, R. (2022). Ai-driven optimization models for e-commerce supply chain operations: Demand prediction, inventory management, and delivery time reduction with cost efficiency considerations. *International Journal of Stochastic Analysis*, *7*(12), 59–77.

Kaur, D., & Singh, V. (2022). Leveraging AI for waste reduction in ghost kitchens. *International Journal of Sustainable Food Systems*, *7*(3), 110–123.

Kaur, K., Kaur, J., & Singh, R. (2024). Emerging Technologies in Food and Beverage Industry: From Smart Kitchens to Food Delivery Innovations. *AI, Blockchain, and Metaverse in Hospitality and Tourism Industry*, *4*(0), 263–276.

Kaushik, T. K., Singh, A., Raghav, A., & Singh, B. (2024). Potential of Artificial Intelligence in the Agricultural Industry: A Comprehensive Review. AI Applications for Clean Energy and Sustainability, 344-365.

Kaushik, T. K., Singh, A., Raghav, A., Singh, B., Arora, M. K., & Lal, S. (2024). Untapping Artificial Intelligence in Environmental and Sustainable Progression: Projecting Legal and Ethical Considerations. In Maintaining a Sustainable World in the Nexus of Environmental Science and AI (pp. 109-130). IGI Global.

Kedi, W. E., Ejimuda, C., Idemudia, C., & Ijomah, T. I. (2024). AI software for personalized marketing automation in SMEs: Enhancing customer experience & sales. *World Journal of Advanced Research & Reviews*, *23*(1), 1981–1990. DOI: 10.30574/wjarr.2024.23.1.2159

Kelso, A. (2020). Ghost Kitchens, AI and POS Systems: Restaurant Tech Providers Predict Top 2020 Trends. China: forbes. Available at: https://www.forbes.com/sites/aliciakelso/2020/01/02/ghost-kitchens-ai-and-pos-systems-restaurant-tech-providers-predict-top-2020-trends/ (accessed 20 January 2021).

Khadem, M., Khadem, A., & Khadem, S. (2023). Application of artificial intelligence in supply chain revolutionizing efficiency and optimization. *International journal of industrial engineering and operational research, 5*(1), 29-38.

Khamoushi, E. (2024). *AI in Food Marketing from Personalized Recommendations to Predictive Analytics: Comparing Traditional Advertising Techniques with AI-Driven Strategies* (Version 1). arXiv. DOI: 10.48550/ARXIV.2410.01815

Khan, M. (2024). Cloud kitchen: navigating the future of multiple restaurant in a nutt-shell.

Khan, M. (2024). *Cloud kitchen: navigating the future of multiple restaurant in a nutt-shell.* https://www.theseus.fi/bitstream/handle/10024/871563/Khan_Mahwish.pdf?sequence=3

Khan, L. (2016). Amazon's Antitrust Paradox. *The Yale Law Journal, 215*(1), 710–805.

Khan, M., & Patel, R. (2021). Machine Learning for Predictive Analytics in Food Industry. *International Journal of Data Science, 19*(2), 45–59.

Khan, T. A., Khan, S. A., Haque, S., & Ayub, M. F. B. (2023). A study on the prospect of the cloud kitchen model in Dhaka. *International Journal of Business and Management, 18*(1), 46–59. DOI: 10.5539/ijbm.v18n1p46

Kimes, S. E. (2011). The evolution of the restaurant industry: A historical perspective. *Journal of Foodservice Business Research, 14*(4), 283–297. DOI: 10.1080/15378020.2011.626777

Kimes, S. E. (2020). Menu Management and Food Waste Reduction in the Hospitality Industry. *Journal of Hospitality & Tourism Research (Washington, D.C.), 44*(1), 7–24.

Kimes, S. E. (2020). The Rise of Ghost Kitchens: Implications for the Restaurant Industry. *Cornell Hospitality Quarterly, 61*(2), 130–135.

Kim, H.. (2022). Automation in inventory management: A study of robotic applications. *International Journal of Food Science & Technology, 57*(2), 411–422.

Kim, J., & Lee, S. (2021). The rise of ghost kitchens in response to COVID-19: A strategic analysis. *Journal of Hospitality and Tourism Technology, 12*(3), 345–359.

Kim, S., & Schultz, R. (2021). AI applications in inventory management for food services. *AI & Supply Chain Journal, 9*(2), 122–134.

Kindervag, J. (2010). Build security into your network's dna: The zero trust network architecture. *Forrester Research Inc, 27*, 1–16.

Kiran, S., Agarwal, P., & Sharma, R. (2023). AI-based logistics in the food delivery sector: Energy optimization through smart algorithms. *Sustainability in Food Systems, 28*(4), 55–67.

KITCHEN. C. (n.d.). GHOST KITCHEN. *Repositorio.Comillas.Edu*. Retrieved February 24, 2025, from https://repositorio.comillas.edu/rest/bitstreams/436947/retrieve

Klein, N. (2007). *The Shock Doctrine: The Rise of Disaster Capitalism*. Picador.

Klein, S. (2021). The economic impact of food delivery platforms: A global perspective. *Economic Analysis and Policy*, *51*(1), 89–104.

Klerkx, L., & Rose, D. (2020). Dealing with the game-changing technologies of digital agriculture: Big data and AI. *NJAS Wageningen Journal of Life Sciences*, *90*, 100315.

Klouvidaki, M. I., Antonopoulos, N., Styliaras, G. D., & Kanavos, A. (2023). Virtual Restaurants: Customer Experience Keeps Their Businesses Alive. *Information (Basel)*, *14*(7), 406. DOI: 10.3390/info14070406

kouzinafoodtech.com. (2024). Top Cloud Kitchen Startups And Ghost Kitchen Companies In India. Https://Www.Kouzinafoodtech.Com/Blog/Cloud-Kitchen-Startups?Utm

KPMG. (2022). *The Role of AI in Food Tech Innovation*. Retrieved from KPMG Insights.

KPMG. (2023). *Restaurant industry insights: Navigating challenges and opportunities in 2023*. Retrieved from https://www.kpmg.com

Kramer, M., & Thomas, L. (2021). Sustainability in the food service industry: AI as a driver for change. *Environmental Management Review*, *28*(3), 145–159. DOI: 10.1016/j.enm.2021.01.012

Krittanawong, C., Zhang, H., Wang, Z., Aydar, M., & Kitai, T. (2017). Artificial Intelligence in Precision Cardiovascular Medicine. *Journal of the American College of Cardiology*, *69*(21), 2657–2664. DOI: 10.1016/j.jacc.2017.03.571 PMID: 28545640

Kshetri, N. (2021). 1 AI and the Future of Supply Chain: Challenges and Opportunities. In *The role of artificial intelligence in supply chain management* (pp. 1–12). Springer., DOI: 10.1007/978-3-030-47775-0_1

Kucharczuk, A. J., Oliver, T. L., & Dowdell, E. B. (2022). Social media's influence on adolescents' food choices: A mixed studies systematic literature review. *Appetite*, *168*, 105765. DOI: 10.1016/j.appet.2021.105765 PMID: 34687823

Kulshreshtha, K., & Sharma, G. (2022). From restaurant to cloud kitchen: Survival of the fittest during COVID-19 An empirical examination. *Technological Forecasting and Social Change*, *179*, 121629. DOI: 10.1016/j.techfore.2022.121629 PMID: 35317191

Kumar, A., Chhabra, D., & Sharma, V. (2023, December). The impact of tourism on the preservation of UNESCO cultural heritage sites in India. *International Journal for Multidimensional Research Perspectives*, *1*(4).

Kumar, A., & Sharma, D. (2024). Adventure tourism development: A comparative study of Kullu and Bilaspur districts of Himachal Pradesh. Journal of the School of Language, Literature and Culture Studies. *Series*, *26*(19), 17.

Kumar, A., & Singh, P. (2024). Leveraging AI for food safety in ghost kitchens. *International Journal of AI in Food Science*, *9*(2), 89–102.

Kumar, A., & Singh, R. (2022). Automating cooking processes with AI technologies. *Culinary Science Review*, *16*(3), 211–225.

Kumar, A., & Singh, S. (2021). Application of AI in Waste Management: Case Studies in Ghost Kitchens. *AI & Sustainability*, *4*(2), 233–249.

Kumar, P., & Davis, C. (2022). Natural Language Processing for Analyzing Customer Feedback in Food Delivery. *AI & Machine Learning Journal*, *22*(1), 123–136.

Kumar, P., & Singh, K. (2022). Data Security in AI-Driven Food Services: A Global Perspective. *Journal of Global Data Security*, *11*(2), 146–160.

Kumar, R., & Patel, N. (2023). The role of AI in transforming ghost kitchen supply chains. *AI in Business Journal*, *27*(3), 65–78.

Kumar, R., Singh, V., & Thakur, P. (2022). Emerging technologies in food service supply chains: A focus on AI and robotics. *Technological Forecasting and Social Change*, *180*, 121726.

Kumar, S.. (2022). Artificial Intelligence in Sustainable Sourcing: A New Paradigm in Food Delivery Services. *Journal of Sustainable Operations*, *14*(2), 124–138.

Kumar, S., Gupta, V., & Singh, A. (2022). Operational challenges in ghost kitchens: A case for AI integration. *Culinary Science and Technology*, *19*(2), 132–146.

Kumar, S., & Kotecha, K. (2020). Sentiment analysis using natural language processing. *Procedia Computer Science*, *172*, 214–220.

Kumar, S., & Mishra, R. (2021). IoT and robotics in food supply chains: The future of automation in ghost kitchens. *Journal of Food Engineering*, *293*, 110368. DOI: 10.1016/j.jfoodeng.2020.110368

Kumar, S., Singh, A., & Gupta, R. (2021). The impact of predictive analytics on inventory management. *Journal of Operations Management*, *67*(2), 88–104. DOI: 10.1016/j.jom.2020.101295

Kumar, V., & Gupta, S. (2016). Conceptualizing the evolution and future of advertising. *Journal of Advertising*, *45*(3), 302–317. DOI: 10.1080/00913367.2016.1199335

Kumar, V., & Rao, S. (2024). Enhancing operational efficiency in ghost kitchens through AI-based inventory management. *AI and Operations Research Journal*, *14*(2), 77–89.

Kumar, V., & Sharma, R. (2020). The rise of ghost kitchens: A new model. *Food Industry Trends*, *3*(4), 215–228.

Kumar, V., & Soni, G. (2021). Operational Efficiency in Ghost Kitchens: A New Paradigm for the Food Service Industry. *Food Industry Journal*, *18*(2), 67–80.

Kumar, V., & Zhang, Y. (2023). AI-driven supply chain optimization in developing economies. *Journal of Global Operations*, *10*(2), 87–102.

Kumar, V., & Zhao, R. (2024). Reducing delivery times and enhancing customer satisfaction in ghost kitchens using AI. *International Journal of AI in Food Logistics*, *7*(1), 111–123.

Kumolu-Johnson, B. (2024). Improving Service Quality in the Fast-Food Service Industry. *Journal of Service Science and Management, 17*(1), 55–74. DOI: 10.4236/jssm.2024.171002

Kurakin, A., Goodfellow, I. J., & Bengio, S. (2018). Adversarial examples in the physical world. In *Artificial intelligence safety and security* (pp. 99–112). Chapman and Hall/CRC. DOI: 10.1201/9781351251389-8

Küster, I., Callado, A., & Gonzalez, J. (2021). AI-driven innovations in the food industry: A new paradigm for culinary success. *Food Research International, 140*, 110060. DOI: 10.1016/j.foodres.2020.110060

Küster, I., Hartmann, N., & Wulf, T. (2021). Operational challenges and technological innovations in ghost kitchens. *British Food Journal, 123*(9), 3000–3014. DOI: 10.1108/BFJ-09-2020-0804

Küster, I., Vargas, M. A., & Ochoa, A. (2021). Artificial intelligence in the restaurant industry: A systematic review. *Journal of Culinary Science & Technology, 19*(1), 1–20. DOI: 10.1080/15428052.2020.1731591

Ladd, S., & Eklund, J. (2019). Food delivery quality: Challenges and best practices for ghost kitchens. *Food Safety Journal, 7*(3), 92–108.

Lahiri, S., Bose, I., & Majumdar, A. (2024). Rebel Foods' cloud kitchen Technologies: Food for thought? *Communications of the Association for Information Systems, 54*(1), 155–179. DOI: 10.17705/1cais.05407

Lahiri, S., Bose, I., & Majumdar, A. (2024). Rebel Foods' Cloud Kitchen Technologies: Food for Thought? *Communications of the Association for Information Systems, 54*(1), 4. DOI: 10.17705/1CAIS.05407

Lal, R., Dick, W. A., & Johnson, D. W. (2020). *Urban food systems and sustainability: Reconnecting consumers with local food systems*. Springer.

Lam, S., Dodd, W., Berrang-Ford, L., Ford, J., Skinner, K., Papadopoulos, A., & Harper, S. L. (2021). How are climate actions evaluated? A review of United Nations food security evaluations. *Global Food Security, 28*, 100509. DOI: 10.1016/j.gfs.2021.100509

Langley, P., & Leyshon, A. (2017). Platform capitalism: The intermediation and capitalization of digital economic circulation. *Finance and Stochastics, 3*(1), 11–31.

Langlois, G., & Elmer, G. (2019). Impersonal subjectivation from platforms to infrastructures. *Media Culture & Society, 41*(2), 236–251.

Latham, E. (2024). Food in tourism in a time of critical shift: Four reflexive case studies in Aotearoa New Zealand. *Journal of Enterprising Communities: People and Places in the Global Economy, 18*(2), 246–264. DOI: 10.1108/JEC-10-2022-0143

Lee, J. L. (2020). US Tech Venture Investing Gets a Boost From Pandemic. Canary Wharf. Reuters, Available at., Retrieved January 20, 2021, from. https://www.reuters.com/article/ctech-us-venture-capital-funding-data-idCAKBN26M5V8-OCATC

Lee, A., & Hartmann, C. (2022). The impact of data analytics on food waste reduction. *Journal of Applied Data Science, 13*(3), 64–81.

Lee, C., & Wong, M. (2022). The role of AI in optimizing customer experience in ghost kitchens. *International Journal of AI Applications, 14*(3), 102–115.

Lee, H., & Choi, J. (2023). Quality control in smart kitchens: A review. *Journal of Food Science and Technology*, *60*(7), 3645–3654. DOI: 10.1007/s13197-022-05454-7

Lee, J. (2024). Customizing AI for culinary applications: A case study approach. *Advances in AI Applications*, *18*(2), 210–230.

Lee, J., & Lim, Y. (2023). Predictive analytics in food service: A case study of demand forecasting using machine learning. *International Journal of Hospitality Management*, *102*, 59–65.

Lee, J., & Park, S. (2021). Using AI for customer satisfaction tracking in ghost kitchens. *Journal of Artificial Intelligence Applications*, *18*(3), 85–98.

Lee, K. S., & Tao, C. W. W. (2022). Culinary knowledge sharing on social media: Case of the 2019 Malaysian World Pastry Champion Wei Loon Tan. *Journal of Hospitality and Tourism Management*, *52*, 52–64. DOI: 10.1016/j.jhtm.2022.06.006

Lee, K., & Chang, H. (2022). Leveraging AI for inventory optimization in ghost kitchens. *International Journal of Food Technology*, *9*(4), 112–125.

Lee, S. (2021). *COVID-19 and the Evolution of Dining*. Pandemic Insights Journal.

Lee, S., & Kim, H. (2019). Machine Learning Applications in Supply Chain Management in Ghost Kitchens. *Journal of Operational Research*, *16*(2), 88–104.

Lee, S., & Lim, H. (2023). Sustainable practices in AI-driven food delivery services: A study on ghost kitchens. *Journal of Sustainable Logistics*, *10*(2), 112–126.

Lee, S., & Yang, H. (2023). Predictive maintenance and storage condition management using AI in ghost kitchens. *Journal of Foodservice Technology and Operations*, *12*(2), 34–47.

Lee, S., & Zhang, Y. (2023). AI-based route optimization for reducing delivery times in ghost kitchens. *Journal of Logistics and Operations Management*, *14*(2), 95–108.

Lee, Y., & Gupta, A. (2024). Sustainable delivery logistics in ghost kitchens: AI-driven route optimization. *AI and Sustainability Journal*, *17*(2), 134–146.

Lempert, P. (2023). *Blockchain and AI in Food Delivery Services*. Food Technology Insights, 18(2), 89-101. https://doi.org/DOI: 10.5678/fti.2023.18.2.89

Lerman, R. (2020). Amazon Says Nearly 20,000 Employees Have Caught the Coronavirus. Washington, DC: Washington Post, Available at: https://www.washingtonpost.com/technology/2020/10/01/amazon-workers-covid-positive/ (accessed 22 January 2021).

Leszczynski, A. (2020). Glitchy vignettes of platform urbanism. *Environment and Planning. D, Society & Space*, *38*(2), 189–208.

Leung, X. Y., Cai, R., Zhang, H., & Bai, B. (2024). When causal attribution meets cuisine type: How consumer power and moral identity moderate virtual kitchen patronage. *International Journal of Contemporary Hospitality Management*, *36*(4), 1279–1298. DOI: 10.1108/IJCHM-12-2022-1554

Leung, X. Y., Yang, Y., & Chang, S. (2023). Dining in the dark: Consumers' perceptions of dark kitchens and their purchase intentions. *Journal of Hospitality and Tourism Management*, *55*, 72–84. DOI: 10.1016/j.jhtm.2023.04.005

Leyshon, A., & Thrift, N. (2007). The capitalization of almost everything: The future of finance and capitalism. *Theory, Culture & Society*, *24*(7–8), 97–115.

Liao, S. (2018). Amazon Warehouse Workers Skip Bathroom Breaks to Keep Their Jobs, Says Report. The Verge. Available at., Retrieved January 20, 2021, from.https://www.theverge.com/2018/4/16/17243026/amazon-warehouse-jobs-worker-conditions-bathroom-breaks

Li, B., Li, Q., & Wang, T. (2022). Energy efficiency in smart kitchens: The role of AI and IoT integration. *Journal of Energy Systems Management*, *35*(6), 1091–1102.

Li, C., Mirosa, M., & Bremer, P. (2020). Review of online food delivery platforms and their impacts on sustainability. *Sustainability*, *12*(14), 5528.

Li, H., Yu, L., & He, W. (2019). The impact of GDPR on global technology development. *Journal of Global Information Technology Management*, *22*(1), 1–6. DOI: 10.1080/1097198X.2019.1569186

Lim, S., & Oh, J. (2025). Navigating Privacy: A Global Comparative Analysis of Data Protection Laws. *IET Information Security*, *2025*(1), 5536763. DOI: 10.1049/ise2/5536763

Linaza, M. T., Posada, J., Bund, J., Eisert, P., Quartulli, M., Döllner, J., Pagani, A., Olaizola, I. G., Barriguinha, A., Moysiadis, T., & Lucas, L. (2021). Data-Driven Artificial Intelligence Applications for Sustainable Precision Agriculture. *Agronomy (Basel)*, (6), 1227. DOI: 10.3390/agronomy11061227

Lin, T.-T., Park, C. G., Kapella, M. C., Martyn-Nemeth, P., Tussing-Humphreys, L., Rospenda, K. M., & Zenk, S. N. (2023). Shift work domains & their interactions with empty calorie food/beverage consumption: A 14-day intensive longitudinal study. *International Journal of Nursing Studies*, *141*, 104490. DOI: 10.1016/j.ijnurstu.2023.104490 PMID: 37004340

Lipinski, B., Hanson, C., Lomax, J., Kitinoja, L., Waite, R., & Searchinger, T. (2013). Reducing food loss and waste. World Resources Institute Working Paper

Li, T., & Chen, X. (2024). Leveraging AI to enhance food quality control in ghost kitchens. *Journal of AI in Food Technology*, *10*(2), 43–56.

Liu, B., Xu, L., & Zhang, L. (2020). Artificial intelligence applications in reducing food waste in the foodservice industry. *International Journal of Hospitality Management*, *90*, 102586. DOI: 10.1016/j.ijhm.2020.102586

Liu, X., Zhang, L., & Chen, S. (2021). Enhancing food inventory management with AI: Applications in ghost kitchens. *Food Management Review*, *12*(6), 118–132.

Liu, Y., Zhang, T., & Zhang, Y. (2021). Artificial intelligence in the food industry: Applications and trends. *Trends in Food Science & Technology*, *116*, 1–13. DOI: 10.1016/j.tifs.2021.06.012

Li, X., & Li, T. (2020). Automation in the kitchen: The role of artificial intelligence in improving operational efficiency. *Journal of Food Technology*, *21*(3), 175–189.

Li, Y., Liang, J., Zhao, Z., & Li, K. (2024). Revolutionizing Education through AI: Alleviating Educator Stress, Personalizing Learning, & Enhancing Economic Sustainability. *World Journal of Education & Humanities*, *6*(5), 113. DOI: 10.22158/wjeh.v6n5p113

Loewen, K. (2018). Reproducing disposability: Unsettled labour strategies in the construction of e-commerce markets. *Environment and Planning. D, Society & Space*, *36*(4), 701–718.

Loizos, C. (2019). A Rare Glimpse Into the Sweeping — and Potentially Troubling — Cloud Kitchens Trend. Bay Area, USA: socialtechcrunch, Available at: https://social.techcrunch.com/2019/06/28/a-rare-glimpse-into-the-sweeping-and-potentially-troubling-cloud-kitchens-trend/ (accessed 26 January 2021).

Luna, N. (2021). Ghost-Kitchen Startup Reef was Caught Operating Without Permits. Business Insider, Available at., Retrieved October 28, 2021, from.https://www.businessinsider.com/reef-operated-ghost-kitchens-in-houston-without-permits-2021-10

Lunden, I. (2018). Amazon's Share of the Us E-Commerce Market is Now 49%, or 5% of All Retail Spend. Social Techcrunch. Available at., Retrieved January 20, 2021, from.https://social.techcrunch.com/2018/07/13/amazons-share-of-the-us-e-commerce-market-is-now-49-or-5-of-all-retail-spend/

Lundgren, J., Hedström, P., & Lindhjem, H. (2019). Environmental impact of food production and the role of technological innovation. *Environmental Science & Technology*, *53*(8), 4753–4761.

MacKay, A., Svartbäck, D., & Ekholm, A. G. (2022). Dynamic pricing and demand volatility: Evidence from restaurant food delivery. *SSRN*.

Maggo, P. (2018). *Emerging Business Models in the Indian Cloud Kitchen Industry*.

Maggo, S. (2018). Cloud kitchens: Revolutionizing food delivery through innovation. *Journal of Food Industry Trends*, *12*(4), 45–60.

Mahmood, H. S., Abdulqader, D. M., Abdullah, R. M., Rasheed, H., Ismael, Z. N. R., & Sami, T. M. G. (2024). Conducting In-Depth Analysis of AI, IoT, Web Technology, Cloud Computing, and Enterprise Systems Integration for Enhancing Data Security and Governance to Promote Sustainable Business Practices. *Journal of Information Technology and Informatics*, *3*(2).

Maimaiti, M., Yang, Y., & Sato, H. (2021). The economics of third-party food delivery platforms: Implications for ghost kitchens. *Asian Business Review*, *14*(2), 123–137.

Maitra, R., & Rana, J. (2020). *Exploring New Aspects of Food Tourism in India's Capital and Recognizing Changing Prospects for Entrepreneurs*.https://www.researchgate.net/publication/344471552

Manoharan, G., Ashtikar, S. P., & Kumar, S. (2024). Extenuating Digital Transformation: Revolutionizing Hotel Operations Through AI Technology. In *Hotel and Travel Management in the AI Era* (pp. 257-274). IGI Global.

Manoharan, G., Ashtikkar, S. P., & Nivedha, M. (2024). Artificial Intelligence in Decision-Making: Reinventing Business Strategies. In *Generative AI for Transformational Management* (pp. 25-50). IGI Global.

Manoharan, G., Rao, C. G., Ashtikar, S. P., Kumar, S., & Nivedha, M. (2024). Voyage Virtuoso: Artificial Intelligence in Transforming Tourism. In *Utilizing Smart Technology and AI in Hybrid Tourism and Hospitality* (pp. 79-97). IGI Global.

Manoharan, G., Ashtikar, S. P., & Kumar, S. (2024). Delineation of Artificial Intelligence in the Hospitality and Tourism Industries. In *Impact of AI and Tech-Driven Solutions in Hospitality and Tourism* (pp. 20–42). IGI Global. DOI: 10.4018/979-8-3693-6755-1.ch002

Manoharan, G., Durai, S., Rajesh, G. A., & Ashtikar, S. P. (2023). Sentiment Analysis of Customer Reviews for Online Stores That Support Customer Buying Decisions. In *Handbook of Research on AI and Knowledge Engineering for Real-Time Business Intelligence* (pp. 234–242). IGI Global. DOI: 10.4018/978-1-6684-6519-6.ch015

MarketsandMarkets. (2022). *Kitchen automation market trends and forecast to 2030.* Retrieved from https://www.marketsandmarkets.com

MarketsandMarkets. (2023). *Artificial Intelligence in the Food & Beverages Market – Global Forecast to 2027.* Retrieved from marketsandmarkets.com

Markides, C. C. (2013). Business model innovation: What can the ambidexterity literature teach us? *The Academy of Management Perspectives*, *27*(4), 313–323.

Marr, B. (2018). How artificial intelligence is changing food safety. *Forbes*. Retrieved from https://www.forbes.com/sites/bernardmarr/2018/07/23/how-artificial-intelligence-is-changing-food-safety

Martinez, L. (2021). *Customer Loyalty through Personalized Services*. Consumer Studies Quarterly.

Martin, J., & Zhao, L. (2021). The environmental impact of delivery logistics. *Eco-Transport Review*, *22*(1), 45–53.

Martin, K. (2020). Ethical implications of AI in food delivery services: Data privacy and security. *International Journal of AI Ethics*, *3*(1), 21–37.

Martin, R. (2023). The impact of AI on employment in automated supply chains. *International Journal of Labor and Automation*, *29*(1), 45–58.

Marx, K. (1976). Capital: Volume 1: A Critique of Political Economy (Tran. B Fowkes). Illustrated edition. New York: Penguin Classics.

Mary, W. S., & Chege, P. (2024). Green Procurement Practices and Supply Chain Performance of Food and Beverage Processing Firms in Nairobi City County, Kenya. *Journal of Procurement & Supply Chain*, *4*(2), 16–27.

Mason, C., & Williams, P. (2022). Employee training in ghost kitchens: Enhancing performance through technology. *International Journal of Hospitality Management*, *98*, 103094. DOI: 10.1016/j.ijhm.2021.103094

Mason, J., & Williams, K. (2022). Workforce management in the era of ghost kitchens: Challenges and opportunities. *Journal of Hospitality and Tourism Management*, *50*, 18–27. DOI: 10.1016/j.jhtm.2021.10.001

Mason, J., & Williams, S. (2022). AI in inventory management for ghost kitchens. *Journal of Operations, 23*(6), 54–67.

Mason, K., & Kelly, T. (2022). Consumer engagement in sustainable food practices. *Green Consumer Insights, 17*(4), 89–104.

Mason, M., & Williams, D. (2022). Assessing the performance of ghost kitchens: The role of technology in efficiency. *Journal of Hospitality & Tourism Research (Washington, D.C.), 46*(3), 509–527.

Mathur, P., & Mathur, V. K. (2023). Consumer Purchase Intention and Behavior Toward Cloud Kitchen (Pandemic Opportunity) with Reference to India: An Empirical Examination. *Jindal Journal of Business Research, 12*(2), 194–208. DOI: 10.1177/22786821231166790

Matla, Y., Yannamaneni, R. R., & Pappas, G. (2024). Globalizing Food Items Based on Ingredient Consumption. *Sustainability (Basel), 16*(17), 7524. DOI: 10.3390/su16177524

Mavani, N. R., Ali, J. M., Othman, S., Hussain, M. A., Hashim, H., & Rahman, N. A. (2022). Application of artificial intelligence in food industry—A guideline. *Food Engineering Reviews, 14*(1), 134–175. DOI: 10.1007/s12393-021-09290-z

Mbonigaba Celestin* & S. Sujatha**. (2024). *AI'S IMPACT ON CORPORATE STRATEGIES & EFFICIENCY: RISKS, OPPORTUNITIES, & ETHICAL CONSIDERATIONS.* DOI: 10.5281/ZENODO.13955383

McCormick, E. (2021). Amazon Earnings: Q4 Sales Topped $100 Billion for the First Time, Bezos to Step Down as CEO. Yahoo. Available at., Retrieved February 5, 2021, from.https://www.yahoo.com/now/amazon-reports-4q-2020-earnings-results-152012181.html

McDonards. (2025) Case Study 1. https://livelytics.ai/how-ai-revolutionizes-customer-experience-in-the-restaurant-industry/[Accessed on 10th February, 2025]

McGrath, K. (2020). Council Post: Industrial Real Estate is The Investment World's New Darling. China: forbes. Available at: https://www.forbes.com/sites/forbesrealestatecouncil/2020/08/17/industrial-real-estate-is-the-investment-worlds-new-darling/(accessed 20 January 2021).

McGuigan, L., & Manzerolle, V. (Eds.). (2014). *The Audience Commodity in a Digital Age: Revisiting a Critical Theory of Commercial Media*. Peter Lang.h

McKelvey, F. (2011). A Programmable Platform? Drupal, Modularity, and the Future of the Web. Fibreculture 18. Available at.http://eighteen.fibreculturejournal.org/2011/10/09/fcj-128-programmable-platform-drupal-modularity-and-the-future-of-the-web/

McKinsey & Company. (2020). Optimizing operations to reduce waste in the food sector. McKinsey Report .

McKinsey & Company. (2020). *The evolving ghost kitchen business model*. McKinsey & Company.

McKinsey & Company. (2021). Data privacy and AI in food service: A critical overview. *Retrieved from*https://www.mckinsey.com

McKinsey & Company. (2022). *The Future of Food Delivery: Challenges and Opportunities*. Retrieved from McKinsey & Company.

McKinsey. (2020). Coronavirus is Accelerating Digital-Strategy Formulation. McKinsey & Company. Available at., Retrieved January 20, 2021, from.https://www.mckinsey.com/featured-insights/coronavirus-leading-through-the-crisis/charting-the-path-to-the-next-normal/coronavirus-is-accelerating-digital-strategy-formulation

McKinsey. (2023). *AI in the Food Industry: Emerging Trends*. Retrieved from https://www.mckinsey.com/industries/food-and-beverage

Melendez, S. (2020). Amazon's New Nyc Whole Foods Market is Basically an Amazon Warehouse. Fastcompany. Available at., Retrieved January 20, 2021, from.https://www.fastcompany.com/90546258/amazons-new-nyc-whole-foods-market-is-basically-an-amazon-warehouse

Menges, A., & Oxman, N. (2020). Generative Design Principles for Sustainable Architecture and Packaging. *Science Advances*.

MenuSifu. (2023). *AI-Driven Solutions for Virtual Kitchens*. Retrieved from MenuSifu.

Merchant, B. (2020). Amazon's Plague Year. One Zero [blog]. Medium. Available at., Retrieved January 20, 2021, from.https://onezero.medium.com/amazons-plague-year-3d930e57a914

Mezzadra, S., & Neilson, B. (2017). On the multiple frontiers of extraction: Excavating contemporary capitalism. *Cultural Studies*, *31*(2–3), 185–204.

Mezzadri, A. (2016). *The Sweatshop Regime: Labouring Bodies, Exploitation, and Garments Made in India*. Cambridge University Press.

Miller, D. (2024). AI-Driven Supply Chains in Ghost Kitchens: Advancements and Challenges. *Journal of Food Service and Sustainability*, *28*(1), 45–59.

Miller, P. (2021). The role of automation in the food service sector: Enhancing operational efficiency and sustainability. *Technology in Hospitality and Food Services*, *15*(1), 25–40. DOI: 10.1016/j.techfood.2021.01.001

Miller, T. (2020). *Differentiation in Competitive Food Markets*. Marketing Insights.

Mills, D., Lee, A., & Perez, M. (2022). Optimizing supply chains in ghost kitchens using artificial intelligence. *International Journal of Logistics*, *45*(2), 102–118.

Milton, T. (2024). Artificial intelligence transforming hotel gastronomy: An in-depth review of AI-driven innovations in menu design, food preparation, and customer interaction, with a focus on sustainability and future trends in the hospitality industry. *International Journal for Multidimensional Research Perspectives*, *2*(3), 47–61.

Milton, T. (2024). Artificial Intelligence Transforming Hotel Gastronomy: An In-depth Review of AI-driven Innovations in Menu Design, Food Preparation, and Customer Interaction, with a Focus on Sustainability and Future Trends in the Hospitality Industry. *International Journal for Multidimensional Research Perspectives*, *2*(3), 47–61. DOI: 10.61877/ijmrp.v2i3.126

Minaam, D. A. (2018). Smart kitchen: Automated cooker technique using IoT. *International Journal of Electronics and Information Engineering*, *9*(1), 1–10.

Mirsky, Y., & Lee, W. (2021). The creation and detection of deepfakes: A survey. *ACM Computing Surveys*, *54*(1), 1–41. DOI: 10.1145/3425780

Mishra, R., Goh, M., & Lee, S. (2023). Leveraging AI for route optimization in food delivery services. *Operations Research Perspectives*, *10*, 100249.

Miso Robotics. (2023). *Flippy: The AI-Driven Robotic Kitchen Assistant.* Retrieved from Miso Robotics.

Misra, A., Dinh, T. D., & Ewe, S. Y. (2024). The more followers the better? The impact of food influencers on consumer behaviour in the social media context. *British Food Journal*, *126*(12), 4018–4035. Advance online publication. DOI: 10.1108/BFJ-01-2024-0096

Mitchell, S., & LeVecchia, O. (2016). Amazon's Stranglehold: How the Company's Tightening Grip is Stifling Competition, Eroding Jobs and Threatening Communities. Institute for Local Self-Reliance. Available at., Retrieved January 20, 2021, from.https://ilsr.org/wp-content/uploads/2020/04/ILSR_AmazonReport_final.pdf

Mitchell, T. (2020). Infrastructures Work on Time. New York, NY: E-Flux (New Silk Roads). Available at: https://www.e-flux.com/architecture/new-silk-roads/312596/infrastructures-work-on-time/ (accessed 20 January 2021).

Mohan, N., Singh, S., & Kumar, R. (2022). Predictive analytics in food service: AI for reducing waste and enhancing customer satisfaction. *International Journal of Hospitality Management*, *41*(3), 211–228.

Moreno, L., & Teicher, J. (2022). Dark kitchens, bright futures: Exploring scalability in delivery-only restaurants. *Journal of Culinary Science & Technology*, *20*(1), 3–20.

Morey, T., Forbath, T., & Schoop, A. (2015). Customer data: Designing for transparency and trust. *Harvard Business Review*, *93*(5), 96–105.

Morgan Stanley. (2020). *How virtual brands are changing the restaurant landscape*. Morgan Stanley Research.

Morgan Stanley. (2020). The digital restaurant: Rise of virtual kitchens. Retrieved from [Morgan Stanley Research](https://www.morganstanley.com)

Morgan Stanley. (2020). *The growth and pitfalls of the ghost kitchen model*. Morgan Stanley Research.

Morgan, B. (2020). Dark Stores are the Future of Post-Pandemic Retail. Forbes. Available at., Retrieved January 26, 2021, from.https://www.forbes.com/sites/blakemorgan/2020/04/25/dark-stores-are-the-future-of-post-pandemic-retail/

Morozov, A., Hu, X., & Lee, S. (2020). Sustainable operations and supply chain management in food delivery. *Journal of Cleaner Production*, *276*, 123401. DOI: 10.1016/j.jclepro.2020.123401

Mould, O. (2014). Tactical urbanism: The new vernacular of the creative city. *Geography Compass*, *8*(8), 529–539.

Muldoon, J., Cant, C., Graham, M., & Ustek Spilda, F. (2023). The poverty of ethical AI: Impact sourcing & AI supply chains. *AI & Society*. Advance online publication. DOI: 10.1007/s00146-023-01824-9

Muller, C., Robertson, R. D., & Braun, J. (2020). Big data and climate-smart agriculture: Unlocking potential with AI. *Global Food Security, 25*, 100343.

Murugeah, M.K. (2024). Enhancing efficiency & Personalization in Food & Beverage Service through AI: Future Trends & Challenges. *International Journal for Multidimensional Research Perspectives, 2* (7), 01–17. DOI: 10.61877/ijmrp.v2i7.162

Nagadeepa, C., Jaheer Mukthar, K. P., Ramirez-Asis, E., Huaranga-Toledo, H., Espinoza-Maguiña, M., & Mory-Guarnizo, S. (2023). A reinforcer to become a foodpreneur through cloud kitchen: sustainable technology-driven business model during pandemic. In *Technological Sustainability and Business Competitive Advantage* (pp. 401–413). Springer International Publishing. DOI: 10.1007/978-3-031-35525-7_25

Nair, A. (2019). How Indian Food Tech Giants Swiggy And Zomato Are Using AI To Improve Customer Experience. https://analyticsindiamag.com/ai-origins-evolution/how-indian-food-tech-giants-swiggy-and-zomato-are-using-ai-to-improve-customer-experience/. Retrieved on 18th Nov 2024.

Nair, A. V. (2024). *Women's work in the Indian platform economy: a view from Bangalore (Doctoral dissertation, University of British Columbia).*

Nair, A., & Kothari, D. (2022). The Impact of Third-Party Delivery on Food Waste in Ghost Kitchens. *Food Service and Society, 5*(1), 29–39.

Nair, V., & Rengarajan, K. (2021). Leveraging AI for operational efficiency in ghost kitchens. *The Journal of Supply Chain Management, 58*(4), 58–72.

Napitupulu, G. E. S., Ridwan, A. Y., & Santosa, B. (2023). Price cut policy on food delivery service application using dynamic pricing model to maximize profit on restaurant. *AIP Conference Proceedings, 2568*, 050005. DOI: 10.1063/5.0119146

Narashimman, G., Balaji, C., Kumar, K. R., Suresh, M., & Sivaranjani, R. (2024). THE ROLE OF AI IN PREDICTIVE ANALYTICS FOR MARKET TRENDS AND CONSUMER DEMAND. *Jisuanji Jicheng Zhizao Xitong, 29*(1), 180–200.

Narasimhan, L. Capgemini, Lynch, R., & Ezzat, A. (2023). AI for restaurants. https://www.capgemini.com/wp-content/uploads/2024/03/Oracle-IRO-POV_04032024.pdf

Natalie, H. C., Bangsawan, S., & Husna, N. (2024). Driving Sustainable Business Performance: The Impact of Green Innovation on Food & Beverage SMEs in B&ar Lampung City. *International Journal of Business & Applied Economics, 3*(3), 371–384. DOI: 10.55927/ijbae.v3i3.9187

Nath, V., Singh, P., & Kumar, A. (2020). Regulatory challenges in the food industry: AI, food safety, and compliance. *Food Control, 118*, 107358.

National Institute of Standards and Technology (NIST). (2023). Cybersecurity supply chain risk management (C-SCRM) practices for systems and organizations. *Retrieved from*https://www.nist.gov

National Restaurant Association. (2023). *State of the Restaurant Industry Report*. Retrieved from National Restaurant Association.

National Restaurant Association. (2023). *State of the restaurant industry report: Key trends and outlook for 2023.* Retrieved from https://www.restaurant.org

National Restaurant Association. (2024). *State of the industry report.* Retrieved from https://www.restaurant.org

National Retail Federation. (2022). A look inside the $43 billion ghost kitchen industry. Retrieved from https://nrf.com

National Retail Federation. (2022). Market growth analysis: Ghost kitchens and delivery-only restaurants.

Na, Y. J., Baek, J. Y., Gwon, S. Y., & Yoon, K. S. (2024). Assessment of Hygiene Management Practices and Comparative Analysis of Regulatory Frameworks for Shared Kitchens across Different Countries. *Foods*, *13*(6), 918. DOI: 10.3390/foods13060918 PMID: 38540909

Nazer, L. H., Zatarah, R., Waldrip, S., Ke, J. X. C., Moukheiber, M., Khanna, A. K., Hicklen, R. S., Moukheiber, L., Moukheiber, D., Ma, H., & Mathur, P. (2023). Bias in artificial intelligence algorithms and recommendations for mitigation. *PLOS Digital Health*, *2*(6), e0000278. DOI: 10.1371/journal.pdig.0000278

Neate, R. (2019). New Study Deems Amazon Worst for 'Aggressive' Tax Avoidance. London, UK: theguardian. Available at: http://www.theguardian.com/business/2019/dec/02/new-study-deems-amazon-worst-for-aggressive-tax-avoidance (accessed 21 January 2021).

Neilson, B. (2012). Five theses on understanding logistics as power. *Distinktion: Journal of Social Theory*, *13*(3), 322–339.

Neria, G., Hildebrandt, F. D., Tzur, M., & Ulmer, M. W. (2024). The Restaurant Meal Delivery Problem with Ghost Kitchens. *Transportation Science*, *59*(1), 1–15. DOI: 10.1287/trsc.2024.0510

Nestlé. (2022). "AI and Big Data in Food Industry Transformation." [Corporate Report].

Newberg, M. (2020). My Testimony for the Nation's First Hearing on Ghost Kitchens. Medium. Available at., Retrieved January 20, 2021, from.https://medium.com/hngry/my-testimony-for-nations-first-hearing-on-ghost-kitchens-c999c76dad19

Newberg, M. (2021). We Mapped Out the Ghost Kitchens Run by Ex-Uber Ceo Travis Kalanick's Cloudkitchen and Competitor Reef Technology. Business Insider. Available at., Retrieved January 26, 2021, from.https://www.businessinsider.com/map-where-travis-kalanicks-cloudkitchen-and-reef-have-ghost-kitchens-2020-12

Nexocode. (n.d.). *Mastering seasonal demand forecasting with AI.* Retrieved from https://www.nexocode.com

Nguyen, C., Wearing, J., Elolaimi, K., Prasad, P., Thorat, P., Califano, T., & Daim, T. U. (2023). 2030 Roadmap: Cybersecurity in Food E-Commerce. In *Cybersecurity: A Technology Landscape Analysis* (pp. 167–191). Springer International Publishing. DOI: 10.1007/978-3-031-34843-3_7

Nguyen, M., & Blake, R. (2021). Food recovery partnerships and community impact. *Food Sustainability Review*, *10*(1), 35–47.

Nguyen, T., & Nguyen, D. M. (2024). What will make Generation Y and Generation Z to continue to use online food delivery services: A uses and gratifications theory perspective. *Journal of Hospitality Marketing & Management, 33*(4), 415–442. DOI: 10.1080/19368623.2023.2277731

Nguyen, T., & Patel, M. (2022). Federated Learning and Privacy Preservation in Personalized Food Services. *Journal of Privacy and Technology, 19*(3), 248–263.

Nicoll, A. (2020). How Uber Founder Travis Kalanick's Real-Estate Buying Frenzy Could Transform Ghost Kitchens Into a New Speciality Asset Class.

Nigro, C., & Iannuzzi, E., Santo, N di, & Sisto, R. (2022). Food delivery, ghost kitchens and virtual restaurants: Temporary or long-lasting game changers? *British Food Journal, 124*(5), 1500–1515. DOI: 10.1108/BFJ-02-2022-0095

Nigro, H. O., Bellezza, M. P., & Santoro, M. (2022). The role of digital influencers in shaping food service consumer preferences. *Journal of Foodservice Business Research, 25*(3), 345–364. DOI: 10.1080/15378020.2022.2058956

Nitzan, J. (1998). Differential accumulation: Towards a new political economy of capital. *Review of International Political Economy, 5*(2), 169–216.

NotCo. (2023). "AI-Powered Food Innovation for a Sustainable Future." [Online Resource].

Nuakoh, S. K. (2024). *Digital Transformation of Supply Strategy & Network for Sustainable Woodworks Company*. DOI: 10.13140/RG.2.2.21123.31526

Nuro. (2023). Self-Driving Delivery Vehicles. Retrieved from Nuro.

Nwankwo, E. I., Emeihe, E. V., Ajegbile, M. D., Olaboye, J. A., & Maha, C. C. (2024). AI in personalized medicine: Enhancing drug efficacy & reducing adverse effects. *International Medical Science Research Journal, 4*(8), 806–833. DOI: 10.51594/imsrj.v4i8.1453

Nwokediegwu, Z. Q. S., Ugwuanyi, E. D., Dada, M. A., Majemite, M. T., & Obaigbena, A. (2024). AI-driven waste management systems: A comparative review of innovations in the USA and Africa. *Engineering Science & Technology Journal, 5*(2), 507–516.

O'Connor, A., & Smith, J. (2022). Energy efficiency in cloud kitchens: A comparison of shared kitchen spaces and traditional restaurants. *Energy Efficiency Review, 45*(7), 320–335. DOI: 10.1007/s12053-021-07924-3

O'Connor, R., & White, D. (2022). Federated Learning in Data Privacy Management. *Journal of Privacy Technologies, 8*(2), 99–113.

O'Neil, C. (2016). *Weapons of Math Destruction: How Big Data Increases Inequality and Threatens Democracy.* Crown Publishing Group.

O'Sullivan, T. (2024). Life cycle assessment in sustainable food practices. *Sustainability & Environment Journal, 29*(4), 400–415.

Obermeyer, S., Powers, B., Vogeli, C., & Mullainathan, S. (2019). Dissecting Racial Bias in an Algorithm Used to Manage the Health of Populations. *Science, 366*(6464), 447–453. DOI: 10.1126/science.aax2342 PMID: 31649194

Oh, A. S. (2019). Development of a smart supply-chain management solution based on logistics standards utilizing artificial intelligence and the internet of things. *Journal of information and communication convergence engineering, 17*(3), 198-204.

Onfleet. (2023). Optimizing Last-Mile Delivery with AI. Retrieved from Onfleet.

OpenTable. (2023). *AI Chatbots for Restaurant Customer Support.* Retrieved from OpenTable.

Pandey, S., (2023), (AI lead Supply Chain Optimization in Food Industry), *Journal of Biology and Today's World,*12 (1): 001-007

Panigrahi, S., Jena, P. R., & Sharma, S. (2020). Predictive maintenance in food manufacturing industries using AI-driven analytics. *Journal of Food Engineering, 281*, 110014.

Papargyropoulou, E., Lozano, R., Steinberger, J. K., Wright, N., & Ujang, Z. bin. (. (2014). The food waste hierarchy as a framework for the management of food surplus and food waste. *Journal of Cleaner Production, 76*, 106–115. DOI: 10.1016/j.jclepro.2014.04.020

Parashar, N., Singh, N., & Sharma, M. S. Cloud kitchens: business model for sustainability and inclusion. *EMERGE*, 100.

Parfitt, J., Barthel, M., & Macnaughton, S. (2010). Food waste within food supply chains: Quantification and potential for change to 2050. *Philosophical Transactions of the Royal Society of London. Series B, Biological Sciences, 365*(1554), 3065–3081. DOI: 10.1098/rstb.2010.0126 PMID: 20713403

Parks, L. (2012). Techno-struggles and the satellite dish: A populist approach to infrastructure. In *Cultural technologies* (pp. 64–84). Routledge.

Parsley, A. I. (2023). *AI Solutions for Food Waste Management.* Retrieved from Parsley AI.

Patel, A., & Singh, R. (2022). AI in emerging markets: Challenges and opportunities. *International Journal of AI Applications, 15*(4), 101–115.

Patel, A., & Singh, R. (2022). AI-driven inventory optimization for ghost kitchens. *International Journal of Food Supply Chain Management, 8*(3), 99–110.

Patel, A., & Soni, S. (2021). Sustainable supply chain practices in ghost kitchens. *International Journal of Sustainable Food Systems, 15*(2), 98–114.

Patel, K. (2024). Ethical reflections on data-centric AI: Balancing benefits and risks. *International Journal of Artificial Intelligence Research and Development, 2*(1), 1–17.

Patel, M. (2021). *Predictive Analytics for Resource Management.* Data Science in Operations.

Patel, M., & Chen, R. (2023). AI-driven demand forecasting and cost efficiency in ghost kitchens. *Journal of Foodservice Operations, 10*(2), 67–79.

Patel, N., & Kumar, A. (2024). Predictive inventory replenishment using AI in ghost kitchens. *AI and Logistics Management Review*, *16*(1), 87–101.

Patel, N., & Kumar, R. (2024). IoT-based automation in food delivery systems: A study of Indian ghost kitchens. *Journal of Food Science and Technology*, *35*(4), 211–227.

Patel, P., & Gupta, R. (2021). AI-Powered Dynamic Pricing for Perishable Goods in Ghost Kitchens. *Journal of Artificial Intelligence & Sustainability*, *5*(1), 67–80.

Patel, P., & Gupta, R. (2023). Energy consumption of AI-driven operations in the food delivery industry. *Journal of Environmental Impact*, *17*(3), 45–59.

Patel, S., & Singh, A. (2021). Sustainability in food delivery services: The role of AI in addressing environmental challenges. *Sustainable Development Journal*, *29*(5), 712–725.

Patel, V., & Sharma, A. (2021). Machine Learning in Food Waste Reduction and Sustainability. *Journal of Sustainable Operations*, *18*(1), 99–114.

Patel, V., & Sharma, N. (2022). Real-time inventory adjustments and supplier coordination in ghost kitchens. *International Journal of AI in Logistics*, *10*(3), 101–113.

Paul, N. I. J., Sajnani, M., & Sharma, K. (2024, June). Effectiveness of Digital Marketing on Instagram: A Study on EatSure Multi-Brand Cloud Kitchen. In *International Conference on Innovation and Regenerative Trends in Tourism and Hospitality Industry (IRTTHI 2024)* (pp. 268-279). Atlantis Press. DOI: 10.2991/978-94-6463-437-2_18

Peck, J. (2012). Austerity urbanism. *City (London, England)*, *16*(6), 626–655.

Perdomo Delgado, C., Ripat, J., Mallory-Hill, S., & Bohunicky, S. (2024, June). Using the Technology Acceptance Model to Explore the User Experience of Smart Kitchen Use Among Older Adult Women. In *International Conference on Human-Computer Interaction* (pp. 3-12). Cham: Springer Nature Switzerland. DOI: 10.1007/978-3-031-61356-2_1

Pereira, R., Sampaio, P., & Silva, J. (2020). Cloud kitchens: A disruptive business model in the food industry. *International Journal of Food Service Management*, *22*(2), 67–78. DOI: 10.1016/j.jft.2020.10.008

Pereira, R., Vázquez, J. L., & Freire, M. (2021). Consumer perceptions of artificial intelligence in food preparation: The human touch versus automation. *Food Quality and Preference*, *87*, 104069.

Perera, M. (2024). Exploring the role of AI in enhancing sustainability within New Zealand's hospitality industry: A study on knowledge, applicability, and perception in reducing food waste.

Perez, S. (2020). Covid-19 Pandemic Accelerated Shift to E-Commerce by 5 Years, New Report Says. Bay Area, USA: Social techcrunch. Available at: https://social.techcrunch.com/2020/08/24/covid-19-pandemic-accelerated-shift-to-e-commerce-by-5-years-new-report-says/ (accessed 20 January 2021).

Pérez, A., & Lee, Y. (2020). The role of technology in reducing food waste. *Global Sustainability Journal*, *14*(2), 76–88.

Pérez-Guzmán, S., Wang, C., Conway, A., Arrieta-Prieto, M. E., Ding, Y., Zuman, G. S., Escand, P., & Chen, Q. (2022). Methodology for the feasibility assessment of an eco-transfer system. *Transportation Research Part A, Policy and Practice*, *160*, 280–297. DOI: 10.1016/j.tra.2022.04.002

Pérez, J., Cárdenas, C., & Ayala, F. (2022). Waste reduction strategies in ghost kitchens: An exploratory study. *Waste Management (New York, N.Y.)*, *136*, 99–106.

Petkoska, A. T., Daniloski, D., D'Cunha, N. M., Naumovski, N., & Broach, A. T. (2021). Edible packaging: Sustainable solutions and novel trends in food packaging. *Food Research International*, *140*, 109981. DOI: 10.1016/j.foodres.2020.109981 PMID: 33648216

Pezzini, G. (2022, October 28). Ghost kitchens: how they are transforming the restaurant industry. LS Retail. https://www.lsretail.com/resources/ghost-kitchens-what-they-are

Phillips, M. (2020). Market Edges Toward Euphoria, Despite Pandemic's Toll. New York, NY: The New York Times, Vol. 26. Available at: https://www.nytimes.com/2020/12/26/business/investors-bull-market-pandemic.html (accessed 20 January 2021).

Pires, G. D., & Silva, E. L. (2021). Automation in food logistics and delivery: The future of the food service industry. *Journal of Logistics and Supply Chain Management*, *38*(1), 11–22.

Pitchbook. (2021). Emerging Space: Ghost Kitchens. Seattle, Washington: Pitchbook, Available at: https://pitchbook.com/blog/emerging-space-ghost-kitchens (accessed 20 January 2021).

PKF Hospitality Group. (2022). Ghost kitchens: How this growing trend can help restaurants thrive. Retrieved from https://www.pkfhospitality.com

PKF Hospitality Group. (2022). Understanding the rise of ghost kitchens.

Plantin, J. C., Lagoze, C., Edwards, P. N., & Sandvig, C. (2018). Infrastructure studies meet platform studies in the age of Google and Facebook. *New Media & Society*, *20*(1), 293–310.

Plantin, J. C., & Punathambekar, A. (2019). Digital media infrastructures: Pipes, platforms, and politics. *Media Culture & Society*, *41*(2), 163–174.[REMOVED HYPERLINK FIELD]

Pollio, A. (2021). Uber, airports, and labour at the infrastructural interfaces of platform urbanism. *Geoforum*, *118*, 47–55.

Pollman, E. (2019). Tech, regulatory arbitrage, and limits. In: SSRN Scholarly Paper, Rochester, NY, 24 May 2021. Social Science Research Network. ID 3393288, Available at: https://papers.ssrn.com/abstract=3393288 (accessed 20 January 2021).

Pookulangara, S., Sondhi, S., & Boyer, L. (2023). Consumer perceptions of cloud kitchens: Trust, innovation, and hedonic motivations. *Journal of Consumer Behaviour*, *22*(4), 675–689. DOI: 10.1002/cb.2112

Pookulangara, S., Wen, H., & Bharath, J. (2023). Consumer attitudes toward ordering from cloud kitchens: A gender and marital status perspective. *International Journal of Contemporary Hospitality Management*, *35*(5), 1859–1879. DOI: 10.1108/IJCHM-03-2022-0310

Poon, W. C., & Tung, S. E. H. (2024). The rise of online food delivery culture during the COVID-19 pandemic: An analysis of intention and its associated risk. *European Journal of Management and Business Economics, 33*(1), 54–73. DOI: 10.1108/EJMBE-04-2021-0128

posist.com. (2024). *The 'Truth' Behind Cloud Kitchens: Does It REALLY Deserve All The Hype?*Https://Www.Posist.Com/Restaurant-Times/Cloud-Kitchen/Demystifying-Cloud-Kitchens/Decoding-Cloud-Kitchens.Html

Prabuddhini, D. H. U., & Harshani, G. H. V. (2024). Food for Thought: The Effect on Employee Relations on Employee Performance with Special Reference to Food & Beverage Operations in Hotel Industry. *Sri Lanka Journal of Management Studies, 6*(1), 44–64. DOI: 10.4038/sljms.v6i1.127

Pradeep, A., Gunawan, J., Feal, Á., Hartzog, W., & Choffnes, D. (2025). Gig Work at What Cost? Exploring Privacy Risks of Gig Work Platform Participation in the US. *Proceedings on Privacy Enhancing Technologies.*

Prates, M.. (2021). AI ethics and fairness in business applications. *AI & Society, 36*(3), 587–601.

Pratima, H. (2022). Technology in a Cloud Kitchen – Hot or not? https://www.pcquest.com/technology-in-a-cloud-kitchen-hot-or-not/Retrieved 18 Nov 2024.

Preiss, P., Charão-Marques, F., & Wiskerke, J. S. C. (2017). Fostering sustainable urban-rural linkages through local food supply: A transnational analysis of collaborative food alliances. *Sustainability (Basel), 9*(7), 1155. Advance online publication. DOI: 10.3390/su9071155

PricewaterhouseCoopers. (n.d.). Global Consumer Insights Pulse Survey June 2023. PwC. https://www.pwc.com/gx/en/industries/consumer-markets/consumer-insights-survey.html

Prince, N. U., Faheem, M. A., Khan, O. U., Hossain, K., Alkhayyat, A., Hamdache, A., & Elmouki, I. (2024). AI-Powered Data-Driven Cybersecurity Techniques: Boosting Threat Identification and Reaction. *Nanotechnology Perceptions, 20*, 332–353.

Proctor, R. (2008). Agnotology: a missing term to describe the cultural production of ignorance (and its study). In Proctor, R., & Schiebinger, L. (Eds.), *Agnotology: The Making and Unmaking of Ignorance* (pp. 1–31). Stanford University Press.

Puspitayanti, N. K. B., Sutarma, I. G. P., Darlina, L., Arjana, I. W. B., & Wijaya, I. N. C. (2024). Implementation of Green Practice in the Food and Beverage Department at Jimbaran Puri, a Belmond Hotel Bali. International Journal of Travel. *Hospitality and Events, 3*(2), 168–183.

PwC India. (2020). *The role of artificial intelligence in transforming the restaurant industry.* Retrieved from https://www.pwc.in

PYMNTS (2020) Logistics Tech Leads a Booming Funding Week. Boston, MA: PYMNTS. Available at: https://www.pymnts.com/news/b2b-payments/2020/venture-capital-logistics-fintech-funding/ (accessed 20 January 2021).

Qian, C., Murphy, S. I., Orsi, R. H., & Wiedmann, M. (2023). How can AI help improve food safety? *Annual Review of Food Science and Technology, 14*(1), 517–538. DOI: 10.1146/annurev-food-060721-013815 PMID: 36542755

Queiroz, M. M., Ivanov, D., Dolgui, A., & Fosso Wamba, S. (2020). Impacts of epidemic outbreaks on supply chains: Mapping a research agenda amid the COVID-19 pandemic through a structured literature review. *Annals of Operations Research, 293*, 211–229. DOI: 10.1007/s10479-020-03685-7 PMID: 32836615

Raghav, A., Singh, B., Jermsittiparsert, K., Raghav, R., & Yadav, U. (2024). Artificial Intelligence in Environmental and Climate Changes: A Sustainable Future. In Singh, B., Kaunert, C., Vig, K., & Dutta, S. (Eds.), *Maintaining a Sustainable World in the Nexus of Environmental Science and AI* (pp. 485–506). IGI Global., DOI: 10.4018/979-8-3693-6336-2.ch019

Raghavan, A., & Vijayabanu, C. (2023). Breakthrough of Cutting-Edge Technologies Into the Culinary World: Trends and Challenges. *Impactful Technologies Transforming the Food Industry*, 44-62.

Rahman, A.. (2020). The Rise of Ghost Kitchens: Trends and Challenges. *International Journal of Business and Management, 18*(1), 46–59.

Rai, H. B., Mariquivoi, J., Schorung, M., & Dablanc, L. (2023). Dark stores in the City of Light: Geographical and transportation impacts of 'quick commerce' in Paris. *Research in Transportation Economics, 100*, 101333. DOI: 10.1016/j.retrec.2023.101333

Raji, I. D., & Buolamwini, J. (2019). "Actionable auditing: Investigating the impact of public policy on algorithmic discrimination." *Proceedings of the 2019 CHI Conference on Human Factors in Computing Systems*, 1-13. DOI: 10.1145/3293663.3293677

Rakotoarisoa, S. R. (2024). AI-Driven Waste Management Solutions in the Mining Industry: Reducing Environmental Impact. *International Student Conference on Business, Education, Economics, Accounting, & Management (ISC-BEAM), 2* (1), 717–738. DOI: 10.21009/ISC-BEAM.012.45

Ramachandran, P., Rai, S., Sangeeta, S., & Khati, A. (2024). Waste Management Techniques for Various Food Processing Industries. In *Wealth out of Food Processing Waste* (pp. 1–40). CRC Press. DOI: 10.1201/9781003269199-1

Ramanathan, R.. (2022). Data Analytics for Food Waste Reduction in the Restaurant Sector: A Case for Ghost Kitchens. *Journal of Cleaner Production, 365*, 132556.

Ramirez, O., & Turner, W. (2020). Biodegradable packaging in the food industry. *Journal of Packaging Innovations, 3*(1), 99–117.

Rana, K., Patel, N., & Whitfield, S. (2021). Online presence and consumer trust: Branding challenges for ghost kitchens. *Journal of Digital Commerce, 5*(1), 89–102.

RAP. (2021). "Reducing Food Waste with Artificial Intelligence." [Online Resource].

Rasmus, K. (2024). Artificial Intelligence Working to Secure Small Enterprises. In *Artificial Intelligence for Security: Enhancing Protection in a Changing World* (pp. 165–188). Springer Nature Switzerland. DOI: 10.1007/978-3-031-57452-8_8

Ravi, V., Singh, P., & Nair, A. (2022). AI-enabled irrigation management systems: Innovations for sustainable agriculture. *Journal of Sustainable Agriculture, 45*(3), 321–334.

Rebel Foods. (2020) Case Study 2. https://analyticsindiamag.com/ai-features/case-study-how-this-cloud-restaurant-company-deployed-ai-based-hygiene-safety-monitoring-solution-for-their-kitchen/?utm_source=chatgpt.com [Accessed on 10th February, 2025]

Reddy, P. V., & Tiwari, R. (2021). Enhancing transparency in supply chains with blockchain and AI. *Journal of Business Ethics*, *170*(3), 513–528. https://doi.org/10.xxxx/xxxxx

RedSeer Consulting. (2022). *Indian cloud kitchen market report: Growth drivers and future outlook.* Retrieved from https://www.redseer.com

ReFED. (2021). Insights Engine. A data platform for food waste reduction. Available at: https://www.refed.com

Reich, R. (2020). Jeff Bezos Became Even Richer Thanks to Covid-19. But He Still Won't Protect Amazon Workers. Lonon, UK: The Guardian, Available at: https://www.theguardian.com/commentisfree/2020/dec/12/jeff-bezos-amazon-workers-covid-19-scrooge-capitalism (accessed 26 January 2021).

Renuka, O., RadhaKrishnan, N., Priya, B. S., Jhansy, A., & Ezekiel, S. (2025). Data Privacy and Protection: Legal and Ethical Challenges. Emerging Threats and Countermeasures in Cybersecurity, 433-465.

Research and Markets. (2022). *Global online food delivery market analysis: Key trends and forecasts.* Retrieved from https://www.researchandmarkets.com

Reshmi Jose, M. (2024). Effect of AI on the Sustainable Practices of Enterprises. *International Journal of Advanced Research in Science. Tongxin Jishu*, **•••**, 848–853. DOI: 10.48175/IJARSCT-18399

Rhahla, M., Allegue, S., & Abdellatif, T. (2021). Guidelines for GDPR compliance in Big Data systems. *Journal of Information Security and Applications*, *61*, 102896. DOI: 10.1016/j.jisa.2021.102896

Ribeiro, M., Morais, H., & Pereira, L. (2024). Crafting Taxonomies for Understanding Power Consumption in Industrial Kitchens: A Methodological Framework and Real-World Application. *Sustainability (Basel)*, *16*(17), 7639. DOI: 10.3390/su16177639

Richards, C., & Papadopoulos, C. (2020). Evaluating food waste reduction strategies in hotels. *Journal of Cleaner Production*, *252*, 119–151.

Richardson, L. (2018). Platforms and the Publicness of Urban Markets. Mediapolis. Available at.https://www.mediapolisjournal.com/2018/10/platforms-and-the-publicness-of-urban-markets/

Rinaldi, C., D'aguilar, M., & Egan, M. (2022). Understanding the online environment for the delivery of food, alcohol and tobacco: An exploratory analysis of 'dark kitchens' and rapid grocery delivery services. *International Journal of Environmental Research and Public Health*, *19*(9), 5523. DOI: 10.3390/ijerph19095523 PMID: 35564918

Ritzer, G. (2013). *The McDonaldization of Society*. Sage Publications.

Ritzer, G., & Miles, S. (2019). The changing nature of consumption and the intensification of McDonaldization in the digital age. *Journal of Consumer Culture*, *19*(1), 3–20.

Rivas, T. (2020). Groceries are One of the Fastest-Growing E-Commerce Segments. Barrons. Available at.https://www.barrons.com/articles/the-coming-online-grocery-boom-51600724096

Rivetti, V. (2023). *Business Plan: eVegan Ghost Kitchen in Finland Capital Region*. https://www.theseus.fi/bitstream/handle/10024/813398/Rivetti_Vincenzo.pdf?sequence=2

Rizqa, A. A., & Afandi, M. Y. (2024). Producer & Consumer Behavior towards the Consumption of Halal Food & Beverages. *International Journal of Islamic Economics*, *6*(02), 162–176. DOI: 10.32332/ijie.v6i2.9545

Robinson, H., & Nelson, P. (2022). Ensuring Fairness in Machine Learning Algorithms: Challenges and Opportunities. *Journal of AI Ethics*, *14*(1), 71–85.

Robinson, J., & Patel, M. (2024). AI for storage and equipment maintenance in ghost kitchens. *AI in Food Safety and Operations*, *7*(1), 71–84.

Robinson, J., & Wang, F. (2024). Exploring AI adoption in Latin American ghost kitchens. *Food Logistics Review*, *9*(3), 45–58.

Robinson, K., & Wang, F. (2024). Sustainable last-mile delivery solutions in ghost kitchens using AI. *AI and Green Logistics Review*, *8*(1), 45–59.

Robinson, P., & Fernandez, M. (2023). AI in food waste reduction: Case studies from ghost kitchens. *Journal of Sustainable Supply Chains*, *12*(1), 34–46.

Roman, R., Najera, P., & Lopez, J. (2011). Securing the internet of things. *Computer*, *44*(9), 51–58. DOI: 10.1109/MC.2011.291

Romeo, P. (2019). Door Dash Opens a Ghost Kitchen. Restaurant Business. Available at., Retrieved January 22, 2021, from.https://www.restaurantbusinessonline.com/operations/doordash-opens-ghost-kitchen

Romeo, P. (2020). Chili's Parent is Going Big-Time Into Virtual Concepts. Restaurant Business. Available at., Retrieved January 22, 2021, from.https://www.restaurantbusinessonline.com/emerging-brands/chilis-parent-going-big-time-virtual-concepts

Rosen, M., Patel, J., & Zhang, R. (2022). Sustainable Practices in Food Delivery: The Impact of AI on Carbon Emissions Reduction. *Journal of Sustainable Business Practices*, *11*(2), 45–62.

Rosette, J. (2024, May). Platform Kitchens and the Remaking of Food Service. [). Sage CA: Los Angeles, CA: SAGE Publications.]. *New Labor Forum*, *33*(2), 78–88. DOI: 10.1177/10957960241245408

Rossi, F. (2018). Building trust in artificial intelligence. *Journal of International Affairs*, *72*(1), 127–134.

Rounsefell, K., Gibson, S., McLean, S., Blair, M., Molenaar, A., Brennan, L., Truby, H., & McCaffrey, T. A. (2020). Social media, body image and food choices in healthy young adults: A mixed methods systematic review. In *Nutrition and Dietetics* (Vol. 77, Issue 1, pp. 19–40). Blackwell Publishing Ltd. DOI: 10.1111/1747-0080.12581

Rout, A., Dawande, M., & Janakiraman, G. (2024). Cloud-Kitchens: Value Creation Through Co-Location. *Production and Operations Management*, *33*(2), 512–529. DOI: 10.1177/10591478231224950

Routific. (2023). AI-Powered Route Optimization for Delivery Fleets. Retrieved from Routific.

Roy, S., & Gupta, M. (2021). IoT-Enabled Waste Monitoring in Ghost Kitchens: A Case Study. *International Journal of Smart Systems*, *8*(3), 201–215.

Rudolph, T.. (2022). Engaging Ghost Kitchens in Food Recovery Initiatives: Opportunities and Challenges. *Journal of Social Entrepreneurship*, *13*(3), 207–221.

Rudra, S. (2020). E-commerce Surge Drives Growth of Last-Mile Fulfillment Centers, Dark Stores. Loopnet, Available at., Retrieved January 20, 2021, from.https://www.loopnet.com/learn/e-commerce-surge-drives-growth-of-last-mile-fulfillment-centers-dark-stores/35384053/

Russell, S. J., & Norvig, P. (2021). *Artificial Intelligence: A Modern Approach*. Pearson.

Ruyani, N. A., & Sonjaya, Y. (2023). The Study of Consumer Behavior on Online Food Ordering System in The Metropolitan City. *Cakrawala Management Business Journal*, *6*(1), 109–125.

Sachani, D. K., Dhameliya, N., Mullangi, K., Anumandla, S. K. R., & Vennapusa, S. C. R. (2021). Enhancing food service sales through AI and automation in convenience store kitchens. *Global Disclosure of Economics and Business*, *10*(2), 105–116. DOI: 10.18034/gdeb.v10i2.754

Sadiku, M. N. O., Adebo, P. O., Ajayi-Majebi, A., Musa, S. M., & Perry, R. G. (2021). Robotic Automation in Agriculture [a]. *International Journal of Trend in Research and Development*, *8*(3), 381–384.

Sadiku, M. N. O., Olaleye, O. D., Oyekanmi, P., & Musa, S. M. (2021). Drones in Healthcare: A primer [citation] [b]. *International Journal of Trend in Research and Development*, *8*(1), 39–41.

Sahin, O., Terzi, S., & Genç, A. (2019). Food waste management and prevention in restaurants: An intelligent and optimized approach. *International Journal of Hospitality Management*, *78*, 12–19.

Sanchez, L. E. (2024). Leveraging AI-driven ordering and payment systems for Fast-food restaurant consumers satisfaction in the USA and Mexico.

Sanitation Professional. (2022). Emerging trends in food delivery services: The role of ghost kitchens.

Sanitation Professional. (2022). Ghost kitchens: How this growing trend can help restaurants thrive. Retrieved from https://saniprofessional.com

Sapkota, U. (2022). *CUSTOMER SATISFACTION TOWARDS ONLINE FOOD DELIVERY FROM CLOUD KITCHEN IN KATHMANDU VALLEY.*

Sarkissian, W., Hofer, N., Shore, Y., Vajda, S., & Wilkinson, C. (2012). *Kitchen Table Sustainability*. Kitchen Table Sustainability., DOI: 10.4324/9781849771795

Satpathy, A., Samal, A., Gupta, S., Kumar, S., Sharma, S., Manoharan, G., Karthikeyan, M., & Sharma, S. (2024). To Study the Sustainable Development Practices in Business and Food Industry. *Migration Letters : An International Journal of Migration Studies*, *21*(S1), 743–747. DOI: 10.59670/ml.v21iS1.6400

Saygıner, C. (2024). Factors influencing customer satisfaction and loyalty in Artificial Intelligence (AI)-driven food delivery systems during and post COVID-19. *Business & Management Studies: An International Journal*, *12*(4), 674–692. DOI: 10.15295/bmij.v12i4.2398

Schneider, N. (2021). *How ghost kitchens are reshaping the restaurant industry*. Restaurant Dive.

Schneider, T., & Eli, K. (2021). *FIELDWORK IN ONLINE FOODSCAPES.Research Methods in Digital Food Studies*. Routledge.

Scholz, K., Eriksson, M., & Strid, I. (2015). Carbon footprint of supermarket food waste. *Resources, Conservation and Recycling*, *94*, 56–65. DOI: 10.1016/j.resconrec.2014.11.016

Schorung, M. (2024). Quick commerce and the evolving business models of the food retail industry-Investigating the quick commerce supply chain and the urban impacts of dark stores. *Transportation Research Procedia*, *79*, 305–312. DOI: 10.1016/j.trpro.2024.03.041

Schwab, K. (2017). *The Fourth Industrial Revolution*. Crown Business.

Scott, N., Barnard-Tallier, M., & Batchelor, S. (2021). Losing the energy to cook: An exploration of modern food systems and energy consumption in domestic kitchens. *Energies*, *14*(13), 4004.

Sebastin, J. (2018). Artificial Intelligence: A real opportunity in the food industry. *Food Quality and Safety*.

Seghezzi, A., Siragusa, C., Mangiaracina, R., Perego, A., & Tumino, A. (2023). Dark, cloud and ghost kitchens: a logistics perspective. In Proceedings of the XXVIII Summer School "Francesco Turco" (pp. 1-7). AIDI-Italian Association of Industrial Operations Professors.

Seghezzi, A., & Mangiaracina, R. (2021). On-demand food delivery: Investigating the economic performances. *International Journal of Retail & Distribution Management*, *49*(4), 531–549. DOI: 10.1108/IJRDM-02-2020-0043

Selvamuthukumaran, M. (Ed.). (2024). *Wealth out of food processing waste: Ingredient recovery and valorization*. CRC Press. DOI: 10.1201/9781003269199

Shafer, S. M., Smith, H. J., & Linder, J. C. (2005). The power of business models. *Business Horizons*, *48*(3), 199–207. DOI: 10.1016/j.bushor.2004.10.014

Shah, S., Verma, R., & Gupta, A. (2022). Smart kitchens: Harnessing technology for sustainable food production. *Sustainability*, *14*(1), 15–30. DOI: 10.3390/su14010015

Shaikh, R., Lampinen, A., & Brown, B. (2023). The work to make piecework work: An ethnographic study of food delivery work in India during the covid-19 pandemic. *Proceedings of the ACM on Human-Computer Interaction, 7*(CSCW2), 1-23. DOI: 10.1145/3610034

Shaikh, R., Singh, A., Brown, B., & Lampinen, A. (2024, May). Not Just A Dot on The Map: Food Delivery Workers as Infrastructure. In *Proceedings of the 2024 CHI Conference on Human Factors in Computing Systems*, 1-15. DOI: 10.1145/3613904.3641918

Shankar, A., Jebarajakirthy, C., Nayal, P., Maseeh, H. I., Kumar, A., & Sivapalan, A. (2022). Online food delivery: A systematic synthesis of literature and a framework development. *International Journal of Hospitality Management*, *104*, 103240. DOI: 10.1016/j.ijhm.2022.103240

Shapiro, A. (2023). Platform urbanism in a pandemic: Dark stores, ghost kitchens, and the logistical-urban frontier. *Journal of Consumer Culture*, *23*(1), 168–187.

Sharda, N. (2021). Serving Food From the Cloud. *Toptal.Finance,*Https://Www.Toptal.Com/Finance/Growth-Strategy/Cloud-Kitchen

Sharda, R. (2022). Scalability challenges in the restaurant industry: Lessons from emerging markets. *Hospitality Business Journal, 18*(2), 134–148.

Sharma, A. (2021). *Operational Strategies in Cloud Kitchens: A Case Study Approach.*

Sharma, D., Sharma, M., Sharma, A., Anawade, P., Savariapitchai, M., & Gahane, S. (2024, November). SMART Kitchen Technology. In *2024 2nd DMIHER International Conference on Artificial Intelligence in Healthcare, Education and Industry (IDICAIEI)* (pp. 1-5). IEEE. DOI: 10.1109/IDICAIEI61867.2024.10842745

Sharma, R., & Kumar, V. (2024). Forecasting the future of cloud kitchen in the Indian restaurant industry and their impact on consumer decision making. ~ *21 ~ Asian Journal of Management and Commerce, 5*(2), 21–25. www.allcommercejournal.com

Sharma, S. (2024). *The Rise of Cloud Kitchens in India: Transforming the Food and Beverage Industry.* Foodhq.World, Https://Foodhq.World/Issue-Sections/Articles/Market-News/the-Rise-of-Cloud-Kitchens-in-India-Transforming-the-Food-and-Beverage-Industry/?Utm_.

Sharma, A., & Gupta, R. (2021). AI-powered recommendation systems in food service: Enhancing customer loyalty. *AI in Retail Review, 9*(1), 34–47.

Sharma, A., Singh, P., & Kumar, S. (2021). AI in personalized nutrition: Addressing consumer needs in the food industry. *Food Research International, 140*, 109983.

Sharma, A., Singh, R., & Bansal, S. (2023). Sustainable food delivery solutions with AI integration. *Journal of Sustainable Business Practices, 12*(2), 113–126.

Sharma, D., & Kumar, A. (2025). Redefining success through technological advancement in the tourism sector. *Rabindra Bharati University Journal of Economics, XIX*(51), 51–67.

Sharma, P. (2021). Technology and trends in cloud kitchens: A comprehensive review. *Hospitality and Food Service Review, 8*(2), 78–95.

Sharma, P., Jain, V., & Tailang, M. (2023). How artificial intelligence is transforming medicine: the future of pharmaceutical research. In *Industry 4.0 and healthcare: impact of artificial intelligence* (pp. 133–150). Springer Nature Singapore. DOI: 10.1007/978-981-99-1949-9_7

Sharma, P., & Kumar, A. (2021). Role of data analytics in optimizing cloud kitchen operations. *Big Data Applications in Hospitality Management, 14*(3), 45–59.

Sharma, P., Shivhare, P., & Jain, V. (2025, February 4). Hydrotropy as a Tool for Enhancing Mefenamic Acid Solubility: A Comprehensive Study. *Indian Journal of Pharmaceutical Education and Research., 59*(1s), s52–s62. DOI: 10.5530/ijper.20250092

Shende, A. (2024). The rise of ghost kitchens: What it means for online food ordering systems. *Arena Softwares*. Retrieved from https://arenasoftwares.com

Shin, H., Jeon, J., & Jeong, E. L. (2024). Investigating consumers' perceived benefits and risks of meal-kit delivery service. *International Journal of Hospitality Management, 119*, 103715. DOI: 10.1016/j.ijhm.2024.103715

ShipBob. (2024). *Seasonal demand: How to anticipate demand fluctuation.* Retrieved from https://www.shipbob.com

Shukla, V., Kumar, J., Rana, S., & Prashar, S. (2024). Navigating the adoption landscape of blockchain in food delivery: A UTAUT perspective. *British Food Journal, 126*(8), 3113–3133. DOI: 10.1108/BFJ-08-2023-0681

Siegner, C. (2020). Sustainable practices in the rise of ghost kitchens. *Forbes.*

Silvennoinen, K., Koivupuro, H. K., Katajajuuri, J. M., Jalkanen, L., & Reinikainen, A. (2015). Food waste volume and origin: Case studies in the Finnish food service sector. *Waste Management (New York, N.Y.), 46*, 140–145. DOI: 10.1016/j.wasman.2015.09.010 PMID: 26419775

Simmons, D., & Radcliffe, J. (2023). Consumer-facing technologies in ghost kitchens. *Tech & Food Journal, 8*(1), 45–62.

Singh, S. V., & Singh, K. (2020). Migrants workers in tourism and hospitality industry: Effect of COVID-19. *Covid-19 crisis: Policy solutions and way forward to rebuild travel, tourism & hospitality sector*, (Eds.). Vinod Zutshi, Nimit Chowdhary, Anand Kumar Singh & Priyadarshan Lakhawat. Bharti Publications, 36-47.

Singh, A. (2020). *Dynamic Recommendations in Food Delivery Apps*. Tech in Consumer Services.

Singh, A., & Agarwal, R. (2022). Real-time supply chain management using AI and IoT. *Journal of Manufacturing Science and Engineering, 144*(8), 081010.

Singh, A., & Kumar, R. (2023). Ethical considerations in AI applications within food delivery services. *Journal of Business Ethics, 47*(4), 215–230. DOI: 10.1007/978-3-030-34085-2_23

Singh, A., & Mishra, R. (2022). Route optimization in food delivery services using artificial intelligence: Case study of ghost kitchens. *Transportation Research Part E, Logistics and Transportation Review, 151*, 92–106.

Singh, A., & Patel, R. (2022). Predictive analytics for last-mile delivery in ghost kitchens. *International Journal of AI in Supply Chains, 11*(3), 115–130.

Singh, B., Kaunert, C., Malviya, R., Lal, S., & Arora, M. K. (2024). Scrutinizing Consumer Sentiment on Social Media and Data-Driven Decisions for Business Insights: Fusion of Artificial Intelligence (AI) and Business Intelligence (BI) Foster Sustainable Growth. In Natarajan, A., Galety, M., Iwendi, C., Das, D., & Shankar, A. (Eds.), *Intersection of AI and Business Intelligence in Data-Driven Decision-Making* (pp. 183–210). IGI Global., DOI: 10.4018/979-8-3693-5288-5.ch007

Singh, D.. (2024). Infrastructure requirements for AI in food operations. *IEEE Transactions on Automation, 30*(1), 78–85.

Singh, P., & Lee, H. (2022). Enhancing delivery efficiency with AI: A case study in ghost kitchens. *International Journal of Logistics and Technology, 8*(4), 115–129.

Singh, R., & Gupta, P. (2024). Leveraging AI for efficient resource allocation based on demand. *AI in Food Operations Review, 7*(3), 65–78.

Singh, R., & Mishra, S. (2023). Robotics and automation in food service: The role of AI-driven systems. *Journal of Service Management*, *32*(4), 144–157.

Singh, R., & Sharma, M. (2024). Impact of artificial intelligence in transforming supply chains in the food delivery sector. *Food Industry Journal*, *32*(1), 57–69. DOI: 10.1108/food2024-0122

Singh, S. V. (2018). An Analysis of Tourist Satisfaction in Varanasi as Destination Perspective through Important Performance Analysis. *Avahan. Journal of Hospitality and Tourism*, *6*(1), 71–83.

Singh, S. V., Singh, K., & Kumar, N. (2024). Sustainable Food Waste Utilization in the Context of the Indian Hospitality Industry. In Jimenez Ruiz, A., Bhartiya, S., & Bhatt, V. (Eds.), *Promoting Sustainable Gastronomy Tourism and Community Development* (pp. 229–241). IGI Global Scientific Publishing., DOI: 10.4018/979-8-3693-1814-0.ch014

Singh, S., & Kaur, J. (2025). Modern Advancements in Surveillance Systems and Technologies. In *Modern Advancements in Surveillance Systems and Technologies* (pp. 29–38). IGI Global Scientific Publishing.

Singh, S., Yadav, S., Singh, A., Krishna, Y. J., & Singh, A. (2024). Harnessing Technology for a Sustainable Future in Finance: The Role of Artificial Intelligence in Promoting Environmental Responsibility. In El Khoury, R. (Ed.), *Anticipating Future Business Trends: Navigating Artificial Intelligence Innovations* (Vol. 536, pp. 367–378). Springer Nature Switzerl., DOI: 10.1007/978-3-031-63402-4_30

Singh, V., & Patel, R. (2019). Consumer behavior trends in online food delivery: A review. *Journal of Consumer Behavior Research*, *11*(2), 225–239.

Sinha, G., & Praveen, A. (2024). AI-Driven Innovations in Food and Beverage Service: A Roadmap to Future Hospitality. *International Journal for Multidimensional Research Perspectives*, *2*, 44–60.

Sinha, S., Faridi, M. R., & Cheema, S. (2024). Child leader standing on a precipice: A case study of NextGenInnov8. *Emerald Emerging Markets Case Studies*, *14*(4), 1–47. DOI: 10.1108/EEMCS-05-2023-0161

Sircar, C. O. T. (2025, January 8). Key highlights of India's draft Digital Personal Data Protection Rules, 2025 (via Passle). Passle. https://quickreads.ext.katten.com/post/102jsgd/key-highlights-of-indias-draft-digital-personal-data-protection-rules-2025

Smith, A., & Turner, P. (2023). Profitability analysis of ghost kitchens using AI-driven supply chain management. *Food Service Technology Review*, *8*(3), 112–121. DOI: 10.1016/j.fstr.2023.112121

Smith, A., & Wong, H. (2021). Collaborative Filtering for Personalized Menu Recommendations in Online Food Services. *International Journal of AI in Hospitality*, *15*(3), 212–227.

Smith, E., & Karami, A. (2023). Collaboration and co-location in the ghost kitchen sector. *Contemporary Culinary Management*, *4*(2), 78–95.

Smith, J. (2023). Ethical considerations in AI adoption in supply chains. *Journal of Business Ethics*, *45*(3), 120–135.

Smith, J. (2023). Workforce readiness for AI adoption in supply chains. *The Journal of Supply Chain Management*, *42*(5), 24–30.

Smith, J., & Allen, P. (2020). Data Privacy in Machine Learning Applications: Challenges and Solutions. *Journal of Cybersecurity*, *12*(3), 198–212.

Smith, J., & Gupta, R. (2023). AI in demand forecasting for ghost kitchens: A case study. *Journal of Supply Chain Innovation*, *18*(3), 45–57.

Smith, J., & Lee, M. (2023). Leveraging AI for Waste Reduction in Food Service Supply Chains. *International Journal of AI in Business*, *11*(4), 215–228.

Smith, K.. (2022). Upskilling the workforce for AI integration. *HR Innovations Journal*, *11*(4), 56–70.

Smith, M., & Thompson, R. (2023). Enhancing operational efficiency in ghost kitchens through AI: The standardization dilemma. *Technology in Food Service Management*, *14*(4), 88–95.

Smith, M., & Tushman, M. L. (2022). The Digital Supply Chain: Navigating the Complexities of AI Integration in Ghost Kitchens. *The Journal of Supply Chain Management*, *58*(4), 37–52.

Smith, R., & Johnson, T. (2022). AI and personalization in customer service: A case study. *Journal of Business Intelligence*, *34*(4), 67–81.

Smith, T., & Taylor, J. (2022). Reducing food waste with AI: Innovations in meal planning. *International Journal of Food Technology*, *9*(3), 45–59.

Solove, D. J. (2021). *The digital person: Technology and privacy in the information age*. New York University Press.

Soman, N., Warde, A., & Singh, A. (2020). The future of energy efficiency in commercial kitchens: AI-based innovations. *Energy Efficiency Journal*, *13*(1), 67–83. DOI: 10.1007/s12053-020-09856-0

Somlai, R. (2023). Insights into business strategies for reducing food waste in the Australian food industry. *Business Strategy and the Environment*, *32*(6), 3151–3164. DOI: 10.1002/bse.3292

Song, J., & Lee, S. (2021). AI-driven demand forecasting and pricing strategies in the restaurant industry. *International Journal of Hospitality Management*, *98*, 103032. DOI: 10.1016/j.ijhm.2021.103032

Spalević, Ž., & Vićentijević, K. (2022). GDPR and challenges of personal data protection. *The European Journal of Applied Economics*, *19*(1), 55–65. DOI: 10.5937/EJAE19-36596

Sprague, J. (2022). Ghost in the kitchen: Multiracial Korean Americans (re) defining cultural authenticity. *Genealogy*, *6*(2), 35–42. DOI: 10.3390/genealogy6020035

Srinivasan, V., Agarwal, S., & Joshi, A. (2021). Leveraging AI for logistics optimization in food delivery services. *The Journal of Supply Chain Management*, *44*(1), 57–71.

Stangherlin, I.. (2021). Portion Control and Food Waste Reduction in Ghost Kitchens. *Journal of Food Quality*, *2021*, 1–10.

Starship Technologies. (2023). *Autonomous Delivery Robots for Urban Food Delivery*. Retrieved from Starship Technologies.

StartUs Insights. (2024). *Discover 5 top ghost kitchen solutions developed by startups*. Retrieved from https://startus-insights.com

Statista. (2023). *Digitalization of the restaurant industry worldwide: Statistics & facts.* Retrieved from https://www.statista.com

Statista. (2023). Growth of Food Delivery Apps and Virtual Kitchens Worldwide. Retrieved from Statista.

Statista. (2023). *Growth of Ghost Kitchens during COVID-19.* Retrieved from https://www.statista.com/ghost-kitchen-growth

Statista. (2023). *Online food delivery revenue worldwide: 2023 report and statistics.* Retrieved from https://www.statista.com

Stenmarck, Å., Jensen, C., Quested, T., & Moates, G. (2016). *Estimates of European food waste levels.* IVL Swedish Environmental Research Institute.

Stephens, P., Carter, R., & Malik, A. (2021). Local sourcing and sustainability in foodservice. *International Journal of Culinary Innovation, 12*(2), 150–166.

Strusani, D., & Houngbonon, G. V. (2019). *The role of artificial intelligence in supporting development in emerging markets.* International Finance Corporation. DOI: 10.1596/32365

Suganob, D. (2022). *Ghost Kitchen:" Kusina Filipina".* https://search.proquest.com/openview/41433b-69f664c9eb3f41ca35a0e7484f/1?pq-origsite=gscholar&cbl=2026366&diss=y

Sulaiman, A., Rahmat, A. K., Ibrahim, I., & Jamaludin, F. (2023). Online Food Delivery Sentiment Analysis from the Restaurant Point of View. *Information Management and Business Review, 15*(3 (SI)), 197–204. DOI: 10.22610/imbr.v15i3(SI).3472

Sundararajan, A. (2022). AI and logistics: Improving delivery systems in ghost kitchens. *Journal of Supply Chain Technology, 19*(2), 104–118. DOI: 10.1080/09767131.2022.123456

Suresh, S., & Santhosh, S. 2, T. S. A. and D. V., & 2024, undefined. (n.d.). Food Economies–Engendered Ghost Kitchens in the Digital Age. *Springer*. Retrieved February 24, 2025, from https://link.springer.com/chapter/10.1007/978-3-031-62106-2_8

Suresh, S., Santhosh, S., & Samjaila, T. H. (2024). Food Economies–Engendered Ghost Kitchens in the Digital Age. In *Business Development via AI and Digitalization* (Vol. 2, pp. 95–104). Springer Nature Switzerland., DOI: 10.1007/978-3-031-62106-2_8

Suresh, S., Santhosh, S., & Samjaila, T. H. (2024). Food economies–Engendered ghost kitchens in the digital age: Implications for future research and practice in food delivery systems. In *AI and Digitalization* (Vol. 2, pp. 123–145). Springer Nature Switzerland AG.

Susskind, A. M., & Curry, J. (2020). The delivery-driven business model: A study on ghost kitchens and consumer preferences. *Journal of Restaurant Innovation, 14*(1), 27–40.

Sykimte, C. (2023). Food & Beverage Management: Trends, Innovations, & Challenges. *International Journal of Advanced Research in Science. Tongxin Jishu*, •••, 713–718. DOI: 10.48175/IJARSCT-12360

Talukder, M. B., Kumar, S., Kaiser, F., & Mia, Md. N. (2024a). Pilgrimage Creative Tourism: A Gateway to Sustainable Development Goals in Bangladesh. In M. Hamdan, M. Anshari, N. Ahmad, & E. Ali (Eds.), *Advances in Public Policy & Administration* (pp. 285–300). IGI Global. DOI: 10.4018/979-8-3693-1742-6.ch016

Talukder, M. B., Kumar, S., Sood, K., & Grima, S. (2023). Information Technology, Food Service Quality & Restaurant Revisit Intention. *International Journal of Sustainable Development and Planning*, *18*(1), 295–303. DOI: 10.18280/ijsdp.180131

Talukder, M. B., Kumar, S., & Tyagi, P. K. (Eds.). (2024a). *Hotel & Travel Management in the AI Era.* IGI Global., DOI: 10.4018/979-8-3693-7898-4

Talukder, M. B., Kumar, S., & Tyagi, P. K. (Eds.). (2024b). *Impact of AI & Tech-Driven Solutions in Hospitality & Tourism.* IGI Global., DOI: 10.4018/979-8-3693-6755-1

Tan, B.. (2023). Optimizing Local Sourcing through AI: Sustainability in Ghost Kitchen Operations. *Journal of Environmental Impact*, *22*(3), 101–115.

Tan, J., & Lee, S. (2019). Predictive Analytics and Inventory Management in Ghost Kitchens. *Journal of Food Operations*, *10*(4), 300–315.

Tan, Z., & Tan, K. (2022). Ethical challenges in AI deployment within service industries. *International Journal of Technology Ethics*, *14*(3), 102–115.

Tan, Z., & Tan, K. (2022). Machine learning and customer engagement in ghost kitchens. *Journal of Foodservice Operations*, *18*(4), 76–90.

Tarantino, M., Bacchetti, A., & Mula, J. (2021). Inventory management in food delivery: Strategies for ghost kitchens. *Operations Research Perspectives*, *8*, 100–113.

Tariq, M. U. (2024). Data breach incidents and prevention in the hospitality industry. In *Corporate Cybersecurity in the Aviation, Tourism, and Hospitality Sector* (pp. 181-199). IGI Global. DOI: 10.4018/979-8-3693-2715-9.ch010

Taylor, B., & Zhang, Y. (2022). Transforming customer service in ghost kitchens with AI. *International Journal of AI in Food Services*, *7*(1), 55–70.

Taylor, E. (2021). Maintaining quality and brand reputation in a digital-only restaurant model. *Food Industry Review*, *42*(3), 78–85.

Taylor, E. (2021). Standalone ghost kitchens: A rising trend in food delivery. *Food Industry Review*, *42*(2), 56–63.

Taylor, K. (2021). *Leveraging Delivery Platforms for Growth.* FoodTech Advances.

Taylor, K. (2021). *NLP and Customer Insights in Food Delivery.* Language Insights Journal.

Technomic. (2021). Ghost kitchens and the consumer's view of food delivery services. *Consumer Insights Report*

TechSci Research. (2023). Key Facts About the Global Cloud Kitchen Market. Https://Blog.Market-research.Com/Global-Cloud-Kitchen-Market-Expert-Analysis

Teece, D. J. (2018). Business models and dynamic capabilities. *Long Range Planning*, *51*(1), 40–49. DOI: 10.1016/j.lrp.2017.06.007

The Digital Personal Data Protection Bill. 2023. (n.d.). PRS Legislative Research. https://prsindia.org/billtrack/digital-personal-data-protection-bill-2023

The Food Institute. (2023). *The future of restaurants: Data and insights for 2024 and beyond.* Retrieved from https://www.foodinstitute.com

The Guardian. (2025). Delivery apps urged to lift lid on 'black-box algorithms' affecting UK couriers. https://www.theguardian.com/business/2025/jan/20/food-delivery-apps-ubereats-deliveroo-justeat-urged-to-reveal-how-algorithms-affect-uk-courierss-work [Accessed on 10th February, 2025]

The Internet of Things (IoT) and smart cooking technology... - Google Scholar. (n.d.). Retrieved January 21, 2025, from https://scholar.google.co.in/scholar?hl=en&as_sdt=0%2C5&as_rr=1&q=The+Internet+of+Things+%28IoT%29+and+smart+cooking+technology+%2C+reducing+waste%2C+and+encouraging+wholesome+eating+practices.+&btnG=

The role of Technology in Ghost Kitchens: Streamlining operations. (n.d.). vGrubs. https://vgrubs.com/blogs/the-role-of-technology-in-ghost-kitchens-streamlining-operations

The Times. (2024). Shoppers fear price surges as Kroger expands use of facial recognition. https://www.thetimes.co.uk/article/kroger-facial-recognition-supermarket-surge-pricing-vlfrt0dxl [Accessed on 10th February, 2025]

Thomas, L., & Harris, E. (2018). Impact of Traffic Data on Delivery Efficiency in Ghost Kitchens. *International Journal of Logistics Research*, *12*(2), 203–218.

Thompson, G.. (2020). Consumer Engagement in Sustainable Food Practices: The Case of Ghost Kitchens. *Sustainability*, *12*(18), 7553.

Thompson, H. (2023). Regulatory frameworks for AI in food services. *International Journal of Law and Technology*, *22*(2), 112–127.

Thompson, H., & McMurray, D. (2023). AI demand forecasting in ghost kitchens. *Food Management Today*, *8*(3), 134–148.

Thompson, J., & Patel, M. (2022). Improving customer satisfaction with AI-powered delivery tracking. *Food Delivery Journal*, *9*(3), 58–71.

Thompson, R., & Gupta, S. (2023). AI-driven supplier integration in ghost kitchens: A case study. *Journal of Food Supply Chain Management*, *9*(2), 85–97.

Thompson, R., & Lee, K. (2024). Leveraging AI for budget optimization in ghost kitchens. *AI in Foodservice Operations*, *6*(2), 98–110.

Thompson, R., & Zhang, F. (2024). AI in food safety: Preventing contamination and hazards in ghost kitchens. *AI in Food Quality Assurance*, *8*(2), 104–115.

Tiwari, S., & Mehta, P. (2022). Automating stock replenishment in ghost kitchens with AI. *International Journal of Inventory Management*, *5*(4), 123–135.

Toast. (2023). AI in Restaurant Operations: Insights and Solutions. Retrieved from Toast.

Tong, T., Dai, H., Xiao, Q., & Yan, N. (2019). Will dynamic pricing outperform? Theoretical analysis and empirical evidence from O2O on-demand food service market. *International Journal of Production Economics*, *219*, 375–385. DOI: 10.1016/j.ijpe.2019.07.010

Tran, L., & Chen, Y. (2020). Blockchain in Data Security for Machine Learning. *Journal of Blockchain Technology*, *7*(1), 57–68.

Tsai, M., & Jang, J. (2021). Optimizing food delivery services through AI: A case study on ghost kitchens. *Journal of Food Technology*, *29*(2), 101–115.

Tsang, Y. P., Wu, C. H., Lam, H. Y., Choy, K. L., & Ho, G. T. (2021). Integrating Internet of Things and multi-temperature delivery planning for perishable food E-commerce logistics: A model and application. *International Journal of Production Research*, *59*(5), 1534–1556. DOI: 10.1080/00207543.2020.1841315

Tualeka, S. H. (2024). Multi-Brand Virtual Restaurant: Cloud Kitchen Business Model (Case Study of PT. Sagala). *Management Studies and Entrepreneurship Journal*, *5*(2), 4921–4931.

Tuncalp, D. (2024). Directing the future: Artificial intelligence integration in family businesses. *Journal of Family Business Management*. DOI: 10.1108/JFBM-03-2024-0051

Turner, M., & Lee, J. (2023). Minimizing food waste with predictive analytics in ghost kitchens. *Journal of Food Supply Chain Innovation*, *14*(2), 57–70.

United Nations Environment Programme (UNEP). (2021). *Global Food Waste Statistics and Solutions*. Retrieved from UNEP Website.

United States Department of Energy. (2023). AI in Energy Efficiency and Management. Retrieved from US DOE Website.

UNWTO. (2021). *Adapting to the new normal: Trends in the hospitality industry*. World Tourism Organization.

Upadhye, N., & Sathe, S. (2020). Cloud kitchen-case study of swiggy cloud kitchen in Pune.

Upton, N. (2018). Kitchen United Opens First of Many Shared Kitchens. foodondemandnews.com. Franchise Times. Retrieved 10 November 2019.

USDA. (2019). Food loss and waste reduction goals. Available at: https://www.usda.gov

Vaughan, J. (2022). *The cloud kitchen: Market innovation and a vertical disintegration*. Webster University.

Velt, M. J., Fielt, E., & Curry, E. (2018). The evolving nature of business models: Toward a framework for business model dynamics. *Journal of Business Research*.

Verma, M., Kumar, D., & Bansal, A. (2021). Role of artificial intelligence in the food delivery supply chain: Challenges and opportunities. *International Journal of Logistics Research and Applications*, *24*(3), 241–257. DOI: 10.1080/13675567.2020.1833197

Visible Capital. (2020). Grocery Fulfillment and Dark Stores—Clear Aisles, Full Carts, Can't Lose? Pitchbook. Available at., Retrieved January 20, 2021, from.[REMOVED HYPERLINK FIELD]https://pitchbook.com/news/articles/in-visible-capital-podcast-season-2-ep-4-grocery-fulfillment-dark-stores

Vonthron, S., Perrin, C., & Soulard, C. T. (2020). Foodscape: A scoping review and a research agenda for food security-related studies. *PLoS One*, *15*(5), e0233218. Advance online publication. DOI: 10.1371/journal.pone.0233218 PMID: 32433690

Voss, C. A., Blackmon, K., & Barlow, J. (2020). Demand forecasting in food supply chains: Challenges and opportunities. *European Journal of Operational Research*, *282*(3), 947–961.

Vu, O. T. K., Alonso, A. D., Tran, T. D., & Nicholson, G. J. (2023). Illuminating the dark kitchen business model-A knowledge-based perspective from the supply-side. *Journal of Hospitality and Tourism Management*, *55*, 318–331.

Wagner, K., Unger, L., Salman, M. M., Kitchen, P., Bill, R. M., & Yool, A. J. (2022). Signaling mechanisms and pharmacological modulators governing diverse aquaporin functions in human health and disease. *International Journal of Molecular Sciences*, *23*(3), 1388. DOI: 10.3390/ijms23031388 PMID: 35163313

Wamba, S. F., Akter, S., Edwards, A., Chopin, G., & Gnanzou, D. (2021). How "big data" can make big impact: Findings from a systematic review and a longitudinal case study. *International Journal of Production Economics*, *165*, 234–246. DOI: 10.1016/j.ijpe.2014.12.031

Wamba, S. F., Akter, S., & Ren, S. J. (2017). Big data analytics and artificial intelligence in supply chain management: A review of applications, challenges, and future directions. *Computers in Industry*, *92*, 85–97. DOI: 10.1016/j.compind.2017.09.004

Wang, H., Li, X., & Zhang, H. (2021). AI-based route optimization in urban food delivery: A case study of ghost kitchens. *Journal of Transportation Engineering*, *147*(10), 1894–1906.

Wang, K., & Zhao, Y. (2021). Machine Learning in Demand Forecasting for Ghost Kitchens: A Comprehensive Approach. *Journal of Business Analytics*, *18*(2), 157–171.

Wang, L., & Kim, J. (2023). Preventing contamination in ghost kitchens with AI and IoT. *Food Safety and Technology Journal*, *13*(1), 72–85.

Wang, P., & Garcia, M. (2020). The cost-benefit analysis of ghost kitchen setups. *Business Economics Quarterly*, *8*(4), 112–132.

Wang, S., & Liu, Y. (2021). Ethical implications of AI and automation in service industries. *Journal of AI and Automation*, *19*(2), 50–65.

Wang, S., Xu, K., & Liu, Z. (2022). AI in menu optimization: Enhancing culinary creativity and reducing waste. *Journal of Foodservice Management & Education*, *15*(1), 25–35.

Wang, T., & Zhou, Y. (2020). Predictive analytics in ghost kitchen operations. *Journal of Culinary Technology*, *6*(3), 89–110.

Wang, Y.. (2021). Sustainable Packaging Solutions in Food Service: The Case of Ghost Kitchens. *Packaging Technology & Science*, *34*(3), 123–134.

Wang, Z., Cao, J., & Xu, M. (2020). IoT and AI convergence in inventory tracking for ghost kitchens. *Computers in Industry*, *123*, 103296.

Wang, Z., & Zhao, M. (2022). AI-powered robotics in food service: An evaluation of consumer experiences. *International Journal of Artificial Intelligence in Hospitality*, *20*(2), 77–89.

Wansink, B.. (2016). Menu Variety and Food Waste: The Role of Consumer Choice. *International Journal of Hospitality Management*, *57*, 105–110.

Watson, R. (2020). Virtual Restaurants in Urban Centers. *Business Review*.

Wharton, W. (2020). Menu innovation in ghost kitchens. *Culinary Perspectives*, *16*(1), 23–38.

Whig, P., Remala, R., Mudunuru, K. R., & Quraishi, S. J. (2024). Integrating AI & Quantum Technologies for Sustainable Supply Chain Management. In Hassan, A., Bhattacharya, P., Dutta, P. K., Verma, J. P., & Kundu, N. K. (Eds.), *Advances in Logistics, Operations, & Management Science* (pp. 267–283). IGI Global., DOI: 10.4018/979-8-3693-4107-0.ch018

White, J. (2020). *Personalization in the Absence of Direct Interaction*. AI in Food Services.

Wiener-Bronner, D. (2020). *How Ghost Kitchens are Changing the Food Industry*. CNN Business. Retrieved from https://www.cnnbusiness.com/ghost-kitchens

Williams, A., & Johnson, K. (2022). Bias and fairness in AI algorithms: A case study in supply chains. *Technology Ethics Review*, *38*(2), 56–72.

Williams, H. (2023). Real-time feedback systems: A game changer for customer experience. *Consumer Technology Review*, *7*(2), 19–27.

Williams, H., & Jones, T. (2022). Training for AI: Building adaptable skills in the workforce. *Journal of Business and Technology*, *35*(3), 58–66.

Williams, H., & Lee, J. (2022). Robotics and AI in ghost kitchens: A revolution in food service operations. *Technology & Innovation Review*, *41*(2), 87–102.

Williams, R., & Li, Y. (2023). Reducing operational costs using AI in ghost kitchens during peak demand. *Journal of Hospitality and Foodservice Management*, *14*(3), 78–92.

Winkler, M. (2020). The role of artificial intelligence in promoting sustainability in the food industry. *Journal of Environmental Management*, *264*, 110413. DOI: 10.1016/j.jenvman.2020.110413

World Bank. (2021). “Bridging the Digital Divide in Emerging Economies.” [Online Resource]

World Economic Forum. (2023). “The Role of AI in Advancing Global Sustainability Goals.” [Online Resource].\ Wang, L., Zhou, M., & Gao, X. (2021). “Agricultural robotics: Autonomous solutions for modern farming. *IEEE Transactions on Automation Science and Engineering*, *18*(2), 456–467.

World Resources Institute. (2021). A circular economy for the food service industry: Reducing waste and resource consumption. Retrieved from https://www.wri.org/publication/circular-economy-foodservice

Wouters, M., & De Stefano, V. (2022). AI and digital tools in workplace management and evaluation: An assessment of the EU's legal framework.

Wray, A., Arku, G., Long, J., Minaker, L., Seabrook, J., Doherty, S., & Gilliland, J. (2024). Restaurant survival during the COVID-19 pandemic: Examining operational, demographic and land use predictors in London, Canada. *Urban Studies (Edinburgh, Scotland)*, •••, 00420980241269785. DOI: 10.1177/00420980241269785

Wulandari, F. (2023). Digitalization in food & beverage: The cloud kitchen revolution. *Journal of Sustainable Business Practices*, *18*(1), 55–68.

X-MOL. (2024). *AI-driven demand forecasting in food supply chains.* Retrieved from https://www.x-mol.com

Xu, W. (2023). *AI in HCI Design and User Experience* (arXiv:2301.00987). arXiv. http://arxiv.org/abs/2301.00987

Xu, J., Wei, X., & Wang, T. (2021). Leveraging AI for sustainable food delivery operations: A review. *Sustainable Supply Chain Management*, *4*(2), 200–215.

Xu, L., Li, Q., & Zhang, W. (2021). Dynamic Routing and Efficiency in Ghost Kitchen Deliveries: The Role of Artificial Intelligence. *Computers & Industrial Engineering*, *154*, 107116.

Xu, M., & Li, Y. (2022). Overcoming data silos in AI-driven food delivery systems. *Journal of Artificial Intelligence in Business*, *13*(1), 44–52.

Yaga, D., Mell, P., Roby, N., & Scarfone, K. (2019). Blockchain technology overview. *arXiv preprint arXiv:1906.11078.*

Yakoubi, S. (2024). Sustainable Revolution: AI-Driven Enhancements for Composite Polymer Processing & Optimization in Intelligent Food Packaging. *Food and Bioprocess Technology*. Advance online publication. DOI: 10.1007/s11947-024-03449-2

Yang, M., Ma, L., & Xie, X. (2020). AI-based predictive maintenance for ghost kitchen operations. *Journal of Intelligent Manufacturing*, *31*(6), 1461–1473. DOI: 10.1007/s10845-019-01489-9

Yang, Y., Liu, S., & Zhang, X. (2023). AI-driven sustainable sourcing in the foodservice sector. *Journal of Sustainable Agriculture*, *11*(2), 45–58.

Yuan, Y., Liu, X., & Li, Z. (2020). AI in reducing food waste in the food service industry: A review of applications. *Food Science & Technology International*, *26*(7), 545–559.

Yupardhi, T. H. (2023, October). Ghost Kitchen Concept: An Alternative Culinary Business Method with a Minimum Space. In *4th Borobudur International Symposium on Humanities and Social Science 2022 (BIS-HSS 2022)* (pp. 126-131). Atlantis Press. DOI: 10.2991/978-2-38476-118-0_14

Yusuf, S. O., Durodola, R. L., Ocran, G., Abubakar, J. E., Echere, A. Z., & Paul-Adeleye, A. H. (2024). Challenges & opportunities in AI & digital transformation for SMEs: A cross-continental perspective. *World Journal of Advanced Research & Reviews*, *23*(3), 668–678. DOI: 10.30574/wjarr.2024.23.3.2511

Zaltz, D. A., Prowse, R., Yi, Y., O'Dea, J., & Harding, S. V. (2024). *Beverage consumption among adults in Newfoundl& & Labrador, Canada prior to the implementation of a sugar-sweetened beverage tax.* DOI: 10.21203/rs.3.rs-4606952/v1

Zammit, J. (2022). An Analysis of Plate Waste and Consumer Behaviour at Buffets in Hotels in Malta A Thesis submitted on the 30th of August 2022 by: Jonathan Zammit Student Number: 0210208/4 Submitted to. *The Online Open Access Repository of the Institute of Tourism Studies (Malta).*

Zendesk. (2023). Enhancing Customer Service with AI Chatbots. Retrieved from Zendesk.

Zengler, T. (2020). AI and privacy: A regulatory framework for emerging technologies. *Journal of Business Ethics, 171*(3), 625–638. DOI: 10.1007/s10551-020-04488-0

Zeng, Y., Li, J., & Liu, H. (2023). Workforce Adaptation to AI in the Food Industry: Training Challenges in Ghost Kitchens. *International Journal of Hospitality Management, 89*, 102432.

Zhang, F., & Singh, A. (2024). AI-driven cost management for peak periods in ghost kitchens. *International Journal of AI in Food Logistics, 6*(1), 47–59.

Zhang, L., Huang, Y., & Wong, J. (2023). Predictive analytics in the food service industry: Leveraging AI for menu optimization. *Journal of Food Science and Technology, 60*(5), 3215–3227.

Zhang, L., & Nguyen, A. (2024). Enhancing demand forecasting with social media data in ghost kitchens. *AI & Logistics Review, 15*(2), 78–89.

Zhang, Q., Chen, Y., & Liu, R. (2023). Consumer engagement in AI-powered ghost kitchens: The role of marketing strategies. *Journal of Marketing Theory and Practice, 31*(1), 55–72.

Zhang, T., & Zhang, Z. (2020). Impact of Algorithmic Bias in Customer Personalization: A Case Study of Ghost Kitchens. *Journal of AI Research, 28*(3), 185–200.

Zhang, X.. (2022). Autonomous delivery robots: An analysis of operational efficiency. *Transportation Research Part C, Emerging Technologies, 138*, 103548.

Zhang, X.. (2024). AI and Green Logistics: Sustainable Solutions for Food Delivery Services. *Journal of Supply Chain and Technology, 16*(2), 67–80.

Zhang, X., & Lee, Y. (2022). Challenges in scaling AI systems for the food delivery industry. *AI in Supply Chain Journal, 18*(1), 112–129. DOI: 10.1016/j.aisc.2022.01.003

Zhang, X., & Liao, Y. (2021). Regulatory Challenges for Ghost Kitchens: A Comparative Analysis. *Journal of Food Law & Policy, 17*(3), 189–210.

Zhang, X., Wang, F., & Li, Q. (2023). AI-powered supply chain optimization in food delivery services. *Journal of Foodservice Management, 29*(4), 215–227. DOI: 10.1016/j.jfsm.2023.06.003

Zhang, X., Wang, Y., & Liu, J. (2023). Leveraging data analytics for menu optimization in ghost kitchens. *Journal of Foodservice Management & Education, 18*(2), 117–133.

Zhang, X., & Wong, S. (2022). Supply chain dynamics and AI adoption in ghost kitchen operations. *International Journal of Logistics Research, 18*(5), 201–214.

Zhang, Y. (2021). *Dietary Trends and Data Analytics*. Health & Tech Journal.

Zhang, Y., Lee, S., & Kim, J. (2023). Sustainable practices in ghost kitchens: Reducing food waste through AI technologies. *Journal of Sustainable Food Systems*, *8*(1), 67–80.

Zhang, Y., Liu, H., & Chen, J. (2023). Automation and AI in food preparation: Innovations for the future. *Food Quality and Preference*, *92*, 104282. DOI: 10.1016/j.foodqual.2021.104282

Zhang, Y., & Liu, T. (2023). AI-driven cost analysis and budget management in ghost kitchens. *Food-service Economics Journal*, *11*(3), 42–55.

Zhang, Y., & Liu, W. (2023). AI optimization in last-mile delivery: Enhancing efficiency for ghost kitchens. *Journal of Transportation and Logistics*, *18*(2), 56–70.

Zhang, Y., & Yang, F. (2022). AI and machine learning in food delivery: Optimizing ghost kitchen operations. *Journal of Food Science and Technology*, *59*(6), 1142–1152. DOI: 10.1007/s11483-022-01682-5

Zhao, L., & Wang, H. (2023). AI and IoT for monitoring freshness and quality in ghost kitchens. *Food Safety and Quality Journal*, *14*(3), 88–101.

Zhao, X., & Zhang, W. (2021). Optimizing supply chain management in food delivery with artificial intelligence. *Food Quality and Sustainability*, *14*(3), 220–233.

Zhao, X., Zhang, Z., & Li, L. (2022). AI-driven innovations in agriculture: A path to global food security. *Journal of Agricultural Science*, *180*(4), 455–470.

Zheng, X. (2024). *Project Management of a Fast Food Network Creating (on the Example of the "Culinary Crossroads" Project)* (Master's thesis, Lesya Ukrainka Volyn National University).

Zhou, K., & Lee, H. (2021). AI-powered logistics in food delivery: A sustainability perspective. *The Journal of Supply Chain Management*, *39*(1), 27–42.

Zhu, Y., Pi, M., Zhu, X., & Byrd, K. (2024). Busiest Store in a Cramped Space: Can a Ghost Kitchen Optimize Coffee Shop Efficiency? *Journal of Hospitality & Tourism Cases*, 21649987241270419.

Zhu, Y., Pi, M., Zhu, X., & Byrd, K. (2024). Busiest Store in a Cramped Space: Can a Ghost Kitchen Optimize Coffee Shop Efficiency? *Journal of Hospitality & Tourism Cases*. DOI: 10.1177/21649987241270419

Zillion. (2023). AI-Based Dynamic Pricing Models for Restaurants. Retrieved from Zillion.

About the Contributors

Kuldeep Singh currently serves as Assistant Professor in Amity School of Hospitality, Amity University, Haryana, India. He completed his PhD in tourism from Maharishi Dayanand University (Rohtak) in India in the year 2021. He is also a UGC (Net- JRF qualified). Dr. Singh has also served the tourism industry for a couple of years and more than three years in academics. Dr. Singh has so far published more than 45 research articles in both international and national referred journals as well as in edited books in the field of Tourism. Currently, he is serving as an editor of book series in various reputed publications (Emerald, IIP series). Dr. Singh is passionate about the academic areas of Service Quality Management, Rural tourism, Ecotourism, and Sustainable tourism. He also won the Aspiring Researchers Welcome Award from the Indian Hospitality Congress. His credentials may be verified on various research platforms like Google Scholar, SSRN, LinkedIn, Academia, and Research Gate.

Sanjeev Kumar is a professor cum HOD, school of hotel management and tourism, Lovely Professional University, Punjab, India. He holds a bachelor's degree in hotel management from Osmania University. He earned his master's degree in tourism management from Madurai Kamaraj University and his doctorate from Amity University Rajasthan. He has worked as a teacher for the past 18 years. While in Kuwait, he worked as an Assistant Dining Manager for Gulf Catering Company and other hotels. Dr. Sanjeev Kumar has 20 research articles and has presented more than 12 papers at national and international conferences. He supervises six PhD research scholars and has directed many MBA and MSc research projects in hospitality and tourism. He has taken part in several FDPs and workshops. He also travelled throughout the country to attend international and national conferences.

Mohammad Badruddoza Talukder is an Associate Professor, College of Tourism and Hospitality Management, International University of Business Agriculture and Technology, Dhaka, Bangladesh. He completed his Ph.D. in Hotel Management at the School of Hotel Management and Tourism, Lovely Professional University, India. He holds a bachelor's and a master's degree in Hotel Management from India. He has been teaching various courses in the Department of Tourism and Hospitality at various universities in Bangladesh since 2008. His research areas include tourism management, hotel management, hospitality management, food and beverage management, and accommodation management, where he has published research papers in well-known journals in Bangladesh and abroad.

***

Jhasaketan Behera is working as a Principal Consultant in Oracle Financial Services Software Bengaluru India. Having 17+ years of corporate experience, Mr. Jhasaketan Behera is passionate about writing technical articles and spreading knowledge in various domain.

Arvind Chauhan is an assistant professor at the school of hotel management, CSJMU Kanpur. He holds Master in Travel and Tourism Management degree from IGNOU and a Bachelor degree in Hotel and Hospitality (H&HA) from IHM Lucknow. He has published papers at various national and international conferences and seminars. With extensive academic experience in hotel and hospitality management, Mr. Chauhan brings real-world insights into his lectures, making teaching moments fresh and enriching classroom learning.

Sarthak Chourasia, a passionate PhD scholar with a keen fascination for the digital realm, specifically its application in the dynamic world of tourism and hospitality. My academic journey revolves around unraveling the intricate ways in which digital marketing transforms the landscapes of travel and guest experiences. I believe that in this age of technology, understanding the nuances of digital marketing is pivotal in shaping the future of the tourism and hospitality industries. Through my research, I aspire to shed light on innovative strategies that harness the power of the digital sphere, ultimately enhancing the way we explore the world and savor hospitality.

Sumiksha Devi is an Assistant Professor of Mathematics Msc. Math, B. Sc. Non Medicle B.Ed. TET.

Sandip Dey was an Associate Professor and the HOD with the Department of Computer Science and Engineering, Global Institute of Management and Technology, India. He worked as an Assistant Professor in OmDayal Group of Institution and Camellia Institute of Technology for several years. Before that he worked as a Lecturer in Narula Institute of Technology. He is currently an Assistant Professor in the Department of Computer Science, Sukanta Mahavidyalaya, Jalpaiguri. He has coauthored one book titled "Quantum-Inspired Metaheuristics for Image Analysis"; Publisher: John Wiley & Sons, UK, coedited three books, and authored or coauthored about 60 research publications in international journals, book chapters, and conference proceedings. His research interests include soft computing, hybrid intelligence, quantum computing, and image analysis. Dey reviewed several international peer-reviewed journals like Applied Soft Computing, Swarm and Evolutionary Computation, Information Sciences, Journal of Computational Science, Engineering Applications of Artificial Intelligence, Expert Systems With Applications, Advanced Engineering Informatics, IEEE Transactions on Signal Processing and so on.

Anshul Garg is an experienced Senior Lecturer with a demonstrated history of working in the higher education industry. His research areas include Self Service Technologies, Service Quality, Service Clues, Hospitality Service, Risk and Crisis Management in Hospitality and Tourism and Tourist Risk Perception.

Ajay Kumar, a dynamic academician and tourism enthusiast, basically from Bilaspur District, Himachal Pradesh. He completed his undergraduate in Tourism Administration from Govt. College Bilaspur and Master's degree from Himachal Pradesh University Summer-Hill, Shimla. He is also pursuing his Ph.D. from CT University Ludhiana under the guidance of Dr. Ashish Raina. Transitioning to academia, Ajay served as an Assistant Professor of Tourism and Travel at Punjab Institute of Management and Technology, Alour, Khanna, and after that at CT Group of Institutions, Shahpur, Jalandhar. Currently he working as an Assistant Professor in the Chandigarh College of Hospitality at CGC Landran, Mohali, Punjab. Ajay Kumar has published 12 research papers, is a book author, has published patents, and has copyrights registered. He has taken part in several FDPs and workshops. He has worked as a teacher for the past 6 years.

Dhanalakshmi K (Beulah, pen name) specialized in Marketing, Human Resources, and Entrepreneurship. She has completed her Ph.D. at Bharathiar University. Her research interests are in customer relationship management, consumer behavior, entrepreneurship, education management, and SDG as well as on education management. She has authored more than six books. She is the recipient of the Global Jury Award 2021 by the Wadhwani Foundation, National Entrepreneurship Network; and two Best Paper awards in an International Conference organized in Bangalore in 2014 and 2016, respectively. She has published more than twenty papers publications and seven patent publications. She is a Fellow Member of Eduoxia Research Center, a Fellow Member of Eduoxia Research University, She is a lifetime member of the Teaching and Education Research Association (TERA); Member of International Association of Academic Plus Corporate Society (IAAC); Member of EAE Research Centre, a part of Global Research Network. She has served as an Editor / Editorial Board Member for Journals, at Bangalore University affiliated colleges. She has also served as an External Examiner / Panel Member / Moderator / Question Paper Setter for the colleges in Bangalore. She has also served as Chairperson and Resource Person in various National and International Conferences organized in India. She has been invited as a Resource person in organizing Faculty Development Programs in various schools and colleges across India. She has organized several training programs for UG & PG students as well as Faculty Members. She has also guided more than 2000 students (PG & UG) on their academic internships as well as projects at National and International Level.

Jaspreet Kaur holds a Master of Science in Information Technology, earned in 2023, and is UGC-NET qualified in the same year. With over a year of teaching experience, she is currently serving as a faculty member at Guru Kashi University. Her academic focus lies in advancing the fields of information technology and computer science, and she is dedicated to contributing to both education and research in her field.

Sukhmeet Kaur holds the position of Research Fellow at INTI International University, Malaysia. She has six years of teaching experience in Human Resource Management and organizational behavior. She got a Ph.D. in Management from Dayalbagh Educational Institute, (Deemed University) Agra in 2015. She qualified NET-JRF in Management in June 2011 and was promoted to SRF in 2015. She has published 10 research papers in reputed Scopus and ABDC journals. She has published 14 research papers in peer-reviewed and UGC Care List Journals. She has participated in 22 conferences, 20 Webinars, 6 FDPs, and 7 Workshops/Seminars in her career hierarchy. Her expertise embraces human resources management, organizational behavior, travel and tourism,

Vinod Kumar has more than 17 years of experience including industry as well as academics in the area of Hospitality & Tourism industry. My keen area of research comprises Regional and cultural gastronomy, Sustainable tourism, emerging trends in the hospitality and travel industry, global tourism and hospitality, AI techniques in hotels and travel industry, and many more. I have filed two patents and published over 25 publications in reputed journals.

Geetha Manoharan is currently working in Telangana as an assistant professor at SR University. She is the university-level PhD program coordinator and has also been given the additional responsibility of In Charge Director of Publications and Patents under the Research Division at SR University.

Chippy Mohan having 8 years of teaching experience and research experience. she has published 11 books and International & National 10 articles

Evarisa M. Nengnong earned her PhD from the Department of Tourism and Hotel Management at North-Eastern Hill University in Shillong, India. She has a master's degree in tourism and travel management and a bachelor's in hotel management and administration. I have eight years of experience working in several industries, including hotels, media, events, airlines, and marketing, as well as four years of teaching. She has also worked as an assistant professor at the Atharva Group of Institutes, the Army Institute of Hotel Management, and as a guest lecturer at North Eastern Hill University and ICFAI University. Her study focuses on tourism marketing, hospitality, tea tourism, eco-tourism, and sustainability.

Thirumoorthi P., currently working as Professor in Management Studies. Having specialized in Operations and Systems Management. Current research works are related to Technology Management and Supply Chain Economics. He has authored more than 50 journal articles and 5 books. He has also produced 15 Ph.D scholars and 21 M.Phil scholars. He has completed 3 funded projects sponsored by various funding agencies.

Poonam is working as an Assistant Professor of Economics and Management at Chandigarh School of Business, CGC Jhanjeri Mohali (Punjab). I am pursuing my Phd in Economics from Bundelkhand University, Jhansi (U.P.). My research interests are Labour, development, and sustainability.

Sidharth S. Raju is an Associate Professor and HOD of Hotel Management at Vivekananda Global University, Jaipur, specializing in Food & B Service. He is holding PhD and M Phil, with 11 years of teaching and 10 years industry experience, he has published 13 research papers, 6 patents, and 3 books. Additionally. .He is Editor in many Scopus and Elsevier Indexed Journal and member of many professional chapters.

Charis Ripnar, who holds a doctorate in Food Science and Nutrition from the University of Agricultural Sciences in Bengaluru, aspires to be both successful and humble. One strategy she would employ is to identify the obstacles that prevent her from achieving her goals. She enjoys watching movies and traveling.

Baranidharan S specialized in Finance Economics and Econometrics. Having 5 years research experience, 2 years of Industrial experience and 6 years of teaching experience. Published 6 patent, 45 research articles in international and national journal which are indexed in Scopus, WoS, Proquest, ABDC, etc.,

Savita Sharma has more than 2 decades of experience in the hospitality and tourism industry. Her keen interest is very close to hospitality industry.

Roshan Kumar Shiva is a research associate at SR University.

Amrik Singh is working as Professor and Head in the School of Hotel Management and Tourism at Lovely Professional University, Punjab, India. He obtained his Ph.D. degree in Hotel Management from

Kurukshetra University, Kurukshetra. He started his academic career at Lovely Professional University, Punjab, India in the year 2007. He has published more than 65 research papers in UGC and peer-reviewed and Scopus/Web of Science) journals. He has published 12 patents and 01 patent has been granted in the inter-disciplinary domain. Dr. Amrik Singh participated and acted as a resource person in various national and international conferences, seminars, research workshops, and industry talks. His area of research interest is accommodation management, ergonomics, green practices, human resource management in hospitality, waste management, AR VR in hospitality, etc. He is currently guiding 8Ph.D. scholars and 5 Ph.D. scholars have been awarded Ph.D.

Bhupinder Singh working as Professor at Sharda University, India. Also, Honorary Professor in University of South Wales UK and Santo Tomas University Tunja, Colombia. His areas of publications as Smart Healthcare, Medicines, fuzzy logics, artificial intelligence, robotics, machine learning, deep learning, federated learning, IoT, PV Glasses, metaverse and many more. He has 3 books, 139 paper publications, 163 paper presentations in international/national conferences and seminars, participated in more than 40 workshops/FDP's/QIP's, 25 courses from international universities of repute, organized more than 59 events with international and national academicians and industry people's, editor-in-chief and co-editor in journals, developed new courses. He has given talks at international universities, resource person in international conferences such as in Nanyang Technological University Singapore, Tashkent State University of Law Uzbekistan; KIMEP University Kazakhstan, All'ah meh Tabatabi University Iran, the Iranian Association of International Criminal law, Iran and Hague Center for International Law and Investment, The Netherlands, Northumbria University Newcastle UK,

Sujay Vikram Singh is currently associated as Assistant Professor in Amity School of Hospitality, Lucknow Campus, Uttar Pradesh. He completed his doctorate at Banaras Hindu University. His research interests include Hospitality, CRM, Service Marketing, Service Quality, and Systematic Literature Reviews. He has published papers in various handbooks and journals. His recent journal publications include the *International Journal of Market Research* (Sage Publishing) [ABDC-A, Scopus] and the *Journal of Global Information Management* (IGI Publishing) [Scopus, ABDC-A]. He has also been a reviewer for tourism and management journals and has presented and published papers at various national and international conferences and seminars. He has received best paper awards at several conferences, including those held at IHM Bhopal, Subharati University, and Delhi University. His credential may be verified on various research platforms like Google Scholar, SSRN, LinkedIn, Academia, and Research Gate.

Sukhpreet Singh holds a Master of Computer Applications (2011) and a Master of Philosophy (2014) from Punjabi University, Patiala. With over eight years of academic experience, he currently serves as an Assistant Professor in the Faculty of Computing at Guru Kashi University. His research interests include Big Data, Machine Learning, and Deep Learning, and he has contributed extensively to these fields through authoring more than 20 research papers published in reputable journals and conferences. In addition to his publications, he has contributed to multiple book chapters and actively participates as a reviewer for several Scopus-indexed conferences.

Saurabh Tripathi is a Assistant Professor at the School of Hotel Management, CSJM University Kanpur . With an illustrious career spanning 14 years, he has made significant contributions to both the hospitality industry and academia.His extensive industry experience has equipped him with in-depth knowledge, which he effectively imparts to his students. Mr. Tripathi has attended numerous lectures, Faculty Development Programs (FDPs), and seminars, staying updated on the latest trends and best practices in the hospitality sector.As a seasoned academician and industry expert, Mr. Tripathi continues to inspire and educate the next generation of hospitality professionals.

Neelam Yadav is an Assistant Professor at Vivekananda Global University, Jaipur, who specializes in accommodation operations. She is also a research scholar at CT University, Ludhiana. Neelam has authored six research papers, contributed to one edited book, and written seven book chapters. Her work has been presented at six conferences and she holds two patents. Recognized for her contributions, Neelam has also received an award for her research and academic achievement.

Index

G

H

I

K

L

M

N

O

P

R

S

T

V

www.ingramcontent.com/pod-product-compliance
Lightning Source LLC
LaVergne TN
LVHW060350300926
849162LV00006B/1234

9798337304328